Eastern Politics
of the Vatican 1917-1979

Pope John Paul II and Soviet Foreign Minister Andrej Gromyko during the private audience on January 24th 1979.

Foto: Felici

Hansjakob Stehle

EASTERN POLITICS
OF THE VATICAN
1917-1979

Translated by Sandra Smith

OHIO UNIVERSITY PRESS Athens, Ohio
London

English translation copyright © 1981
by Sandra Smith and Ohio University Press.
Printed in the United States of America by Oberlin Printing Company.

Originally published as:
Die Ostpolitik des Vatikans, 1917-1975
© R. Piper & Co. Verlag, München, Zürich, 1975.

Library of Congress Cataloging in Publication Data

Stehle, Hansjakob, 1927-
    The Eastern politics of the Vatican, 1917-1979.

    Rev. translation of Die Ostpolitik des Vatikans,
1917-1975.
    Bibliography: p. 429
    Includes index.
    1. Catholic Church—Relations (diplomatic) with
Eastern Europe. 2. Europe, Eastern—Foreign relations
—Catholic Church. 3. Communism and Christianity—
Catholic Church—Europe, Eastern. 4. Europe, Eastern
—Church history. I. Title.
BX1490.5.S7413   261.7   80-15236
ISBN 0-8214-0367-2
ISBN 0-8214-0564-0 (pbk.)

Table of Contents

Introduction

"Truth does not allow us to despair of our opponents."

John Paul II
January 1, 1980

I

This book does not intend to either accuse or defend, but rather to clarify what is widely discussed and often disputed as Vatican "eastern policy," by writing its history. When this book, here presented to the English-speaking public revised and updated to the end of 1979, first appeared in Germany in 1975, it evoked a broad, largely positive echo, and even more, a certain amount of surprise: more than I as the author had been conscious of, the book had demystified—in a positive and negative sense—conceptions of Vatican diplomacy. Papal policy did not appear to be as clever, moral, and farsighted as many of its admirers had thought, but also not as sly, opportunistic, and shortsighted as many of its detractors had insinuated.

In fact, diplomacy, since the disappearance of the Papal States (1870), was no longer an instrument of temporal power for the church, or an end in itself, but rather always an agent of its apostolate, i.e., its spiritual-pastoral mission. For other, perhaps power-political goals, the church was lacking—not least in military divisions. "A diplomat of the Holy See is first and foremost a priest," said Paul VI, on April 24, 1978, to graduates of the pontifical Diplomatic Academy. His successor, John Paul I, also left no doubt, right from the beginning of his short pontificate, that "Our opportunities for diplomatic intervention are limited and of a peculiar nature—above all in the pastoral area, which is the true obligation of the church" (address to the diplomatic corps, August 31, 1978). And John Paul II, the Pope from Poland, strengthened the continuity of this line: He even broached the subject of broadening the diplomatic relations of the Vatican (especially with Catholic countries, "but also with others"), declaring his "openness" (*ouverture*) to all nations and regimes, and he confirmed this

1

during his historical visit in communist-governed Poland in June 1979 (see chap. XI).

From the beginning the Polish Pope made it clear that Vatican diplomacy would speak out for freedom of religion and conscience, but that it also "is always prepared to take into account the transformations of social realities and mentalities." Like his predecessors, Pope John Paul II also spoke of "satisfactory results," but also stated "that the religious freedom of certain local churches, certain rites, leaves much to be desired, if it is not completely deplorable" (cf. addresses to the diplomatic corps, October 20, 1978 and January 12, 1979). And in relation to the East, where today over 70 million Catholics are ruled by atheist Communists, Vatican "policy" (it never calls itself that) can accordingly only be *pastorally* motivated. And this means *conservatively* in the broadest sense of the word: it tries to preserve and protect the existing possibilities and to restore what has been damaged or destroyed. Efforts of this kind go back to the inception of the Soviet Union, and use diplomatic methods as old as the states *in* which and *with* which a church always has to live. In just this way has the Catholic church for centuries withstood all those storms from which its sanguine opponents, as well as its timid adherents, expected its demise. The will to religious survival has always proven itself stronger— even at a high price.

Without doubt, questions must be raised here about the limitations of such "pragmatic" behavior. Like all history, church history too is stamped by the tensions between morals and politics, between means and ends. The only ones to be outraged by this are certain "spiritualists." They believe that, in history, the wind must blow with the flag; anyone who, realistically, refuses to rely on such a possibility is in their eyes an opportunist who lets his flag blow with the wind. . . . The theme of this book, however, is neither moral-philosophical nor theological: not because the author is insensitive to these questions but because as a historian, he tries to limit himself to two analytical points of view: "practically," to the question of the *usefulness* of Vatican eastern policy for its pastoral goals, and "ideological-ly," to the question of the *effectiveness* of ideas in the history of this policy.

This methodological limitation, however, rooted in a "historicism" (with which the author became acquainted through Benedetto Croce and Otto Vossler), allows us to make two statements at the beginning: a *philosophy*, even one like the Marxist, which presumes to be "turned from head to foot," can be blind to historical realities—for example, to the phenomenon of religion and church. A *religion*, however, that claims—like the Catholic—to be more than private piety or spiritual community, in an atheistic environment cannot create itself any breathing space through academic dialogue or a retreat into "pure" spirituality but only in the arena of political history: and this is the field of action, interaction, and negotiation. "The Christian faith is not a secret cult; it needs publicity. Therefore the church has always done everything it can, and will do everything in the future, to guarantee publicity for the exercise of faith," said Cardinal Franz König[1], who was confirmed by Pope Wojtyla as president of the Vatican "Secretariat for Non-Believers" in 1978. Soon after his election, the new Pope John Paul II thus let it be known that he would not allow the diplomatic threads woven by his predecessor to be broken: ". . . The Catholic church is not seeking special privileges, but it needs living space (d'espace vital) in order to fulfill its religious mission, and also—in accordance with its particular nature and with its own means—to be able to work for the integral and peaceful development of the whole person, of all people," said Pope John Paul II on December 14, 1978, to Petar Mladenov, Foreign Minister of Communist Bulgaria, to whom, at the same time, he declared the continuation of a "mutual and not sterile search for solutions of various problems between church and state."

The publication of his address (Osservatore Romano, December 15, 1978)—previously not customary in a private audience with a minister—showed that the Pope wanted to signal to Eastern Europe in this way. For the Communists, above all the Soviet, the election of a Pole as Pope had been just as great a shock as it was grounds for erroneous expectations in many Western observers. The beacon that Poland's powerful Catholicism could send out through this Pope (which might even be "ideologically destabilizing") could have a frustrating and inhibiting effect on Communist church policies—especially since Pope John Paul II, even more strongly than his predecessors, accentuated humanitarianism and human rights (in the sense of a Christian personalism). But Vatican pastoral diplomacy as such could not be negatively affected by this: for its goals remained centered on the "practical"—that is, assuring the existence of the church—and sought points of contact in the realism which also motivated atheistic politicians to take religion into account as a permanent factor. This was often not understood since the Vatican, at the beginning of the 60's, began to follow the international political trend of East-West detente, after having followed the cold war trend in the 50's. Many misunderstandings were fostered by different interpretations of the Second Vatican Council, which opened the Catholic church to the "modern world" but simultaneously also exposed its long-smoldering crisis of creed and discipline. The reforms and renovations which arose from the Council were thus accompanied by "conservative" attempts to return to the lines of proven church diplomacy and above all to introduce security measures where, as it turned out, religious substance, in spite of—or indeed because of—all attack from outside, had remained almost devoid of crisis: in the atheist-governed East.

II

Lenin had believed that religion could only exist in connection and symbiosis with a particular social system, feudal or capitalist; if the system fell, then religion—with only a little push—would collapse of itself. This supposition, however, was not realized, even where—as in the Soviet Union—the Orthodox church as a "cult church" had seemed to be little capable of resistance; even in its sphere of influence it turned out "that religion is very vital, and has a tenacious hold in the consciousness of millions of people," as Okulov, the Soviet sociologist of religion, admitted at a scientific conference in June 1965.[2] One reason for this was that "unresolved individual conflicts and personal problems (sorrow, misfortune, illness, loneliness) continue to exist as possible sources of religion," as East German sociologist Olof Klohr stated at the same conference. But another reason was that the separation of church and state, as the Russian revolution pretended to put it into practice 130 years after the French revolution, resulted in the opposite: the revolutionaries elevated their atheism to a state ideology. Because Lenin, Stalin and their successors could only conceive of religion as a social evil which—like prostitution—could be pragmatically or tactically tolerated, they remained incapable of debating it intellectually, much less exposing it to a quiet and dangerous process of secularization. While they morally despise the western "consumer society," at the same time making it a goal of their own economic plans (without actually being able to satisfy the most basic needs in goods and freedoms)—religion remains the "sigh of the oppressed creature" (Marx).

Signs of a remarkable revival of religiousness, becoming increasingly visible since the mid-seventies in the Soviet Union, led, primarily among the followers of the Orthodox church, to the question of whether an illegal religious catacomb existence would not be preferable to a legal existence controlled, discriminated and discredited by collaboration. The writer Alexander Solzhenitsyn, in a 1972 letter to Moscow Patriarch Pimen, became a spokesman for such reflections. Hadn't Patriarch Tikhon, after the October revolution, refused any accommodation and assumed an uncompromising position?

Catholic church historian Johannes Chrysostomus (OSB), a Russian who grew up in the Soviet Union and now lives in the West, has pointed out that it was precisely Patriarch Tikhon who—without losing the confidence of the believers—introduced an understanding with the Soviet government, as soon as he recognized that his church was threatened with total destruction if it refused the offered minimum level of existence.[3] Every act of resistance by the Orthodox church, as Chrysostomus demonstrates, resulted immediately in massive closings of churches. Any church authorities who would accept this simply to preserve their attitude of protest would be "robbing the congregation entrusted to them of the protective walls of the church and exposing it to plunder, to the 'wolves and thieves' " (thus the opposition priests Esliman and Jakunin). For the overwhelming majority of the faithful, "only one thing [was] important: that in the closest church still existing, the divine service is carried out in its customary order. . . . Here, however, this is only possible under the one indispensable condition, that there is a *legal church organization*," wrote opposition priest Sergei Zeludkov to Solzhenitsyn in 1973. Zeludkov defended accommodation as the natural "attitude of a living organism," without denying the "great mystical significance" of martyrdom, which however was not to be expected of the simple believer.[4] (See also documentary appendix no. 9.)

It was not least such considerations that encouraged Vatican eastern policy not to make unpromising "intellectual approaches" to the Communists, but rather to try to secure, to save, or to reconstruct those ecclesiastical *structures* that were or still are endangered or threatened with destruction. Certainly, for the Vatican it remains incomparably more difficult than for western states to draw a sharp line between *ideological* and *practical* coexistence (i.e., the existence of the church within the Communist state). A regulated situation can never arise only between the Vatican dwarf state and a Communist government. Since the Catholic church is supra-national, but at the same time exists within concrete states, Vatican policy also always affects domestic affairs of the countries with which it attempts to reach agreements. This complicates its relationship with mistrustful partners insistent on their own sovereignty.

III

Papal eastern diplomacy or "policy"—seen as a technical means, as the art of the possible—follows, as we shall see, the same basic pattern which underlies all international intercourse: defense of one's own interests through *confrontation* where coexistence is impossible, through *compromises* where they seem to be tolerable, through *cooperation* where there are partners for it. Like every policy, it oscillates between allegiance to principles and expediency, and—often with no alternative—is entangled in national and ideological contradictions. A strange mixture of worldliness (*per saecula saeculorum*) and priestly unworldliness characterizes its relative breadth—and narrowness. Its active anti-Communism was never an end in itself but a reaction to the situation. "Its attitude has always hardened only to the degree that its hopes for possible agreement were destroyed," I was told by Professor Federico Alessandrini, longtime anti-Communist commentator for the *Osservatore Romano*. I also asked Alessandrini whether the Holy See, which (as this book shows) had Eugenio Pacelli negotiate with the Soviets over a long period in the 20's, and then concluded concordats with Mussolini and Hitler, would also have signed an agreement with Stalin if he had ever been willing to do so. Alessandrini's answer: "I believe so. Do not forget that the Holy See finally agreed on a concordat even with the French Revolution!"[5]

In this way, the Popes of this century from Benedict XV to John Paul II have always oriented themselves to the contemporary situation and tried to exploit it for the church in the East: the Russian famine, the German Rapallo policy, Hitler's anti-Communism, Stalin's defeats and victories, the various phases of the Cold War and detente politics—from Kennedy to Carter, from Khrushchev to Brezhnev. They have negotiated with Lenin and Stalin, made demands and offered concessions, written to Khrushchev, received Podgorny, Kadar, Gierek and Tito, talked, kept silent, fought, prayed and sometimes reached a *modus vivendi*. They were all neither "reactionaries" nor "progressives," but very human, strategically cautious, sometimes clear-sighted, often erring pastoral politicians.

Such behavior can be presented historically only by also touching the so-called "sore points" and not avoiding taboos. For it would be the end of any historiography if indulgence were to rank before truth, as a cardinal once recommended to a church historian.[6] Political and human tragedies, too, may not be excluded—for instance, that of the Jesuit d'Herbigny and his unfortunate attempts with secret bishops, or the fates of Bishops Profittlich and Schubert, Cardinals Mindszenty and Slipyj. The papal church is also paying today for earlier errors; its eastern policy is "in a certain sense an homage to those who, by their loyalty, made it possible for the church to survive, and who have thereby convinced others to resume a dialogue with it"—thus did Casaroli, the Vatican's "foreign minister," formulate it; to which one must note that—pastorally speaking—many of these faithful were sacrificed needlessly. The metaphysical significance of a martyrdom did not replace priests and bishops for the faithful.

The unsuccessful chapters of the "old" eastern policy in particular show why there is no other choice for the "new"—which often must begin from the ashes— than to rebuild on renewed attempts at negotiations, as well as through concessions, institutional assurances. Today it is doing this with no crusade ideology and no visions of ideological coexistence (both of which are in any case much farther from its mind than many in the East desire or in the West fear.) It has also given up that narrow sense of "Catholic" which for much too long was aimed only at "conversion of schismatics" in the East. Today the recognition has grown that even a very relative freedom for other Christian churches is an asset that must be protected; for the security of the existence of "religion as such" (a concept with which Protestant American diplomats were alarming Vatican diplomats as late as 1941!) increasingly ranks before confessional positions and theological dogmatism—at least in the East.

Such an eastern policy can no longer regard "religious freedom" as isolated; for religious existence is hardly practicable without assurances for human existence, without a minimum of civil rights and liberties, of tolerance (not concordance), of coexistence between politically hostile states as well. And therefore the Vatican's attempt to have a voice, to participate, wherever international peace efforts are in motion, where the great powers sit down to negotiate. Only to the degree that the latter make progress can Vatican eastern policy also count on progressing. It immediately enters a phase of difficulties when—as it appeared in 1979—the relationship between Moscow and Washington, between East and West, becomes more complicated. (Cf. Casaroli's and Silvestrini's speeches in the documentary appendix no. 7 and 8, confirmed by Pope John Paul II on January 12, 1979.)

IV

Cardinal Casaroli, for many years the Vatican's most prominent diplomat, rejected as "unjust, indeed almost calumnious," the suspicion that the Vatican was striving for agreements with Communist states "at any price."[7] He sees the risks, and also the difficulty, in "applying the principle of choice of the lesser evil to the individual case." With a "wisdom that remains open to venture," Casaroli set priorities according to papal instructions: the primary goal is freedom for religious life, but "it would not be wise to reject what is possible today [i.e., partial steps], provided that this is no hindrance to the final goal. . . . The policy of 'all or nothing,' or 'now or never,' cannot be morally defended even in emergencies. . . . There can be standstills and setbacks. . . . In the short run, no comprehensive results may be reached, but dialogue complies with what seems to be the course of history—determined for Christians by Providence. . . . The action is designed for the long run, and there is no alternative to it."[8] Nor was there one for a Pope from Poland.

But are "structures," bishops for example, really so important? It is for theologians, not historians, to analyze this concept critically. Still, it may be useful to the understanding of this book to sketch briefly the theological guidelines of all papal policy confirmed by John Paul II.[9]

"Salus animarum suprema lex"—salvation of the individual soul as the supreme law—remained for the Roman Catholic church, even after Vatican Council II, a purpose that transcends all history. The Catholic church will not be a "slave of historicism," neither in the sense of identification with the *Zeitgeist* nor as a resistance movement. Also, its biblical charge to be "leaven," and thus to contribute to the humanization of the world, ultimately serves the eschatological purpose and, as long as the earth exists, is "disturbed by sin." The church is not bound to any political or social system, but, as a "sign of the transcendence of the human person," it intercedes in all systems for human rights—above all for religious freedom. According to Catholic doctrine, the church can fulfill its mission only as a "*visible* community," as a "society constituted and ordered in this world": the dispensation of the sacraments necessary for salvation is reserved to ordained priests only (except for baptism in emergency cases); but the continuity of the priesthood is assured only within a hierarchy whose "keystones" are bishops. Therefore: without a Pope, no bishops, without bishops no priests, without priests no sacraments, without them no eternal salvation. The installation of bishops is therefore "indispensable for the survival of the church, at least in the long run" (Casaroli). It must therefore be the duty of the Vatican, as central "government" of a church active all over the world as an "organically structured society," "to create the possibility of its own survival through dignified and loyal relations with the established powers, and to contribute to the general welfare in the confident expectation that the seed of Christianity will bear the fruit of freedom for all mankind." (Thus the Archbishop of Florence, Cardinal Giovanni Benelli, who as a longtime "sostituto" [undersecretary] in the Vatican Secretariat of State was often erroneously viewed as an opponent of Casaroli.)

From the point of view of a non-Catholic church concept, such argumentation is certainly questionable. Protestant free churches, e.g., which can do without "structures," can survive under the rule of state atheism with no relationship with the "powers that be"; however, as soon as their existence becomes evident to the state organs, they are all the more defenselessly exposed to attack. But, where adherents and priests live in diaspora (especially in the Soviet Union), the pressure burdening the official churches—the Catholic as well as the Orthodox—has awakened a certain nostalgia for the "primeval church"; behind this, unconsciously, lies the church concept of the Reformation. Such tendencies, however (which are also unconsciously oriented toward religious-socialist community models), should not be overestimated. All known experience shows that "success" or "failure" of a church-state *modus vivendi* is viewed critically only by those believers who think primarily in political categories (and thus view the church as a basis for resistance or collaboration). But for their private religious life too, the decisive element is ultimately whether access to the sacraments and liturgy remains open to them. According to Catholic doctrine, even a subjectively unworthy but validly ordained priest can exercise this function. In the frontier situation into which religious existence is often driven by state atheism, such a formal legitimization becomes an objective asset.

The Christian catacomb church existed historically in an epoch when this church—statistically—was no more than a small Jewish sect in the great Roman Empire. In such circumstances, it was viable. But catacombs are no religious home for the masses—at least not for Roman Catholics. That is why militant state atheism has always tried first and foremost to destroy or limit the *visible* structure of the Catholic church. Eastern European Stalinists, in particular, have understood the structure of the papal church better in this regard than many (rightist or leftist) Catholics. The latter, of course, forgot their "spiritual" church concept when they wanted to mobilize their church—in the East or the West—for very tangible interests: for political collaboration or opposition. . . .[10]

V

The theme of this book is *not* the history of the Catholic church in Communist countries; that is reflected here only to the degree to which it is necessary for understanding and for background to Vatican policy in Eastern Europe. It is just as little concerned with presenting an exhaustive study of the church policies of Communist governments. (It must be observed that these policies were strongly centralized by Moscow in the fifties, gained greater national latitude in the sixties and seventies, and today their guiding principles are discussed and coordinated in annual conferences of the directors of all church offices of the Warsaw Pact States.)

Like any work of contemporary history, this book must remain fragmentary until all the archives are opened. I am indebted to the helpful accommodation of many institutions and persons in West and East in allowing me to utilize many unknown or little developed sources, above all for the period 1917-1945. They are named in the notes and bibliography; sometimes, for obvious reasons, they could not be named. I should mention here in first place the Political Archive of the Foreign Office in Bonn, the Bavarian and Austrian State Archives, the Archives of various orders in Rome, as well as the Archive of the Vatican Secretariat of State, whose documents from this century are not yet open to research but which gave me oral answers to essential questions concerning the twenties and the ability to corroborate documents from other sources. Without the laborious and distinguished work of Robert A. Graham, Angelo Martini, Pierre Blet and Burkhardt Schneider (who died all too prematurely), who have published nine volumes to date of the "Papers and Documents of the Holy See on World War II," the period 1939-45 could not have been presented. These volumes have been systematically utilized here for the first time on the theme of "Eastern policy."

My journalistic experience—thirteen years in Eastern Europe, more than nine years in Rome—has been very helpful to me as a historian.[11] Many documents and much information have only come to light thanks to this professional "combination"; I hope that it also contributes to the readability of this book. Wherever it appears too "journalistic" to the scholarly reader, please bear in mind that even the apparently unimportant "colorful" and atmospheric details are researched and documented. Errors and inaccuracies called to my attention by reviewers of the German edition have been corrected.

And not least I have to thank the translator, Sandra Smith, the Director of Ohio University Press, Patricia G. Elisar, and copy editor Thomas DeWitt, without whose painstaking and sensitive work this updated English edition of my book would not have been possible.

Rome, November 1979

I

Misunderstandings: Missionaries to Revolutionary Russia, 1917-1922

Hopes for Conversion—to "Opium"?

The Bolshevik Revolution seemed to hold its breath. On May 30 of 1918, a strange procession of several thousand people was moving down the Nevski Prospect, the grand boulevard of Petrograd (soon to bear Lenin's name). They were not singing political songs, but rather hymns, and the flags glowing in the spring sunshine were not red, but embroidered in gold with crosses and madonnas. Hardly seven months after the October revolution, which Orthodox Patriarch Tikhon had damned, on January 19, 1918, as "the work of Satan," the capital of the victorious proletariat was experiencing the first—and to date the last—public Corpus Christi procession of the Roman Catholic church in the history of Russia.[1]

The gazes of tens of thousands of astonished but respectful spectators were turned to the Archbishop, the Baltic Baron Eduard von der Ropp, who was carrying the monstrance with the consecrated host past Communist placards. Beside him under the canopy strode his Polish Suffragan Bishop Jan Cieplak, and—for the first time in company with Catholics of the Latin rite—the Russian Exarch Leonid Feodorov, leader of the small congregation of the Eastern Rite, which had ties with Rome. Under the czars, they had all been victims of discrimination and exile. Had a new hour of freedom arrived for them—now that Lenin, who professed himself "a resolute enemy of all religion," had with his decree on the separation of church and state also cut the bonds between throne and altar and deprived the intolerant state religion of its power? As the procession reached the Liteiny Bridge over the Neva, the bells of even the Orthodox churches began to ring.

What hopes and misunderstandings this scene reflects; what appears to be the beginning of a self-deception, was actually the end of an illusion which had a long history in the Vatican, the center of the Roman church. As an enthusiastic French missionary had written as early as 1879: "The revolution will open the gates of Russia to the church. . . . The Russian colossus is moving toward collapse. We must be prepared. On the field swept clean by revolutionary storms, we will erect the true cross."[2]

From the viewpoint of Vatican diplomacy, of course, this would never seem quite so simple. To be sure, on the one hand papal policy toward Russia had always been aimed at a "conversion" of Russia—that is, at overcoming the schism to Rome's advantage—and this meant conflict with the Caesaropapism of St. Petersburg. On the other hand, however, this Russian policy could not be separated from the papacy's great apprehension about the liberal and social-revolutionary movements of the 19th century, those "monstrous errors" among which Pius IX had specifically numbered Communism in 1846 (encyclical "*Qui Pluribus*"). This was two years before Marx and Engels had begun their "Communist Manifesto" with the words:

> "A spectre is haunting Europe—the spectre of Communism. All the powers of old Europe have united into a holy alliance to exorcise this spectre: the Pope and the Czar. . . ."

The first meeting between a Pope and a ruler of Russia had occurred in December 1845 (between Nicholas I and Gregory XVI). A concordat between St. Petersburg and Rome even materialized, somewhat laboriously, two years later. But this had all vanished again within twenty years. The Poles, since the division of their nation the majority of the Czar's Catholic subjects, revolted against his rule in 1863. Although the Pope—vainly—instructed the Polish revolutionaries to respect "authority established by God," the Czar nevertheless renewed his discrimination against the Catholics. Monasteries were dissolved, church property confiscated, acquisition of land forbidden to Catholics, and conversion from the Orthodox to another confession was even made punishable. In 1866, Russia withdrew her ambassador to Rome; in 1867, the Catholic church administration in Russia was subordinated to a "Spiritual Council," which was controlled by a "Department for Foreign Confessions" within the St. Petersburg Ministry of the Interior—actually by the Czar's Secret Police. In this year, 1867—exactly fifty years before the October Revolution—the

Pope appealed for prayers for the "persecuted church in Russia" (encyclical "*Levate*").

Had the united "holy alliance" against Communism, denounced by Marx and Engels, already collapsed? In the papal "Syllabus" of 1864, Communism, along with Liberalism, Socialism, Freemasonry and Bible societies, figured among the "pestilences" of the day. This almost medical description, conversely, corresponded to the Communist view of religion: Marx wrote in 1843, in the introduction to his critique of Hegel's Philosophy of Law, that religion was "the groans of oppressed creatures, the soul of a heartless world" and the "spirit of spiritless conditions," an "opium of the people"—thus clearly a medicine for human suffering: A narcotic, and not a cure. For the Russian Marxist Lenin, who not only wanted to theorize but also to engage in politics, religion of course also constituted a theoretical error, but, more importantly, was an obstructive social narcotic. He saw in religion primarily the Orthodox state church, which supported the autocratic regime. Lenin and his friends were as little concerned with the enmity of the Russian Orthodox Church toward Rome as with the Popes' mistrust toward Russia; one didn't have to be a Marxist to realize that their common conservative interests would always build new bridges across their differences.

This was proven again in 1905, during the first attempted Russian revolution, which was violently quelled in St. Petersburg. It began with a workers' demonstration led by the Orthodox priest Gapon (an *agent provocateur* for the police, as it later turned out). With a sure feeling for the discord which thereupon threatened to arise between Czar and Orthodoxy, Pope Pius X, in a pastoral letter to the (Polish) Catholics in the Russian empire, recommended that they were to "stand on the side of order," should not join the "pernicious sect" of the Socialists, and have no contact whatsoever with "parties of crazy people" (encyclical "*Poloniae Populorum*"). The Czar rewarded the gesture from Rome with a decree of tolerance, which for the first time curtailed the privilege of the state church, granted more rights to the Catholics, and even allowed a change of confession.

However, hardly had such relief been granted—which could also be interpreted as a weakness on the part of the Czar—than hopes for "conversion" stirred again in Rome, as did the manifold ethnic diversities within Russia herself, which had been hidden under the cloak of religion.

The pro-Polish Archbishop of Vilna, Baron von der Ropp,[3] who was faced with a rebellion of Lithuanian Catholics, was relieved of his office in 1907 by the Russian government, without protest from the Pope. But at the same time, Archbishop Andreas Count Sheptyckyi of Lemberg[4] (Metropolitan of the Uniates, the Rome-affiliated Ukrainian Catholics of the Eastern Rite) undertook two journeys to Russia under an assumed name to ascertain the political climate and the prospects for missionary work. In 1908 he reported in Rome. Although the Pope was negotiating again with the Czar at the time, he secretly conferred full powers upon Sheptyckyi to be prepared for a future "count-down" in Russia—a two-track diplomacy that would often encumber the Eastern policies of the Popes in decades to come.

Sheptyckyi's secret instructions, which were not very precise, would not become topical until the end of the First World War, when not only the "schismatic" Czarist empire but also the loyal Catholic Austro-Hungarian empire (of which Sheptyckyi was a citizen) collapsed, and the Archbishop himself was freed from Siberian internment. With circuitous tactics, he had approached both the Kaiser in Vienna and the Czar in St. Petersburg, always with his double goal in mind: the catholicization of Russia, and the establishment of an independent Catholic nation of the Ukraine. Due to historical misfortune, but also through his own overzealousness, the Metropolitan repeatedly failed to attain his goals. In 1918, he and his Ukrainian-Catholic Archbishopric landed in the new Polish republic, which was as ill-disposed toward the Ukrainians as toward the Russians.

The figure of the Metropolitan Sheptyckyi, whose almost quixotic life will be featured frequently in this book, symbolically embodies that knot of national and religious frustrations that has repeatedly embarrassed papal policy toward the East; especially because after the First World War the map of Europe was radically altered in ways that none of the countries concerned could accept. The old idea of the union of churches, the re-unification of the "western" and the "eastern" churches, thereby became proportionately more complicated as it seemed to become a topic of great interest again. The question of the religious ritual—Latin or Slavic—which for Rome could actually only have technical missionary significance, played a more and more important and confusing role because in this question national resentments clothed themselves in religious colors.

"Revolution in Russia"—from Rome's viewpoint that certainly meant all kinds of possibilities, but it was by no means clear how to take advantage of them. Should the Vatican commit itself to the new Catholic Poland—and thus immediately come into conflict with the new Catholic Lithuania, and also with the new Russia, where after the February Revolution of 1917, Kerenski's Social-Liberal government temporarily held out the prospect of greater freedoms for Catholics? On the other hand: wouldn't a settlement with Russia disturb Rome's relationship with the new Poland *and* with the Ukraine? Consideration of Sheptyckyi's Ukrainian desires, on the contrary, would have annoyed both Poles *and* Russians. ·

The particular dilemma in which the Vatican found itself was only mitigated by the fact that it was very difficult in general to draw a clear picture of the situation in Eastern Europe; it was nowhere near clarified by the middle of 1917, when Kerenski's government wanted to establish relations with the Holy See. Nor was the World War over yet.

In Petrograd—as the former St. Petersburg was now called—by April 1917 not only had Lenin arrived (the German government had sped him from his Swiss exile to Russia in order to increase her war-weariness by continued revolutionary activity), but also the Lemberg Metropolitan Sheptyckyi appeared in the capitol at this time and, calling upon his papal authorization from 1907, established his "disciple" Leonid Feodorov[5] as Exarch of the small converted congregation of the Eastern rite. It counted hardly a hundred members, but was comprised mostly of prominent intellectuals and was regarded by Sheptyckyi as the nucleus of future Catholic expansion in Russia, which he considered hopeless under the Latin rite. At the same time, however, Baron von der Ropp, who had been removed by the Czar, also appeared in Petrograd as Bishop of Mogilev with a mandate from Rome to shepherd the 1.6 million Catholics of the *Latin* rite (primarily Poles living in Russia). While the Kerenski government regarded with some suspicion the Russian-Catholic Feodorov, who before the war had studied in Italy under an assumed name, they favored the "Latin" Catholics, and in the summer of 1917 came to an agreement with Archbishop Ropp which seemed to assure the formation of five dioceses (Mogilev, Minsk, Kamieniec, Zhitomir, and Tiraspol) with 600 priests for about 600 churches. Even the Jesuits, exiled from Russia, could dare to be seen again. The "separation of church and state" which was on the Kerenski program—although little was accomplished in that direction—disquieted the Orthodox church; however, it held out hope for the Catholics.

And nothing changed at first, as Lenin's October revolution undertook a radically antireligious course. "In the attitude of the Bolsheviks toward the Catholic church, there was not only tolerance, but even a certain preference—if one can call it that—in comparison to their attitude toward the Orthodox priesthood, which they persecuted." This was reported four years later by a theologian who taught at the Petrograd Ecclesiastical Academy.[6] He explained this peculiarity by the fact that "in the Catholic clergy the Bolsheviks saw victims of the earlier czarist regime"; and "six Catholic priests had been martyred in various rebellions."

Still, as early as 1905, Lenin had recommended caution, especially in regard to "Catholic workers"; an alliance "between Jesuits and proletariat" had to be opposed, "not with police methods, of course." In his essay "Socialism and Religion" (1905), Lenin demanded that religion should be "a private matter as far as the *state* is concerned; however, we can by no means view it as a private matter in regard to our own *party*." But what if the state party—following the Russian tradition of a state religion—should elevate its ideological monopoly to the level of a new "state religion"? Would then the separation of church and state as Lenin foresaw it in 1905 really mean that "the religious fog would be fought with purely intellectual, and *only* intellectual, weapons, that is, with the press, with words"?[7] Lenin later boasted that, as a "by-product" of the revolution, he had achieved the separation of church and state that the "petty bourgeois democracy" had only talked about. However, the corresponding "Decree of the Council of People's Commissaries" of Jan. 23, 1918, which has remained in force to this day, made clear how important an ideological opponent Lenin considered the churches, and how determined he was to oppose them not only "intellectually," but with state administrative measures as well.

"Freedom to embrace any religion whatever, or even none at all," was of course guaranteed (§ 3), also freedom of worship "as long as it does not disturb public order" (§ 5); however, religious instruction was forbidden, not only in the schools, but also, practically speaking, in the churches. "Citizens may teach and study their religions in private" (§ 9). Not only were the churches deprived of any state support, they were not even allowed to demand any contributions from their members (§ 11); indeed, they were deprived of all material foundation:

> "No church or religious community has a right to possessions or property. They do not possess the rights of legal persons." This was true not only for landed property; "buildings and objects which specifically serve religious worship" were also ceded to religious communities only by special governmental decrees "for use without charge" (§§ 12 and 13).[8]

"Come to your senses, you madmen! Stop your bloodbaths! What you are doing is the work of Satan, which will earn you eternal fire after death and the terrible curse of coming generations!" With such words the Orthodox Patriarch Tikhon had already flung anathema against the new rulers of Russia four days before Lenin's religious decree.[9] The Catholic Archbishop von der Ropp, however, behaved quite differently: he avoided any vehement public utterances against the decree, and even remained silent when at the end of April 1918 all religious instruction—even private—was forbidden "for persons under 18 years of age."[10] As yet, Catholic church life hardly seemed to be affected by the decree; the main blow was to the old state church. The Catholics did not really wake up until the 24th of August, 1918, when the People's Commissariat of Justice issued a regulation whereby the right to use (nationalized) church buildings and objects of worship could only be obtained by a contract between a congregation of "at least twenty faithful (*dvatchatka*)" and the local soviet, after this congregation had produced an appropriate inventory.

Such a demand contradicted all precepts of Catholic canon law. Von der Ropp protested in a sharply-worded, but unpublished, letter to Moscow. But the fact that the religious department of the Commissariat of Justice invited Ropp to Moscow for "consultation" about the decrees led him to believe that the dictatorship was not completely master of the situation. Perhaps the Bolshevik rule was only a revolutionary episode? Therefore Ropp avoided any violent confrontation and tried to bring his church safely through the confused course of events by means of caution and shrewdness.[11] Anyway, everything still seemed to be in a state of flux: Lenin, against intense resistance in his own camp and against the opposition of the Orthodox church, had forced through the peace treaty with Germany in Brest-Litovsk. However, having escaped the World War, Russia was now being swept into the whirlpool of civil war, which the other powers did not watch idly. So it seemed that everything was still open; no door should be closed.

The untroubled and unmolested Corpus Christi procession at the end of May, 1918, with which Archbishop Ropp and his Catholics demonstrated both their desire for religious survival and also their relative freedom, must be seen against this background. This flexible attitude also conformed with the policy of the Vatican and its representatives, which it now sent to the center of events.

On Outpost Duty: Ratti and Pacelli

The two key diplomatic figures that Pope Benedict XV sent to revolutionary central and eastern Europe both followed him into office: Achille Ratti, later Pius XI, and Eugenio Pacelli, later Pius XII. They determined almost forty years of Vatican policy toward the East. General opinion is that both were confronted so drastically at that time by the "revolutionaries" that their implacable attitude against Communism was formed for all time. But historical documents paint a different picture.

Slender, pale, with the majestic carriage of a Renaissance prince, which surely also concealed certain insecurities—this was the picture in 1917 of 41-year-old Eugenio Pacelli, papal nuncio in Munich and later in Berlin. His efforts on the Pope's behalf to negotiate a prompt peace treaty remained unsuccessful. Kaiser Wilhelm had told him ominously that the "Red International would fill the vacuum" if the World War did not end soon;[12] for Pacelli, this was soon no longer only a theoretical certainty. He could observe much of it from the windows of his nunciature at 15 Brienner St. in Munich.

Kurt Eisner, leader of the revolutionary-socialist majority government in Bavaria, had courteously notified the Vatican of his accession to power. However, the nuncio, on orders from Rome, soon had to retreat to Rorschach, in Switzerland, because machine gun fire had been whistling around his head. After the assassination of Eisner, a "Soviet Republic" was acclaimed in Munich; it replied proudly to a congratulatory telegram from Lenin, who misunderstood the very un-Leninistic "Schwabing" constituent of this anarchistic-romantic adventure. The socialist government, which had fled to Bamberg, published a declaration (*Bayerische Staatszeitung*, April 10, 1919)—in Italian, no less—that they regarded it as a "sacred duty" (*sacro dovere*) to guarantee the inviolability of the nuncio.

Pacelli returned to Munich. He was soon provided with a document from People's Delegate for Foreign Affairs Dietrich, which assured him of the "protection of the *Räteregierung* [Soviet-like government]." But that didn't help much.

On the afternoon of April 21, the "Red Guard"—heavily armed, half-uniformed soldiers and sailors—broke into the nunciature. Although the nuncio showed his "letter of protection," an officer named Pongratz put a pistol to his chest. What was it all about? The Red Guards wanted nothing less than: the nuncio's big Daimler-Benz automobile. When Pacelli telephoned the Ministry of War to protest, a chaotic reply came over the line that "they would shoot down the nunciature and everybody in it." Finally the nuncio had his servant open the garage. The climax of the farce: the luxury convertible wouldn't start. The "revolutionaries" didn't tow it away until the next day, only to return it meekly a few days later.[13]

Could this Bavarian-style "comedy" form Pacelli's whole image of Communism? Germany's Catholic press dramatized the incident into a confrontation with "Godless Bolshevism"—to the great displeasure of the nunciature, as is shown by documents in the Bavarian Secret State Archives. Pacelli's representative, Monsignore Scioppa, assured the Bavarian envoy to the Holy See that the occurrence had had "no antireligious nature." And Pacelli himself made light of the affair, as the envoy reported:[14]

> "Nevertheless, Mons. Pacelli is not at all put out, because he is intelligent enough to realize that under the existing conditions, proper attention is not being paid to diplomatic amenities."

As we shall see, Pacelli would need such patience and good spirits in the years to come, when he became the Vatican's most important intermediary with the Soviet Communists.

The second key figure that Pope Benedict XV sent to the "revolutionary" parts of Europe, Achille Ratti, was made from a different mold, although he was just as relaxed in dramatic moments. Let us sketch his initial experiences here; they were also the first contacts between the Vatican and Lenin's Russia.

More a scholar than a politician, with not much experience of the world, Ratti assumed his post as apostolic delegate in Warsaw on May 29, 1918. Ratti, who held three doctorates, had previously distinguished himself less by diplomatic talent than by scholastic zeal as Prefect of the Vatican Library. Now—at the age of 61—he was placed into a completely different world, one shaken by the fever of radical transformation. He was the Vatican's representative not only for the New Poland, but also for all regions previously part of the Czarist empire—from Lithuania to Siberia. From the beginning, he was particularly oriented toward Russia. "My greatest joy would be to shed my blood for Russia," he wrote somewhat overenthusiastically to Benedict XV.[15] To be sure, he probably never met Lenin—as he once apparently claimed[16]—but he certainly had direct contact with him by telegraph. The Pope, who needed Ratti as a diplomatic representative and not as a martyr, forbade his trip to Russia, because the Russian limitations on his route were unacceptable. Nevertheless, Ratti soon became active in this direction. In the summer of 1918, he made a vain appeal to the Soviets for the release of the Czarina and her daughters; soon thereafter, by telegraph, he pleaded for the life of Grand Duke George.

These and other humanitarian actions—Ratti's "eastern contacts," as we would say today, in general—did not make his position in Warsaw any easier. Hatred toward anything Russian was perhaps even stronger here than antipathy toward Communism. Warsaw had also not forgotten that the Vatican, two years earlier, had considered the idea of an independent Poland "unrealistic,"[17] and people knew that the papal Cardinal Secretary of State not only deplored as immoral the Versailles Treaty, to which Poland owed so much, but that he even regarded as silly[18] the overall Polish policy, which now came into conflict with both Russia *and* Germany (in Upper Silesia). Thus, no matter how honorably Ratti attempted to prove himself a friend of Poland, political Warsaw, and particularly the anticlerical and national-democratic factions, increasingly gave him the cold shoulder, and at the end of 1920, after Ratti's neutrality had come into question in the Upper Silesian plebiscite, they forced his inglorious departure. This left a long-lingering bitterness in him.

A Polish priest who was close to the nuncio later pleaded[19] that he had not been scorned by the true Warsaw, but rather by the "dissolute, dancing 'Warszawka' that glowed with naked female bodies, bathed in champagne, flirted with every worthless Prussian or Muscovite (as long as he had a title)." Besides leftist agitators, Freemasons and Jews (!), Ratti had also been denounced, according to the priest, by that fine society whose salons, "populated by shamelessly dressed women," the nuncio had avoided. "Basically, these charming daughters of Eve were only trying to slander a man who had dared to ignore them," his contemporary biographer proclaimed. This was an allusion to rumors that claimed that the nuncio had been deterred from flight only by the plea of a woman of the high aristocracy when the Red army threatened Warsaw in July 1920. The terror spread by the Cossacks at that time as they neared the Vistula was described by Isaac Babel, who could scent the "fragrant fury of the Vatican" even in the biscuits he discovered in a plundered Polish rectory kitchen. In truth, it was not any transport of emotion that kept the nuncio in the Polish capital, but sober instructions from Rome: Ratti was to stay at his post so that even if the Bolsheviks occupied Warsaw, he could immediately establish contact with them.[20]

We have somewhat anticipated events here, because it was important to gain an impression of the two diplomats the Pope had sent to the "outposts." Ratti and Pacelli were both—despite their differing temperaments—thoroughly suited to introduce this phase of Vatican diplomacy, one of the most difficult in its history. Neither one possessed any practical recipe, no more than did the Vatican itself, which could not give them any unequivocal concepts, except one: to assure to Catholics the greatest possible measure of religious freedom in a world out of joint; perhaps even to win new terrain in areas apparently lost. To be sure, hope and trouble could not long stay in balance; every prospect for the future ran up against a historical novelty: militant atheism as state policy.

Papal Telegrams to Lenin and the "Ropp Case"

"One must proceed with extraordinary caution in the battle against religious prejudice. We do great harm if we injure religious feelings." Thus Lenin warned his comrades in the fall of 1918.[21] He had reason to do so, for zealots were becoming enraged. And it was just this that provided a pragmatic point of departure for Vatican diplomacy, which was feeling its way carefully. Humanely intended measures basically only had a chance if they were above suspicion of "counter-revolutionary" sympathies—unlike, for example, the telegrams on behalf of the Czar's family. A persecuted Catholic bishop, on the other hand, concerned the Vatican itself—the Soviet functionaries should be able to grasp that more easily.

Thus on Feb. 3, 1919, by Ratti's intercession, the first direct telegram from the center of the Roman church reached Lenin:

> "Pope Benedict XV has learned, with great sorrow, that Monsignore Ropp, archbishop of Mogilev, has been taken hostage by the Bolsheviks in Petrograd. He beseeches Mr. Lenin to order his immediate release. (Signed) Cardinal Gasparri."

And indeed, on Feb. 6, Lenin inquired of the Petrograd police: "Is it true that you have arrested the Mogilev Archbishop Ropp? Please inform me what conditions would be necessary for his release; this is a request from the Pope."[22] And Lenin promptly telegraphed back to the Pope:

"Upon receipt of your telegram, I requested information from Petrograd, which replied to me that Archbishop Ropp was never arrested, but rather his nephew Egon Resilevitch Ropp, a young man of 22, who was arrested for speculation, but was entrusted to Jamnsen Gobaret[?]. (Signed) Lenin."

It was unfortunate that the Vatican was relying upon a rumor in this first "summit contact." However, it proved to be an error only for a short time: two and a half months later, on April 19, Ropp actually was arrested—the same day that Józef Piłsudski, Poland's chief of state, undertook a *coup de main* against Vilna. Ropp was accused of collaboration with Poland.

Actually, however, it was Ropp's delaying, tactically evasive resistance against Lenin's church decrees that was more and more a thorn in the side of the Bolsheviks. Since December 1918, Ropp had called his clergy together regularly for conferences to discuss the defensive moves of the moment. Despite misgivings of many of the priests, based on canon law, he had arranged—with Rome's support—the creation of "Parish Committees" which, if the political pressure became too strong, could sign "contracts of utilization" of church property with the authorities. It was the only way to prevent the confiscation of altar vessels and the closing of churches. Ropp formed a Catholic "central committee" in Petrograd from representatives of these Parish Committees to act as partner in negotiations with the central authorities.

This clerical "soviet"-system, which seemed to fit the political vogue but was difficult to reconcile with canon law, still did not please the Soviets. They naturally sensed in this arrangement a clever attempt to circumvent one of the main goals of their religious legislation: the isolation of congregations (in groups of twenty) and the disappearance of "the" church as one legal person. This suspicion was certainly strengthened by the fact that the overwhelming majority of Roman Catholics in Russia was Polish, and that the Pope had just posted his representative for Russia in Warsaw. Another aggravating factor was the beginning of the Civil War and the open intervention of anti-Communist foreign countries which did not leave the Pope untouched. He could no longer avoid taking a position when, on Feb. 7, 1919, he received a telegram from the Orthodox Archbishops Sylvester and Benjamin, via the headquarters of "White" Admiral Kolchak (whose troops certainly fought no less cruelly than the "Red"):

Where the Bolsheviks reign, the Christian church is more cruelly persecuted than in the first three Christian centuries. They are violating nuns, they are proclaiming the socialization of women and allowing the most disorderly passions. Everywhere there is death, cold and hunger. . . . It is with deep sorrow, Reverend Father, that we inform you of the evils that millions of Russians of the True Russia are suffering. We hope to be able to count on your sympathy by force of human solidarity and Christian brotherhood. . . ."

Benedict XV telegraphed back that he "sympathized with all my heart with the troubles and fears" and prayed heaven that "peace and quiet will return to Russia as soon as possible." And on March 12 he had his Cardinal Secretary of State telegraph to the "Red" side—in French:

> To Lenin, Moscow. We have heard from reliable sources that your followers are persecuting servants of God, particularly those belonging to the Russian religion called Orthodox [!]. The Holy Father Benedict XV beseeches you to give strict orders that clergy of every religion be respected. Humanity and religion will be indebted to you. (Signed) Cardinal Gasparri."

Lenin's answer, in a telegram to Rome, also in French, from his People's Commissar for Foreign Affairs Georgiy Vassilyevich Chicherin, deserves to be reproduced in detail in spite of its prolixity. It shows very graphically the amalgamation of antireligious, confessional, political and national resentment that the Vatican's eastern policy has had to deal with from the beginning—and fundamentally until today.[23]

> "To Cardinal Gasparri, Rome. In receipt of your telegram of March 3, I am in a position to assure you that the reliable sources you mention are misleading you. After the separation of church and state was realized in Russia, religion has been regarded here as a private affair. It is absolutely wrong to speak of persecution of servants of religion. Nothing is happening in our country that compares with what was customary against the Orthodox where the Roman Catholic Church ruled. Since you show particular interest in the religion that, up until now, the Roman Catholic Church has branded heretical and schismatic and which you now qualify as Orthodox, I can assure you that no priest of this religion has had to suffer because of his religious convictions. We treat those who have conspired against the Soviet government and against the power of the workers and peasants just as we do other citizens. . . . You inform us that the head of the Roman Catholic Church beseeches us to alter our attitude toward the Orthodox clergy; such a sign of solidarity reaches us in the very moment when open and decisive action by the power of the people has exposed the betrayals with which the clergy deceived the masses, by basing its influence on lies. The gilded and bejeweled graves which contain what the clergy has called indestructible holy relics were opened, and there where relics of Tikhon of Sadonsk, Saint Mitrofan of Voronezh and others were supposed to be, were found dust-covered and mouldy bones, padding, materials and even ladies' stockings. I consider it necessary to point out that, although our actions in regard to the clergy right now have the misfortune of displeasing you, it is on the other hand regrettable that the uncounted atrocities our enemies are perpetrating upon the Russian people—by the governments of Kolchak, Denikin and Petlyura,[24] by the parties presently ruling in Poland, which have Catholic Archbishops among their leaders and which horribly torture those fighters for the cause of the people who fall into their hands, yes, who even

murdered our Red Cross mission in Poland[25]—that all this has called forth no protest from your side. The voice of humanity that our revolution is fighting for is not respected by those who consider themselves your followers; not a word has been heard from your mouth in favor of that voice. (Signed) People's Commissar for Foreign Affairs Chicherin."

Would the Vatican also be tempted to be so vehement? The Pope arranged to have this malicious telegram, which bore more resemblance to Lenin's writing than to that of his Foreign Minister (whom we will soon meet in more well-mannered dialogue), published in detail, along with all the other telegrams. The sole commentary added to it was:

ANNO CINQUANTANOVESIMO · · · MERCOLEDI' 2 APRILE 1919

La Santa Sede

è il Governo Massimalista russo

Avendo alcuni giornali accennato ad uno scambio di telegrammi fra la Segreteria di Stato di Sua Santità ed il Governo Massimalista di Russia, ed anche riprodottili in parte, crediamo opportuno di pubblicare il testo dei detti documenti.

In seguito a comunicazione del Rev.mo Visitatore Apostolico della Polonia, Monsignor Ratti, il quale partecipava l'avvenuto arresto, come ostaggio, dell'Arcivescovo di Mohilew, Monsignor Ropp, la Santa Sede si occupò subito del modo onde venire in aiuto del povero Arcivescovo, vecchio e malato. Dopo avere pertanto preso a tale scopo consiglio col Ministro di Russia presso la Santa Sede, Signor Lyssakowsky, l'E.mo Cardinale Gasparri, d'ordine di Sua Santità, in data 3 febbraio p. p. faceva pervenire, per mezzo di radiotelegramma, al Governo russo il seguente dispaccio:

Lenin

Moscou.

« Le Pape Benoit XV a appris avec une immense douleur que Monseigneur Ropp, Archevêque de Mohilew, a été pris comme otage à Petrograd par les Bolsceviks. Il prie instamment Mr. Lenin de vouloir bien donner des ordres, à fin qu'il soit mis aussitôt en liberté ».

Cardinale Gasparri.

A questo telegramma il Signor Lenin rispondeva col dispaccio seguente:

Cardinale Gasparri

Rôme.

« Après avoir reçu votre télégramme j'ai démandé explication de Petrograd on vient de me repondre que Archevêque Ropp n'a jamais été arrêté; c'est son neveu Aigon Resilewissch Ropp jeune homme 23 ans qui à été arrêté pour speculation mais il est affidé Jamusen Gobaret ». Lenin.

data 12 marzo p. p., faceva, a mezzo dello stesso E.mo Cardinale Segretario di Stato, pervenire al Signor Lenin il seguente telegramma:

Lenin

Moscou.

« De source serieuse on rapporte que vos partisans persecutent ministres de Dieu surtout ceux qui appartiennent a la religion russe appellée ortodoxe. Le Saint Père Benoit XV vous conjure donner des ordres sévères afin que ministres de n'emporte quelle religion scient réspectés. L'humanité et la religion Vous en seront reconnaissantes ».

Cardinal Gasparri.

A questo telegramma veniva risposto dal Ministro degli esteri del governo massimalista, signor Cicerin, nei termini seguenti:

Cardinal Gasparri

Rome.

« Ayant reçu votre radiotélégramme 12 Mars, je suis en mesure de vous assurer que la source serieuse mentionnée dans ce radiotélégramme vous a induit en erreur. La séparation de l'Eglise et de l'Etat ayant été accomplie en Russie, la religion y est traitée comme une affaire privée. Il est donc absolument faux de parler de persécution des ministres de la religion. Il ne se produit dans notre pays aucun fait analogue à ceux qui étaient la règle à l'égard des orthodoxes là où dominait l'Eglise Catholique que Romaine. Vu l'intérêt spécial dont vous faites preuve à l'égard de la religion que l'Eglise Romaine Catholique considerait jusqu'à présent comme schismatique et hérétique et que vous qualifiez comme orthodoxe, je puis vous garantir qu'aucun ministre de cette religion n'a souffert pour ses convictions religieuses et quant à ceux d'entre eux qui ont participé à des conspirations contre le Gouvernement soviétiste et contre le pouvoir des ouvriers et des paysans, nous avons procédé dans le traitement que nous leur avons infligé du point de vue qu'ils doivent être soumis aux mêmes lois que les autres citoyens et qu'aucune situation privilégiée par rapport aux laiques ne doit leur appartenir. Vu l'esprit de solidarité témoigné

"Mr. Chicherin's answer deserves to be read with the greatest caution in several respects—for example, where he claims that the Orthodox were persecuted by the Catholics, while the truth, as is well known, is just the opposite. But it is not our intention to carry on a controversy with Mr. Chicherin. . . ."

Benedict XV and his secretary of state had nothing to gain by an aggravation of the atmosphere. Especially after Archbishop Ropp's arrest, they did not want to cut all ties with the Bolsheviks. On the other side, Moscow also apparently had no desire to burn all its bridges, as was shown by an occurrence on May 25 which sounds almost unbelievable under the conditions of a "dictatorship of the proletariat" as we know it today: More than 10,000 Catholics marched in Petrograd from St. Catherine's Church to the headquarters of the "Cheka," the secret police, and demonstrated at the tops of their voices for the release of their Archbishop. Ropp was thereupon moved to Moscow, as a precaution, but held under house arrest there, in a rectory, not in prison. He was allowed to correspond with his representative Cieplak, and even with Ratti, the nuncio in Warsaw. Ratti tuned himself in to the discussions being conducted by the Polish and Russian Red Crosses about a large exchange of prisoners. However, Ropp's case could not be connected with this transaction, since he himself—with good reason—set great value on being considered a Russian, not a Polish, citizen. Foreign Commissar Chicherin, with whom Ratti exchanged several telegrams, finally suggested this solution to the nuncio, which would also allow Moscow to save face: at the Polish-Soviet border, which Ratti could reach only on foot, he delivered a note to the Soviets in which he designated the leader of the Catholics in Russia as: "a subject of the Pope (*suddito del Sommo Pontefice*), with whom the Soviet government is not in a state of war." This and the "friendly disposition of Mr. Chicherin" (as the *Osservatore Romano* praised it) sufficed to have Ropp freed on Nov. 17, 1919.[26] But where did he go? To Warsaw. . . .

Ropp entered the Polish capital "truly in triumph," as the Vatican newspaper reported. Not only the papal nuncio and the Warsaw archbishop, but also the military bishop and the commander of the city (!) had appeared at the train station to welcome him. They accompanied Ropp through a large crowd of people, many moved to tears. "He seemed to have aged; this appearance was also emphasized by his white beard, which he had to let grow long, according to Bolshevik custom—they like beards and long, uncut hair," so wrote the *Osservatore Romano* with unintentional humor.[27]

Although there was little reason for triumph, Archbishop Ropp soon continued his activities unabated from Warsaw. Above all, he tried to convince the nuncio, Ratti, and through him the Vatican, that the reign of the Bolsheviks could not continue much longer in Russia, and for that reason they could not—without endangering principles—make any delaying compromises. Ropp and the nunciature joined in, to this end, with the Polish-Russian peace discussions in 1920-21. after the "miracle on the Vistula" (cf. p. 20) had proven the apparent weakness of wartime Communism; Lenin's land of Soviets had survived the end of the civil war, but now, starving and bleeding to death, it appeared to be heading toward economic and political chaos.

Ropp was even hoping to return to Petrograd, and was also disseminating publicly his illusionary opinion that the great masses of Russians were more and more inclined toward Catholicism, toward recognition of the Roman Pope.[28] Although the Vatican did not succeed, in spite of Ropp's and Ratti's efforts and the help of Polish peace negotiators, in pushing through extensive demands, still they regarded it as a measure of success that Article 7 of the Polish-Russian peace treaty, signed in Riga on March 18, 1921, contained the following provision:

"Neither party to the treaty will interfere with the religious concerns of the other. Within both countries, the religious communities of national minorities will enjoy full freedom."

How this "freedom" would manifest itself in daily life was of course not defined. Ropp's representative in Russia, Archbishop Jan Cieplak, and his vicar general Konstanty Budkiewicz, recognized the unpromising reality. They reckoned with the possibility that the Soviet regime could be permanent, and were more inclined toward determined opposition than toward compromise. As early as the fall of 1919, Budkiewicz, who in this respect was even more inexorable than Cieplak, gave strict orders to the Catholic faithful: they were to refuse in every case—appealing to lack of permission from the Vatican—to sign any arrangement with the local authorities about church properties. Cieplak secretly organized the forbidden religious instruction for children, and even clandestine theological training.[29]

This was doubtless all known to the police, if only because the two Catholic dignitaries, who always affirmed their loyalty as citizens, at the same time made no secret of their ties to anti-Russian Poland. The secret police surely also knew that there were severe differences among the Catholics: Cieplak and Budkiewicz (with Ropp's support from Warsaw) adhered tenaciously to the Latin rite, and wanted at all costs to missionize with the help of the so-called "Biritualism," that is, that the eastern church rite would be kept only as an appendage, secondary to the Latin. In contrast, the Russian-Catholic Exarch Feodorov—following his teacher, the Lemberg Metropolitan Sheptyckyi—believed that any future hope lay only in a Russianized, "de-Polonized," Catholic church.[30] Although they were both under pressure from the regime, and they both finally were arraigned in court together (cf. p. 46), the two Catholic alignments battled with a macabre nationalistic zeal. Feodorov, whose Russian congregation consisted of only 100 members, had already vainly attempted in a letter, at the beginning of 1919, to arouse Lenin's political interest in Catholicizing the Orthodox. Feodorov described how useful the sympathies of a universal church could be for the prestige of Soviet Russia all over the world; he pleaded in a letter to the Pope "to make an end to all Polish interference in our affairs." Budkiewicz, however, complained to the Papal Nuncio in Warsaw that Feodorov, in his inclination toward the Russian, "goes so far as to give the sacrament, in his church, to schismatics who have not yet converted."[31]

The Bolsheviks at least had other problems at the moment. For them, of course, "all religions, no matter in what language they celebrate their rites, were counter-revolutionary,"[32] but Lenin recognized now that the revolution had over-exerted itself. At the tenth party congress, in March 1921, he changed its whole course with an ingenious stroke: the "New Economic Policy"—called the NEP—which was now proclaimed, signified a domestic as well as a foreign policy reorientation. The resumption of economic, but also political, relations with the capitalist world was now to be urged; it was to free Russia from her isolation, and prevent the total ruin of the country, especially the threatened famine. At the same time, socialization and collectivization in the interior was to be sharply slowed down, the dictatorship loosened. Would this also take effect in the area of religion?

Lenin criticized the May appeal of the Central Committee, which still demanded the "unmasking of the lies of religion": "This is tactically wrong. Especially at Easter, we must recommend one thing: not to unmask the lies, but whatever happens, to avoid any injury to religion." A new circular to the party shortly thereafter warned them "not to allow, under any circumstances, any occurrence that could injure the religious feelings of the masses."[33] Was this only a tactic, or also a more far-seeing strategy? To ascertain this, and also to take advantage of the smallest possibility if conditions were favorable, the Vatican opened a new phase of its Russian policy.

Secret Agreement with "Mental Reservations"

"I'm so hungry, that my hands and knees are trembling . . ." wrote Exarch Feodorov from Moscow.[34] Russia was starving; two million people starved in 1921-22. Consequences of the World and Civil Wars, drought, mismanagement and a bad harvest overshadowed everything political and ideological. It was now a question of simple survival. Hundreds of thousands were living on grass; according to well-authenticated reports, in many places the flesh of the dead was eaten. The poets Maxim Gorky and Gerhart Hauptmann, and polar explorer Fridtjof Nansen, called on the world for help. Orthodox Patriarch Tikhon of Moscow was allowed to apply to church leaders, even the Pope. Benedict XV had $50,000 remitted to Petrograd—to Archbishop Cieplak. And on August 5, 1921, the Pope appealed to the entire world, in the curial form of a letter addressed to his Cardinal Secretary of State:[35]

> "Millions of people in the Volga area who are facing a terrible death are crying for help to all of humanity. This cry of distress has pierced Us deeply. We are dealing with a people that has suffered enough under the lash of war, a people under the luminous sign of Christ, who have always chosen with great determination to belong to the great Christian family. No matter how much they are separated from us by barriers that the centuries have erected, still the greater their misfortune, the closer they are to Our fatherly heart. . . . Thus, Your Eminence, We invite you to do everything in your power to awaken the governments of nations to the necessity of initiating a rapid and effective common action. . . . "

The signal that Benedict XV gave with this letter had an especially electrifying effect on Lenin's man in Rome. This was Waclaw Worowski, a literary man and *bel esprit* of Polish descent, 51 at the time, who had already become friendly with Lenin in 1904, in his Swiss and Parisian exile. Although a Bolshevik, he had at first considered the October Revolution only an "amusing adventure." Nevertheless, Lenin made him his representative in Stockholm, then in 1920 the leader of the first Soviet Russian "trade commission" in Rome.[36] As a former Catholic, Worowski recognized from the beginning how valuable it would be for Russia's return to world politics if he could succeed in effecting any act of "recognition" of the new regime by the Pope. Worowski had also not failed to observe the interest with which the Vatican and the leaders of the Catholic orders contemplated possibilities for "missionary work" in Russia. Lenin's new policies (the NEP), the famine, and the Pope's appeal now offered Worowski unexpected points of departure.

To this day, a veil of secrecy lies over the beginnings of his contacts; however, recent discoveries of documents[37] allow us to lift it a little. To get closer to the Vatican, Worowski made use of a strange German middleman, Doctor of Law Wilhelm von Braun, who was 38 at the time. The son of a Protestant estate owner near Frankfurt on the Oder, Braun had studied in Rome, become Catholic in 1912, had served as a captain for Turkey in the World War, had been a Russian prisoner of war, and had re-emerged in Rome after the war. He liked to converse with ecclesiastics, whom he assured that he wished to become a priest; and he would mention in passing his father's fortune of a million marks, to which he claimed (falsely) to be the sole heir.[38] That Braun—for whatever reasons—was a confidant of the Soviet representation to Rome was no secret. Why he was also trusted in the Papal Secretariat of State, where caution is valued as a cardinal virtue, is unknown. He was probably vouched for by the clerical consultant to the German Embassy to the Vatican, Prelate Johannes Steinmann of Breslau, who may have known the von Braun family. Steinmann was at any rate the second, less mysterious key figure who made possible Soviet Representative Worowski's connection to the Vatican.[39]

Aid from America to starving Russia had already begun; at the end of August, 1921, Herbert Hoover had come to an agreement with the Soviets that put the action into gear, without the USA thereby recognizing the Lenin government. Would it not now be proper for the Pope to follow the example of the ARA (American Relief Administration) and also send off a contractually guaranteed mission of aid to Russia? This suggestion was urged upon the Vatican by Braun and Steinmann. The first meeting between Worowski and Giuseppe Pizzardo,[40] the Under-Secretary of State for Extraordinary Affairs in the Papal Secretariat of State, occurred on December 16. Polite, charming and elegant—not at all as Rome had imagined a Bolshevik—Worowski painted absolutely fantastic possibilities for the Vatican Prelate:

> "Former errors of the Soviet government are no longer in force. There will be not only full freedom of religion, but freedom for foreign missionaries. Catholic missionaries would be welcome, if they are properly endowed financially. . . . Overall, Catholics are trusted much more than the Orthodox, because the Catholics would certainly have no nostalgia for the Czarist regime. . . . Members of Catholic orders could distribute foodstuffs, and also establish model farms, artisan workshops, vocational schools. . . . only an oath of political neutrality would be required from the missionaries. . . ."[41]

Such attractive prospects could not fail to have their intended effect upon Benedict XV. Pizzardo was instructed to strike as quickly as possible, while the iron was hot. After scarcely a week of negotiations shortly before Christmas (and two days before the conclusion of the first Italian-Soviet trade protocol), Worowski and Pizzardo prepared the outline of an agreement, in French language, which seemed to confirm the unbelievable: They were actually talking about "missionaries" being allowed to enter Russia, so long as they did not belong to any "anti-Soviet nationality or political group" (that meant, no Poles). They would not be allowed to spread any political propaganda, but could dedicate themselves to the support of the population "by distribution of foodstuffs to the hungry, by agricultural and vocational schools, etc., and by *moral and religious education.*" The missionaries would be assured of freedom of movement, exemption from taxation, and other privileges, if they would take an oath to renounce any kind of anti-Soviet activity.[41]

Had starvation really taught the Soviets, if not to pray, at least some flexibility? Were the decrees about religious instruction no longer in effect? Or had Worowski—apparently or in fact—overstepped his authority?

Such skeptical questions were drowned in the exuberance of the moment. Father Carl Friedrich, the Roman representative of the Society of the Divine Word Missionaries (SVD), wrote on Dec. 21, 1921, to the General of his order in Steyl, the Netherlands, that they should ready members of the order as missionaries as quickly as possible:

> "The general belief in informed circles is that the hour of grace will soon strike for Russia. Many people would like to have us believe that perhaps there may even occur a kind of mass conversion to the Catholic church. . . ."[43]

The old pious phantom of the "conversion" of Russia, which had raised so many hopes back in 1917-1918, was coming to life again. To be sure, in October the Pope was still denying the suspicion that he was trying to do religious "business" with his famine relief; but many of Benedict XV's utterances show how strongly the existing curia was trapped, so to speak, in a narrowly confessional way of thinking.[44] The hope that the Catholic church could still become the heir of the Orthodox in Russia motivated this Pope to the very end. Even during the night when he died of a sudden pneumonia, Jan. 22, 1922, Benedict XV called Monsignore Pizzardo to his bedside three times, to ask him, "Have the visas come yet from the Bolsheviks?"[45]

For Worowski was taking his time. He had gone to Moscow to get authority to sign the draft treaty. When he returned, he brought new instructions along. In the meantime, however, there was also a new Pope: Achille Ratti had ascended the throne of St. Peter as Pope Pius XI. This former nuncio to Warsaw not only had "eastern experience"; he was also open to the influence of Archbishop Ropp, who now hurried to Rome from his exile in Warsaw and warned against a hasty conclusion of the treaty. Ropp too dreamed of a "systematic missionizing of Russia," but he also wanted to gain some other concessions from the starving Bolsheviks at this opportunity; in addition, he resisted the Russian demand that no Polish clerics be sent.

Here—as would often happen in the future—not only Polish and Russian interests were clashing, but also Polish and German. Prelate Steinmann of the German Embassy to the Vatican was working toward a Vatican-Soviet rapprochement, under orders from Berlin, as we shall see later. A Silesian who was not fond of Poles to begin with, he now found his efforts endangered by the Polish interests. Steinmann therefore did everything in his power to convince the Vatican of the "utopian" nature of Ropp's demands. What he heard from Worowski he not only relayed secretly to the German Foreign Office in Berlin, but also to the Vatican:

> "Ropp is a clever rogue; you can't catch him, because he behaves not like a Pole but like a Russian, and is extremely careful not to lose his Russian citizenship. His whole plan is to pretend to be purely a Catholic, but in the eyes of the Bolsheviks he is purely Polish. He wants restitution of the Catholic schools, libraries, church property—but these were and are confiscated not as Catholic institutions, but rather as Polish ones."

This is what Steinmann learned from Worowski. The German Monsignore found the representative from Moscow to be a "moderate Bolshevik" who wanted to prevent extreme measures against the church "and is with good reason opposed to the brazen behavior of Poland, which is posing as the protector of Russia's Catholic church."[46] Monsignore Steinmann's counterattack was successful: Archbishop Ropp, he proudly announced, had finally "left the Vatican in a fury" (cf. document in appendix).

But what had Worowski brought back from Moscow? To begin with, he heavily watered the wine of enthusiasm that he himself had poured. Worowski had received orders from the Kremlin to reach at least a *de facto*, if not a *de jure*, recognition of the Soviet government by the Vatican in contracting the treaty. In addition, he was to ascertain how much money the Vatican—so fabulously rich—thought to put into the relief operation. (After all, the ARA had started right out with $20 million!)

Monsignore Pizzardo, now, had to be extremely careful in this very essential point. After the death of Benedict XV, it had turned out that the Vatican was "very nearly bankrupt."[47] Collections from Catholics all over the world could only be successful if there was also visible hope for the religious interests. But it was in this very respect that Worowski brought something of a disappointment. Moscow had cancelled the word *missionaires* throughout the draft treaty and replaced it with *envoyés* (emissaries). In Article 3, the reference to agricultural and vocational schools, and above all the possibility of "moral and religious instruction," had disappeared. In addition to all this came the report that the Soviet government had authorized the confiscation of all valuable ecclesiastical objects made of gold, silver and jewels, including the chalices and monstrances used in the divine service and the sacraments. Worowski insisted that this was only a consequence of the famine; the Soviet government, in view of its empty state treasury, needed gold to buy grain abroad. In truth, ideological zealots also naturally wanted to use this opportunity to destroy ecclesiastical life.[48]

Under these conditions, was any kind of a treaty possible? Cardinal Gasparri nevertheless, on March 12, 1922, secretly put his signature next to Worowski's and thereby concluded the first and to this day the only "Agreement between the Holy See and the Government of the Soviets" (for text see appendix). This was possible because the Roman curia as well as the Kremlin calculated an advantage in spite of everything—and set their hopes (and mental reservations) on certain unofficial agreements.

The Vatican had refused the Soviets a *de jure* recognition; *de facto*, of course, it had signed the agreement with the *gouvernement des Soviets*, not with *la Russie*, as Gasparri had wished. And the Holy See had issued in advance a separate, strictly confidential avowal that the "imperial Russian legation formerly accredited to the Holy See did not represent the present government of Russia." This was not much, but to judge by the furious attacks and accusations against the Vatican made at that time by the Russian emigrés, it was no minor matter either.

On the other hand, Worowski and his diligent go-between, Wilhelm von Braun, had succeeded in keeping alive the missionary and ministerial expectations of the Vatican, in spite of all ill tidings. On March 11, one day before the signing of the treaty, Worowski delivered to the Vatican an assurance in writing that the Soviet government would give the Holy See land concessions, for the establishment of agricultural and artisan teaching and production facilities.

To this day, we do not know the exact text of this document, but we do have the accompanying text, a memorandum that Braun also delivered to the general of the Steyl missionary society (SVD) on the same day. It opened apparently fantastic prospects:

In order to realize the land concessions that Worowski had assured on the basis of "a secret authorization," "the most productive agrarian and factory objects" were to be chosen, according to Braun's memorandum. For this purpose a financial syndicate would be formed under the leadership of Director Alexander of the German Orient Bank Co. in Berlin. Experts from this syndicate would enter Russia at the same time as the Vatican mission for famine relief. The church and the order would only invest 50% of the capital, but they could pay their contributions by installments. For the banks concerned, on the other hand, it would be important that "active and self-sacrificing participants as well as an exceptionally tractable corps of workers are available" (by this was meant the Brothers!) It should also be taken into consideration that "collections were being taken in the entire Catholic world." With this project "the Church, Russia and Germany would be served"; its advantage lay in the fact that "a squandering of Catholic monies in unprofitable undertakings would be avoided"; however, the prerequisite would be that they should "speak as loudly as possible about the famine relief and as little as possible about the financial syndicate." (Point A, b)

At first glance, one could think that this document came from the arsenal of Marxist propaganda, which prefers to view church policy and "capitalist exploitation" as going hand in hand. Or could it be a pure figment of von Braun's imagination, who on the one hand, on Worowski's orders, wanted to attract the Roman church circles, and on the other, wanted to feather his own private and perhaps also religious nest (we can't completely exclude this latter)? However, this busy friend of Russia, whose strange double-dealing will concern us again later, was by no means building his castles on sand.

As early as the end of 1920, at the 8th Party Congress, Lenin had developed a policy of economic concessions which contemplated relinquishing useful land, or even whole regions (for instance the Kamchatka Peninsula) to foreign capitalistic enterprises. Under the "New Economic Policy," Lenin broadened the possibilities of foreign capital participation to the area of industrial production. Lenin felt that this was the "tribute" that Russia had to pay for her backwardness. In January 1922 the Supreme Council of the western War Alliance (the "Entente") had picked up this idea at a conference in Cannes, and decided in turn to make capital out of the Russian famine. The watchword was: help for the Soviets, and investment credit and participation, only if Moscow takes over the pre-war debts of Russia and returns foreign private property they had confiscated.

Thus the Worowski-Braun offer would not seem only frivolous to the Vatican. The German ambassador to the Holy See, Diego von Bergen, also took it seriously. In a confidential letter that he enclosed with a report of Prelate Steinmann's, Bergen recommended "participation by wealthy German financial circles in the Catholic missionary undertaking" (for full text of the letter see appendix); however, the Vatican, as Steinmann reports, did not want to make use, "*for the moment*," of the Russian concessionary offers. The Russians should be convinced that "the church is not acting from egotistical motives, but from Christian love, and is far removed from allowing beneficence to degenerate into exploitation."

This wise "asceticism" was made easier for the Roman curia by the fact that it lacked the necessary means. At the end of March there was only 1.5 million lira available in the Vatican for Russian relief (about $75,000 at that time), while the American ARA had already spent a million. Pius XI therefore sought contact with the "rich" Americans, whose mission was already in Moscow, under the direction of Colonel Haskell. A week after the conclusion of the Soviet-Vatican agreement, the Pope sent the American Jesuit Edmund Walsh—a friend of Haskell's—to Moscow to feel out the situation.

Walsh looked around for four weeks, also naturally spoke with Archbishop Cieplak, and noted that religious "liberalization" or missionary possibilities were out of the question. Russia was starving, the ruling party was seeking a way out of its economical and political isolation, and apparently only this was assuring a brief respite for a religious minority like the Catholics. On March 20, shortly before the arrival of Walsh, Cieplak had openly requested Catholic parents, in a pastoral letter, to give their children religious instruction. A week earlier, he had instructed the priests, by telegram, to resist the decree about delivering objects of worship: "Demand unjustified. Do not deliver inventory." Nothing, or very little, had happened since then.

The Papal relief works—it could not be more at the moment—had still not made an appearance. When Walsh returned to Rome from his reconnaissance, the number of "missionaries" was established—five Jesuits, three Steylers, three Salesians, and two Claretians; thirteen Brothers in all. But the financing still looked very sparse; departure for Russia could not yet be discussed. The Pope sent Walsh on another trip: to Washington, with a letter to President Harding. American Catholic donations were to be collected, and support from the ARA, particularly the purchase of foodstuffs from them, to be contracted; because completely on its own, the tiny group from the Vatican would hardly be able to distribute a crust of bread. In the meantime, so the Pope hoped, perhaps better political conditions for the whole undertaking would develop after all, even for the religious-missionary aspect. For on April 10, 1922, a World Economic Conference was convened in Genoa. Here Communist Russia would appear on the international stage for the first time as a full-fledged participant. Lenin's foreign politicians—Chicherin, Litvinov, Worowski, Krassin—packed frock coats and tails in their suitcases. What would they concede to become politically fit for society? And how would the others accept them? Vanquished Germany, under the leadership of the Catholic-Center chancellor Josef Wirth, was also invited to the conference for the first time as an equal partner, just like Russia. The name for what was in the air, which produced new considerations even in the Vatican, only later became a political catchword: *Rapallo*. Although only the name of a beautiful place on the Italian Riviera, it is still haunting Europe's chancelleries today.

II

On The Rapallo-Course:
Attempts At Co-existence,
1922-24

Backstage Talks—Arranged by Chancellor Wirth

Several of the formally-dressed gentlemen at the long, candlelit table leaned forward so as not to miss the scene: Soviet Commissar for Foreign Affairs Chicherin and Monsignore Giosue Signori, the Archbishop of Genoa, had just lifted their champagne glasses with a friendly smile and toasted each other; now—following proper etiquette—they were autographing their gilt-edged menus and exchanging them. Even the always unsuspecting host, Italy's King Victor Emmanuel, who had invited the delegates of the World Economic Conference to his flagship *Dante Alighieri* this April 22, 1922, could hardly conceal his astonishment: "The extremes have met," he said. In the general tumult of voices in lively conversation during the meal, of course, no one had heard what the man of the church and the representative from Moscow (whom accident of alphabetical seating order had placed opposite each other) had to say to each other.[1]

Archbishop Signori had tactfully offered for the consideration of his Soviet neighbor that in the USA too there was separation of church and state, though religious life there was completely unfettered—in contrast to Russia.

"In our country religion is a private matter and is as free as in America," Chicherin had asserted without hesitation. Of course, he had added, a

34

Catholic bishop in Moscow [he meant Cieplak—or had it been Ropp?] had once suggested to the Soviet government that it should "sign a concordat with the Holy See."

Archbishop Signori sat up alertly, but Chicherin had already diplomatically dismissed the idea he himself had voiced: Why would they need a concordat, when religious freedom was guaranteed for all confessions anyway. . . . !?

When the royal guests, late in the evening, left the brightly-lit cruiser in the Genoa harbor, only one person recalled the Catholic-Soviet toast without astonishment: German Chancellor Wirth. For he had not only devised, the previous week in Rapallo, that German-Soviet agreement which, to the unpleasant surprise of the Western powers, strengthened the position of the two defeated nations of the World War; he had also, through his Roman confidant, Monsignore Steinmann of the German Embassy to the Vatican, seen to it that the Vatican took great interest in the Genoa conference.

Controversial in his Catholic Center Party (*Zentrum*) as "leftist," nationalistically and democratically oriented, Wirth was convinced that a Soviet Russia in need of economic contacts could perhaps be "tamed" and used to assist in breaking the "circle of Versailles": the stranglehold of astronomically high reparations that the peace treaty had imposed upon Germany and that now, with inflation and perhaps even revolution, could throttle the young Weimar Republic. The main point of the Rapallo pact, much puzzled over later, thus signified nothing other than a mutual German-Soviet waiver of financial compensation for war damages.[2]

By the beginning of April, when Chicherin travelled to Genoa and during a break in his journey in Berlin made first contacts with Wirth, the Vatican already had an idea—probably through Steinmann—of the emerging possibilities. A discharge of Germany's debts was quite in line with the sympathies of the Roman curia, which had never considered the Versailles Treaty a masterpiece of wisdom. The "best guarantee for peace is not a forest of bayonets, but rather mutual trust and friendship," the Pope wrote to Archbishop Signori in an open letter of April 7, 1922; Pius XI welcomed the conference of Genoa as an opportunity to "facilitate for the vanquished the rapid fulfillment of their obligations, which in the end will also prove advantageous to the victors"; it now behooved them to "sacrifice at the altar of the common good."

He was not referring directly to Russia here; however, since Russia belonged to the vanquished, and her first appearance upon the international stage was the main news on everyone's lips, the Pope must have also been thinking of Russia. A remark of Cardinal Gasparri's at this time has been transmitted, though recorded only much later, which coincides with the basic position that the Vatican actually assumed in the following decades towards *all* authoritarian regimes—even the fascist and national socialist:

> "The church has—theoretically speaking—no prejudice against a communist form of government (*nulla da opporre pregiudizialmente ad una organizzazione statale comunistica*), in economic matters she is completely agnostic and indifferent; her spiritual interests lie beyond and above economic systems and can be maintained in any political and social climate. The church requires only that states, regardless of what kind, do not attempt to hinder or attack the free development of the religious and sacramental life that is the purpose and obligation of the church."[3]

One may question whether a sociopolitical "climate" that determines the extent of freedom of a society is such an insignificant matter for a church; but certainly her apostleship is not directly tied to specific constitutional systems—any more than is finding like-minded partners in international relations.

The Catholic Josef Wirth arrived at Rapallo in this Spring of 1922 from a similarly pragmatic premise. On April 16, to the unpleasant surprise of the French and English and also of the Social-Democratic Reich President Ebert, he signed the German-Russian pact. On April 22 came the Catholic-Soviet champagne conversation on the cruiser *Dante Alighieri* (see page 34); on April 29 the Pope, in an open letter to Gasparri, commented "with concern" upon the "progress of the conference," which after all must work to the advantage of the victors *and* the vanquished,

> "but especially those unhappy peoples on the borders of Europe who, already afflicted by domestic wars and religious persecution, are now also being decimated by famine and epidemics, whereas they possess so many sources of riches in their lands and could be strong elements of social reconstruction. . . ."

What Pius XI feared was not only the collapse of the conference, which—as he hinted—could drive starving Russia to desperation and thus move Europe toward catastrophe; the Pope also believed that the proper moment had arrived to play the "Russian card" himself. A few days after his letter to Gasparri, he sent his under-secretary of state, Monsignore Pizzardo, to Genoa and had him deliver a memorandum to the European heads of government; it was to make clear that Soviet Russia could no longer be outlawed, and that the German "sin" of Rapallo should thus not be taken as occasion for a break in relations; at the same time, however, the Pope wanted to see the opportunity used to tie the Bolsheviks to the rules of international law. Entry into the community of nations was to be granted to them for a religious-political price.[4]

Before Pizzardo left for Genoa on May 5, Secretary of State Cardinal Gasparri assured the Austrian ambassador, "We will be the last to have

dealings with the new Russia."[5] The *Osservatore Romano* too on the same day denied any kind of "new relationship" with Moscow; but all this served only to appease those souls who were startled by wild rumors in the press about a "Vatican-Soviet plot." Russian emigrants everywhere were especially enraged that "the Vicar of Jesus Christ is preparing to bless the empire of the Antichrist."[6] On the other hand, Palmiro Togliatti, in the party newspaper of the recently founded Communist party of Italy, had to deal with the fact that "many comrades were turning up their noses" at the Vatican-Soviet toasts on the royal ship; he apprised these critics that Communists were not anticlericals like the Freemason Socialists of Italy and France. "It is now important to consolidate the workers' state. If this requires that we deal with the Vatican, make and receive demands of them, there is nothing bad about that. . . . The Vatican is a power like any other. . . . The workers' state reckons with them, tolerates them or uses them for its own purposes. . . ."[7] The only sure thing was that Pizzardo went to Genoa with the explicit task of taking up direct contact with the Soviet Russians. The text of the following papal memorandum referred to it:

> "In this historic hour, when the reentry of Russia into the community of civilized nations is being negotiated, the Holy See hopes that the religious interests that are the basis of every true culture be protected in Russia. Thus the Holy See demands that in the agreement to be made among the powers represented in Genoa, the following three clauses be explicitly included, in some form:
> 1. Complete freedom of conscience be guaranteed in Russia for Russian citizens and for foreigners.
> 2. Private and public practice of religion and worship also be guaranteed. (This second clause is in agreement with declarations that the Russian delegate, Mr. Chicherin, made in Geneva.)
> 3. The properties that belong or belonged to a religious community shall be returned and respected."[8]

About Pizzardo's mysterious meeting with the Soviet delegation there has been as yet only a fragmentary report, intent on playing it down, published in the *Osservatore Romano* a week later (May 15/16, 1922), to quiet all kinds of press rumors. It is significant that Pizzardo himself—so I was told by the archive of the papal Secretariat of State—left no record at all of his Rapallo conversations with the Soviets. However, from German archival material, some of which was opened for the first time to me, the occasion may be largely reconstructed:

Chancellor Wirth, who twenty years later still commended himself as an "imaginative Baden Aleman," had used one of his private strolls with Chicherin on the Italian Riviera to impress upon the Soviet Commissar for Foreign Affairs, who liked to talk about music and literature, the importance of the Vatican as well; Wirth himself placed importance upon ecclesiastical blessing for his controversial Rapallo pact. Monsignore Steinmann of the German Embassy in Rome had already previously (by-passing the embassy) played the mediator between Wirth, the Vatican and the Russians. Early in the evening of May 9, Pizzardo visited the Chancellor in his Genoa hotel and delivered the papal memorandum; Wirth immediately made clear that point three of the document—the demand for the return of church property—would only encumber the realization of the other two points (religious freedom), especially as the questions of property were the main theme of the conference of Genoa anyway.

But why was Pizzardo so quickly persuaded to give up his point 3 altogether (see facsimile of the Maltzan report, p. 39), or at least to empha-size only the first two points, as the *Osservatore Romano* later reported to play it down? For the first time, the answer can be given here: because Pizzardo had gotten the apparently clever idea from the German chancel-lor of making the return of church property more acceptable to the Rus-sians by exchanging it, "tit for tat, for the support vouchsafed by the Holy See"; that is, to tie the intended famine relief from the Vatican to the return of church property—a rather extraordinary "deal."[9]

May 12, 1922
Under Secretary of State Pizzardo yesterday evening delivered the memoran-dum attached in copy to the Reich chancellor as well as the chiefs of the other delegations. Mr. Pizzardo concurrently expressed the desire to call on Mr. Chicherin, together with Mr. Steinmann, in order to discuss with him the further development of the wishes of the Holy See in Russia. It was called to the attention of the two gentlemen of the clergy that Nr. 3 of the memorandum would greatly encumber their wishes. It was pointed out that dropping Nr. 3 would only simplify the position of England and Italy toward Russia. Mr. Pizzardo then declared himself willing to designate Nr. 3 of the memorandum as "non avenu."

The gentlemen were in Rapallo after that yesterday evening and had a conversation of several hours with Mr. Chicherin which, as they told me today, proceeded completely satisfactorily. In particular, Russia gave extensive assurances concerning Nr. 1 and 2 of the memorandum, and declared itself very satisfied with the renunciation of Art. 3.

Hereby
for the kind attention
of the Foreign Office.   K480058
Genoa, May 10, 1922

Thus "prepared," Pizzardo, accompanied by Steinmann, drove to Santa Margherita, at that time a suburb of Rapallo. In the magnificent hotel "Imperial Palace," where the Soviets had their quarters, the two spoke first

Aufzeichnung.

Herr Unterstaatssekretär Pizzardo hat gestern abend abschriftlich beigefügtes Menorandum den Herrn Reichskanzler ebenso wie den Chefs der übrigen Delegationen übergeben. Herr Pizzardo hat daran anschliessend den Wunsch geäussert, mit Herrn Steinmann zusammen Herrn Tschitscherin aufzusuchen, um mit ihm die weitere Entwicklung der Wünsche des Heiligen Stuhles in Russland zu besprechen . Die beiden geistlichen Herren sind darauf aufmerksam gemacht worden , dass Nr. 3 des Menorandums ihre Wünsche sehr belasten würde. Sie sind darauf hingewiesen worden , dass ein Fallenlassen von Nr.3 die Stellung Englands und Italiens zu Russland nur erleichtern würde. Herr Pizzardo hat sich daraufhin bereit er - klärt, Nr. 3 des Menorandums als "non avenu" zu bezeichnen .

Die Herren sind darauf gestern abend in Rapallo ge - wesen und haben mit Herrn Tschitscherin eine mehrstündige Unterredung gehabt, die, wie sie mir heute mitteilten, voll- kommen befriedigend verlaufen ist. Insbesondere hat Russland eine weitgehende Zusicherung hinsichtlich Nr. 1 und 2 des Menorandums gemacht und hat sich hinsichtlich der Aufgabe des Art. 3 sehr befriedigt erklärt .

        Hiermit
     den Auswärtigen Amt

zur gefälligen Kenntnisnahme .
     Genua, den 10.Mai 1922.

K480058

Ago Baron von Maltzan (1877-1927), ministerial consultant in the Foreign Office, sent this report about the Vatican-Soviet meeting in Rapallo to Berlin.— Monsignore Steinmann wrote to Maltzan on July 19, 1922: "Monsignore Pizzardo still often speaks of Genoa, and remembers you with particular affection. . . ." (PAAA, Secret Acts, B20/3/IV.Ru/Pol. 16/K 105156) with their familiar Roman negotiating partner Worowski, who was now acting as Secretary General of the Soviet delegation. Then Chicherin greeted the two ecclesiastical gentlemen and chatted with them most charmingly until late into the night, literally "about God and the world."

The most astonishing thing was that Chicherin by no means rejected the "tit for tat solution" to the problem of church property (could it be that he had suggested it to the German chancellor?), and he left his visitors with the impression that the discussion had progressed "most satisfactorily." Not just because Chicherin had succeeded in a simple deceptive maneuver, but because this educated diplomat of the revolution, who was descended from the old Russian aristocracy, was of the personal opinion that a *modus vivendi* with the Catholic church and the Vatican would be extremely useful for the fledgling Soviet power struggling for acceptance, and would also be worth a certain price. This opinion, which Chicherin defended for years, as we shall see, seems to have been shared to a degree by Lenin too (see p. 55). However, the majority of the Moscow party leadership at that time, and Chicherin's deputy Maxim Litvinov, did not consider Catholicism worthy of such regard.[10]

Thus it came about that, at a press conference in Genoa three days after his meeting with Pizzardo, Chicherin praised the "high moral authority of the Pope," and did not even exclude the possibility of presenting himself personally at the Vatican, while on the same May 12 a communiqué of the Soviet delegation replied rather coolly to the papal memorandum: with reference to Soviet legislation, especially to the Decree of Separation of 1918, in which "complete freedom of religion, as well as the use of buildings and objects necessary for worship" was formally guaranteed.[11] In Moscow, the Orthodox Patriarch Tikhon had just—on May 10—been placed under house arrest; he was accused of being responsible for bloody clashes in which Red Army soldiers had shot at believers who opposed the confiscation of liturgical objects.[12] From the Russian Catholics too, cries for help reached Rome, just as Pizzardo had returned from Genoa. The under-secretary immediately used his new friendship to write to Chicherin in Rapallo on May 14:[13]

> "It has pained the Holy Father to discover that Patriarch Tikhon and other priests have been arrested in Moscow. His Holiness would be particularly grateful to Your Excellency if through your gracious intervention these priests were to be released, which under the present circumstances would make a most favorable impression in the most diverse circles.—On this occasion I have the honor of informing you that—according to a telegram from Monsignore Cieplak to the Holy Father—the authorities in Petrograd insist that valuable sacred objects be surrendered so that the proceeds from their sale may alleviate the sufferings of famine. Thus I hasten to inform you that the Holy Father is prepared to purchase these holy vessels in order to deposit

them with Monsignore Cieplak. The agreed-upon price will be immediately remitted to Your Excellency or to any other person named by your government. I request Your Excellency to inform me as soon as possible in order that I may transmit the necessary arrangements to Petrograd."

Chicherin replied politely from Rapallo three days later:

"In reply to your letter of May 14, 1922, No. 3605, I request that you assure His Holiness that the Patriarch Tikhon, although court proceedings against him are pending, is not in prison. Concerning the very interesting suggestions in the second part of your letter, I transmitted them immediately to Moscow, and they will certainly be studied by the government with all the benevolence that they deserve."

This was a gleam of hope for the diplomats of the Pope; they tried to "strike while the iron was hot." Thus on the same day Monsignore Pizzardo wrote to Chancellor Wirth in Genoa, and as thanks for his help in the negotiations sent him a photograph of Pius XI with a personal dedication from the Pope—with the injunction, however, to maintain strict silence about the gift and its occasion (*Secretariato di Stato, No. 3981* of May 17, 1922). Pizzardo's letter also was not sent through diplomatic channels, but included in a private letter dictated by Monsignore Steinmann to a discreet nun of the "Grey Sisters" (with whom he was staying in Rome). Steinmann notified Wirth "in confidence" that the Vatican was hoping for "further kind intervention" from the chancellor, while he, Steinmann, was striving for more understanding in the Vatican for the cooperation of the Catholic Center Party with the Social Democrats in Germany. . . .[14]

The reservations harbored in Rome against the domestic "leftist course" of Wirth's Center Party by no means prevented the Vatican from discreetly making use of the palpably improved post-Rapallo German-Soviet relations. Thus Wirth's "kind intervention"[15] was soon in demand again as the offer transmitted to Chicherin to buy the liturgical vessels remained unanswered by Moscow. Archbishop Cieplak and his vicar general Budkiewicz had submitted the suggestion once again, in writing, to the authorities, but finally gotten the answer that a sale was impossible "because it is no longer known where the objects are to be found." Indeed, much had fallen victim to the fanatical iconoclasts or simply to black marketeers.[16]

However, it is doubtful whether the Pope could have raised the money to buy back the sacred vessels at the world market price of gold. The famine relief for Russia—contractually agreed upon three months earlier!—had not even swung into action yet; Father Walsh was still travelling through the United States, inviting American Catholics to the collection plate. When he returned to Rome at the end of June 1922, he did not have all too much to show for his efforts. The Soviets, meanwhile, were realizing ever more clearly that, compared to the American, the material assistance of the Vatican would turn out to be rather paltry, and in addition was "ideologically" encumbered. The question of a legal recognition by the Vatican had thus become all the more interesting for Russia after the discussions at Genoa and Rapallo. And only this prospect moved Chicherin to engage in any kind of consideration of church property.

In the spring of 1922, when Worowski and Pizzardo had negotiated the relief agreements, the question had still been whether the papal envoys to Russia could be *missionaries* or only *dispensers of charity*. Now in the early summer, after their international debut at Genoa and Rapallo, the Soviets were urging more and more strongly that the famine relief workers become the *vanguard of a diplomatic representation*.[17] The problem of church properties, apparently still hanging in the air (Archbishop Cieplak had not yet been forced to sign the legally required document), was well suited as an instrument of pressure.

The Pope was thus confronted with a difficult alternative: either he met the Soviets' desires half way in order to bolster a very uncertain chance of the church's survival in Russia; or he refused any political cooperation, thereby risking the accelerated destruction of the Catholic church in Russia and beyond that the failure of any religious secondary intentions of his famine relief mission, but also preserved his political-moral authority in the eyes of the anti-Communist world.

The decision depended very strongly upon the "life expectancy" accorded at that time to the Soviet regime; whether one predicted its imminent demise from the famine, or its probable consolidation through the "New Economic Policy." There were many indications for both possibilities.[18]

The Vatican tried—as it often would—to escape the dilemma by not deciding in favor of either possibility, but rather juggling the two to gain time. To the Roman curia, it seemed most important at the moment that the door to Russia not be slammed. Even if it did not want to use it, and avoided the back doors for the time being as well, it had to at least keep a foot in the door.

Famine Relief with Obstacles

A lump black as coal, a few kernels of grain baked with straw and bran— it was a piece of "Russian bread" that Father Walsh had brought back from Moscow. Cardinal Gasparri held it in his hands like a frightening object; he showed it to the brothers who were to go into the famine-stricken areas of Russia, for the time being not as "padres," but as simple "signori," furnished of course with Vatican diplomatic passports. They should know what awaited them. A short time earlier on that day, July 24, 1922, the thirteen missionaries—or "agents," as they were somewhat misleadingly called in the contract—had been received by the Pope himself. He had obtained their solemn vow to refrain from any political or religious activity, "or else all is lost."

Two weeks earlier, Monsignore Pizzardo had called the group into the Secretariat of State and given them instructions that had the effect of a cold shower on the enthusiastic young priests:

> "Even if Catholic churches are plundered and native Catholic priests arrested, you may not do anything nor say anything, instead you must watch with folded arms. . . . if someone comes to you with a religious matter, then say: I cannot hear, I cannot understand anything; but if you need a new coat—that I can give you. . . ."[19]

Of course, this temperance being impressed upon the travellers to Russia was not an end in itself, it had a tactical motive: it was hoped that this purely charitable activity "will in time form a basis [for more]; naturally, that could take a while," Pizzardo said, mentioning also that the nomination of "a papal delegate to Moscow" was being contemplated. Pizzardo had consoled the Soviet representative Worowski with this possibility when the latter, early in the summer, was urging not so much the departure of the papal relief mission any more as the recognition of the Soviet government by the Vatican.

Finally, on July 10, the Pope had issued a proclamation to the Catholic bishops all over the world[20] that they should encourage all the faithful to give donations for Russia. Pius XI himself donated 2.5 million lire from the Vatican coffers—$125,000 at that time; "as much as present circumstances will allow us," he wrote. When the padres of the "mission" finally embarked in Bari on July 24, reaching the Crimean peninsula three weeks later, their financial situation was extremely limited. "We are living from hand to mouth. . . ," one of them soon wrote home. And so it continued for the ensuing two years of their activity; 292 million Catholics all over the world contributed not much more than $2 million for the starving Russians, while the American relief organization ARA in the same period distributed food and goods worth $66 million.[21]

At Sevastopol already, the missionaries to Russia, who were travelling under the papal flag, were met by a destroyer carrying a representative of the Moscow government come to welcome them respectfully. But it soon became apparent that there was lingering Soviet mistrust. The Soviets would have liked to concentrate all the Catholic "gentlemen" in the Crimea to keep them under closer control. But Rome insisted that they spread out; three in the Crimea, two in Rostov, three in Krasnodar, one in Orenburg in

**Католическая Миссия Помощи
в России.**
————◄■►————

РИМСКИЙ ПАПА =
= РУССКОМУ НАРОДУ   *Briefkopf der Katholischen Hilfsmission in Rußland*

the Urals, however five in Moscow, where the "director general" of the group, Jesuit Father Walsh, also set up his quarters.

In Moscow alone, a hot meal was distributed daily to 40,000 people, primarily children, invalids and students.[22] Wherever they were active, the Roman representatives did their utmost to relieve misery; since they were committed to "religious asceticism," they advertised the benefactor in other ways: "The Catholic mission of the Roman Pope is helping the Russian people" said large, garlanded posters above the distribution centers, usually with a photograph of Pius XI making a gesture of blessing (see first page of illustrations). The Pope was becoming "more and more popular" with the Russians, some of the members of the mission could report; it was for just that reason that the authorities viewed the undertaking with mixed feelings, especially since after the fall of 1922 a slight improvement in the food supply was becoming visible and it became clearer that the papal assistants had arrived rather late.

It was now most important for the Vatican, however, to have a representative in Moscow, even if only a semi-official one. Outwardly, to be sure, they claimed until the very end that the charity work had "nothing to do with the political system of Russia,"[23] but Father Walsh possessed formal authority as a quasi-diplomatic representative for contacts with the political authorities in order to ease the religious situation of the Catholics in Russia. "He is authorized to negotiate in the name of the Holy Father with all competent authorities (*autoritées competentes*) concerning matters that the Holy See has entrusted to him," read the document issued by Cardinal Gasparri on July 5, 1922.[24] Walsh was in continuous telegraphic contact with Rome, via the German embassy in Moscow and the Berlin Foreign Office; he reported and received his instructions by German secret code.

In Petrograd, on July 22, 1922—two days before the departure of the Vatican mission from Rome—Archbishop Cieplak had received an ultimatum to sign the prescribed contract for the utilization of "buildings and objects of worship" within one month; otherwise, the Catholic churches would be closed. Walsh now transmitted the text of the contract to Rome; Cardinal Gasparri telegraphed back that the Holy See could not allow such a contract, since it would constitute an indirect approval of

nationalization of church property. Gasparri also urged the German chancellor Wirth to warn the Russians that they could expect a public protest from the Vatican if they—"ungratefully and unwisely"—persisted in their actions.[25] Chicherin had, after all, in Rapallo, held out the prospect of a "tit for tat" settlement of property matters for famine relief!

The Soviets hesitated. While they extended Cieplak's ultimatum again and again, finally until January 2, 1923, they also again raised the old idea, launched long ago by their middleman Wilhelm von Braun, of economic enterprises on a concession basis (see p. 31). Why not have the papal relief group now establish vocational schools, they proposed. Then came the idea of a children's sanatorium in the Crimea, for the support of which the Roman "missionaries" were to acquire two large estates, one with 2500 hectares of farmland.[26] Rome was not averse to this. The Pope said in private conversation that the assistance of his representatives "in the intensive cultivation of the fields" would be useful, because the missionaries could then "establish roots in Russia, so that they will not be expelled when papal donations finally cease."[27] But the "missionaries," who had experienced more official mistrust than cooperation on the spot, were skeptical.[28]

It was also obvious that the foreign policy and the religious policy of the Soviets were by no means completely "synchronized." Even while their Roman representative Worowski was negotiating with the Holy See about all pending problems, in Petrograd, three weeks before Christmas 1922, all the Catholic churches except the French congregation were closed by the police. The Pope nevertheless, in the consistory on December 11, complained only in very careful language about the lack of religious freedom in Russia. And when Archbishop Cieplak finally received Rome's permission at the end of February 1923 to sign the contract of church utilization in a milder form, Comrade Krassikov of the 5th department of the Commissariat of Justice, which was responsible for questions of religion, suddenly appeared to be uninterested, or hard of hearing.[29] For the agitators in the Party did not want anybody to "steal their show" any longer: they wanted court proceedings against the Archbishop of the Catholics in Russia.

The Cieplak Trial, a Shot in the Neck— And No Break in Relations

"Sub tuum praesidium—under your protection, Holy Virgin," thousands of Catholic Poles sang in Latin at Petrograd's central railroad station as the train to Moscow slowly pulled out with its first-class compartments reserved for the clerics. It was the beginning of March, 1923;

Archbishop Cieplak, his Vicar General Prelate Budkiewicz, Exarch Feodorov and twelve other clerics were not exactly arrested, but had been summoned to proceed to Moscow—at their own expense—to their trial. They were to defend themselves before the highest court against the accusation of opposition to the decree on the separation of church and state and to the decree on the confiscation of church treasures.

Not until three weeks after their arrival in Moscow were the clerics arrested and driven in an open truck to the former Aristocrats' Club, where the trial stage had been erected. From the 21st to the 26th of March a trial was staged which, though still far removed from the perfection of the later Stalinist show trials, was no less unfair and fanatical. It has been described in detail by witnesses who took minutes, among them Father Walsh as an observer.[30]

"The government did not understand us. . . . For us, the canon law of the church is absolutely sacred, for the highest spiritual authority of the Roman Pontiff is a dogma of our Catholic faith," Exarch Feodorov defended himself. "According to the constitution I may preach my religious convictions—why not to children too? And you—don't you yourselves teach young people under eighteen?" the Exarch turned to the Communists in the hall.

What had not yet dawned on Feodorov, one of the few non-Poles among the accused, quickly became apparent: for this tribunal and the Party leaders which it obeyed, the primary target, among Russia's Catholics, was—the Poles. While Feodorov, with mystical-religious fervor, practically begged for a martyr's death,[31] the judgment "let him off" with ten years' labor camp; however it condemned Cieplak and Budkiewicz to death by firing squad on Palm Sunday 1923 . . . because of "counterrevolutionary activities."

The cry of indignation that was raised, not only in the press, but in government chancelleries all over the world, delayed the execution and saved at least Cieplak's life; Cardinal Gasparri too had intervened by telegraph to the president of the "All-Russian Central Executive Committee," Kalinin. A decision of this committee on March 28 took into consideration "that citizen Cieplak is a representative of that community of worship that was suppressed under the czars and the bourgeois republic . . ." and changed his sentence to ten years' imprisonment. Pardon for Budkiewicz, however, was denied because of his "counterrevolutionary activities in direct contact with a foreign bourgeois government unfriendly to the Soviet power." They meant Poland.

Prelate Budkiewicz, who considered himself a Polish patriot, had indeed been so careless as to request the Warsaw government, in a letter, to intervene with the Russians against the religious decrees on the basis of the

Treaty of Riga, (see p. 25).[32] Commissar for Foreign Affairs Chicherin, to whom the whole proceeding was extremely repugnant, had openly admitted how strong an effect the anti-Polish resentment had had in the Cieplak trial when Father Walsh called on him on March 21 to plead for the lives of the two clerics. On the same day, the Polish Communist Julian Marchlewski polemicized in *Isvestia* (either from ignorance or perhaps to confound Chicherin) against the "foreign Pope," who, by inciting Cieplak to disobedience, had had the sole object of "forcing the Soviets into direct negotiations with Rome about religious questions in Russia and thus having occasion to meddle in the domestic affairs of the Soviet Republic."[33] It was just such negotiations that Chicherin's Roman representative Worowski had long been conducting with the Vatican; Worowski had also assured Rome that the sentences would not be carried out if only the curia, but above all the Poles, "kept quiet."

In vain did Cardinal Gasparri admonish the Poles, via the Warsaw nuncio, to be moderate; the Polish prime minister Sikorski still delivered an almost threatening speech in parliament and openly quoted the Soviet ambassador to Warsaw, who, on Chicherin's orders, had assured him very confidentially that none of the condemned would be executed. "Why don't they open proceedings against the Pope?", railed *Pravda* on March 31. Nevertheless, had Lenin, the cool tactician, not been out of action at this point due to illness, things would probably never have come to a triumph of political stupidity over reason.[34] But as it was, everything impelled events toward judicial murder: on Easter night, March 31, 1923, Prelate Budkiewicz was executed by a shot in the neck in Moscow's Lubianka prison.

Would the Vatican now indignantly break off all negotiations? Would it recall its relief mission and cry its protest to the world? Nothing of the kind occurred. In "strictly secret" instructions which the Pope himself composed on April 9 and the German embassy to the Vatican cabled in code to Walsh in Moscow, he retracted—incidentally also on German advice—his original harsh protest:

"1. We have been informed of the mood in Moscow. If this is correct, it seems opportune to postpone the démarche ordered in the telegram of March 31 for a while.
2. It is urgently requested that the prisoners be given all possible help.
3. Inform us as quickly as possible whether the political accusations the condemned prisoners have been charged with may be considered as proven.
4. Continue the distribution of foodstuffs."[35]

The Vatican was convinced that Budkiewicz had done nothing that deserved death, but—according to the April 10 report of German Ambassador von Bergen—they had heard of "overwhelming evidence,"

and knew that politically, Poland had a hand in the matter. For that reason
the curia even hesitated with a solemn requiem for Budkiewicz; it was
celebrated later (in Gasparri's presence), but in the Polish National Church
in Rome, not in St. Peter's Cathedral, as the Poles had wished.

"It is very easy for others to demand condemnation, when they do not
have to bear the responsibility of such a step in the ecclesiastical and
religious domain," Cardinal Gasparri defended himself against a reproach
that was now—and oftentimes in following decades—raised against the
Roman curia. The church was more circumscribed in its judgments than
secular governments, "which also incidentally have cannons at their
disposal," the Cardinal reminded the Bavarian ambassador. But the latter's
Austrian colleague, the pious church historian Pastor, at the same time
heard a "more optimistic interpretation of the conditions in Russia." And
on what did the cardinal base such "optimism"? On "the principle that the
blood of martyrs has always been the best seed of Christianity."[36]

Strangely contradictory remarks. But the conflict that they disclosed is
almost as old as the Catholic church itself; it is rooted in her dual nature as
spiritual and historic community: martyrs, no matter whether victims of
Nero, Stalin, Hitler, or the church's own judicial errors, as in the case of the
Maid of Orleans, are really necessary to this church, according to her
theological perception, for her inner consecration. At the same time,
however, in times of external oppression, martyrdom cannot be raised to a
moral imperative for every single believer, and even less to a guiding
principle of church policy: the latter is dictated, especially in such cases, by
the historical will to survive, which tries to "save what can be saved."

Thus, as Archbishop Cieplak wrote, an objective understanding between
church and Communists was still desirable, not least because "the faithful
otherwise will become tired of resisting—especially if they remain without
that spiritual fortification that arises from the community of
worshippers."[37]

And that meant: closed churches, or churches without priests, cannot be
replaced by any romantic ideas about martyrdom; these do not by accident
grow most fruitfully where no one sows "seeds of blood," but rather where
the creed can be preached unmolested behind baroque façades.

Father Walsh—An American in Moscow

What to do? That was the question when, on May 14, 1923, Cardinal
Secretary of State Gasparri, his under-secretary Pizzardo and Jesuit
General Ledóchowski met to discuss the situation of the papal mission to
Russia. Walsh, the director of the mission, had sent a Salesian brother from
Moscow as his reporter, who described the course of the Cieplak trial, all

the bureaucratic but also financial difficulties in the famine relief, and then repeated Walsh's personal opinion: that now would be the right moment to leave ungrateful Russia under protest.

Was this solution not attractive for another reason as well? "The violence in Moscow has had the effect of a much scantier flow of donations for the papal relief work . . . ," thus a confidential report from Monsignore Steinmann of the German embassy to the Vatican.[38] The famine relief could therefore not be continued in its previous proportions anyway. But: "If we give up everything now, we can hardly expect that another opportunity to get back into Russia will present itself in the foreseeable future." This was Gasparri's main argument, which finally prevailed with the Pope's approval.

The money for the famine relief would, however, only suffice until the middle of July at the latest; but the American relief organization ARA, which the Vatican depended on, was to leave in the middle of June already, and the Soviet authorities had also announced the termination of the Vatican-Soviet agreement for this date. Would it be possible to stay in Russia without giving way to Soviet pressure for diplomatic recognition? Jesuit General Ledóchowski, who as a Pole regarded such a possibility with particular aversion, warned against illusions; he also defended his Jesuit brother Walsh, whose somewhat brusque (the Russians said "American") manners had caused complaints to reach Rome. The German embassy to the Vatican was under the impression that Walsh was "not the right man" in the Vatican's eyes either. But was a change conceivable right at this moment? The ecclesiastical diplomats at the conference table in the Vatican were aware that at present they had no Russian negotiating partner in Rome: Worowski, the "moderate Bolshevik," had been murdered by an emigrant four days previously in Lausanne; among the Russian trade representatives left in Rome were only "dyed-in-the-wool Bolsheviks," Steinmann complained. Thus for the time being, only a temporary solution could be sought:

> "We shall attempt to find another basis for activity after July 15; it does not matter whether this is done through the establishment of vocational schools or other institutions."

These were finally the words of a Vatican instruction to the famine relief mission in Moscow; and at the same time, Father Walsh was ordered to Rome. For two weeks, from the middle of June to the beginning of July, Walsh tried to clarify events for himself and the rather perplexed papal secretary of state. Not only the situation of the relief mission had deteriorated (the notice to vacate lay on the table now); the international situation also looked threatening. The occupation of the Ruhr by France and culmination in the inflation of the mark seemed to make Germany "ripe for revolution" in the eyes of the Communists, in this summer of 1923. When the former Reichs Chancellor Wirth, who had smoothed the path for the Vatican in Rapallo, called on Gasparri in Rome on July 17 and described the danger that "seeds of Bolshevism could probably very soon sprout" from the struggle in the Ruhr, he received from the Cardinal Secretary of State, to his astonishment, detailed information about the "position and development of the Russian army," which was a direct danger for Poland:

> "He [Gasparri] continued, verbatim; *Suppossons nous que dans cette année ou dans l'année prochaine l'armée de la Russie marche contre la Pologne, et à la fin* . . . [let's assume that this year or next, the Russian army marches against Poland and finally . . .]—then there was a long pause and he described somewhat the clash between Russia and Poland, and asked me what I had to add, whereupon I remarked quite drily: 'Then Germany has become Russia's neighbor.' We then discussed this eventuality for some time. . . ."[39]

Where had Gasparri gotten his political and even military knowledge of Russia? He made no effort to conceal it from Wirth: from the papal mission in Russia, from Walsh. Because Gasparri took Communist Russia very seriously and considered the future uncertain, he did not want to ignore any possibility. The Vatican's expectations from the Rapallo policy had not been fulfilled up to now, and Gasparri saw very well that they also contained risks for Germany; but he suspected (or perhaps he knew) that there was a secret cooperation between the Reichswehr and the Red Army which set limits—at least tactical—to the ambitions of the Communist International.

Since November 1922, Germany had had an ambassador in Moscow, Count Brockdorff-Rantzau, a passionate conservative. He had gained the reputation of being a "Red Baron," but in truth supported the Rapallo policies from purely nationalistic motives—as being anti-French and anti-Polish.[40] Rantzau had assured the Berlin nuncio Pacelli, even before moving to Moscow, that—although Protestant himself—he would also be of assistance to the Vatican. Brockdorff-Rantzau did not, however, have complete trust in Walsh, who was more inclined toward the Catholic Poles, but he indebted the Vatican mission by taking care of their telegraphic communication with Rome. When in the summer of 1923 the continuation of the mission seemed to be in jeopardy, even Walsh recognized that "in the present political constellation" it was only with Brockdorff-Rantzau's support that anything could be salvaged. As soon as Walsh, in June, discovered in Rome that the curia by no means wanted to break with the Soviets, he himself suggested that the German group of the relief mission— the Steyler Divine Word Missionaries under the direction of Father

Eduard Gehrmann, who were working in the Crimea—be called to Moscow:

> "In case of an overthrow or threatening circumstances, the German group, thanks to the present good relations of Germany and Russia, is in the safest position."[41]

But that was not the only consideration; in Rome Walsh received a whole package of instructions, though it is hard to say whether they arose from flexible tactics, or simply from Vatican indecision. Walsh was, namely, to attempt the continuation of the relief mission—for the time being only in the form of medical aid—and to propose a new contract to the Soviets for this purpose; he was also to hold out the prospect, with no commitment, of a kind of *de facto* recognition, perhaps even a "formalization" of relations, however only at the price of concrete concessions. Among these were not only the release of Archbishop Cieplak, but above all a demand that would repeatedly play an important role in coming years: religious instruction for children, at least in church buildings, should be allowed, and the Soviet legislation be revised on this point.

In July, Walsh presented the Soviet "Commission for Foreign Aid," which was directed by Mme. Kameneva, Trotsky's sister, with the outline for a new eight-point contract, which was however kept rather vague, and the last two points of which, dealing with diplomatic privileges, were subject to a special agreement "from Rome."[42] The Soviets reacted reservedly, most especially to the demand for free appointment of the relief personnel of the Vatican mission.[43] The promise of even a limited recognition was of course tempting as it always had been, even if they were not quite comfortable with Walsh's double role as "charity director" and "relief diplomat." The fact that Walsh now even wanted to rent a house in Moscow (Vorovskaja 44), with the explicit remark that it could perhaps one day serve for an apostolic delegate, made just as much of an impression as the transfer of the German fathers to Moscow; Father Gehrmann hardly knew what was happening when the local government of the Crimea gave him a "great banquet" on August 5, 1923, before his departure:

> "A toast was drunk to His Holiness Pope Pius XI too, and it moved me strangely when the twenty government representatives (all Communists) rose and emptied their champagne glasses to the health of the great monarch of Rome."[44]

But outward appearance was deceptive. On August 1, Walsh had brusquely ordered all the relief stations of the mission to halt distribution of foodstuffs—even where there were still some supplies. Publicly, he was demonstrating a "policy of strength" toward the hesitant negotiating partners. In reality, however, he wanted to conceal the weakest point of the mission: its acute lack of funds. This latter had of course not remained a secret from the Soviets; they now insisted on concrete agreements before they would even discuss religious concessions. Walsh adhered all the more to these very demands; Father Gehrmann complained that the contract had not materialized solely because Walsh was demanding "too much freedom of movement" in the question of religious instruction.[45] Walsh, however, decided to bluff financially too: on October 17, he submitted to Mme. Kameneva a relief plan based on $900,000, without having discussed it with Rome or having received any kind of assurance of such a sum.[46] But all this only provoked anger on the Soviet side and finally the demand, sent directly to Rome, that Walsh be recalled from Moscow.

In mid-November Walsh appeared excitedly at the German embassy and declared to Count Brockdorff-Rantzau that a break in relations between the Vatican and Moscow "was imminent"; the Soviets were playing such tricks on him personally that he had demanded his papers and would leave on November 23.[47] Actually it was the Vatican that had recalled Walsh.[48] And Commissar for Foreign Affairs Chicherin, who used to chat away whole nights with Brockdorff-Rantzau over their favorite cognac (the only thing "French" that they both appreciated), assured him (according to a telegram from the ambassador):

> "Russian government absolutely wishes to preserve good relations with Vatican. But [Chicherin] has refused for weeks to receive Walsh; says he is dishonest and intriguing, with Yankee manners; he hopes the curia will decide on change in personnel to avoid endangering relations. . . . From what I know from a definitely reliable source, he [Walsh] has even said in intimate circles that there *must* be a break, and *he* would incite it. Professor Walsh's attitude is transparent; having mixed politics equally with works of Christian charity, he now wants to justify his position and arising animosity by a break in official relations."[49] (These remarks Brockdorff-Rantzau cabled to Berlin.)

The German ambassador advised that the Vatican be informed of this quickly, before Walsh arrived in Rome. Immediately—under telegraphed instructions from the Berlin Foreign Office—the ambassador to the Vatican von Bergen went to the Cardinal Secretary of State. Gasparri, however, reacted casually: the question of personnel was of "secondary importance"; on the other hand, it was lamentable that the Soviet Russians had not fulfilled their promises, "for example, concerning a modus for the property of the Catholic church."[50]

The question of personnel was by no means as insignificant as Gasparri thought, Brockdorff-Rantzau contradicted: "Chicherin has personally told me of several cases in which Walsh has given provedly biased reports and claimed promises from the [Soviet] government that were never made in the distorted form in which he presented them."[51] How far the personal differences had blossomed became clear when they literally "turned off the taps" on Walsh: after Walsh had refused, in mid-November, to formally take possession of the house he had rented for $12,000 a year in the Vorovskaja in Moscow because the authorities had not dislodged a sub-tenant, they cut off his water and electricity. However, the same evening, after the angry American had left Moscow almost head over heels, without any goodbyes, and his successor, the German Father Gehrmann, had moved in, the water was running again and the lights burning. . . .[52]

A Martyr to Rome—A Priest to Lenin

Red Army soldiers guarded the lead-sealed car that was attached in Moscow to the regular train to Odessa. Its peculiar freight consisted of only one single crate. Its accompanying papers could have confused any worthy Bolshevik: "Valuable statue! Gift to the Vatican Museum!"

But this freight declaration was a camouflage, it revealed only a part of the truth. What was loaded onto a Russian ship bound for Constantinople, there in the harbor of Odessa in November 1923, then taken by an Italian freighter to Brindisi, and finally to Rome, were the relics of a Polish national saint, the Jesuit Andrzej Bobola.[53] As a "soul-catcher" (*duszochwytacz*) who wanted to Catholicize the Orthodox, the missionary had been killed by Cossacks in 1657, and canonized by the church almost 300 years later. In 1919, the Red revolutionaries had wanted to open the grave of the martyr in the White Russian city of Polozk and present his remains for ridicule at one of those anti-religious exhibitions so fashionable at the time (see also p. 22). An urgent telegram of protest from the "Catholic Central Committee" and Archbishop Cieplak to Lenin had prevented this, however.

Not until three years later was the reliquary shrine finally brought to Moscow and put on exhibition—in the Museum of Hygiene. Here the papal relief mission discovered it and after extended efforts arranged that Bobola's remains be sent, not to Poland, but to Rome; this was happening at the same time that Walsh had to pack his bags and give up the direction of the Vatican mission in Russia. Foreign Affairs Commissar Chicherin had spoken out in favor of this gesture—it cost nothing—and also obtained Lenin's consent to it.

In October 1923, Lenin, who after his second stroke suffered from speech impediment, had surprisingly returned once more to his desk in the Kremlin, if only for a short time. Clandestine power struggles for his succession and also for the future "line" of the Party and the Soviet state had already begun. Certain ideological "relaxations," which resulted in Lenin's "New Economic Policy," (NEP) but which were still controversial, also had an impact on cultural policy. A general interest had arisen in religious questions.[54] Two atheistic publications appeared in 1923, *Besboshnik* (The Godless) and *Besboshnik u stanka* (The Godless at the Workbench), which polemicized not only against religion, but against each other. The one appealed to Lenin's thesis that the struggle against religion must be conducted "scientifically," if possible without administrative measures, above all without insulting the simple believer; the other wanted to "strike (religion), knock it to pieces, root out this riff-raff like weeds,"[55] especially by means of offensive caricatures and satire. Lenin personally, toward the end of his life, leaned increasingly toward a more serene approach: "The transformation of the peasant psyche and custom is a matter that takes generations. The use of force does not help."[56]

Not only the extraordinary release of St. Bobola as a "gift for the Pope" can be explained by this general atmosphere, but also a second remarkable episode, little known until today: a private meeting of Lenin with a "soul-catcher." It was the Catholic priest Dr. Viktor Bede, who visited Lenin several times in the autumn of 1923 and published the conversations *anonymously* a year later. Bede's somewhat florid description, which sounds almost incredible, would hardly deserve consideration had it not appeared in the official Vatican paper *Osservatore Romano* as the "personal memoirs of a foreign priest of our acquaintance and frequent contributor to this paper," and had I not succeeded in unveiling the secret of the author's identity.[57]

"Your Pope must have sent you to me!?", Lenin cried mistrustfully, when Bede tried to convince him that a more just social order could arise, not from the destruction, but rather on the foundation, of religion.—Bede insisted, as was true, that he had no instructions, that not even his friends knew about his private trip to Moscow. Bede, about fifty years old at the time, was a native of Hungary, a French citizen, and had been a journalist in Paris from 1909-1912; there he met the Russian journalist Ilitch Ulianov (Lenin), who wrote for the emigrant paper *Proletari*. The memory of this professional friendship from his years in Paris opened the door to Lenin for Bede, who in the meantime had become a Catholic priest. He entered the Kremlin in civilian clothing, "provided with the best papers by the powerful dictator."

Bede reports that Lenin received him simply and reflectively, quite without any tyrannical airs, although marked by his illness. "Humanity is going the path of sovietism; in a hundred years, there will be no other form of government," Lenin announced, and added consolingly, "I believe, though, that among the ruins of present institutions, the Catholic hierarchy will still continue. . . . In the next century, there will be left only *one* form of government, the soviet, and *one* religion, the Catholic—it's a pity that we won't live to see it."

It seemed to Bede that Lenin's error consisted in the equation of the soviet form of government (*il soviettismo*) with Communist ideology. And thus Bede tried to champion the cause of religious freedom by mentioning—in allusion to the papal relief mission—the "pure communism" of the Catholic monasterial orders, whose religious educational work also had social effects.

"You would probably like me to allow the peasants to be incited against the Soviets by your monastic brothers? No, that is impossible!", Lenin replied sharply, and then suddenly reflected almost gently—so Viktor Bede reported—"I sense that I have only a short time to live; what you contemplate is too beautiful for me to bring to realization. There will be others, I hope, who instead of bloody coercive measures, will employ the ones you are talking about to inspire humanity. . . ."

Of course, Soviet policy was not so sentimentally inclined as this sounds. The fact was that daily decision-making had already to a large extent slipped out of Lenin's hands, even though he had begun to govern again for a short time this autumn of 1923. However, not a few indications imply that Lenin himself—and above all "his" foreign politician Chicherin—were more concerned with improving relations with the Vatican than destroying them. This was closely connected with Soviet efforts toward diplomatic recognition, and paradoxically it was favored by a thesis current in Western Europe: that the Soviet regime itself might not survive Lenin's imminent death—at least not in its present form—and for that very reason one should have a diplomatic presence in Moscow.

This assumption played an important role especially with that government which, more than any other European regime, considered its vocation to be the "fight against Communism": the Italian government of Benito Mussolini. The fascist leader, even before his "march on Rome" (October 1922), had taken the death of Benedict XV as occasion to ingratiate himself with the Vatican, although a-religious himself. Laicism, liberalism and Marxism were dying, Mussolini announced; the only "universal Idea" that still possessed any radiant force emanated from papal Rome. In March 1922 in Berlin, and in July 1923 in Rome, Mussolini had met with the German Catholic "Rapallo" chancellor Wirth. In the summer of 1923 the Vatican had brought about the resignation of the priest Luigi Sturzo as chairman of the Catholic People's Party of Italy and thereby taken the first step toward an understanding with Mussolini. The latter declared on November 30, 1923: "The fascist government sees no difficulty in a *de jure* recognition of Soviet Russia." Which actually occurred nine weeks later.[58]

Immediately after Mussolini's announcement, the Kremlin also submitted a new proposal to the Vatican; its essential content was revealed in several diplomatic reports from Rome,[59] but its intention became tangible in the altered atmosphere that Father Eduard Gehrmann observed as new director of the Vatican Relief mission: on December 1, Gehrmann heard from Ambassador Brockdorff-Rantzau, who had invited him to dinner, how important a normalization of relations was to the Soviets; they even wanted a press interview from Gehrmann about the relief mission (probably to prepare public opinion for the rapprochement). Father Gehrmann, very inexperienced in diplomacy, very simple and easily led,[60] allowed the German ambassador to guide his pen. In his interview, the Soviet citizen discovered for the first time officially the extent of papal aid in the Crimea, but also that Gehrmann was in "constant communication" with official powers "who gladly fulfill my wishes." This was rather optimistic, and had not been discussed with Rome, but it fit very well with the cordiality with which Gehrmann was shortly thereafter received by Ambassador Theodor Rothstein in the Soviet Commissariat of Foreign Affairs:

> "The government very much regrets the misunderstandings that have occurred now and again and . . . have impeded a cordial relationship. . . . We have instructed our representative in Rome that we desire good relations with the Holy See . . . . We regard the mission . . . as a quasi-representation of the Holy See. . . ."[61]

The kernel of the Soviet proposal that Jurenev, Worowski's successor and soon to be representative to the Quirinal, submitted to the Vatican Secretariat of State at the beginning of December 1923, concerned above all the question of diplomatic relations: Moscow seemed prepared to make certain concessions, if the Holy See would upgrade its Moscow mission into a nunciature and at the same time conclude a new relief agreement (with concrete promises!). In this case Moscow promised guarantees of "freedom of worship" for the Catholics, release of sentenced clerics through an "act of grace," and what sounded rather new: certain possibilities for Catholic religious instruction of young people; thus concessions on the very issue that in previous months—when Walsh was negotiating—had always proven the most difficult. Could this be taken seriously?

In fact, at the end of December 1923 a Soviet government decree was issued that forbade "religious instruction of minors outside of school through the formation of groups larger than three," but at the same time seemed to make possible the formation of such "larger groups" under qualified pedagogical direction, if "previous permission" had been obtained and this instruction "registered with the proper authorities." A later official elucidation said that not only parents, but also "persons invited into the home" were allowed to give religious instruction "if this action is not transformed into a group activity."[62] These conditions were probably anticipated in the Soviet offer that was presented to the Vatican, without being spelled out.

Secretary of State Cardinal Gasparri considered the offer from Moscow worthy of "most careful consideration." He called a special session of the "Holy Congregation for Extraordinary Ecclesiastical Affairs" for December 17, 1923, which at that time consisted of eighteen cardinals. Discussion, however, began before that. The diplomats in Rome pricked up their ears.

"From various indications I conclude that Jesuit General Ledóchowski, a Pole, would offer resistance to a plan to recognize the Russian government, as he has also suspected highly-placed Vatican personalities of over-friendliness toward the Soviets," Ambassador von Bergen telegraphed, "top secret" and in code, to Berlin.[63] His Bavarian colleague also reported that there were "people in the Vatican" who accused the curia of "too conciliatory an attitude" toward Moscow.[64]

But what did "friendly" or "conciliatory" mean at this moment? Cardinal Gasparri regarded the situation objectively. He considered it a "gross error" to believe that anything like a counterrevolution had any chance in Russia. He told Ambassador Pastor[65] that the Russian people were "too passive" for that, and besides, one should not forget that the Russian peasants owed the possession of their own land to the new regime (collectivization was not yet the order of the day). Gasparri, who was an old hand at canon law, believed in the utility of institutional protection almost as deeply as in divine assistance; for him there was basically no question that the church would still be confronted with Soviet Communism even after Lenin. The argument launched by another cardinal, that they hadn't sent a nuncio to the National Assembly in Paris during the French Revolution either, had no effect on Gasparri first of all because, to his knowledge, the Paris National Assembly had never submitted a proposal to the Pope or asked his help for the starving masses.

But in Moscow, in mid-December 1923, Vatican missionaries sat in nervous, worried anticipation of an answer from Rome. For the Bolsheviks, it could only mean a diplomatic plus or minus, but for the Catholic church in Russia it was linked with the question of survival.

Father Gehrmann Quits—Pacelli Negotiates

"I consider it my conscientious duty to most humbly inform the Holy See that numerous Catholic priests of the Ukraine, the Crimea and also here in Moscow (20 to 30 priests) have expressed to me the sincere and positive wish that the Holy See may find a way to keep the mission here and thereby offer strong backing and moral support to the religiously oppressed."

With only a faint, but fearful, idea of what was being intensely discussed in the distant Vatican around the New Year of 1923/24, Father Gehrmann wrote these lines at the beginning of January.[66] Doubtless, a permanent representative of the Holy See in Moscow would have been welcomed by the Catholics of the Soviet empire "like a Messiah."[67] Hadn't the Pope, months before, declared himself prepared, "wherever possible, to make concessions and sacrifices in order to make existence less burdensome for the church"?[68] To be sure, the Pope had also spoken of an "insurmountable line" of principle; however, *where* this line was to be drawn was the main point of contention at the conference of Cardinals that had met on December 17, 1923 and with the consent of the Pope would finally produce only a half-decision.

The offer from Moscow (see p. 56) was not directly rejected, but it was answered with an evasive proposal: no legal recognition of the Soviet government, and no nuncio for Moscow, but instead an *apostolic delegate* was offered, a papal emissary who—according to canon law—is only authorized to supervise and report on the local church; this is primarily in states that do not wish to maintain diplomatic relations with the Vatican (like the USA to this day). The papal delegate in Moscow, however, was also, according to this proposal, to negotiate on the spot with the Soviet government about a *modus vivendi* for the church; in the event of a successful outcome of such talks, the Vatican held out the prospect of recognition for the Soviets, even if only in very vague formulation. For internal use, the Pope issued the watchword: "If the Soviet government proves itself worthy. . . ."[69]

What did "worthy" mean in this situation? Naturally in the Vatican the first thought was of the liberation of the imprisoned priests, Archbishop Cieplak above all; but also of greater freedom of movement for the relief mission in the distribution of (now rather scanty) donations for food provisions. There was a growing, prolonged discord again between Mission Director Gehrmann and the Moscow authorities on this very point. Tens of thousands of hungry Moscow students, who suffered particularly badly in these winter months, were waiting for help. Gehrmann, on the other hand, had been waiting for six weeks for instructions—and for new resources from Rome. But in the Vatican they were debating primarily about "wide-reaching policies," about legal clauses and strategems. Finally Gehrmann distributed, on his own authority, some of his remaining stores of flour, rice and sugar; but this could hardly impress the Soviet authorities, who for their part were just as concerned with clauses and strategems: while Gehrmann was supposed to, and wanted to, seek out needy students at his own discretion, the Moscow authorities insisted upon selecting the "chosen ones" themselves—a macabre tug-of-war for the growling stomachs of students who certainly, at this moment, ranked food *above* marxist or Catholic morality. . . .

Finally, on January 7, 1924, Gehrmann received his long-awaited instructions from Rome, via the German diplomatic telegraph; but they hardly relieved him, but rather were "frightening,"[70] because they restricted his possibilities even more:

"Holy See renounces none of the demands previously made by Walsh concerning reorganization of relief work. . . . (It is) necessary to refrain from obligation to government of any kind on any question without prior information from Holy See. . . . Please use great care to protect rights of Holy See concerning provisions and house. . . . Remittance follows as soon as you have reassured Holy See through report concerning preceding points."

Thus Cardinal Gasparri telegraphed to his man in Moscow. Of course, what he did not tell Gehrmann was the fact that the Vatican counterproposal—the offer of an Apostolic Delegate—had been made to the Soviets and also that the choice had been made as to who this future delegate should be. It was not to be Gehrmann himself, who with his upright manner seemed poorly suited as a diplomat, but rather another member of the Vatican relief mission, in Rostov at the time: the Jesuit Father Giulio Roi. He too was no diplomat, but—18 years older than Gehrmann—he had proved himself deserving as rector of a seminary in Northern Italy, and was an unknown quantity for the Russian observers in Rome.[71]

Roi was now called to Rome at the beginning of January 1924 to prepare for his duties. As an Italian, the curia figured, he would not have a bad start if only because the assumption of diplomatic relations between Italy and the Soviets was imminent (February 8). The Pope, who would not permit himself such a step, was by no means unhappy about this connection; Mussolini would "keep a sharp eye" on the new Soviet embassy in Rome and "if necessary, step in with his usual energy," said Cardinal Secretary of State Gasparri.[72]

It was an iron rule of the Vatican, since the end of the Papal States (1870), to maintain no contact with the foreign representatives who were officially accredited to the Quirinal (i.e. the Italian Head of State). Therefore, after the Soviet trade representative in Rome, Jurenev, had received the rank of Ambassador to Italy, Gasparri insisted on transferring further contacts to Berlin. The papal nuncio in Munich, Eugenio Pacelli, had not yet moved to the Reich capital; this took place only in August 1925. But Pacelli's frequent visits to Berlin served, from February 1924 on, for confidential meetings—usually in the Franciscan Sanatorium—with the Soviet chargé d'affaires Bratmann-Brodowski, and soon also with his superior, Ambassador Nikolai Krestinski. It was probably here that the Vatican's temporizing reply to the Soviet proposal of December 1923 was delivered,[73] which occasioned Foreign Affairs Commissar Chicherin's angry remark:

"Perhaps we will have to get along without the assistance of the (Vatican) mission; they are making great demands, and no recognition by the Roman curia has been forthcoming."[74]

Basically, both sides demanded "pre-payment": the Vatican did not want to extend legal recognition without previous, documented, Soviet concessions; the Soviets refused to negotiate about concessions without this recognition. Before that they would neither admit an apostolic delegate nor alleviate the situation of the church. Even Father Gehrmann's relief kitchens, which had long been cooking on low flame, would only be allowed to continue if the Vatican would write clear assurances—financial as well as temporal—into a new contract.[75] Father Gehrmann, in Moscow, who was hardly aware how heavily his Russian charity depended on the outcome of a diplomatic game, was still hoping for a new, solid foundation. On February 20, however, a second "cold shower" hit him in the form of a telegram from Cardinal Gasparri:

"concerning contract Holy See wishes continuation of work but can settle neither termination nor amount stop will give as much as it has at disposal and receives. . . ."

On the other hand, the imaginary $900,000 that Father Walsh had bluffed with were still haunting the mind of President Kameneva of the Soviet "Commissariat for Foreign Aid" (see p. 52). When Gehrmann now appeared before her with this telegram from Rome, which sounded almost like an oath of manifestation, she still could not believe that the Pope's coffers were empty; she suspected instead that part of the diplomatic tug-of-war for recognition underlay it. For that reason, but also because with Lenin's death on January 21 Soviet policies had taken an erratic course, Mme. Kameneva reacted crossly, but did not order the departure of the mission. Not until a month later, on March 22, did she inform Gehrmann that the Vatican mission had been removed from the list of licensed relief organizations, while in Rome on that day there was a meeting of the same men who, two years earlier, had laboriously brought the mission to life: Monsignore Pizzardo, Prelate Steinmann of the German embassy to the Vatican, Father Friedrich of the Steyl Order, and the mysterious Dr. Wilhelm von Braun, who was emerging ever more strongly as middleman for the Soviets (see p. 27) and who, after Father Walsh's recall from Moscow, had offered himself as his successor. They discussed what should happen now;[76] Braun recommended meeting the Soviets half-way and repeated his offer to go to Moscow himself to help the "moribund mission" to its feet again. Pizzardo, however, disagreed: "If the Russians make everything dependent on recognition, we don't even have to talk about it any more; then it's all over. Never ever can the Holy See recognize such a government. . . ."

Then Dr. von Braun let fall a remark that betrayed him; namely, he almost threatened, "If *I* don't get to Moscow, then no missionaries will stay there at all. . . ."

This remark must have alarmed the Secretariat of State, for shortly thereafter this coded telegram was sent via the German embassy to Gehrmann in Moscow:[77]

"As the danger exists that Russian government will expel members of papal relief mission, it is advisable that agents prepare for possible departure, especially regarding archives. Cardinal Gasparri."

Things had by no means gone this far. At this time[78] Mme. Kameneva would turn irresolutely to Chicherin: She personally no longer attached importance to the continuation of the almost inactive Vatican mission, but perhaps it was in the interest of the Foreign Affairs Commissariat to keep it up for the time being? Chicherin, who was still playing the Berlin line to Pacelli, asked her to wait. Certainly the situation had changed since, in the first months of 1924, England, Norway, Austria, Greece and Sweden had, in addition to Italy, recognized the Soviet government:

"*De jure* recognition by the Vatican would have been incomparably more valuable for the Soviet government two years ago than now. In spite of that, it [the government] hopes to arrange a religious peace with the Vatican, and is completely prepared to negotiate to attain this goal. . . ."

Thus Chicherin informed the German ambassador Brockdorff-Rantzau on March 31, 1924, who immediately relayed this remark "top secret" to Pacelli in Berlin. In Rome they understood exactly where the impediment lay:

"The main stumbling block has simply not yet been removed: '*de jure*' recognition. The Vatican remains firm in its policy that it cannot give its recognition under the existing circumstances without causing a great scandal among the faithful. . . . A compromise was not accepted (by the Russians). So now what? An additional, perhaps complicating, circumstance has arisen, that Dr. von Braun has gone over to the service of the Soviets and that he is very much put out by the four-time rejection of his plans in the curia. . . . He sees himself as the creator of the mission and also believes that one word from him would suffice to have it thrown out of the country. . . ."

So Father Friedrich reported,[79] and Cardinal Gasparri telegraphed Gehrmann succinctly: "I warn you against Braun." This extraordinary friend of the mission had namely disappeared very suddenly from Rome at the end of April, in the direction of Moscow.[80] Not only did Wilhelm von Braun boundlessly overestimate his own influence, he apparently also deceived himself about the Soviets whom he served.

In Moscow, in these first months after Lenin's death, the "Diadochian" struggle for power had not yet really broken out. What Karl Radek entrusted to the German ambassador was still valid: the leadership was being held together "by common hope for victory or by the certain prospect of a common gallows."[81] But at this time one could not really speak of a consistent line in Soviet domestic and foreign policy[82]—and that also had its effect on relations with the Vatican. While Chicherin was making great efforts to bring the Vatican to an agreement in the Berlin Pacelli-Brodowski discussions, and to this end not only bridled the zealous Mme. Kameneva (Trotsky's sister), but also cautiously included in his diplomatic calculations the release of Archbishop Cieplak, as a symbolic "pre-payment," the GPU played him a nasty trick: the secret police, without Chicherin's knowledge, suddenly removed the Archbishop from prison and quite informally put him on the express train to Riga at the Lettish border on April 9, 1924; and this at the mere request of the tiny Communist party of *Ireland*, for whom the Cieplak case had become extremely unpleasant propagandistically, in their Irish Catholic milieu.[83] With the same special authority it had received on April 2, which made possible such "kindnesses," however, the GPU also set in motion a new wave of arrests: during April and May, numerous Catholic priests and nuns, among them 37 Russians of the Eastern Rite in Moscow,[84] were arrested and sentenced without trial, via "administrative channels," to prison and exile. When the so unexpectedly released Archbishop Cieplak arrived in Rome at the beginning of May, Cardinal Gasparri declared, shaking his head, "Russia is still a great enigma."[85]

In the face of such contradictions and uncertainties, was it not advisable to delay as long as possible the withdrawal of the Vatican mission from Russia? Its duties now shifted—with ever more limited means—to helping Catholics in Russia:[86]

On the same day that Archbishop Cieplak arrived in Rome and could present the Vatican with the latest reports on the actual situation, the Cardinal Secretary of State sent another coded telegram to Moscow:[87]

From the watchword given here may be seen how strongly the Roman curia still hoped to be able to combine the incompatible: conciliation with intransigence. The Vatican was evidently also strengthened in this tactic now by Archbishop Cieplak, who had been treated strictly, but not inhumanely, in the GPU prison; he had been able to receive packages, books, newspapers, and even visitors.[88] While Cieplak, in the intimate circle of his Roman acquaintance, made no secret of his attitude, and complained that the European governments were "blind to the Bolshevik danger," and that the Soviet diplomatic representatives—the sixty-man embassy at the Quirinal in Rome as well—were composed of "nothing but agents,"[89] still he emphasized simultaneously that he wanted to "forgive and forget" his personal bitter experiences. He carefully avoided any public

Berlin, den 26. April 1924.   zu IVa Rm 2678

B Diplogarma

M o s k a u.   Nr 161   T e l. i. Z.
                                        (Geh.)

                        Gasparri bittet Weitergabe an Gehr-
                        mann:

                                "Bitte klug aber reichlich katho-
                        lischen Klerus unterstützen, der über-
                        all in sehr großer Bedrängnis.

                        Aufheimstelle Weitergabe.
                                H a u s c h i l d

                                        K480342

Abgesandt

("Gasparri requests delivery to Gehrmann: Please support, sensibly but abundantly, Catholic clergy, which is in great distress everywhere. Gasparri.")

polemics against the Soviets. Even the Soviet ambassador Jurenev was favorably impressed by that. At a diplomatic reception he let his Polish colleague know how highly the Soviet government respected such behavior, and how much he personally would like to talk with the Archbishop sometime. Shortly after that, Cieplak "quite privately," but with the approval of the Vatican, visited the Soviet ambassador to Rome. Jurenev revealed to him that the whole problem of the imprisoned priests could be swept aside if the Vatican would at least recognize the Soviet government *de facto* and take up negotiations in Rome.[90]

To this day we have no assurance that Cieplak did not simply misunderstand this conversation as he reported it to the Cardinal Secretary of State. Why should Moscow come down a peg and suddenly give up on *de jure* recognition? *De facto*, the Vatican had been in contact with them for a long time. But maybe Jurenev had simply wanted to start a new round of negotiations. After all, the Soviets were still just as concerned as the Vatican not to burn all bridges.

At any rate, Gasparri now intensified the Berlin contacts between Nuncio Pacelli and embassy counselor Bratmann-Brodowski again.[91] Two weeks later, at the end of May 1924, the Jesuit Giulio Roi, who had been in Rome for four months preparing for his supposed new duties (see p. 59), travelled back to Moscow; he was to be there, on the spot, as apostolic delegate, in case an agreement should be reached in the Berlin discussions.

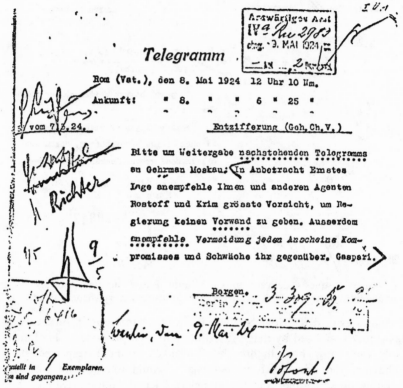

("Please deliver the following telegram to Gehrmann in Moscow: In view of the serious situation [I] urge greatest caution upon you and other agents in Rostov and Crimea; don't give government any pretext. Also recommend avoiding the appearance of any compromise or weakness vis-á-vis government. Gasparri.")

In his pocket, however, Roi also carried the cancellation of the relief mission. It was formally presented on May 31 to the impatient Mme. Kameneva. Why? Was that not in contradiction to the current negotiation?

By no means; with clever tactics, the Vatican, which could no longer completely support the relief mission financially anyway, anticipated a Soviet order of expulsion with this notice, pulled the rug out from under Soviet accusations of "deviation from the intentions" of the aid, signaled its preparedness to change its charity representation into an apostolic delegation, and—gained time. For at the same time, the Vatican representatives assured the Soviets that they would still distribute the remaining 367 tons of provisions, and perhaps send "fresh supplies" later, and that furthermore they needed another few weeks to wind things up. This stretched to three and a half months. . . .

"Right now, a persecution of Christians is raging through Russia," Father Gehrmann wrote on June 17, 1924, to his superior in the Order. On the same day in Moscow, Mme. Kameneva's secretary tried to clear the air: "I would like to say, Herr Gehrmann, that we don't want to mention the past—all that shall be forgotten!" If the Vatican would guarantee aid amounting to at least $8,000 to $10,000 a month, then one could discuss an extension, the secretary gave him to understand. After all, in May alone, the mission had gotten $9700 to imprisoned Catholics![92] But on June 28, another reticent report arrived from Rome: since the provisioning situation had improved in Russia, the Holy See could not issue another call for contributions, and could not guarantee $10,000 from its own resources; however it would

> "very gladly continue relief works, especially for children and invalids . . . without any definite commitment, however. [The Holy See] hopes to *continue* [!] *good relations with government*, which could even be improved by presence of apostolic delegate. Monsignore Pacelli is working toward this end. . . ."[93]

As amicably packaged as this telegram of Gasparri's was, the Soviets would no longer go along with such a vague offer, but did not refuse it until six weeks later. The first Vatican emissaries had already left the Crimea. "The population, in tears, surrounded our house," one of them reported about the departure. On July 29 Cardinal Gasparri telegraphed the fathers in Moscow to "protract their departure"; from this the German ambassador Brockdorff-Rantzau suspected that Pacelli's Berlin negotiations with the Russians were perhaps nearing a successful conclusion, especially as Father Roi already had presented himself to the ambassador as the prospective apostolic delegate.[94]

But now, as many aspects became known by rumor, severe resistance to and criticism of the Vatican's Russian policy was again raised in Rome by "international Catholic circles."[95] Did the Holy See want to "draw nearer" to the Russians? The archival documents presently available for this phase of Pacelli's negotiations (in contrast to later ones) offer only very sparse indications of the actual situation. It is certain that Pacelli spoke with Brodowski not only about the replacement of the relief mission by an apostolic delegation, but also about many particulars, for example religious instruction for young people (see also p. 113). The Vatican by no means insisted here on the "establishment of *confessional schools*," as was claimed by Chicherin, and even 50 years later by the East German historian Eduard Winter (who prefers to quote documents one-sidedly or incorrectly, and neglects to mention "unsuitable" ones). In reality—as Cardinal Gasparri communicated to Moscow—the Pope requested *"only permission for the clergy to teach the catechism in the churches."*[96] Unrealistic enough to demand more than such a minimum the Roman curia was not. Of course, the latitude for concessions that the Vatican thought it could allow itself was also minimal. The Berlin discussions were interrupted at the end of August. Even a decidedly anti-Communist observer in Moscow had the impression at the time that the Vatican could have assumed an "impregnable position" for the defense of its religious interests in Russia if it had established itself with a stable, permanent representation in Moscow by means of a legal-diplomatic act of recognition, like other governments.[97] The opportunity that the famine relief mission offered would perhaps never reoccur.

Cardinal Gasparri seems to have had this uneasy impression when at the end of August he finally did give the mission the signal for an orderly retreat; he telegraphed:

> "Gehrmann, Vorovskaya 44, Moscow. Before your departure I request that you convey to the vicars general words of encouragement for the priests and believers of the Mogilev and Tiraspol dioceses. . . . Tell them that the Holy Father is thinking of them, follows their difficult tasks with a fatherly heart, and blesses them. . . . Give them . . . everything you possess. Assure them that the Holy Father will do everything possible to serve them *by other means*. . . . Cardinal Gasparri."

There were still about a million Catholics in the Soviet sphere of influence at this time, and 127 priests, of whom 111 could still officiate, while the other 16 were in prison.[98] "Somehow the Vatican must keep in touch with Russia," Father Gehrmann wrote anxiously before his departure, and was almost happy when, shortly before his final exit from Moscow with Father Roi on September 18, 1924, Chicherin asked him around to take assurance to Rome that the Soviet government nevertheless wanted to maintain contact with the Vatican.[99] And was that not also Rome's wish?

It was no accident that the Vatican paper *Osservatore Romano*, on August 23—that same day that Cardinal Gasparri ordered the retreat from Moscow—published those strange memoirs of the priest Viktor Bede of his conversations with Lenin (see p. 54), in which the deceased creator of the Soviet state was respectfully invoked as a witness for the enduring strength of Catholicism and—of Communism. The German embassy to the Vatican already knew on August 27 that papal Rome, true to a centuries-old tradition, in spite of everything did not intend to write a historical finis:[100]

> "Even though the curia is leaving Russian territory at the moment, it has not thereby given up the hope of continuing its activity in the east. It will seek new avenues, and wait for that moment with its own innate tenacity in the pursuit of its grand designs—which are independent of time and person. . . ."

III

On A Double Track:
Confidential Contacts And
Secret Bishops, 1924-1926

To "Intervene" against Moscow?—A Memorandum

Anyone with an important matter to discuss, after panting up the steps of the Vatican palace from the Damascus Court to reach the third loggia—at that time the present-day elevators did not exist—and then somewhat anxiously awaiting an audience in the magnificent antechambers of the papal apartments, had to resign himself to a great uncertainty: one could never be sure of the reaction, the reply, the final decision of Pius XI. This Pope, whose reputation as a passionate mountaineer, as well as an aloof, reflective historian possibly lacking in decision-making ability, had preceded him at his accession to the throne of St. Peter, had since then made a kind of virtue of this weakness: more and more often, he let himself be carried on a wave of momentary emotion to the peak of passionate enthusiasm—only to change his mind later after all. Some observers called him choleric or impatient, and even respectful admirers complained that "on almost every occasion [his decision] ran contrary to suggestions."[1]

Not only the Ratti Pope's closest associates had this experience, but also occasional, less experienced visitors such as Fathers Eduard Gehrmann and Giulio Roi on their return from Moscow. On the very day of their arrival in Rome, September 26, 1924, they had been received by Cardinal

Gasparri and Monsignore Pizzardo to deliver their reports, and had learned that the Pope, after the unpleasant end of his Russian relief mission, no longer wanted to keep silence, but rather to take an open stand against Moscow. Father Gehrmann was alarmed; for as inauspicious, even gloomy, as his report from Russia had to be, he also clearly recognized that "an open declaration of war by Rome would produce frightful outbursts of rage by the Communist rulers, and surely cost a lot of blood."[2] But when a week later, on October 2, he was able to report to the Pope by himself— without Roi—for an hour and a half, he met with a very different, very calm atmosphere: the Pope seemed to have an open mind for Gehrmann's idea of a "reconciliation with Soviet Russia," and also received favorably Gehrmann's advice that they might withdraw ecclesiastical jurisdiction over the Russian dioceses from the Catholic bishops who were now living outside Soviet Russia—that is, those who had emigrated (like Ropp and Cieplak), but also the Eastern Polish ones—and install apostolic administrators; only this plan would allow the re-establishment of a hierarchy and contribute to an understanding with the Moscow government.

This suggestion of Gehrmann's, which Pius XI later tried to realize in a different and rather dilettantish form (see p. 83f), touched on a problem which occupies Vatican eastern policy to this day (cf. the formation of the Oder-Neisse dioceses in Poland, the administrators in East Germany or the dismissal of Cardinal Mindszenty in 1974). In that autumn of 1924, when the Pope regarded things as "very bleak for Russia," even saw a "terrible danger for European culture" in the Soviet Union[4]—as it was now called— a letter had reached him from an imprisoned cleric, the deacon vicar of Zhitomir, Andrzej Fedukovicz. This letter, probably brought back by Father Roi, had been influenced by the Soviet police, perhaps even extorted, but it also contained—Gehrmann could vouch for this—some bitter truths:[5]

"... For five years we have been orphaned, without a shepherd, because the Bishop of Zhitomir emigrated to Luck, which now belongs to Poland. ... To communicate with the bishop the priests must use various go-betweens: speculators and spies who cross the border by forbidden paths; or the Polish consulate. ... Unfortunately, the situation of the Catholic church in the Ukraine is constantly deteriorating, because the gentlemen of the Polish consulate even force matters upon the clergy that have nothing to do with their religious functions. Thus Mr. Swirski, the consul in Kiev, in 1923 sent me monies to be used for the material support of the Polish teachers in the Soviet schools in Zhitomir. ... Mr. Swirski informed me, in Prelate Teofil Skalski's apartment (see p. 123), that he had received various reports on the actions of the government of the Soviet Ukraine: about armed attacks on Catholic churches and chapels in the beginning of May. ... Swirski charged me with verifying these facts. ... Thus I became an agent of the Polish consulate. ...

"I implore Your Holiness on bended knee to use your apostolic authority to influence the Polish government so that it does not exploit clergymen for political purposes. The Catholic church must be the bearer of the pure Christian ideal, without any adulteration. I firmly believe that Your Holiness will hear my lowly voice, will not leave the weak without protection, and will come to an understanding with the local government concerning the establishment of an apostolic vicarate, to be put on the level of a bishopric. . . ."

Such a document, in all its ambiguity, could only underline Gehrmann's desire that "contact had to be maintained with Russia"—in spite of everything. Chicherin's message,[6] brought by the returnee from Moscow (see p. 66), but also Gehrmann's determination to do everything within his power "to find a formula that conforms to the interests of both sides" could not have failed to have an impact on the Pope. He instructed Gehrmann to write down, in addition to his detailed reports on the accounts and experiences of the charitable activities of the relief mission, also his political impressions, perceptions and opinions.[7] But now something quite strange happened:

In the six weeks that Gehrmann spent in Rome, his opinion on the Vatican's Russian policy appears to have changed radically—if one accepts the twenty-page political memorandum that he wrote as proof of this. This document, dated November 12, 1924, and intended for the Pope alone, lies unpublished to this day in the Vatican secret archives, but a duplicate can be found not only in Gehrmann's private papers (in the Roman archives of his order, the "Society of the Divine Word"), but also in the archives of the German Foreign Office, to which Gehrmann, who always wanted to show that he was "patriotically oriented," delivered it in Berlin four months later (facsimile of first page, p. 70). The Foreign Office advisor noted in long-hand on the margin that Gehrmann had stipulated that the document "not be transmitted to Moscow." Gehrmann probably did not want his patron Brockdorff-Rantzau (with whom he had up to now had quite a different opinion), to discover it, and he certainly also feared that it could fall into the hands of the Soviets.

Right at the beginning, Gehrmann openly called upon the Pope to "intervene" against Communism in Russia, and at the end of the memorandum he comes to this conclusion: since the "dismal fact" of the identity of Soviet government with Communist party was now "established with complete certainty," there was no longer any reason to abstain from an "official and public condemnation of Bolshevism." As reasons for this counsel, Gehrmann named—in rather unusual order for a theologian—"1. reasons of expediency; 2. reasons of principle."

Among the first sort of motives Gehrmann counts not only the applause that a condemnation of Moscow would find among conservatives as well as social democrats all over the world (see facsimile), but also the *internal,*

A. Prolegomena.

Aus mehrfachen Gründen ergibt sich für den Heiligen
Stuhl die Notwendigkeit, gegen den jetzt herrschenden Kommunismus in Rußland einzuschreiten, ihn   als verwerflich hinzu-
stellen und zu verurteilen. Die Gründe hierfür sind:

    I. Opportunitätsgründe,
    II. Prinzipielle Gründe.

I. Opportunitätsgründe.

    1.)   Viele konservative Kreise der ganzen Welt, nicht
nur katholische, würden für den Heiligen Stuhl gewonnen werden,
wenn eine solche Aktion unternommen würde; und viele nichtkatho-
lische Kreise haben schon mehrfach danach gerufen, da sie den
Papst als einzige Autorität von genügender Bedeutung und Er-
leuchtung ansehen.

    2.)   Auch unter den Arbeitern der ganzen Welt, und selbst
der Sozialdemokratie (II.Internationale) herrscht eine große
Feindschaft gegen Sowjetrußland, weil sie einsehen, daß die Bes-
serung der Lage der Arbeiter durch das Vorgehen der Sowjets
aufs schwerste gefährdet und diskreditiert wird.. Wenn die Aktion des Heiligen Stuhles nach der bestimmten Richtung geführt
wird, wie es später auseinandergesetzt wird. Von einer solchen
Aktion des Papstes würden selbst diese sozialistischen Kreise
so befriedigt sein, und die Stellung der christlichen Arbeiter-
verbände würde eine ganz bedeutende moralische Festigung er-
fahren.

L233273

3.)

intra-party situation in the Soviet Union. He analyzes the beginning
struggle for power for Lenin's succession, although—as we can recognize
today—with some false emphasis:[8]

"The extreme faction consists of Zinovieff, Dczerczinsky (director of the
GPU), Stalin (party secretary), Bucharin (party chairman), Kamenev (president
of Moscow). . . . The opposition leaders are Trotsky, Radek, Rykov, Krassin
(members of the Foreign Office are closer to this movement). . . . The
opposition has given up the idea of a world revolution and is seeking its fortune
in holding its own in Russia. . . . The opposition is supported primarily by the
old idealists, the (non-Jewish) intelligentsia in the party, a large fraction of the
students, and the army which is completely devoted to Trotsky. . . .

". . . Trotsky's and his supporters' time has not yet come, but certainly will
sometime, and then he will not spare his opponents as they have spared him. The
following may serve to characterize this tendency: Trotsky made a speech in July
[1924] in which he proposed that they should harass religion indirectly, and not
directly, as they do now. . . .

"Unless completely unforeseen circumstances arise, Communism in Russia
will not be replaced by the old Czarist system, nor can an armed invasion by its
other powers [?] be expected in the near future. But if this case should arise, it
would be highly desirable that the Holy See had undertaken an action against
the Soviets, because these new rulers would accuse the Holy See of having kept
silence, or even of having entered into closer relations with the Soviets. . . .

". . . It is however more probable—and the diplomatic delegations in Russia
also confirm this—that not a new ruler, but rather the . . . *moderate faction
within Communism will be successful.* . . . Thus the Holy See, in its steps
against the present Soviet government, also has *this* reassurance, that it has not
begun a hopeless course of action but on the contrary a very promising
one. . . ."

Father Gehrmann accordingly wanted the Vatican to intervene in the
Kremlin power struggle, wanted it to condemn Bolshevism—and not
because the position of the church in Russia had become untenable (up to
now this had been the only conceivable motive that influenced the Pope
even to consider such a condemnation!), but on the contrary, because this
would favor a "moderate Communism," according to Gehrmann. He
supported his analysis of the situation with dramatic descriptions of police
terror and economic decline, but also of the collapse of morals, to which he
contributed his own observations that today seem almost comical; for
instance, when we discover from him that apparently the "bikini" bathing
suit was invented at that time in what is today a very prudish Moscow:

". . . [Bolshevism] has abolished monogamous marriage and the
family . . . the struggle against any kind of morality begins even with
children . . . boys and girls are brought up together, taken for walks together
to sing their blasphemous songs in the streets. . . . They are taken swimming
together, where they wear no bathing suits. . . . The boys run around in the

streets of Moscow clothed only in swimming trunks, and the girls have an additional little covering over their breasts, the rest of the body is naked. . . ."

For the author of this memorandum, this was as depressing as the social and other injustices of the Soviet system, which—as he emphasized—were passed off as a necessary transition to permanent justice. This seduction was dangerous in that it came from fanatical young people; it caused Gehrmann to cry out:

> "Europe has taken a terrible responsibility upon itself by allowing these devils to continue to exist."

Where was the circumspect, always compromise-seeking friend of Russia, the Gehrmann whom we know from his reports from Moscow? Had he not himself feared "frightful outbursts of rage" against the church from an open challenge? Even now, in his memorandum to the Pope, he took into consideration the possibility that the Kremlin leadership might feel provoked by "a forceful action of the Holy See," "and would then proceed to a merciless persecution, harassment and execution of Catholics in Russia." But: "When it is an enemy that threatens all of Christianity, indeed all of mankind, it seems that even the otherwise praiseworthy consideration for the few does not release us from our duty to confront these enemies of all," Gehrmann advised the Vatican.

Was Gehrmann himself really the author of this document, so contradictory to his previous and also his later attitude? Many formulations, especially the more naive ones, witness that he wrote most of it himself. He writes in a note, however: "During my entire stay in Russia I have never concerned myself expressly with all these matters. First, I had no desire to, and second, this would have endangered the position of the mission." —Gehrmann thus had no special political interest; he was, as everyone who knew him testifies, not an analytical, intellectual person, and for that very reason was also easily influenced. In the Foreign Office in Berlin he later related proudly that during his six weeks in Rome he had "worked through all the relevant secret material concerning Russia."[9] This may have impressed him; but probably more important was a meeting with his prominent monastic brother Wilhelm Schmidt, an ethnologist and missionary scientist, who happened to be in Rome at the time.[10] Schmidt may have helped to guide Gehrmann's pen.

Apparently, though, Gehrmann had also gotten into the middle of the discussions that had flared up again within the papal curia about future policies toward Russia. The old questions arose—accommodation? continued negotiations? disengagement? condemnation?—whereby the memorandum of the "Russia specialist" Gehrmann would be used by one faction against the other.

An Exchange of Notes and Table Talks in Rome

"The strongest opponent to establishing relations with Russia in the autumn
of 1924 was Cardinal Ragonesi. Gasparri was in favor of it; Merry de Val was at
least for an apostolic delegate."

So noted the Austrian Ambassador von Pastor after a conversation with
Archbishop Cieplak, who ought to know.[11] Opposition among the
cardinals was strengthened not only by reports like Gehrmann's, but also
by the fact that Moscow—even in Pacelli's contacts with Brodowski in
Berlin—up to now had never made a formal, written reply to the counter-
propositions from the Vatican (dispatch of an apostolic delegate, see pp.
63-4). When Nuncio Pacelli met Ambassador Brockdorff-Rantzau at a
diplomatic breakfast in Berlin, given by the Reich President, he asked him
to make discreet inquiries of the Soviets. Rantzau thereupon addressed the
Soviet Commissar for Foreign Affairs in Moscow on the subject on
November 5, "as if it came from me."

"Chicherin replied that the actual negotiations had not yet begun; now that
Ambassador Krestinski has returned to Berlin, they will begin at an accelerated
pace. —I accordingly do not have the impression that there is any intention to
obstruct on the Russian side, but am still of the opinion that negotiations on the
basis so far adopted by the Vatican will meet with great difficulties."

Such was Brockdorff-Rantzau's report to Berlin, with the request that
Pacelli be "speedily" informed of it.[12] Shortly thereafter came Pacelli's first
meeting with Ambassador Krestinski. Even now, the Soviets still gave no
written answer, but repeated orally—as did Pacelli, by the way—their
familiar positions; much like the Czar in his time, they would gladly have
established their own delegation at the Holy See, but were reluctant to have
a papal representative at home. The subtle question, "nuncio or delegate,"
over which the Vatican was still racking its brains, of course interested the
Soviets much less now—as their urging of "recognition" had also tangibly
cooled. In the meantime, France too had recognized the Soviet Union (end
of October 1924); the price for this legal act was falling. . . .

Had the last chance been passed up then with the withdrawal of the relief
mission? Was a challenge, in the sense of the Gehrmann-memorandum, all
that was left, as the pessimists, but also the "idealists," in the Vatican
thought? Or couldn't they, even now, break the tie, as the diplomats—led
by Gasparri—advised? Pius XI, torn in both directions, played to both
sides. First he announced:

"No one can have thought that, because we have shown benevolence toward
the Russian people, we wished to support in any way a form of government (*una
maniera di governo*) which we are very far from endorsing. On the contrary, we
consider it our duty—after having tried for so long, with all our heart and with

all our strength, to ease the immense affliction of this people—, . . . to admonish everyone, and especially the statesmen, . . . that they try to fend off the extremely great danger and very certain evil of *socialism and communism* with their strength and that of their fellow citizens, without, however, relaxing their dutiful concern for the improvement of the situation of the workers and the disadvantaged. . . ."[13]

With these sentences in his Christmas address to the cardinals (Dec. 18, 1924), the Pope conformed to the mood of the majority of this body. His mention of socialism and communism in the same breath was clearly observed at the time. This was above all a warning to the Catholic People's Party of Italy, which (after the murder of the socialist Matteotti by Fascists, which almost brought about Mussolini's fall) had moved somewhat closer to the socialists; at the beginning of October 1924, the Vatican had applied for an Austrian entry visa for their party chief, the cleric Don Sturzo—he could not be allowed to become a hindrance in the negotiations between the Vatican and Mussolini, which were taken up at the beginning of 1925.[14] However, the warning was also meant for the Catholic Center Party of Germany, whose Reich Chancellor Marx governed with the support of the Social Democrats.[15] But finally (and this may even have been the primary motive for the papal communism-socialism warning), Pius XI wanted to buy some ideological insurance, so that he could quietly continue his own Russian policies. It could hardly escape careful readers of his address that he distanced himself only from the Soviet *form* of government and only excluded an "endorsement" of it, but not legal recognition of it.

Thus it is hardly astonishing that the Pope at the same time gave his Berlin nuncio Pacelli instructions for further negotiations with the Soviets. However, Father Eduard Gehrmann was appointed as Pacelli's advisor on Russia. He wrote—"confidential!"—to his superior on Nov. 24, 1924 (Orig. SVD Archive, Rome):

"Confidential!!!

Thus it will come about that I shall stay in Rome about a month longer; a difficult, but also pleasant time for me, as I can put my abilities at the direct disposal of the Holy Father. The same applies to Father Roi S. J., my Moscow companion. The reason for our stay is the approaching negotiations in Berlin between Russia and the Berlin Nuncio Pacelli. We are regarded and employed here as advance workers and as having quasi-competence *in rebus russiacis* (in Russian affairs)."

Had Gehrmann perhaps recommended himself for this advisory position by the militant memorandum he had delivered to the Pope hardly two weeks earlier? We shall notice how little, even now, Gehrmann was suited for "militancy," how strongly, in accordance with his basic beliefs, he was in favor of conciliation. . . .

Pacelli was called to Rome right at the beginning of the new year; on Jan. 8, 1925, the Pope gave him instructions for the new phase in negotiations with the Russians—provided that it would finally result in a clear, written position.

On Feb. 2, by telephone, the Soviet ambassador in Berlin, Nikolai N. Krestinski, informed the papal nuncio—who had arrived in the Reich capitol from Munich the previous day—that he had received instructions from Moscow and wished to discuss "important questions of church policy" with the nuncio.

On Feb. 3, Father Gehrmann—whose order had only reluctantly released him—arrived in Berlin; Pacelli was visibly relieved to have an expert assistant at his side at this moment. He asked Gehrmann to stay "until the negotiations have either reached a conclusion or come to a deadlock." Pacelli would have preferred to take the priest along the next day to his meeting with Krestinski, but Gehrmann advised against it,

"since the Russians probably know my face, but certainly my name, and could thus draw conclusions and [retroactively] discredit the relief mission. I also did not want a possible breakdown of negotiations to be linked to my name. . . ."[16]

For three weeks—from Feb. 4 to 24, 1925—Pacelli and Krestinski negotiated, without even the fact of their meeting reaching the public. Right at the beginning, on Feb. 4, Krestinski delivered a document of so-called *theses*[17]:

Moscow again wanted the Holy See to promise recognition of the Soviet Union at least in the foreseeable future; that it accept the Soviet version of "separation of church and state" and thereby also the Soviet legislation on the formation of "religious associations." In accordance with the instructions of the Commissariats of Justice and the Interior of April 27, 1923, "registration" of communities of worship and the presentation of a "statute" for authorization by the authorities were required. In return, Moscow was prepared to affirm the "principle of freedom of religion and conscience" for the Catholic church, to allow financial support of Catholic communities by the Holy See—under control of the state bank—and also the exchange of letters between these registered communities and the Vatican, including the transmission of papal encyclicals—everything under state censorship, of course. The "directors" of the individual communities (in Soviet terms, "religious associations," for the "church" as a whole had no legal existence) were to be "elected" by the members of the communities.

Perhaps the bishops should be elected, too, as well as the priests? Pacelli, holding on to his temper, asked the Soviet negotiator, and received an answer that would soon conjure up a momentous misunderstanding: it was the church's private affair what they wished to entitle the individual "directors"; the government would not meddle in that, they were indifferent as to whether someone was called "priest" or "bishop," so long as everything proceeded according to law.

"These negotiations are difficult, because the Soviets simply cannot change their nature [aus ihrer Haut heraus]," Gehrmann wrote his superior on the third day of negotiations. "I do not know whether I can be of that much help to His Excellency Pacelli. I believe that he does not want to carry sole responsibility for a possible failure. This is in my opinion the strongest reason why he will not let me go. . . ."

Here a characteristic of Pacelli's comes to light that we will often see in him—even later as Pope. This very sensitive ecclesiastical diplomat, who, when confronting his negotiating partners, seemed to "step out of a Titian painting like a renaissance prince,"[18] hid behind this exterior a hesitant nature, always weighing the pros and cons, which usually made him nervously avoid unequivocal decisions and expressions of opinion.[19]

His negotiations with Krestinski—to this day a carefully guarded Vatican secret—were probably a torment for Pacelli by the very fact that he was only too aware of the narrow latitude for negotiation existing for both sides on grounds of principle. But Pacelli was too much of a diplomat to consider insurmountable the hindrances that confronted him as a priest. Concordatory politics were for him as for Pius XI the contemporary means of ecclesiastical self-assertion vis-à-vis the modern state of whatever color. He had just achieved a concordat with Bavaria (1924), he was negotiating one with Prussia; with the Russians no concordat could be reached, but perhaps, if one could use their own manifest interest, one could arrive at a modus vivendi.

Of course, if Krestinski insisted on a "community election" of bishops, Pacelli quite openly told the Soviet ambassador, the Holy See had hardly any basis for discussion left; the canon law of the church simply did not allow that sort of thing.

At the meeting on Feb. 11, 1925, Krestinski surprisingly presented new clarifications from Moscow of the "theses"; this second Soviet negotiating document stated—not very clearly, to be sure—that the Vatican was to have the right of proposition, discussion and confirmation in the naming of bishops, and the bishops in the naming of priests. It was not much, but Father Gehrmann, who informed the German Foreign Office under the seal of secrecy, was hopeful:

> "I believe that the negotiations will proceed favorably. . . . I have now strongly advocated conciliation, and am trying to save what can be saved. . . ."

So wrote Gehrmann on Feb. 15 from Berlin to his superior. (One can see now how little this had in common with his adamant memorandum!) Pacelli may have also reported accordingly to Rome, when he interrupted the discussions on Feb. 24 in order to obtain new instructions from the Pope. The nuncio reckoned with a pause in negotiations of two or three weeks, but half a year passed until the next meeting.

For Pius XI was anything but encouraged by the result of this round of negotiations. It did not escape him that the small concession in Krestinski's second paper had been offered exactly one day after the signing of a concordat between the Holy See and Poland (Feb. 10, 1925). In this concordat with Warsaw, the Vatican had received many privileges for the church, but it had also ceded to the state president a veto in the nomination of bishops (art. XI), and to the government a right of veto over appointments of politically undesirable clerics to parishes (art. XX). A new bishopric was founded (Pinsk), according to the concordat, directly on the Soviet border of White Russia.[20] All this must have been a thorn in the side of the Soviet government, which was still allergic to Poland. The Polish concordat of course also showed how far the Vatican could accommodate particular state interests, if it received some concessions in turn. In addition, during these weeks of Feb. 1925, the first contacts had been made toward an agreement between Italy and the Vatican, and Pius XI said: "Naturally, only God knows the heart, but it seems that Mussolini means well. . . ."[21]

By contrast, the Soviet offers not only appeared paltry, but seemed to be tantamount to the curia giving its blessing to state control over a church already extremely limited in its possibilities. On March 6, 1925, after a conversation with the Pope (ex Aud. SS mi), Cardinal Gasparri noted on the Soviet suggestions: "unacceptable."[22]

But this was internal judgment; toward the outside, they kept a diplomatic silence, and waited. The Soviet embassy in Berlin several times urged a written answer, and Pacelli himself advised the curia not to allow the contact to break; that would not help the Catholics in Russia. In the spring and summer of 1925, new ill tidings arrived from the Soviet Union. On instructions from Rome, the nuncio asked for German help in a telegram from Munich dated August 14—shortly before his permanent move to Berlin:

gesandter graf zech
auswaertiges amt berlin

Telegramm Nr.
Aufgenommen den 14 AUG 192

Telegraphie des Deutschen Reichs

Berlin, Haupt-Telegraphenamt

Telegramr 965/14 muenchan c + 6385 25/14/8 9.10 n ar - Min.

= morgan sonnabend soll petersburg katholischer priester
dmowski erschossen werden bitte anweisung an reichsbotschaft
um begnadigung zu intervenieren = nuntius pacelli +

"Ambassador Count Zech, Foreign Office, Berlin. Tomorrow Saturday Petersburg Catholic priest Dmowski to be shot. Request instructions to German embassy to intervene for pardon. Nuncio Pacelli."

But it was too late to help the Polish priest of St. Catherine's in Leningrad. The Pope, however—on Aug. 12, 1925—now authorized Nuncio Pacelli to draw up a reply to the Soviets immediately after his arrival in Berlin; the Eastern Church congregation in Rome supplied material for it. To this day we do not know the exact wording of this letter from Pacelli to Ambassador Krestinski; it was dated Sept. 7, 1925, reference number 33518 (as revealed in a message from the nuncio to the German Foreign Office, see p. 85).

The letter contained a dispassionate statement of the reasons why the Vatican could not accommodate the Kremlin in certain points. It also, however, named points—primarily concerning the national loyalty of the clerics—in which the Holy See could make concessions, if the Soviet government were interested in a genuine normalization of relations. Two problems remained at the center: 1. appointment of bishops; 2. freedom of evangelization, i.e. religious instruction, also to minors under 18 (at least inside the church).

Three weeks later, on September 30, 1925, Reich Foreign Minister Stresemann gave a dinner for his Soviet colleague Chicherin, who was passing through on his way to the spa at Baden-Baden. Pacelli was also invited. He sat next to Chicherin, who politely acknowledged receipt of the nuncio's letter in Moscow; he had passed the matter on to his representative Maxim Litvinov for study. But Pacelli knew exactly that Litvinov, in

contrast to his superior, was only minimally interested in the "line to the
Pope." Was it therefore not advisable to use Chicherin's stay in Berlin for
an exhaustive tête-à-tête discussion? The nuncio found opportunity for this.

A week later, on the evening of October 6, 1925, two inconspicuous cars
drove up to the house at 34 Viktoria Street in Berlin. No one suspected that
it was the Foreign Minister of the Soviet Union and the papal nuncio—in a
simple black suit—who got out of them. In the apartments of Chamberlain
Count Ernst von Rantzau, the twin brother of the German ambassador to
Moscow, the two gentlemen dined "quite privately" and spoke—less
privately—with each other in great detail: Chicherin, the Communist from
the Russian aristocracy, and Pacelli, the Roman priest and diplomat. The
common language was German. There was no agreement in the matter, but
only in their perception to represent two opposing, but respectable, worlds.
They duelled not with the saber, but with the foil.

Rome had noticed, Pacelli said, that in the Soviet suggestions certain
limitations on the Catholic church had been "taken over from the era of the
Czars."—That could be possible, replied Chicherin, for in the so-called
"Renovated Church," which had close ties to the Soviet government, many
individuals had come from the era of the Czars.

This allusion to a separate group (see p. 81) of the Orthodox church was
more than a diversion; it was also a hint which indicated that the Orthodox
church, loyal to the regime, had a voice in the treatment of the Catholics.
Was a new hope being offered here? Pacelli probably pricked up his ears at
this argument. His first meeting with Chicherin, at any rate, was not his
last. . . .

Father d'Herbigny's Fact-Finding Mission: Dispute about God

Hands casually in his pants pockets, pushed-up tie jammed into his
much-too-short vest, pointed beard cut in the Lenin style—thus, on the
evening of October 6, 1925—the same time that Pacelli and Chicherin were
meeting in Berlin—Anatoli Vasilyevich Lunacharski, People's Commissar
of Education, stood in the glow of the spotlights on the stage of the
Moscow "Experimental Theater." Is it a comedy or a tragedy in which he
has assumed one of the leading roles? Six thousand people are listening to
him spell-bound—workers, students, soldiers, functionaries, aristocrats,
priests, a fascinated audience with divided sympathies. Two thirds of the
hall applaud Lunacharski's thesis, which he defends with an almost
romantic pathos: namely, that labor has become the true religion, the
proletariat the true God.

Yet immediately thereafter, a not insignificant minority in the hall celebrate a bearded Orthodox bishop, the Metropolitan Alexander Vvendensky, on whom the spotlights now focus and who replies with equal eloquence: God is a verity which continues to prevail unchanged even under the dictatorship of the proletariat—just like the multiplication table in mathematics. "And if Comrade People's Commissar thinks that the end of Czarism was the triumph of atheism, then we must differentiate among three categories of Russians who no longer go to church: those few like Comrade Anatoli Vasilyevich, who is a very well-educated man; then those who are not so well-educated, but who tell themselves that Comrade Anatoli Vasilyevich is a very strong man . . . and finally those who consider the livelihood of their families and—rightly or wrongly—are afraid. . . ."

"You are insulting us! Down with him! Stop!" come cries from the audience. Lunacharski smiles, chews unmoved on his pencil; then he himself returns once more to the podium: "We will gladly leave God, Christ and the saints to the Vvendenskys; for us remains the real creator—labor!"

Ten years before the revolution, Lunacharski had already gotten on Lenin's nerves with this sort of aphorism.[23] "Scientific socialism is the most religious of all religions . . . The search for a divine truth is an essential characteristic of humankind," Lunacharski had written. However, Lenin, although he had only scorn for this "God-building," entrusted Lunacharski with the Ministry of Public Education. And the Muscovites had him to thank that on this autumn evening of 1925—for a half-ruble admission—they were able to experience a spectacle that would be denied them in the next fifty years of Soviet history: a public intellectual duel between religion and atheism.

"What a surprise!", remarked a strange, beardless cleric in a black suit with a Roman collar sitting in the first row of the audience between two Orthodox bishops and observing Lunacharski with astonished eyes: it was the French Jesuit Father Michel d'Herbigny, the president of the "Papal Institute for Eastern Studies" in Rome, an intimate of Pius XI.[24]

How did this new emissary from the Vatican get to Moscow?—In d'Herbigny we meet the most puzzling, interesting, and tragic figure in the modern history of Vatican eastern policies.

His path, as we shall see, will lead from the peak of influential positions to the deepest humiliations of ecclesiastical exile.—At this moment, at the end of 1925, the 45-year-old d'Herbigny stepped into the spotlight of church politics for the first time. He had entered the Jesuit order at 17, had studied in Paris and Trier (Germany) and made his mark in 1911 with a work on the Russian religious philosopher Solovyov, which won the prize of the "Academie Française"; Solovyov's mystic-politically tinted conversion from Orthodoxy to Catholicism and his predictions of a "mongol storm" upon Europe had fascinated the young d'Herbigny.[25] The

Russian Revolution and the apparent missionary opportunities that it offered fired his imagination and his spirit of enterprise. In the autumn of 1922 he waited in vain in Berlin and Riga for a Soviet visa to join the famine relief mission in Russia; in a brochure on "Soviet Tyranny" he said: "The suicide is complete, this great nation is dying. . . ."[26]

When Pius XI entrusted the Papal Institute for Eastern Studies (*Pontificio Istituto di Studi Orientali*) to the Jesuit order in September 1922, d'Herbigny was called to Rome and named president; at the same time, the Pope appointed him consultant (*Consultor*) to the Eastern Church congregation. D'Herbigny not only kept in close contact with the Russian emigration in France and Germany,[27] he also observed intently the events in the Russian Orthodox church: after Patriarch Tikhon had been placed under house arrest in May, 1922 (see p. 40) and subjected to intense interrogation,[28] a so-called "Renovated Church" had formed in 1923 which attempted to preserve its religious existence by reforms within the church and by political concessions to the Soviets; it was at first favored by the Bolsheviks because a schism in Orthodoxy was very convenient for them just then. In order to prevent the threatening schism, however, Patriarch Tikhon suddenly, in June 1923, made a political confession of guilt with an oath of loyalty—and was set free. When he died in April 1924, the rise of the reformist "Renovated Church" had been stifled, already split into a small "red" group of bishops (the "Church of the Revival") and a "concordatory" moderate one (the "Church of the Renovation").

The differentiation between "red" and "concordatory" comes from Michel d'Herbigny, who also thereby revealed where his sympathies lay. For in the summer of 1925—even while the secret exchange of notes between Pacelli and Krestinski was taking place in Berlin—the Jesuit Father had received an invitation from the head of the "Renovation," Metropolitan Vvedenski, to the council of this Orthodox splinter church (which had surely not been extended without the agreement of the Soviet authorities and was interpreted by d'Herbigny as evidence of a certain interest in Catholicism).[29] Since the Berlin discussions were making no progress, the Pope was agreeable to a "private journey for vacation and study" for d'Herbigny, which would serve to reconnoiter the situation. When issuing his visa in Paris, Soviet Consul Aussem told the Jesuit traveller to Russia on September 29, 1925:

> "We are now practicing a new religious policy, for we have ascertained that millions of people, the majority of the Russian population, are bound up with religious ideas, and thus we have decided to cease the direct struggle with these tendencies, so long as there is no political agitation hiding behind them."[30]

Indeed, the XIIIth Party Congress in May 1924 had put forward the slogan, "spare the feelings of the believers"; blasphemous processions like those at Christmas 1923 (when they had a masquerading Pope appear with the Virgin Mary) had gone out of fashion. Commissar of Public Education Lunacharski taught that priests were to be viewed as comic figures, but not to be made into martyrs. So d'Herbigny, who came to Moscow for only 6 days on October 4, 1925, found a relatively relaxed atmosphere, "less hostile than in the tragic period from 1917 to 1923." Most of the Moscow churches were open, he remarked; things had not come to the desecration of churches as they had during the "barbarism of the French Revolution."

D'Herbigny received a devastating impression of the conditions in the patriarchal church of the late Tikhon, with whose vice-regent he had a long conversation. Still they had the majority of believers behind them; d'Herbigny, however, found them theologically rigid, religiously and politically implacable and absolutely passive. But the "red" hierarchy also received a low rating: Their Metropolitan Antony, said d'Herbigny, was "a charlatan, he had no influence any more in Russia."[31] On the other hand, d'Herbigny was deeply impressed by the church of the "Renovation," whose leader Vvedenski he observed on the above-mentioned evening of discussion with Lunacharski. Theologically, in terms of an understanding of liturgy and church, he heard a lot that was "Catholic" from Vvedenski during the "Renovation" council too.[32] Was there perhaps a common point here?

D'Herbigny was aware of the main difficulty: the patriarchal church was "reactionary," the "Renovation" on the other hand had "no hopes of establishing permanent roots among the population," he remarked to western diplomats in Moscow.[33] The travel report that he first published in the French Jesuit journal *Etudes* in December 1925 contained none of this skepticism, but rather a picture of the "Renovation" bordering on optimism, which was politically very welcome to them.[34] By contrast, the rather sketchy picture that d'Herbigny drew of the life of Catholics in the Soviet Union showed no bright side, but only a poor church, quite harmless to the regime:

> "Its position is more painful than all of the Orthodox, who at least are not without a bishop. . . . I found out, for example, that one priest has to care for five parishes, namely Archangelsk, Vologda, Jaroslavl, Kostroma and Rybinsk—that is an area nearly as large as the total area of Italy. . . . "

What purpose did d'Herbigny have with his so differently accented reports? Was he trying to generate an atmosphere for negotiations? He asserted later that he had not "visited" any high Communist functionaries or People's Commissar; but he had *met* Lunacharski, and the latter had assured him that he saw no hindrances to the entry of Catholic monastic clergymen into the Soviet Union, whether Benedictines, Dominicans,

Jesuits or Assumptionists.[35] D'Herbigny had also heard the opinion of another People's Commissar from the French ambassador in Moscow, Jean Herbette (whose name Herbette had not mentioned): as a result of modern means of communication, humanity was approaching a general centralization; three universal currents were competing in this—the materialistic-communist one of Moscow, supported by Asia, the materialistic-capitalist one of London, supported by America, and finally the idealistic one of papal Rome; since this last depended on "God," it was the hardest to tackle. . . .

A vision of the future—for the nineteen twenties, a fantastically daring one! It fired d'Herbigny's own rather productive imagination: It was conceivable, he wrote, that the two materialistic powers would not continue their rivalry to the triumph of one over the other, but "someday change it into a mutually beneficial community." Even then, the Catholic church—"which is not engaged in this struggle and is not sending out any propagandists against progress"—will spread Christian spiritualism "without political titles"—just as it christianized the "two forms of materialism," the Roman Empire and the barbarians. . . .[36]

One can see how strongly the concepts of the Orthodox "Renovation" (which d'Herbigny not without reason called "concordatory") had seized the Jesuit priest. A visionary streak becomes obvious, which actually seems to negate the thought that d'Herbigny had journeyed under instructions from the more sober Vatican diplomats, or that he had even prepared the way for "a concordat with the Soviet Jews" (as the newspaper of the German Hitler party claimed at the time in screamer headlines[37]).

And actually d'Herbigny had not been instructed to do more than reconnoiter the situation on this first trip to Russia; his quickly publicized, somewhat romantic conclusions would not have been discussed here in such detail if they had not had astonishing results: They not only offered Pius XI eye-witness information which decisively influenced his next decisions; they also qualified Michel d'Herbigny in the Pope's eyes as the right man for what would probably be the most adventuresome action of the Vatican's eastern policy, now in preparation. The Jesuit Father's travel report served as a "ticket of admission" to the Soviet Union.

Behind Closed Church Doors: Three Consecrations of Bishops

For five months already the Vatican had been awaiting Moscow's answer to Pacelli's note of September 7, 1925 (see p. 78). Pius XI, who had little hope that the stalled talks would really get going again, became more and more impatient after hearing d'Herbigny's travel report. Back in 1924, after the departure of the relief mission, the Pope had seriously considered sending clerical support to the Catholics in Russia "clandestinely."[38] Now, at the beginning of 1926, he no longer wanted to limit himself to the diplomatic route. First he conferred with the Superior General of the Assumptionist order. Gervais Quénard, an experienced missionary to Russia in prerevolutionary times. Quénard himself describes his conversation with Pius XI:[39]

> "He wanted to dispatch priests at any price and erect at least a *provisional hierarchy*. He asked me whether there were no monks in our order who had once been engineers or technicians whom we could send as civilians to one of the many factories that the Germans were building all over (in Russia), —out from under the control of the Allies—to serve German rearmament. . . ."[40] The Pope remembered having read that, during earlier persecutions in Russia, the mass had even been read out in the deep forest, and perhaps one could start again this way.—However, I presumed to remind the Holy Father that the 'Ochrana,' the secret police of the Czars, were not like the Soviets' 'GPU'. . . ."

Finally, in this conversation with Father Quénard, the Pope remembered another monk who had been living nearly twenty years in Russia and had survived the revolution: the Assumptionist Father Pie Eugene Neveu. In 1907 he had become pastor of a congregation of French and Belgian mining specialists, who were then managing coal mines and iron foundries near Makejevka in the Donetz basin. In 1922, Neveu, half-starved, had sent a sign of life to Rome and requested a new pair of pants and a new map of Europe. . . . His superior, Quénard, described him to the Pope as a man as pious and peaceable as he was stalwart and cunning, who as a Frenchman probably had stayed out of the local (Polish-Russian-Ukrainian) quarrels, and in addition was familiar with the Eastern as well as the Latin rite. There were also reports that Neveu had successfully extricated himself from numerous police interrogations and searches, by representing his and his followers' solidarity in poverty as primitive Christianity: "We are really communists, for we possess everything in common."

Was then Neveu, now 49, the right man for a future Catholic bishop in the Soviet Union? Quénard recommended him, and the Pope agreed. But how could they notify Neveu and consecrate him as a bishop? With or without the consent of the Soviets?

Once again the Vatican urged an answer from Moscow: before the German ambassador Brockdorff-Rantzau returned to the Soviet capitol from his Christmas vacation in Berlin, Pacelli called on him and asked him to make inquiries of the Russians. On February 9, 1926, the ambassador spoke with Chicherin, who acted quite surprised: on the contrary, the Soviet government was waiting for the Vatican; their note of spring, 1925, had never been answered. That was of course simply not true, and Pacelli

hastened to point this out—with proper dates and document numbers. A
telegram from the Berlin Foreign Office—marked urgent—was sent to the
embassy in Moscow (KO 11985/86):

"*Strictly confidential!* For the ambassador personally. Nuncio Pacelli, who
received in confidence the contents of your telegram nr. 169 of February 10,
declared, Chicherin's assumption the Vatican had not yet answered Russian proposals of spring 1936 based on error. . . ."

Brockdorff-Rantzau informed the deputy foreign commissar, Litvinov,
and also spoke with Chicherin himself, when he met him at a diplomatic
reception on February 28. Now Chicherin admitted his "error" and
excused it by his absence of several months. Affairs had, in fact, to a certain
extent slipped out of Chicherin's hands when he spent an extended period
in German sanatoriums with diabetes, and his deputy Litvinov was little
interested in the Vatican negotiations. In the meantime, the Soviet embassy
secretary Stange had appeared in the Berlin nunciature to clear up the
matter. They were polite; Chicherin even had Brockdorff-Rantzau asked to

inform Pacelli that, in spite of strong differences, "the divergences [were] no longer unbridgeable";[41] but there was still—after half a year!—no concrete answer to the Vatican paper.

The Pope was in a hurry, because on February 11 he had decided in favor of the long-contemplated secret action, if no positive reply came from Moscow. On this day he revealed to the—very astonished—Jesuit Michel d'Herbigny that he had selected him to become a bishop[42] and would send him to the Soviet Union, furnished with special authority so that d'Herbigny could consecrate several other new bishops there, but at least one: Pastor Neveu of Makejevka. The French Ambassador in Moscow, Herbette, had been informed through the friendly mediation of French Foreign Minister Aristide Briand, who had just relaxed the tension between the Vatican and France and at the same time opened relations with the Soviet Union.

At the beginning of March, d'Herbigny went to Paris and applied for a new entry visa to Russia—this time not for a study tour but for a "ministerial journey." This declaration was not false, strictly speaking, even though d'Herbigny kept silent on the main purpose of his visit and claimed that he only wanted to attend to the spiritual needs of the French, English, Italian and German Catholics, above all the members of the embassies, during the Easter holidays. But before he made use of the touristic back door, so to speak, to carry out his mission, the Vatican made one last attempt:

On March 20, 1926, Cardinal Secretary of State Gasparri directed the Berlin nuncio to deliver a verbal note to the Soviet Embassy, asking why they had still not replied to the September note. A week later, on March 27, the Soviets sent Pacelli a laconic letter in which they only affirmed the receipt of that note, now seven months old, and added that they were in the process of "studying" it.[43]

Did the Soviets sense something already? Had they become suspicious from the completely harmless-sounding letter in which Ambassador Herbette had invited Pastor Neveu to Moscow—a letter that never reached Neveu!—that there was something special behind d'Herbigny's trip to Moscow? Or did they just want to wait and see what the resourceful Jesuit would do now? In any case, d'Herbigny's visa was from the beginning limited to the Moscow city area; he had been told that he could later request its expansion through the French embassy and the Commissariat of Foreign Affairs.[44]

However, d'Herbigny first stopped in Berlin; but not to gather information on the state of diplomatic contacts, about which he knew nothing. On Monday, March 29, 1926, in great secrecy behind the closed doors of the house chapel of the nunciature at Rauchstrasse 21, d'Herbigny was consecrated as a bishop by Eugenio Pacelli, himself a titular bishop. A sealed "Motu proprio," dated March 10, 1926 and signed by Pius XI, authorized d'Herbigny as "*Delegatus ad fines Nobis notos*" (delegate for aims known to us) with all faculties necessary to his mission (*cum omnibus opportunis et necessariis facultatibus*). But now, after the secret ceremony in Berlin, he also possessed the theological prerequisites, indispensable in the eyes of the Catholic church, to pass on to priests and bishops the full authorization without which valid sacraments could not be given to the believers. The Pope assigned him the formal title of "Ilio" (today Hissarlik), a long-extinct bishopric in Turkey, a name with roots in the classical name of Troy. Perhaps the Pope—an educated humanist—was thinking of the Trojan horse now, as he sent his secret emissary on the German train into the land of unbelievers and iconoclasts.

D'Herbigny arrived punctually in Moscow for the Easter services on Maundy Thursday, April 1, 1926. He assiduously began to take great pains with the Catholic diplomats and even had "the peculiar taste" to call on Otto von Radowitz, a German Catholic diplomat, to remind the Catholic personnel in the German embassy of the fulfillment of their Easter religious obligations (confession, communion). Ambassador Brockdorff-Rantzau, who reported on this, was annoyed primarily, however, because he sensed that the Vatican's Russian policy was being taken up on a parallel track without his own knowledge—and with the help of the French, which he did not like. He summoned the Jesuit priest right after Easter, to "sound him out." D'Herbigny "thereupon became quite candid" and admitted that, although without official orders, he had tried "by private means" to make contact with the Commissar of Foreign Affairs; but they had snubbed him there with the comment that the relationship with the Vatican (or with the church?) was a domestic matter. But Chicherin must know, d'Herbigny claimed, that these were questions of international importance. . . .[45] Now Brockdorff-Rantzau was even more astonished: could d'Herbigny not have been informed by Pacelli in Berlin about the existing contacts?

It sounds unbelievable, but neither the Pope nor Pacelli had initiated d'Herbigny into the state of the negotiations;[46] they probably wanted him to undertake "unencumbered" his pastoral mission, the political explosiveness of which could not be mistaken. D'Herbigny, who in his later publications always denied that he tried to meet with any official of the Soviet Commissariat of Foreign Affairs, much less spoken with one, did meet—as we know today—with a Soviet functionary who occupied an even higher office: this was P.G. Schmidovitch, the member responsible for matters of religion of the Central Executive Committee (ZIK), to which the Council of People's Commissariats was subordinate. From Schmidovitch, who later (1929) also became chief of the Permanent Commission for

Church Questions of the ZIK,[47] d'Herbigny heard sybilline pronouncements: the state did not concern itself with any church in the Soviet Union; the church could—"under observance of constitutional regulations"—establish itself however it wanted to. The questions of designation of bishops, establishment of priests' seminaries, and entry of foreign clerics were also regarded in the same light, although Poles were of course undesirable.

That did not sound harsh, could even—if one wished—be interpreted as accommodating; but those very legal regulations to which Schmidovitch referred set narrow limits. It was also apparent that the jurisdictional competency among Soviet organs was not yet clearly settled. The Commissariat of Foreign Affairs refused to receive d'Herbigny, and referred him to the Commissariats of Justice and Interior, which usually enacted decrees on questions of religion, for example: "Every religious group is to freely select its bishop or priest. . . . No religious organization has the right to intervene in the activity of another against the latter's will, for example by installing priests."[48] Did this apply to the relations of congregations of the same confession *among each other*, or only *between* different confessions (religions), or perhaps also *within* one whole church, which did not exist for the Soviets as a legal entity?

The idea of a church whose leader resided in another country and ordered church administration within Russia was foreign even to traditional Russian thinking, much more so to the Soviets—and remains so to this day. Chicherin, a clever politician and "man of the world," was probably the only high Soviet functionary who was capable of thinking beyond this barrier. In contrast to Litvinov, he could completely comprehend "the *international* significance of an understanding with the Vatican," he repeatedly assured Brockdorff-Rantzau, his partner in evening fireside conversations over cognac. To translate this into practical politics, however, was becoming more and more difficult for Chicherin, especially since it was as clear to him as to the secret police that the Vatican was initiating a kind of self-help action. D'Herbigny knew exactly why he had to keep his intentions secret not only from the Soviets, but also from the German ambassador. . . .

"You are interfering with my correspondence with my countrymen!" complained France's Ambassador Herbette on April 13, 1926, in the Commissariat of Foreign Affairs, after his second letter to Father Neveu in Makejevka also remained unanswered. Finally, when Herbette telegraphed with a paid return, Neveu announced his arrival on the night train from Kharkov on April 21, at 5 a.m. Even now efforts were made to obstruct his meeting with d'Herbigny, or at least to intimidate him; on his journey, he was twice taken from the train and detained by the police; he did not arrive in Moscow until late morning.

D'Herbigny had received a summons from the Moscow city soviet for the same day at 2 p.m. that made him uneasy. In great anxiety, he now decided to act quickly. In the very early morning, he sneaked out a back door of his hotel (unobserved, so he thought), and slipped through the gate of St. Ludwig's, the only Catholic church in Moscow which—being French—was still "working."[49] Right across the way was the infamous Lubianka prison, where the GPU brought in prisoners every night. . . . Four hours later a robust, bearded peasant in a sheepskin jacket entered the church: Father Neveu. They barred the entrance; under the seal of confession d'Herbigny revealed himself to the bewildered priest:

> "I am a bishop, sent by the Holy Father to order religious affairs in Russia to the best of my ability (*régler la jurisdiction religieuse en Russie le plus possible*). But this must remain a secret for now. I need your advice, your help. . . ."

D'Herbigny first had Neveu give him the names of several other priests whom he considered worthy of consecration as bishops. Then he told the astonished Neveu that the Pope had already named him, Neveu; the consecration must take place immediately: "For I have been summoned to the city soviet today, and Ambassador Herbette thinks that they could arrest or deport me, or at least put me out of action. . . . So, kneel down at the altar and meditate. . . . I will give you half an hour to prepare yourself!"

So d'Herbigny quotes his own words in his memoirs. D'Herbigny had invited two witnesses to the consecration: the faithful church servant of St. Ludwig's, Alice Ott, who had also procured the oil for the ritual anointing, and the Italian military attaché Lieutenant Bergera, an intimate acquaintance of the Pope from the latter's service as nuncio in Warsaw.[50] When d'Herbigny, at the end of the ceremony, placed a copper bishop's ring on Neveu's finger and handed him the letter of appointment (facsimile p. 90), Neveu said, overwhelmed but with a touch of gaiety, "You have made me a successor to the apostles!"

But there was no time for emotions. Quickly d'Herbigny gave orders for the event that the Soviets were to deport him the same day; he revealed to Neveu:

> "By virtue of the authority I have received, I name you *Apostolic Delegate in the Soviet Union;* in case I do not return, you shall consecrate the priests Sloskans and Frison as bishops and decide together with them when you consider it advisable to openly declare yourselves as bishops. Here are instructions from the Holy Father, the rights and obligations, and the money he gave me. . . ."

Thus an attempt was made to realize "conspiratorially" what Vatican policies had been struggling for officially since the end of 1923, but had not yet attained in negotiations with the Soviets. And this without breaking off diplomatic contacts!

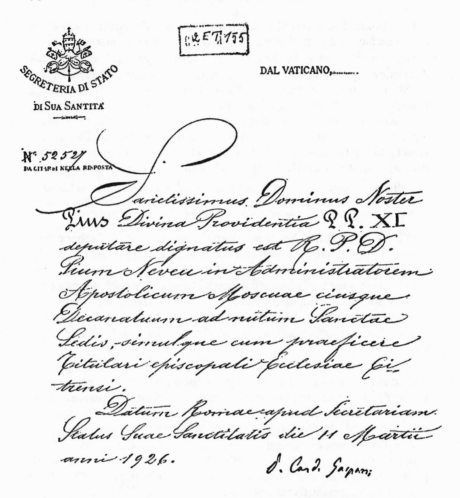

Bull of Appointment of the first secret bishop, which d'Herbigny brought to Moscow: "Our most Holy Father, by divine providence Pope Pius XI, has the grace to appoint the very Reverend Father Pius Neveu as Apostolic Administrator of Moscow and of its deanery "ad nutum Sancta Sedis" and at the same time head of the titular bishop's church of Citro. Given at Rome in the Secretariat of State of His Holiness on 11 March 1926, Signed Cardinal Gasparri." (Original in Neveu papers, "Archivio dei Padri Assunzionisti," Rome.)

But can one really assume that this action remained a secret from the Soviets? The bishop's consecration as such was of course not an illegal action in their eyes. But with the consecration, canonically effective jurisdictional acts had become possible. D'Herbigny had good reason to enjoin Neveu not to attempt any episcopal actions for the time being. Only if Neveu heard nothing from d'Herbigny within six months should he consult with the others, whom he was to consecrate as bishops at that time, on how they could exercise their episcopal function "without being arrested immediately." "We were completely in accord about the danger and the necessity for caution," d'Herbigny writes in his memoirs.

But the officials of the Moscow city soviet received the Jesuit with more curiosity than the hostility that he had feared. They handed him a letter which he himself could deliver to the directorate of the Ukrainian Soviet Republic: in it, Moscow asked them to issue a travel pass for the Ukraine to the gentleman from Paris (his clerical function was not mentioned), whom the French ambassador had vouched for, and permission to stay until May 16.

On April 22, d'Herbigny and Neveu got on the express train to Kharkov together; there d'Herbigny met for the first time the pastor Vincent Ilgin, who had been proposed as apostolic administrator here. From Kharkov both went to Makejevka, where Neveu would first remain in his parish. Then d'Herbigny went on alone; on April 26 he was in Nikolayev on the Black Sea; from there he reached Carlsruhe, a Volga-German village, in a horse-drawn wagon. There he met two German clerics, Augustin Baumtrog and Johann Roth, who were proposed as apostolic administrators for the Volga-German territory and the Caucasus. On April 29/30, d'Herbigny stopped in Odessa and informed the German deacon of Sevastopol, Alexander Frison, who was working there, that in the middle of May he would be secretly consecrated as bishop in Moscow. On May 1, d'Herbigny arrived in Kiev and immediately appointed the Polish vicar general of Zhitomir, Teofil Skalski, who lived in Kiev, apostolic administrator of the (since the Peace of Riga, 1921) Soviet part of the diocese—an honor that would have fateful consequences for Skalski more quickly than for any other of the appointees (see p. 96).

But could the purpose of d'Herbigny's visitation—to build up a new Catholic church hierarchy—remain hidden from the Soviets? They probably gave d'Herbigny relative freedom of movement because they thought they could "find out his tricks" better that way. Moving with the conspicuous inconspicuousness of the "amateur conspirator " (a peaked cap with his modest Roman collar, he reported proudly), he himself did some things that must have aroused mistrustful notice.

The last destination, after a short stop in Mogilev, was Leningrad, where d'Herbigny arrived on May 4, 1926, and took a room in the parsonage of the French Dominican Maurice Jean Amoudru. Amoudru, who had ministered to the St. Petersburg French since the years before the revolution, reported that in and around Leningrad there were still twelve

Catholic parishes and fifteen clergymen. D'Herbigny met them all on that same evening in the main Catholic Church, St. Catherine's, in the Nevski Prospect. D'Herbigny discovered with surprise: hundreds of children and youths were gathered to go to confession. A young chaplain, Boleslas Sloskans, was bewildered when suddenly an unknown foreigner addressed him and invited him into the parsonage.

Sloskans, now 33 years old, had given up his Latvian citizenship in the spring of 1924 and by means of a large bribe had acquired Soviet citizenship, so as not to have to leave Leningrad. He was—as Neveu described him—"simple, but holy." In contrast to two other Leningrad clerics, Malecki and Matulionis, who would later become bishops but had just now finished serving their three-year sentences from the Cieplak trial of 1923 (see p. 45ff.), Chaplain Sloskans also was probably not burdened with a "record" in the eyes of the Soviets. D'Herbigny had thus selected him for the third bishop's consecration.

(In 1972 and 1973 I was able to consult the sole surviving witness of these actions of d'Herbigny's, Mons. Sloskans, who lives in a Belgian cloister. In the library of the Papal Institute for Eastern Studies I discovered an unprinted manuscript of the diary he kept in great detail from 1917 to 1933.)

Hardly had d'Herbigny returned to Moscow from his grand tour than there stirred again those uninformed critics in the world press who for fifty years have been constant companions of Vatican Ostpolitik (to be sure, also partly as a result of the Roman curia's inadequate information policy). The fact that it was a Jesuit who had a finger in the pie in this year 1926 was enough to warm up some old legends—for instance, that for this order a pious end justified any means. For example, a newspaper made noises along these lines in Catholic Poland, where people observed d'Herbigny's efforts in Russia with particular suspicion and even in later years continued efforts to intrigue against d'Herbigny. "Respect for the Catholic church demands that we protest energetically against the methods of her representatives. . .", wrote the above-mentioned paper (Za Swobodu, May 9, 1926).

Naturally, it had not escaped Poland's notice that the Soviets, in negotiations with the Vatican, had excluded Polish priests from the beginning, and that Rome was not disinclined to go along with this condition. A Soviet diplomat, G. Bessedovsky, for example, got to hear about this when in May/June 1926, through the offices of an Italian embassy advisor, he came in contact with the apostolic delegate in Tokyo, Mario Giardini. The delegate informed him that, in order to lay to rest the Soviets' suspicions against foreign clerics, the Vatican would be happy to build a seminary for native priests.[51] But Bessedovsky's superiors quickly whistled him back—on the one hand, because they already had contacts with Pacelli in Berlin, on the other, because they were in the process of testing the intentions of the Vatican by d'Herbigny's actual behavior.

D'Herbigny stayed in Moscow nearly two weeks after his tour. He was determined to secretly consecrate more bishops, but also wanted to insure himself politically and diplomatically. Without revealing any of his intentions, he attempted to establish a favorable climate in his conversation with Schmidovitch (see p. 87). At the same time—following the basic pattern of Vatican Eastern policy—he made every effort to exploit the current European situation:

On April 24, 1926, the same day on which d'Herbigny had received permission for his tour, the "Berlin Treaty" was signed by Reich Foreign Minister Stresemann and Ambassador Krestinski, which was intended to strengthen the German-Soviet Rapallo agreements. With the Berlin Treaty, Stresemann had balanced the "Treaty of Locarno," signed in the autumn of 1925, in which Germany had recognized the western, but not the eastern borders of Germany (to Poland's discomfort). Against this background it is understandable that d'Herbigny was able to meet the creator of the German Rapallo policy, the former Catholic chancellor of the Reich Josef Wirth, at a luncheon in the house of the French Ambassador Herbette. The complete guest list of this dinner is not known; it is only certain that a high Soviet government official was present, if not Chicherin himself.

Wirth, who at this time had no official position, and had even temporarily turned his back on the Catholic Center fraction in the Reichstag (because it was too "rightist" for him), was staying in Moscow privately, so to speak: as chairman of the board of directors of the "Mologa" corporation—one of those concessionary enterprises of the kind that had been promised the Vatican in 1922 (see p. 31). Although Wirth's own financial interests were involved[52] and the enterprise was approaching a crisis, he considered it a "symbol of German-Russian cooperation." And as in Rapallo, (see pp. 37-8), he was also now prepared to place this connection in the service of his church. Of course, there is to this day no exact documentary evidence for Wirth's efforts at mediation in Moscow at the beginning of May 1926. It is well-founded that Chicherin gave him the same information about Soviet Vatican policy as he did Brockdorff-Rantzau shortly thereafter:

"The [Soviet] government will not hear about a *treaty* with the Vatican and *direct* relations; therefore he [Chicherin] is about to prepare a circular to be sent shortly to Nuncio Pacelli. The Soviet government does not intend to appoint a Russian representative to the Vatican, no more than it will allow a papal delegate in Russia; it does however wish to come to an understanding with the

Vatican and hopes for the agreement of the curia to this circular. . . . As he told me in confidence, Chicherin also informed the former Reich chancellor Dr. Wirth about his general plans. . . ."[53]

What was meant by the ominous word "circular"—a simple declaration of intention, or a "ukase" the Pope would just have to accept, or a negotiable position paper—would only be clarified months later. The hardening on the Soviet side, however, was now as evident as were Chicherin's efforts not to let things come to a breach in relations; however, the "question of recognition" was at this point no longer an object or matter for negotiation. Thus, even Josef Wirth could give d'Herbigny no favorable information about the *legal* possibilities. The only thing left for the "Rapallo" Chancellor, the friend of Russia and of the church, who naturally knew nothing of d'Herbigny's secret program, was a gesture of solidarity: on Sunday, May 9, during his mass in St. Ludwig's, d'Herbigny saw Josef Wirth's Herculean figure kneeling in the first row. . . .

On the very next day, May 10, d'Herbigny moved into action: again behind closed church doors, with Madame Ott and Lieutenant Bergera again as sole witnesses, he performed the second and third bishops' consecrations. Boleslas Sloskans and Alexander Frison, who had arrived from Leningrad and Odessa, knelt at the altar of St. Ludwig's and received from d'Herbigny, by virtue of papal authority, that power of consecration that according to Catholic teaching alone makes possible the continuance of the sacramental religious life. But d'Herbigny warned them also to remain silent for the time being, not to reveal themselves as bishops, but rather to return immediately to their congregations as simple priests.

The secret action had, in d'Herbigny's opinion, succeeded well but he still tried—even though revealing only half his cards—to obtain a little official insurance: two days before the double consecration and three days before his departure he met once more with Schmidovitch. The conference—he believed—proved to be so positive that he wrote about it enthusiastically from Moscow, by regular mail, to Neveu in Makejevka:

"Mr. Schmidovitch, whom I saw again yesterday, told me that he sees no difficulty in [d'Herbigny's] return which—as I told him—would have the purpose of installing Father Neveu, in the name of the Holy Father, as a French bishop in Moscow. He [Schmidovitch] added that his comrades in the various [People's] Commissariats found this solution to be "good for everyone." He also agreed in principle that two French parish priests be installed. The idea of a theological seminary in Odessa was also favorably received, and we may hope to realize it this year. . . . You may notify the south of this good news. I will probably have an opportunity then to come. . . ." (*D'Herbigny's letter of May 13, 1926; Neveu papers in "Archivio dei Padri Assunzionisti," Rome.*)

This document, which has remained unknown for almost half a century and (like many others) is published here for the first time, is particularly noteworthy, for it reveals exactly the fatal mixture of diplomatic and conspiratorial methods that d'Herbigny used: d'Herbigny obtains Schmidovitch's agreement to the installation of a bishop in Moscow, even assurance of another entry visa for that purpose, but conceals from the Soviet official that he had already consecrated Neveu. He guarantees Schmidovitch's promise by informing Neveu of it by regular mail (knowing very well that the censors and thereby also the competent authorities will learn of it); in the same letter, however, in a naively-coded form he informs the bishop-priest of Makejevka that two more bishops have already been consecrated.

Did d'Herbigny really imagine that he could deceive the Soviets with this sort of craftiness? He thought so. Convinced of his success, and of an even more successful return visit, he left the Soviet Union on May 15, 1926. When the train stopped at the border, a border guard gallantly distributed twigs to the female passengers. "They have no leaves or buds yet, but in the damp dewy air of this evening, seed was already beginning to sprout over the last vanishing snow," noted d'Herbigny, who was always ready to describe a romantic atmosphere. Unmindful of the dangerous situation in which he had left several of his brethren, he added almost ecstatically: "Leaves and flowers are near. . . . O my beloved Russia, you faithful souls of the Russian people . . . is a season of flower and fruit dawning for you too after your winter. . . ?"

A Deceptive Success: D'Herbigny's Last Trip to Moscow

"My return to Moscow met with scant approval from certain official personalities. . ." With this delicate intimation Michel d'Herbigny begins the report on his third journey to the Soviet Union, which he began from Paris on July 30, 1926, after two and a half months' preparation in Rome.[54] Again he traveled by way of Berlin and Riga, avoiding the direct route through Poland; for political changes had taken place there in the meantime that further aroused the Soviets' suspicion of their western neighbor:

On May 14, the same day on which d'Herbigny had left Moscow after his second visit, Jozef Pilsudski had succeeded in a coup d'état in Warsaw, with the help of the socialists, and even the communists. Six years earlier, the Marshal had performed the legendary "miracle on the Vistula" and defeated the Soviet army. And now, he had not become a "leftist Mussolini," as many of his friends had believed, recognizing their error too late. Pilsudski's democratically-laced rightist dictatorship was meant from the beginning as an anti-Soviet "bulwark." It was an open secret that Pope Pius XI admired the Marshal.

In the Soviet Union the struggle for power was also coming to a head in the early summer of 1926. Unlike Pilsudski in Warsaw, Trotsky in Moscow did not dare a coup d'état, but in the Central Committee session in July, with his followers, for the first time he openly formed an oppositional "bloc" again Stalin's increasing power.

Naturally, for the Kremlin, church problems now more than ever were at the bottom of the list; they had still not replied to Nuncio Pacelli's note, now nearly a year old (see pp. 63-4). Chicherin, whose diplomatic action in this question was already under suspicion within many party circles, was irritated by the duplicitous Vatican behavior that was revealed in the d'Herbigny action. But the continuance of this procedure seemed advisable to the Pope in view of the Eastern European situation. D'Herbigny's first successes—after all, he had managed to install three bishops—strengthened the Pope in his conviction that they could and must establish a hierarchy in the Soviet Union even without permission from Moscow, and thereby prevent the "complete dissolution" of Catholicism in Russia.

But already, on June 9, only three weeks after d'Herbigny's departure from Moscow, his work in building up the church received its first blow: the newly-installed apostolic administrator of Zhitomir, Teofil Skalski, was arrested on this date, together with other Polish priests.[55] The GPU accused them of "espionage" for Warsaw; as it later turned out (see p. 68), significant facts in this indictment had been known for years. They were now dragged up because—after Pilsudski's seizure of power—this could serve to intimidate Poles in the border areas.

All this by no means prevented the Vatican from sending d'Herbigny to Moscow once more; on the contrary: this time he even had instructions to consecrate a bishop of that very nationality that was more objectionable to the Soviets than any other: a Pole. Of course, this was to be kept strictly secret, as was the redistribution of the dioceses in the Soviet Union. The German consul in Odessa, who reported on June 17 that the Tiraspol diocese had been divided into four apostolic administrative districts (with sees in Odessa, Saratov, Pyatigorsk and Tiflis), asked that the information be treated as confidential, "as the Catholic church is very concerned that the Soviet government not receive premature knowledge of the Holy See's arrangements."[56]

At the same time, the Vatican was rather cleverly attempting to arouse the impression that they were playing with a full deck: on June 20, 1926, the Pope established a special commission on Russia (*Commissio pro Russia*) in the Eastern Church congregation, the practical direction of which was assigned to d'Herbigny—with the title "Relatore." To underline this promotion of the Jesuit, who up to now had been a kind of "private tourist for ministry to foreigners," d'Herbigny's episcopal incognito was also revealed: when application for his third visa to Moscow was made in July, through the French government, the Soviet consul in Paris was quite openly informed that d'Herbigny was a bishop. But this did not seem to influence the diplomats at all: church "service ranks" were irrelevant to the Soviet government; by the same token d'Herbigny could also not expect "any extra consideration". . . .

The reasons for this afterthought soon dawned on d'Herbigny. When he arrived again in Moscow on August 3, 1926, he immediately sensed that his return "was not popular with several official personalities." Not only did the police restrict his visa to the Russian SSR; his Communist contact from the spring, the ZIK official Schmidovitch (see p. 87), whom he visited again also, appeared less friendly: "misunderstandings had arisen," said Schmidovitch, who in the meantime had become quite aware that d'Herbigny had not told him the whole truth in their conversation of May 12; now Schmidovitch told him coolly that the Commissariat for *Foreign* Affairs felt itself entirely competent for d'Herbigny's concerns; but neither Chicherin nor any other official of this department wished to receive the Jesuit bishop. D'Herbigny suspected, quite correctly, that (as he told the German embassy's chargé d'affaires Hey[57]) behind this lay Chicherin's intention to negotiate all church questions with the Vatican via official diplomatic channels (through Pacelli), and not with a semi-official visitor. D'Herbigny was "disquieted by this threat to his successfully-begun mission," Hey reported to Berlin. His ambassador, Brockdorff-Rantzau, vacationing in Germany at the time while still keeping his hands on the reins, sneered when he read this report that "Father d'Herbigny was politically active in Russia under the pretence of a ministry"; Chicherin, "in spite of difficulties within the party," was still interested in an agreement with the Vatican, he said.[58]

This again reveals that d'Herbigny—whose zeal surpassed his assignment—did not possess complete insight into Soviet-Vatican relationships. For had he been completely aware of the duplicity of the Vatican procedure, he would not have viewed Chicherin's negative attitude as a "threat" to his goal, but rather as a warning that Moscow had seen through the Vatican's tactics. The Commissariat of the Interior and the GPU were doubtless interested in using this visit of d'Herbigny's to Russia to collect material on the "illegal activities" of the Catholics; for that reason alone they had not refused a visa for the Jesuit bishop's third trip. For Chicherin, on the other hand, the relationship to the Vatican was a problem of some importance to Soviet foreign policy, which he did not want to have complicated by domestic ideological and police trivia.

For that reason Chicherin did not close his mind to Brockdorff-Rantzau's request that he intervene in a death sentence pronounced at the beginning of August 1926 against a priest by the name of Zilinski, who had been arrested together with the apostolic administrator Skalski in Zhitomir. Although Brockdorff-Rantzau was reluctant, as a "German" ambassador, to intercede with Chicherin for an "apparently Polish" cleric, he let Nuncio Pacelli's "urgent requests" prevail upon him to do so. The death sentence was in fact not carried out. But when d'Herbigny made the same requests, at the same time, in Moscow (running on the "second track" again), his words fell on deaf ears even with the German chargé d'affaires.

The Skalski proceedings, which stretched over months, showed d'Herbigny how sensitive, even hysterical, the Soviets continued to be about anything Polish, especially in the religious realm. For that reason he now decided to carry out his primary mission as quickly as possible. On August 11 he was still assuring the German chargé that the Catholic church would "use neither Polish citizens nor people of Polish descent" as bishops,[59] but on the very next day he made a thirty-hour "lightning visit" to Leningrad and consecrated a Pole as bishop: the priest Antoni Malecki, who was born in that city (then St. Petersburg) in 1861, the son of a Polish engineer, and had attended the German St. Anna high school in the Russian capital. Malecki was not unknown to the Soviets: in 1923 he had been sentenced to three years' imprisonment in the Cieplak trial (see p. 45), but had gotten an early amnesty. On August 13, 1926, he was consecrated bishop behind the locked doors of the French church "Notre Dame de France," whose priest, the Dominican Father Jean Amoudru, and his vicar Dominic Ivanov, served as witnesses. Bishop Sloskans, the Latvian cleric whom d'Herbigny had already consecrated in May, assisted at the secret ceremony.[60]

Along with the sacral authority, d'Herbigny also conferred upon them canonical authority that he had brought from Rome: Malecki was named apostolic administrator for Leningrad, Sloskans for Mogilev and Minsk. The only thing lacking in the provisional re-establishment of the Catholic hierarchy in the Soviet Union was the transferral of Bishop Neveu from Makejevka to Moscow and his installation as apostolic administrator of the capitol. But was all this to remain a secret from the Soviets?

D'Herbigny sensed that he was being watched even more closely than before on his return from Leningrad to Moscow; perhaps he was becoming conscious of that vicious circle that would repeatedly be so fateful for Vatican eastern policies in the following decades: fear of persecution forced conspiratorial methods, but this secretiveness in turn aroused suspicion and persecution.

D'Herbigny now decided, without consulting Rome, on a "flight to the front": since the Soviets already knew anyway that he was a bishop, and since he had fulfilled his duty, he saw no reason any longer to keep this honor hidden from the faithful in Moscow. The romantic self-confidence that filled him at the time echoes in his own words:

"On the morning of August 15, after I had put on the purple socks in my hotel room for the first time, I dressed in the sacristy (of St. Ludwig's) in bishop's robes, the purple soutane. . . . When the choir boys carried a mitre to the altar . . . an astonishment, a curiosity, an emotion seized the crowd. . . ."

From the pulpit d'Herbigny proclaimed: "The Holy Father—in order to prove his great love for his Catholic children in Russia—has decided to have a bishop minister to them. . . . It is not a question of a diplomatic or political mission, for my visit will be only a few weeks long. I hope, however, that St. Ludwig's church will soon have another priest. . . ."

This first public appearance of d'Herbigny as a bishop had an electrifying effect not only upon the Catholics of Moscow, about 30,000 at that time; the tidings spread with astonishing speed to far-distant regions of the Soviet Union too, although a Leningrad newspaper was the only one to report on the arrival of a "Cardinal Derbini." Volga Germans traveled over a thousand miles to have themselves and their children confirmed; the French came from the Donetz basin, Poles from White Russia and the Ukraine, but also many Russians; many had secretly converted to Catholicism, as for example the Orthodox Bishop Bartelemy.[61] D'Herbigny avoided any contact with the Orthodox hierarchy, who were still entangled in internal dissensions. But he did not hesitate to celebrate a second solemn pontifical mass the next Sunday in Moscow's Polish church, Sts. Peter and Paul. For days he listened to confessions in Russian, French, German and Italian—the languages he knew. The faithful crowded in for hours to receive the sacraments, above all confirmation, from the hand of the bishop, to have the ill and infirm blessed, candles, rosaries and pictures consecrated. Catholic church life seemed suddenly to awaken—and the Soviet officials rubbed their eyes: was this "religious worship" or a "political demonstration" by a foreign power?

Since d'Herbigny now only came to his Moscow hotel, the "Savoy," late at night to sleep, the GPU had difficulties in applying their usual tricks. Still, he had to resist many clever or not so clever visitors who wanted to entrust to him letters to foreign countries, messages for Russian emigrants, or even "military secrets." On August 27, supposed reporters from *Komsomolskaya Pravda* appeared before d'Herbigny and asked him for an "interview," which naturally was never published. According to d'Herbigny's notes, it proceeded as follows:

"Are you an emissary from the Pope?"

"No, I am director of the Institute for Eastern Studies in Rome and have come as a bishop, with no diplomatic or political mission, to help Catholics in their spiritual need, especially the French, Italian, German and English."

"But what relationship have you established with the Orthodox clergy, with the priests and bishops of the various churches?"

"On this trip none, I have not met or spoken with any of them."

"But you surely are saying that the Catholic church in Russia is not free, that it is persecuted?"

"No one has heard such a remark from my lips. Only this is certain: If the Catholic church could not have either a regular hierarchy or a seminary for priests here, and if the arrests and sentencing of priests should continue, then naturally your enemies would say that church was being persecuted, and even your friends would not know how to answer."

The hidden barb in this elusive answer could hardly be missed, especially as d'Herbigny now turned the point around and himself asked the "journalists" some questions: "Are young people allowed to read for example Plato here? May they concern themselves with the philosophical concepts of truth, freedom and justice?" As answer he received party slogans, and probably the same word lit up in the minds of the visitors that had occurred to d'Herbigny under *their* questions: provocation.

The Jesuit bishop wanted to know the consequences as quickly as possible: the next day—August 28—he left his passport at the Moscow city soviet, applied for an extension of his visa, which expired September 4, and its expansion to include the Ukraine. He received a *temporary* permission until September 12; they said the final decision could be expected in four days.

D'Herbigny now attempted once more to speak with the ZIK member Schmidovitch; this official seemed even cooler than at their last meeting.[62] The comrades of the "Central Executive Committee" had not been able to sympathize with any of d'Herbigny's wishes, he said; religious instruction for minors could not be authorized even in the French church (he, Schmidovitch, had pleaded for this exception); a seminary for priests could perhaps be allowed in Odessa or Leningrad, but that too seemed rather improbable. And incidentally, this sort of question must be cleared through diplomatic channels. . . .

D'Herbigny had again run up against the limits of his "unofficial" possibilities. He was thus little astonished when the city soviet, on August 31, gruffly refused him permission for travel in the Ukraine. "I shall report this to the French ambassador!" he cried just as gruffly to the official, and left without taking his passport or inquiring about the extension of his visa. After all, he had his "temporary" extension until September 12 in his pocket! But even this strategem did not help for long. Shortly after midnight on September 4, there was a heavy knock on the door of his hotel room:

"Mr. d'Herbigny! Open in the name of the Moscow city soviet!"

An official in elegant civilian clothing entered, excused himself for the lateness of the disturbance, and came right to the point:

"We are amazed, sir, that you are still here!"

"But I have permission until the twelfth!" d'Herbigny bluffed, but his visitor was not impressed with the paper he was shown:
"Excuse me, I am not here to negotiate with you, but to tell you that your continued presence is unwelcome. This is not an expulsion; you have until eight o'clock this morning to tell us where you wish to cross the border. You may select your own route—only you may not stop anywhere else. We will send your passport to the hotel this afternoon."

This was unequivocal. Did they want to prevent the Pope's emissary from meeting again with Bishop Neveu, whose arrival from Makejevka he had been expecting for days? Neveu, wearing a black leather suit, entered St. Ludwig's quite suddenly, while d'Herbigny was still reading the morning mass. Immediately d'Herbigny handed him four documents, written in Latin calligraphy, that the Pope had signed six weeks earlier, on July 26, 1926. The first authorized Neveu to install "whomever he wished" as apostolic administrator in urgent cases, without waiting for the decision of the Holy See (". . . *facultatem habet eligendi vel nominandi Administratorem Apostolicum quem voluerit.* . . ."), with the condition that there should never be more than three consecrated bishops in Russia besides himself. The second authorization promoted Neveu, practically speaking, to sole negotiating partner with the Soviets: in order to present the most unified front, the other bishops should only with Neveu's approval "*negotiate with state officials about better conditions for the faithful.*" Two further papal decrees subordinated even the Exarch of the Eastern Rite, Feodorov, to Neveu's jurisdiction, and provided for the possibility of allowing Orthodox priests who wanted to become Catholic to keep their conversion secret—if necessary.[63]

With these canonical documents, which he delivered to the new bishop of Moscow on September 4 in the sacristy of St. Ludwig's in Moscow (their existence and contents are published here for the first time), d'Herbigny supposed his work completed for the moment. He packed his bags to leave as quickly as possible—in accordance with the Soviets' wishes. However, he had overestimated the GPU or underestimated the old Russian bureaucracy. No one brought him his passport that Saturday afternoon, nor on Sunday. He was still able to formally introduce their new priest to the congregation of St. Ludwig's, without revealing that Neveu was also a bishop. For the last time, d'Herbigny also celebrated a pontifical mass in the Moscow Polish church on that Sunday, and with an outdoor procession such as the Moscow Catholics had not experienced even in the time of the Czars:

> Hundreds of people, many amazed and curious Communists among them, stood crowded about as d'Herbigny entered the great square of the Sts. Peter and Paul church behind white-robed girls strewing flowers, behind banners,

singing choir boys and a great number of Polish believers. "As I carried the heavy monstrance with both hands, I could feel the tears running over my cheeks onto my clothes . . . ," he reminisced later.

This scene was just what the secret police needed in their records. Now the "French-Polish-Vatican" conspirator—as he would be titled years later in the newspapers—was completely "exposed." The next morning, September 6, 1926, his passport was at the hotel porter's. "Immediate departure is ordered," said the attached notification. A man with no luggage, but with that sad-sour expression by which the "inconspicuousness" of this profession is so easily recognizable all over the world, got on the train with d'Herbigny and accompanied him to the Finnish-Soviet border. From there, d'Herbigny was the only passenger to Helsinki. "The Passport control went quickly, and in this last corner of Russian territory I was able to pray the complete Hail Mary without the slightest disturbance," the episcopal traveler noted, and he remembered: "Back in May, when I was returning home, I could see only bare branches from the train; today I saw the beautiful Russian fruit. . . ."

A symbolic picture, the kind d'Herbigny loved, but unfortunately only a pious illusion. This ministerial traveller reading contemplatively in his brevier, who had not even the "slightest disturbance" to complain of and would soon arrive safe and sound in Rome, had left behind him in the Soviet Union an edifice that—by the very nature of its structure—was destined to destruction.

Chicherin's "Circular" and the Jesuit Scare

Hardly had d'Herbigny left the Soviet Union when the Vatican *Osservatore Romano* revealed to its readers for the first time, in a 35-line notice (datelined Moscow), that the Jesuit Father d'Herbigny had celebrated masses in the Soviet capitol in the middle of August and disclosed his identity as a recently-consecrated bishop. "Edifying ceremonies in Moscow," the headline read.[64] The Roman headquarters of the Jesuit order, on the contrary, found this information by no means edifying; the general of the order Ledóchowski, who had considered d'Herbigny's secret mission an annoyance anyway, found it completely superfluous that d'Herbigny's position as bishop—which after all had only been conferred "ad hoc," for a one-time practical goal—had been blazoned abroad in such a fashion.[65] Above all, Ledóchowski feared that d'Herbigny, calling upon his "secretum pontificium" (his vow of silence to the Pope), would evade his duty of informing his order, or—with his bishop's mitre—even become a rival to the Jesuit General.

Ledóchowski, and above all his compatriot Polish bishops who were

SCHWEDEN

FINNLAND

Weißmeer

Solowjezki-Inseln
(Priester-Lager)

Leningrad ♁

ESTLAND

D'Herbigny-Geheimaktion
(1926)

Charkow unterstrichene Orte: Sitze von
       Apostolischen Administratoren

♁   Bischofssitze

Ostsee

LETTLAND

LITAUEN

Kazan ●

■ _Moskau_ ♁

●_Witebsk_

DEUTSCHES — REICH

●_Minsk_

Kaluga ●

Mogilew♁
Weissrussland

● _Warschau_   _Pinsk_●

POLEN

Saratow ●

S O W J E T U N I O N

●_Kiew_

Lemberg   _Schitomir_
(Lvov)

Charkow

TSCHECHOSLOWAKEI

Ukraine

UNGARN

Makejewka

Tiraspol
      Odessa♁

RUMÄNIEN

Simferopol

Sewastopol

Pjatigorsk●

JUGOSLAWIEN

Schwarzes· Meer

BULGARIEN

Tiflis●

TÜRKEI

⊢——⊣ 100 km

questioning him, would very much like to have known what d'Herbigny had actually done in the Soviet Union, what was true or false in the rumors in the press that were now buzzing around the world—usually polemically and with anti-Jesuit barbs. But d'Herbigny was silent, at least toward his order. To the outside he issued denials: "There were no new dioceses nor episcopal sees created in Russia; I also did not undertake a single ordination of *priests*."[66] That was true, but as we know, not the whole truth.

To Monsignore Steinmann of the German Embassy to the Vatican, however, d'Herbigny was more communicative, partly because he knew Steinmann to be an advocate of an active eastern policy (see p. 37), partly because Steinmann had already been oriented by the German consulate in Odessa. Ambassador von Bergen, in any case, could soon report to Berlin that d'Herbigny had in fact carried out the "hierarchical reorganization" of the Soviet Union. The ambassador added:[67]

.· *Ich darf noch die Notwendigkeit betonen, daß diese Maßnahme des Heiligen Stuhles ganz geheim behandelt wird. Monsignor d'Herbigny hat darum ausdrücklich gebeten mit dem Hinweis auf die großen Gefahren, die im Falle des Bekanntwerdens den mit der Verwaltung der Sprengel beauftragten Geistlichen seitens der Sowjetregierung ohne Zweifel erwachsen würden.*

Bergen

(Let me emphasize the necessity that this measure of the Holy See be treated as *completely confidential*. Monsignore d'Herbigny expressly requested this, alluding to the great danger to the clergymen entrusted with the administration of the dioceses that would doubtless arise from the Soviet government if it were to become known. Bergen.)

This new "scaffold" of church structures that d'Herbigny had erected was however by no means so insignificant that it could be easily hidden. After all, there were ten apostolic administrators, among them four bishops.

Could one seriously believe that such an organization could be established in a dictatorial state without its knowledge? To be sure, this question, which is also of importance for Vatican eastern policy since 1945, has never been discussed officially in the church, in the last fifty years, let alone historically researched; still most specialists agree today in their

Secret Hierarchy in the Soviet Union, 1926	
Archdiocese Mogilev (Archbishop: Eduard von der Ropp, in exile in Poland since 1919) *Apostolic Administrators: Mogilev:* Boleslas Sloskans, Titular Bishop of Cillio *Moscow:* Pie Eugen Neveu, Titular Bishop of Citro *Leningrad:* Antoni Malecki, Titular Bishop of Dionisiana *Kharkov:* Vincent Ilgin *Kazan:* Michael Iodokas *Diocese Minsk* (Soviet part, separated from Poland) *Apostolic Administrator:* Bishop Boleslas Sloskans	*Diocese Tiraspol* (Bishop: Alois Kessler, in exile in Germany since 1920 *Apostolic Administrators: South Russia (Odessa):* Alexander Frison, Titular Bishop of Limira *Central Russia (Saratov):* Augustin Baumtrog *North Caucasus (Pyatigorsk):* Johann Roth *Georgia (Tiflis):* Stefan Demurof *Diocese Zhitomir* (Soviet part, separated from Poland *Apostolic Administrator:* Vicar General Teofil Skalski

judgment. "A state can send in its agents like that, but not a church its priests and bishops," Father Josef Olsr, SJ, of the Roman "Russicum," for example, told me in a conversation in 1973, while Father Wilhelm de Vries, SJ, of the Papal Institute for Eastern Studies, is of the opinion today that it is simply incredible that d'Herbigny lifted his episcopal "incognito" in Moscow in August 1926.

Of course, d'Herbigny by no means did this from a lack of concern or from simple egotism, although he was no stranger to these emotions. All of the bishops and administrators that he installed were aware—and were instructed accordingly—that they too sooner or later would have to give up their "incognitos" if they had any hope of exercising their functions in a larger sphere and really becoming available to the masses of the faithful.[68] "Naturally we soon had to appear openly before the congregations—even if it was dangerous!", the only survivor, Bishop Sloskans, told me. But why not right away, why only later, why the game of "hide and seek" at all?

The answer must have two prongs: on the one hand, the repeatedly ruptured and unpromising Berlin negotiations with the Soviets gave rise to the impatient feeling that "something would have to be done" soon in any case; on the other, the Vatican wanted to avoid having its "self-help action" revealed prematurely and thus cutting off the last thread of negotiation. All attempts at legalization would then be destroyed. The only error in all these calculations was the belief that such an action could remain covert for any length of time. Political and national friction in which the action was caught up precluded that. For although the old division of the dioceses had not been touched formally, in particular those that crossed the new Soviet-Polish borders (much like at first after the Second World War, along the new German-Polish borders—see p. 346); but *de facto*, the jurisdictional territories of the new administrators in Minsk and Zhitomir were naturally the cores of new dioceses. Thus the Holy See had now done what Father Gehrmann had advised it to do on his return from Russia in 1924,[69] and what the unhappy Pastor Fedukowicz had begged the Pope to do (see pp. 68-9); only it had not occurred "with the agreement of the government," and had also by no means freed the church from the encumbrance of the Polish-Soviet antagonism, as the case of Prelate Skalski in Zhitomir will show.

An additional handicap was the delicate question of the rite: all the administrators and bishops installed by d'Herbigny were priests of the Latin rite; Exarch Leonid Feodorov, the only Catholic dignitary of Russian nationality following the Slavic rite, although he had been granted a pardon in 1926 after his sentencing in the Cieplak trial (see p. 45f.), had been arrested again three months later, after he had settled in Kaluga (south of Moscow) and begun to officiate in Mogilev; most of his priests had been sentenced to hard labor. His few, and small, Uniate congregations no longer existed. D'Herbigny had of course brought a papal decree to Moscow that removed Feodorov from the jurisdiction of the Metropolitan Sheptyckyi (in Poland) and subordinated him directly to Neveu (in Moscow) as "Vicar General for the Believers of the Eastern Rite," but in view of the real situation, this had no effect.

The question of the rite therefore did not arise *practically* when d'Herbigny made his third tour—which could only please the Poles. In its concordat of 1925 with the Vatican, Warsaw had insisted that the eastern rite be confined to the areas of Poland that were settled by Ukrainians and White Russians. The ambitions of the Lemberg Uniate Metropolitan Sheptyckyi had thereby been strictly limited, and his old hopes for a Catholicization of Russia without Latinization (and Polonization) could then no longer even be pinned to the Russian Catholic circle of his disciple Feodorov.

But still, the question of the rite encumbered the d'Herbigny action at least *theoretically:* for it was well-known that the Jesuit bishop was not only an admirer of Russian culture and piety, but also a friend of the eastern rite and—independent of rite—of the "Russification" of the local church. In the Frenchman Neveu, d'Herbigny had installed a bishop in Moscow who, since he had come to Russia in 1907, had always proven himself as a clergyman for *all* nationalities, although himself of the Latin rite. As pastor in the Donetz district, he always read the gospel in Russian too, and preached in the vernacular, although—as the then Volga German Bishop Kessler (of Tiraspol) complained—Russian in the church was so repugnant to the Poles "that they even considered an absolution of sins given in Russian to be a blasphemy."[70]—But now Neveu presented himself for the first time publicly as a bishop, of all places, in the *Polish* church of Sts. Peter and Paul in Moscow, on October 3, 1926 (one month after d'Herbigny's somewhat sudden forced departure)—and in the *Russian* language:

> ". . . We do not serve, and do not wish to serve, any earthly power, for we are—like St. Paul—ambassadors of Christ. But since we live in the bosom of the great Russian nation, which shelters us as guests, we are grateful to it and wish it peace, prosperity and respect. . . ."

Pius XI had quite consciously given this Assumptionist Father and Moscow bishop episcopal jurisdiction over the clerics of *both* rites, and very great authorizations—"greater than I have myself," as the Pope said in jest to Neveu's superior.[71] This probably also happened because Rome correctly assumed that Neveu, as a French citizen (he was formally included in the embassy personnel two years later as "librarian"), would have a more stable position than all the other bishops and administrators. In fact, Neveu was the only one able to maintain his position, which he did for ten years. But "Biritualism," which was embodied in his person and which also in following years continued to determine the Vatican's eastern-political activities, and especially those of d'Herbigny, was an encumbrance from the beginning: what was intended, by this position, to be practically reasonable, supra-national, "catholic" in the literal sense, for that very reason did not inspire trust in the midst of the Eastern European stew of nationalities—not in the Poles nor the Russians, not in the Orthodox and far from it in the Communists. . . .

Thus, although d'Herbigny's constructive work in the church had from the beginning carried the seeds of destruction within it, at first this was not very evident. It could still be argued whether the unpleasantness surrounding d'Herbigny's departure from Moscow, which came close to an expulsion, was the prelude to the storm. Some seven weeks later the Vatican newspaper still polemicized strongly against the malicious remarks of a Polish prelate who had observed that d'Herbigny had left Moscow "in a huff."[72] As we know today, something very strange and not easily explainable had happened:

The first official Moscow reaction following the d'Herbigny action came on September 11, 1926, exactly 72 hours after d'Herbigny had left the Soviet Union. On this day[73] the Soviet chargé d'affaires in Berlin, Bratmann-Brodowski, finally delivered to the papal nuncio Pacelli the answer to the Vatican note of September 7, 1925, which had been awaited for over a year (see p. 78). It was that "circular" that Chicherin, in his discussion with Pacelli and Brockdorff-Rantzau, had promised repeatedly.

The concept of "circular," in the Soviet religious legislation of the time, was customary for orders that the People's Commissariat of Justice (NKJ) or of the Interior (NKVD) issued. Thus the paper that the Soviets delivered to the Vatican was not a draft of a legal agreement, a *modus vivendi* or concordat, but rather a set of guidelines—applied to the Catholic church— of *domestic* legislation on religion, as it had evolved since 1918.[74] The Vatican's objections to the Soviet "theses" that had been delivered to Pacelli in February 1925 (see p. 75) were considered only insofar as Moscow was prepared to allow a certain controlled communication between the Soviet Catholics and their Roman leader. However, the Catholics (like all other religious groups) were denied, now as ever, legal personality, any property, religious instruction for minors, and also the formation of a central body or conference of bishops.

Now Moscow was not suggesting a bilateral agreement to the Vatican, but rather endorsement of a unilaterally-issued decree. "The legal position of the Catholic church in the (Soviet) Union was to be regulated and *safeguarded*" thereby, as Chicherin later elucidated.[75] The Soviet government was apparently also still prepared to negotiate certain points of its suggestion and to maintain a dialogue, especially since it recognized that its proposal was "not far-reaching" (Chicherin). But basically its position had become more obdurate.

Even if the "circular" and its bearer did not refer to d'Herbigny's visits by a single word, it was still obvious that this paper was the answer to the Vatican attempt to enact canon law on its own, behind the back of the Soviet authorities. For a whole year Moscow had delayed this answer and closely supervised and observed d'Herbigny's three visits. The test had turned out negative, but not so devastating that Moscow wanted to burn all bridges immediately. Chicherin, in spite of his annoyance,[76] remained quite conscious of the importance of an understanding with the Catholic universal church.

In the Vatican too, where the circular was naturally a disappointment, they did not miss the catchword "legal safeguard" which was offered the Catholic church in the Soviet Union—even if it was only a minimum existence. Therefore the Pope decided to use the same tactics as the Soviets: to send Moscow no reply at all for the time being, but rather first to test the minimum of good will on the Soviet side.

An opportunity was offered by the fact that the question of the seminary for priests, which d'Herbigny had already discussed with Schmidovitch, was not presented wholly negatively in the circular. With the ban on religious instruction of minors in 1921 had been combined this concession: "Special theology courses for the education of priests may be organized for persons over 18 years of age, under the condition that the courses of instruction are limited exclusively to theological subjects."[77] Since the beginning of 1925 there had been a Protestant preachers' seminary in Leningrad.[78] Could one not also establish a seminary for Catholic priests?

At the beginning of October 1926, two young Jesuits appeared at the Soviet consulate in the Via Gaeta in Rome, applied for visas for a "study tour" through Russia and—received them, to their great astonishment. Most surprised of all was d'Herbigny, who had selected the two theologians, of whom the one spoke hardly any Russian, the other none at all: the 30-year-old Father Josef Schweigl, a Tirolian Austrian, and the 28-year-old Josef Ledit, a Frenchman with a U.S. passport.[79] D'Herbigny himself was "skeptical that it would succeed" when he sent the two off. But, as he confided to the Bavarian Ambassador Ritter, one had to try, as only 120 Catholic clerics were presently still active in the Soviet Union.[80]

The two Jesuits, whom the Pope had personally seen off, went by ship from Bari to Odessa, then to Moscow and Leningrad. Since after the failure of their undertaking—four weeks later—they were much more silent than d'Herbigny (only in 1974 did Ledit tell me a few details), almost nothing was known about their journey until now. In any case, they presented themselves at all the German diplomatic delegations:[81] in Odessa they declared candidly that they were foreseen to be teachers at a future seminary in Leningrad; in Moscow, where they stayed five days and visited Bishop Neveu, they were a little more careful and claimed, on their visit at the German embassy, that they possessed "neither letters of introduction nor any commission at all" from the Vatican; in Leningrad, where they stayed with Father Amoudru, they made an "impression of inexperience and complete unworldliness" on the German consul. This was probably due above all to the fact that Schweigl delivered a written request to the city soviet to open a seminary, and seriously thought that they could thereby "steal the jump on Chicherin, who wanted to use this in exchange for a recognition of the Soviet Union." The two Jesuits also had no idea of Pacelli's Soviet contacts in Berlin. However, since the Soviets found it difficult to believe their naiveté, instead of answering, they ordered them to leave the country within 24 hours. Even decades later, Schweigl, in remembering this conclusion, felt his "heart contract."[82]

Had the Vatican seriously "tested" the Soviets with this amateurish mission of Schweigl and Ledit? In contrast, for the Soviets the appearance of the two Jesuits became the last link in a "chain of evidence"; now they drew their final conclusions about d'Herbigny's journeys too. On October 15, 1926, a resolution of the Council of People's Commissariats was given to the German Embassy in Moscow, which said:[83]

> "The government of the USSR has come to the decision not to admit [into the country], until further notice, foreign servants of religion who wish to enter for religious purposes or for the direction of religious unions or organizations existing in the USSR."

It was not xenophobia, and not only communist policies on religion, but also a Jesuit-phobia that now put a stop to "ministerial tourism." The Russian Dominican Sister Abrikosova, who belonged to the congregation of the Uniate Exarch Feodorov, had already written at the time when the Jesuit Father Walsh had so unfelicitously directed the famine relief mission in 1922/23 (see p. 42f.):

> "Doesn't Rome understand the terrible aversion to the Jesuits? . . . If Jesuits enter Russia in civilian clothing, it can only mean the worst; their arrival here will be regarded as a gigantic Catholic conspiracy. . . . In spite of my complete respect for this order, I must admit that it should not come to Russia. . . ."[84]

Even now, at the end of 1926, Moscow did not yet raise its hand for the final blow; there was still the belief that in spite of the Jesuits, one could "somehow" come to terms with the Vatican, as with other "capitalist" countries. They even let the secretly consecrated bishops act freely for a while. Boleslas Sloskans appeared as a bishop for the first time on November 14, 1926, in St. Anthony's church in Vitebsk and celebrated a pontifical mass. However, when he was arrested—not until ten months later—one of the first questions of the GPU in Minsk concerned the activities of d'Herbigny—"that charlatan." A Comrade Grodis, a specialist in the combat of "counterrevolutionary intrigues," began the interrogation:[85]

> "Do you know who the Black Pope is?"
> "No, I do not."
> "Then you don't know that the Jesuit General, the Black Pope, appoints bishops and makes policies independently of the leader of the Catholic church? That the Pope is an instrument in his hands?"
> "You may be assured that there is not a kernel of truth in anything you are saying. . . . The Jesuit General does nothing against the will of the Pope."
> "But was it not d'Herbigny who consecrated you as a bishop? And you must know that he is a Jesuit and has no papal authority, but wants to make you an instrument of Jesuit policy."
> "D'Herbigny consecrated me on the Holy Father's orders."
> "But he had no authority, and you saw no document, you only believed his jesuitical word!"
> "No, he first showed me a paper in which he was named as an emissary of the Holy Father, it had the Holy Father's signature. . . ."

These trick questions of the Sloskans interrogation in Minsk were of course part of police tactics; they also revealed an ignorance of the legal as of the personal position of Jesuit General Ledóchowski; there was, however, mirrored in them a sense of the wilful role that this Polish count actually played in papal Rome. That d'Herbigny himself was much more the Pope's man than his Jesuit superior's, remained difficult for Moscow to grasp.

With this allusion to the Sloskans interrogation of autumn, 1927, we have somewhat anticipated events, because at the same time it represents the tragicomic epilogue to this period of papal eastern policies in the twenties. What was really the awkward two-track procedure of Pius XI and d'Herbigny's pious dilettantism, the Soviets could only explain as the expression of jesuitical deceit and cunning.

IV

From The End of The Dialogue To The "Crusade," 1927-1932

Pacelli Speaks with Chicherin: Last Attempts

Two high black automobiles stopped one behind the other before the house at 34 Viktoria Street in Berlin.

From each one stepped a dark-clad man—without looking around: the one tall, slender, with gold-rimmed glasses, the other short, with a goatee. Both gentlemen obviously did not want to be seen; they quickly disappeared into the house entrance, where a young man was awaiting them and greeted them with "Your Excellency." It was a mild evening in early summer, June 14, 1927, around eight o'clock. Chamberlain Ernst Count von Rantzau[1] had unusual guests for dinner: the papal nuncio, Eugenio Pacelli; the Soviet Commissar for Foreign Affairs, Georgi Vasilyevich Chicherin; and his own twin brother Ulrich, the ambassador of the German Reich to Moscow. The young man who had greeted the guests at the door sat there too, quiet and unassuming, but with open ears and a discreetly-drawn notebook: Andor Hencke, personal assistant to the ambassador, who today (1974), almost 80 years old, lives in Bavaria and from his lively memory told me of this historic meeting—the third and last between Chicherin and Pacelli.[2]

> "After dinner we retired to the parlor, and Rantzau said: now let's talk 'business'—for during the meal they had not gone beyond the Berlin society chat. In fluent German, an immensely spirited skirmish took place between two such intelligent men as Chicherin and Pacelli, who—as I saw it—were not uncongenial."

After the first mutual assurances of good will for better relations, the conversation (according to Hencke's recollection) converged on two points: the nomination of bishops, and religious instruction. Chicherin avoided mention of d'Herbigny's activities; and it would have been difficult for him to explain why the Soviets had temporarily tolerated the Jesuit bishop's activity. Instead, Chicherin pointed to his "circular" of September 11, 1926, to which he had been vainly awaiting a reply from the Vatican. Pacelli politely promised to inquire in Rome, but let it be known how difficult it would be for the Vatican to accept the Soviet conditions: the form for nomination of bishops in the Soviet proposal amounted to the Holy See's being allowed at most to "give its blessing" after the fact. Chicherin was obviously more flexible in this question, and thought that in negotiations, a modus acceptable to both sides could surely be found.

> "The conversation then ran aground," Andor Hencke recollected, "on the problem of religious instruction. That could not get through in Moscow, Chicherin said. Religious indoctrination of youth in any form was unacceptable to the Soviet government. And the conversation of about three hours ended thus: A pity—we cannot come to an agreement!"

Had Pacelli not perhaps put in a word for the imprisoned priests in the Soviet Union at this opportunity? He had indeed mentioned the situation, Andor Hencke remembered, but not named any names nor expressed any concrete wishes. That is all the more astonishing because this problem had played a rather large role in the prologue to the Berlin meeting, which was shrouded in secrecy. This prologue, which shall be reconstructed here, of course also shows the "change in climate" that had taken place in the first months of 1927:[3]

On January 3, Pacelli had a list of the names of 39 imprisoned Catholic clerics sent to Ambassador Brockdorff-Rantzau in Moscow; in first place among them figured the Polish Prelate Skalski, apostolic administrator of Zhitomir; right after him, Prelate Ilgin of Kharkov, the second of the dignitaries installed by d'Herbigny, who had been arrested back in December 1926 under a trifling pretext (he had possessed foreign newspapers). Could the German Embassy do anything for them?

The ambassador wrote back to his cousin Count Zech of the Foreign Office, on January 12, that he found Pacelli's request "rather extensive." "Since Chicherin is away,[4] and Litvinov has rejected any intervention on behalf of Catholic priests for over a year, declaring that these questions belong exclusively to the department of domestic affairs, I advise waiting for the return of Chicherin, who personally takes another point of view, and discussing the problem confidentially at my brother Ernst's house. . . ."

Zech wrote back to Moscow on January 14:

> "My dear cousin, . . . Pacelli emphasized at least twenty times that you had always so extremely amiably espoused Catholic interests in Russia. . . . He accepted with pleasure your suggestion that he discuss things with Chicherin, indeed he seemed to be greatly looking forward to the forthcoming breakfast at Ernst's house. . . ."

For the greatly ambitious Brockdorff-Rantzau, "not being able to do anything" was hardly endurable; he begged for understanding in a private letter to the nuncio's secretary, Father Gehrmann: "You know me well enough to know that, in addition to many undesirable qualities, I possess at least one good one, that is, determination. . . . However, circumstances here [in Moscow] are particularly difficult now. . . ." Pacelli would be able to discuss "the whole complex of problems unobtrusively and undisturbed" at his brother Ernst's house, but in Moscow—as Gehrmann knew from his own experience—there were "very narrowly-drawn limits and difficulties that are absolutely insurmountable," he wrote.

Did Rome not see these limits—or did it now want to consciously strike against them? On March 10, Cardinal Secretary of State Gasparri wrote to the German Embassy to the Vatican ("very personal") that they should procure a Soviet visa for the German priest Alois Mauderer, so that he could devote himself to the care of souls in Saratov. Did the Vatican not know that since d'Herbigny's activities there had been a travel ban for foreign clergy? Gasparri recommended Mauderer with the somewhat irrelevant comment that he had been active in Germany "amongst the Social Democrats" (*impiegato in mezzo ai social-democratici*).

Chicherin's visit in Berlin was not yet within view (the Foreign Commissar remained ailing in Wiesbaden); Brockdorff-Rantzau and the Foreign Office could do nothing. Then the Catholic *Augsburger Postzeitung*, doubtlessly as "mouthpiece," wrote: "The German official representation in Russia seems to know and to recognize a religious interest only when it is a Protestant matter. . . . We will not discuss for the present whether it is only the personal inclination of the German representative Brockdorff-Rantzau that is at work here."

"An impertinence bordering on blackmail," the ambassador raged in a letter of May 2 about this article, and he was even more offended by the fact that immediately after this attack in the press, on March 29, Pacelli had sent a note directly to the Catholic Reichschancellor Marx and asked him to intervene with the Russians in the cases of Skalski, Ilgin and Mauderer. This action of the nuncio's had pained him greatly, Brockdorff-Rantzau wrote; as German ambassador he had represented "the extremely difficult-to-defend wishes" of the Vatican, often up to "the extreme limits of the admissable"; now—especially after the aforementioned newspaper article—this had been made very difficult, because it had now become "a dangerous question of prestige" for the Soviets. He was not willing to tolerate "such vulgar methods with the connivance of the Vatican. . . ."[5]

As false and unjust as it was to accuse the ambassador of inactivity, the basic reason for the ill feeling was neither that nor his oversensitivity: in truth, the Vatican was about to break off the dialogue with Moscow, and thereby also to withdraw from the "neighborhood" of German eastern policy.

And more: Herbert von Dirksen, the director of the Eastern Division of the Foreign Office, on March 23, 1927, "confidentially and personally" informed his brother-in-law Diego von Bergen, the ambassador to the Vatican, that the Catholic Center Party ". . . wants to gradually bring us to the point of giving up our hitherto existing policy of a cordial coexistence with Russia, and seeking contacts with England; in the same vein, a decided pressure seems to be arising from the Center that we should strive for a political reconciliation with Poland, perhaps at the expense of national demands. . . ."[6]

As a symptom of such a turn, Dirksen mentioned among other things that the Center Party had proved to be "completely disinterested" in the question of the financial salvation of the "Mologa," the largest German concessionary enterprise in the Soviet Union. The party also simply "dropped" the personal interests of its own ex-chancellor Wirth.[7] Basically, the Vatican too had already given up hope for an agreement with Moscow. Not that the Pope was attempting to form a "political front" with England—as Chicherin would soon suspect—rather, international political events in the spring of 1927 had their effects upon the Vatican's attitude toward Moscow:

The British Empire at that time felt itself threatened by Communism in Asia, especially in China, while Stalin, who was still struggling with Trotsky, suffered a heavy defeat in China in the spring of 1927. The nationalist Kuomintang Party had namely (under British influence, as Moscow believed) suddenly turned against their allies, the Chinese Communists, had defeated them devastatingly, and practically put them out of action for the next two decades. Motive: fear of the Chinese revolution that Mao Tse-tung already wanted at that time but that Stalin, who had backed Chiang Kai-shek, did not. Of course, this only became known much later; London saw only that the leadership of the Communist International in Moscow was inciting revolution, while the Soviet government talked of a "peaceable foreign policy." On May 12, 1927, a sudden house search of the Soviet trade center "Arcos" in London brought to light whole truckloads of Communist propaganda material and proof of espionage activities. Great Britain thereupon brusquely broke off diplomatic relations with the Soviet Union. Moscow, however, felt itself suddenly threatened, even encircled, from East and West. When in addition, on June 7, the Soviet ambassador to Warsaw was murdered right out on the street, the Soviet leadership was swept by an almost panic fear of war. The terror of the civil war was still deeply rooted in the Kremlin leaders.

Chicherin interrupted his cure and hurried to Berlin to keep at least the Germans on a course friendly to the Soviets; Brockdorff-Rantzau came from Moscow for the same reason, and also took this occasion to speak his mind to Pacelli—somewhat vehemently, but finally conciliatorily. The long-planned evening "breakfast" with Chicherin at Chamberlain Ernst von Rantzau's house could now finally take place—but in such an atmosphere?

Brockdorff-Rantzau and Reich Foreign Minister Stresemann considered it important, especially right now, to keep the Vatican out of the anti-Soviet campaign, also to assuage somewhat Chicherin's fear of Catholic Poland. (Pilsudski is "both a romantic and an adventurer," a concerned Chicherin told Stresemann on June 7). But what position did the Vatican take at this moment of international tension and agitation? Following is an excerpt from the report of the Bavarian Ambassador to the Vatican, Ritter von Groenesteyn (*Secret State Archives, Munich*, Holy See, Fasz 1009/MA 104 467).

This report, written five days after the dramatic break between London and Moscow, signalled the turning point. Cardinal Gasparri not only showed understanding, he even sent congratulations! And on June 9—five days before the already arranged secret meeting between Pacelli and Chicherin—the *Osservatore Romano* wrote that the church had long ago recognized the abyss of Bolshevism, for which "embassies, trade delegations and consulates are centers of propaganda." Conflict of interest and political calculations had unfortunately resulted in a refusal to listen to the church, lamented the Vatican newspaper, while Cardinal Gasparri advised the Bavarian ambassador that it was dangerous "to conspire with the present Russian government for reasons of expediency."[8]

But wasn't the Vatican itself doing exactly that when several days later, on June 14, 1927, it sent its nuncio, Pacelli, to that secret meeting with Chicherin in Berlin's Viktoria Street?

"I consider any idea of a crusade against Russia to be foolish and senseless. It would weld Russia together and only weaken Europe," Reich Foreign Minister Stresemann cried to the Western Powers on June 15 at the League of Nations in Geneva.[9] Chicherin had been waiting in Berlin for this declaration. When he then returned, relieved, to Moscow two days later, he did of course take along an equivocal impression from his fruitless

. *N.* 68   *Rom, den 30. Mai 1927.*

**BAYERISCHE GESANDTSCHAFT
BEIM PAEPSTLICHEN STUHLE**

B. Staatsministerium
d. Aeusern
empf. 1-JUN. 19. 7
..... Beil. 13276

Betreff:

*Abbruch der diplomatischen Beziehungen
zwischen England und Rußland.*

> *Der Herr Kardinalstaatssekretür hat sich zu mir
> sehr erfreut darüber gezeigt, daß England die diplomati-
> schen Beziehungen zu Rußland abgebrochen hat, und er sag-
> te mir, daß er den Englischen Gesandten bitten werde, sei-
> ne Regierung zu diesem Entschlusse zu beglückwünschen. Das
> Unheil, das die bolschewistische Propaganda in schamloser
> Weise überall in der Welt anrichte, indem sie den inneren
> und äußeren Frieden gefährde, die Grundsätze der christ-
> lichen Moral untergrabe und Kirche und Religion bekämpfe,
> nähme derartige Dimensionen an, daß man England allgemein
> dafür dankbar sein müsse, dagegen energisch Stellung ge-
> nommen zu haben. Freilich seien es für England in erster*

In re: Break in diplomatic relations between England and Russia.

The Cardinal Secretary of State was evidently very pleased that England had broken off diplomatic relations with Russia, and he told me that he would ask the English ambassador to convey congratulations to his government on this decision. He said, the mischief that Bolshevik propaganda was shamelessly inciting all over the world, by endangering domestic and international peace, destroying the principle of Christian morality, and fighting church and religion, was assuming such dimensions that one must be universally grateful to England for taking such an energetic position. . . .

meeting with Pacelli: on the one hand, the fact of this conversation showed him that the Vatican still by no means wanted to burn all bridges and also had no immediate thought of a "crusade"; on the other, the course of the meeting did strengthen Chicherin's suspicions of a "Vatican-British rapprochement." Count Brockdorff-Rantzau had hardly returned to Moscow from his vacation in August when Chicherin told him this;[10] indeed, the Soviet Commissar for Foreign Affairs admitted to his friend the

German ambassador that another spectacular event of this summer could be understood as a direct reply to this: a sudden declaration of loyalty from the Orthodox Patriarchal Administrator Sergius, whom the Soviets had released from imprisonment in the spring.

"We want to be Orthodox Christians, and at the same time recognize Russia as our earthly fatherland. . . . Any blow against the Soviet Union, whether war or boycott, any public misfortune, and even a murder on a street corner—as recently occurred in Warsaw—will be taken as if it had been directed against us," read a pastoral letter from Metropolitan Sergius dated June 29, 1927.[11] Sergius used the international tension and the Kremlin's fear of war as a chance to gain a little breathing space for his church by making himself patriotically useful. The mention of the murder of the Soviet Ambassador to Warsaw—the only concrete reference—also contained an anti-Catholic dart. Another key sentence of the pastoral letter could even be interpreted as an allusion to d'Herbigny's unfortunate secret action: only "unworldly dreamers" could imagine that a large church could exist within a state "by hiding itself from the eyes of the authorities," Sergius wrote.

With the declaration from the Metropolitan, which aroused notice all over the world, "the Orthodox church was standing on its own two feet," Chicherin explained the event to the German ambassador.[12] The Vatican could now no longer hope to win over these "lost sheep," and had to realize that the Soviet Union would not do "the Vatican's job"; for that reason the Vatican had now moved on to "drastic methods," and was attempting to "battle [the Soviet Union] politically," Chicherin claimed, adding: the advances by the Vatican to the British government could also be explained by those reasons.

Brockdorff-Rantzau thereupon turned the tables: "Perhaps a certain forthcomingness on the part of this regime vis-à-vis the Holy See could pull the rug out from under the rapprochement between Rome and London!" Even German Catholic circles were disturbed about the state of Vatican-Soviet relations.

Chicherin replied—"without irritation," as the ambassador remarked: "The Soviet government is prepared, as it has been, to negotiate with the Vatican; it of course does not mean to reach a concordat, but is not disinclined to agree with Rome upon a 'circular'. . . ." Appropriate proposals had been made about a year earlier, Pacelli had promised him an answer in Berlin, which however was still outstanding. If the Soviet government "was not honored with a reply" for nearly a year, it could not attempt on its own to begin new negotiations.

Brockdorff-Rantzau described this conversation with Chicherin in an extensive secret report of August 29, 1927 (complete text in appendix). He would leave to the Foreign Office whether any part, and if so what part, of it should be passed on to Pacelli; he did not want to tender any unasked-for advice and also felt no inclination to advise indulgence, much less conciliation, wrote the ambassador, who had now apparently become more skeptical.

"Only orally and in excerpts" did Count Zech of the Foreign Office transmit some of Chicherin's remarks, on September 8, to the Berlin nuncio. In doing so, Zech passed over all of Chicherin's polemical remarks, so that Pacelli got to hear only the Soviets' readiness to negotiate and their insistence on an answer to the note of September 1926.[13]

Pacelli did not deny that a formal reply from Rome was still outstanding; he had reminded them of it after his Berlin discussion with Chicherin. (After all, the Russians had also let the Vatican wait for a year in 1925/26!) Perhaps Rome now believed that "nothing could be done anyway," the nuncio said in a conversation with Zech; for reports had arrived in the meantime that "painted such a black picture" of the treatment of Catholics there.

"I had the impression that Pacelli personally does not believe the argument he was advancing. On the contrary, I am beginning to consider much more probable, after my conversation with Pacelli, Chicherin's thesis of an English-Vatican alliance against Russia," Zech wrote on the same day in a private letter.[14] "However, I did tell Pacelli very clearly, as my own personal and quite private opinion, that ignoring the Russian proposals was not quite comprehensible to me as a tactic. In any case, neither the lot of the Catholics in Russia, nor the Vatican's position in any possible future press discussion about the treatment of Catholics in Russia, would be improved."

The half-truth of the "Vatican-English alliance" haunted the diplomatic papers. The Vatican Secretariat of State could describe it as an "invention"[15] simply because there were no anti-Soviet "agreements" (what about?) between the papal curia and the London government, but only a concurrence in their judgment of the Communist International and the gloomy prospects of coming to an understanding with its Moscow leadership. The friendly relations that Michel d'Herbigny had established in Moscow with the French ambassador Jean Herbette, in addition, increased the probability that Herbette's opinion of the situation was also known, and carried influence, in the Vatican. However, in August 1927, Herbette was of the opinion that the Soviet leadership suffered from "paranoia"; but because Stalin was now talking about the "unavoidability of war," Herbette advised against following England's example: "I cannot convince myself that diplomatic removal from Russia is the best method to impress the Soviet government. . . . Basically a rupture also means a retreat. . . ."[16]

And therefore the Vatican finally also did not "ignore" the Soviet circular, as the East Berlin historian Eduard Winter erroneously maintains.[17] Furthermore, Pacelli certainly did not believe they would be able to gain "more through combat than through negotiations without pressure." How could the Roman curia have applied "pressure" on Moscow?! In any case, they held the shorter end of the stick; this was not the least reason why Pacelli had repeatedly proposed discussions and had been sent to private meetings (of which Winter seems to know nothing). Even now, at the beginning of September 1927, it was Pacelli who in his reports to Rome advised one last attempt. To be sure, the Pope himself expected little from it; somewhat reluctantly, as Cardinal Gasparri noted in his audience minutes, he gave instructions that they should now follow the Soviet example and "demand the maximum."[18] But the "maximum" in this last Vatican proposal looks more like a "minimum," if we take into consideration the political concession it involved.

Nuncio Pacelli thus, on October 6, 1927, disclosed to the Soviet ambassador in Berlin, Krestinski, that

> "the Holy See is prepared to take into account objections of a political nature that the Russian government may have against candidates for the office of bishop, and requests permission to
> a) open seminaries,
> b) send to Russia clergymen agreeable to the government,
> c) support these clerics and their works."[9]

This last proposal came much too late—and the Vatican sensed it. However, if the content of this verbal note had become publicly known, probably many cries of incredulous indignation would have been raised. As is the case today, church circles that considered themselves conservative then also did not like to have their idyllic conception of a straight-marching "ecclesia militans" disturbed by the picture of a worldly-wise church that in the end always thinks in terms of pastoral Realpolitik, even if it does not always act so consistently.

The Break with Stalin—Hope on the Right?

Again a dark automobile drives up before 34 Viktoria Street in Berlin, again a man in dark clothes gets out, tall, slender, with gold-rimmed glasses, and quickly disappears into the entrance. But on this September 8, 1928, Nuncio Pacelli is not meeting a Soviet politician in Herr von Rantzau's home: he has come to express his condolences to the chamberlain Ernst on the death on his twin brother. Ulrich Count von Rantzau had succumbed that day to a malignant cancer of the larynx. The ambassador of the Soviet-German understanding, the mediator between the Vatican and Moscow, is dead.

The Soviet government—in a deviation from the strict atheist rule in effect at that time for Soviet diplomats—instructed its Berlin chargé d'affaires Bratmann-Brodowski to participate in the funeral services for the ambassador. Pacelli, on the other hand, had opposite instructions; unfortunately, he explained, as a Catholic bishop he was not allowed to attend the rite in the Protestant Church of the Trinity; but he would not neglect to pay his last respects at least privately to the man who had stood up so strongly for the interests of the Holy See in Moscow. . . .

"The nuncio stepped up to the closed casket, which was laid out in the parlor, and offered a silent prayer," Brockdorff-Rantzau's secretary Andor Hencke remembered.[20] "I then accompanied him on foot down Tiergarten to the nunciature in Rauch Street, and Pacelli questioned me about the situation in Russia. . . ."

The conversation is as gloomy as the autumn day. Chicherin, a year ago still a halfway obliging partner in discussions, had been in Wiesbaden again for months, ill not only with diabetes, but also with melancholy. Andor Hencke can report—and Pacelli is not very surprised—that Chicherin is opposed to the kind of Communism that Stalin is now practicing; that the Commissar for Foreign Affairs had earlier expressed himself in confidential conversations with Brockdorff-Rantzau in such a way that the ambassador was concerned: "I hope he doesn't speak that openly with anyone else!" Now there are even indications that Chicherin does not want to return to Moscow. When his Moscow friends finally do persuade him to return from Germany, he is put on ice, and spends his last years as a poor pensioner with his own piano compositions and Mozart records, until he dies in July 1936—shortly before the murderous show trials that Stalin staged against the old Bolsheviks. . . .

Since the autumn of 1927, Stalin's struggle for sole power had been decided. In November, Trotsky and Sinoviev were excluded from the party. At the XVth Party Congress, at the beginning of December, Stalin forced the radical collectivization of agriculture, which constituted the actual prologue to his reign of terror.[21] Now the connection of church and village became an obvious point of attack. In an interview he accused the "reactionary clergy" of poisoning the minds of the masses: "The only unfortunate thing is that they (the clergy) were not completely liquidated." And he demanded before the congress that everyone conquer any weariness in the anti-religious struggle.[22] France's Ambassador Herbette, who analyzed the Party Congress in great detail, reported on December 10 of the Kremlin leaders: "They are preparing for some adventure. . . . I am however convinced now as ever that we cannot break off relations with Russia. . . . No church ban can kill a person, no wall can check an idea. . . ."[23]

During these days Pope Pius XI made a decision, which he revealed to his Secretary of State Cardinal Gasparri on December 16, 1927:[24] "As long as the persecution continues in Russia, we can no longer negotiate with the Soviets."

Moscow had not answered the last laconic proposal from Rome anyway, that Pacelli transmitted in October (see p. 120). Rather, the Soviets had begun to present the bitter reckoning for d'Herbigny's secret action:

Bishop Boleslas Sloskans, whom the newspapers had accused for months of being "an agent of Poland and Pilsudski" (he was of Latvian nationality!) was arrested in Minsk on September 16, 1927. His examining magistrate in Moscow, a man named Rybkin, even at the interrogation in Lubianka prison made no secret of the actual reasons:[25]

"The Catholic church is mixed up in politics, it does not want any legal relations with the Soviet Union. Proof: according to canon law, all those who send their children to atheistic schools, i.e. Soviet ones, are excommunicated. The Catholic church has formed a state within the Soviet state. A Catholic bishop travels around in his dioceses without the knowledge of the government and transfers priests without asking for permission. . . ."

"Is that forbidden?" Sloskans asked.

"No, but one must take into consideration the wishes of the government. All other denominations coordinate their activities with the government, only the Catholic church continually defies the Soviets. Therefore we shall persecute it until it submits or is completely destroyed. If the Pope would write something favorable to the Soviets, one could make concessions, but the Pope shows only hostility. . . . But we will not make the same mistakes as the French revolution and accuse the priests for being priests, we will always be able to find a crime against the state for them. . . ."

Bishop Sloskans knew from experience how that worked: in his absence, the police had hidden military maps in his rooms and then "found" them; the examining magistrate admitted that openly. He was primarily concerned with finding out from Sloskans something about the background of the Vatican's behavior. In order to incline the bishop to co-operate, he even supplied him with religious literature[26] and suggested—in vain—that he write a translation of the "Codex Iuris Canonici." Later, when Sloskans was sentenced without trial to three years' prison camp in the Solovetski Islands, he learned from a GPU official that his sentence was for military espionage ("paragraph 58/6"). "But you may put your mind at ease," the official added, "if you had really been a spy, they wouldn't have given you such a mild sentence, they would have had a big trial and executed you, or at least given you a ten-year sentence."

That is what happened in the case of Prelate Teofil Skalski, the apostolic administrator d'Herbigny had installed for Zhitomir.[27] After a long proceeding, Skalski was sentenced on January 27, 1928, to ten years' imprisonment, after he had confessed that Catholic priests had crossed the Polish-Soviet border illegally with his knowledge and that he had assigned them to parishes without permission. Of the charge of espionage that had also been made, however, suddenly no more was heard. Why? Responding to a request from the Polish [!] embassy in Moscow the trial was held *in camera*. The *Osservatore Romano* protested against the sentence, but when Skalski was exchanged four years later and went to Poland, he never appeared publicly again.

The German consulate reported from Odessa that Bishop Alexander Frison—following d'Herbigny's instructions—had tried on May 1, 1928, to move from Simferopol to Odessa to take up his office as apostolic administrator. But the GPU had stopped him "at the last moment."[28] A year and a half later he was arrested "under the pretext that he was secretly consecrated as bishop," as Cardinal Gasparri informed the German Ambassador to the Vatican (see facsimile p. 124). The Cardinal Secretary of State asked whether Bergen would be so good as to "interest" his brother-in-law Dirksen, who was now the German Ambassador to Moscow, "in the liberation of Monsignore Frison, who is being held *for no reason*." But any such attempt, since the death of Brockdorff-Rantzau, had been doomed to failure, because since then every contact between Rome and Moscow had been broken off, and because the Pope had not only changed the course of his eastern policy, but had simultaneously begun to come to an understanding with another dictatorship: the Fascists in Italy.

At about the same time that the contacts between the Vatican and the Soviets were gradually drying up and the papal nuncio in Berlin was undertaking his last vain attempts, his brother, the lawyer Francesco Pacelli, was conducting secret negotiations on behalf of the Holy See with a representative of Mussolini. While the demands (and the hopes) of the curia's Russian policy had to be reduced more and more, they were coming closer and closer to fulfilling all their desires in discussions with the Fascists. When finally, on February 11, 1929, the Lateran treaties were signed "in the name of the most holy trinity" (as the preamble read), the Pope two days later praised the Fascist Duce as the man "with whom providence has brought us together."[29] Mussolini—in spite of his basically a-religious, anti-clerical attitude, had cut the nearly sixty-year-old Gordian knot of the "Roman Question": he confirmed the Catholic religion as the "sole state religion" with all the consequences thereof, and returned to the Pope at least symbolically a miniature Papal State, the Vatican City.

To the reproach that the Pope had now after all associated himself with a "revolutionary movement," Pius XI replied with the strangely naive

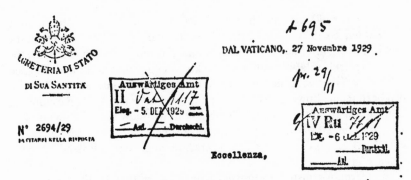

A 695

DAL VATICANO,. 27 Novembre 1929 .

N° 2694/29

Eccellenza,

Il Rev.mo Prof. Dr.Pietro Pal di Jassy in Romania, a mezzo della Nuhziatura Apostolica di Berlino, ha fatto pervenire alla Santa Sede la dolorosa notizia che Monsignor Alessandro Frison, verso il principio di questo mese, è stato arrestato dai Soviety e deportato in luogo finora sconosciuto, sotto pretesto che fu consacrato segretamente Vescovo.

Essendo attualmente Ambasciatore di Germania in Mosca l'Eccellentissimo Signor Von Dirksen, cognato dell'Eccellenza Vostra, Le sarei veramente grato se Ella avesse la bontà d'interessare personalmente il menzionato Ambasciatore alla liberazione del suddetto Monsignor Frison, detenuto senza alcun fondamento.

Nell'anticiparLe, Signor Ambasciatore, i miei ringraziamenti per quanto avrà modo di fare al riguardo, ho l'onore di profittare dell'opportunità per esprimere all'Eccellenza Vostra i sensi della mia più alta e distinta considerazione.

A. Ca.d. Gasparri

A Sua Eccellenza
IL SIGNOR DR. DIEGO VON BERGEN
Ambasciatore di Germania presso la
Santa Sede

Cardinal Gasparri's letter to Ambassador von Bergen.

remark: "But this revolution [Mussolini's] came about legally, under the king's supervision!"[30]

"That such transactions leave a bitter taste especially in the mouths of the most faithful is neither new nor illogical," Alcide De Gasperi, who as

Secretary General of the dissolved Catholic People's Party had been sentenced to four years' imprisonment in 1927 and now received as charity a position as a writer of index cards in the Vatican library, wrote at that time. "The settlement is a success for the regime, but from a world-historical point of view, it is a liberation of the church. . . . The Pope could not do other than open to a Mussolini who was knocking at the bronze gates. . . . The danger is rather in concordatory policy. . . . A concordat is one thing, an agreement (*la concordanza*) another. . . . At this moment, a breeze of mediaeval romanticism is blowing. . . . But the reality of the 20th century will soon make itself felt, the great masses will appear on the scene again: let's hope that the men of the church do not lose sight of them, for they are the reality of today and tomorrow. . . ."[31]

De Gasperi, the man who, 15 years later, as head of the Christian Democratic government, shaped the anti-Fascist constitutional compromise with the Italian Communists without allowing them to come to power, in this letter was able, over and above his own melancholy, to objectively recognize and understand the basic problem of papal policy toward modern dictatorships. When Pius XI shortly thereafter had his first run-in with the Fascists, he cried out in a speech:

"If it were a question of saving a few souls, of preventing greater evil, we would have the courage to deal even with the devil in person."[32]

Mussolini was furious about this unflattering comparison. But this was and remains the position—contradictory and still unavoidable—that motivates the Vatican Ostpolitik of this century. In 1928/29 this involved a fateful fallacy to which not only the papal church succumbed, namely:

Hardly anyone recognized at the time that the "diabolical" forms developing more and more strongly in the Communism of Stalin's Soviet Union were no longer at all an expression of world-revolutionary intentions, that on the contrary, Stalin's domestic terrorism was a sign of his long-term *abandonment* of *foreign*-political adventurism, the expression of a self-isolation. It made possible—under the supposed pressure of "capitalist encirclement"—the use of the strongest coercive measures for building up the Soviet Union as a great power. But it also favored the growth of Fascism and National Socialism in Europe, those right-totalitarian movements that appeared—even to the church—as "protectors of order" against the Communist threat. In reality, they—formally no atheists, but inhuman—then upset the European order and helped Soviet Communism to attain world power status.

"Fascism is a monstrous power, but also one limited in time. What will the papacy do when it finally collapses?" asked Carl von Ossietzky in the Berlin *Weltbühne* on the day the Lateran treaties were signed; Mussolini, this "former Marxist," he said, knew that "class groupings" also involve the church, and one could "trust Roman diplomacy to be clever enough to have reached similar conclusions even without Marxism." When *Germania*, the paper of the German Catholic Center Party,[33] reported soon after the Lateran treaties that the same sort of thing was now being explored between the Vatican and the Soviets, the German Embassy in Moscow made inquiries and received a quite clear reply from Litvinov:

". . . that the Soviet government has no intention of entering into negotiations with the Vatican, since similar earlier attempts have shown the hopelessness of such exchanges of ideas. Mr. Litvinov said that no third power had made any attempt to mediate between the Soviet government and the Vatican, but asserted that the latter, after the conclusion of its agreement with Italy, had put out feelers to the Soviet Embassy at the Quirinal through private mediators; but the mediator had been informed that the Soviet government did not wish to enter upon negotiations."[34]

"Various telegraph agencies in Europe and America have spread the news of imminent negotiations of the government of the USSR with the Holy See for the purpose of a religious pacification in the USSR." So began a notice in the *Osservatore Romano* of April 7, 1929, edited by the Cardinal Secretary of State. It would be desirable, of course, it went on, that the Soviet government renounce religious persecution, but "in informed circles of the Vatican nothing was known about it to date," on the contrary: in March alone, fourteen Catholic priests had been arrested in White Russia. . . .

It is not impossible that one of the "private mediators" that Litvinov mentioned was that Hungarian priest Viktor Bede, who had aroused notice in 1924 through his "Conversations with Lenin," which he described in the Vatican paper (see p. 54). Bede was heard from now on August 8, 1929, in the *Oberschlesischen Kurier* (Königshütte/Chorzów), with the announcement that he would try to travel to the Soviet Union as a journalist "to report on the religious situation," in order to pick up again, "for now very noncommittally and very inofficially," the threads that had been torn since d'Herbigny's expulsion. The solution of the "Roman question" between Vatican and Fascist Italy, he said, had also been viewed as impossible, while he, Bede, had predicted it long in advance. Of course, in the case of Moscow, he was not that sure, but recognition by the Holy See must still be desirable to the Soviets, Bede thought, as he fantasized an "alliance between Communism and the greatest moral power, the Papacy." His long-range goal was the entry of Catholic monks as "examples of true Communism" in the land of the Soviets. . . .

Certainly, these fantasies of the 60-year-old Bede were not "rewarded" with a Soviet entry visa. Nor would they be worth remembering if they had

not been taken completely seriously by the Catholic Center paper
Germania, which attested to Bede's "astonishing political acuity." On
August 22, 1929, the Vatican saw itself obliged to take an official position in
the *Osservatore Romano:*

> "The article by the Very Reverend Bede, which is based on unfounded
> optimism, contains such unusual opinions and considerations that we will not
> stop to discuss them, for that would be a waste of time. We will also overlook the
> fact that the newspaper gives him, gratis, the title of Monsignore, as well as a
> commission that no ecclesiastical office ever dreamed of according him; still we
> cannot conceal our astonishment that a Catholic newspaper like the *Germania*
> repeats such an article with a commentary that arouses fears of sympathies in an
> extremely dangerous area."[35]

That was of course quite a false suspicion. The Catholic Center Party,
which since December 1928 had been led by Monsignore Ludwig Kaas, the
closest friend and advisor of the Berlin nuncio Pacelli, had already turned
away from the old "Rapallo policy" and friendship with Russia. Instead,
back in June 1927—to the lively displeasure of the German Foreign
Office[36]—Kaas had spoken in favor of easing relations with Poland and
proposed making the controversial German-Polish border "invisible"
through the common administration of the Polish corridor. Thus it was no
wonder that it was from Upper Silesia, where they were especially sensitive
to "pro-Polish tones," that Bede's article was launched into the *Germania*;
it was ammunition, so to speak, in an intra-party altercation that had
basically already been decided.

Prelate Kaas, an admirer of a Catholic form of government such as
Prelate Ignaz Seipel, the Austrian chancellor, attempted with unhappy
results at that time, called for a "leadership in the grand style" at the
Freiburg Catholic Conference of 1929, while his leftist counterpart, the
former Rapallo-chancellor Wirth, warned against the "harbingers of
Fascism." But Kaas was more inclined to see salvation on the right from the
party quarrels that were tearing apart the Weimar Republic. Carl von
Ossietzky commented maliciously: "The party leadership has long ago
wrenched the bells of democracy away from Dr. Wirth and in return placed
the silent altar candle in his hand. In the person of the weasel-nosed Prelate
Kaas from Trier, the German Seipel, in perfect, dyed-in-the-wool
Catholicism, has entered that region where alone better politics is
brewed."[37] Foreign politics too, one must add. The time when Berlin served
as a discreet stage for Kremlin-Vatican contacts, and German diplomacy
rendered "good services" for it, was at an end.

Now, in October 1929, the Vatican could in good conscience label as
"pure invention" reports that Pacelli and Soviet Ambassador Krestinski
were negotiating;[38] that the two diplomats had previously been in contact

for years was not publicly known; now that the thread was broken, its existence could easily be denied. At the same time, even now there were still helpless attempts at contact: the unfortunate traveller to Russia Father Schweigl, S. J. (see p. 109), at the beginning of August 1929, betook himself with a written commission from Pius XI to the Soviet Embassy in Rome and asked the Russians to pass on scientific publications of the Vatican astronomical observatory to the Soviet astronomical center in Nizhny Novgorod (Gorki). But Schweigl was politely referred to the mails, as he remarks in a documentary note of August 14, 1929 (*Neveu Papers*). The next day the Pope announced the establishment of his Russian College (*Russicum*) with an explanation that mentions "diabolical snares" with which the Soviets were so encircled that. . .

". . . in human terms, no hope exists that the situation will improve in the foreseeable future."[39]

At the end of 1929, the world economic crisis lay like a nightmare on people's consciousness; at the same time, fear of the "Red Peril" was growing everywhere, and a simple Bavarian pastor asked in the title of an anti-Communist/anti-Semitic brochure: "When will the blood tyranny of Satan begin here?"[40] Eugenio Pacelli too spoke of a "dark, combat-ridden future" in the address with which he departed from Berlin at the end of December 1929, soon to take the helm in Rome as the new Cardinal Secretary of State, and ten years later as Pope. Prelate Kaas wrote this address for him, which also spoke of an "*intensified intellectual struggle* with a world increasingly rebellious against the Kingdom of Christ."[41] Stalin issued the watchword of *intensified class struggle*. . . .

Missionary Battle Cries: Atheistic from Moscow,
"Non-Political" from Rome

"We must work as if Russia will soon be open to us!" cried Michel d'Herbigny in a festive address when the cornerstone for the "Russicum," the papal Russian college, was laid on February 11, 1928, not far from the Piazza Santa Maria Maggiore in Rome. Here prospective priests would now be educated who were intended in the future to revive the Christian faith of those 140 million people between the Baltic and the Black Sea who were to be led back "to the unity of the true Church of Christ." D'Herbigny did not speak of the political conditions, but if one wished to follow the lofty vision he presented, one could believe that the "missionization of Russia," on which so many illusory hopes had been placed ten years earlier—after the collapse of the Czarist empire (see p. 12)—had suddenly become of immediate interest again. Catholic missionaries would one day "penetrate southward from the Asiatic North" and then together with the native clergy which had converted from the Orthodox to the Catholic confession would "enlighten the still heathen peoples." That was a great plan, he said, which of course would stretch over centuries. . . .[42]

No doubt, the Pope—after he was finished with his "diplomatic Latin" with the Soviets at the end of 1927—had been won over by a new enthusiastic conception of d'Herbigny's. It cannot be established exactly to what degree it was the result of the false expectation or assumption that Stalin would destroy the Soviet Union or embroil it in fatal foreign-political adventurism with his domestic terrorism; this thought surely had some influence. D'Herbigny, who now told his many tales as the mysterious traveler in Russia, and cloaked himself with the aura of the expert, gradually became one of Pius XI's closest collaborators, even though he was never incorporated into the curial hierarchy. Many an old Roman prelate can still remember today that the Jesuit bishop had "free access to the papal chambers."

The oath of loyalty to the Soviet leadership by the Moscow patriarchal administrator Sergius (see p. 118) had released a wave of outrage among the West European Russian emigrants, and produced not a few conversions to the Catholic church. For this reason, the Pope in 1927 sent his "eastern expert" d'Herbigny on a great reconnaissance and recruiting trip to almost all the centers of Orthodoxy existing outside the Soviet Union: Velehrad (in Moravia), Vienna, Belgrade, Bucharest, Sofia,[43] Istanbul and Alexandria were his travel stops. The Greek Orthodox Patriarch in Alexandria asked d'Herbigny whether there were relations between the Vatican and Moscow. "Yes," said the Pope's emissary, "relations that are characterized by arrests and sentencing of Catholic priests, without there ever having been the slightest attempt on the side of the Holy See to establish diplomatic relations. . . ."[44]

This again—as we know—was correct in word, but not exactly in fact. D'Herbigny was exclusively concerned with arousing trust among the Orthodox hierarchy of the West by creating a convincing distance from the Soviets. Not Christian "unity" (as Catholic ecumenicalism understands it today after the second Vatican Council), but rather "reunification" of all schismatics with the Roman church was the goal that the presentation of a united front against Communist atheism was to serve. Also to this purpose was the adoption of the "Russian," the accomodation in language, liturgy and religious life style of Eastern Christianity, which d'Herbigny now more and more zealously pursued as president of the papal "Commissio pro Russia," with no idea that he would thereby land in the hornets' nest of nationalism.

The Russian College in Rome was d'Herbigny's very own achievement. He procured the money for its construction from the wealthy sister of the

French Carmelite nun Therese Martin (1873-1897), who had been sainted three years earlier and was revered as "little Theresia of the Child Jesus." The "Russicum" bears the saint's name to this very day; built onto the papal Institute for Eastern Studies and connected with a "Russian-Catholic" church, it was placed entirely at the service of preparation for an imaginary future. Here only Russian was spoken and dress was in the style of the Orthodox priests. D'Herbigny himself, shortly before his trip to the Orient, grew a beard, because—so the Pope had told him—"for the Russians a beard is also a medium of apostleship. . . ."[45]

D'Herbigny's man in Moscow, Bishop Pie Eugene Neveu, took care of direct communication with the land of heart's desire. For eight years, from 1926 to 1933, he sent a letter to d'Herbigny every two weeks via the French embassy's courier post, reporting not only on the religious situation, but also on political developments. They were so detailed and exact that today they constitute a more valuable historical source than many diplomatic reports. Neveu circulated in Moscow as a Russian among Russians, he commanded innumerable personal contacts,—partly because not only Catholics, but also believers in other faiths, even Communists, confided in the papal delegate, in spite of surveillance. He was a sharp, often sarcastic, observer: many of his letters were datelined "Kremlin-Bicetre" (a Paris suburb with a mental institution!). In return, d'Herbigny used to tell him in long, hand-written letters about the situation in the Vatican, in the "Commissio pro Russia," in the "Russicum"; in this way d'Herbigny gave instructions and advice, and acquired for himself and his institutions newspapers, new and old books, also devotional objects (like icons) that would have been difficult or impossible to export legally. Only to the Pope did d'Herbigny read selected parts of Neveu's letters in his weekly audiences—for the rest, the Jesuit bishop held the line to Moscow in his own hand. He alone determined what part of it got into the official documents of the "Commissio pro Russia." And he also later took care that the correspondence did not land in the Vatican secret archives.[46]

Via Neveu's reports from Moscow, the first news reached Rome about the fate of 22 Catholic priests, Bishop Sloskans and Exarch Feodorov among them, who were detained in a hard labor camp in the Solovetski Islands in the White Sea. For a few months in the summer of 1928, the GPU allowed them to celebrate services in both rites in the chapel of a deserted Orthodox monastery; Sloskans even ordained a priest here on September 7, 1928. But at the beginning of 1929, the situation of the priestly prisoners, especially the Catholics, deteriorated.[47] This was the moment that the announcement of the Lateran treaties between the Pope and Mussolini went around the world. . . .

D'Herbigny had already written to Neveu at the beginning of December

1928, on the Pope's behest, that he should, as soon as possible, secretly consecrate as bishop the Lithuanian priest Teofilus Matulionis in Leningrad, as a "substitute," so to speak, because Bishop Malecki—whose rank the Soviets were aware of—was being harassed more and more. On February 9, 1929, Matulionis came to Moscow, and Neveu now performed the same kind of consecration he himself had experienced three years earlier, behind the barred doors of St. Ludwig's. However, the event was probably not a secret from the Soviet authorities (which had sentenced Matulionis, like Malecki, to three years' imprisonment back in 1923 in the Cieplak case). The entrance of St. Ludwig's was under constant surveillance—even with cameras—from the Lubianka prison across from the church. Matulionis was arrested in Leningrad shortly thereafter and exiled to the Solovetski Islands.[48] In the summer, it was Monsignore Naskreski's turn, the deputy of Skalski, the administrator of Zhitomir who was in prison in Moscow; in autumn, the same fate overtook Bishop Frison in Odessa (see p. 123). Stalin was ready for the great blow against religion.

On April 8, 1929, under the direction of Schmidovitch—d'Herbigny's former contact!—the "Permanent Commission for Questions of Religion" was formed in the Presidium of the Central Executive Committee, and at the same time, the previous legislation on religion was unified and sharpened in a decree. This decree, which is valid to this day, and also influenced religious legislation in the Eastern European countries with Communist governments after the Second World War, subjugated religious communities to a rigorous state control—quite contrary to the classical concept of the separation of church and state. This not only gave a stronger legal base for compulsory registration of the parishes and contractual use of buildings of worship (see p. 16), it also enabled, above all, the creation of legal pretexts to restrict religious life and to close the churches:[49]

The church communities must guarantee in the contracts for the use of buildings and objects (which remain state property) that they will bear all costs of repairs, heating, insurance, custody, taxes "and so forth"— otherwise the right of usage will be withdrawn; they are responsible for all depreciation and must allow "periodic inspections" (§29 b-f).

Buildings of worship must be insured against fire; however, in case of a fire, the local executive committee shall decide whether the compensation shall be used for the reconstruction of the church or for "social and cultural purposes" (§33).

If "not enough persons can be found who are interested in acquiring the rights of usage to satisfy their religious needs"—and under the above-named conditions!—the churches shall be closed (§ 34-37).

The decree regulated such a "liquidation of buildings of worship" down to the smallest detail, from the candelabras to the sacramental wine (Bishop Neveu later reported to Rome that in the liquidation of Sts. Peter and Paul in Moscow, he was allowed to save only the "Sanctissimum" from the tabernacle and take it in a taxi to St. Ludwig's).

The activity of the "servants of religion" shall be limited to the town where their church is located (§19)—a limitation that must especially affect a small, often widely-scattered congregation like the Catholic.

The decree forbids religious communities from "granting to its members any kind of material aid," it forbids them to "form religious or any other assemblies, groups, divisions, working groups—no matter whether these concern themselves with the Bible, literature or any other theme, whether they undertake handicrafts or religious instruction." Even in the churches themselves, only such books may be kept "as are necessary for the performance of the respective worship service" (§17a-c).

The crowning touch of this legislative edifice, with which atheistic caesaropapism established itself, was the alteration of the constitution passed by the Greater Russian Executive Committee (WZIK) on May 18, 1929:

Freedom of "religious *and* antireligious propaganda," as it had been established in Article 13 of the constitution of 1918, was now changed into "freedom of religious *confession* and of antireligious *propaganda*." Any dissemination of faith, any evangelizing in word or script, any preaching that was not a direct part of the "worship service," was thereby made illegal. Theory followed practice—and vice versa. Now the non-stop work week (without Sunday) was introduced; clerics were denied suffrage, the right of domicile, the right to purchasing-permits for food. An ambiguous prohibition against "fraudulent activities for the purpose of misleading the masses into superstition" was introduced into the penal code (§123). In a massive campaign, the closure of churches was advocated, especially in the villages. The "Atheists' Alliance" mobilized all the union and party organizations, cultural clubs and factory councils, to this purpose. "The collection of signatures to support the closing of churches is allowed, the reverse is regarded as counter-revolutionary and will be punished," announced the *Besboshnik*, the paper of the atheist organization.[50] The "spontaneous" will of the people demanded a prohibition on bell-ringing, then the confiscation of the "unused" bells; those of the German Protestant church in Tiflis, for example, were ceremoniously presented to the zoo to be melted down—for a monkey cage.

The over-zealousness of the atheists, which Stalin coolly exploited for the forced collectivization of agriculture, outdid itself at Christmas 1929 in an orgy of carnivalistic processions; western diplomats in Moscow watched in revulsion as young Communists, dressed in liturgical robes, publicly spat upon crosses. There were scenes such as would not be seen again until the

Chinese "Cultural Revolution" decades later. The Kremlin leaders, who were now occupied only with themselves and their fanatical plan for a revolutionization of Russia, were no longer concerned by the echo of the world, indeed by the entire rest of the world. But shocked foreign observers drew exactly the opposite conclusions: "Perhaps people abroad do not sufficiently comprehend what is happening here and is being prepared for the rest of the world. This is the most terrible danger that we have experienced since the World War. . .", said French Ambassador Herbette in a letter from Moscow,[51] and Bishop Neveu's reports to Rome conformed to this mood—even though they erred in their reasoning concerning foreign policy.

D'Herbigny considered this a propitious moment to advise the Pope that he must finally break his silence with a public protest, with a moral-political outcry such as Father Gehrmann had recommended back in 1925 (see p. 69). A few months earlier, Pius XI had admitted in a conversation that at the beginning of the twenties he had "raised an open protest" against the situation in Russia, "which however had done more harm than good."[52] Now Pius XI hesitated no longer to sign a text that was obviously d'Herbigny's writing. On February 2, 1930, in the form of a letter to the Roman Cardinal Vicar Pompili, the Pope summoned the faithful all over the world to a *crusade of prayer*.[53] This was to expiate the "vicious attacks" that "are being organized systematically in the immense regions of the Soviets, which exceed, yes even violate, the wording of the revolutionary constitution, which is itself so anti-religious."

However, the Pope did not content himself with condemning the excesses of the anti-religious campaign and complaining about the oppression of the Catholics (he mentioned by name only Sloskans, Frison and Feodorov), but even reproached the Western European governments for having neglected, back at the conference of Genoa in 1922, to proclaim, "as a precondition for *any* recognition *at all* of the Soviet government, respect for the conscience of the individual, freedom of religious practice and of church properties." In Genoa at the time, these demands had been

"sacrificed in favor of worldly considerations, which however would have been better preserved if the various governments had made allowances above all for the rights of God and his justice. . . ."

Anyone familiar with the actual occurrences at Genoa and Rapallo (see p. 38) can at this point only read the papal epistle with mild astonishment. Had the Pope, had the Roman curia itself not attempted, in 1922 and for years thereafter, to reach compromises with the Soviets? Had Vatican diplomacy not gratefully made use of the diplomatic relations of other countries to Moscow—especially the German and French embassies?

D'Herbigny, the composer of the papal letter, seems to have banished that from his consciousness; but Pius XI, whose temperament it was occasionally to slam his fist on the table, had shortly before gotten a new Secretary of State: Cardinal Pacelli, by nature more a diplomat than a missionary, stepped into action. While the anti-Soviet/anti-Communist counter-campaign of the Catholic church was already in high gear (on February 17, 1930, the *Osservatore Romano* appeared with the headline "Roman Light Against the Moscow Darkness"), the Berlin papal nunciature suddenly turned to the German Foreign Office on February 15 with a strange request: would it explain to the Soviets, via its ambassador in Moscow, that the Pope's crusading letter was intended purely religiously and not at all politically? The Reich Foreign Minister Curtius thereupon telegraphed immediately to Moscow:

Monsignore Luigi Centoz, the chargé d'affaires, was in such a hurry that on the same afternoon he made sure again that the communication had been sent to Moscow. The Vatican departmental head of the German Foreign Office simply couldn't resist "pointing out that the Pope's 'religious' letter did indeed contain political elements, especially where he had spoken of the negotiations in Genoa. Mr. Centoz seemed to admit this readily, but then again underlined the fact that the letter had actually been intended to be purely religious. *It would be terrible if because of this greater persecutions should arise again in Russia. . . .*"[54]

However, the explanations that Monsignore d'Herbigny gave to the German Ambassador von Bergen at this time about the Pope's "crusade letter," whose author he admitted himself to be—not without pride—were quite politically tinged: its importance lay in the fact

"that the Holy See has given up the hope of reaching an understanding with the present [!] rulers of Russia. The Pope now hopes for Russia's salvation only by means of prayer, by means of the spiritual alliance of all Christian nations against the moral and religious dissolution that Bolshevism has written on its banners. Seen from this point of view, the Pope's letter signifies not only a certain conclusion to the history of relations between Russia and the Holy See, but perhaps also an *important turning point* in the struggle of all civilized nations against Bolshevism. . . ."[55]

Were two different tendencies in the Vatican expressed in the diplomatic attempts at appeasement by the papal Secretariat of State on the one hand and in this radical summation by the president of the Papal Commission on Russia on the other? Or was it only the usual confused duplicity again?—D'Herbigny himself assured that it was a "materialistic interpretation" to claim that the Pope was preaching a *military* crusade.[56] Even Ambassador Bergen warned against such an interpretation: "According to my knowledge of the circumstances, official Vatican policy—although its representatives may not always be in agreement in their judgment of the

Abschrift.

Berlin, den 15. Februar 1930.

Kilt sehr !

Diplogerma

M o s k a u

Nr. 93

Tel.i.geh.Ziffern.

Im Anschluß an Telegramm Nr.92
Für Botschafter persönlich !

Hiesiger vatikanischer Geschäftsträger hat uns soeben
mitgeteilt, der Brief, den der Papst an den Generalvikar –
Pompili – Rom geschrieben habe, trage einen rein religiösen
Charakter und habe keinen politischen Einschlag. Andere religiöse Gemeinschaften seien bereits vor dem Vatikan in
ähnlichem Sinne an die Öffentlichkeit getreten. Der Vatikan
regt an, Sie entsprechend zu unterrichten, damit Sie bei
sich bietender Gelegenheit die Russen informieren und darauf
hinwirken könnten, daß nicht etwa im Zusammenhang mit dem
nach Ansicht des Vatikans falsch interpretierten Papstbrief
weitere Verfolgungen in Rußland einträten.
Ich bitte Sie, Obiges gelegentlich bei Herrn Litwinoff
zu verwerten und mir über das Ergebnis zu drahten.

C u r t i u s .

K503460

(Berlin, February 15, 1930. In connection with telegram no. 92. For the
Ambassador personally! Local Vatican chargé d'affaires has just informed us,
the letter that the Pope wrote to the Vicar General Pompili in Rome was of a
purely religious nature and had no political element. Other religious
communities have stepped forward before the Vatican with similar intentions.
The Vatican requests us to inform you accordingly, so that at the proper
opportunity you may inform the Russians and thereby effect that no further
persecutions arise in Russia as a result of what the Vatican feels is a false
interpretation of the papal letter.

May I ask you to bring this up at your convenience with Mr. Litvinov and
telegraph me about the results. Curtius.)

measures to be used in fighting Soviet policies—is very far from any attempt to produce an alteration by forceful or even military methods."[57] But then how was d'Herbigny's working hypothesis that he had prescribed to the "Russicum" (". . . as if Russia would soon be open to us. . .") to be realized?

Only someone who could empathize with d'Herbigny's remarkable frame of mind, this mixture of missionary mysticism and church-political fantasy, or who, as a believer, considered prayer an effective powerful factor in this world, could perhaps be able to regard the papal challenge as "purely religious." Neither the one nor the other could be expected from the Soviet Communists. On the contrary, they saw their crassest prejudices confirmed, and—this was the paradoxical result—the papal rage not only provoked them to even wilder outbursts, it even frightened them. . . .

Mass of Atonement, Diplomatic Tricks, and Plans for Conversion

"The Pope is assuming the role intended for him by the international plutocracy as leader in the struggle against the Soviet Union," the Moscow government paper *Isvestia* announced on February 18, 1930. After Pius XI, in his crusade letter, had extended an invitation to a ceremonial "mass of atonement for Russia" in St. Peter's cathedral on March 19, party and atheists' alliance in the Soviet Union pulled all the stops on agitation for four weeks. Protest demonstrations, abusive articles, caricatures, posters were offered; philosophers, literati, even the Moscow astronomers delivered impassioned declarations; tanks, planes and submarines were named "Answer to the Roman Pope." The Orthodox patriarchal administrator Sergius was induced to deny any persecution of the churches and to accuse the Pope of "inciting his flock against our land and thus igniting the pyre from which the flame of war is to spread against the Soviet Union."[58] Even Nikolai Bucharin, Stalin's rival who was removed from power in 1929 but had just been half-restored to grace (until he was shot in 1938), sprang to the barricades. He wrote a pamphlet for *Pravda* that was soon disseminated abroad too:[59]

Accompanied by the clanging of censers, a moral preparation for an attack on the Soviet Union was taking place—this was the bogeyman Bucharin held up to his readers, and offered anticlerical literature from Ulrich von Hutten to the "*Pfaffenspiegel*" to morally disqualify the papacy. "The Vatican knows what it is doing. . . . Now it is forming a bloc with Mussolini. . . . The alliance of the Fascist clique . . . is a glaring symbol of the fact that the highest sacrificial priest and arch-strategist of the Catholic church has now become a main agitator of the international counter-revolution. . . . The peoples of the Soviet Union are transforming the fabric of the village from the ground up. . . . They are marching out of the gloomy cells of superstitious belief in witches and magicians onto the broad avenue of the construction of a socialistic society in which there will be neither capitalists nor exploitation, neither Popes nor Patriarchs. For that very reason the parsons are mobilizing for a new crusade. . . . For that reason the reactionary challenge of the Pope will be met by the revolutionary challenge of the workers of all lands: Down with the Pope and all his archbishops!"

Papst-Karikatur aus der Moskauer Prawda *(1930)*
Cartoon of the Pope, *Pravda* (1930)

Besboshnik, the paper of the Atheists' Alliance, dedicated a special issue to the debate with the papacy, which up to then had been publicly rather ignored.[60] France's ambassador to Moscow, Herbette, reported: "The Pope's letter has especially upset them. Why this agitation, if they were already decided at this point to challenge the whole world?" The ambassador, who himself only a month earlier had seen a danger of war (see p. 133), now recognized in the sensitivity with which the Soviets reacted to Pius XI's attacks, that Litvinov had probably been right when he assured the western diplomats: "All our strength—strained to the utmost— is employed in *domestic* reconstruction; we have none left over to go adventuring. . . ."[61] —The anti-religious campaign was only part of a great *domestic*-political adventure, with which Stalin was trying to finally stabilize the Soviet state; for this state could only live and become a great power in the long run according to the law it had come to power with: by the collectivization of 137 million peasants, by the destruction of the traditional rural structures, to which church and clergy also belonged.[62] Any disturbance from outside hampered this immense process, especially because it was only with difficulty that Stalin could keep it under control. He himself on March 2 warned in *Pravda* for the first time against the "dizziness of success". . . . Five days before the demonstrative mass of atonement that the Pope wanted to celebrate as the acme of his prayer crusade, the Central Committee of the Soviet Communist Party, on March 14, 1930, criticized "unacceptable deviations from the party line in the struggle against religious prejudices. . . , above all the administrative closure of churches without the agreement of the overwhelming majority of the village inhabitants." Point 7 of the ZK resolution now even said: "In case of injurious attacks upon the religious feelings of the peasants, the guilty are to be strictly called to account."[63]

"The Communist leaders have recently recognized that the domestic situation in the USSR was overstrained. . . . [They] have succeeded, or are not far from it, in making opponents of the whole world. They can still claim *one* relatively favorable factor: up to now, the Vatican is the *only* power that has attacked them directly. However, since they are intelligent, they will not imagine that the other powers are so unintelligent as to keep silent forever. . .", wrote Ambassador Herbette to Paris on March 10.[64] His German colleague Dirksen, in the meantime, had complied with the strange request of the Vatican and informed the Soviet government that the papal cry for a crusade was "not meant politically" (see p. 139). But Litvinov naturally disputed that: this was a "political action," he replied, and on the whole, with the Catholic church "everything [is] more or less political," wherefore any agreement with the Vatican was "rather hopeless. . . ."[65] Nevertheless, Litvinov tried to come round. He pointed to the ZK resolution against "anti-religious excesses," and Dirksen sensed how important it was to the Soviet Commissar for Foreign Affairs to erase the bad impression the atheist campaign had made; but above all, Litvinov wanted to dull the political edge of the approaching mass of atonement in St. Peter's. . . .

Rome, however, could not and would not turn back the clock anymore. When Ambassador von Bergen, on orders from Berlin, informed the Vatican that out of regard for German-Soviet relations he would not attend the mass of atonement, Cardinal Secretary of State Pacelli tried to convince at least the Bavarian ambassador, Ritter, to take part; if even Catholic Bavaria turned its back on the papal crusade against Russia, it would displease the Pope very much, Pacelli hinted. Ritter thereupon anxiously asked the Munich state chancellory how he should behave. Bavaria's prime minister, Heinrich Held of the Catholic People's Party, hesitated: he did not want to provoke either the Pope or the Berlin Reich government (which for a long time had been looking for an excuse to end Bavaria's special representation at the Holy See.)

"Your inquiry is not officially acknowledged. In your place, I would certainly take part," the Bavarian secretary of state, Baron Stengel, telegraphed on March 17 to Ambassador Ritter, who was however not much enlightened by this all-too-clever answer. He immediately hurried back to Pacelli and assured him that he would gladly attend the mass of atonement for Russia if the Pope set great store by it, but that in that case the continued existence of the Bavarian legation would be placed into question. And now this danger carried more weight for the Vatican than any anti-Soviet solidarity. Because—and this makes this Bavarian episode especially noteworthy—in the final analysis, the "opportune" still ranked above the "principle". . . . On the afternoon of March 19, Ritter—visibly relieved, but also full of diplomatic pride—telegraphed in code to Munich:

Ambassador Ritter's only misfortune was that *that* was not at all how Munich had meant it. For while Ritter was bragging, not quite honestly, to his Berlin colleague Diego von Bergen that he—"loyal to the Reich"—was resisting the temptation to take part in the anti-Soviet proceedings in St. Peter's, his prime minister Held ascended the podium of a demonstration in the Munich Löwenbräukeller and together with Cardinal Faulhaber, spoke against the godless Soviet Union. When the papal mass of atonement was finally celebrated on March 19 and the choir of St. Peter's struck up the 59th Psalm ("Deliver me from mine enemies"), whereby everyone was supposed to think of the Russian Communists, there knelt in the diplomatic loge of the basilica—as the only German—the chairman of the Center Party, Prelate Kaas (whose party governed together with the Social Democrats in Berlin!). The German Foreign Office assured the Berlin Soviet Embassy, which protested that day against Held's speech in Munich, that the Bavarian head of government had spoken only as a

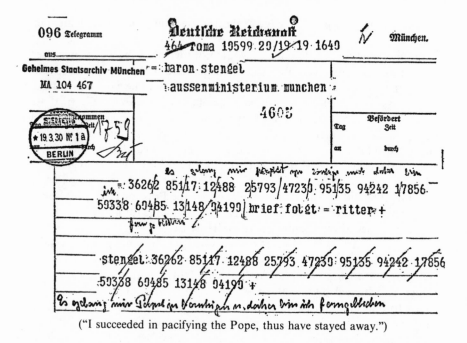

("I succeeded in pacifying the Pope, thus have stayed away.")

"Catholic and a private citizen." No—the Bavarian state chancellory publicly contradicted and thereby embarrassed not only the Reich government but also its own Vatican ambassador: Held had expressed the feelings of "by far the predominant majority of the Bavarian population. . . ."[66]

However, no emotional exuberance or diplomatic tricks influenced the Soviet leadership, but rather the unmistakable danger of its international isolation at a time when the country was drifting toward a new catastrophic famine—the result of the precipitous collectivization. The Vatican, which no one in the Kremlin except Chicherin had ever understood, suddenly appeared to be an uncanny crystallization point of this danger. Among the 65 slogans of the Soviet Communist Party on May 1, 1931, the almost comical cry "Down with the Pope!" stood in fourth place.[67] The impression that the papal protest had "not missed its mark," even that "a certain shift for the better could not be denied" in Soviet church policies, was not entirely wishful thinking by the Berlin Foreign Office.[68]

The church celebrations of Easter 1931 suddenly proceeded without the usual disturbances. "The churches were thronged. In Moscow even the midnight procession took place outside the church." In April the German embassy in Moscow reported 27 Catholic priests imprisoned, among them the apostolic administrators installed by d'Herbigny, Baumtrog and Roth (who had both been in a labor camp since August 1930). In the following months, however, no new arrests were reported; Bishop Alexander Frison (Simferopol), in prison since 1929, whom the Pope had mentioned in his crusade letter, was even released—for the next four years. Bishop Sloskans too was very surprised when he was given his release papers in the middle of October 1930 in the camp in the Solovetski Islands, even given the freedom to choose his own place of residence. Naturally he selected his bishopric Mogilev. The police there did not believe their eyes when the bishop duly reported to them; this must be an "error," they said, and advised Sloskans to disappear immediately, even offered him a free ticket to Smolensk. But Sloskans stood on his rights, and—surrounded by believers as deeply stirred as they were fearful—celebrated a solemn pontifical mass in his cathedral. A week later he was arrested again, the "error" was explained: only a plodding bureaucracy had prevented the administration of the Solovetski Camp from receiving on time his "administrative" sentence (that is, without trial) to three more years of exile in Siberia. . . .[69]

Thus one could not really speak of a true détente; also because the Roman curia sent out a few signals that meant "fight." The unfortunate traveller to Russia of 1926, the Jesuit Josef Schweigl, on April 10, 1930, opened a series of lectures that the Pope had decreed in his prayer-crusade letter with a lecture in the Papal Bible Institute on the theme "Moscow against the Vatican."[70] On the same day, the Moscow government paper *Isvestia* wrote that the capitalists were already dividing the skin of the Russian bear: some wanted land, others oil and coal, "the Roman church wants souls." It said that the most important role in this was played by the "repeatedly exposed French-Polish-White-Guardist agitator *d'Herbigny*," who in his "Commission for Russia" and the "Russian College" was training emigrants for positions in a future "liberated Russia," had grown a beard as a disguise, and was now celebrating the mass in Russian, supported by a Slavic church choir consisting of "White Guardists and prostitutes from the Roman bordellos. . . ."

"With all the obscenity of its tone, the article is noteworthy in that it proves that the policy of the curia in regard to Russia is followed very carefully and in great detail," the German ambassador in Moscow said to this.[71] There were reasons why d'Herbigny was the particular target of the Soviet attacks. He was better known in Moscow than almost any other Roman dignitary; they quite correctly saw in him the driving force of Vatican Russian policy. It was not by accident that the Jesuit bishop was reaching the high point of his ascent now, just at the moment of the prayer crusade:

On April 6, 1930, the Pope separated the "Commissio pro Russia" from the Eastern Church congregation and its president Cardinal Sincero and made it independent. D'Herbigny, already its actual director as Sincero's assistant, now formally became president of the "Papal Commission for Russia," with jurisdiction over all Catholic Russians (of both rites) within and outside of the Soviet Union.[72] Its offices were transferred from the Borgo Nuovo directly into the apostolic palace; the Pope wanted to have his advisor on Russia in close proximity.

When the secret archives of the Commission were also moved on this occasion, rumors first arose in Rome that there was also a special reason for this removal to behind the Vatican walls: important documents had been *stolen*.[73] What was behind this? Had something really happened? Or was this the beginning of that fatal mixture of levity and intrigue that d'Herbigny now began to get caught up in? This would cause more trouble for Pius XI's eastern policies than even his Soviet antagonists could have dreamed of.

For now the greatest consequences did not arise from the theoretical-intellectual discussions, nor from the diplomatic tug-of-war as in the twenties. Even an encyclical as important for Catholic social doctrine as "*Quadragesimo Anno*" (of May 31, 1931), in which Pius XI announced that "no one could be a good Catholic and at the same time a true socialist,"[74] had very little influence on the Vatican's Russian policy (partly because Pius XI was unable to define exactly where "true" Socialism was to be found—with Stalin, with Trotsky, or with western social democracy). The historically decisive event (and fate) for this eastern policy at the beginning of the thirties was that—although it was as always directed toward securing pastoral freedom—it landed in the maelstrom of nationalism: Polish, Russian, Ukrainian and—most catastrophical in its later implications—German nationalism.

This process crystallized around the figure of Michel d'Herbigny, the political-mystical Jesuit bishop. The fact that it was he who was suspected as a "*Polish* agitator" in Moscow at the beginning of 1930 was a particularly paradoxical, but—as we shall see—not accidental misunderstanding.

Soviet Spy in the Vatican?—The "Deubner Affair"

Shaking their heads, Roman prelates whispered the unbelievable to each other, there was malicious gossip in anti-clerical salons from Paris to Warsaw, newspaper boys cried it on the streets of the European capitols: "Soviet spy Deubner flees the Vatican! D'Herbigny's secretary a GPU agent! Monsignore marries Russian Communist! To Moscow with stolen documents!"

At the turn of the year 1932/33, these thrilling headlines were nowhere so avidly noted—with a mixture of horror and glee—as in Catholic Poland;[75] Pius XI had shortly before warned his faithful d'Herbigny: "You have many enemies, people are intriguing against you, it is even reaching Our ears . . . !"[76] When the Pope soon thereafter received the Polish ambassador to the Holy See, Vladislav Skrzyński, Pius XI could not easily suppress the rancour which he had loudly vented somewhat earlier—as the ambassador learned; it was the "Deubner affair" that so enraged him.[77] What had happened? What did it have to do with Poland?

Alexander Deubner, a Russian priest 33 years old at the time, who lived in the Roman "Russicum" and was employed by d'Herbigny as translator and office aide in the "Commission for Russia," had very suddenly—and at first without trace—disappeared from Rome at the end of 1932. Immediately everyone said that he had been "a Bolshevist agent disguised as a priest"; that through his confidential knowledge he had turned in Catholic clerics in the Soviet Union to the GPU. A Vatican announcement denied this accusation, but described him as "morbidly inclined" and said nothing about his whereabouts.[78] Deubner had "returned" to the Soviet Union,[79] "things had gotten too hot for him in Rome"[80]—one can read this even today in Communist-influenced publications, and this also remains the conviction of many older clerics in Rome who can remember those times. The historical truth was different.

The young man called Alexander Deubner, who had come to d'Herbigny in Rome in 1928, already had a lively past. He carried a recommendation from Archbishop Count Sheptyckyi, the Ukrainian-Catholic Metropolitan in East-Polish Lemberg (Lvov). For Sheptyckyi had been connected with the Deubner family (russified Germans from the Baltic provinces) long before the First World War, since the time when he had adventurously attempted to build up in Russia a Catholic church of the Eastern Rite with ties to Rome. At that time Leonid Feodorov's little Catholic-Russian congregation was formed in St. Petersburg (see p. 15). One of its most prominent members was the school inspector Ivan Deubner, who had also at times worked as secretary to the later Russian prime minister Stolypin and had secretly become Catholic. In 1906, after the Czar had granted the Catholics greater freedoms, Ivan Deubner, who was married to a French woman, Marie Panet, was ordained as a priest by Sheptyckyi, entered the "Studite" order, and took the name Spiridon. Soon after the revolution the Bolsheviks arrested Deubner, sentenced him, and exiled him to Siberia, where he was shot by bandits in August 1937. His son Alexander, however, who was born in 1899, had already been sent to Belgium in 1911 to an Assumptionist convent-school, which sent him to study theology in its missionary seminary in Kadiköy (Turkey) from 1921 to 1926.

Unstable, sensitive and religiously irresolute, Alexander Deubner seemed to his superiors unsuited for a priestly vocation. Hardly had they told him this than he went to Poland, where his father's friend Archbishop Sheptyckyi in Lemberg recommended him for ordination in 1926. However, instead of ministering to a Uniate congregation in Nice on the French Riviera, as he was assigned, Deubner went to Paris and—converted to the Orthodox exile church there. Shortly thereafter he repented of this, came to Rome and was received graciously, thanks to Sheptyckyi's intercession, but also because his father was regarded as a "persecuted believer." Bishop d'Herbigny installed him in the "Russicum," charged him with a small scientific-theological work[81] and was happy to have found a Russian helper, with French as mother tongue, who could analyze and translate newspapers and in addition had a good knowledge of the life of the Russian exiled Orthodoxy.

Certainly, many of Deubner's idiosyncracies had not been kept a secret from d'Herbigny; above all his nervous restlessness. But probably d'Herbigny did not regard this as serious, partly because he himself, driven by missionary zeal, displayed an assiduous, almost hectic, activity.—But first let us examine the politico-religious background that fostered the "Deubner case."

In January 1931, d'Herbigny, *together with Deubner*, authored a long, thoroughly documented book about the controversial bishops of the Orthodox emigration.[82] Although the authors wanted to be objective, their real concern was to prove that Orthodoxy no longer offered any real hope for Russia. What the book left unspoken—the Catholic alternative in Russian clothing as the only hope for the future—d'Herbigny advocated all the more openly as president of the papal Commission for Russia. Here is an example:

". . . Instead of preparing themselves mentally for the revival of monastic life in Russia, as is the intention of the Holy See, many are propagating, with a zeal more ardent than clear-seeing, . . . another goal, that they call by a very inexact expression, 'union of the churches'," so wrote d'Herbigny on January 31, 1931, in official instructions to the apostolic visitator, whom he sent to the Benedictine convent in Amay-sur-Meuse (Belgium);[83] there a Father Lambert Beauduin had founded, solely with the resources of his wealthy family, a kind of "experimental monastery" for the eastern rite, but opposed the complete russification of the monastic society as d'Herbigny wished.

"The Holy See would like to have monks who are capable, in that they accept their eastern rite, of someday educating other monks whom they recruit from the populace of the regions of the earlier czarist empire," so d'Herbigny's visitator defined the assignment to the rebellious Belgian fathers. Their prior was finally subjected to a secret penal interrogation in the Russia Commission in Rome, removed from office, exiled from Belgium, forbidden to settle in certain cities of Europe, and finally sentenced to two years' stay in a cloister under vow of silence. . . .

Anyone reading the documents of this case today cannot escape the impression that d'Herbigny and the Roman curia employed many of the methods usual in Russia under the white as well as the red czars. . . . However, the Jesuit bishop d'Herbigny did not yet sense that he himself was nearing a fate similar to the one he helped to cast for the Belgian Benedictine prior. For what had only been a test case in distant Belgium developed in Russia's neighbor Poland into political gunpowder:

Disunified both nationally and religiously, the Poland of the interwar period suffered continuously from the tensions between its 20 million Latin (Polish) Catholics, its 3.5 million Uniate (Ukrainian) Catholics, and the almost 3 million (Ukrainian and White Russian) Orthodox. It lay in the nationalistically interpreted state interest of Poland to gradually de-nationalize the eastern border areas settled by "foreigners"; church-political methods were not unwelcome to this end. Catholicization through latinization furthered polonization. Nevertheless, many of the actions that—with the support of the episcopacy—not only led to church expropriation trials in the thirties, but often even ended with the burning down of Orthodox churches, met with little applause in the Warsaw government, which after all was also concerned with law and order in the country.[84] But the attempts to have the Polish-Catholic influence prevail in the east with some concessions to the *eastern* rite (through compromise solutions in the sense of "Biritualism" and a so-called "Neo-Union") were also a thorn in the government's side. These experiments were at first supported by Archbishop Eduard von der Ropp, who was formally still bishop of the Soviet diocese of Mogilev and since 1919 had been waiting in vain, in his Warsaw exile, for his hour to strike. . . .

Warsaw's mistrust and aversion against the "Neo-Union" experiment of a "mixed rite" grew stronger as it became clearer that d'Herbigny's Roman Commission for Russia by no means wanted to use this model in a Polish national sense—as Ropp, for instance, long believed. For d'Herbigny the Neo-Union was not a *tactical* compromise between the rites, but rather the means to a missionary *strategy*. It could only succeed if the *outward* differences between the Uniate and the Orthodox church disappeared entirely. Any consideration of Polish national interest was only a hindrance here. According to his experiences with the Belgian Benedictine experiment, d'Herbigny now wanted to build on the same model on a large scale in Poland: beside the existing Ukrainian-Catholic church of Sheptyckyi, a *Russian*-Catholic church of an individual stamp, in which except for the dogma, nothing else would recall the western-Latin element. Eastern Poland was designated as a testing field for the future catholicization of *Russia*, and the Neo-Union was the vehicle for that aim—but no longer an instrument for polonization.

The Warsaw government, the clerical and anti-clerical Polish nationalists, could perhaps put up with having simply lost the instrument of the Neo-Union; but they feared that it would now be reversed *against* their interests:

Given these circumstances, the Neo-Union—as it was conceived by the papal "Commissio pro Russia"—would "*conserve* the Russian culture in the eastern regions," wrote the Catholic nationalist Lubienski, who in the summer of 1932 published a polemical, sensational book about the "Roman Road to the East."[85] Lubienski said that the point in question was "that the closer influence of Moscow on the believers of such a (russified) church can be stronger than Rome's influence—as was the case twice already in the past, in the 15th and 18th centuries."

This fear was strengthened after d'Herbigny's Russia Commission, "in which we know our enemies, but not our friends" (Lubienski), had the Ukrainian priest Mikolaj Czarneckyj installed as bishop and apostolic visitator in Kovel (Volynia), in February 1931: bishop for "all Catholic Slavs" of the eastern rite in Poland—except those of the pure Ukrainian dioceses. The "Neo-Unionists" thus suddenly had their own leader, who was naturally closely connected with the Lemberg Metropolitan Sheptyckyi. However, except for him, a few bishops, and a Krakow Jesuit group,[86] no one in Poland supported this development. And its importance was basically small: 45 pastorates with 18,000 believers.[87] Nevertheless, the problem stirred up national resentments more and more seriously. Even the name of d'Herbigny's commission gave offence in Warsaw: "*Pro Russia*" was incorrectly and maliciously translated as "in Russia's favor" (*na rzecz Rosji*). And so naturally d'Herbigny's next strike against Poland's interests, when he liquidated the archepiscopal secretariat of Mogilev, which was in exile in Warsaw, was interpreted the same way:[88] on December 9, 1931, the papal Commission for Russia informed the thoroughly surprised Archbishop von der Ropp that there was no further need for such an office in exile; it was to transfer its archives from Warsaw to Rome. Ropp himself (who had just turned 80) was allowed to retain the title of Mogilev, but his 151 priests of the Latin rite who had also emigrated from Russia to Poland were given the choice of joining a Polish diocese. Thus there was no more thought of using them again on a future "Day X," because in d'Herbigny's vision of the future there was only a de-polonized, non-Latin Catholicism in the Soviet Union.

The ancient archbishop himself was not so sorely stricken by this decision as his nimble vicar general Antoni Okolo-Kulak; he had once been deacon in Smolensk and could pride himself on having later, in Berlin, instructed Eugenio Pacelli in Russian. He had also been able to fill to overflowing the purses of the fictive Mogilev diocese in Warsaw, by imposing high assessments on the emigrant clergymen who were functioning as priests in Poland. Protests from these priests, who viewed Okolo-Kulak as the archbishop's "evil spirit," also contributed to the Roman decision to stop this source of revenue. We may accordingly assume that Monsignore Okolo-Kulak also had personal ill feelings toward Monsignore d'Herbigny, and that for this reason too it was difficult for him to resist the temptation to avenge himself. . . .

Opportunity for this arose several months later, in the middle of 1932, when a co-worker of d'Herbigny's came to Poland, from whose history we have only seemingly deviated in the last pages: Alexander Deubner. D'Herbigny had sent the young Russian priest to Lemberg, to his "spiritual father," Metropolitan Sheptyckyi, perhaps as a "constant observer," but at least to reconnoiter the situation. But questions were now raised about him: the Polish state police were interested in the fact that a man with the reputation of a certain instability had arrived from d'Herbigny's suspect Commission for Russia. They knew that the Soviets had exiled Deubner's father to Siberia, but it was also known that a sister of this father—lived in the Kremlin! Her second husband, who was employed there, was the son of the prominent German Communist Clara Zetkin.[89] The attention of the police was also drawn to the fact that Deubner was accustomed to write to his family in the Soviet Union (for example, to his French mother, who lived in Moscow until her arrest in 1934). And finally, Deubner had not only seen Clara Zetkin, but also met a young Polish woman while passing through Berlin—a "purely platonic" liaison, as he declared.

All this sufficed—with Okolo-Kulak's considerable assistance[90]—to devise a sturdy intrigue; the police denied Deubner an extension of his Polish visa.

Deubner, even more nervous than before, returned to Rome, just at the moment that the news flew through the world press (again launched from Poland) that important secret documents had disappeared from the "Commission for Russia." There was some truth in this, and some suspicion had arisen, which however did not touch Deubner;[91] but he was stricken by a panic fear, because he was sure that everything was only aimed against him.[92] He fled Rome on a December day in 1932, without leaving even a line of explanation for his superior d'Herbigny.

However, perhaps the occasion for his dramatic departure was subconsciously not entirely unwelcome to Deubner. For his flight was by no means, as the Polish press would have the world believe, to Moscow as an exposed spy, but rather—to his Polish girlfriend in Berlin, with the firm intention of marrying her.

Of course, the Vatican *Osservatore Romano* withheld this curious but true point when it denied any theft of documents on February 2, 1933. Deubner's role in the Commission for Russia was played down as "temporary," it was labelled as "absurd" that Deubner could have had anything to do with the Moscow GPU, but the Vatican still owed the public an answer as to where Deubner had gone, if Moscow was not the correct destination.

Actually, the Vatican had known everything since the middle of January, for Deubner had reported in Berlin to the "Papal Relief Work for Russians in Germany," whose secretary was the secretary of the nunciature, Father Eduard Gehrmann. "Unfortunately, the confusion has also involved a Russian-Uniate priest, Father Deubner. . . . It would seem that he intends to marry. Father Rittmeister S. J.[93] has taken care of him. Whether he will dissuade him from the course he has taken is more than doubtful," Gehrmann noted on January 19, 1933.[94] Was this simple truth of the affair too embarrassing to the Vatican to be published? Or were there also interests in Rome for which the "Deubner affair" was just the thing to shake d'Herbigny's position, and above all the Pope's trust in his eastern expert?

"The whole story of Deubner's theft of documents, his espionage, etc., was thought up in Warsaw, with an only too transparent goal in mind. I have heard names named . . . ," intimated Father Jan Urban, the editor-in-chief of the Krakow Jesuit monthly *Oriens*, which was the only Polish paper to take the part of d'Herbigny and his concept.[95] "Perhaps someday a historian will come upon the real origin of this 'Deubneriad,' " Urban hoped.

But even he could hardly have been aware that this checkered story was not only a part of the Polish-Vatican tug-of-war about the proper Russian policy, that its dimensions spread out much farther because it got caught up in a moment of world history: Hitler's seizure of power in Germany.

For the Vatican this event threw a new light on the question of whether the Soviets should be fought or converted, whether eastern atheism should be met with "prayer crusades" or with a "dike policy." As the painful farewell to an illusion took place in the "Deubner-d'Herbigny" case, another now arose.

Joachim Fest, in his biography of Hitler, characterized the basic anti-Communist mood of liberal-conservative, bourgeois Europe, and the attraction of the authoritarian model, as the decisive factors that enabled the German dictator to evade the objections and antipathies confronting him.[96] Hitler also succeeded in this with the Vatican, which—after comparatively harmless experiences with Mussolini—now became fascinated by another, much more dangerous "ventriloquist of the Zeitgeist."

V

Hitler's Anti-Communism: False Hopes With Fatal Consequences, 1933-1939

Polish Intrigues and Deubner's Penance

Flames shot out of the Reichstag building in Berlin. Whoever had set this fire, it was made to order for the National Socialists on this February 28, 1933, hardly four weeks after Hitler's election as Reich chancellor: Finally they had an excuse to suspend important basic rights of the democratic constitution, in order to forestall, by terrorism and arrests, the supposed planned uprising of the "Reds." The facts that the German Communists' potential for revolutionary upheaval was a legend of their own making, that their party, the KPD, had crippled itself by its foolish battle strategy which directed "the main thrust against Social Democracy" (Walter Ulbricht on January 18, 1933), that Stalin had given up hopes for a world revolution in favor of his Russian ambitions[1]—all this disappeared for contemporaries behind Hitler's impressive pose as savior; in his first speech as chancellor on January 31, he had spoken of "Almighty God," may "His divine grace bless our labors."

Although on the day of Hitler's accession to power, Secretary of State Cardinal Pacelli was still of the opinion that this was "more fatal than a victory of the socialist left,"[2] a reversal of mood soon swept in at the Vatican. The antipathy against the Hitler movement had been based more on its neo-pagan, anti-clerical tendencies than on its anti-democratic

150

character anyway. The Catholic Center Reich chancellor Heinrich Brüning had remarked back in 1931 that "to the Vatican bureaucracy, an authoritarian form of government seems the most stable and reliable." When Brüning, who was himself an admirer of Mussolini and a secret monarchist, called at the Vatican on August 8, 1931, Pacelli felt "compelled to advise a union with the Nazis"—naturally not out of any affection for them (as Brüning was told immediately thereafter in his subsequent conversation with Pius XI), but because the Vatican hoped for a "restraint" on the Hitler movement, and above all for a parliamentary majority for a concordat with the Reich.[3] The example of the Lateran treaties with Mussolini (see p. 125) floated before the curia's eyes.

Now, in 1933, Hitler was dropping heavy hints of such a concordat, and offered himself as a guarantee against "Bolshevism," which the *Osservatore Romano* naively threw together into one pot with all other kinds of heresies: "Protestantism, schism, laicism and Bolshevism are basically the same thing (*sono in sostanza sinonimi*)" wrote the Vatican paper in a commentary to the consistory of March 13, 1933.[4] At this assembly of the college of cardinals, the Pope violently attacked the "Missionaries of the Antichrist," whom the peoples of Christian civilization must oppose. And on the same day, the German Ambassador to the Vatican von Bergen sent a dispatch to Berlin (PAAA, Vat. IIa, Pol. 19, Bd. 1) (see facsimile p. 152).

There is other evidence that Pius XI actually was trying to compliment Hitler's anti-Communism in his address of March 13. Five days previously, on March 8, the Pope had told the French Ambassador Charles-Roux that Hitler was the "only head of government who not only shares his [the Pope's] opinion about Bolshevism, but challenges [Bolshevism] with great courage and clarity."[5] And in an audience on March 9, Pius XI surprised the Polish Ambassador Skrzynski with the remark that "He had to reconsider his opinion of Hitler, '*not quite reverse it, but modify it significantly,*' for he had to admit that *Hitler is the only head of government in the world who recently 'speaks of Bolshevism the same way the Pope speaks of it.*' The Holy Father maintains that to speak thus is an expression of personal courage, which could only spring from a well of deep conviction that does not fear even the noble sacrifice of his own life. He repeated that this altered the image that he had previously had of Hitler, since he saw that Hitler shared his view that Bolshevism is not one of the difficulties or one of the opponents, '*mais que c'est l'ennemi. . . .*' "

"*The* enemy"—i.e., Satan. The Polish ambassador wrote this formulation in French—as the Pope had spoken it—in the report that he sent to Warsaw on March 11, 1933, "strictly secret, for the minister's eyes only" (original: *Archiwum Ministerstwa Spraw Zagranicznych, Warsaw*).

Actually, if we look at it this way, what was more obvious than a

Vppl ℸ Vof 10? ⁱ⁷/₅.r.

Telegramm (Geh.Ch.V.) ⁱ.ₐ Soll Vo.ᵉ

Rom, den 13. März 1933,   12,20 Uhr

Ankunft, 13. "   "   14,35 ".

Nr. 11 vom 13.5.   Im Anschluss an Telegramm vom 12.Nr.10.

Heutige Allokution Papstes an Kardinäle
wird einen Satz enthalten des Inhalts, dass
bis vor kurzem allein Papst seine warnende
Stimme gegen die schwere Bedrohung der
christlichen Zivilisation durch die umstürz-
lerischen Kräfte und Bestrebungen erhoben
hätte.

Im Staatssekretariat wurde mir nahege-
legt, darauf hinzuweisen, dass diese Worte
als indirekte Anerkennung des entschiedenen
und unerschrockenen Vorgehens Reichskanzlers
sowie der Regierung gegen den Kommunismus
zu deuten wären.

Bergen.

(Nr. 11 of March 13, 1933. In reference to telegram nr. 10 of the 12th. Today's allocution to the cardinals will contain a statement to the effect that until recently the Pope alone had raised a warning voice against the grave threat to Christian civilization from revolutionary forces and strivings.

The Secretariat of State urged me to point out that these words were to be interpreted as an indirect recognition of the decisive and unflinching actions of the Reich chancellor [Hitler], as well as the government, against Communism. Bergen.)

common defense front? Cardinal Pizzardo, the Secretary for Extraordinary Affairs within the Secretariat of State, had tried twice in February 1933 to make clear to the Polish ambassador to the Holy See that—in spite of all their differences—Pilsudski, Mussolini and Hitler could work together "on the same course of a containment of Communism."[6]

Mistrustful, the Poles hesitated; Pilsudski had just guarded against the unpleasant consequences of German-Soviet cooperation by a non-aggression treaty with Moscow in July 1932 (which for example enabled the release from prison in September 1932 of Prelate Skalski, who had been sentenced in 1928, see p. 123). Pilsudski was an anti-Communist, but not an

Polish Ambassador to the Vatican Skrzyński's report on his papal audience

ideologist. As a politician, he thought above all in terms of mutual French-Polish preventive measures against a Germany which now, 1933, was ruled by the most irreconcilable opponent of the Versailles peace treaty. On the other hand, it had also not escaped Pilsudski that the "Austrian" Hitler, in his book *Mein Kampf*, had always mentioned only Russia, never Poland, as the goal of his "Lebensraum" conquests. Indeed, from May 1933 on, advances by Hitler to Poland became visible that finally, in January 1934, led to a—short-lived—rapprochement and non-aggression pact. Pilsudski viewed it soberly: Hitler was waiting to see whether Poland—like Italy—would be better suited as a satellite or a victim of his expansionist policy.[7] The Soviet Union, upon which the Vatican was fixated as the primary danger, actually stood on the sidelines, weakened by self-induced overexertions. Only six years later did Hitler bring Russia into the game—first through a pact with it, then by attacking it.

The Vatican—like almost everyone else—did not see through Hitler's cold Machiavellianism until very late, or only partially. Of course, here too there were some cool, if false, calculations: in return for a concordat in which Hitler apparently accommodated the Catholic wishes farther than any honorable Reich chancellor before him would have dared, the Pope gave up the Center Party—the political home of German Catholicism.

The haste with which the Center chairman Prelate Kaas himself arranged for this[8] may be explained by his quite correct realization that Hitler would liquidate the Center in any case; therefore there was the hope of saving something by timely self-dissolution. Kaas and his friend Pacelli consoled themselves in this with the hope that "the Nazis would sooner or later be forced to resign," and they both indulged in the fancy that Hitler's non-atheist National Socialism was the "lesser evil" when compared with Stalin's Communism.[9] But the decisive element was that Hitler needed the "kind understanding" of the church for the "struggle to defeat Bolshevism," as he wrote Cardinal Bertram, and that "the new Germany" was fighting "a decisive battle against Bolshevism," as Pius XI joyfully confirmed to Hitler's vice-chancellor von Papen.[10] In foreign policy, Prelate Kaas had already led the Center Party away from the pro-Russian Rapallo policies anyway (see p. 38) and prepared the rapprochement with Poland that Hitler was now apparently carrying out and that the Pope recommended most warmly.

After the Lateran treaties of 1929, Alcide De Gasperi thought he could encourage his friends in the Italian People's Party: "We have at least the consolation of being the last to be sacrificed." But now, four years later, he saw his German friends of the Center Party vote for Hitler's Enabling Act [*Ermächtigungsgesetz*] and for their own demise. He commented sorrowfully: "Fear of Communism has gripped everybody and almost convinced them—as if it were not a matter of the suppression of essential freedoms. . . ."[11]

Was any Vatican eastern policy, in the sense of saving and guaranteeing pastoral possibilities, even conceivable in this climate of irrational fears and exorcisms?—Let us return from the heights of "high politics" to the lower regions:

Berlin, February 28, 1933. On the day after the Reichstag fire, Hitler's propaganda minister Goebbels noted in his diary: "Now the red plague will be rooted out lock, stock and barrel. . . . The worst is over. . . . It is a joy to live again."[12] But in this Berlin there are people who have lost their joy; for example the Russian priest Alexander Deubner, who actually had only a private problem: church or marriage? His name haunts the press and certain offices as a "red agent," who had fled the Vatican. Even the girl he loves is named: she is probably the actual agent, they say—Polish or

Soviet—to whom Deubner has betrayed Vatican secrets; in addition, this Deubner is related to Clara Zetkin, the German Communist (see p. 147). A dreadful event occurs: the girl's father commits suicide in Berlin. We do not know the circumstances, we only know that at this moment Alexander Deubner is again seized by panic, so that he suddenly leaves Berlin— heading South, not East. . . .

But in the meantime, the German ambassador to the Vatican, Diego von Bergen, has sent a report to Berlin in which a question mark is placed after the Vatican's version of the "Deubner case":[13]

"Despite all official denials, it may not be out of the question that he [Deubner] was active as a Bolshevist agent, and as a translator he likely also found opportunities to examine important documents and to evaluate them in his own lights."

This hint from Bergen arrived in Berlin on the day of the Reichstag fire. The Communist-hunt reached a peak in Germany: 4,000 arrests in 24 hours. Under the pretext of threatening danger, the National Socialists take over the governments of the German states. "Gentle pressure is enough to bring them to their knees. . . . In the evening it is decided that now it is Bavaria's turn," Goebbels noted in his diary on March 8. On this day (when the Pope speaks admiringly of Hitler to the French ambassador),

". . . Alexander Deubner, stateless, born August 15, 1899, in Ilienski-Tobolsk [is] taken into protective custody by the Bavarian border police station in Passau . . . before his planned departure for Austria on suspicion of political intrigues [*Umtriebe*]. . . ."[14]

That is what the official documents say. The Vatican soon knew what was up. Bishop d'Herbigny, in a letter to Bishop Neveu in Moscow, sighed: "Poor Deubner!"[15] Father Gehrmann, advisor to the nunciature in Berlin, concerned himself with the prisoner, "who is presently in prison in Passau."[16] Two and a half months later, the political police freed Deubner. On May 26, 1933, the Prussian Ministry of the Interior even informed the German embassy at the Vatican:

"According to the inquiries that were instituted, the assumption that in Deubner we had a Bolshevist-oriented individual was *not* substantiated. It also could *not* be ascertained that he is an agent of the GPU."

The cauldron of intrigues in the meantime bubbled right along. The Pope's trust in d'Herbigny was still almost unbroken; indeed, in the consistory of March 13, he even considered elevating the president of the Commission on Russia to the rank of cardinal. Only the annoying echo of the Deubner affair, the reverberations of which refused to die down, kept the Pope from granting this consolation to his eastern expert (whose "greater and greater nervousness" the Polish ambassador Skrzyński noted with satisfaction). On March 11, Skrzyński received the "confidential, but accurate, information" that no one had ever had such great influence on the Pope as d'Herbigny, indeed, that his position was even expanding, although d'Herbigny himself did seem "somewhat disoriented."[17] Fortunately, however, Cardinal Pacelli's influence was also increasing "in other ways." The papal nuncio in Warsaw, Marmaggi, had also finally been won over to the Polish position; they should therefore do "something nice" (cos milego) for the nuncio, so that he could present it to the Pope. Skrzyński was also delicately cultivating the Cardinal Secretary of State; on April 9, he said to Pacelli:

"Certainly Monsignore d'Herbigny had the best intentions, but he generated such a catastrophical confusion that now one does not know how to extricate oneself, and all this simply as a result of insufficient knowledge of the very difficult circumstances in Eastern Europe and their entanglement with the general problems. . . ."

Naturally Pacelli guarded against telling the Polish ambassador his own opinion of d'Herbigny; nor did the Cardinal want to defend the president of the papal Commission on Russia. It was Pacelli who strengthened the Pope in the concordat policy toward Hitler, and it was also Pacelli's influence if the Pope—who basically did not have a very good opinion of the Poles[18]— now more often expressed the desire for a Polish-German modus vivendi, so that Poland could continue to play "its traditional role as the outer wall of Christianity" (against atheistic Russia).[19] However, d'Herbigny's "Neo-Union" efforts in fostering a russified Catholicism on Polish territory did not fit in at all with this bulwark-function of Poland. This was the "confusion" that the Poles were attempting to "disentangle" by playing up the entanglements of the unfortunate Russian priest Deubner. However, their intention of tripping up d'Herbigny with this was thwarted for the time being.

The Pope, who sensed the intrigue but did not see through its inner logic, did not play along. He did begin to weigh what Pacelli was trying harder and harder to impress upon him: that the mystical-political concepts of a "conversion of Russia" had to fail, that a defensive alliance of anti-Communist powers in Europe was now much more important. But Pius XI was still fascinated by d'Herbigny's personal charisma, by his missionary political romanticism. On the same day on which the report of Deubner's release arrived from Passau, May 25, 1933, d'Herbigny, as a sign of confidence, was given the honorary title of "assistant to the papal throne."

Alexander Deubner, dismayed at the lack of scruples with which his private fall was used politically, now came forward himself. He went to Ljubljana (Yugoslavia), asked advice from the theology professor and prelate Franz Grivec, an expert on the eastern church, and with his support composed an open statement which he sent to numerous European newspapers on June 9. However—as far as I can ascertain—only the Catholic *Tablet* in London (!) printed Deubner's dementi in full:[20]

> "It is true that I left Rome without the authorization of Mgr. d'Herbigny, President of the Papal Commission for Russia, and that I went to stay with relatives in Berlin. I am of course in touch with my family in Russia now, as I always was while in Rome. My mother, my brother and my sister are in Russia, and so is my father, who is a priest and also was an intimate friend of the late Vladimir Soloviev, the great thinker and protagonist of Christian Unity. It would be in contrast to the honor and tradition of my noble Russian ancestry to steal documents from one party in order to hand them over to another, or in general to play the part of a spy. This would be more especially dishonorable towards His Lordship Mgr. d'Herbigny, whose self-sacrifice and devotion to the Russians, without distinction of creed, is well-known. The accusations said against me are not only unfounded, but they were invented for a purpose which is condemned not only by Christian-minded persons, but by all decent people in general. The purpose was to compromise and if possible destroy the work of the [Church] Reunion in Poland, and more particularly of the Russian Commission and its President. . . ."

For all the dust that Deubner's disappearance from Rome at the end of 1932 had kicked up, his return at the beginning of July 1933 was greeted by the same degree of silence. It seems that it even embarrassed d'Herbigny. Father Ledit of the Papal Institute for Eastern Studies gave d'Herbigny the idea of sending the contrite home-comer to the remote mountain monastery of St. Benedict near Subiaco "for penance"; also in the hope of avoiding Deubner's reappearance on the Roman stage that in the "holy year" 1933 was populated by pilgrims—genuine or pretended—from all over the world. In Subiaco, Deubner then even received visitors: d'Herbigny came with Bishop Boleslas Sloskans, whom the Soviets, in exchange for Latvian Communists, had finally freed at the end of January and deported to Latvia. From this—probably his last—conversation with Deubner, d'Herbigny gained the impression that the fickle Russian had learned something, "but not much," from his experiences. . . .[21]

Had the great intrigue against d'Herbigny really collapsed with Deubner's penance? To assume this would be to underestimate the zeal with which Poland was fighting d'Herbigny's eastern-political conceptions at a moment when the Pope was more enthused about Hitler's anti-Communism than about the missionary ideas of his "house sovietologist". . . .

Litvinov's Road to Rome and D'Herbigny's Fall

Summer heat brooded oppressively over Rome; after months of excitement, even the papal curia seemed to be on vacation. Embassy

Counselor Klee, who had to hold out in the German embassy to the Vatican even on the hot "Ferragosto," August 15, was all the more surprised when he was bidden to Cardinal Pacelli's office for the next day. Did it perhaps concern the first protests against violations of the concordat, which had been hastily signed on July 20, 1933, but was not yet ratified? When Klee returned from the Vatican in the late afternoon, he was relieved and concerned at the same time; Pacelli had not raised any complaints; he had only requested him to transmit a friendly warning[22] (see p. 159).

What was this "secret agreement" that so acutely interested the Soviets? It was an addendum to the concordat, which the German bishops had desired, but which—as vice-chancellor von Papen correctly assumed—would make Hitler "particularly happy": a provision in case of the introduction of compulsory military service, that is, the rearmament of Germany that Hitler was planning.[23] We do not know how Moscow's curiosity about this document was reported to Pacelli. It cannot be excluded that the embarrassing question was asked in a direct contact. For no matter how hopelessly all Soviet-Vatican negotiations had been broken off since 1927, and especially since 1930, no matter how sharply the Pope spoke against Communist and Soviet atheism, this did not completely exclude occasional contacts. Thus—as only became known 45 years later—Cardinal Pizzardo had met with Embassy Counselor P. M. Kersentchev of the Soviet Embassy to the Quirinal in 1932 and had sounded out the possibility of exchanging Catholic priests imprisoned in the Soviet Union for the most important philosopher of the Italian Communists, Antonio Gramsci. (The attempt miscarried; Pizzardo, on Mussolini's orders, was only allowed to leave his card at the prison in Turin where he had wanted to speak with Gramsci.)[24]

It is also possible that the Soviets, who—undismayed by Mussolini's Fascism—had signed a non-aggression and friendship agreement with Italy on September 2, 1933, had gotten wind of the appendix to the concordat during their negotiations in Rome. Foreign Affairs Commissar Litvinov had announced his arrival in Rome for December to sign a trade agreement with Italy.

Naturally the Vatican was not exactly delighted by such maneuvers; as little as it was by the efforts of Pilsudski and his resourceful Foreign Minister Jozef Beck, who not only were trying to come to an arrangement with Germany—with the Pope's blessings—but also, at the same time, were sending out personal feelers to Moscow (where the Russians were prepared to prolong their non-aggression pact with Warsaw). The greatest surprise came in autumn, when the new American President Franklin D. Roosevelt, on October 10, formally suggested negotiations with the Soviet Union concerning diplomatic recognition and shortly thereafter invited Litvinov

Telegramm (geh.Ch.V.)

Rom (Vatikan), den   16.August 1933   18 Uhr 20 Min.
    Ankunft: 16. "   "   20 " 20 "

Nr.57 vom 16/8.   Im Anschluß an Tel.vom 11. Nr.56.

    Kardinabtaatssekretär sagte mir heute
vertraulich,nach ihm zugegangenen Nachrichten
versuche Sowjetrußland sich in Besitz Kon -
kordatsanhanges zu setzen. Er machte darauf
aufmerksam, daß bereits Presse sich mit Geheim-
abkommen beschäftige,wofür er als Beispiel
Journal de Genève vom 12.August anführte.
                                        Klee

("The Cardinal Secretary of State told me confidentially today, according to
reports he had received, Soviet Russia was trying to obtain concordat appendix.
He called attention to the fact that the press was already engaged in the secret
agreement, mentioning the August 12 *Journal de Genève* as example. Klee.")

to Washington. Stalin now even forced his way into the Geneva League of
Nations, while Hitler declared Germany's withdrawal.
    It was clear that the Soviet Union—although very occupied with itself—

was urgently trying to escape its threatening isolation in Europe. Especially in the USA, a public opinion stood in its way that was sensitive to any violation of tolerance, and demanded assurances of religious freedom. The Jesuit Edmund Walsh, of whom Moscow had unpleasant memories from the Famine Relief Mission of the twenties (see p. 48), now straightaway started a campaign against the assumption of relations with Moscow, because secure guarantees could not be expected.

The Soviets thus had reason in autumn of 1933 for launching reports that they were not only prepared to discuss religious guarantees, but were even already holding discussions about them with the Vatican. A laconic four-line notice in the *Osservatore Romano* on October 1, 1933, denied that. "Having learned by experience," they were "particularly on guard" against official or inofficial contacts with the Soviets—thus the German Ambassador von Bergen was advised in the Vatican.[25]

When Litvinov then actually arrived in Rome on his return trip from America in early December 1933 and the rumors would not die down that—with the intervention of Mussolini, who received him—he was to take up contacts with a papal representative, the Vatican assured the foreign diplomats:[26]

> "The curia considers it pointless to negotiate with the Soviet government, because one cannot believe any eventual assurances. The agreement with America has only strengthened it in this belief. . . . The terms of religious freedom were only on paper. . . . So many pieces of evidence could be found for this in the Vatican archives that any attempt at denial by the Russians would be regarded as senseless. . . . Negotiations with Russia about freedom of religious practice, according to its [the Vatican's] opinion, could never be based on the foundation of Russian legislation, but would have to proceed from entirely new preconditions. Up to now there have been no indications that the Soviet government is prepared for this. . . ."

Still, even in this adamant denial, one can hear the echo of a basic willingness to negotiate—even if only under "new preconditions." These would have included an actual offer from Stalin, which was not forthcoming; in the case of the concordat with Hitler, however, not only had an extensive proposal been presented, but Pacelli had "felt a pistol at his head," so to speak: he had had to choose—with no other alternatives— between Hitler's offer of a concordat, and the "practical elimination of the church," he told the British *chargé d'affaires* Kirkpatrick on August 19, 1933.

It is characteristic of this consistent line of behavior and the reasons that motivated it (which were never quite buried by ideological enmity) that a bishop participating in the Reich concordat negotiations argued thus:[27]

"The government of a country is by no means identical with the Weltanschauung of a party. Thus the case could also arise that the Pope could come to an agreement with Stalin without thereby recognizing Bolshevism."

Following this principle of course leads again and again to difficulties with political systems that identify their state interest with a total prevalence of a party ideology; for the object of negotiation in Vatican concordatory policies must always be a certain measure of philosophical freedom that totalitarian systems can only admit for reasons of political opportunism, never from ideological motives. Similarly, the church's return concession—civic loyalty of priests and believers—must always be limited to practical daily relationships and cooperation, and can never include a profession of the state doctrine. All the actions of Vatican Ostpolitik moved, and still move to this day, within these limits.

The so-called "religious clause" upon which the American government insisted for international recognition of the Soviet Union, was from the beginning very modestly framed and by no means directed at "religious freedom" as such. In an exchange of notes with Litvinov of November 16, Roosevelt put through "the open exercise of freedom of conscience and religion" only for *American citizens.*[28] The above-quoted Vatican criticism of this agreement thus missed the point of the matter, because the Soviets did not promise more than they would keep. In contrast to the religious clause of the treaty of Riga (see p. 25), which promised religious freedom to the Polish minority in the Soviet Union, the question here was only of religious freedom for a group of foreigners. Only in one practical point did the agreement go beyond that: the Soviets agreed to the dispatch of an American Catholic priest for St. Ludwig's church in Moscow. And for this the Vatican had actually tuned in to the negotiations—in contradiction to all its denials:

"At the right moment, I alerted friends in New York; they convinced the President [Roosevelt] through his son that the acceptance of a Catholic priest in the Moscow embassy personnel would prove, better than any other argument, a certain willingness on the part of the Soviets to show religious tolerance," so reports Gervais Quénard, the Superior General of the Assumptionist Order, who was a member of d'Herbigny's Commission on Russia.[29] "For a whole week Litvinov fought against this undesired visitor—like the devil against holy water—by protesting that this was completely unnecessary, because religious freedom prevailed anyway. And finally he found a totally unexpected objection: there was a Catholic bishop in Moscow, and his approval would be necessary if they wanted to send him a priest.—Now what?

Concerned, the apostolic delegate in Washington, Amleto Cicognani, telegraphed to Rome; Cardinal Pacelli inquired of the Commission on Russia how they could most quickly obtain Bishop Neveu's consent from Moscow. Father Quénard hurried to the French embassy at the Vatican to send off a coded telegram to Moscow. "No, that would cause trouble in Paris," said Ambassador Charles-Roux, like a timid clerk, but he also came upon the saving idea: "Just telegraph to Washington yourself!"—And so they did:

"NEVEU AGREES WHOLE-HEARTEDLY," Quénard cabled to Cicognani, and immediately thereafter the dispatch lay on the negotiating table in the White House before Litvinov and Roosevelt. . . . Shortly thereafter the 30-year-old Assumptionist Father Leopold Braun[30] set out for Moscow together with the first US ambassador to Moscow—as "curate" to the bishop-parson of St. Ludwig's. . . .

How did it happen that only a "consultant" of the Papal Commission for Russia, this Father Quénard, was active in all this, and not its president, d'Herbigny? The anti-Soviet press in the USA, which protested furiously against Roosevelt's negotiations with Litvinov, suspected that d'Herbigny's "Jesuit intentions" lay behind all this. "Naturally denials—especially if they are cabled from Rome—will not drive out of people's heads this false assertion that doubtless comes from the same 'friends' who maneuvered the Deubner affair too," d'Herbigny wrote in a private letter of November 13, 1933.[31] "Other newspapers, above all in central Europe and in Switzerland, describe for many columns the passionate discussions in which I am supposed to have turned against the Holy Father—some write, because he wanted to conclude a concordat with the Soviets, the others write, because he did not. These are all pure inventions."

In fact, at this point d'Herbigny had already been "put on ice." The above-quoted letter is not dated from Rome, but from Brussels. What had happened to d'Herbigny? His downfall, of which he himself was as yet hardly aware, had been brought about in such a gentle and clever way, and so hidden from the public, that even four decades later the veil of mystery lying over it seemed to be impenetrable. After long investigations it is possible to lift most of it.[32]

"For a reason whose secret I could never penetrate, the director [of the papal Commission on Russia] fell into disgrace," writes Charles-Roux, who was the French ambassador to the Vatican from 1932 to 1940 and certainly kept up a close contact with his compatriot d'Herbigny.[33] The German Ambassador von Bergen, who observed the Roman scene attentively, noticed only that at the end of 1933, d'Herbigny was received twice within a few days by the Pope. Later, after d'Herbigny had disappeared and rumors about the political background were buzzing, Bergen was "confidentially" informed by the Vatican Secretariat of State that d'Herbigny was suffering from "incurable cancer of the intestine. . . ."[34]

Nevertheless, d'Herbigny lived for 24 more years! He did indeed suffer from intestinal complaints, and in July 1933 a doctor had advised him (but without any urgency) to have an operation to remove an obstruction that was not exactly diagnosable.[35] The Polish bishops and Cardinal-Primate August Hlond had announced their arrival in Rome for the beginning of October. Rome knew that they were resolved to assault d'Herbigny's "Neo-Union" endeavors, that they would demand a change of name for the Commission for Russia, if possible also the deposition of its president—and not least by alluding to the Deubner affair. The Warsaw government, with the same intention, had turned confidentially to the General of the Jesuit order, the Pole Wlodzimierz Ledóchowski; supposedly Marshal Pilsudski had even furiously threatened to "deport to Russia" all the Jesuits in Poland if d'Herbigny were not "put out of commission. . . ."

The Pope instructed d'Herbigny to communicate with the Polish bishops immediately after their arrival in Rome, in order to explain to them the Holy See's eastern policy. But this was not to come about. Jesuit General Ledóchowski stepped into action. His busy monastic brother d'Herbigny had been a source of displeasure to him for a long time already (see also p. 102). At the end of September, Ledóchowski went to the Pope and described to him how fatal it would be for the welfare of the church, and also for the Eastern Mission, if a direct confrontation should now arise in Rome between d'Herbigny and the Polish episcopacy. Would it not be better to first let some grass grow over the Deubner affair and take d'Herbigny out of the line of fire—under an elegant pretext, as believable as possible? . . .

On September 29, 1933, as friendly and patronly as usual, Pius XI conversed with d'Herbigny, who had no idea that this papal audience would be his last. . . . Long and thoughtfully the Pope contemplated several photographs that d'Herbigny had received from Bishop Neveu in Moscow via courier post: they showed the Uniate Exarch Feodorov and the apostolic administrator Ilgin in Soviet labor camps. . . .Then the Pope surprised his Russia expert with a request that sounded like a command:

"According to a report that our Father General gave him, he [the Pope] decided that I absolutely need some time for rest and recuperation, perhaps surgery might be necessary. . . . It seems that this cannot be delayed, and I shall leave for a Brussels clinic within a few days, probably on October 12, . . . if the experts do not recommend that I leave even earlier. . . . People will look for political grounds for this departure. . . . But many here and in Poland will be immensely pleased, . . ." so wrote d'Herbigny the next day in his weekly letter to Neveu in Moscow.

And in fact: d'Herbigny obeyed immediately when Ledóchowski asked him to leave Rome earlier, on October 2—the day on which the Polish bishops arrived. . . . Only ten days later did d'Herbigny undergo his operation in a Catholic clinic in Brussels. (Relatively harmless hemorrhoidal excrescences were removed with a local anesthetic). He was still hoping to be back in Rome in two or three months at the latest. He took as a good sign the fact that the Pope entrusted the "temporary" direction of the Commission for Russia to Monsignore Tardini of the Secretariat of State and not—as it first appeared—to Monsignore Margotti, with whom d'Herbigny had quarreled at the beginning of 1930;[36] he also took as equally promising the fact that at the Pope's command, Neveu's letters from Moscow were still sent to him—now to Brussels.

But on October 27, 1933, Ledóchowski struck his second blow; he wrote to d'Herbigny:[37]

"It will be humble and thus conformable to the constitution [of the order] and to the spirit of St. Ignatius, and also convenient (commode) for the Holy See if, through the mediation of the Father General, you would offer the Holy Father your written resignation from all your employments in Rome."

This letter from the Jesuit General contained no reasons, but also no direct order (which Ledóchowski could not give to a bishop under the Pope's authority). It was "only" an unmistakable appeal to that spirit of blind self-denial for which the founder of the order Ignatius of Loyola had set up the rule: ". . . to believe that the white that I see is black, if the hierarchical church so decides. . . ." (Exerc. Spirit.)

In order to resume life in Rome "in this climate," one needs good health, d'Herbigny wrote with a bitter undertone to Neveu on October 28; he did not tell the Moscow bishop of Ledóchowski's demand, and represented his resignation request as his own decision:

"I am in doubt, and since I know that many people will be happy with this decision, but also in the hope that it will all turn out for the best for the Russian souls, who need a leader in good health, who is not confronted with an over-sensitive national opposition—for these reasons I am writing this morning to the Holy Father that he should most graciously keep in sight only the welfare of the Russian souls and release me from the presidency [of the Commission for Russia]. . . ."

But at the same time, d'Herbigny can still not imagine that the Pope could drop him: "I suspect that he will not accept [the resignation]." D'Herbigny is even hoping for "frequent trips between Brussels and Rome," and clings to the fact that they are still passing on "secret mail" from Rome, even confidential information of Vatican congregations. This showed that "they are not yet sure whether they want to be rid of me completely, as some have proclaimed" (letter of November 13, 1933).

The Pope was actually hesitating. Only as more and more new facts, half-truths and rumors were brought to him (collected primarily by the busy Jesuit General into an imposing "dossier," which we will have to discuss later), and when finally a persistent report turned up in the serious press that d'Herbigny had met secretly with Litvinov[38]—only then, at the beginning of *December* 1933, did the Vatican give to understand that d'Herbigny had been released back in *October* from the directorship of the Commission for Russia "for medical reasons" and had left Rome.

Very certainly, d'Herbigny and Litvinov did not meet *in Rome*. But had there perhaps been contact when Litvinov—before and after his trip to America—traveled via Paris, where d'Herbigny—before and after his operation—had been staying with his sister? He himself commented rather sibyllinely, in a letter to Neveu of December 8, 1933, on the "insinuations about myself" that Litvinov's visit to Rome had elicited. "It seemed that they knew nothing yet [?]. Suddenly—in a kind of see-saw—many people who criticize me have become advocates of my kind of actions."

Had d'Herbigny perhaps—dismayed and confused over the inglorious end they were trying to prepare for him and his Russia policy—in a kind of eleventh-hour panic tried to make the breakthrough on his own, by—either orally or in writing—making contact with Litvinov? Was the curt "no" with which, at the beginning of December, Moscow itself denied any Vatican-Soviet contact[39] a sign that the Soviets had rebuffed d'Herbigny? Did they too want to expose the unhappy russophile, whom they knew as their old adversary, after he had already lost much of his prestige as a result of the Polish intrigues?

The available documents give no final answer to these questions. It is certain that no basic differences existed between d'Herbigny and the Pope. For instance, when Pius XI, in his Christmas 1933 address to the diplomatic corps, deplored that some governments maintained good relations with Moscow without demanding guarantees for the end of all religious persecution and Communist propaganda abroad, this certainly corresponded to d'Herbigny's opinion. Only his views on the proper church-political and diplomatic *methods* were controversial. And finally, d'Herbigny's *personal style* offered his opponents points of attack that made it easier to shake his position. Let us mention here only a few of the background details that can be corroborated by d'Herbigny's papers and other sources and were probably also included in Jesuit General Ledóchowski's "dossier":

Surrounded by the reputation of a mysterious traveler to Russia, d'Herbigny in the Rome of the early thirties had become much in demand socially. Charming and eloquent, the imposing prelate with the patriarchal beard, who with some vanity always wore episcopal violet with his simple

Jesuit black, became a bit of what one might call today a "cocktail lion." He liked to be provocative—and to be provoked. For example, at a reception he asked the Polish military attaché—in the presence of others—how they could drop priests by parachute over the Soviet Union. . . . In (at least) one case, he used his episcopal authority without the knowledge of the Vatican and casually ordained as priest a layman travelling to Russia, who seemed worthy to him, so that he could "carry the eucharist into the vast expanses of the Soviet empire." Conspiratorial and naive behavior were mixed in d'Herbigny's official activity in the Russia Commission as they had been in his travels in Russia in the twenties; here is one example that only became known in the Vatican at the beginning of 1933, when the liberated Bishop Sloskans came to Rome and several prelates read his diaries:

A priest by the name of Piotr Awglo, whom Sloskans, for the period of his incarceration, had installed as vicar general in Mogilev, after the Pope's appeal in 1930 for a crusade of prayer (see p. 133) made a written declaration, under the threats and promises of the GPU, to the effect that there was no hindrance to religious life in the Soviet Union. Awglo at the same time sent word to Rome via Neveu's diplomatic channels in Moscow that he had been forced to make this declaration, that he rued it bitterly, and asked for release from his office. D'Herbigny, however, sent his answer—that he should remain in his position and name a deputy in case of his arrest—not via the same confidential route, but rather—on an open postcard written in Latin (as "camouflage"?). . . . (Awglo died in prison in Mogilev.)[40]

D'Herbigny's missionary zeal, which fed on a genuine, but mystical, piety removed from reality, at times rose to ecstatic fancies. For instance, he once confided to his correspondent Neveu: he was sure that a Soviet Jewish woman whom he had secretly baptized when she was in Rome on business had been "shot in the Kremlin": he had experienced this in a nocturnal vision.[41] At the same time, he took pleasure in external activities; he was passed around in Russian emigrant circles (which were of course infiltrated by the Soviet and other secret services), he gave lectures and hours of devotion, was happy to be admired and adulated, not least by pious aristocratic ladies who surrounded him every week (since 1929) during edifying meetings in the British "Holy Child" monastery in Rome. There the young Russian wife of a Turkish diplomat, whose mother—it was later rumored—worked for the Soviets, made him pathetic declarations of love, but when he rejected her, she made him the talk of the town. Supposed Soviet engineers came to him with offers that he could buy "relief" for the church by trade in armaments—which he refused. By finally accepting Deubner's repentant return to Rome, he nourished new doubts about himself, especially when it became known in the autumn of 1933 that Deubner had again left the Benedictine cloister in Subiaco without permission and returned to Rome—seventy miles on foot!—where it was then said that he was in contact with the Soviet embassy. . . .

However, all this never led to any church disciplinary proceedings against d'Herbigny (even in the Holy Offices there is no "file" on him). His fate was of a different kind, and could not be reduced to a theological, moral, or canon law denominator. There was also no one single cause, but rather a number of causes finally adding up to an excuse—welcome to many. A contemporary and fellow sufferer of d'Herbigny's, the Benedictine Father Beauduin (whom d'Herbigny had sent into exile, see p. 144-5), probably touched the heart of the matter when he wrote to a friend:

> "You know what they called him [d'Herbigny]: *'Monseigneur m'as-tu vu'* (Monsignore Did-you-see-me). His name was mentioned in the press—of the 'La Croix' sort—every day; there was no clerical dinner at which he did not appear. . . . The climate of Rome is deadly to all-too-busy foreigners: the microbe of 'Prelatism' kills them."

Not without gloating, Beauduin noted at the beginning of December 1933 that "d'Herbigny's role in Rome is nearly played out." It had been the Polish government that "finally blew him up," Beauduin discovered at the beginning of January 1934 in his silent cloister, and reflected: "Why don't they send him here? We could then make observations together about eclipses of the sun and the laws of falling bodies. . . ."[42]

But it had not yet come to this. Of course, a private dream of d'Herbigny's had ended, namely to become a member of the Académie Française (as successor to the former Jesuit Bremond[43]), but he did not think of leaving his order; indeed, he still believed in an indirect sign of sympathy from the Pope, when the latter on March 30, 1934, officially accepted and announced d'Herbigny's resignation. The fact that Pius XI had chosen a Good Friday to do this, d'Herbigny thought, showed how painful the decision had been for him.[44]

The final disgrace did not come until three and a half years later, when the Vatican's Russian policy lost its orientation completely and for some time to come.

Encyclical Against Moscow, Popular Front Inclinations, and d'Herbigny's End

Full dress uniforms, black frock coats, red and violet draped soutanes— the reception committee at the little railway station of the Normandy village of Lisieux offered a colorful picture; many-colored also in political hues: Catholic local dignitaries next to those of the French Popular Front parties, Free-thinkers, Socialists, atheists, bishops. . . . An honor guard presented arms, military trumpeters sounded their horns: first the papal hymn, then the "Marseillaise," the anthem of the French revolution. . . .

The papal legate who stepped out of the Pullman car late in the afternoon of July 10, 1937, to be received joyfully by almost 300,000 people, was Secretary of State Cardinal Pacelli. He was not merely formally representing the Pope at the "Eucharistic Congress" of Lisieux. Pius XI, if he had not been hindered by illness, would actually have gone to France himself, and it would have been the first foreign journey of a Pope since Napoleonic times, to a France governed by the Popular Front— Socialists, supported by Communists, allied militarily since 1935 with the Soviet Union, sympathizing with that "red," republican Spain that for a year (since July 1936) had been involved in a bloody civil war with the Fascists (who were supported by Hitler and Mussolini. . .). Leon Blum, the head of the French Popular Front government, had already informed Rome that he would put the palace of Versailles at the Pope's disposal. . . .[45]

Of course, it did not come to this, but Pacelli by no means satisfied himself with dedicating the new, kitschy basilica of St. Thérèse in Lisieux. He let himself be honored like a head of state in Paris and was greeted with loud applause in the Notre Dame cathedral when he assured: "The church does not intend to favor nor to oppose any political group; it stands above and beyond politics."

This was of course more an expression of embarrassment than a real intention. For in this summer, the Pope's dream, nourished for years, of a moral-political anti-Communist front in Europe had vanished. To be sure, the Spanish bishops, on July 1, 1937 (a year after the outbreak of the civil war, a week before Pacelli's trip to France), had blessed Franco's "national uprising" as a "crusade against the enemies of the faith."[46] The German Catholic bishops, on January 3, 1937, also still thought it was necessary to assure the "Führer and Reich Chancellor, who long ago foresaw the advance of Bolshevism," of their support against the "Bolshevist arch-enemy," because it was a "satanic force"—as Spain testified.[47] The Vatican, however, had begun to analyze the situation more soberly and reflectively, with growing concern and perplexity in view of the incongruous European scene.

In July 1935, at its VIIth World Congress, Stalin's Communist International (Comintern) finally dissociated itself from the absurd thesis that had equated social democracy with fascism; an anti-fascist, democratic "popular front," open not only to Marxists, was now on the program. Was this an opening toward the "right"? 1936, the year that Spain and France form their first popular front governments and Poland (after the death of Pilsudski) again begins to distance itself from Germany and from Hitler's plans for expansion to the east, is also the year in which the great Moscow show trials begin: "We served Fascism!", even Kameniev, one of Lenin's old comrades-in-arms, accused himself. In the same year, Hitler, to the alarm of the French, occupies the demilitarized Rhineland, forges the "Axis" alliance with Mussolini, and mobilizes for a decisive intervention in the Spanish Civil War, in which Stalin, for a long time, is only hesitatingly engaged. Hitler concludes an "anti-Comintern pact" with Japan, which Italy then also joins. While the Comintern—in accordance with its popular front line—tries to win the "honorable and upright Catholic priests" as allies in the struggle against Fascism, in Germany the conflict between church and regime is intensifying. The regime, against all concordatory promises, wants to enforce as a monopoly its confused "Weltanschauung" and refuses to allow its anti-Communism to be consecrated as Christian, let alone Catholic.[48]

Soon after the outbreak of the Spanish Civil War, the Pope's insecurity, indeed—as he himself said—his "mood of despair," became evident in view of the confused fronts: he spoke on September 14, 1936, to Spanish refugees about the "satanic preparations" for a "conquest of the whole world on behalf of absurd and destructive ideologies" that threatened to begin in Spain. "This is what will happen if all those whose duty it is do not hasten to a defense that is perhaps already too late." Of course, the Pope was also dissatisfied with those who were arming for intervention with bombs and grenades—Mussolini and Hitler—because they "confuse all ideas and blacken religion, even to the point of preaching Christianities and religions of a new character." On the other hand, Pius XI saw in the tendency of the popular front to approach the Catholic side from the left, an "extremely dangerous trap, invented and intended solely to deceive and disarm Europe and the world. . . ."[49]

"In recent times there has been very strong pressure on the Vatican, even from some French bishops, aimed at compromises with the Communists. It seems that there were moments when even one or another of the advisors here attempted to influence the Pope in this direction," Polish Ambassador Skrzyński reported two weeks after Pius XI's Spanish address[50] and added: "Cardinal Pacelli is absolutely against these tendencies toward reconciliation regarding Communism."

It was also Pacelli who behaved remarkably tolerantly toward a book with which Bishop Alois Hudal, an Austrian "greater Germany" advocate who lived in Rome, later brought himself into great disrepute:[51] Hudal undertook again an acrobatic attempt to offer the National Socialists a partnership with the Catholic church against Bolshevism—on the condition that they give up the anti-Christian parts of their Weltanschauung and free their—as Hudal thought—not altogether unwarranted anti-Semitism from "racist exaggeration." Should the "synthesis of Christianity and Deutschtum" not succeed, Hudal feared,[52]

Bolshevist Russia, "whose entire middle and lower party apparatus is *Judaized*," would take over the leadership of Europe, and he prefaced his book with a dictum of Molotov's to the Comintern session of January 22, 1934, as an encouraging motto: "The world revolution is in the greatest danger, if an ideological and organizational agreement between the Catholic and the Fascist internationals should arise. . . ."

What Molotov feared and Hudal desired, however, could no longer become a reality if only because Pius XI, in all his perplexity, was clear on *one* point: that Hitler was not the anti-Communist "hero" he had considered him as late as 1933 (see p. 151). The Pope thus began a difficult, unpromising balancing act. As early as the autumn of 1936, when the French Cardinal Jean Verdier came to Rome to receive instructions for the attitude of the church vis-à-vis the Popular Front, these instructions proved to be "more moderate and broad-minded" than expected.[53] Of course, an explanation from the archdiocese of Paris concerning the *Semaine religieuse* warned that the moderation of the Communists was "only a tactic," but also conceded that there were, among the Communists, "men of sincere and high-minded views." In the spring of 1937 the Pope then sent out two encyclicals—against the National Socialists *and* against the Communists: a double blow that was to forge the virtue of distributive justice from the necessity of the two-front struggle. . . .

First, on March 14, 1937, the encyclical "*Mit brennender Sorge*" [*With Burning Sorrow*][54] was published, which accused the Hitler regime of breach of contract, even of the intention of a "war of extermination" against the church, reproached its idolization of race and state, and questioned its "godliness." The echo of the world to this papal outburst of rage (which Pacelli would have liked to soften) was so loud that the second attack, in the opposite direction, following only five days later, gained somewhat less of a hearing (as the Vatican had deliberately calculated. . . .)

The encyclical "*Divini Redemptoris*,"[55] published on March 19, 1937, not only settled accounts with Communism as an ideology, rejecting it not merely as a "pseudo-ideal of justice, equality and fraternity," as an atheistic theory of salvation, but as a "*Moscow* world organization." For the first time, the Soviet Union is condemned without circumlocution. Communism had not, even economically, created a "Soviet paradise." Of course it had achieved "a few material successes," but it had replaced moral responsibility by a "terrorism that We see in Russia, where old comrades in struggle and conspiracy are now mutually annihilating each other"—a reference to Stalin's show trials, for which in this spring of 1937 Nikolai Krestinski is being prepared, the man with whom Pacelli had once negotiated in Berlin. (In 1938 he is shot as a "German spy" and "mangy dog."[56])

"We by no means wish to condemn en masse the peoples of the Soviet Union, for whom We have a strong fatherly affection," writes the Pope. "We know that not a few of them are groaning under the hard yoke inflicted upon them by men who are predominantly strangers to the true interests of the country. . . . We are accusing the system, its creators and those who support it. . . ."

Without differentiating, the Pope names Mexico and Spain too as showplaces of Communist "horrors," in addition to Russia; he seems to take into account the fact that Mexico's Social Revolutionary party at this time is already in the process of winding down its battle against the church[57] as little as he does the fact that the atrocities against the church in Spain (4000 priests murdered) are being perpetrated almost exclusively by the anarchists (FAI) and Trotskyites (POUM), while the Communists led by the Moscow Comintern are much concerned with averting an extremism that would disturb its popular front tactics. The encyclical also does not take notice of the partisanship of Basque Catholics and clerics for the Popular Front republic—on the contrary: it warns against the "hypocrisy with which Communism leads very pious nations to believe that it is assuming a more mild aspect, that it will not hinder religious worship and will respect freedom of conscience. Beware, reverend brothers, don't be deceived! Communism is *perverse through and through* and no one who wants to preserve Christian culture can engage in any kind of cooperation with it. . . ."

It had taken twenty years before *such* a fanfare resounded from the Vatican for the first (and to date the only) time. It reflected the temperament of Pius XI, but much less the diplomatic caution of his Secretary of State Cardinal Pacelli, whom this same Pope, as we know, had sent on many attempts to achieve an agreement with the Soviets. Pacelli, to be sure, considered Soviet Communism a *greater* evil than German National Socialism, but he probably recognized more clearly than the Pope the dilemma the Vatican had gotten into by the fact that Hitler at least embodied the more *immediate* evil for the church. Therefore he not only put up with, but actually encouraged—by delaying the release of the two encyclicals—the fact that the relatively milder, but more sensational, one against National Socialism to a certain degree paralyzed the other, stronger one against Communism.

This was so successful that even the ambassador to the Vatican von Bergen, in the German protest note that he delivered to Pacelli on April 12, 1937, proceeded from the erroneous assumption that the anti-Communist encyclical had been issued "shortly *before*" the anti-Nazi one. That the latter had "*dealt a dangerous blow to the defensive front against the international danger of Bolshevism*"—as Bergen, following his instructions, complained[58]—was difficult to deny, if one understood this "front" in

Hitler's sense. . . . But this was just what the Vatican refused to do; indeed, the Berlin protest note gave it a cue that Pacelli took up with a finely-honed diplomatic pen.[59]

"The Holy See does not mistake the great importance that the formation of inwardly healthy and vital political defensive fronts has against the danger of atheistic Bolshevism," the Cardinal Secretary of State wrote in his answering note of April 30, 1937 (N. 1625/37) and immediately distanced himself from a power-politics interpretation: the church worked with "spiritual means" for a "*spiritual* conquest of the errors and misdirections inherent in Bolshevism." In the Holy See's opinion, nothing was more fatal for the "longevity of a defensive front against the international danger of atheistic Communism than the erroneous belief that this defense could be based solely upon external forces, and that the place due to spiritual forces in it be withheld. . . . The Holy See is not unaware that the present German government has successfully eliminated Communism as a public organization. To what degree German Communism, at the time of the National Socialist seizure of power, represented an immediate danger that could not be overcome by other means is a question of facts that the Holy See has not to decide on its own. . . ."

And if there was still any doubt as to how far the Vatican had come in breaking with its illusions about rightist-authoritarian forms of government, Pacelli dispersed it with the words:

"If the [German] note of April 12 of this year [1937] thinks it must remind the Holy See that 'the authoritarian German state has finally broken, in all areas of public life, with the concepts of liberal-parliamentary democracy,' it mistakes the intentions of the papal encyclical in an unusual way. . . . The Holy See, which maintains friendly, correct, or at least tolerable relations with states having all kinds of constitutional forms and directions, will *never interfere in the question of which concrete form of government a certain people will view as the most appropriate for its character and its needs. . . .*"

This did not imply anything different from what Pacelli's predecessor Gasparri had formulated for the Soviet-Vatican Rapallo contacts back in 1922 (see p. 36). And it also provided a basis for the readiness of the Vatican—arising in spite of all hesitations—to put up with the "Popular Front" in France, which showed itself friendly to the church. The German bishops, whose ponderous provinciality is so often embarrassing to Vatican world-church diplomacy, were still laboring at changing the mind of the anti-clerical National Socialists by anti-Bolshevist insinuations,[60] while the Roman curia was already quite pragmatically thinking of seeking affiliation with the democracies—even at the price of compromises with the left. Of course, a Hitler party paper was exaggerating when it maliciously wrote: "For several years, the Vatican has been seeking a diplomatic road to Moscow. . . . The encyclical against atheistic Communism was intended to camouflage this great coup." But the paper was quite correct in declaring: "The Vatican refuses to instruct the Catholics in France and Czechoslovakia to stay away from a government that cooperates with Bolshevist Russia. . . . The Pope refuses to bless the anti-Comintern pact."[61]

Pacelli's trip to France in the summer of 1937, above all his appearance in Paris, were calculated to strengthen this impression, certainly without any propensity for Socialists, let alone Communists. However, a scarcely-noticed occurrence on this trip, almost unknown until today, in retrospect attains an almost symbolic importance for this phase: the closing ceremony of the Eucharistic Congress in Lisieux saw the last public appearance of the Jesuit bishop Michel d'Herbigny. There a silent Cardinal Pacelli was assisting at the final "degradation" of the Pope's former leading expert for anti-Communism.

Let us remember: d'Herbigny had obediently remained in Belgium at the end of 1933. He was forbidden to return to Rome. For years he attempted in letters to Ledóchowski, the Jesuit General, to get explanations why he had fallen into disgrace (see p. 164). In the summer of 1934 his longtime protégé and correspondent Bishop Neveu of Moscow had come to Rome for a short vacation. In an audience on June 21, 1934, Neveu openly asked the Pope what had actually happened to d'Herbigny. Pius XI only raised his hands mutely and dismissed it . . . (thus Neveu reported in a letter to d'Herbigny in Paris). One night, at the door of the Assumptionist General Offices in Rome, where Neveu was staying, the spectral figure of Alexander Deubner appeared, that unhappy Russian whose self-inflicted misfortune had contributed so much to d'Herbigny's downfall (see p. 157). Now he wanted to speak with Neveu, probably to find out something about his family in Moscow, but Neveu did not receive him. The bishop was afraid. Perhaps, he thought, Deubner was a spy after all?

(Deubner stayed only a short time in Rome; he was suspended as a priest, went to Paris, then to Prague. There he lived sparsely on a tiny pension sent him by the Lemberg Archbishop Sheptyckyi, and as a singer in the choir of the Catholic Uniate congregation of Prague. He always swore that he had never worked for the Soviets. He was last seen in 1945, then all traces are lost. . . .[62])

Although d'Herbigny's portrait as bishop (see illustrations) could no longer be seen in the Papal Eastern Institute after 1934 and his name could no longer be mentioned, he was still formally the "honorary president" of the institute, figured as "consultant" to the Eastern Church congregation and as an assistant to the papal throne.[63] At the "Semaine Sociale" in Versailles (1934) he appeared before a large auditorium with his verbose rhetoric[64]; then he was seen once more on lecture tours that he undertook in 1935/1936 through France, England, Ireland and Switzerland. He not only appealed to the Europeans to "let the example of Soviet Russia serve as a warning," he also shared many details known only to him about the situation of the church in Russia (cf. "*Schönere Zukunft*" Nr. 30/1936, pp. 785/86). And this at the time when Bishop Neveu had come to France from Moscow on medical leave and was impatiently awaiting a return visa . . . (see p. 179). Did this loquacity of d'Herbigny's give occasion for the last blow against him? Or was it his lecture in Dublin, where his anti-Soviet polemics turned into such strong criticism of the French Popular Front that the Paris government supposedly complained to the papal nuncio?

Still, on March 22, 1937, Pacelli replied to a report about his tour of lectures with a written benediction: he was happy about d'Herbigny's activity, which "warns the faithful against the many and grave dangers of the Communist heresy."

S. Ex. Mgr CHALLIOL, évêque de Rodez.

S. Ex. Mgr ROUSSEAU, évêque du Puy.

S. Ex. Mgr D'HERBIGNY, évêque titulaire d'Ilion.

S. Ex. Mgr NEVEU, évêque administrateur de Moscou.

S. Ex. Mgr HARSCOUET, évêque de Chartres.

S Ex Mgr SIEFFERT évêque titulaire de Polybotus .

D'Herbigny and Neveu stood among the French bishops at the Lisieux train station when Cardinal Pacelli was received with the strains of the "Marseillaise" and the papal hymn. The two bishops were sharing a room in a church hospice; the next morning—Sunday, July 11, 1937—d'Herbigny participated in Pacelli's pontifical mass for the consecration of the Teresa-basilica; he ardently hoped for an opportunity to speak about his case with the Cardinal, who had even embraced him. On the Vatican radio station, over loudspeakers, he heard the voice of Pius XI, so familiar to him, but sounding fragile and ill, as he wished for peace and tranquility for the peoples "who are oppressed by the sorrows of the present and fears for tomorrow. . . ."[65]

D'Herbigny was suddenly missing at the dinner in the episcopal residence. Shortly after the papal address, as people were getting lost in a vast crowd, Bishop Neveu was requested over the loudspeaker to call at his lodgings immediately. There, d'Herbigny was waiting for him: he had to pack his bags and leave Lisieux immediately—even before the great sacramental procession. Neveu is nonplussed. What has happened?

Not until forty years later was the secret, for the most part, revealed. At the end of 1976, the Catholic private scholar Paul Lesourd (Paris), on behalf of the d'Herbigny family, published large excerpts from an autobiography from the estate of the Jesuit bishop and documents from d'Herbigny's papers (*"Le Jesuite Clandestin,"* Ed. P. Lethielleux, Paris). Lesourd, who had already three years previously given me oral information for the German edition of this book, never concealed his intention of defending a rehabilitation, indeed even a canonization, of d'Herbigny; his book, written at an advanced age, contains no historical-political background analysis, it suffers from a confused chronology and much vagueness of fact, but it conveys some information with documentary verification which—together with other sources—allows an extensive clarification of d'Herbigny's end:[66]

Months before d'Herbigny's last official appearance in Lisieux, i.e. since March 1937, Jesuit General Ledóchowski had initiated an investigation of d'Herbigny's "private life." This was occasioned by a denunciation: that he had been seen several times in 1936 "with two nurses"—at a Belgian beach and in Brussels—and had been wearing civilian clothing (the so-called "clergyman's") at the time; both women had testified to this. Included in the investigation were also older events of the same banality: for instance, that d'Herbigny, in his preparations for the secret baptism of the Soviet Jewess (see p. 166), had given her religious instruction in a closed room and not kept a proper distance thereby—an assumption as little provable as was its contrary. The level of such "moments of suspicion" apparently sufficed for Ledóchowski to have d'Herbigny subjected to weeks-long embarrassing interrogations at the hands of an "inquisitor" of the Order, Pater Adélard Dugré, during which the complete "dossier" that the Jesuit General had collected against d'Herbigny ever since 1933 (see p. 163) was also brought up. The goal was to prevail upon d'Herbigny to give up his episcopal regalia and functions now, and thus—most important to Ledóchowski—to "return to obedience to the General of the Order," that is to give up his direct subordination to the Pope (as the latter's "bearer of secrets").

"Before God and man, I am completely innocent of everything I am accused of now and since 1933," d'Herbigny wrote on July 5, 1937, to the Pope and at the same time to the General of the Order: "My impotences and inabilities are greater than ever; age is becoming highly noticeable in my body and in certain faculties. . . . I beg the Society [the Jesuit Order] for forgiveness for all my deficiencies, of which the Lord God knows I am guilty, He Who knows that I am innocent of all the accusations that have been made since 1933. . . ."

Nevertheless, d'Herbigny obediently signed his request for resignation. However, his attempt five days later to discuss everything once more with Pacelli in Lisieux was defeated by Ledóchowski's having him called back to the religious house in Paris during the ceremonies. Here his accuser Dugré delivered the formal reproof of the Order to him and then made an astonishing announcement: the investigation against him would begin all over again on the basis of "new material." However, d'Herbigny was supposedly never directly confronted with this material, which—according to Lesourd—came from "Polish-Soviet" sources. After Pacelli, with express friendliness and even with papal benediction, had told him on June 27, 1937, that Pius XI accepted his renunciation of the miter, the Secretary General of the Jesuit Order, Louis Dumoulin, opened a new series of interrogations. They ended (as far as can be deduced from Lesourd's somewhat confused description) on December 11, 1937, with d'Herbigny's finally signing the required confession—not as a convicted sinner, but rather (as emerges from his private notes of that time and later) still convinced of his innocence. Then why the confession?

All signs point to the fact that his fanatical nature, which had stamped not only his religiousness, but also his political style, for two decades, made possible a paradoxical, although theologically-based, "salto mortale" out of the web of intrigue: in mystical identification ("*imitatio*") with the guiltlessly condemned and humiliated Jesus Christ, d'Herbigny wanted to take guilt and punishment upon himself—as a sacrifice for that "conversion of Russia" on which he had foundered in church politics. D'Herbigny's contradictory reactions during the interrogations were a result of this spiritual disposition, and even brought the "Inquisitor" Dugré to the conclusion that d'Herbigny was simply mad ("*un détraque*").

Obediently and silently, without ever once considering an obvious flight from the Order and the church, d'Herbigny submitted to Ledóchowski's judgment, which—as "*suspens ad nutum Patris Generalis*"—on January 17, 1937, forbade him all priestly functions with the exception of reading the mass, prohibited any public appearances, preaching or speeches, as well as any travel without an escort (determined by the Order), indeed any correspondence (except with members of his family) and any publication.

D'Herbigny obediently moved into his assigned place of forced residence: from 1937 to 1940 in Florennes (Belgium), then in the castle of Mons (Departement Gers), a fortresslike, remote Jesuit novitiate in Southern France. The novices in Mons are instructed to address him as "Father," not as "Your Excellency." He spends the last twenty years of his life in religious contemplations—and with a butterfly collection. Sometimes he takes up his pen. On August 20, 1955, when the Jesuit order gives up the Mons castle, he writes: "Rome must find a new hiding place for me." It is the novitiate in Aix-en-Provence (Bouches-du-Rhône). To the end he pleads, he hopes, to be called once more to Rome to justify himself. His refuge remains that mysticism which was his political undoing: "The greatest gift of the Lord is to be able to unify oneself with Him in what He suffered on the cross: in the last agony of His holy heart, in that so dreadful feeling of having been abandoned by His Father," he writes in February 1956.

Pacelli, Pope since 1939, does not think of ending d'Herbigny's exile. He once remarked that this Jesuit was as great a mystery to him as the mysteries of faith. On the day before Christmas 1957, d'Herbigny dies at the age of 77. His "dossier" to this day belongs to the most strictly guarded documents of the Jesuit General Offices. D'Herbigny's former students and friends in the Papal Eastern Institute in Rome are even forbidden by the Vatican to announce publicly his requiem mass; only a short notice in an internal publication is allowed.[67] Friends and relatives have a memorial picture printed that portrays the missionary to Russia as a bishop . . . (see illustrations). Only his title could be taken from him; the consecration as bishop, according to Catholic doctrine, remains effective sacramentally: its "*charakter indelebilis*" was a sign for d'Herbigny that— even if disowned by the Pope—he was not abandoned by God. . . .

Even fourteen years later, when the Roman synod of bishops was considering the theme of "justice" in October 1971 and Cardinal Josef Slipyj, for very personal reasons (see also p. 367), wanted to bring up the forgotten case of d'Herbigny, the synod secretariat ordered him not to. . . .[68]

The tragic figure of the Jesuit bishop, who without complaint let himself in effect be buried alive, although he was conscious of no wrong, surely— even if sometime *all* the archives were to be opened—would arise no less iridescently than it sank. What happened to him was certainly not in any proportion to what he could be accused of; his end is no credit to modern Catholic church history, but nor is it merely an episode of a "*chronique scandaleuse.*" It is an exemplary expression of a specific historical moment:

D'Herbigny's gradual downfall, his visionary improvised actions in Russia, and his shipwreck on the political realities of the thirties—all this reveals the occasionally disturbed sense of orientation of papal Ostpolitik at the time. In the charged atmosphere between the desirable and the possible, its thrust—in spite of continuity of purpose—began to waver. It is an experience from the contradictory epoch of Stalin, Hitler and Mussolini. It serves as a lesson to this day.

Dismantling the Commission for Russia; Pius XI's Last Missionaries

Soon after d'Herbigny's ungentle removal from Rome, the Vatican began a fundamental alteration of its practical Russian policy; the organizational changes simultaneously indicated a conceptual limitation of its expansionist-missionary goals: the Commission for Russia, which Pius XI had only freed in 1930 from the Eastern Church congregation, "made to measure" for d'Herbigny and entrusted with jurisdiction over *all* Catholic Russians or missionaries to Russia of *all* rites in *all* countries (see pp. 141-2), was now robbed again of its independence, even of its own offices, by a decree of December 1934.[69] Since then it has existed only as a *formal* appendage to the Secretariat of State in the "Congregation for Extraordinary Affairs of the Church" (today "Council for the Public Affairs of the Church"), whose secretaries (1934: Pizzardo, 1974: Casaroli) became its formal presidents. All Catholic believers of the eastern rite, including the "Neo-Unionists" and "Biritualists" in Poland, were again, as earlier, placed under the Eastern Church congregation.

"The remainder of the Commission for Russia's sphere of activity that was transferred to the Secretariat of State is very small, since it actually only involves the Catholic bishoprics of the *Latin* rite that still exist in Russia," reported the German Ambassador to the Vatican von Bergen, and referred to the success that pressure from Poland had had in this question.[70]

But this dismantlement of an establishment all too concerned with Russia was not only out of regard for Polish sensitivities. The Vatican also wanted to make allowances for the situation in the Soviet Union itself: there—for domestic and foreign political reasons—a short, relatively quiet period was beginning.[71] The anti-religious campaign had passed its peak, the Atheists' Union was complaining about a loss of membership; its paper, the *Besboshnik*, ceased publication for four years at the end of 1934. The Catholic hierarchy that d'Herbigny had built up was, of course, already almost destroyed. After Boleslas Sloskans had been traded at the beginning of 1933 for Lithuanian Communists, and Antoni Malecki, the administrator of Leningrad, for Polish ones in April 1934 (Malecki died eight months later as a result of his Siberian imprisonment), two of the four secret bishops installed by d'Herbigny were still in office: Neveu in Moscow and Frison, who had temporarily been released from prison again, in Sevastopol. Neveu was able to spend a holiday in Rome in 1934; the Pope instructed him, at his earliest opportunity, to install the French pastor of "Notre Dame de France" in Leningrad, the Dominican Jean Amoudru, as apostolic administrator and consecrate him as bishop—once again in secret. Had the experiences of d'Herbigny's secret consecrations in 1926 not been enough to renounce this method?

The beginning of 1935 seemed a propitious time: France was negotiating with the Soviet Union about a mutual assistance pact (which materialized in May). The Pope was not pleased with this alliance; in a conversation with the French ambassador to the Vatican, he compared it ironically with the meaningless calling cards that private persons exchange. In fact, the alliance proved to be ineffective when Hitler unleashed the Second World War. But skepticism and anti-Communism by no means hindered the Pope from making use of this line to Moscow—as he had used others earlier: in January 1935, a second French Dominican father, Michel Clovis Florent,[72] was allowed to enter the Soviet Union and settle in Leningrad for the next six years. The Soviets had insisted on only *one* condition: Father Florent was not allowed to preach in Russian!—It was symbolic of the shift of Vatican Russian policy away from the old missionary ideas (of d'Herbigny) that Rome accepted this condition. Of course, the double-track *method* had still not been abandoned.

Soon after Father Florent's legal installation on April 30, 1935, when it could be assumed that, on the eve of the May Day parade and two days before the ratification of the French-Soviet mutual assistance pact, the GPU's attention would not be too sharply focused on the Moscow French, Neveu performed the consecration of Amoudru as bishop behind the locked doors of St. Ludwig's. Fathers Florent and Braun were witnesses.[73]

Amoudru's elevation in rank, for which no permission had been asked, had naturally not escaped the Soviets. They left Amoudru unmolested, but immediately urged his recall, through energetic diplomatic maneuvers. The French government finally bowed and asked the Vatican to "transfer" Amoudru. Several months later, the Dominican bishop quietly left Leningrad, where he had been active for three decades and had survived all the events by extreme caution and attention to all Soviet laws, and also thanks to his citizenship.[74] Amoudru came to Rome just at the time when the news arrived there, months late, of the death of Exarch Leonid Feodorov, who had died in March 1935 in exile in Siberia. Thus the last representative of the Russian-Catholic rite had disappeared—an unfortunate idealist whom the Roman curia, out of regard for the Poles, had never dared to endow with the bishop's mitre. . . . Did it not seem to be a sign of a lost hope that the Pope now, in autumn of 1936, had a converted former Czarist diplomat, Alexander Evreinov, consecrated as "bishop of the Eastern Rite" with his seat in—the Roman "Russicum"?

When he got on the train in Moscow on July 31, 1936, Bishop Neveu still had no idea that he too would never return. He was to go to France for an urgent operation, it was arranged with the Soviet Commissariat for Foreign Affairs, for four months at the most. His return visa was promised. Without it ever being expressly refused him, he waited for it for years—until his death in 1946.

Finally even the last Catholic bishop in the Soviet Union was overtaken by the worst kind of fate: Alexander Frison was shot on August 2, 1937. He was born in the Volga German town of Baden (near Odessa) in 1875, the son of an Alsatian. Six weeks after Soviet Marshal Tuchachevski, he was also executed—like the marshal—as a "German spy."

As late as 1936, Stalin was still endeavoring to support the Popular Front tendencies in the western democracies, by introducing certain democratic forms as part of a new constitution for the USSR, for example *universal* and *equal* suffrage. Political parity was thereby also established for "servants of religion," who had been denied the right to vote up to then (e.g. according to Art. 69 of the RSFSR constitution of 1925)—and thus the right to purchasing-permits for foods, to public housing and lower taxes. But Article 124 of the new Stalin constitution of 1936—valid until 1977—also stated: ". . . The freedom of religious *worship activities* and the freedom of anti-religious *propaganda* is granted to all citizens." Even in the constitution of 1925, only atheists had been allowed to disseminate (propagandize) their beliefs, but the believers were still allowed to *confess* theirs; now, in the supposedly more democratic constitution, they retained only the freedom "to practice religious worship" (*swoboda odprawlenija religiosnych kultow*).[75]

Of course, constitutional law had only followed a custom already in practice. A church like the Catholic, which cannot be nearly as satisfied as the Orthodox with simply a liturgical-service existence nor dispense with doctrine, sermon and evangelization, was struck particularly hard by this. In the future it was at the discretion of the Soviet state organs whether and to what extent they would allow and tolerate expressions of religious life as "worship activities."

Basically the constitution sealed the end of an organized papal church in the Soviet Union of the thirties: if there were still about 50 Catholic priests active in 1936 within the USSR, in 1937 there were 10 priests and 11 Catholic churches open, and in 1939 only 2: the Moscow one with the American Assumptionist Father Braun and the one in Leningrad with the French Dominican Father Florent.[76]

"As we view the situation, it would be unwise to send anyone to Russia at the moment," said Jesuit General Ledóchowski at the end of 1937 to the Polish-American Walter Ciszek, who had been ordained in the Roman "Russicum" according to the eastern rite and like other Jesuits in the "Russicum" was naively yearning "to be in Russia soon." Ciszek, who later adventurously attempted to make his dream come true (see p. 220), describes the disappointment and depression that reigned in the "Russicum" at that time because the Vatican was opposed to any experiments.[77] There was absolutely no talk of "conquering" the Soviet Union or of preparing "for the coming march (!) into the Soviet Union," as the East Berlin historian Eduard Winter misleadingly reads into the Ciszek memoires.[78] The "eastern missionaries" in Poland were increasingly "detoured" into

Top: Discussion partners in the 1920s: Eugenio Pacelli, later Pius XII, as Nuntio in Berlin (left), and G. W. Chicherin, Soviet Minister for Foreign Affairs (Photo: Archive).

Bottom: Vatican aid in Moscow, Christmas 1922: left, Father Walsh SJ. The writing under the garland: "The Roman Pope's Catholic mission is helping the Russian people." (Photo: Pont. Ist. Orient.).

Top left: Archbishop Jan Cieplak (Mogilev), right: Archbishop Sheptyckyi (Lemberg).

Bottom left: Pius XI. (Achille Ratti), right: d'Herbigny before death.

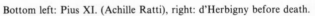

NISI UT ACCENDATUR

ANNO MCMXXVI

Michel d'Herbigny (1880-1957). After travelling in Russia as a "secret" Bishop he asked the Russian painter Malzew in 1929 to make a portrait of him while in Rome. The portrait was painted showing the snowcovered Kremlin towers against a red sky background. With the permission of the "Pontifical Institute for Eastern Studies" (Rome), where it has been kept under lock and key, the icon-like picture is published here for the first time.

D'Herbigny's picture to the left was made shortly before his downfall in 1933, and was printed in 1957. The obituary picture of the removed Bishop was distributed among his friends without the permission of the Church.

Top: Msgr. Domenico Tardini at his desk in the Vatican (approx. 1943)

Bottom: The "secret" Bishop of Bucharest Josef Schubert at his first and last meeting with Pope Paul VI, on the 23rd February 1969.

The beginning of the 'new' Eastern politics

Top: Signing the Vatican/Hungarian protocol in Budapest on 15th September 1964 (left) Msgr. A. Casaroli, (right) Minister Prandtner, behind him J. Miklos, Government Officer for Church Affairs since 1971. Bottom: Paul VI welcomes Nikolai Podgorny. The Soviet head of state visited the Vatican on January 30th 1967; to the right beside the translator Msgr. A. Casaroli. (Photos: Archive 4).

An example illustrating the differences in the Catholic church in east Europe: The residence of the Polish Archbishop Cardinal Kominek, who died 1974 in Wroclaw (Breslau).

The residence of the Apostolic administrator in south Bulgaria, Bishop Simeon Kokov, who died 1974 in Plovdiv. Both pictures were made during a journey through east Europe by the author and *Stern* magazine photographer Hilmar Pabel.

State visit by Yugoslavian President Tito and his wife Jovanka to Paul VI on 29th March 1971. The usual bestowing of orders was omitted.

domestic ministry; a Vatican instruction of May 27, 1937, made "Biritualism" dependent on special papal authorization. Of course, there was occasional mention of a "return of Russia" to the Catholic church—as for example in a papal letter on the occasion of the 950-year anniversary celebration of the baptism of the Grand Duke Vladimir (a jubilee, incidentally, that even Stalin, indicative of his growing pan-Russian nationalism, allowed to be celebrated as a "cultural event.") Even in the farthest eastern mission station, in Albertin, which had been such a stumbling-block for the Polish nationalists, there were only 4 Jesuits in 1939, and these were not forging any dark plans of conquest, but rather were active as "horse-and-carriage preachers" ministering to the peasants.[79]

Uncertainty and fear, and not lust for attack, now characterized the Vatican anti-Communism, upon which was increasingly superimposed the concern unleashed by Hitler's expansionist policies. For the Vatican had again withdrawn from the "conviction that the danger of all-destroying Bolshevism was being headed off by the impact of the National Socialist movement," as Austria's bishops argued in their "Anschluss"-declaration of March 18, 1938. The relentless manner in which Hitler repressed and then swept away the Catholic "corporate state" [Ständestaat] in Austria, without regard to its staunch anti-Communism and ideological relationship with Fascism, contributed to the further disillusionment of the curia. Vienna's Cardinal Innitzer brought a harsh reprimand from the Pope upon himself for his—later much regretted—"Heil Hitler!"[80]

"How is it that Comrade Thorez [the French Communist Party leader], six months after the papal encyclical against atheistic Communism, can still stretch out his hands to French Catholicism with hopes of success? How is it possible that even today General Franco must demand intervention from the Vatican against clerics, even against a bishop and a Jesuit Father, because they have taken the side of the Spanish Bolshevists? Why are there still priests in Prague who propagate political cooperation with Moscow?" So fulminated an organ of the Hitler party.[81]

The answer to such overstated questions arises from the greater and greater embarrassment and plight into which Hitler's policies were bringing the European states and with them the Vatican as well. After Austria, Hitler begins to destroy Czechoslovakia. The "Munich Agreement" with which France and England try to appease Hitler in 1938 is not greeted by Pius XI as a peace saver, but rather seen as Hitler's "bluff",[82] Pius XI sees only a poor consolation in the fact that the Soviet Union, which is after all allied with Czechoslovakia and France by mutual assistance pacts, is thereby kept out of play. And he greatly resents the Poles' participation in the dismemberment of Czechoslovakia. Of course, it is not the political Popular Front that interests the Pontiff; it is true, he does allow Vatican contacts with Italian Communists (the under-secretary of the Vatican Study Commission, Monsignore Mariano Rampolla del Tindaro, meets in Switzerland in August 1938 with two representatives of the CPI, through the mediation of Christian Democratic anti-Fascists[83]), but the Pope is moved above all by the thought of making his last moral contribution with a new encyclical against the Hitlerian ideology—now that his pontificate is approaching its end under dark political storm-clouds.

But this will no longer come to pass. On February 10, 1939, Pius XI dies, the man who during his whole reign saw himself confronted with the great totalitarian movements of the century, torn between coexistence diplomacy and challenge. Would his successor Eugenio Pacelli, whom he had himself educated and who now ascended the throne almost like a crown prince, as Pius XII, overcome the contradictions more easily?

Pius XII, a man of quite a different stamp, not a man of erratic decisiveness, but rather of a scrupulously examining, elegant, hesitating diplomacy, was from the first moment faced with the same difficulty as his predecessor. And in the final analysis—as we shall see—no other attempts at a solution occurred to him than those in keeping with the continuity of Vatican policies.

At first, of course, Pacelli's watchword was "caution." The two confidential conferences he held with the German cardinals shortly after his election, on March 6 and 9, 1939, the minutes of which are available to us in the Vatican documentary publication on the Second World War, already show the basic orientation of the new Pope. His predecessor, he told the cardinals, had once thought of recalling his nuncio from Berlin. . . .

"I answered: Your Holiness, what shall we do after that? How can we then maintain communication with the bishops? He understood and calmed himself. . . . It is easy to destroy. But then if you want to build again, God only knows what concessions you must make. . . . We are not against Germany and *not against any particular form of government*. I also emphasized in Budapest that the church, as long as God's law is observed, lets every people choose its own form of government. . . ."[84]

At the Eucharistic Congress in Budapest in May 1938, to which he had been sent as Pius XI's legate, however, Pacelli had also called upon the Congress "to oppose the revolution of clenched fists with the peaceful re-formation of the hearts"—which was to be understood as an anti-Communist reference.[85] This was still valid in principle. But this Pope, who had negotiated in the twenties with the Soviet Communists, and in the thirties with the National Socialists, now on the threshold of the forties saw that Hitler was steering toward a war which would more than once fundamentally alter the fronts between the powers, as well as between ideological opponents: first through the German-Soviet alliance, then due to the German attack on the Soviet Union and the American-Soviet alliance, and finally as a result of the East-West "cold war."

Thus it was not astonishing that Pius XII, who in the handwritten draft of his letter to Hitler in which—according to protocol—he informed him of his accession to the throne, in the address first wrote the word "Führer," then crossed it out, but then used it after all,[86] began his pontificate with two external precautionary measures: he forbade the *Osservatore Romano* to polemicize against the National Socialists, and took care that the words "Communism" and "Socialism" disappeared for the next ten years from official communiques of the Holy See.[87]

The "Dike" Breaks: "Every Word Against Russia Would Be Avenged"

The enthusiasm of over a hundred thousand people on the Castle Square in Warsaw is mixed with tearful emotion; on the platform the papal nuncio crosses himself, beside him Marshal Edward Rydz-Smigly, who has assumed Pilsudski's heritage as "Supreme Leader," salutes. At this moment the formal state president of Poland, Professor Ignacy Moscicki, stepped up to a silver casket laid out in a sea of flowers. The President, with an expansive gesture, takes the grand cross of the order "Polonia Restituta" from his own breast and lays it on the casket. With this he honors, on this June 17, 1938, not some recently deceased national dignitary, but rather the Polish Jesuit Andrzej Bobola, murdered almost 300 years earlier in Russia, whose relics had been transported to Rome in 1923 as Lenin's "gift for the Pope"—under the express condition that they should never return to Poland (see p. 53).

In the middle of April 1938, the Pope had canonized the Blessed Andrzej Bobola; now, in June, the silver reliquary, after an eleven-day train procession through Italy, Slovenia and Hungary which was repeatedly interrupted by new ceremonies, has reached Poland[88] and serves for a common church-state demonstration. Its anti-Russian accents cannot be overlooked, if only because, simultaneously with the tribute to the controversial missionary to Russia, a wave of destruction against the Russian Orthodox is beginning in Poland: in conjunction with a Vatican-Polish agreement of June 20, 1938 (about the return of Catholic church possessions expropriated during the time of the Czars), in July and August alone 138 Orthodox churches are burned to the ground in the region of Chelm. Even the Catholic-Uniate Metropolitan Sheptyckyi, who is worried about the credibility of his eastern mission, protests to the Warsaw government on July 20 against these "acts of vandalism and terrorism" and thus again reveals how inextricable the national antagonisms in this corner of Europe still remain, even if they appear to be bridged by presentations of a common ideological front.

Even the better understanding between the Vatican and the Warsaw government that appears to be arising after the d'Herbigny conflict, under the impact of the Spanish Civil War in 1936/37, is fragile; Poland's function, as seen by the Roman curia, as a "bulwark against the Bolshevist danger," is proving more and more an empty slogan.[89] As among the German clergy, among the Polish too not a few are losing their moral orientation: anti-Communism is becoming an excuse for nationalism and even anti-Semitism—for example when the Catholic theologian J. Pastuszek writes in 1938 about the "metaphysical perspective" of the Jewish share in Communism.[90]

In addition, the domestic political importance of the "Communist Party of Poland" is actually nil, and is rated as such by the Soviets themselves: in June 1938—at the same time that state and church are demonstratively celebrating the relics of Saint Bobola as a symbol of resistance against the "danger from the east"—the tiny "Communist Party of Poland," at the command of the Comintern, has to dissolve itself, after Stalin has already enticed its top functionaries to Moscow and had them murdered.[91]

Stalin was namely preparing for his grand gamble with Hitler. For hardly had Hitler liquidated Czechoslovakia than he turned in the spring of 1939 to Poland—that much-vaunted anti-Communist "dike." If it would not open voluntarily as a "sally-port" for Hitler's further expansion to the east, then he would simply break it down. What can arrest him in this decision? Compliance or resistance? Stalin, sly and without ideological scruples, discovers a third possibility for himself: sharing the Polish booty with Hitler.

Poland neither wants to bow to the German pressure nor save itself with the help of its awesome eastern neighbor. While France and Great Britain are seeking, in negotiations with the Soviet Union, to put together a coalition that could perhaps effectively scare off Hitler, Poland still prides herself on making these efforts more difficult.

"It is the Polish policy that makes it possible to leave Russia out of the game," boasts the Warsaw Foreign Minister on May 9 in a conversation with the papal nuncio Cortesi.[92] The Vatican too does not want to recognize that the effect will be exactly the opposite. Far from advising the Poles to form a contact with the Soviet Union as well (without whose cooperation an English-French assistance would not be at all practicable), the new Pope Pius XII repeatedly exhorts the Warsaw government only to "moderation and calm" toward their extortionary German neighbor. Prevent war at any price—this is the Pope's watchword, arising from a basic love of peace, but also from the fear that a war would confuse even more the "spiritual fronts" in Europe, especially the anti-Communist one. At the beginning of May the Pope attempts to arrange a new European Five Conference—like the Munich conference—to settle the German-Polish dispute; consciously—and to London's regret—he excludes the Soviet Union from the invitation.[93] However, Hitler tries to convince the Berlin nuncio, Orsenigo, on May 6 that he does not yet see any grounds for war, that he could wait—"perhaps until 1945." He hypocritically adds: if Mussolini and he had not intervened in Spain, "the empire of Bolshevism" would now exist. The nuncio seems to be not unimpressed by all this: if Poland would "calm itself and be quiet," time could be won for negotiations, he says.[94] But only eleven days later, the nuncio hears something quite different from the mouth of Reich Foreign Minister von Ribbentrop: there is the anti-Comintern pact against the Bolshevik world revolution, "but if Russia ceases this propaganda, nothing hinders us from approaching each other. . . ."[95]

So the Vatican is not much surprised when, three and a half months later, Ribbentrop startles the world with his trip to Moscow to sign the Hitler-Stalin pact on August 22, 1939. On the morning of the same day, the Polish Ambassador Kazimierz Papée appears in the Papal Secretariat of State with "information" from his government which can only evoke astonished head-shaking in the Vatican: "The news [of the German-Soviet pact] proves the desire of the Soviets to retire from the European field," Warsaw imagines. At least, Papée seems to have noticed two days later that the Soviets have given Hitler a free hand (the public as yet knows nothing about the secret partition agreement): "Poland has never trusted in Russian help. It opposes force and offers resistance to aggression. It would desire that the Holy Father condemn aggression. . . ."[96]

Hitler is not yet on the march; but would this not be the moment for the Pope to raise his voice—now that the two powers hostile to the church, who up to now were antagonists and whom Pius XI in 1937 had condemned simultaneously, had suddenly gotten together? This question is asked in these August days by many moralists who are not familiar with the involved mechanism of a diplomacy housed between metaphysics and pastoral politics. Perhaps Pius XII's predecessor would have spoken some strong words, if his Secretary of State Cardinal Pacelli had not been able to deter him—but the latter is now Pope himself. On the evening of August 24, during the very hour when Ribbentrop is reporting to his "Führer" how he had toasted Hitler with Stalin, Pius XII speaks on Radio Vatican from his summer residence:[97]

". . . Empires that are not based on justice are not blessed by God. Politics that cuts itself loose from morality betrays those who refer to it. . . ."

In order to make this indirect reference a little clearer, the Pope had also written this sentence in his manuscript: "Woe to those who play nation against nation. . . , oppress the weak and break their given word." But he had timidly crossed that out in the last moment from the draft text. Then he cried:

> "The danger is great, but there is still time. Nothing is lost with peace. But everything can be lost with war. May people come to an agreement by resuming negotiations. . . ."

Something of a despairing powerlessness lies in these words. What was left to be negotiated about? For at least a week the Vatican had had reports that the whole "Danzig question is only an excuse for Germany and that a war of extermination against Poland has been decided upon. Opinion is that there is an understanding with Russia about the division of poor Poland" (*note from the Secretary of State Cardinal Maglione of August 16, 1939*). France's ambassador asks the Vatican for a public word supporting threatened Poland. "His Holiness says that would be too much," noted Monsignore Domenico Tardini, the Secretary for Extraordinary Affairs in the Secretariat of State. "One cannot forget that there are 40 million Catholics in the Reich. What would they have to suffer after such a step by the Holy See! . . ." In Poland there are 30 million Catholics; the Pope tries for long uneasy days to influence their government to make concessions to Hitler, although the Warsaw nuncio Cortesi considers this hardly reasonable, although Monsignore Tardini reports serious reservations, and Nuncio Orsenigo reports from Berlin: "Here, with a frightening callousness, everyone is decided on war."[98]

Doesn't all this concern the Pope? On the contrary. If Monsignore Tardini fears that people might draw the conclusion that the Holy See wanted to bring about "a new Munich," it is exactly this that Pope Pius XII considers the lesser evil. Of course, the Pope's own notes of his thoughts have not been found in the Vatican archives, but his behavior actually permits only this interpretation: that he prefers an appeasement of Hitler— even if only temporary—to a war, a certain division of Poland and thereby the advance of the Soviet Union toward the West. As soon as this becomes unavoidable, however, the Pope immediately adjusts to the altered situation: he is steadfastly silent when Hitler attacks Poland on September 1, and is just as silent when the Soviet Union marches into East Poland on September 18 under the pretence of having to protect its White Russian and Ukrainian brothers (but actually on the basis of the secret agreement with Berlin). Editor in Chief Count dalla Torre of course writes in the *Osservatore Romano* on the same day: "That is a cowardly act. . . . Is this the end of Poland? No, Poland has a double right to live, because it is offering heroic resistance." But from the Pope himself—who in May 1940 will not hesitate to condemn clearly Hitler's attack on Belgium and Holland—no word toward the East is to be heard.

Charles-Roux, the French Ambassador to the Vatican, on October 2, 1939, delivered a memorandum from the Prime Minister Daladier: "The Holy See has up to now attempted to explain its refusal to condemn the German aggression against Poland with the fear that this would expose the Catholic Germans to repression by the Nazi regime. There is no such reason to justify silence with respect to the Soviet action. . . ."

However, there was a reason, indeed exactly the same one; Monsignore Giovanni Montini (the future Pope Paul VI) explained it to the ambassador:[99]

"Every word against Germany and Russia would be bitterly paid for by the Catholics who are subject to the regimes in these countries."

For the first time since Lenin's October Revolution, about 11 million Catholics in East Poland were now ruled by the Soviets. This was a new reality for Rome—and for Moscow. Would the instruments (and weapons) from the arsenal of the past two decades—somewhat rusty—suffice to cope with it?

VI

The Crusade Does Not
Take Place, 1939-1944

Soviet Advance: Rome is Silent—Moscow Hesitates

"The world is now awaiting Your Holiness' first encyclical. With what concerned anticipation the tearful eyes of the trampled Polish people will read this historic document, a people that in better times . . . followed an appeal from Pope Innocent XI and crushed the power of the crescent near Vienna, then in our times, under the eyes of the future Pius XI, routed the Bolshevist hordes marching toward the west in the miracle on the Vistula! [see p. 20]. This bulwark of Christianity and of Latin culture is now in the hands of the enemies of the cross. Therefore, Holy Father, have the goodness to include in the so eagerly anticipated encyclical a word of lamentation about the fall of Poland. . . ."

The Polish Primate Cardinal Hlond directed this request to Pius XII in autumn of 1939.[1] On the day after the Soviet entry into East Poland, on September 18, the Primate—who had fled Poland with the Warsaw government—had arrived in Rome. Immediately thereafter he had presented to the Vatican a situation report that considered the fact that now 11 million Catholics had come under Soviet rule, and feared the worst. "Making an attempt with the Russians to see whether the dispatch of an apostolic visitator or delegate would be possible seems to the Holy See an almost impossible undertaking."[2] With these words Hlond practically advised against such an attempt.

Rome still had no news about what was actually happening in the Soviet-occupied areas; only from German-occupied Poland came the first reports about repressive measures, because the Berlin nuncio Orsenigo had at least been able to send his secretary to Warsaw for two days to secure the nunciature's archives there. The Pope was determined to bide his time and to compose his first encyclical, which he had already begun before the outbreak of the war, with the utmost caution: against "unlimited state authority," which withdrew the basis for international law and "makes peaceful mutual relationships difficult"; against the war which was spilling "the blood of innumerable people, even non-combatants, in a beloved nation, which is Poland"—a nation that "has a right to the human and fraternal sympathy of the world, and trusting in Mary, the patron saint of Christians (*auxilium christianorum*), awaits the hour of its resurrection in justice and peace. . . ."

The Pope went no further in his Christmas address two months later than he did in this encyclical ("*Summus Pontificatus*" of October 20, 1939[3]). He did of course lament the "deliberate aggression against a small, industrious and peaceable people,"[4] but he left open whom he meant by this. Later, when Hitler's Foreign Minister Ribbentrop visited the Pope (see p. 207), Monsignore Tardini took the following minutes:

> "His Holiness reminded him that in his encyclical he had taken pains not to insult Germany, although—in keeping with his mission—he had to tell the truth. He added that the small nation that he had referred to in his Christmas address is *Finland* (in Germany they thought that it was Poland)."[5]

Finland was far away; it was able to resist the Soviet attack at the end of November 1939 with some success, and—there were hardly any Catholics there. However, in the meantime news had reached Rome from Soviet-occupied Eastern Europe that made discretion seem opportune. The first to report was the Lemberg Archbishop Sheptyckyi, of whom Cardinal Hlond had erroneously reported to the Secretariat of State on October 12 that he had been "transported to Russia."[6] But back on October 10, Sheptyckyi, who sat in his Lemberg bishop's castle with crippled legs, but as active as ever, had dispatched a dauntless Jesuit: after six weeks of adventuresome travels over the Carpathians and many "green borders," the courier, Father G. Moskva,[7] arrived in Rome with Sheptyckyi's letter. The Vatican learned something astonishing from this letter, although at first only in allusions that were not clear until later:

Abruptly and without asking the Pope, Sheptyckyi, on the day of the Soviet entry into East Poland, September 17, 1939, had immediately "partitioned" the entire Soviet Union, so to speak, into Catholic divisions. Calling upon the legendary, supposedly "unlimited" authority conferred upon him by Pius X in 1907 [!], and faithful to his nationalist-romantic missionary ideas that had never faded since the days of the Czars, he had installed four apostolic exarchs: Bishop Czarneckyi (see p. 146) for the

Volynian and Podolian section of the Ukraine (with Luck and Kamenec); Father Klement Sheptyckyi (his brother) for "greater Russia and Siberia" (with Moscow); the Jesuit Antonin Niemancewycz for White Russia; and finally the most important figure, Josef Slipyj, the rector of the priests' seminary in Lemberg, for the "greater Ukraine" (with Kiev).[8]

What did this mean? Sheptyckyi regarded the incorporation of eastern Poland with its large White Russian and Ukrainian population into the Soviet Union as, on the one hand, a danger for the church, but at the same time, as a kind of opportunity. "The Russians had occupied Poland—so we were, in effect, already in Russia," enthused the Jesuit Walter Ciszek. Although as an American citizen he could have emigrated, Ciszek prepared himself this autumn, with Sheptyckyi's permission, to undertake a missionary trip to the industrial area of the Urals disguised as a worker, with falsified papers.[9] The Lemberg Archbishop, who all his life had used conspiratorial methods with a certain naiveté, right at the beginning seized a hope that had betrayed him once before (after 1917). Did he have any idea that Rome had learned something from its experiences and that the Pacelli Pope would not let himself be guided by the emotions of his predecessor?

The embarrassment that Sheptyckyi's first sign of life called forth in the Vatican was probably so great that the official document publication of the Holy See even today conceals the exact wording. Only one laconic sentence from Cardinal Tisserant, the prefect of the Congregation for Eastern Rite Churches, with all sympathy for Sheptyckyi's awkward situation, betrays the cool reaction of the curia vis-à-vis Sheptyckyi's insistence on his "authorization" from 1907: "Other extraordinary and ordinary authorities, it is the opinion here, are not necessary for the moment," Tisserant wrote back to him on November 27, 1939.[10] The delicate mode of expression also takes into account the danger that the letter could be intercepted along the way. . . .

Anyway, at the end of November the Pope had conferred certain special canonical powers on *all* bishops in the Soviet-occupied areas,[11] above all the possibility of secretly naming two reliable priests as possible successors in case they were unable to carry out their office, so that the episcopal succession would never be interrupted. The Lemberg Archbishop too was allowed to consecrate his "beloved pupil" Slipyj as bishop. However, all of the Lemberg Metropolitan's other far-ranging plans—although Sheptyckyi urged them repeatedly—seemed to the Vatican all too fantastical, even dangerous; partly because the behavior of the Soviets toward the papal church in these months was by no means unequivocal, but at least not as revolutionarily destructive as had been feared.

The priests were "granted complete freedom in their functions within the church, so long as they do not preach against the Soviet regime," Prelate

Peter Werhun, a confidant of Sheptyckyi's, reported to the Berlin nuncio after his return from Lemberg in the middle of January 1940.[12] The monastics on the contrary were expelled from the cloisters, their property confiscated, whereby the Latin Catholics were worse off than the Ukrainians, who "because they are anti-Polish have less fear of the Russians"; in Galicia, "Nazi elements" were trying to stir up unrest against Russian Communism. ("I fear that the Ukrainian clergy is not keeping a proper distance from these intrigues.") The rector of the "Russicum," Philippe de Régis, who by chance had been in Poland at the outbreak of the war, reported similar impressions: "The Communists have been careful not to be imprudent, and have shown themselves to be lenient with religion."[13]

Sheptyckyi himself, who in December 1939 is even able to convene a diocesan synod, draws a rather contradictory picture in a letter to Cardinal Tisserant (which he sent along with a German military deputation in Lemberg):[14] On the one hand he reports disorder, anti-church chicanery, arbitrary arrests, and complains that the Jews, who have fled to East Poland en masse (before Hitler's anti-Semitism), are favored by the Soviets. . . . On the other, he confirms that "the clergy is still able to work in all parishes and churches," and thinks there is even a growing interest in religion in the Soviet army and among the Communists: "It seems that all these areas are becoming a sphere of action for an apostolate that could be very fruitful."

The contradiction may be explained by the fact that Sheptyckyi cannot reconcile the determination of the new rulers to sovietize East Poland with their hesitation toward the church. It did not quite dawn upon the 75-year-old Lemberg Metropolitan that Stalin was simply being tactically more clever in this regard than Hitler in "his" part of Poland. In the new system, which especially to the Jews appears—and very rightly so—to be a lifesaver, he thinks he has discovered a "diabolical mass possession" (*une possession diabolique en masse*), and asks the Pope in all seriousness to summon monastic orders to carry out—an anti-Soviet exorcism of devils (*d'exorciser la Russie sovietique*). Even his first letter of October 10 contained this request; now the Ukrainian-Catholic Metropolitan repeated it and combined it with the request that the Pope formally delegate him (*designer, deputer et deleguer*), "to die for the faith and the unity of the church", because it would be good "if someone became a martyr of this invasion. . . ."

Such mystical longings for martyrdom are usually valued in the Vatican, at the most, for a later beatification process, but not for the requirements of present pastoral policy. Pope and curia thus answered the unusual request from Lemberg with indulgent silence.

In the second great arena of Soviet occupation, the Baltic states, the

Vatican could orient itself more easily, since it had its own observers at its disposal in two nunciatures. But here too there are difficulties that do not arise solely from the Soviet presence. At the time, the Polish Archbishop Romuald Jalbrzykowski sat in Vilna, the city populated predominantly by Poles, the possession of which Poland and Lithuania had been disputing for two decades. The Lithuanian government accused him, unchallenged, that when the Soviets marched in, a red flag had flown from his cathedral, but when the Lithuanians entered (to whom the Soviets awarded the city on October 10, 1939), there was no Lithuanian flag. Jalbrzykowski also forbade the ringing of the bells for the Lithuanian liberators.[15] Perhaps the archepiscopal palace sensed that the apparent concession to Lithuania, which was paid for with Soviet military strongpoints, would not last long. The aversion of many Lithuanian nationalists against the just as nationalistically inclined Polish bishop was so great that the editor of a Christian Democrat newspaper in Kaunas had turned to the Soviet city commissar in Vilna—and requested the Archbishop's arrest. The Soviets, who during this their first short sojourn in Vilna preferred to rely on Polish Communists and leftist Catholics rather than on Lithuanians, refused.[16] Then, when Vilna came under Lithuanian sovereignty (for only eight months until the liquidation of *all* of Lithuania by the Soviets!), the government in Kaunas had no other concern than to demand of the Vatican that it forbid Archbishop Jalbrzykowski to invoke Mary as *regina Poloniae* (the Queen of Poland) in the litany. . . .

The Vatican, greatly perturbed by the senseless quarrel between nationalisms, exhorted both sides to moderation—with little success. The discord ended only when the Red Army, in the middle of June 1940, after an ultimatum to the Baltic states marched into Lithuania, Estonia and Latvia without a struggle. For the first time, a papal nuncio experienced with his own eyes a Communist seizure of power. The documents about it that are available today reveal a reactive mechanism which was repeated in similar manner after the Second World War (about which far less source material is available).

"Capital and country are quiet, although immensely depressed," Nuncio Centoz wired from Kaunas on June 17, 1940, with the news of the Soviet invasion. The Pope, who had at least condemned Hitler's attack on Belgium and Holland in May with solicitous telegrams to the crowned heads of those countries, was silent. Not even the *Osservatore Romano* commented on the event. Moreover, as recently as May 13, when the Italian Ambassador Alfieri criticized the papal telegrams to Brussels and The Hague, Pius XII had declared with quiet dignity: "We had no fear when they once held a revolver on Us [allusion to Pacelli's experience in "red" Munich, see p. 18], and We would have no fear the second time either,

not even of the concentration camp. The Pope, under certain circumstances, cannot keep silent. . . ." (il Papa in certe circonstanze non
puó tacere).[17]

The "circumstances," which lead to the Sovietization of the Baltic States,
nevertheless give the Vatican no occasion for loud complaint; again it
observes with a cautious waiting attitude. In Lithuania there are about two
million Catholics (87 percent), in Latvia half a million (25 percent). A week
after the occupation, Nuncio Centoz asks Rome whether he should now
convey to the Baltic bishops the extraordinary authority "that has already
been granted to the Polish bishops under Russia." This telegram crosses
another from the Secretary of State Cardinal Maglione, who leaves to the
nuncio whether it is already necessary to dispense this authority, "which is
only foreseen for the case of Russian occupation and a Bolshevist
regime."[18] The nuncio observes how "events precipitate themselves," and
acts accordingly. The primary concern of the Roman curia is that the
country approach the new situation with its hierarchy as intact as possible:

The hasty appointment of a Lithuanian suffragan bishop for Vilna, who
is to support the Polish Jalbrzykowski, of course does not dispose the new
Soviet-dependent government in Kaunas any more favorably. On July 6 it
cancels the concordat of 1927. Poland's exile ambassador to the Vatican
meanwhile calls the bishop's appointment "distressing." Secretary of State
Cardinal Maglione tries to reassure him: "In Vilna, the Lithuanians and the
Poles are now united by the Russian oppression. . . ."[19] Actually,
however, the Polish archbishop and his Lithuanian suffragan bishop will
mutually avoid each other in Vilna.[20]

Bishop's Consecration in Soviet Lithuania—With Nuncio

In a lively exchange of coded telegrams with Nuncio Centoz in Kaunas
and Nuncio Arata in Riga, the Vatican made its last arrangements before
the formal incorporation of the Baltic states into the Union of Soviet
Republics. "Your Excellency will take care to stay as long as possible,"
Maglione wired on July 17 to Centoz, and gave him orders to consecrate
the priest Padolskis as suffragan bishop of Vilkaviškis without waiting for
the papal bull of appointment. While the Metropolitan in Soviet-occupied
Lemberg could only in secret consecrate his co-adjutant Slipyj as bishop,
Padolskis' consecration is celebrated openly:

"On the morning of August 4, 1940, I drove there in the car," reports the
nuncio.[21] "Although the religious celebration took place on the day after
the official annexation of Lithuania into the USSR, thus on Soviet
territory, it was carried out in a completely peaceful and deeply devout
atmosphere. The bishops walked from the parsonage up the main street to
the cathedral in full vestments. . . . The pontifical mass was celebrated

with good liturgical music before a devout crowd. The population that filled the plaza before the cathedral knelt down and received the blessing. A group of only sixteen men and eight women who meanwhile came out of a neighboring street in six rows crossed the main street with red flags and Communist songs. Half an hour later a much larger Soviet demonstration took place to celebrate the annexation of Lithuania by the USSR. A procession of about 400 people, men and women, the great majority Jews [notice the "sharp" eye of the nuncio!], filed through the main street with flags, pennants, pictures of Stalin, and sang songs praising Communism. The people watched the procession quietly: not the slightest incident could raise complaint. . . ."

It apparently does not occur to the Vatican to establish any kind of contact with the new Soviet rulers of the country. On August 13 all diplomatic representatives in the Baltic capitals are bidden to depart within two weeks. Nuncio Centoz leaves Lithuania on August 25, not without exhorting the bishops to exercise "great caution."[22] Still, the Vatican's restraint seems to be paying off a little. At the end of August the suffragan bishop of Kaunas, Vincentas Brizgys, sends news via confidential paths to Centoz, who in the meantime has arrived in Rome:

> "The bank account of the nunciature has been divided up, according to Your Excellence's wishes. . . . The seminary will begin its work on September 16. . . . The archepiscopal palace has not yet been occupied. We have hope. . . . A parents' movement for religious instruction is beginning. . . . One must recognize that the priests are realistic, but not pessimistic—they are conscious of their surroundings, but they do not lose courage. The government is satisfied with their behavior up to now. . . ."— And finally—as if this were a special consolation: "In the new council of Commissars there are no Jews. . . ."[23]

Four months later, at the beginning of January 1941, the picture that Bishop Brizgys sends to the Vatican via the detour through the Berlin nunciature seems more serious, but also more complicated:[24] Twenty priests have been arrested, four without any cause, the others on trifling grounds. "Among the high officials of the GPU are Poles, which the Polish minority takes advantage of to obtain exaggerated rights in the church. . . . I know that four or five priests have pledged themselves in writing to deliver information to the GPU 'within the limits of conscience'. . . ."

Brizgys reports on the abduction and arrest of many people, on the dwindling sympathies of the working class for Communism. "The Russian political functionaries are very fanatical against religion. . . . The military are not anti-religious; in conversations without witnesses they occasionally even show interest and sympathy for religion." And again missionary hopes are stirring in Brizgys—as with the Lemberg Metropolitan Sheptyckyi; he would like to send selected young priests to the "Russicum" in Rome for appropriate education, and requests the arrangement of entry visas. (In a later letter on March 21, 1941, Brizgys asks that popular religious literature in the Russian language be sent to him.) But at the same time he warns against a Russian-Catholic cleric whom the Soviets had sent to Rome, "probably so that he can inform the USSR embassy about what is happening among the Catholics in Rome, especially in the Russicum."

"Under the tyrannical regime of the Bolshevists, the Christian life, led by the clergy, has not been diminished," the Riga Archbishop Springovics reports to the Pope in retrospect from *Latvia*.[25] Aside from the deaths of eleven priests—of whom most were victims of the GPU only shortly before the German entry in June 1941—he deplores primarily the confiscation of church property, dissolution of the cloisters, and obstruction of religious instruction. "The religious situation is more and more assuming the imprint that it has in Russia," the Jesuit Bishop Eduard Profittlich, who lives in Tallinn (Reval) as apostolic administrator for *Estonia*, writes to Rome on January 14.

This was accurate, for the existing Soviet religious legislation (see pp. 131-2) was now to be gradually carried over to the new Baltic Soviet republics. But only in the case of Estonia, where there were hardly more than two thousand scattered Catholics, was this almost synonymous with the end of *all* pastoral possibilities. And for that reason too, Bishop Profittlich, who held German citizenship, decided in 1941 to depart together with the Estonian ethnic Germans, who were being resettled. He felt no "inner inspiration from God" to stay, as he openly wrote to Rome, and common sense told him "that my continued presence here would be senseless." Back in October he had asked this question of his superiors in Rome—and received the sibylline answer that the Pope would leave to him what he considered best "*in Domino*" (in the Lord). Now at the beginning of February 1941, Profittlich repeated his inquiry—and again Pius XII spoke like the Delphic oracle: he had left the decision to him and trusted that he would make it "inspired above all by the welfare of the souls entrusted to him." Profittlich interpreted that as a papal request that he stay; he hoped that his sacrifice "in any case would not be completely fruitless," he wrote. Five months later, when Hitler's armies attacked the Soviet Union, Profittlich was arrested as a "German spy" and deported to Siberia, where all traces—in spite of later investigations—were lost forever. . . .[26]

In the personal tragedy of this man is reflected the psychodrama of the diplomat-Pope Pacelli, who in grand politics, as in the smaller human realm, repeatedly recoiled from taking full responsibility and making decisions in situations that did not seem to him to be easily or at all comprehensible. It was rather self-evident that Soviet politics of the years 1939-41 in the Baltic and in East Poland did not want to disturb "atmospherically" the consolidation of their new "forefield" by directly destroying religious life. But it was just as clear that the sovietization of these regions—the openly declared goal—in the long run could not be attained by any other method than the abolition of all traditional structures, thus also the ecclesiastical. And that unavoidably amounted to at least a gradual reduction of church life to simple "worship."

The Vatican was rather helpless in the face of these proceedings. It avoided provoking the Soviets. But it also undertook no new attempts to reduce the points of friction of their—for them quite new!—intercourse with predominantly Catholic regions through clarifying contacts. Did the reason for this lie in the fact that the Pope was convinced of the "temporary nature" of the situation, or even reckoned with Hitler's aggressive intentions? A document from the only official Soviet-Vatican contact of that time shows, instead, the opposite:

With no small astonishment, the papal nunciature in Berlin at the beginning of January 1941 received a telephone call from the Soviet embassy asking whether Mr. Vladimir Georgievitch Dekanosov, the new ambassador of the Soviet Union, could make a first visit to the nuncio in his capacity as the doyen of the diplomatic corps. Since Pacelli's conversations with Krestinski (see p. 73) there had been no more such visits; new Soviet ambassadors had always been content with cool written notification of the doyen. Then what did Dekanosov want?

"The conversation proceeded in a very polite tone," Orsenigo reported on January 11, 1941, to Rome.[27] "He asked me whether I wished to ask him anything—for example about the war; but just because he invited me to do so I feared that it might be a trap, and I said no. However, I asked about the situation of the Catholics in the three republics—Lithuania, Estonia and Latvia—that a short time ago came under the rule of Russia; he answered with surprising candor that the situation of the Catholics was unchanged. Although my information did not agree with this, I did not believe that I should expressly contradict him, in order to avoid the danger that I would be challenged to produce proof of the opposite, which would have given grounds for repressions against possible informers. Therefore I only added that it was sometimes necessary for the Catholic church to transfer clerics, monks, and nuns into other areas, and I asked him to support me in such a case in obtaining the necessary permissions. He did not refuse this, but added that it was now better to stay in countries that were not scourged by the iron heel of war. I said that my vision was *far beyond the war*, which would surely not last forever. . . ."

Was the Vatican then—or at least Orsenigo—counting on an extended

Soviet presence in the Baltic? After all, the fact had not escaped Orsenigo—as he writes in the same report—that Stalin's Foreign Minister Molotov (with whom Ambassador Dekanosov came to Berlin for the first time in 1940) this time had not come to terms with Hitler about the division of the future booty. Through an agent of the German military secret service chief, Admiral Canaris (who considered Hitler's war a crime), Pius XII had been informed earlier than many other European politicians about Hitler's plans for attacking the Soviet Union.[28] There were also attempts by opposition circles of the German political secret service to sound out through contacts with the Jesuit General Ledóchowski—whose anti-Communist attitude and international connections were well known—whether a peace treaty with the West and cooperation against the East were possible in return for a moderation of the domestic German regime (also in regard to the church).[29] In the spring of 1941 the Sudeten-German Count Khuen-Belasi-Lützow called on Ledóchowski, and made such suggestions in the name of the secret service. Back in the autumn of 1940, the Bishop of Passau had received a surprise visit from an old acquaintance, the SS officer Albert Hartl of the *Reichssicherheitshauptamt* (the Main Office for Security)—a renegade Catholic theologian who now offered the church cooperation in the struggle against "materialism" for the price of "an unreservedly positive" attitude toward National Socialism. . . .[30] It is thus completely possible that the Soviet ambassador in Berlin, himself a functionary of the secret service, had orders to ascertain on his visit to the nuncio how the Vatican, where so many threads came together, assessed the war perspectives and above all Hitler's intentions.

However, the Pope did not allow himself to be tempted out of his reserve by all this. Just because—like many serious observers all over the world—he feared in the spring of 1941 that a victory by Hitler and Mussolini was probable, any further expansion of the war—even against the atheist Soviet Union—was no reason for enthusiasm. And all the less so when the National Socialists during these very months intensified their anti-Catholic church struggle. Their chief ideologist, Alfred Rosenberg, by derivation a Baltic German anti-Communist, had noted in his diary on May 10, 1940, the day on which Hitler attacked France: "The struggle against Rome, after a German victory, will be carried to its conclusion in Germany."[31] What a "liberation" of East Poland and the Baltic by Hitler's armies would mean for the church there was plain to see. But what would happen if Hitler, after France, now also defeated Great Britain with backing from the Soviets? Pius XII saw "in the complete destruction of our opponents, or in an all too long duration of the war, a further advance of Bolshevism with its anti-religious concomitants. . . ," reported German Ambassador to the Vatican von Bergen on February 15, 1941.[32]

Far from openly declaring for or against any side,[33] the Pope, two weeks before Hitler's attack on the Soviet Union (the date of which he already knew), wrote to the Passau bishop in answer to the offers of the SS-officer Hartl: "The Pope thinks only of . . . a peace for everyone that does not oppress or destroy any nation. . . ."[34] And to the bishops of the Baltic Soviet republics he directed a Latin document that avoided any political accent. There were general words of consolation, but also warnings against—laziness and avarice among the clergy (not without reason, as the author of the draft of the letter noted in a comment for the Pope!), finally admonitions to persevere in the faith and as motto: "*Contra turpidam impietatem pura religio*"—against vile ungodliness, pure religion. But the word "*turpidam*" (vile) the Pope cautiously crossed out of the final version of the text. . . .[35]

After Hitler's Attack: "Help the Soviets—But Not Too Much"

"Robbers have thrown themselves upon our Russian Fatherland. . . . The Church of Christ gives its blessing to the defense of the holy homeland of all the Orthodox. May the Lord grant us victory. . . !"

The Moscow Metropolitan Sergius directed this proclamation to the faithful in the Soviet Union[36] on June 22, 1941—the same day as the assault by Hitler's armies on the Soviet Union. Stalin, who up to the last moment did not believe in the possibility of a German aggression, was literally speechless: not until ten days after the Metropolitan did he direct his first appeal to his people.

In Germany, however, on June 29 the Catholic military bishop Franz Josef Rarkowski wrote to the soldiers of the German Wehrmacht: "Be confident in your mission! Then victory will be yours, a victory that will allow Europe to breathe again. . . . Many European states know that the war against Russia is a European *crusade*. . . ."[37]

Again—and this time in dead earnest—the ominous slogan haunted Europe. Even if it could hardly become the catchword of the Pope, did it not still demand a tribute from him too?—Vatican document publications reveal no immediate initial reaction from the curia. (Perhaps the corresponding documents were among those that Pius XII, toward the end of the war, had his confidant Prelate Kaas burn for days in a fireplace in the Palazzo San Carlo.) Not even the demand from Hitler, delivered by Ambassador von Bergen, that the Pope declare himself in favor of the anti-Communist crusade can be adequately documented.[38] Ambassador von Bergen reports on June 24 about a "certain relief" in the Vatican, since they had feared that Bolshevism could emerge from the war "untouched, indeed even strengthened"; in any case, the advance into Russia had "not surprised" the papal Secretariat of State.[39]

There could really be no talk of surprise; not only because there had been an indication from German secret service circles (see p. 205), but also because the Reich Foreign Minister had given the Pope a hint a year and a quarter before: Ribbentrop, in his seventy-minute audience of March 11, 1940, had "talked a lot against Communism." He had attempted to convince Pius XII that in Germany, without the victory of the National Socialists, just as in Russia "not even *one* church would have been left—as he, Ribbentrop, had been able to ascertain with his own eyes. . . ." The Pope replied dryly that one could not know what would have happened "if".

. . . And he had taken Ribbentrop's allusions to his Moscow trip of 1939 as occasion to ask "whether Germany had nothing to fear from this alliance with Communism? Ribbentrop rejected this: the alliance is only external and for the war. . . ."[40]

Ambassador Bergen's observation that there was "relief" in the Vatican when the Red Army—especially in the first days after Hitler's surprise attack—was thrown back toward the east, was certainly not altogether false. After all, the secretary of a papal congregation, Archbishop Celso Constantini, had blessed the Italian soldiers whom Mussolini sent to the east as warriors against "the Red barbarism."[41] The Pope also had "no reason to bemoan the fate of the Soviet Union, which was exposed to a blow from the Wehrmacht after it had divided the hide of Poland with Hitler" (the editors of the Vatican document publications were still formulating it thus in 1969[42]). Many Roman prelates—for example the Anima-rector Bishop Hudal, whose "unfortunate affection" for the Hitler movement we already know (see p. 169), now thought that they could perhaps advance Hitler some trust once more. The Jesuit Leiber, one of the closest papal advisors, objected in a letter that "Russia, in a way, is fighting a holy war for the Fatherland" (Hudal, "Römische Tagebücher, Graz 1976," p. 213). But others wondered what would happen if Hitler, who had just "rolled up" the Balkans, after a victorious campaign against the Soviet Union should then pounce on Britain with full strength? And if Hitler should run aground in the vastness of Russia, could not then the western powers, above all the USA, which was beginning to get more and more involved in Europe, turn around and proclaim an anti-Nazi crusade? And would this not also again confuse the ideological fronts?

The Pope decided—as always when he was torn between moral feelings and political understanding—in favor of the principle of "caution." Of course, five years later he could boast that in 1941, in spite of "certain pressures," he had spoken not a word of approval or encouragement for the war against Russia.[43]

But he did not condemn this attack either, as little as he had the previous attack by Hitler on Yugoslavia and Greece. Rather, the Pope took refuge in

"Reflections on Divine Providence in Human Events." Pius XII gave this title to his radio message for the feast of Sts. Peter and Paul on June 29, 1941, when Hitler's armies had already reached Minsk—in one week!—and with the help of armed Lithuanian Catholics[44] had driven the Soviets out of Kaunas. He felt his heart contract at the thought of the sufferings and fears of the present-day world, the Pope said, but there was also a

> "consoling sight that opens the heart to great and holy expectations: the high-minded value of the defense of Christian culture and reliable hopes for its triumph. [There is] great love of fatherland and heroic deeds of valor. . . . But on the other hand: a decay of the sense of justice, peoples plunged into the abyss of misery, human bodies torn apart by bombs and cannon. . . . Prisoners. . . . Displaced persons. . . . Hunger. . . . And in addition unspeakable sufferings and persecutions that many of Our beloved sons and daughters—priests, monastics, laymen—have to endure in several places ["countries" the Pope first wrote—and crossed it out again]. . . . How can God permit all this? . . . Trust in God means . . . to believe that God sometimes allows the supremacy of *atheism* and wickedness for a while here on earth . . . in order to purify peoples and individuals through penitence. . . . As rough as the hand of the divine surgeon may appear when it pierces living flesh with the sword, still it is always only active love that directs and moves. . . ."[45]

Who was being addressed with such strange "medical," moral-theological interpretation of the war? The papal representative in London reported that in the Anglo-Saxon countries, people were happy that "not a word of the Pope's could be interpreted as favorable to German propaganda, which praises the German chancellor as the savior of the world from atheistic Bolshevism."[46] The chargé d'affaires of the German embassy to the Vatican, on the other hand, heard "from informed sources" that Pius XII, in this address, had wanted to express the hope "that the great sacrifices that this war demands . . . according to the will of providence would lead to victory over Bolshevism." And in Berlin, Nuncio Orsenigo told the German Secretary of State on August 20, 1941: "Anyone who talks peace now is a Stalinist!"[47]

The Pope's actual train of thought is contained in the notes of Monsignore Tardini concerning a conversation with the Italian Ambassador Attolico, who on September 5—shortly after a trip by Mussolini to Hitler's headquarters—called upon the Vatican to finally make a clear anti-Bolshevist statement, especially since, in spite of everything, the church was much better off in Germany than in Russia. Tardini answered:

> . . . that the attitude of the Holy See to Bolshevism needs no new declarations . . . , that I for my part would be very happy if Communism were put out of action. It is the worst, but not the only, enemy of the church. Naziism did practice and still practices a real persecution of the church. The swastika is thus not the cross of the crusades. . . . *I see the crusade, but not the*

crusaders. . . . If the Holy See were to call attention to the errors and horrors of Communism, it could not pass over the aberrations and persecutions of Naziism. . . . For that reason, I am at the present moment not making use of the crusade doctrine, but rather of the saying 'Set a thief to catch a thief' (*un diavolo caccia l'altro*). All the better, if the other is the worse one. . . ."[48]

How strongly the Pope was in agreement with these thoughts is proven by the fact that he returned the minutes with only *one* modification: the situation of the church in Germany has deteriorated. In a semi-official article for an Italian government journal, however, he also lets "Vatican circles" assert that a "crusade" would be out of the question, because the Holy See, "as much as it wishes the Bolshevist plague eradicated from the world, could not have wanted this to happen at the price of such a monstrous martial bloodbath" (*cf. Relazioni Internazionali, Milano, of August 2, 1941*).

More than his energetic collaborator Tardini, the Pope might have been aware that the "two evils"—Communism and National Socialism—could be of different gravity: it depended on whether one weighed them on the scales of a church or a state, of a temporal or a transcendental order—and whether the two always could be separated. In the autumn of 1941, through the intervention of the USA in the European war, the Vatican was confronted with this intrinsic difficulty. Because President Roosevelt, at the beginning of September, sent his special ambassador Myron C. Taylor to Rome with instructions to convince the Pope of the necessity of rescuing the Soviet Union and to keep him away from any ideas of an anti-Soviet crusade—if not to convert him to ideas of an anti-Nazi crusade.

For Roosevelt too, Germany and the Soviet Union were both dictatorships, but, as he wrote to Pius XII on September 3, 1941, "I believe that this Russian dictatorship is less dangerous to the safety of other nations than is the German form of dictatorship." This could not be rejected out of hand, because after all, Hitler had begun the war, in two years had subjected eight European states and made satellites of five others, while Stalin—after long isolation only brought into play by Hitler—up to now had only advanced as far as the old borders of the Czarist empire (in the Baltic, Finland and East Poland). The Vatican also saw clearly that Roosevelt's thesis "is true, if one looks at it politically and militarily" (Tardini). But Roosevelt's second thesis was quite another matter: "I believe that the survival of Russia is less dangerous to religion, to the church as such, and to humanity in general, than would be the survival of the German form of dictatorship." Since the President sensed that this— and finally *only* this—point of view was decisive for the Roman curia (for after all there were dictatorships, for instance in Spain, about which the church had nothing to complain!), Roosevelt added an argument that he considered effective, but that especially in Vatican ears must have sounded incredibly naive:

"In so far as I am informed, churches in Russia are open. I believe there is a real possibility that Russia may as a result of the present conflict, recognize freedom of religion in Russia, although of course without recognition of any official intervention on the part of any church in education or political matters within Russia."[49]

The sermonizing in these sentences almost grips the temperamental Monsignore Tardini with rage: "Aren't these the same kinds of hypocrisies, fictions and lies that present-day politics are full of?" he noted in disgust.[50] "For anyone concerned only with the moral and religious interests of the Russian people, there is only one way to save it: the destruction of Communism. But that is not Roosevelt's idea. . . . For him, as a good American, religion is quite apart from politics. That is the liberal and democratic theory. It is wrong, for even the state as such has duties to God. . . ."

Tardini—in contrast to Roosevelt—is convinced that Stalin is not only a Russian dictator, but also an atheistic Communist, who recognizes no compromises in the area of religion, "even if he is now waving the flag of the Fatherland instead of the banner of the International." Is Hitler's Germany perhaps more dangerous? "Divine service is less obstructed in Germany than in Russia," noted Tardini. Then is Russia more dangerous? "That is only the momentary situation. . . . As soon as Naziism were internally and externally sure of its powers, it would proceed mercilessly with its anti-religious program. . . ."

Then what remains? The hope "that providence in its goodness and mercy will bring to pass out of the present tragedy the destruction of *both* great evils threatening humanity, culture and religion: Communism *and* Naziism," Tardini writes, and he repeats it once more in the notes that he sends to the Pope with his draft reply to Roosevelt.

But can that be more than a "pious" wish? How does Tardini actually picture this in practical political terms? This prelate, who as secretary for "extraordinary affairs" in Pius XII's Secretariat of State is something like the Pope's foreign minister, angrily and restlessly turns this dilemma facing Vatican politics over and over like a cumbersome boulder. He is far too much of a diplomat not to know that in high politics one cannot avoid decisions—especially not the choice between two evils. He senses, if only faintly, that perhaps a church, but no state can afford this luxury (an uncomfortable one at that). Tardini thus clings to the possibility—in the autumn of 1941 not improbable—that Stalin ("that war mongerer who was forestalled in his criminal plans by a more daring criminal") would be defeated by Hitler and that Naziism would come out of this battle "weakened and defeatable." And how will this come about? Tardini notes down his recipe on September 15, 1941, without those unctious disguises that so often turned curial style into enigmatic code:

"If I were close to Roosevelt and Churchill, I would give them something like the following advice: help the Russians—but within limits. And the limits would be to help them *only as much* as is necessary to shift the theater of war from the west to Russia and to weaken both Communism and Naziism as much as possible; but do *not* help them enough to avoid a defeat of the Russians which— under the present circumstances—is the desirable defeat of Communism. (To tell the truth, I hope that Roosevelt basically also has this program. . . .)"[51]

After the Second World War, Stalin will accuse his western military allies of just this intention and make it an excuse for the "cold war." But the papal "foreign minister" writes it this clearly only in his own private notes. He knows that the Pope, even if he thought it out this consistently, would never write it down or speak it, much less discuss it with his advisers. Pius XII needs no "*collaboratori,*" only "*esecutori*"—executive organs (Tardini recollects twenty years later). So the Pope also rejects out of hand the sketch of an answer to Roosevelt, only half-clear anyway, which refers to *both* evil systems. The Pope thinks it is better not to get to the essence itself (*non entrare in merito*), but to reply with a letter that is polite, but kept general—"especially when writing to a combatant!"[52] And that is what happens. But at the same time, Tardini hands the American special ambassador Taylor a note—"strictly personal"—in which he warns of the danger of an "enormous Communistic bloc" that would arise after a Soviet victory, and which would then "unavoidably provoke a war with England and America, regarded by the Communists as a Capitalistic bloc."[53]

We do not know whether the Pope saw this memorandum of Tardini's, or whether the prelate acted on his own—which is difficult to imagine. There are also no notes about what Pius XII really said to Ambassador Taylor in the three private audiences of September 1941. But it is certain— and that is what mattered to Roosevelt and Stalin—that the Vatican finally did not obstruct American military aid to the hard-pressed Soviet Union, which was highly controversial among American Catholics.[54] For, as Tardini informed the American bishops through the apostolic delegate in Washington, "the encyclical *Divini Redemptoris* of 1937 [see p. 170] wanted to condemn only atheistic Communism and not the Russian peo- ple." That the encyclical forbids any cooperation with Communists must be interpreted according to the "exegetical basic norm," namely from the "natural connection" of the Popular Front tactics of the thirties, i.e., do- mestic policy, not foreign policy. The nuncio, however, was to give this interpretation only orally to the American bishops and impress upon them that they should use it "as if it was their own" and "without basing it on the Holy See in any way."[55]

Under the seal of silence, the apostolic delegate in Washington, Cicognani, thereupon asked the Archbishop of Cincinnati (whom he considered the most discreet among the American bishops) to declare in a pastoral letter to be distributed to the press that the anti-Communist encyclical *Divini Redemptoris* "is *not* to be applied to the present moment of armed conflict."[56]

Once again, it was shown in the practical actions of the Vatican's eastern policy that pragmatic considerations had a greater effect upon them than considerations of principle. Of course, not without mixed feelings and scruples—a pang of conscience out of which Pius XII, especially to the outside, laboriously tried to make a virtue: neutrality.

Digressive Remarks: Pius XII's "Impartiality"

Over the Piazza Colonna marched a troop of Italian soldiers— emaciated and wearing thin coats—looking like crumpled cardboard. A woman wept aloud. The crowd looked like a starving, collapsing horse. . . . In the early mass in Maria Sopra Minerva a stranger spoke to me: I was to wait at a certain place, at a certain time, on the plaza of St. Peter's. There the stranger appeared again among the hordes of people. "Excuse me for walking on the right side, and let's go quickly. We must not call attention to ourselves."—Inside, on the steps, I had to ask. "There is treason—even in the Vatican."

A snapshot of Rome, June 1941, shortly before Hitler's armies invaded the Soviet Union. It is described by the German Catholic poet Reinhold Schneider.[57] The Bishop of Berlin Konrad Count von Preysing, who on January 17, 1941, had asked in a letter to Rome whether the Pope could not issue an appeal in favor of the persecuted Jews, had arranged a private audience with Pius XII for the poet, who was close to resistance circles. The poet—as he writes—was deeply moved by his meeting with the Pope: the Pontiff seemed to him to be "only an office," reflecting high spiritual refinement, elevated to the supra-personal. "A man like a ray of light," burdened by sorrow. "Behind him gloomed the night."

From Reinhold Schneider's literary circumlocution and from other information we discover that the poet dared to raise objections to the attitude of the Pope; also to express hope for "change from within"; that he mentioned the "almost devastating" intra-church contradiction between the office of St. Peter and freedom, between obedience and conscience. And what did the Pope answer? He looked upward: "But the power!"

After this audience Reinhold Schneider avoided the "Eternal City" to the end of his days. Two decades later, another poet and moralist, the Protestant Rolf Hochhuth, did not get much farther than Grottaferrata, where the strange Alois Hudal spent his last embittered years—that bishop who had once hoped for salvation from Bolsheviks, Jews and liberals out of a reconciliation of the Hitler movement with the church (see p. 169); who then helped to save many Jews from their murderers, later many murderers from their judges, by obtaining Red Cross passes for them. . . . Only when he spoke of the Pacelli Pope, who had once inspired him, and then dropped him again, did Hudal's *"caritas"* get a little lost. . . . And this was the origin of Rolf Hochhuth's *The Deputy;*[58] the picture of an icy skeptic, of a Pope who—together with the institution that he embodied—no longer allowed himself the luxury of emotions, but only made cold and sober political calculations, with confident arrogance: Hitler's crimes may not be condemned, so that Germany remains "worthy of negotiation" for the West, so that the front against the East does not collapse. . . .

The moral outcry of the Hochhuth drama, at the beginning of the sixties, strengthened the self-righteousness of those Germans who had long been looking for an alibi. But it also acted as a beneficial shock to the self-image of the papal church; archives in Germany and the Vatican were opened. After the radiant Pacelli legend that Hochhuth helped to destroy, the dark one also belongs to the past. This Pope, who outwardly sometimes styled himself as a super-human oracle, was deeply insecure, intimidated and discouraged by the political world in which he lived, by this "most terrible and *complicated* of all wars"—as he called it.

Pius XII's above-average intelligence, which also became a filter of his trust in God, allowed him to fully recognize the moral-political dilemma in which he was entangled—even if for him it was more a theoretical, abstract problem than a practical one, surrounded as he was by unrealistic splendor and Byzantine veneration. He wrote to Archbishop Frings in Cologne:

> ". . . The *superhuman* exertions that are necessary to keep the Holy See *above parties*, and the *sheer inextricable merging* of political and philosophical currents, of power and justice (in the present conflict incomparably more so than in the last World War), so that it is often *painfully difficult to decide* whether reticence and cautious silence are called for or frank speech and strong action: all this torments Us *more bitterly* than the threats to peace and security in Our *own* household. . . ."[59]

Church rationale, which—like reason of state—is more susceptible to the drive for self-preservation than to commands of individual conscience, enabled this priest-diplomat to seek a way out that corresponded to his professional talents: his goal, which he never lost sight of, "not for a moment and in none of Our actions," was to "preserve intact *the impartiality* of the Holy See"[60] —a kind of anxiously preserved virginity in the midst of torn souls and bodies. . . .

This was how Reinhold Schneider met the Pope in June 1941: an iridescent, luminous figure, that in the eyes, tuned to apocalyptic visions, of the pious, historicizing literat, solidified to a Christian manifestation—in its shattering contradiction. Pius XII wrote on September 30 to the Bishop of Berlin, who had recommended Schneider to the Pope (Hitler's armies were just approaching Moscow), that "the general political situation by its difficult and often contradictory character imposes due reticence upon the leader of the universal church in his public statements."[61]

In 1940, when Hitler was only waging war in the west, it did not disturb the Pope if his standard behavior "from which no considerations of any kind will turn Us aside," was called *neutrality*.[62] Two and a half years later, on the day the Germans had lost the battle of Stalingrad, he preferred the expression *impartiality*, because "neutrality could be understood in the sense of passive indifference, which would ill suit the leader of the church in the face of such events. Impartiality means for Us to judge things according to truth and justice, whereby, however, when public statements from Us are concerned, We would take into fullest consideration the situation of the church in the separate countries, in order to spare the Catholics in those places any avoidable difficulties. . . ."[63]

On May 12, 1942, the Pope was informed for the first time about the system of *mass* extermination (*uccissioni in massa*) of Jews from Germany, Poland and the Ukraine.[64] At the end of August 1942, Archbishop Sheptyckyi wrote to him from Lvov (Lemberg) that the German regime was worse than the Bolshevik; the number of murdered Jews in the Ukraine alone had passed 100,000.[65]

On September 18, 1942, Under-Secretary of State Montini, the later Paul VI, noted after a conversation with Count Malvezzi, who had been in the occupied east as an official of the Italian public holding company IRI: "The massacres of the Jews have assumed atrocious and frightening forms and proportions."

On September 26 the American special ambassador Taylor delivered an analogous report of the Geneva office of the Jewish Agency for Palestine. "I believe we have no information that corroborates in particulars this very serious news, do we?" asked Cardinal Maglione. "Yes, there is Count Malvezzi's report," Montini answered.[66]

On October 6 the Pope instructs Monsignore Montini to prepare a short note in answer to the Americans, which states "that the Holy See received news of severe treatment of the Jews, but cannot check the accuracy of all these reports."[67]

On October 7 Father Pirro Scavizzi, who as a military chaplain had on several occasions accompanied an ambulance train of the Knights of Malta to the occupied east, reported to the Vatican: "The elimination of the Jews through mass murder is almost total, without regard for children, not even for infants. . . ." Scavizzi declared in 1964 that he had also reported to the Pope orally about the crimes. "I saw him weep like a child. . . ."[68]

On October 10 Cardinal Maglione nevertheless delivered the note ordered by the Pope to the American chargé d'affaires with the remark that the Holy See knew nothing verifiable, it was using all its resources "to alleviate the sufferings of the non-Aryans."[69]

On April 30, 1943, in a letter to the Bishop of Berlin, Pius XII gives the reason for his silence: "*Ad maiora mala vitanda*"—to prevent greater evil. "The inhumanities that have reached our ears for a long time now, that lie completely outside the realm of serious military necessity, are gradually having a *paralyzing* and horrible effect." Only "refuge in prayer" gives strength to "resist spiritually" such impressions. "Never in the far-reaching and shocking contests among the powers of this earth have the honorable desires of the Popes been put to such a test as now to confront *all* with full impartiality, while simultaneously being careful to uphold the interests of the holy church."[70]

In 1929, in the Lateran Treaties (Art. 24), the Vatican had assumed the obligation "not to interfere in worldly power struggles between other states." Did that exonerate it from any concrete statement even when the immoral character of certain "military actions" of the states was only too clear? Since the opening of the Vatican Archives on World War II, we know that it was not primarily the anti-Communist, anti-Soviet motive that kept the Pope silent. He was also silent, for example, when the anti-Hitler coalition developed terror bombings of civilians as a systematic weapon of war, when the Germans attacked Norway, occupied Denmark, assaulted Yugoslavia, when the Soviets liquidated the Baltic states, the Americans occupied Iceland, the Japanese attacked Pearl Harbor out of the blue.

"I am afraid history will reproach the Holy See for following a policy of convenience for itself, and not much more," wrote Cardinal Tisserant, Prefect of the Eastern Church Congregation, in June 1940 in a private letter,[71] and added: "That is extremely sad, above all for those who lived under Pius XI. . . . Our superiors (*nos governants*) will not comprehend the nature of the real conflict, and they stubbornly insist on imagining that it is a war like in the old days. . . ."

But even when Pius XII had the "nature of the true conflict," deeply disturbing and frightening, clearly in view, he still held back. Not for convenience; the position that he laboriously and rigidly tried to hold on to while he was called upon to bless now an anti-Soviet, now an anti-Nazi crusade was anything but convenient. It would have been simpler to take the part of the probable victor. Of course, one could also be seriously mistaken in this, as the repeated turns of the fortunes of war showed.

But not acting, not taking a stand, is no protection against error either. Perhaps it is for that reason that the Pope, during the entire duration of the Second World War, allowed organs of publication that were more or less close to the curia, with which they identified, but from which they could also distance themselves, to use a more open, often harsher, language. Many post-war authors who *before* the publication of the Vatican documents wanted to set right the criticism of papal "impartiality" relied on them.[72] Thus harsh anti-Soviet and anti-Fascist judgments could be quoted from the *Osservatore Romano* that for the most part stemmed from the initiative of one of the editors, the later long-time Christian Democrat Minister of Justice of Italy, Professor Guido Gonella. The assistant director of the paper, Federico Alessandrini (in the seventies the head of the Vatican press center), attacked the National Socialists under the pseudonym *Renano*—in the mask of a German collaborator. And Radio Vatican, under the direction of the Jesuit General, repeatedly delivered such strong blows in all directions that the Pope—as we know today—often found it necessary to apply the brakes.

How problematical even such non-official statements were is shown by an example that leads us from this digression directly back to the theme of Ostpolitik and at the same time invalidates reproaches that to this day come primarily from those conservative Catholic circles that never tire of accusing the Vatican of a too soft, too careful position regarding Communist regimes. At the beginning of 1941 the suffragan bishop of Kaunas repeatedly requested, by direct post and also by confidential routes via the Berlin nunciature, that the Vatican radio station

"... might cease its Saturday programs in the Lithuanian language; they only cause us misfortune and are useless. ... Above all we ask that no anti-Bolshevik propaganda be broadcast in Lithuanian (lectures on Marxism, Leninism, anecdotes, etc.). ... Such broadcasts only provoke the state authorities here and greatly damage the already oppressed church in Lithuania. ... This 'information' is after all very far removed from true, exact reality. What we expect are reports from the Catholic world, commentaries on Catholic doctrine. ... What is happening here, we already know. ..."[73]

No "Harvest" for Rome in Hitler's Russia

Exactly a week had passed since the German armies had attacked the Soviet Union, supported by Slovakian, Hungarian, Rumanian divisions and soon also by an Italian army corps, when on June 29, 1941, Tardini noted at the Vatican Secretariat of State:

"It would be not only necessary but urgent for the Holy See and for the welfare of souls that someone go to Russia, to the Baltic countries and the Ukraine. When the Germans have finally penetrated there, it will be impossible for a representative of the Holy See to enter these regions. Therefore almost the only way is to use the Italian (or Hungarian) troops. ... We must move very quickly in order not to miss any opportunity that offers itself now and that shortly may no longer exist."

Five days later the preparations are already in high gear, under the title "Apostolate in Russia." Cardinal Tisserant of the Congregation for Eastern Rite Churches and Jesuit General Ledóchowski are alarmed. They are in the process of seeking out suitable priests and—with the cooperation of the Capuchin and Basilian Generals—working out a "plan of action." The Pope himself gets involved on July 4; Ledóchowski, for the record, remarks after a conversation with him that one "must be very careful not to arouse the impression of any connection between the dispatch of the priests and the entry of the army, and not to injure the patriotic feeling of the Russians."[74]

Did the Vatican then after all have the intention of following Hitler's military footsteps? In the west, the rumor even arose that the Vatican had made a "secret agreement" of this sort with the Germans, a tale that still in recent times—and even in scientific garb—was disseminated in the east.[75] Secretary of State Cardinal Maglione could deny it in good conscience to the British government back in March 1942. Also the German documents available today show unequivocally how right Monsignore Tardini was when from the beginning he set no store by any concessions from the Germans. Naturally, even if there could be no question of a Vatican-Hitler agreement about a dispatch of priests, it was still clear that the Vatican would have gladly jumped at it if Hitler had offered even a "little finger."

Hitler was no "crusader," and the Vatican had no intention of supporting his supposed "crusade"—as we have seen. But it suited the always pragmatic calculations of the curia and church reasoning to at least make the most of opportunity: would it not be an "act of justice" if they could send twenty Catholic priests from the Baltic into the occupied Soviet territory, after that number of Orthodox had been allowed in? Nuncio Orsenigo in Berlin had so impressed this argument upon Secretary of State von Weizsäcker that the latter made inquiries to the "Reich Ministry for the occupied eastern territories."[76]

This was the "right" address, for the chief of this new ministry was— Alfred Rosenberg, the most determined foe of Christianity among the top Nazi functionaries. His appointment had already "called forth consternation" in the Vatican, as Ambassador Bergen reported.[77]

On July 16, at a conference which Rosenberg also attended, Hitler had already decided that "any missionary activity (by the church) was absolutely out of the question";[78] he had raged violently against Franz von Papen, his former vice-chancellor and concordat signatory who (as ambassador to Ankara in close contact with the nuncio there, Roncalli, the later Pope John XXIII) had pleaded for the opening of Catholic churches in the occupied Soviet Union. Five days later, the chief of the Reich Security Office, Reinhard Heydrich, could report on a "large-scale" plan of the "anti-German curial Cardinal Tisserant." Heydrich had learned something about the fact that they wanted to send along with the Italians, and other allies, military chaplains with special instructions:

"These priests are on the one hand to prepare the ground for Vatican work in occupied Russian territory, but on the other, simultaneously to explore the field in order to work out further plans for the Vatican's work abroad." The long-term goal was to encircle Germany with Catholic countries and "to prepare a later aggressive front against German territory"[79] from Russia.

As fantastically grotesque as the reasoning process was, the German secret service had apparently received such exact particulars from an agent in the Vatican about its plans. In a whole series of orders in August, September and November 1941, the supreme command of the Wehrmacht then forbade the field chaplains "any official church activity or religious propaganda toward the civilian population," and even forbade civilians to participate in field services. One must watch out, among the Italian, Hungarian and Slovakian military chaplains, that "none of the Catholic priests remain in the country." The danger was, so said a memorandum of the Reich Security Office, that a catholicization of Russia "would result in a polonization" [!] and that the Vatican "will become the actual war profiteer in Russian territory that is being fought for with German blood."

Still, all this ideological hysteria was not altogether without cause. The Foreign Office in Berlin discovered through an advisor in the Rosenberg ministry: "Orthodox and Catholic priests were allowed to enter the occupied Russian territory temporarily by *permission of Wehrmacht units which however were not competent*. By order of the Eastern Ministry these priests were deported again." The actual motive for this, he said, was that "the Catholics should not be allowed to break new ground in the former Russian territory," but it would be well "not to reveal the real reason" to the papal nuncio.[80] He should instead be convinced that the Vatican could not "reap any fruits" only because it did not sanction the anti-Bolshevik war.[81]

What could become of the "Tisserant plan" under all these circumstances can be imagined. The Cardinal, who—as a former officer—to the end of his life loved willful bravura gestures, according to his own later statements (to the historian Robert A. Graham S. J.) had only been able to send *eight* priests of the eastern rite, in all, into the occupied Soviet regions, disguised as civilian "interpreters" for the Italian army in Russia. Only five of them probably became active at all, but even they could not dare even to hold the mass publicly. The uniformed Italian military priests were soon subjected to the same restrictions as the German. They had to be satisfied with passing out religious pictures here and there that were printed in Russian and Ukrainian, on the Vatican's orders, and had also been given to the Italian soldiers.

Only the Rumanian Monsignore Markus Glaser, a Russian German by birth and a Rumanian citizen, had a little success: The Rumanian dictator Antonescu, at the request of the Bucharest nuncio, allowed him to install himself in the old Catholic church in Odessa. (He died in 1950, after interrogation by Rumanian Stalinists, in a prison in Jassy.) Naturally the survivors of the Vatican Ostpolitik of the twenties and thirties also hoped to get back to the Soviet Union from their exile in the Baltic. Bishops Sloskans and Matulionis (see pp. 94 and 131) attempted this at the end of 1941, at the suggestion of the Vilna Archbishop Jalbrzykowski, to whom the Vatican had assigned ecclesiastical jurisdiction for White Russia. But: "In practice only Orthodox priests (*solum sacerdotes schismatici*) are allowed in there. In the past year many priests whom I sent to the regions of Minsk, Mogilev, Vitebsk and Smolensk were removed again by the German civil authorities. In Minsk itself there are over 17,000 Catholics, in the surrounding area over 50,000. . . . Two priests who were active there were deported for political reasons to a destination unknown to me. The situation of the Catholics who live across the Dvina River is better, where the administration is not in civilian, but in military hands. . . . An example is the Jesuit Father Mirski, who has his seat near the St. Josefat church of Polock, in the building of the Jesuit college that the Orthodox had occupied for over a hundred years. . . . Between August and December 1941, 6,892 people were baptized, 114 marriages solemnized, and 39 people, after instruction, brought into the true church from the schism. . . ."[82]

This is from a report that Jalbrzykowski wrote on February 14, 1942, from Vilna to the Secretary of State Cardinal Maglione. When the letter reached Rome via roundabout routes four and a half months later, the zealous Polish archbishop had already been banned from Vilna to a village. The German authorities removed the inconvenient Bishop Sloskans to a cloister in Bavaria. Matulionis was entrusted with a Lithuanian bishopric and did not get back into the Soviet Union until the Stalinists, after their return in 1946, sent him to Siberia for ten years. . . .

Archbishop Sheptyckyi, the Ukrainian-Catholic Metropolitan, informed the Pope from Lemberg in August 1942 that "we will support the German army which freed us from the Bolshevik regime, until it brings the war to a good end that—God granting—once and for all will conquer atheistic and militant Communism." But he soon had to realize as well that his admiration for the "liberators" was not mutual. As early as November he indicated that "our trials are not yet over" and that the possibilities of "leading our separated brothers of the Greater Ukraine into the unity of the church. . . . are almost zero." Still, in the group around the Lemberg Uniate Metropolitan Sheptyckyi, sparks of the old missionary hopes glowed again. His episcopal coadjutor Slipyj, whom the Vatican had only reluctantly and provisorily approved as "exarch of the Greater Ukraine" (see pp. 197-8), wrote to Cardinal Tisserant in Rome on April 12, 1942, that conditions in the Ukraine were of course extremely difficult (*nimis difficiles*), but he had nevertheless succeeded in installing two parish priests in Kiev; he himself was trying to get to Kiev. He soon gave up. The "exarch of White Russia," the Jesuit Antonin Niemancewycz, was arrested right after his arrival in Minsk by the German police and executed soon thereafter. The "exarch of Volynia" Nicholas Czarneckyj's attempt to get there also came to nothing. And Archbishop Sheptyckyi had to admit to the Pope, in a letter (dated August 29/31, 1942) that is among the most moving documents of Catholic church history, how terribly he had deceived himself:

> "Today the whole country is agreed that the German regime, perhaps to a higher degree than the Bolshevist, is evil, indeed even diabolical. For half a year not a day has passed that the most horrible crimes have not been committed. The Jews are the first victims. . . . The Bolshevist regime is being continued, spread and intensified. . . . The village inhabitants are treated like colonial negros. . . . It is simply as if a band of madmen or rabid wolves were throwing themselves upon the poor nation. . . . It will take much freely sacrificed blood to atone for that shed as a result of these crimes. Your Holiness three years ago refused me the grace of an apostolic blessing, by which You were to have dedicated me to die for the salvation of my diocese. . . . I did not insist upon it. . . . I believe that I lost the best and perhaps the only opportunity for it under the Bolsheviks. . . . These three years have taught me that I am not worthy of such a death. . . ."[83]

The Lemberg Metropolitan, who wrote these lines with a trembling hand, was not yet at the end of his eventful life; but in the last-quoted documents is reflected something of the last act of a tragedy that had begun in 1917, under the proud title of "Missionization of Russia," with the illusion that Lenin's revolution would somehow prepare the ground for the Roman church. Now it was approaching its end—with the destruction of a different illusion: that Hitler's predatory war could create space for religious conversion and renewal (see also documentary appendix, Nr. 4).

Stalin Needs Religion—Not Rome?

On the very same day that the German armies attacked the Soviet Union, the two Jesuits Nestrow and Ciszek (a Russian and a Polish-American) were arrested in the Urals. On Sheptyckyi's orders, they had let themselves be recruited in Lemberg in 1940 as forestry workers, with false names and papers, in order to get deep into Russia. Their hopes of somehow being able to practice ministry were bitterly disappointed. And now they sat in the Lubianka prison in Moscow (across from St. Ludwig's), where no one would believe that they were not "German spies." And when the secret police finally believed they had exposed them as "spies for the Vatican," because they had actually wanted to conduct secret ministerial and missionary work,[84] the Kremlin leadership, hard pressed by Hitler, was already trying to persuade its new American allies of something of which the Americans were also trying to convince the Vatican: that there was religious freedom in the Soviet Union, even for Catholics.

What did it actually look like on the other side of the military front in the east? With a list of simple facts, the Vatican had disclosed to the American special ambassador on September 20, 1941, that—contrary to President Roosevelt's optimistic assumptions (see p. 209)—the "anti-religious attitude amongst the Bolsheviks [had persisted] at least until a few weeks ago"; in the entire Soviet Union there were only two Catholic churches open, in Leningrad and Moscow, of which the latter—although it lay across from the central police station—"in the course of a few months was violated five times by nocturnal thefts and sacrilegious profanations."[85]

Taylor thereupon asked his colleague Averell Harriman, who was negotiating about war aid with Stalin and Molotov in Moscow for a week at the end of September, to "bring about a modification" in Soviet religious policies. Harriman made an effort. "They all agreed at least by nodding their heads," he reported by wire to Roosevelt. Soviet Ambassador Umanski had even assured him that the restrictions on freedom of worship would be "moderated." Umanski's further promise of an official gesture in this direction was kept: the Moscow government spokesman Salomon Abramovitch Losovski agreed on October 4 with Roosevelt's opinion that the "religious element" within and outside the Soviet Union had significance for the power of resistance in the country. Not exactly a Marxist admission! Nevertheless, Harriman left Moscow with the impression that "the Soviets are putting us off with fair words . . . without, however, really changing their present practice." At a dinner in the Kremlin, Molotov had asked the ambassador confidentially whether Roosevelt, as an intelligent man, was really so pious. . . . But from Stalin's toast, in which he literally cited "God's help," no one drew such conclusions. . . .[86]

Before his departure from Moscow, Harriman spoke with Father Leopold Braun, the American pastor of St. Ludwig's; two letters from Braun, of the 5th and 27th of October 1941, were transmitted to the Vatican by the apostolic delegate in Washington. We do not know their wording (the Vatican document publication is withholding that secret), but we do know their content—also through unpublished memoirs of Braun's.[87] The pastor in Moscow could report few, but still remarkable, changes in the situation:

Many Orthodox churches were opened; the Soviet press now also reproached the Germans with destroying "religious monuments"; the papers of the Atheists' Union (*Besboshnik, Antireligiosnik* and *Atheist*), suspended publication; *Pravda* suddenly mentioned religious events unpolemically; the former private residence of the German ambassador was given to the Moscow Metropolitan—his appeal for resistance, which the Russians followed enthusiastically, had apparently impressed Stalin. On the whole, the nationalistic and patriotic was now taking over more and more from the Marxist-Leninist, to such a degree that the American special envoy Taylor, a year later, thought he could convince the Vatican that "Communism, as such, is passing."[88]

Father Braun did not abandon himself to such deception; he clearly saw the opportunistic element in Soviet behavior, but he now recognized a process that had begun years ago—basically since Stalin's victory over Trotsky: the development of the Soviet Union from a great world-revolutionary, international power to the "national Communist" Russian one. And in this Father Leopold Braun saw at least a "favorable chance" for the Vatican to undertake direct steps with the Soviet government, a new attempt at a *modus vivendi* for the Catholics—especially now that Stalin found it so necessary to make a good impression.

It was questionable whether Stalin's modified attitude, his war-inspired return to the Russian tradition, really offered the Vatican a starting point; for the Orthodox church, which gained a little breathing space from this, saw itself, now as always, as "anti-Roman." Could Stalin then have any interest in frightening them with "Catholicism"? But it was not this consideration that held the Vatican back. Pius XII and his curial diplomats did not in the least recognize the significant ideological—by no means only tactical!—change. They refused to even test its seriousness and magnitude. Father Braun had advised it, but Monsignore Tardini attributed this to only a "nationalistic emotion" of the American priest and sighed in the memorandum: "It is unfortunate when missionaries interfere in political questions!"[89]

Thus the French Dominican Michel Florent, who had wanted to settle in Moscow in the middle of December 1941 as a "representative of General de Gaulle," could not count on much understanding, either. He had had to leave his parish in Leningrad (see p. 79) when the Germans approached. Now the Vatican detained him from returning to the Soviet Union: "The good people will take offence at seeing a priest accredited to Stalin; Moscow's opponents will blame the Holy See and let it take the consequences," Monsignore Tardini feared.[90] Later, in July 1942, the representation of "Free France" offered to negotiate a rapprochement between the Vatican and the Kremlin. Had there been any inspiration for this from the Soviet side?

Even decades after the Second World War, a supposed "letter from Stalin to the Pope" haunted many history books. The leader of the Kremlin supposedly gave Pius XII assurances for the Catholic church and suggested the assumption of relations—as compensation for the fact that the Vatican had just exchanged ambassadors with an Axis partner of Hitler's, Japan. The news had first been given to the world on March 3, 1942, by the Italian news agency "Urbe" (an appendage of the state agency "Stefani"). The Anglo-Saxon press greedily snatched it up (to demonstrate Stalin's good will), but so did the German press (to cast a shadow on the Pope). Still, the church of the Uniate Catholics in Kiev, which had been closed before Easter by the Germans, was opened again on the basis of "Stalin's letter to the Pope."[91]

The Soviets themselves were silent, the Vatican made denials in all directions and was convinced—as internal documents show today[92]—that the false information had been launched with the intention of luring the curia out of its reserve. But by whom? The perpetrators could be as varied as the motives were conflicting. We cannot even completely rule out that someone in the Vatican had given the rumor to the Roman agency—be it to force the Secretariat of State to deny it and thus prevent the Soviets from taking such a step, or be it with the intention of giving Moscow a hint that such a Soviet initiative was expected.

Whatever the shape of the speculation behind it, the event fit the current picture in 1942: wouldn't the western allies be acutely interested in such a step by Stalin?—Up to now there is no indication that they would have directly urged him to do something of the kind. Stalin himself, hard-pressed by Hitler's offensive which in the summer of 1942 advanced the Germans up to Stalingrad and the Caucasus, could only have *one* reason for putting out feelers to the Vatican: he was about to equip the Catholic Poles, whom he had put into prison camps or deported beyond the Urals in 1939/40, as auxiliary divisions. The Polish army bishop Gawlina, with his seat in London, prepared in spring 1942 for a trip to the Soviet Union to visit these troops. (We will report on this unusual event in the next chapter.)

"The Vatican is valued by the Soviet leadership for its moral strength," said Professor Stanislaw Kot, a Polish cultural historian who had spent a year in Moscow as ambassador of the exile government in London. On his return trip at the beginning of August 1942 he met the apostolic delegate Marina in Teheran and shared this judgment with him orally.[93] Kot also gave this advice: "I myself assume that the moment would be favorable for a rapprochement. . . . And if you asked me 'why,' since there is no religious freedom anyway and the priest must live practically on the edge of society, then I would say: You are right, but the mission of the church often is fulfilled under greater difficulties, and if the representatives of the

Vatican really stay out of domestic politics (Stalin will not endure anyone interfering in the domestic affairs of the country), then a step forward can be taken for the welfare of many Catholics who live there. . . ."

Whether Kot's remarks can be traced to Soviet intentions of sounding out the situation cannot be definitely ascertained. In any case, during the same summer of 1942, the apostolic delegate in Syria, Leprétre, also reported that the Soviets had given the French representation (de Gaulle's) in Moscow to understand that they were interested in an agreement with the Vatican. The head of the French mission in Moscow, Roger Garreau, even offered himself as mediator. For the Roman curia—with all its skepticism—this was still worth consideration. For the first time, Under-Secretary of State Tardini drew up a rough draft. In a documentary note for the Pope he wrote on August 8, 1942:

After so long a period of persecution, the "almost complete destruction" of Catholicism and "the repeated strengthening of atheism as a basic tenet of Communism," it would be absolutely necessary "to establish in practice *how* religious freedom is really being respected and protected by the Russian government. When an adequate test period (*periodo di esperimento*) has expired, the Holy See could decide on its position in full knowledge of the circumstances. Naturally, such a decision—per se and as viewed from the outside—would have to appear and be solely motivated by higher religious interests, not by political advantage or favors."[94]

A *modus vivendi* with Moscow was thus not totally excluded—and this corresponded to the continuity of Vatican Ostpolitik. But it was not the Soviet *willingness* to make concessions (which Father Braun had stimulated) that was to be tested, but rather a *proof* of good will from the Soviets—"payment in advance," we might say today. To be sure, the over-cautious Pope considered it advisable not to tell the apostolic delegate in Syria exactly even these very reserved thoughts for transmission to Moscow; he ordered only an abridged version sent to him as a directive.

Thus an agreement by the Vatican with the Soviet side of the Russian front was as little in sight as one with the German. But here too, not only Pius XII's officious "neutrality" was to blame, but also the lack of an obliging, friendly partner. Or was Moscow indeed more favorably inclined than Berlin?

VII

For Fear Of Stalin's Victory: No Dialogue, 1944-1949

"Papal Divisions" and a Priest Close to Stalin

"The Pope! The Pope! How many divisions has he got?", Stalin is supposed to have asked a French head of government back in the thirties, and at the Yalta conference in 1945 he repeated the ironic question, which was probably one of his favorite sayings. However, in 1942, when the Germans were 130 kilometers from Moscow and beginning to advance from the Don to the Volga, and the Soviet Union desired nothing more ardently than a second front, the Western Allies, at Hitler's back, there was something almost akin to "papal divisions" in the Soviet Union: those Polish divisions under General Wladyslaw Anders, which Stalin permitted not only 32 Catholic military chaplains, but even a visit from an episcopal visitator vested with papal commissions and mandates.

On April 28, 1942, a Catholic bishop re-entered the Soviet capital for the first time since Michel d'Herbigny's last trip to Moscow. It was Józef Gawlina, the Polish army bishop, who had come from London via Teheran. He spent a few days with Father Leopold Braun, the sole Catholic priest in Moscow, then informed himself about the situation in Kujbyšev (to which the Soviet government had withdrawn), and settled for a few months in the summer in Jangijul, near Tashkent.[1]

Here, in the Uzbek capitol, General Anders had set up his headquarters nearly a year earlier. At the beginning of August 1941, a few days after the Polish exile prime minister General Sikorski had signed an agreement with

225

the Soviets in London, Anders had been released from the Lubianka in Moscow and metamorphosed from a prisoner into an ally of Stalin's. With this rapid reversal, made possible by Hitler's attack on Russia, General Sikorski had achieved something for his country that could really no longer be hoped for: Not only were tens of thousands of prisoners of war released, but also almost 1.5 million Poles who had been deported from East Poland in two great actions—in 1939 and 1941—and held in penal or labor camps in the far reaches of the Soviet Union, could now take heart again.[2] General Anders was to muster six divisions with almost 100,000 men, which he promised to put into action on the side of the Soviets—who would equip them. When Anders met with Sikorski in Teheran at the beginning of December 1941, the papal delegate Marina used the opportunity to also inquire about the military ministry.[3]

"That will be just as at home," answered General Anders.

"Did you agree on that with the Soviet authorities?" asked Monsignore Marina.

"That was not even necessary; no one ever questioned it. Anyway, although we are fighting alongside the Russians, in our divisions everything is Polish: language, organization, religion; we can practice our religion in complete freedom and independence. It even occurs, not infrequently, that I have a high Russian official visiting on a Sunday, and must excuse myself for half an hour to fulfill the duties of a good Christian with my soldiers; out of consideration, my guests then come along to mass as well. . . ."

Bishop Gawlina, who arrived at Anders' headquarters on June 7, 1942, came with the firm intention of regulating and guaranteeing the civilian ministry for the Polish Catholics in the Soviet Union too. He brought along 50 field altars, 572 Bibles, 53,500 crosses, 784,000 pictures of saints, and a lot of money. The pious pictures showed Saint Andrzej Bobola beside Mary—which may not have exactly delighted informed Soviets (cf. p. 191).

Of course, everything had already become more difficult for the Poles by this time. While the Soviets wished to engage them as quickly as possible at the retreating front, General Anders kept his army behind the lines with the argument that the mustering was not yet completed and that he wanted to deploy his soldiers only as a unified army corps, and not dispersed at various sections of the front. Probably this was more of a pretext; the mood in the Anders army was a mixture of lust for battle against the Germans, and malicious joy at the Soviet defeats. Stalin, who now put the Poles on shorter rations (like the non-combatant Red Army members), was finally not all that displeased by the desire of his troublesome allies to be transferred to the western front against Hitler, via Persia. As early as March, 44,000 Poles left the Soviet Union—many of them filled with a "wild hatred," as the papal delegate in Teheran, who met them, reported.

Bishop Gawlina could nevertheless report to the Cardinal Secretary of State in Rome, on July 1, 1942, that for the moment they had managed to have about half of the Polish priests released from Soviet prisons, 107 of whom were available for family ministry. One would probably have to declare them military chaplains as well. Some were prepared to remain as priests in Russia even after the withdrawal of the Polish army—*"sub omni conditione"* (under any conditions).[4]

The bishop, who traveled around between Jangijul and Samarkand for almost a month, administered the sacrament of confirmation not only to 1100 soldiers, but also to 1496 children. He saw with astonishment that even in the Sóviet Union, there were now schools with religious instruction for the displaced Poles, but the summation that he sent to Rome—in Latin—was this:

> "Nevertheless, the religious situation is as it appears to the Holy See (*talis qualem videt S. Sedis*). The Orthodox request baptisms from our priests, which our army chaplains refuse them, for fear that religious work in favor of Catholics would be completely forbidden to Catholics. . . . To illuminate the situation, I would like to add: NKVD officials asked me whether I am a Jesuit and whether I am bound to the Holy Father only in the faith or also in political questions. In the city of Kermin, a major of the NKVD greeted me during a dinner with our officers with a long address—but he closed the window first. Still, the next day there was much discussion among the inhabitants of Kermin that he had titled me 'Wasze Preswiaszczenstwo' [Your Grace]. In other places, the NKVD officials conducted themselves correctly, but reservedly. . . . To NKVD questions as to when I intend to leave, I did not give very clear answers. For I also want to visit the civilian population that lives far outside the military areas."

Gawlina does not seem to have thought for a moment of negotiating with the Soviets. The only instructions he had from the Vatican which would have made such contacts necessary concerned the question of the Italian and German prisoners of war. The nuncio in Teheran, who delivered these instructions to Gawlina, regretted that he could not undertake anything himself, since he had "no contact whatsoever with the Soviet embassy"; the Polish ambassador, however, who knew his Soviet colleague, had discouraged him: "My dear Monsignore, don't have any illusions. . . . The Russians themselves do not know how many prisoners they have. . . ."

The apostolic delegate in Turkey, Angelo Roncalli (later Pope John XXIII), had previously not let himself be deterred from seeking contacts "with people from both sides of the river," in the hope that "my little ship will stay afloat between the opposing currents." Of course, it was not on his own initiative that Roncalli sought contacts with the Soviets, but on direct instruction from the Vatican. A handwritten note of Tardini's was found in the archive of the Secretariat of State (ADSS, vol. 9, doc. no. 100):

Copies of your letters have been forwarded to the
Department of State.

It is noted that your letters of December 12 and December 16, touching on internal political problems of Hungary,
requested the assistance of the United States Government in
altering certain conditions which Your Eminence deplores.
In this connection you are of course aware of my Government's
long standing policy of non-interference in the internal
affairs of other nations. This policy has proven over a
long period of time and through many trying situations the
best guarantee of spontaneous, vigorous and genuine democratic development. It will be clear to Your Eminence that
it necessarily precludes action by this Legation which could
properly be construed as interference in Hungarian domestic
affairs or which lies outside the normal functions of diplomatic missions.

I should like to take this opportunity to assure Your
Eminence that I shall continue to welcome the expression of
your views on any matters to which you may desire to draw my
attention.

". . . inform the Russian government through Mons. Roncalli that the
Holy See—in order to fulfill its charitable mission—would be grateful for
lists of the Italian prisoners of war in Russia?—Mons. Roncalli is a
'*pacioccone*' [Italian dialect expression for a man who is popular with
everyone] and has good relations with diplomats, even the Russians. . ."

Roncalli even visited the Soviet Consul Nikolas Ivanov in Istanbul on
March 22, 1943 and suggested exchanging lists of prisoners; the Polish
ambassador had arranged the contact.[5] But only a month later, all hope of
such a contact disappeared. The discovery of mass graves in Katyn (near
Smolensk), where thousands of Polish officers, prisoners of war in Soviet
camps since 1939, were murdered, led to the rupture of relations between
Moscow and the Polish government in exile in London. What Bishop
Gawlina had tried to establish, and what was surprisingly easy in favor of
the Polish civilian population in Soviet Uzbekistan, now collapsed: after
the withdrawal of the Anders army, pastoral possibilities fell back to the
"normal" condition in Soviet Russia (that is, no religious instruction and
high, hardly affordable payments for the maintenance of the church
buildings).

"We have now begun the battle against the Bolsheviks, and we hope that
we have the Vatican on our side." This pronouncement of the Polish Exile
Prime Minister General Sikorski on June 16, 1943, was reported by the
apostolic delegate in Baghdad.[6] Sikorski had flown to Iraq in order to calm
down the Polish troops in the Near East that had withdrawn from the
Soviet Union, and ready them for action. After the "Katyn case," they
feared contributing to a Soviet victory if they fought against the Germans.
Sikorski had even been warned that because he had formed the Polish-

Soviet alliance in June 1941, he could not be sure of his life among his compatriots. Politically, he was still convinced even now that Poland, in the end, could not re-emerge *against* the will of the Soviet Union, especially now that Hitler's defeat had become almost certain after the battle of Stalingrad. Was Sikorski's remark to the Vatican delegate, then, perhaps only tactical? The delegate gave an evasive answer to Sikorski's anti-Soviet outbreak and promised only "moral support."

Two and a half weeks later Sikorski was dead. Under circumstances that were never quite explained, his plane crashed on the return flight from the Near East, over Gibraltar. Shortly thereafter, on July 15, 1943, the western correspondents in Moscow were invited to a pine forest on the banks of the Oka, where 12,000 Polish soldiers, freshly equipped with national uniforms and Soviet weapons, were to be put under oath: the "Kosciuśzko" division. Stalin finally had "his" Poles. The commander was a colonel who had not withdrawn with the Anders army, Zygmunt Berling. The political tone was set by a temperamental woman, Wanda Wasilewska, of the Communist-led Moscow "Union of Polish Patriots." The two mistrusted each other, because the image of a Poland friendly to the Soviets, but free, which the colonel entertained honorably, was only a tactic to the Communist woman. But they were agreed that nothing Polish could be "performed" without Catholicism.

Thus the swearing-in ceremonies, to the astonishment of all the foreign guests, began with a solemn mass in the open air. No one knew that Franciszek Kubsz, the young Polish priest who celebrated it, had been abducted from a village parsonage in East Poland by Soviet partisans. To his own astonishment, they did not harm him, but promoted him—to a Polish captain, as befitted an army chaplain. It was Father Kubsz who administered the oath to the soldiers in which they promised to fight for the liberation of Poland—and remain loyal to the Soviet allies. . . .[7]

Alexander Serow (specialist for "church affairs" in the Soviet Ministry of the Interior) had worked in vain on the Jesuit Walter Ciszek, who was a prisoner in Moscow's Lubianka, to go to the "Kosciuszko" division as an army chaplain. As a Pole, an American, and a "Vatican spy," he would perhaps have been able—so the Soviets thought—to establish the necessary relationships. . . . But Ciszek, more honorable than clever, even refused the tempting offer to "go to Rome and arrange a concordat between the Pope and the Soviet Union." The wireless apparatus they wanted him to take along made him suspicious. . . .[8]

Was Stalin really interested in a serious contact with the Vatican? The closer his armies came to Poland in 1943/44, the more urgently arose the question of the future of this Catholic country which—there was no doubt in Moscow about this—the Vatican had always regarded as a "bulwark" against the heretical or atheistic East. Given his sober political calculations, but also in consideration of his Western allies, Stalin had every reason to handle the "Polish question" with kid gloves. Determined never again to endure a Poland hostile to the Soviet Union, he had to try to "neutralize" Catholicism without engaging the Vatican, which would not be responsive anyway. Therefore he did *not* turn, as the situation suggested, to Father Leopold Braun, the only actual, even if inofficial, representative of the Vatican in Moscow, but rather, after Father Ciszek had refused, used another Polish-American priest whom chance offered to him:

Muscovites did not believe their eyes when they opened *Pravda* on April 28, 1944; there they saw a photo of Stalin and Molotòv with a Catholic priest, Pastor Stanislaw Orlemański from Springfield, Massachusetts, who had come "to study the problems of the Poles and the Polish army in the Soviet Union." In the evening of the same day, the American parish priest was interviewed by Radio Moscow; he had not only found a friend in Stalin, he said; he also had to "make the historical observation that—as the future will show—Stalin is a friend of the Roman-Catholic church." Even sympathetic observers—for instance the British BBC correspondent in Moscow[9]—had the impression that Orlemański was "either a fool or a joker"—if the latter, then someone who was playing a practical joke on the Kremlin. . . .

Actually, Orlemański meant it seriously; the ingenuous cleric, whose three brothers were also Catholic priests, was quite unsuspecting. He had applied for an entry visa at the Soviet general consulate in New York to study the "religious question in Poland." Thereupon Stalin had invited him to discuss "religious persecution all over the world" with him. On April 17, 1944, with the permission of the U.S. Secretary of State Cordell Hull, Orlemański had flown to Moscow via Alaska and Siberia, and had twice spoken with Stalin for over two hours. In a letter to President Roosevelt, of course, Stalin had confirmed that Orlemański was regarded by the Soviet government as a "private citizen," but on May 6, Stalin even sent his "dear friend" Roosevelt a special telegram of thanks that he had made Orlemański's trip possible. For Stalin had every reason to be satisfied:

Orlemański had no sooner returned than he gave a press conference in Detroit on May 12 and related how "openly and democratically" Stalin had treated him. He had spoken "man to man" with the Kremlin ruler and pointed out to him that the most important question at present was religion. Stalin had answered with a question:

"How would you proceed in this? what would you do?"

Orlemański: "Do you think that collaboration with the Holy Father, Pope Pius XII, is possible in the struggle against oppression and persecution of the Catholic church?"

Stalin: "I believe that that is possible."

Orlemański: "Do you consider it admissible that the Soviet government is conducting a policy of force and persecution in regard to the Catholic church?"

Stalin: "As a defender of freedom of conscience and worship, I regard such a policy as inadmissible and out of the question."

Surprisingly quickly, on May 14, *Pravda* picked up Orlemański's statements and thus gave them an official stamp. But this did not help the poor pastor from Massachusetts either; on the contrary: his bishop, Thomas O'Leary in Springfield, suspended him from priestly duties, sent him to a cloister for penance, and thus documented before the world that Stalin had wasted his time on an outsider. Of course, to this day we do not know whether the Pope or his delegate in Washington, Amleto Cicognani (later Cardinal Secretary of State), insisted on Orlemański's being disciplined; it is certain that the Vatican discounted Stalin because they considered his "gesture" completely unserious, especially because it could hardly be assumed that Stalin should have been so foolish as to not see through the insignificance of the person he was talking to. Had the Kremlin ruler, to whom other confidential and diplomatic channels had been completely available, not quite deliberately preferred the propagandistically effective, but ultimately non-committal conversation with the unsuspecting American pastor?

For Stalin had certain things to consider; since 1942 he had been supported in the "Great Patriotic War" by the Russian Orthodox church, which in 1943 he had allowed to elect a patriarch. The Moscow patriarchate was not unaware of the missionary ambitions—still countenanced by the Vatican—that were being pursued by the Lemberg Metropolitan Sheptyckyi (see pp. 197-8), who was now fearfully watching the return of the Red Army.[10] Of course, Stalin was not disinclined—and could also afford—to hold out the prospect of certain concessions to the Catholic church of the Latin rite in Poland and the Baltic. In the Western Ukraine, after its recapture by the Soviets, a few churches of the Latin rite had even been opened, and the Germans, when they saw that, two weeks before they had to surrender Minsk to the Soviets again had admitted another Polish Catholic priest there.[11] But the fate of the Catholic *Eastern* church of the Slavic rite was already sealed. For how could Stalin better (and for himself more cheaply!) reward the wartime loyalty of the Orthodox church than by raising its hopes for the return of its sons lost to Rome in the Ukraine and White Russia?—For even Stalin, the "renegade" seminarian, believed the old traditional equation: Catholic=Polish, only Polish.

However, the fact that the Vatican could not negotiate the planned liquidation of the Uniate church in Eastern Europe (which would accompany the shifting of the Polish national territory toward the West) was just as clear to the Kremlin as what it had already recognized, that the Pope did not exactly consider the great alliance against Hitler a "holy" one. —Vatican foreign policy, because it supported Fascism, had drawn the "hatred of the Italian masses," Moscow's *Isvestia* wrote on February 1, 1944. And in April—the month of Orlemański's visit!—the Moscow Patriarchate's newspaper gave this theological rebuff to the Pope: the spiritual marriage between Christ and his church did not need any mediating deputy on earth. . . .[12]

"Spare the Russians—Considering the Germans"

A book entitled "The Truth About Religion in Russia," a splendid, sky-blue, richly illustrated volume of 457 pages, appeared in Moscow in August 1942;[13] the editor of this volume, of which 50,000 were distributed, was the Moscow Patriarchate. In the preface, Metropolitan Sergius wrote that "not persecution, but rather a return to the time of the apostles" had been the church's lot in the 25 years of Soviet rule.

Father Braun reported to the Vatican from Moscow that the book was originally to have been published by an anti-religious publishing house, but then at the last minute had been left to the Patriarchate.[14] It was—as the Vatican established—the first publication of the Orthodox church since its wretched synodal calendar had had to cease publication in 1936. And it was the most spectacular sign that Stalin had decided to make the church an ally too, as a part of the Russian national tradition. As favorably as this affected the Soviet Union's ability to resist Hitler's still advancing armies, it made just as good an impression in the West, especially in America—but not in the Vatican.

The "particular way" in which Stalin now rose up as protector of the old Orthodoxy and at the same time invoked pan-Slavism, also awakened "the traditional mistrust against the Catholics," Father Braun reported from Moscow, nevertheless recommending an attempt at a rapprochement. But the notion that there was now a basis for an effort to be "earnestly made to bring Russia more and more completely into a world family of nations with identical aims and obligations," as President Roosevelt's personal representative Taylor tried to explain on his second visit to the Vatican on September 22, 1942, met with deep skepticism in the Roman curia. The Americans had the illusion that a victorious Communist government would behave "like a tame lamb" after the war, noted Monsignore Tardini. "I told Taylor: If Stalin wins the war, he will be the lion that devours all of Europe. . . ."[15]

To be sure, it does not exactly appear that way in September 1942; Hitler's armies are still in the Caucasus, near Stalingrad. Ambassador Taylor also attempts to explain in the Vatican that Stalin will never win the war *alone*, that America would remain stronger than ever in Europe and help to regulate things. But Tardini sees only ignorance, naiveté and "nationalism" at work in the Americans. . . . In November 1942, however, the turning point of the war is becoming evident: the German Stalingrad army is encircled. And now the Vatican feels that its worst fears could be realized.

In Pius XII's 1942 Christmas address the ominous word "crusade" suddenly resurfaces, indeed becomes the central thought: the Pope calls for a "holy crusade for the purification and renewal of society," he speaks of "voluntary crusaders" who are to declare war on the "darkness of alienation from God." The corrected typed manuscript of this papal address, which perhaps could have given us interpretive hints, no longer exists in the Vatican archives[16] (Pius XII probably had Prelate Kaas burn it, along with other important notes). Naturally the Pope used the word "crusade" without any current political, let alone military, reference, but it was not accidental that this message also contained a reminder that "the church, for religious reasons, has always condemned the various systems of Marxist socialism." Is this after all an encouragement to the Germans, who have their backs against the wall at Stalingrad?

Ambassador von Bergen tried to find this out shortly thereafter at the New Year's reception in the Vatican: he addressed the Pope on the "world-historical significance of the heroic German battle in the East," about the "absurdity of Stalin's announcement of religious freedom," but the Pope did not say a word; only when a possible threat to his own person was mentioned was he drawn out of his reserve.

"The Pope expressed explicit approval of a statement I made in allusion to the famous fresco painting in the Stanzas, Raphael's 'Pope Leo the Great Repelling Attila,' that Stalin's hordes would surely not pass by Rome like Attila's troops, nor spare St. Peter's and Vatican City. . . ," Bergen telegraphed to Berlin.[17]

On the other hand, the Pope boasted to Roosevelt's representative that he had now finally spoken up against the German National Socialists. In the same Christmas speech of 1942, Pius indeed dared to mention that "hundreds of thousands have suffered death or a progressive wasting away through no real fault of their own, only because of their nationality or descent." He did not mention the guilty by name—as little as he let himself be persuaded, in spite of his concern, to speak out against the Soviets in the following months.

Dal Vaticano, 9 Septembris 1947

SUA SANTITA

N. 162086

Eminentissime ac Rev.me Domine,

Apostolicus Delegatus Foederatarum Americae Civitatum ad me misit exemplum epistulae, quam Dominus Kenneth C. Royall ad Eminentissimum Cardinalem Spellman reddidit: id ad Sacram Hungariae Coronam spectat.

Nolo adiunctum, id Tibi mittere studeo, sum de re agatur, quae Tibi cordi est.

Sacram Purpuram Tuam humillime deosculatus, summa qua par est observantia, me profiteor

Eminentiae Tuae
addictissimus ac deditissimus

J. B. Montini

Em.o ao Rev.mo Domino
Card. Josepho Mindszenty
Archiepiscopo Strigoniensi

(adiecto documento)

September 1947 letter from Mons. Montini (later Pope Paul VI) to Cardinal Mindszenty, in which he transmits an answer from the War Department to Cardinal Spellman concerning the Hungarian crown—without any formal opinion from the Vatican. (The USA returned the Crown of St. Stephen to the government in Budapest in 1977.)

A week after the capitulation of the German army at Stalingrad, on February 10, 1943, Swiss Foreign Minister Pilet-Golaz met with the nuncio in Bern to describe to him the danger of a "conversion of Germany to Communism" and the "Bolshevization of Europe"; the neutral countries, including the Pope, must now quickly attempt to establish peace.—"The

C O P Y

WAR DEPARTMENT

Washington, D.C

August 11, 1947

His Eminence Francis Cardinal Spellman
Archbishop of New York
452 Madison Avenue
New York 22, N.Y.

Your Eminence:

Your letter dated 26 July 1947, addressed
to Judge Patterson interceding on behalf of Cardinal
Mindszenty, Primate of Hungary, with respect to the
Sacred Crown of Hungary, now in the custody of the
military authorities in Austria, was duly received.

Since the restitution of sacred relics
other than to the government of origin is not properly
within the discretion of the Military Government authorities,
I have taken the liberty of forwarding a copy of your letter
to the Department of State requesting its careful consideration
of your request.

Sincerely yours,

Kenneth C Royall (signed)
Secretary of War

Holy See will wait and see what happens. . . ," noted Monsignore Tardini in the margin of this document.[18]

In the meantime, a dramatic letter of February 24, 1943, from the Hungarian Prime Minister Miklos Kállay had reached the Pope. Kállay, who was vainly trying to release his country from the alliance with Hitler and get it into the Western camp before it was too late, also saw the danger of a "union of Russian and German Communists," if Bolshevism "swept over a National-Socialist Germany proletarianized by the war." For pages, Kállay quoted all the papal utterances against Communism since 1846, in order to convince Pius XII to "deign to continue the struggle against

Communism and . . . to assert his almighty [!?] influence so that Communism . . . at least is stopped at the borders of the Christian states. . . ." Kállay even called to mind Pacelli's Munich experiences with the—as he said—"true face of Communism" (see p. 18). But even this could not move the Pope to change his attitude. The answer that he himself gave orally to the Hungarian ambassador on March 7 was recorded by the Secretary of State Cardinal Maglione. It contains, with an almost startling clarity, Pius XII's basic motive:

> ". . . 1. that the Holy See does not have its eyes closed to the Bolshevist danger. . . 2. that it could not publicly repeat the condemnation of Bolshevism without simultaneously speaking of the persecution now occurring through the deeds of Naziism. . . ."[19]

Did the "indulgence" in Hitler's Germany then take precedence of a sort? Perhaps from a preference of the Pope for the Germans, whom the Soviets thus had to thank indirectly for papal lenience? The Pope disclosed the true motives more clearly to the Hungarian Premier on April 3, 1943, when Kállay himself came to Rome and was received in private audience; there is no record of this meeting in the Vatican archive, but in the "National Archives" in Washington, D.C., Kállay's own memorandum after the audience may be found, captured by American troops (Hungarian Collection, T 973/1/1-201; 1153 ff.):

"He [the Pope] is aware of the terrible dangers of Bolshevism, but he has the feeling that in spite of the Soviet regime, the *great masses of the Russian people have remained more Christian than the poisoned soul of the German people.* . . . Germany, by abandoning every human mode of behavior, has aroused total mistrust on the other side [with the allies]. . . . Thus, as long as these inhuman tendencies continue, the church sees no possibility of mediating between the combatants." The Pope asked Kállay to inform Mussolini of this also, however "*not* to tell [him] that this was his [the Pope's] personal conviction," but that the Pope had heard this from the West. . . .

That the Pope himself did not want to appear publicly as accuser of the Germans had of course another quite pragmatic, so to speak "moral-opportunistic," motive: "Do not forget, there are millions of Catholics in the German army!" the Pope told Eduardo Senatro, the Berlin correspondent of the *Osservatore Romano*, and drew the conclusion: "Should I throw them into a conflict of conscience? They have taken an oath; they owe obedience."[20] Indeed, there were no such Catholics in the Soviet Union, but there probably were among their western allies. From London, for instance, the Catholic Archbishop of Westminster Cardinal Arthur Hinsley was heard to remark during the battle of Stalingrad:

"On the Pope's orders we pray publicly every day for Russia. [He meant Pius XI's order of 1930 on the 'crusade of prayer.'] The fact that the Russian people are now heroically defending their country against its violators increases the fervor of our prayers." They had to "pray every day for Bolshevism," the German radio twisted Hinsley's words, and three German bishops urgently requested clarification from the Vatican, since there was "great disturbance in Catholic circles."

The Pope himself had already taken up pen—"*propter bonum animarum*" (for the good of souls)—to pacify the German Catholics: he and his predecessor had "*repeatedly condemned atheistic Bolshevism with unmistakable clarity*"; indeed, the Pope even referred to his Christmas address of 1942. But hardly had this reply left for Berlin than a telegram arrived from Nuncio Roncalli in Istanbul with the information that, as a result of a conversation with the Soviet representative, he had formed certain hopes of receiving a list of Italian prisoners of war (see p. 227). Pius then immediately telegraphed the nuncio in Berlin to replace the all-too-sharp anti-Soviet paragraph of the clarification with the following more moderate one: "Pius XI and Pius XII have favored the Russian people with the same love and concern as other peoples and countries. *Furthermore, everyone is familiar with the doctrine of the Holy See concerning atheistic Communism.*"[21]

Thus Pius XII, with all diplomatic finesse, tries to keep up his moral-political balancing act between the fronts of the Second World War—as a sign of impartiality at least *outwardly*. Today, however, as we know much more about the *internal* considerations of the Roman curia from published documents, it is clear to what degree this attitude was only a majestic façade hiding its actual impotence, helplessness and pure fear. —Let us remember Monsignore Tardini's frank hope of 1941, that Hitler might first defeat Stalin, and weakened in the process, become "defeatable" himself. The Vatican had not placed exclusive trust in this desired sequence of events; in any event—as always—it had not closed off all possibilities toward the East either. But events since 1941 had destroyed the silent hope that Tardini had written down: Hitler and not Stalin would be the vanquished in the Second World War; the German defeat was now, in 1943, almost mathematically calculable. But will Germany be the only loser—or will the aforementioned sequence perhaps be reversed: Hitler defeated, Stalin weakened and defeatable. . . ?

Many people in Europe, especially among the "neutrals," are clinging to such considerations. But the Vatican does not surrender to *this* illusion for a moment. On the contrary, it rather overestimates the strength of the great eastern power after its immense loss of blood. Secretary of State Cardinal

Maglione, on March 27, 1943, declares to the British Minister Osborne, "privately and as a historical observer" (*a titolo personale come studioso di storia*), that now

> ". . . the danger of a Russian hegemony in Europe exists, a supremacy as terrible as the German, perhaps more so. . . . Bolshevist Russia has assumed political expansionist tendencies that have been entertained by the Czars ever since Peter the Great. . . . They have industrialized their immense land, they possess all the raw materials. . . . If they won political and economic supremacy in Europe, the balance in Europe that was so valuable to the English would be destroyed, perhaps for centuries. . . . Basically, the British Empire must want a bloc of western powers strong enough to prevent a German or Russian hegemony; a restored France, an unweakened Italy, a peaceful Spain."[22]

One may easily indulge in such reflections from the "church tower perspective" of St. Peter's, if—like the Vatican—one is above any concrete military-political decision and the need to win a war. But, as the British Foreign Office declares to the Vatican on April 20, 1943, "the choice is *not* (as some would have us believe) between the preservation of European culture and an exclusively Russian victory, between a Christian Europe and a Communist Europe. The choice is between the Nazi domination of Europe and a joint victory of the United Nations. . . . The final victory will not be that of a single Ally, but of all the Allies. . . . Moreover, Russia will need a long period of reconstruction and recovery. . . . There will then undoubtedly be great British and American armies on the Continent. . . ."

"It is true. . . , that Communism would not be the *only* victor," Monsignore Tardini replied in a verbal note of May 30, 1943. "Nevertheless, there are reasons to fear: [Tardini wrote the following in English]

a) that the war will end in a *preponderantly* Russian victory in Europe, and

b) that the result will be a rapid diffusion of Communism in a great part of continental Europe and the destruction there of European civilization and Christian culture. . . ."

For the Vatican believed, as Tardini told the British chargé d'affaires Montgomery, that the allies, after a victory in Europe, would use their main strength to end the war in the Far East (the early defeat of Japan by the dropping of the atom bomb on Hiroshima is not foreseeable in 1943!). Tardini also seriously held an opinion that may even have gone beyond Stalin's fondest hopes: that the military resistance of the Russian people would "win over the working masses of other countries to Communism," that the Germans, French and Italians "will be easy prey for Communism" and that "all [?] the Slavs naturally harbor sympathies for Russia and [?] Communism."

And if the Western allies reply to all this that their armies will remain in Europe, "then one must ask whether it is true peace that rests only on the fear that one ally instills in another?", so ends the verbal note from the Vatican Under-Secretary of State on May 30, 1943. The British chargé d'affaires—as Tardini noted later—was "struck" by this argument: He replied "that the importance of British and American military strength is that it will facilitate *mutual respect* with the Soviet Union." Tardini's commentary: "I would like to have answered that such strength is the basis of *fear* and not of respect; but I refrained. . . ."

This confidential exchange of opinion of 1943, only known in 1973 as a result of the Vatican document publication,[23] refutes the legend—circulated above all in the East—that the Vatican's intention was to persuade the western powers to do a military *volte-face* and "prepare for a new war against the Soviet Union." No one in the Roman curia had such primitive ideas. On the contrary, in spite of many errors in assessing the situation, the Vatican predicted (completely correctly, as we know today) the coming "cold war" between the victors of World War II—and feared it; indeed, just as much as the advance of Communism. In his perplexity, the Pope knew only *one* answer to this situation—handsome, of course, but ambiguous: Peace.

Just as, in 1939, when Hitler had made Stalin an accomplice in his war plans, Pius XII had considered a *prevention* of the war to be the only salvation—even at the extorted price of Poland—he now believed that a speedy *end* to the war could perhaps still prevent an excessive advance of Soviet Communist influence into central Europe.

Was the Pope then in favor of a "separate peace" between the West and Hitler's Germany? Since their conference in Casablanca (January 1943), the western powers had answered Hitler's slogan of "total war" with a determination for "total victory." The Vatican considered the demand for "unconditional surrender" that resulted from the conference as "practically unreasonable," because it would rouse the defeated to a desperate resistance (Tardini).[24] As Bishop of Rome and as an Italian, the Pope understandably had a special interest that Italy, where the western allies had successfully landed in the summer of 1943, be spared any further military destruction. The danger of experiencing the war right on his own doorstep even brought the Pope out of his diplomatic reserve for a moment: he favored Mussolini's fall and Italy's change of alliance. However, the occupation of Rome by the Germans and the bombing of the city by the western allies caused him new embarrassments and fears.

"Please, no speeches!" Tardini begs the former Secretary of State in the

Berlin Foreign Office, Baron von Weizsäcker, who assumes the post of German ambassador to the Vatican on July 5, 1943—replacing Diego von Bergen, who had held the office for over twenty years. Tardini returns to Weizsäcker the text of a speech he was to give in his first audience with the Pope; it speaks of the "gigantic struggle" of the Germans against "Bolshevism that threatens the whole world with destruction. . . ."[25] The Pope conducts his private discussion with Weizsäcker "with an undertone of spiritual zeal which assumed a recognition of common interests with the Reich only in discussion of the fight against Bolshevism"—so the new ambassador reported to Berlin.[26]

Weizsäcker could henceforth repeatedly report "anti-Bolshevist" things from the Vatican (see facsimile), for now he was also told what the English ambassador and the American special envoy had already heard. Weizsäcker personally quietly hoped for a peace mediation by the Vatican: "But the only important thing for me is whether the curia will stay fearfully in its snail shell, or will finally leave it and raise its voice against the flood from the East," he writes (private letter to his mother, January 9, 1944), and hopes that the Vatican will step out of the "moral-political fog" in which it hides.[27] In his reports to Berlin too, Weizsäcker tries to make the idea of Vatican mediation palatable by packaging the Vatican's fear of Communism in supposed compliments for the "German engagement against Soviet Russia."

In truth, the Pope cared nothing about this "engagement," which was useless anyway, but rather about the idea of a "*Verständigungsfrieden*" ("peace of reconciliation"): the anti-Hitler coalition should reject the question of war guilt and reparation, and Germany renounce all conquests. The Pope knew very well that Hitler would not be interested in such ideas; but he did count on agreement from the "*maior et sanior pars*" (the greater and healthier part) of the German population; so he wrote to Breslau Cardinal Bertram on January 6, 1944, but prudently crossed this sentence out of the draft of the letter.[28] For the Vatican sensed something of the conspiracy that was in progress against Hitler. The Pope, with weak hope, had clung to such a possibility, which—as he thought—could spare Germany total destruction or a resurrection as part of Stalin's empire—this Germany of Pius XII's romanticized private affection, which he also, however (incidentally, with Stalin and in contrast to Roosevelt!) considered a power that should be preserved in central Europe.[29]

It had already been very questionable whether the allies would have spared an unconditional surrender to a German government *without* Hitler. After the failure of the assassination attempt on Hitler on July 20, 1944, any outlook for that (which the Pope had estimated as "extremely small" anyway) disappeared completely. Pius XII—true to the Lateran treaties—could only have engaged in a formal mediation effort at the request of at least one of the combatants anyway. But was such a suggestion made?

More exact information about a late, hesitant, subsequently retracted probe from Berlin has been revealed for the first time by Weizsäcker's private notes, published in 1974 from his literary remains: and by war-time American Intelligence material declassified in 1978.[30]

Reich Foreign Minister Ribbentrop instructed Weizsäcker in February 1945 to approach the Vatican with the idea, for noncommittal transmission to the western allies, that they, together with Germany, should turn against Communism: "If the West misses this chance, then option for the East"—then Germany would voluntarily "bolshevize" herself. Although Weizsäcker considered the suggestion a "product of fear," he presented it to the Pope in a private audience on March 1, 1945 (when the Red Army had already reached the Oder). He subsequently noted: Pius XII "took it all in and assured me repeatedly of his love for the German people, *without indicating what he could do, if anything.*"

Since Weizsäcker had been instructed from Berlin anyway not to allow this sally to appear to be a "peace maneuver" or a direct request for mediation, the Pope saw all the less reason for involvement; in addition, although there were differences between the Soviets and their western allies, "at the moment these are not profound, at least none about the struggle against Germany," Pius XII told Weizsäcker. And Tardini had already made the Vatican's principles clear to the Berlin ambassador:

"1. It could not do anything that would aggravate the situation;

2. it must not compromise itself as an advocate of political or military interests;

3. it must not behave in a utopian manner."

What then remained for the Vatican in the face of inexorable events? Nothing but moral appeals to the—now very obvious—victors: calls for renunciation of hatred and revenge, for generosity, for mercy to those without direct guilt—appeals that seemed very abstract in the Europe of 1945. . . .

Probably only one who had spent the period of the Second World War in the "ivory tower" of the Vatican palace, surrounded by an apparently intact world, would be able to give any political hope to such a noble-minded sermon. The "ocean of blood and tears," the "unspeakable brutalities," the "portrait of Hell"—these words that the Pope had used in his Christmas address of 1944 were no abstract metaphors, however, but a reality beside which the Communist danger—in spite of all its horrors—had to pale in the eyes of suffering contemporaries. (And this was precisely the concern of the Vatican!) A German dictator, no one else, had unleashed this hell, from

Abschrift für die Akten XV 176 XXv.

uswärtiges Amt   **Geheim!**   Berlin,15.Februar 1944.
r.Pol.XV 138
a Anschluß an das Schreiben
om 4.ds.Mts. - Pol.XV 99 -.

ur zur Information:

Die Botschaft beim Heiligen Stuhl berichtet unter dem
11.ds.Mts.Nachstehendes:

"Römische Kurie leidet unter einem Alpdruck; sie sieht
das Gespenst des europäischen Kommunismus auf sich zukommen,

Ich habe bereits geschildert wie die Kurie das Vacuum
fürchtet, das in Italien da entstände, wo die Deutschen ihre
schützende Hand wegzögen. Wo aber, wie im Süden, die italie-
nischen Linkselemente und Herr Wyschinski zusammenspielen,
sieht es nicht besser aus.

Außenpolitisch ist die Kurie gleichfalls in Nöten.
Soeben hat sie von Sowjetrussland eine öffentliche Strafpre-
digt bekommen, weil sie faschistenfreundlich. Man weiß in
Moskau natürlich genau , wie Rom über den Bolschewismus denkt.

Diese Angst stammt aber nicht erst von heute. Ganz unab-
hängig vom militärischen Verlauf glaubt der Vatikan, der europäische Krieg werde sich, wie nach einem inneren Gesetz
zwangsläufig deformieren. Je länger,je mehr müsse er von der
nationalen auf die soziale Ebene hinüber gleiten. Schließlich
werde er in Europa in einen allgemeinen Bürgerkrieg ausarten.

Das ist der Grund,weshalb der Papst in seiner Weihnachts-
ansprache sagte, man müsse ohne Rücksicht auf Kriegsschuld,
Wiedergutmachung oder Kräfteverhältnisse "das ganze Halt"
blasen. Das Echo hierauf von den Westmächten war wenig ermu-
tigend. Aus England kamen sogar recht unfreundliche Worte
an den Papst.

Dieser ließ aber nicht locker. Er hat wie ich zuverlässig
erfahre,den Westmächten weiter ins Gewissen geredet, da sie
ja im Begriff seien, unseren Kontinent aus Zweckmäßigkeits-
gründen Sowjetunion in die Hand zu spielen.

Die Antwort muß grob etwa so gelautet haben:" unmittelbar
vor dem Tor,wünschen wir keinen Rat, den Sieg preiszugeben."
Also keine Bereitschaft, die Front zu wechseln oder einzulenken.

Die Antwort hat den Papst enttäuscht, seine Haltung aber
nicht verändert."

Vorstehender Text darf unter keinen Umständen im Wortlaut
weitergegeben werden.

Im Auftrag
gez. Reinebeck.

as Reichsministerium für die kirchichen Angelegenheiten,
Oberkommando der Wehrmacht - Agr.Ausland-,
Reichssicherheitshauptamt

Copy for the Records XV 176 XXv

Foreign Office   No. II 224/44
r. Pol. XV 138   Berlin, Feb. 15, 1944
Relative to the correspondence of
4th of the month—Pol. XV 99

SECRET!

Only for information:
The embassy to the Holy See reports for the 11th of this month the following:

"The Roman Curia is suffering from a nightmare; it sees the phantom of European Communism coming toward it.

I have already described how the curia fears the vacuum that would arise in Italy where the Germans withdrew their protective hand. However, where the Italian leftist elements and Mr. Wyschinski are working together, as in the south, it does not look any better.

The curia is also having problems in foreign policy. It just received a public admonition from Soviet Russia for being pro-Fascist. Moscow naturally knows exactly what Rome thinks about Bolshevism.

But this fear did not arise just today. Quite independently of military events, the Vatican believes the European war, as if following an inner drive, will necessarily become more deformed. The longer it continues, the more it will be transformed from a national to a social level. Finally it will degenerate into a general civil war in Europe.

That is why the Pope said in his Christmas address that one must cry "a complete halt" without regard to war guilt, reparations or balance of forces. The echo to this from the Western powers was not encouraging. From England came even quite unfriendly words directed at the Pope.

But he did not let go. As I have discovered from reliable sources, he continued to pound into the Western powers that they were on the point of playing our continent into the hands of the Soviet Union, out of mere expediency.

The answer must have been roughly thus: Right outside the gates, we don't want any advice on how to relinquish the victory." Thus no willingness to alter the front or to relent.

The answer disappointed the Pope, but did not change his position."
The preceding text may under no circumstances be passed on.

On Instructions,
Signed: Reinebeck

To the Reich Ministry for Church Affairs,
The High Command—Foreign Affairs—,
Reich Main Security Office

whose abysses, filled with murder a million times over, the survivors were now staggering: Jews, Christians, Communists, anti-Communists. . . . In this war, that Stalin in 1939 had wanted to stay out of, letting the "imperialists fight against each other," the Soviet Union, attacked by Hitler in 1941, had suffered the greatest losses: 20 million dead.

Now, in the moment of victory, could Christian benevolence and reconciliation be expected—especially when the summons came from a side that, although it considered itself the highest moral authority, had never pronounced a clear sentence against the guilty?

The Curtain Falls in Eastern Europe—Not Iron

In full vestments, his flowing beard surrounded by white chrysanthemums, the dead Archbishop Andreas Count Sheptyckyi lay in the casket carried by the priests from St. George's Cathedral in Lvov. The Galician metropolis with its Ukrainian-Polish-Jewish-Austrian colorations, this city that had suffered so much and understood so little of what passed over it, on this November 5, 1944, was honoring the man whose life and works mirrored the city's whole unhappy fate.

A sudden attack of measles, from which the eighty-year-old man had died four days earlier, had spared him the last bitterness. Before closing his eyes, he could even hope that he had again—perhaps—helped his church survive a dangerous turn of events. And in truth: in the funeral procession now passing through the main streets of Lvov (Lemberg), again occupied by the Soviets, walked not only the bishops of the Latin and Eastern rites, 150 priests, 200 theology students, and tens of thousands of the faithful, but the Soviet authorities as well—represented in the person of the Ukrainian party secretary, one Nikita Khrushchev, of whom we shall hear a lot more ten years later. . . .

In a Latin letter posted from Moscow, Sheptyckyi's successor Archbishop Slipyj also informed the Vatican about the remarkable funeral procession—"with the agreement of the Soviet government" (*annuente gubernio Sovietico*).[31] For shortly before his death, Sheptyckyi had attempted the last of his great maneuvers; back in the summer of 1944, shortly before the Soviet entrance into Lemberg, he had declared to his synod that his archdiocese was nearing, "with giant steps," the greatest catastrophe of its history, and this "as a result of Our own conduct"—thus did Sheptyckyi acknowledge in retrospect his original erroneous judgment of the Germans (whose Ukrainian SS "Galicia" division had not gone without the church's blessing). But now, on October 14, 1944, three months after the Soviet entry, in which not a hair was harmed of Sheptyckyi or his church, the Metropolitan wrote a pastoral letter: "Every parish is to collect at least 500 rubles for the sick and wounded of the Red Army and send them by December 1 to the Metropolitan consistory, which will forward them to the Red Cross." At the same time, Sheptyckyi writes in a letter to Stalin:

"The whole world bows its head to you. . . . After the victorious advance from the Volga to the San, you have reunited the West Ukrainian regions with the Greater Ukraine. For the fulfillment of those attested wishes and desires of the Ukrainian people, which for centuries has seen itself as *one* people and wants to live as a united nation, this people thanks you. This brilliant event arouses the hope, in our church as in the whole people, that the USSR, under your leadership, will have complete freedom of work and development. . . ."[32]

Slipyj also immediately aimed at a *modus vivendi*, which was not unwelcome to the Soviets (who needed peace behind their front, which was advancing toward the Oder). "In the spirit of divine justice, the church does not involve itself in political, military and worldly things. . . ," Slipyj assured the Soviet government in a letter, and attached a list of requests in which religious instruction in the schools, forbidden in the Soviet Union, was also mentioned.

Could Stalin's tactical needs be brought into harmony with Slipyj's tactical behavior? The new archbishop zealously hammered the commandment "Thou shalt not kill" into the right-radical partisans (the Ukrainian underground movement); they not only raided Soviet transports, but also "bestially murdered thousands of Polish Catholics," as the bishop of the East Polish diocese Luck could only report to Rome two years later.[33] Thus again, on the fringe of the martial genocide, and supported by it, regional nationalisms also collided and confused all future perspectives.

At first it also seemed to the Bishop of Luck, Adolf Szelazek, that Soviet behavior promised freedom for the church (. . . *multa signa videbantur ostendere plenam libertatem ecclesiae in Statu sovietico*). This even encouraged him to send three priests of the Latin rite to Zhitomir and Kamieniec in the Ukraine, those Polish dioceses that had become Soviet after the First World War and over which there had been so much friction in the twenties (remember the Skalski affair!—see p. 123). Now the Bishop of Luck thought he could regain a footing in the Ukraine—citing an agreement with the Czar of 1847 (!).

"I could not suppose that such a delegation would violate Bolshevist law . . . ," he later wrote to Rome.[34] At the beginning of January 1945, he and the three priests landed in prison in Kiev. While his cathedral chapter was able to rescue the entire church fortune (*omnia aurea et argentea utensilia*) to the West over the new Polish-Soviet border on the Bug, the Soviets were frantically trying to discover political motives for the bishop's activity in the Ukraine. They naturally also suspected that there were connections with the Polish anti-Communist underground, which at this time was just as active as the Ukrainian (and the two also fought each other!).

Of course, the Polish ("Latin") bishop of Luck did not suspect that he had also encroached on the territory of his Ukrainian colleagues of the Eastern rite. For Archbishop Slipyj, whose ceremonial enthronement had proceeded without disturbance, hoped that the Uniate church, thanks to its

Eastern rite, could survive better than the Latin. He had hastened to conclude the collection of money for the wounded Red Army soldiers ordered by the late Sheptyckyi. Sheptyckyi's brother, with two other clerics, took 100,000 rubles to Moscow, and was very disappointed that the delegation was not received by Stalin himself; still, the Kremlin assured him how greatly the Soviet government appreciated Slipyj's contribution to the battle against the Ukrainian underground movement. . . . Nevertheless, the delegation left Moscow with the impression that a church of the Eastern rite, connected with Rome, was uncomfortable for the Soviets.[35] Why?

"Now that, by the grace of God, the Russian land has been reunited along its old borders, you too are united with us forever," wrote the new Orthodox Partriarch Alexji in a special pastoral letter of March 1945, addressed "to the priests and faithful of the Greek[!]-Catholic church who live in the western regions of the Ukrainian Soviet Republic."[36] Alexji had been ceremoniously elected—also with Stalin's "blessing"—on February 27, 1945, as Patriarch of all Russia, in place of the deceased Sergius. Now he informed the Ukrainian Uniates that—since their predecessors had submitted themselves to the Pope in Rome—they had preserved the Orthodox rite, but lost its spirit and even the "apostolic succession" (validity of the office of bishop!). And more:

> "Behold, beloved fathers and sons, where your spiritual leadership has led you in these historic days. . . . The Lord has clearly blessed the weapons of those who have risen against Hitler. . . . The finger of God points before all the world to this cannibal whose last hour is approaching. But where have the late Metropolitan Sheptyckyi and his closest collaborators led you? He brought you to submit yourselves to Hitler's yoke, they taught you to bow your heads before him. *And where is the Vatican leading you?* In his Christmas and New Year's message [see p. 243], the Pope spoke of fraternity with the Fascist bandits, of mercy toward Hitler, the greatest evil-doer in the history of humanity. . . . Thus we beg you, brothers, to unite yourselves with us in spirit, in peace. *Break and sever the union with the Vatican*, which with its religious errors is leading you into darkness and to spiritual downfall, against freedom-loving humanity. . . ."

After this epistle, one could calculate what then actually happened: on April 11, hardly a month before the end of the war, Slipyj and four other Ukrainian bishops who were not prepared to break with Rome were arrested; their residences were searched, and enough material was found— from the period of their illusions—to accuse them of "collaboration" with the German occupation forces. In March 1946 Slipyj was sentenced to a long period of forced labor; he was not freed until seventeen years later, through Pope John XXIII (see p. 308).

One of the best-known theologians of the Uniate church, Gabriel Kostelnyk, who back in 1925 in an address honoring Metropolitan

Sheptyckyi,[37] had deplored the hybrid nature of Rome's half Latin, half "eastern"-leaning ideas of union, now took over leadership of those who hoped to be able to retain at least the religious and pastoral substance of their church by a separation from Rome. With the massive participation of the Soviet authorities, who in spite of their theory of the "separation of church and state" made themselves executors of Orthodox wishes as in the czarist era (because it was politically opportune), a Uniate synod—without bishops—revoked the union with the Pope in March 1946. It had arisen, the argument now went, exactly 350 years ago "under pressure and force, in the interest of Poland"—an assertion that, even in the opinion of Catholic church historians today, was "not completely unfounded."[38]

In the Carpathian Ukraine, which had belonged to Czechoslovakia and whose eastern portion was now annexed by the Soviet Union, the advancing Soviets had met an especially clever and moderate Catholic-Uniate bishop, Theodor Romsha; the Red Army had been greeted amicably there not only by the people, but also by the bishop, and at first behaved likewise. Bishop Romsha even appeared as a speaker at the celebration of the anniversary of the revolution in November 1944. Since the Soviets found no political objection to the bishop, who had only recently been installed, he succeeded for two years in resisting the pressure for "reunification" with the Orthodox (after the example of Lvov [Lemberg]), until in October 1947 he was killed in a—probably staged—traffic accident. Thus, only in February 1949 was the final break with Rome enforced.[39]

Even in Lithuania, where at the entry of the Soviet troops in 1944, 30,000 men had taken to the woods as anti-Soviet partisans, there was at first "a short period of limited tolerance," as even decided anti-Communists concede. That changed only when the bishops refused, in 1946, to condemn the partisan movement that later boasted openly that it had "wiped out smaller units of the Red Army, destroyed depots and supplies, liquidated Soviet-Lithuanian opportunists, [and] blocked the collectivization of agriculture until 1951."[40]

Then if Stalin assumed a wait-and-see attitude even in those areas certain to be incorporated into the Soviet Union and did not at first touch the Catholic church, how would he act in the countries to whose independence the western allies had committed themselves? In Rumania, whose capitol the Russians entered on August 23, 1944, after the king himself had gone over to them, the Catholic church, with its 1.2 million followers of the Latin rite and 1.5 million Uniates of the Eastern rite, was left unmolested the whole year of 1944. The same was true of the 57,000 Catholics of both rites in Bulgaria, which the Red Army entered at the beginning of September 1944. The secretary of the papal nuncio in Bucharest, Monsignore Guido del Mestri, and the representative of the apostolic delegate in Sofia, Monsignore Francesco Galloni, remained at their posts and made reports—among others, about the beginning attempts of the tiny Communist Parties of Rumania and Bulgaria, supported by the Soviets, to gain control of the state.*

* From this point in the book, insofar as no documentary sources are expressly cited, personal reports of contemporary eye- and ear-witnesses are also used. These informers, for reasons of discretion, cannot always be named; but the author has tested their credibility just as carefully as the historical source material documented in this book.

But what was happening in *Poland*, where 22 million Catholics of the Latin rite had come under Soviet control? Pius XII told General de Gaulle, who visited the Pope on June 30, 1944, of "events in Galicia, where persecution of the faithful and the priests has begun with the entry of the Red Army"[41]—which, as we know (see p. 244f.), was not precisely true. A Vatican note that was passed to the German Ambassador Weizsäcker said Poland "was intended as a future Soviet Republic. . . ."[42] Actually, the Vatican had not been in possession of "dependable news" from Poland for a long time. It did not know that the Soviets, who were advancing from the Vistula to the Oder, in spite of many local excesses were determined not to touch the church, and that this was also the motto of the "Provisional Government" of Poland formed in Lublin, in which the tone was set by Polish Communists who knew exactly how weak their position was in the country.

Cardinal Sapieha of Krakow was just as amazed at this as Archbishop Slipyj had been; only—in contrast to Slipyj—he was not threatened in the slightest. Just as he had earlier received Hitler's Governor General Frank (and demonstratively served him dry bread), in January 1945 he received a formal call from the Soviet General Koravnikov and did not hide his astonishment "that the Bolsheviks were not burning down all the churches."

"Why should we not accommodate this 'Krakow Pope' if it costs us nothing?", General Koravnikov said later.[43] "The visit to Sapieha was the dethronement of reactionary superstition."

Would the obvious thing not have been for the Vatican itself to get hold of some information about the situation in Poland? Nuncio Cortesi was still officially in office, although of course his seat was in Rome; he was represented by a chargé d'affaires—though not in Warsaw, but rather with the Polish exile government in London. Only it, and not the "Lublin committee," was recognized by the Vatican. "We must wait and see whether America will have the strength to resist the absorption of Poland into the great Soviet Union," said the above-quoted Vatican documentary note of July 24, 1944.[44]

Not the slightest attempt was made at this delicate moment in 1944 to finally seek contact with the Soviets in order to utilize the favorable initial climate—for instance in the Ukraine or in Poland—to save what could perhaps be saved. Still, a Soviet representative by name of Miskievitch in the meantime sat with the Allied Control Commission in Rome. His meeting with Bishop Alexander Evreinov, the prelate of the Catholic Russian exiles, who was directing a papal relief work for Soviet prisoners of war in Italy, briefly gave the impression that there was after all something in the works. But Miskievitch only expressed his polite thanks, and to the question from a "Russicum"-scholar whether it would be possible to go to the Soviet Union, he replied: "If only you were an engineer, or a doctor! But as a priest there is nothing for you to do there."[45]

"Certain developments have been noted with interest; we assume that one can observe certain signs of change," Vatican spokesman Jacques Martin commented in the summer of 1944 to reports released in the west about the cautious religious policies of the Soviets. "But up to now there are, to be precise, no new facts for the Vatican. . . ."[46] In the middle of August 1944 (while the non-Communist Polish underground army [AK], with its Warsaw uprising, was trying to liberate the capital from the Germans itself, before the entry of the Soviets), the *Osservatore Romano* denied in striking detail reports about a "memorandum from Marshal Stalin to the Pope."[47] The British agency Reuter had reported that Stalin had assured the Pope that Moscow had no intention of introducing the Soviet social order anywhere else. The Vatican, for its part, had no doubts "that Poland will have close friendly relations with Russia after the war"; the pre-war nuncio Cortesi would presently remove to Warsaw. . . .

Why did the Roman curia not only flatly deny these reports, but at the same time quote them extensively?

In this summer of 1944, Pius XII saw only two possibilities: either Poland and the rest of eastern Europe would become Soviet republics— with all its hopeless consequences for the church; or (and this he considered less probable) the West would enforce non-Communist regimes in these countries. In order to strengthen the West's resolve in this direction, the Pope thought it necessary to demonstrate that he personally was not considering any compromise with Stalin, that indeed he did not even want to send a nuncio to Warsaw.

After an attempt to send an American prelate to Poland as an incognito Vatican observer had failed, the Secretariat of State finally asked the British at the beginning of 1945 to make discreet inquiries about the situation via their embassy in Moscow, "without approaching the Soviet authorities." Thus Rome finally learned, even if at second hand, that "the Catholic church in Poland is being treated very carefully" and that for example the Krakow Cardinal Sapieha, in the meantime, had been honored by the "red"-Polish General Żymierski as an exemplary resistance fighter against the Nazis. (Rola-Żymierski, a Polish pre-war general, who placed himself at the Communists' disposal, became the first minister of defense in post-war Poland.)[48]

"The news reaching the Holy See is anything but welcome," replied Monsignore Tardini on April 25, 1945, to this report by the British. He probably meant primarily the proceedings in East Poland (see p. 246), because Rome had learned in the meantime from central Poland that all surviving bishops had returned to their sees. One of them, Wlodziemierz Jasiński, the 73-year-old Bishop of Łódz who had been exiled by the Germans and given high honors by the Pope, on May 1, 1945, without orders, even raised the red flag next to the national one on his cathedral. . . .[49]

This sort of news was naturally also unwelcome to the Vatican, although it signaled a by no means hopeless situation. The fact that the Provisional Government in Warsaw, in which the Communists held four important ministries, immediately invited Cardinal Primate August Hlond (whom the Americans had liberated from German custody) to return to Poland, may have rather astonished the Roman curia. Still, they used this happy circumstance—as we shall see—to spare themselves direct contact with the new masters of the largest Catholic nation of Eastern Europe. . . .

Papal Error and First Consequences in Poland

Posterity, always more clever than contemporaries, has reproached the American President Roosevelt for making too many major concessions to the Soviet Union in February 1945, when the victorious Allies divided the European continent among themselves at the Crimean conference at Yalta; the Pope has been praised for advising against it when Presidential Advisor Hopkins visited him at the end of January on his journey to Yalta.

It was not as easy as it looks for Pius XII to say this. Given that Stalin's armies were already in western Poland and far into the Balkans, he too, like Roosevelt, only had a choice between compromise and war. The only difference was that for Roosevelt (even if he had been less naive politically) there was really no alternative; or should he have marched against Stalin alongside the murderer of Auschwitz?![50] For the Pope, on the other hand, about whose "divisions" Stalin had so mockingly asked at Yalta, "war" was no bloody alternative—aside from possible martyrs (who are theologically easily rationalized when one lives in secure freedom). The Pope could only engage in a spiritual-political confrontation. That he was willing to do. He was not looking for this quarrel, to be sure, but he also did not wish to avoid it at the price of concessions, especially not in Poland, where he felt his church to be strongest and most resistant.

Twenty-two years later, Pope Paul VI's "foreign minister" Monsignore Agostino Casaroli declared in retrospect that the Holy See in 1945, "true to its tradition of taking no initiative toward a break . . . had not withdrawn its representatives from the countries that now belonged to the Socialist realm, indeed it did everything possible so that they could remain there."[51] That is formally correct, and we shall still have to consider this side of the Vatican's behavior in Prague, Budapest, Bucharest, Sofia, Belgrade and Tiranë. Only Warsaw was not mentioned by Casaroli in this connection, for indeed Pius XII did not need to avoid breaking off diplomatic relations there—because they were never even established.

The decision of the Great Powers Conference at Yalta to "enrich" the Provisional Warsaw Government with exiled Poles from London, and thereby to legitimatize it democratically, was not a very promising compromise: the Pope did not trust it even when on March 21, 1945, Edward J. Flynn, Roosevelt's Catholic advisor, flew directly from Yalta via Moscow to Rome to convince the Vatican to cooperate. To this day we do not know the wording of the assurances that Flynn delivered;[52] still, the April edition of the Moscow *Bolshevik* said that the Vatican was a "world power, even though it possesses no vast territory." The dispatch of a nuncio to Warsaw and thus the recognition of the new government of Poland would doubtless not have avoided later frictions, but it would probably have softened Soviet pressure on Poland while at the same time strengthening those nationally-minded forces in Polish Communism that—as became clear later—did not regard a compromise with the church solely as a temporary tactical maneuver.

The Pope, however, who back in the summer of 1944 in a conversation with de Gaulle had already set his hopes on a "union of pro-Catholic nations" and besides Italy, Spain, Portugal, France and Belgium, mentioned Germany as well—but not Poland—was not prepared to place any prior trust in a Communist-led government in Warsaw. For his judgment of the situation was based on two—apparently established— facts:

1. He was convinced that the Communist seizure of power in Eastern Europe would proceed according to the same revolutionary, radically anti-religious model as in Russia after 1917. He did not recognize that Stalin, in spite of his imperial, czarist desires—or perhaps because of them—was

more concerned with security in his eastern frontier than with rapid bolshevization, more with neighbors friendly to the Soviets than with new Soviet republics.

2. He was sure (and many eastern and western Europeans agreed with him) that the survival of Communism and the Soviet Union in the Second World War "would make friendly and orderly mutual relationships among the nations of Europe impossible and that in the not too distant future they would face a new tragic war" (so noted Monsignore Tardini back in 1943).[53]

The Pope was in error on both counts—like many of his contemporaries: Stalin, who had dissolved the Communist International in 1943, first used the glowing expression "People's Democracy," which had in common with the "Dictatorship of the Proletariat" that Communists would not be driven from power by elections, but which left room for "national roads," also for ideological non-conformity. The Soviet model of government was not yet made compulsory—not even in regard to religion.[54] Danger of war arose only when Stalin, driven by the necessities of his internal system of terror, but also by a genuine fear of America's atom bomb and the policy of "containment," in autumn 1947 revived the Communist International as "Cominform" (against the opposition of Tito and Gomulka), and thus made the "People's Democracy" an empty formula and a sure instrument of his ambition to build up his "empire." However, since the atomic age had dawned and the great powers had to avoid military confrontation, a "balance of fear" remained, somewhat as Domenico Tardini had foreseen back in 1942. Not an armed conflict, but a "Cold War" began.

Without doubt, the foundation for this development was already laid by the decisions of the victorious powers at Yalta and Potsdam, of which the most spectacular were the division of Germany and the shifting of Poland's borders from east to west. The fact that the Pope's pastoral policy initially still proceeded from incorrect assumptions, and that he did not join the short-term trend toward Soviet-western fraternization, could this time not be blamed solely on his usual caution, but probably also on pangs of conscience aroused by this very caution during the war. Now he wanted to keep his hands and mouth free, or at least not let himself be bound by premature compromises. In retrospect, however, it seems self-evident that the Vatican—simply as a result of its temporal impotence—would also in this way end up following the trends of the epoch: now it was engaged in the Cold War, just as it had once used the Rapallo policies, subscribed to Hitler's anti-Communism, and then denied any crusade ideology.

Thus the Pope did not send a nuncio to Poland; instead, the Polish Cardinal Primate August Hlond returned on July 20, 1945—while the summit conference of the victors in Potsdam was still in progress. On his journey through a war-devastated Europe, Hlond was accompanied by a

34-year-old Communist, as honor- and security-guard, who held the office of deputy minister of defense in the new, slightly more rightist, "Government of National Unity" in Warsaw: one Piotr Jaroszewicz, who 25 years later, as head of government, would initiate a new attempt at a *modus vivendi* between church and state. We do not know in detail the contents of their conversations on the journey; in any case, Jaroszewicz in 1970, at his meeting with Hlond's successor Cardinal Wyszyński, referred to the fact that he had at that time announced the intention of the Communists to adhere strictly to the concordat of 1925, but that other "non-Communist anti-clericals" had pressed for a break.

That did not help a great deal. Hlond had been prepared by the Pope for that "emergency." In his luggage was a papal epistle to the Polish bishops for which Hlond himself had suggested such formulations as: it is necessary to "save the nation from the infiltration of insidious theories (Bolshevism)." The Pope—as usual—had moderated it and only written of "new truths" by which people should not be deceived.[55] Even that was clear enough. But above all, Hlond was equipped with those plenary powers for bishops in Communist countries which the episcopate in the Baltic states and East Poland had received back in 1940 (see p. 201), and which Neveu in Moscow, for example, also possessed (see p. 101). Wherever Communists began to rule, the Vatican granted such authorities; the wording has never been published, but we may conclude rather precisely the nature of these powers from what we know about the authorizations of the twenties and thirties, and also from the events themselves as well as other reports:

The main purpose was to safeguard pastoral care, even under conditions of chicanery and repression, and if necessary under illegality. The primary precondition was thus to secure the succession of bishops. Therefore the local chairman of episcopates (where there was no nuncio) above all had to be able to install bishops, if necessary without asking Rome and by secret installation. At the same time, they had to draw up a confidential list of successors (administrators, vicars general) who could assume their functions immediately—also secretly—in case the actual official was obstructed or arrested.

After 1945, the Vatican thus fell back on the emergency model that had been tested in the twenties and beginning thirties (primarily by d'Herbigny). At that time—as we know—it had proven a failure (see pp. 83–102), partly because it was handled dilettantishly and ambiguously. Still, after the breakdown of negotiations with Moscow, it seemed the only alternative. Was this method useful after World War II? Now it was a matter of protecting not a relatively small Catholic minority, but millions of Catholics in Eastern Europe, among them a whole Catholic nation like Poland.

To be sure, Cardinal Hlond's powers had not only to face a great persecution of the church; they did not exclude negotiations between episcopate and government. But they assumed the probability of an isolation of the Polish church from Rome; the Vatican's presuppositions were also that a Communist government in Poland

1. would forcibly and totally bring about the disappearance of the church;

2. would itself be of only temporary duration.

Perhaps Cardinal Hlond sensed that both premises did not apply in exactly that way; because directly after his arrival in Poland he used his unusual authority issued by the Sacred Congregation for Extraordinary Church Affairs on July 8, 1945, not for precautionary measures against Communist repression (that were not at all pressing at the moment), but—in accordance with Polish national interests:

Hardly had the Potsdam conference been concluded, which ceded the "former German territories" across the Oder and Neisse to Poland, than Cardinal Hlond issued decrees on August 15, 1945, installing five Polish prelates as apostolic administrators in the Oder-Neisse areas: Karol Milik in Breslau (Wroclaw), Boleslaw Kominek in Oppeln (Opole), Teodor Bensch in Allenstein (Olsztyn), Andrzej Wronka in Danzig (Gdańsk), and Edmund Nowicki in Landsberg (Gorzów). In doing so, Hlond expressly referred to his special authority (*facultas specialis*) for the whole Polish territory "*in tutto il territorio polacco*" as Tardini's document from July 8 stated in Italian. This enabled Hlond to vest these administrators with the rights and duties of resident bishops (*iura et officia Episcopi residentialis*), including the right to administer confirmation and the lower ordinations.[56]

Hlond could claim this legal act, which established the Polish church administration in the Oder-Neisse region—only ten days after Potsdam!— as a national, patriotic step, and it was regarded as such by the entire Polish nation. However, his effort to present it simultaneously as the Vatican's recognition of the new situation would remain unsuccessful, if only because the Roman curia kept completely out of the whole thing and was not even prepared to recognize the Warsaw government internationally, even though it had the blessing of all the great powers.

"La Polonia farà da se"—Poland takes care of its own affairs, was the Roman motto. Hlond had been given a free hand; what he did was his concern. The Holy See kept out of it—and in this way not only isolated itself, but also (to the lively satisfaction of all anti-clericals and Communist extremists) caused the Polish church embarrassment and moved it into the twilight.

And this at a time when millions of Poles could breathe again after five and a half years of brutal repression and were streaming into the churches; at a moment when soldiers of the People's Army had marched in the

Corpus Christi procession and the—nominally non-partisan (in reality Communist)—state president Bierut was seen at church ceremonies!— Hardly a month later came the answer:

". . . In consideration of the fact that the Apostolic See, in contrast to the majority of states, has not yet recognized the Provisional Government of National Unity, and therefore no normal diplomatic relations exist between it and the Apostolic See, the Government of National Unity does not officially recognize the nomination of apostolic administrators that the Apostolic See undertook on August 15," read a decision of the ministerial council of September 12, 1945, which also took a much sharper shot:[57]

"The government of Poland has ascertained that the *concordat* entered into by the Republic of Poland and the Apostolic See [1925] has ceased to be binding, since it was unilaterally broken by the Apostolic See during the occupation by legal acts of the Apostolic See which were in opposition to the provisions."

The reason given for this cancellation of the concordat was the installation of the *German* Bishop Splett and the *German* Monsignore Breitinger as administrators in the Polish dioceses of Chelm and Gniezno-Poznan, which contravened Art. 9 of the concordat. (The Vatican had regarded these nominations in 1940—like the 1945 installation of *Polish* administrators in the Oder-Neisse regions—as pastoral emergency solutions.)[58] However, the government carefully and reassuringly appended to this blow against the Vatican:

"The Government of National Unity declares that, as heretofore, it will not hinder the activity of the Catholic church, and it assures the Catholic church of continued full freedom of activity within the framework of existing laws."

Nevertheless, a non-legal situation had arisen—at least in regard to the Vatican. Of course, it was not yet clear to whose disadvantage the consequence would be. (Many Polish Communists to this day characterize the cancellation of the concordat as a serious mistake.) Abolished were the provisions of state co-determination in the nomination of bishops (Art. 11) and the loyalty of priests to the state (Art. 19) contained in the concordat; before the war, the church had never been able to fill its offices so independently as now with no concordat.[59] The protest which the Pope did not raise until January 17, 1946, in a letter to the Polish bishops, probably for that reason sounded rather unruffled and condescending: he would "not refute" the accusations, "for they are invalid and unjust"; the cancellation of the concordat had "filled him with pain, with a regret equal to the aversion which some of your statesmen show toward religious institutions and toward the essential well-being of their own people."[60]

Thus the Vatican indicated no readiness to negotiate a new legal fixation of the Polish church's position—which was still by no means hard-pressed—not even when Warsaw attempted a direct sounding-out: the Polish writer Ksawery Pruszyński, a left-liberal Catholic, who had returned to Poland from the West and entered the diplomatic service of the new government, was selected for this. To publicly "accredit" him, State President Bierut gave an interview on November 20, 1946, saying: "We have never withdrawn from discussions about a *new concordat*. . . . It would doubtless contribute to regulating many things in Poland." With this declaration of intention, Pruszyński came to Rome twice in 1946/47 on a secret mission; at a private dinner, he met with Professor Federico Alessandrini, the respected columnist of the *Osservatore Romano*. Alessandrini did not get him any contacts. Other avenues proved no more successful for Pruszyński in securing an audience with Monsignore Antonio Samorè, the Secretariat of State's advisor on Poland. The Vatican suspected that the Warsaw Communists wanted to bypass the Polish episcopate and negotiate directly with Rome. However, there was a very similar attitude in the Vatican itself: Pruszyński was indirectly given to understand that, if the Vatican ever did enter into discussions or negotiations at all, "then not with Warsaw, but with Moscow. . . ."[61]

The minister of the London Polish government in exile, Wladyslaw Folkierski, received a similar message when he, conversely, wanted to *prevent* the Vatican from establishing relationships with the new Warsaw regime. Pius XII told him: "The question now is not Poland, my son, but Russia. We would like to have relations with Russia, but Russia does not want them. . . ."—As we know, a declaration only half-correct, but one which moved the ashen Polish minister to the reply: "God grant that at least the Russians don't want to. . . !"

Mindszenty in Action—Disappointment with Tito

"It is the Lord's grace that we are not entirely destroyed! The report that Russian troops intended to destroy the churches did not prove true. Indeed, we were even able to observe many courtesies from their commanders regarding church life. Our churches are standing, and divine services are held unmolested. . . ."

Thus read a pastoral letter from the Hungarian bishops of May 24, 1945, three months after the Soviets had conquered Budapest.[62] The author of the letter: Jósef Mindszenty, who had been bishop of Veszprém for only a year. Just three years earlier he had written about the Bolshevists: "Hell has never gone to battle with such strength. . . . In 1928, Stalin wrote a letter to the Vatican in which he officially informed it that he had condemned the papacy to death. . . . Every compromise gives new sustenance to the persecutors. . . ."[63] During the last months of the war, this bishop had been imprisoned by Hungarian Fascists and the German military because he had pressed for a rapid end to the war, after first having wanted to organize "resistance against both sides." Mindszenty's appointment as bishop had been a compromise solution; Cardinal Primate Jusztinian Seredi had registered doubts in 1943 in a letter to Pius XII: Mindszenty, who has been a small-town pastor for 27 years and had no university education, indeed has great talents for organization, but his vehement temperament, which prevents him from showing his superiors proper respect, while being all too strict toward subordinates, makes his nomination in such difficult times seem risky. . . .

This was the man whom the Budapest apostolic nuncio, Angelo Rotta, recommended to the Pope as successor to the cardinal-primate of Hungary, who had died in March 1945. The nuncio had experienced the siege of Budapest and the entry of the Russians; he had observed how a temporary government had been formed in Soviet-occupied Debrecen under General Miklos—who had gone over to the Russians—even including a Catholic priest, István Balogh, in the cabinet. Soviet Marshal Malinowski had cordially received two Jesuits who visited him and requested protection for Catholic organizations; shortly after the occupation of Budapest he had allowed a Catholic peasants' congress.[64] But it was also known that along with the Soviets had come those Hungarian Communists from Moscow who had been waiting—since the abortive "soviet" revolution 25 years before—for this moment. Together with the rest of the diplomatic corps that had been accredited to the old Fascist government of Hungary, Nuncio Rotta had to leave the country in April 1945—but not without assurances of how glad Hungary would be to see a new representative of the Pope. . . .

The Vatican waited a few months. In the Budapest coalition government, the tone was still being set by the Smallholders' Party, which would also soon win the (last) free election. It needed the skilled, moderate backing of Hungarian Catholicism if the Communists, who were advancing step by step with their "salami-tactics," were to be held within bounds. Was Mindszenty the right man for this? Not a few Monsignori in the papal Secretariat of State doubted it, for they considered cleverness the least clearly-defined characteristic of this bishop. Others thought that Hungary was lost anyway; that Mindszenty, as the only tested anti-Fascist and anti-Communist as well, was the right man for the "finale."

On September 16, 1945, Pius XII named him cardinal-primate of the See of Esztergom. Mindszenty immediately made the government aware that this was no merely formal title: "The first common-law dignitary of the land is at the service of his homeland," he telegraphed in reply to the government's congratulations.[65] According to Hungarian common law (*ius communis*), the primate was president of the Privy Council and permanent member of the Upper House, in practice first to the king (who since the First World War no longer existed). "We live in a lawless abyss— but the prince-primate stands at his post!", Mindszenty exclaimed in his inaugural sermon, and called himself a "pontifex, bridge builder, and first dignitary of the state, vested with 900-year-old rights."[66] Did he perhaps consider himself "regent" for the Kingdom of Hungary—like Admiral Horthy in the inter-war period? On November 1, shortly before the elections, he had a pastoral letter read that the "Allied Control Commission" (composed of Russians, English, and Americans) released only after its western members insisted upon it; Mindszenty agreed with the words of the British Foreign Minister, that Hungary's situation "looks as if one totalitarian tyranny is being replaced by another"; today it wants to force the vote in the elections, "tomorrow it would lead to forced labor, and after tomorrow it would lead them to war."[67]

To describe in *detail* the fates of the Catholic church in the countries within the Soviet sphere of influence is not the theme of this book; only insofar as they are significant for understanding *Vatican eastern policies* must they be repeatedly illuminated—even if only through catchwords.[68] It would thus exceed the parameters of this study to analyze the confused political situation of post-war Hungary, or the clash between the totalitarian ambitions of the Stalinists and the traditional claim of the Hungarian church for recognition of its role (in school and culture, even in agriculture). It is essential to see how the personality of the cardinal-primate selected by the Vatican radicalized and accelerated the process of the Communist seizure of power by offering the Left, even the non-Communist Left, far more excuses for limiting the church's position than it probably desired at the time. For Hungary's Stalinists under the imprint of Matyas Rákosi, who are dying to throw out the baby with the bath water, have not yet received the go-ahead from Moscow. . . .

On November 30, 1945, Mindszenty flies to Rome for three weeks in the plane of the American mission, which continuously assures him that Hungary "will not be left in the lurch." "The Holy Father was very pleased with the report that Hungary is requesting the resumption of diplomatic relations with the Holy See; it pleased him even more that I was able to report this on behalf of the government," said Mindszenty after his return in an interview for the Catholic newspaper *Uj Ember*. Actually—as he disclosed only in 1974 in his memoirs—he had advised the Pope, who "immediately wanted to arrange for the return of Nuncio Angelo Rotta," against it and persuaded him to wait. Nevertheless, Mindszenty announced in the interview: "I have brought the Vatican's answer, which was in agreement, to the Prime Minister's attention."[69] That was, at the moment,

Zoltán Tildy of the left-wing Smallholders' Party—a pastor of the Reformed Church. His deputy is the Communist leader Rakosi. But does Mindszenty make it easy for the non-Communist head of government? On the day before he was elevated to cardinal (December 24, 1945), he proclaimed to Budapest workers: "How many rulers have already reigned on this earth: caesars, Napoleon, Hitler, Mussolini—they are gone! And how many things disappeared!" A week later, in a letter to Tildy, he protested "by virtue of the constitutional position due the Hungarian prince-primate" against the introduction of a republican constitution and against "the plan for the dissolution of the thousand-year Hungarian kingdom."[70]

As early as February 1946, Mindszenty again flew to Rome for four weeks in an American Air Force plane, this time to receive his cardinal's biretta. The question of diplomatic relations was still hanging fire, "although an agreement had already been reached concerning the form and the person," as he later reported.

In reality, with his reports in Rome, Mindszenty convinced the Pope that the dispatch of a nuncio was not feasible; probably the cardinal wanted to keep the reins in his own hands anyway. After all, he had also caused the government to take a dislike to the nuncio question by publicly representing—with long historical flashbacks—the function of such a papal delegate as exclusively one of *domestic-political* arbitration. As Mindszenty remembers it, the Pope supposedly had already prophecied to him at the presentation of his cardinal's biretta that among the 32 cardinals, he would be "the first to suffer martyrdom." Whatever Pius XII may have meant by that, he had made a correct psychological judgment of the new Hungarian primate. . . . And the Pope decided to stay out of Hungarian affairs for the time being.

Things were quite different in *Yugoslavia*. Here Tito's Communists had already come to power without direct Soviet help and assumed the difficult heritage of an ethnically heterogeneous state, whose Catholic part— Croatia—had openly collaborated with Hitler. Tito did not stick to Stalin's "people's democratic" moderation tactics, but immediately began an independent radical-revolutionary church policy, which could only welcome the opportunity to stamp a part of the clergy in Croatia with the mark of Cain, of "collaboration with the enemy." During World War II the fascist "Ustasa" organization of the Croatian leader Pavelic had kindled a bloody religious war against the Orthodox Serbs. The Catholic church and its Zagreb Archbishop Aloys Stepinac, who sympathized with the regime for nationalistic reasons, indeed tried to put on the brakes; the Vatican warned against the kind of forced conversions of the Orthodox that were being carried out by over-zealous monks. But the national passions thus inflamed finally backfired.[71] In 1945 the Vatican realized that it was imperative to make contact with Tito and pacify him.

But was it a happy idea to send an American, of all people, to Tito as the first nuncio? The Vatican believed it had made a particularly clever choice in Monsignore Patrick Hurley—that bishop from Florida who in 1941, to the concern of his clerical brothers, had so vigorously espoused American aid to the Soviet Union (see p. 211). On October 22, 1945, Hurley arrived in Belgrade and was received cordially by Tito. But the head of state also immediately confronted him with a demand: "Get rid of Archbishop Stepinac, take him back to Rome, install another one in Zagreb, or we will have to arrest him," said Tito.

The Pope rejected that, but avoided breaking relations with Yugoslavia even when Stepinac was arrested in autumn 1946, the first bishop in Eastern Europe to be brought to trial (on October 13), and was sentenced to sixteen years of forced labor. Pius XII contented himself with expressing his "great sorrow" about the trial and proving the Vatican's innocence in the forced conversions in Croatia.[72]

Tito's break with Stalin (1948) and America's friendly advances toward "non-aligned" Yugoslavia may have promoted this forbearance. Disappointment was thus all the greater that Tito's refusal to incorporate himself into the "eastern bloc" by no means had the anticipated consequences, but rather paradoxical ones:

"We have broken with Moscow, why can't you break with Rome?" Tito asked a group of priests at the end of 1949.[73] To be sure, in the summer of 1951 he offered the Vatican the release of Stepinac under the condition that the archbishop leave the country, and when the Pope refused that, he released Stepinac from prison anyway at the end of 1951 and exiled him to his home village. However, Tito then considered the Pope's announcement that he would raise Stepinac to cardinal as a "provocation": on December 17, 1952, the chargé d'affaires of the nunciature in Belgrade, Monsignore Silvio Oddi, finally had to pack his bags: Tito broke relations with the Vatican. But even now the Pope was prepared "forgivingly to ignore [Tito's] offensive language," as he told the cardinals on January 12, 1953.

Any other nation would have recalled its representative long ago anyway, wrote the *Osservatore Romano* on January 2, 1953, and explained the "infinite patience" of the Vatican thusly: the existence of diplomatic relations "was to have made possible a *modus vivendi* as soon as the necessary preconditions for it had been created by an act of good will or by understanding." That Belgrade had now "cut the cord" was "completely unnecessary. . . ."

This argument sounds astonishing when one knows how slim the prospects of a *modus vivendi* with the Communists were estimated by the

Vatican itself at the end of World War II, and how little inclination it felt for a dialogue with them. Yugoslavia—because of its soon palpable distance from Moscow—may have been an exception there.

And incidentally, Albania too; the head of government Enver Hoxha in March 1945 asked the apostolic delegate in Tiranë, Monsignore Leone Nigris, who was bound for Rome, to "greet the Holy Father in his name and express to him his admiration for his humanitarian work."[74] Nigris unfortunately did not even get a chance to return the greetings; on his return on May 24, 1945, Hoxha only allowed him to land in Tiranë,—and sent him off with the next plane. Albania, which only broke with Moscow much later and finally—in 1967—proclaimed itself the "first nation in the world totally cleansed of religion," thereby already showed signs of a certain independence.

For from 1944 to 1947/8, almost all of the governments of Eastern Europe oriented toward Moscow were still concerned—as we have seen—with displaying a certain degree of religious tolerance and entering where possible into discussions with the Vatican. The Soviet government itself repeatedly sent out feelers until 1947; two Hungarian priests with Vatican passports made several trips between Moscow and Rome (as the French Father Jean de Matha reports, who from 1947 to 1949 was Father Braun's successor as pastor of Moscow's St. Ludwig's).[75] Supposedly the Soviet diplomats Pushkin and Ossukin suggested a "framework for an agreement" at that time, which was to have been followed by appropriate agreements with the "People's Democracies." A further attempt was set in motion from Berlin: Josef Müller, the Catholic founder of the Bavarian Christian Democrats (CSU), at the request of Soviet General Leonid Georgiev, arranged a conversation in 1946 between the Berlin episcopal vicar-general Prange and the Soviet diplomat Smirnov; Müller himself, in a private audience, then delivered to the Pope a Soviet offer of agreement from Moscow which Pius XII told Müller was "worth serious considera-tion."[76] (See also p. 293).

Similar probes were made through the later Bishop of Meissen, Heinrich Wienken (1883-1961). As head of the commission ("*Kommissariat*") of the Fulda Conference of German Bishops he had 35 meetings with first the Soviet General Chuikov, then with the general's political advisors Lieutenant Tulpanov and the later High Commissar Semionov. He negotiated very quietly essential guarantees for the Catholic church in the Soviet-occupied area of Germany that still exist for her today in the German Democratic Republic (GDR). Not only the retention of religious instruction and the possibility of educating priests, but also public processions, pilgrimages, and religious radio services, a Catholic publishing house (St. Benno in Leipzig), as well as the never-broken contact with Rome, and above all the unquestioned nomination of priests and bishops, were among the arrangements that Wienken arrived at (supported also by Otto Nuschke, the Protestant leader of the East German Christian Democrats). To this end he had special instructions from the Vatican, which however itself abstained from any contact.[77] On the Soviet side there was at that time still an interest in demonstrating a relatively tolerant religious policy, especially in Germany—which was not yet completely divided.

Such beginnings soon miscarried in the rest of Eastern Europe, not only as a result of the Vatican's skepticism and unwillingness to negotiate, but also largely because of Stalin's decision to introduce the rapid Sovietization of Eastern Europe after all. Its instrument was to be the "Communist Information Bureau" (Cominform), under which guise Stalin reanimated the old "International." As at the end of the twenties (if more convincingly in view of the American policy of "containment"), Stalin now used the phantom of an *external* threat in order to pull in the reins *domestically*— this time within the zone of his satellite states. The conflict with religion and the church again belonged to the "intensified class struggle." Still: what had been possible in the Union of Soviet Republics could not as easily be repeated in countries with a predominantly western tradition as Stalin— and the Vatican—thought.

VIII

On A "Cold War" Course: Secret
Bishops Again, 1949-1955

The Schubert Case and the Tragedy of Rumania

Bent, sunken-cheeked, breathing heavily when the
memory of his suffering almost choked off his voice—this
is how, after a detective-like search, I found a 75-year-old
man in a worn suit with dark shirt in the little Rumanian village of Timisul
de Sus on July 1, 1965. On his hand, with the callouses of a heavy laborer,
gleamed a gold bishop's ring: Joseph Schubert, Rumanian-German,
apostolic administrator of Bucharest, titular bishop of Ceramussa. His
name was never noted in the *Annuario Pontificio*, and only once in the
Osservatore Romano: on February 23, 1969, a month before his death,
when the Pope received him for the first and last time. Bishop Schubert's
fate, in his own words, will serve as a model for a broader historical
examination, whereby the author of this book must act as witness for the
reader.[1]

"I have something important to tell you," said the papal nuncio, Bishop
Gerald Patrick O'Hara, when the pastor of the Bucharest cathedral,
Schubert, visited him on June 30, 1950—shadowed by suspicious security
police. The nuncio glanced at the clock: "This very night, let's say in two
hours, I shall consecrate you as bishop."

Schubert paled: "But Your Excellency! Even my nomination as
apostolic administrator of Bucharest in May was not cleared with the

263

government; if the authorities now find out about a bishop's consecration—and surely it cannot be hidden from them—I'll go to prison!"

The nuncio, a stalwart American bishop who had been transferred directly from his diocese in Savannah, Georgia, to distant Rumania,[2] looked at the cathedral priest in amazement; then he said, striving for a solemn intonation: "Then you must simply go to prison as a bishop—the church needs martyrs everywhere!"

Thus Pastor Joseph Schubert was secretly consecrated bishop in the chapel of the Bucharest nunciature—like six other Rumanian Catholic priests before him.

Only a week later, O'Hara, denounced by the press as a "spy in priest's clothing," but quite unmolested thanks to diplomatic immunity, left Rumania forever. The government had accused him, in a trial that was staged against his chauffeur, of collecting "military information." We can establish today, however, that only this much was true: the Catholic clergy of this country (in which all Catholics were Hungarians or Germans) repeatedly reported to the nunciature about harassment, chicanery and arrests—and also about infringements by the Soviet troops stationed in Rumania. The nuncio usually passed on such reports, which naturally allowed conclusions to be drawn about camp locations, to his American compatriots in the "Allied Control Commission." This commission and the nunciature were obviously surrounded by eavesdroppers.

The Cold War between East and West had reached a high point at this time (on June 25, 1950, the "hot" war in Korea had begun, which was seen as a dangerous test of strength between Stalin and the USA). Nowhere in Eastern Europe did Stalin pursue the sovietization of a country as radically and with less regard to national character as in Rumania; nowhere did he find among the native Communists such fanatical, partly hysterical, partly cynical stooges; in this situation the underground seeds of the later nationalistic "heresy" of the Ceausescu era were also being planted.[3] The atmosphere of police terrorism simultaneously favored intimidation of and pressure on the national minorities of the country—and that meant on the non-Orthodox religious communities as well. The Rumanian-Orthodox church, under its clever Patriarch Justinian Marina, succeeded, by means of absolute, demonstrative loyalty to the new regime, in "slipping in under" its anti-religious policy; to this day it has preserved its position, and also its religious substance, to a degree attained by no other Orthodox church of Eastern Europe.

From the very beginning it therefore allied itself with the Communists against "alien" Catholicism. Following the Soviet example in the Ukraine, the 1.5 million Catholics of the eastern (Rumanian) rite were reunited, with

the help of strong police pressure, with the Orthodox church in 1948—
exactly 250 years after their union with Rome under the gentler pressure of
the Habsburg empire. Four of the five bishops who resisted died in prison,
the fifth, Juliu Hossu, in 1970 in an Orthodox cloister; after his death, Pope
Paul VI honored him with a cardinalship. . . .

In order to facilitate the liquidation of the Catholic Uniates, Rumania on
July 17, 1948, cancelled the old concordat (of 1927), which had guaranteed
their existence. First there was a campaign against the Vatican, "whose
imperialist activity is well-known" (Party Leader Gheorghiu-Dej). On
August 3, 1948, the government issued a decree on religion containing
Article 41, which had grave implications for the 1.2 million Hungarian and
German Catholics of the Latin rite: "Foreign religious cults may not
exercise jurisdiction over faithful on the territory of the Rumanian state."
Every religious denomination had to present "its own organizational,
directive and administrative *statute* together with the creed" to the Min-
istry of Culture for examination and approval.

The Soviet model of the twenties is becoming evident. Like Bishop
Cieplak previously (see p. 45), the Catholic bishops of Rumania now
nevertheless try to negotiate an acceptable law with the government.
Apparently they are in a better position than Cieplak, for there is still a
nuncio in Bucharest who could help and could at least try to arrange a
tolerable text with Rome too. But the misfortune is that this emissary of the
Pope is not only inept, but also has instructions that amount to the same
two-track methods we know from the twenties, when Pacelli was
negotiating with the Soviets in Berlin and d'Herbigny simultaneously was
supposed to produce secret *faits accomplis* (see pp. 67-102).

If it was not too clever to send an American as nuncio to the delicate post
in Bucharest in the first place—right under the Soviets' nose and in the
middle of the Cold War—now O'Hara was proving rather uninterested in
actual diplomatic business. The nuncio rejected a statute for the Catholic
church which the bishops—who were already somewhat handicapped in
office—had laboriously worked out and which the government was willing
to accept with few alterations. Article 1 of this statute would have at least
specified that the Catholic church would "carry out its activity in
accordance with its dogmas, legal instructions and traditions, in agreement
with the laws of the state"; Article 2 stated that "the Pope is its highest
authority in matters of faith, morals and spiritual jurisdiction"; and Article
13, that the nomination of bishops "is the prerogative of the Holy See on
the recommendation of the Catholic church of Rumania, based on the
concurrence of the Rumanian government."

Could one not at least have tried to survive the Stalinist period on this
basis? The Vatican saw this statute only as a "clever instrument for the

subjugation of the church." Probably the Communists meant it that way—but could the Vatican not take the risk (as the Rumanian-Orthodox church did successfully) and so at least try to save the pastoral possibilities? Or was there another alternative? Pius XII thought he saw one. He had Nuncio O'Hara prepare not a *modus vivendi*—but a catacomb church. Within a few months O'Hara secretly appointed a total of twenty apostolic administrators, drawing up lists of replacements whom he considered worthy of succeeding each other as *Ordinarii substituti* if the predecessor went to prison. In place of the five imprisoned Uniate bishops he consecrated six secret bishops, who were all arrested only two months later. (The five of them who survived were released in 1964 after 18 years in prison and had to live in secluded villages with no priestly function.[4])

Besides Schubert, O'Hara also consecrated the pastor Adalbert Boros of Timisoara as secret bishop for the Latin church. Pastor Joseph Schubert was first on the nunciature's list for the (Latin) diocese of Bucharest, whose Archbishop Cisar[5] had resigned and been exiled to a village. Schubert had earned this honor by supporting the uncompromising position of the nuncio—even against some members of the episcopal curia. In addition to external oppression came—as is so often the case—internal intrigues within the clergy, differences of opinion that were played up with moral pathos and used accordingly by the Communists. Only his secret installation as bishop made Schubert doubt the rightness of the nuncio's action, and the whole uncompromising attitude in general. After the nuncio's departure he found himself more and more isolated, and what he had feared came to pass only half a year later:

On February 17, 1951, Schubert was arrested in Bucharest, Boros in Timisoara. Proceedings were initiated against them and all the priests on the nunciature list. They were condemned as "Vatican spies," Schubert even to death. Then his sentence was commuted to life imprisonment; for years he was mistreated, put in chains, forced to perform the heaviest labor. Only when the Rumanian regime began to change at the beginning of the sixties was he treated somewhat more gently and finally, after *thirteen* years, released in July 1964 to compulsory residence in that village where I found him soon thereafter, a broken man.

"If I had known what I know now, that in other places, in Poland, in Hungary, they were trying to compromise! If the Holy Father had only given me a little hint!" Schubert said bitterly. He had repeatedly been presented with loyalty oaths to sign, in which he was to pledge civic loyalty and promise to follow Vatican instructions only in religious and moral questions. He had always refused, although they had offered him the archepiscopal see of Bucharest, whose rightful administrator he was anyway according to the Vatican.

But perhaps it was lucky at least for Bishop Schubert's peace of mind that he never assumed this seat with the permission of the Rumanian government. For other prelates who had been on the afore-mentioned nunciature list received black marks for this in Rome: the first had been Monsignore Traian Jovanelli (no. 3 on the nuncio's list). He was released from prison shortly after Schubert's arrest in 1951 and allowed to assume his office in the archepiscopal curia after he had signed the desired loyalty oath. He was followed later by Franz Augustin (no. 5 on the list), who got out of prison on the same conditions. Both were considered apostate by the Vatican. As late as 1965, Petru Plesca, who was consecrated as bishop in Rome (now with the government's agreement), was asked mistrustfully by Vatican prelates why he had never been in prison. . . .

Anyone who got off must have paid the Communists some price—that was current opinion for a long time in the Roman curia, and in Rumania as well. One would have to have ridden a white horse through the country (which no one can forbid)—like the Hungarian Bishop Aaron Marton in Rumanian Alba Iulia—and played all kinds of legal tricks on the government to find favor in Rome and with some of the faithful after a pardon from the state. That began to change slowly only after John XXIII and the Second Vatican Council. Even the sly Franz Augustin, who had brought his cathedral parish in Bucharest through the worst times (with ministry, religious instruction for children and better church attendance than in any parish church in Rome!), received a papal blessing in Rome in 1964—even though he became a representative in the Rumanian parliament. He financed the living expenses of Bishop Schubert, banned from Bucharest, and is countenanced by Rome to this day (1979) as Substitute Ordinary. His dream of an archepiscopal see, of course, will probably never be realized. . . .

Joseph Schubert, however, the unyielding, who was senselessly (and for the ministry quite uselessly) exposed to thirteen years imprisonment without any attempt to free him, finally—as one can understand—could no longer comprehend the world and his church. When Monsignore Giovanni Cheli of the Vatican Secretariat of State, after discussions with the government church office in Bucharest, brought him the offer in 1966 to become archbishop of the capital—but with Franz Augustin as vicar general—he replied what he had told me earlier: "I'd rather be dead than . . . with that . . .!"

Bishop Schubert died in Munich on April 4, 1969, and was buried in the Frauenkirche. Only when he was already fatally ill could he leave Rumania, at the beginning of 1969. On February 8 he arrived in Rome. He waited two weeks before Paul VI embraced him—that Pope who, as Monsignore Montini, had become "Pro-Secretary of State for Ordinary

Affairs of the Church" at the beginning of the fifties. Montini knew, as few others did, the derelictions through which Pius XII had allowed Eastern European Catholicism to come to an impasse, that made the game all too easy for the Stalinists. "The only attitude recognized in Rome is that of Monsignore Schubert," wrote Domenico Tardini (the Secretary for Extraordinary Affairs in the Secretariat of State) as late as May 10, 1951, to the doubtful Bucharest cathedral chapter, when Schubert had already been in prison for three months and no other Rumanian bishop remained free. That "attitude"—honorable and obedient—of course also gave those in the West who spoke of the "silent church in the East" with a pious shudder, an alibi for their own political sloth. . . .

The Pope Speaks—Budapest and Prague Become Silent

And was the Pope again silent on all this? Did he preserve the same reticence vis-à-vis the Eastern Europe of the fifties that he had so scrupulously observed through five years of war ("to avoid even worse")?

By no means. As if to free himself from prolonged pangs of conscience, he now found strong, sharp words. But because he had always paraphrased the war crimes carefully or deliberated on them is silence, his words now sounded strangely out of proportion and suggested the question: did that rule that loud battle cries and protests would only bring still greater afflictions upon the faithful suddenly no longer apply? Pius XII may have felt this himself, but he turned the question around when he said in October 1947:

"What was in the opinion of many a duty of the church, and what they demanded of her in an unseemly [!] way, is today, now that these people have come to power, a crime in their eyes and a forbidden interference in domestic affairs of the state: namely resistance against unjust restraint of conscience by totalitarian systems and their condemnation all over the world. . . ."[6]

The Pope of course hereby called attention to the contradictions of others, but had not cleared up his own. He, the cautious one, now minced no words about the new regimes in the East. He differentiated "between the peoples, who are often robbed of every freedom, and the systems that rule them"; but he also testified to the "knavish dependence" on the Communists of the "so-called Orthodox" churches (Christmas address 1948).[7] In an almost Manichaean way, he began to sketch a picture of a historic battle between good and evil, in which on the one side were only "the good in radiance of virtue," on the other only the "machinations of the infernal foe."[8]

He cries to the imprisoned Ukrainian bishops: "Even if you are now in chains, these speak more loudly and clearly, and proclaim Christ."[9] He consoles the Rumanian bishops, after they have all been incarcerated: "Remember that a reward awaits you in the other world. . . . Know that all Catholics are fervently praying with Us to God that He end your sufferings quickly. . . . Better to continue to bear exile and prison rather than to deny your faith and loosen or dissolve the strong ties that bind you to the Holy See." Now that it is too late, the Pope assures Rumanian Communists that the Catholics "are second to none in respect for civil authority and in obedience to the laws, insofar as these do not demand anything that contradicts natural law, the law of God and the church."[10]

In *Hungary*, where the Communists throttle legal political opposition and assume sole power in 1948, Cardinal Mindszenty considered himself the last leader of a resistance—in the political sense too. The Pope praised Hungary on May 30, 1948, as a "weathered oak that nothing can uproot"; faith strengthens the Hungarians especially "when the enemies of the name and dominion of God waylay you with craft and treachery."[11]

The nationalization of the predominantly parochial schools became a test of strength; the episcopate asked the government to recognize "that a final regulation of this so important question is impossible under present circumstances without the intervention of the Holy See." Party Chief Rákosi—Hungary's "Stalin"—who not incorrectly saw in the disputatious cardinal his most dangerous opponent, wanted to eliminate him: on December 26, 1948, he had Mindszenty arrested, which the Pope only a week later pilloried as a "wicked audacity." Pius XII reacted especially bitterly to Rákosi's irresponsible maneuver in announcing three days after Mindszenty's arrest that

1. the cardinal had already admitted to being a spy and conspirator (which was not true);

2. the government wanted to make an agreement with the Vatican;

3. Hungary's bishops should take up negotiations immediately.

"Do not be led astray by that illusory appearance of truth with which they are deceitfully and enticingly trying to lure your hearts," the Pope warned the Hungarian bishops in an open letter.[12] And the *Osservatore Romano* (on January 2, 1949) called it inconceivable that, after the treatment of Mindszenty, an agreement between the Vatican and Hungary could still be realized.

On February 8, three days before the show trial[13] against Mindszenty in Budapest ended with a sentence of life imprisonment, the Pope (in an address to the curial cardinals) refers to the "insidious cunning" of the accusations and to the broken condition of the confessing cardinal, which would hardly be thinkable "without secret influences, that do not permit mention" [an allusion to brainwashing by drugs].[14]

There is no doubt that the vengeance of Rákosi and his Moscow principals affected the cardinal most brutally; it is just as certain that the cardinal never conducted political opposition on the Vatican's orders or inspired by the "U.S. imperialists"—as the charges stated, substantiated partly with absurd exaggerations, partly with false proofs. Mindszenty did this in his very own stiff-necked, naive and unworldly way—as many of the prelates in the Roman curia had feared from him from the very beginning. (See the letters of the American Minister in Budapest and Monsignore Montini's letter on pp. 234-5.) He hoped for the possibility of a world-political change, for "salvation from America," and regarded the fact that the Pope was no longer silent—as he was during the war—as an affirmation of this hope. It was, as the Pope now asserted,

". . . quite contrary to truth if during the course of this trial the claim is made that the Apostolic See, out of a will to power, had given commands and directives against the republic of Hungary and its leaders. . . . Everyone knows that the Catholic church is not guided by earthly motives, that it *tolerates every form of government* as long as it does not contradict divine and human rights. . . ."[15]

Cardinal Mindszenty, however, who regarded himself as a state dignitary (see p. 256), certainly had "earthly motives" too, which he identified with the religious. Afraid of assuming partial responsibility, the Vatican had actually to a large extent left it to him to determine the church-political course in Hungary (see also p. 259). But Pius XII, with his public speeches between 1945 and 1948, had helped to form the general atmosphere of this course. Such scorching words as the Pope directed at the Roman people in St. Peter's square on February 20, 1949,[16] *after* the judgment against Mindszenty, had not been heard from his lips at any terror verdict of the years 1939-1945. However, they not only conformed to his post-war policy line, but also revealed how the old "silence complex" tormented him, how much this trauma influenced the behavior of an innately hesitant Pope:

"Romans! The Church of Christ does not interfere in purely political or economic questions, it is not concerned with the quarrel over the utility or harm of one or the other form of government. . . . However, it is only too well known what the totalitarian, anti-religious state . . . demands of the church as the price of its tolerance: a church that is silent when it should preach; . . . a church that does not oppose the violation of conscience and does *not protect the true freedom of the people and its well-founded rights*; a church that, with a dishonorable, slavish mentality, closes itself within the four walls of its temples. . . . Can you imagine a successor to Peter who would bow to such demands?"

Four times in succession, like a public orator, Pius XII asked the faithful on St. Peter's square the question: "Can, may the Pope be silent?" And the echo of the crowd, the shrill "No" that resounded to him, may have strengthened him, but would hardly have freed him from his trauma. . . .

For Eastern Europe's Stalinists, in any case, such words were fuel for the fires with which to further intensify the battle against the church. But there was more to come: on July 1, 1949, the Pope, through the Holy Office (once the Inquisition, now called the Congregation for the Faith), for the first time in this century excommunicated members, supporters and followers of Communist parties, indeed even mere readers of their newspapers—in any case, that was how the decree was loudly interpreted by the anti-Communist *and* Communist propaganda of the day.

On closer examination, to be sure, there are precise differentiations in the document: "conscious and voluntary" *membership* in Communist parties, support of them and the reading and dissemination of their publications, is punishable by *exclusion from the sacraments*; the threat of *excommunication* because of apostasy, on the other hand, is valid only for those "believers" [!] who espouse the doctrine of materialistic and anti-Christian Communism (*fedeli che professano la dottrina del comunismo materialista e anti-christiano*).

Now, one could ask what kind of "believers" those are who *profess themselves as anti-Christians*, and still placed any significance on exclusion from the church?! Basically, this anti-Communism decree expressed a very self-evident conclusion which said nothing new. Archbishop Casaroli, Pope Paul VI's "Foreign Minister," even delicately intimated this in a lecture 23 years later.[17]

However dull a theological, canon-law instrument the decree was, (even the Italian CP worried only briefly about it), it had a sharp effect as a political weapon in Eastern Europe. It permitted opponents of the church, if they simplified it, to cast doubts on the civil loyalty of Catholics and to confront the clergy with the painful question as to whether it was not a foe of any kind of "socialist system," indeed of every practical cooperation for the welfare of the general public.

With this decree, the Pope had aimed at that hybrid collaboration of well-meaning or merely adaptable believers, who as "friends of peace," "progressive Catholics," and "priests of peace" under Communist rule were confusing rather than bridging the intellectual fronts. He had probably also thought that by drawing a sharp canonical line he could steady the bishops in Eastern Europe and prevent them from making what he considered too sweeping agreements. In reality, he caused the clergy in Eastern Europe great embarrassment (except for clergymen who were seeking total confrontation and martyrdom). The Roman decree—as we shall see—in fact accelerated the attempts of the bishops in Hungary and Poland to quickly salvage what they could. Only in Czechoslovakia was it already too late even for this. . . .

It was a coincidence, but for Prague Communists a lucky one, that the anti-Communism decree was issued on July 13, on the same day that the last representative of the Vatican was forced to leave Prague: "On the evening of the day that [Monsignore Gennaro] Verolino left forever the land he wanted to prepare for civil war, a decree was issued over Radio Vatican that threatens the Catholic Communists [sic!], and those who cooperate with them, with excommunication. . . . Without doubt, anyone who carries out the orders of the Vatican will become a traitor to state and people," announced the CSR Minister of Justice Čepicka,[18] the son-in-law of state president Klement Gottwald who a year earlier had set great store on the Archbishop of Prague's intoning a "Te Deum" at his accession to office. . . .

Never during the inter-war period had relations between Czechoslovakia and the Vatican been as good as immediately after 1945. It seemed possible to many people, even in the Vatican, that Stalin would have to respect the strong western democratic traditions of this country. The large Communist party, which participated in the government, even had a chance to come to power legally. On May 13, 1946, relations with the Vatican were re-established; Archbishop Saverio Ritter came to Prague as nuncio. The Pope, with prudent foresight, named an anti-Nazi resistance fighter, Joseph Beran, who had spent three years in German concentration camps, as the new Archbishop of Prague. A Communist Minister of the Interior pinned an Order of Merit on Beran's soutane right at his installation.

The situation in Slovakia was politically-psychologically encumbered; from 1939-1944 it had been a republic by grace of Hitler—with the Catholic priest Josef Tiso as state president.[19] Using anti-Communist arguments, Tiso had strongly supported Hitler's policy of extermination of the Jews. He paid no attention to the Vatican, which indeed had its nuncio in Bratislava protest, but did not initiate any church discipline against Tiso.

"That the Holy See cannot stop *Hitler*, everyone understands, but that it can't put the brakes on a *priest*—who can comprehend that?" noted Monsignore Tardini in 1942 with an unmistakably critical reference to his "boss," the Pope.[20] In a collective pastoral letter by the Slovakian bishops, the Jews were represented as "anti-national" murderers of Christ; their steadfast attitude had been seen "in the bloody persecutions of Christians in Russia and Spain in which the Jews played an important part;" still one should not forget "that even a Jew is a human being. . . ."[21] The nuncio considered one of the Slovak bishops, Jan Vojtassák of Zips, a "great chauvinist" because this prelate had characterized humanity toward Poles and Jews as "almost sinful" (*humanitas nostra esset fere peccaminosa*).[22]

This same Vojtaššák was the first Catholic bishop who already in April 1945—on orders of the chairman of the Slovak National Council, the anti-clerical Communist Gustav Husák—was imprisoned, but in consideration of the national mood was freed again. A few years later, both of them—Vojtaššák *and* Husák (the later Party Chief of the CSSR)—were put on trial: for Stalinists there was hardly any difference. After acceding to sole power in spring 1948, they thought any excuse to strike at the church as such was justified.

For this very reason, should one not avoid giving them excuses? This was the question the Vatican asked itself about Czechoslovakia, as everywhere else, without arriving at a conclusive answer. Archbishop Beran was prepared to negotiate; but he would not and *could* not do so without the assistance of the Holy See, which was represented in Prague—in contrast to Budapest and Warsaw—by a chargé d'affaires. In February the discussions were broken off because the government refused to allow the participation of the papal representative, and because it not only insisted on a loyalty oath from the bishops, the text of which seemed unacceptable to the Pope, but also demanded the rehabilitation of the priest Josef Plojhar, who had become Minister of Health without the church's permission (and who supported the Communists with his pseudo-Catholic "People's Party"). Had the Vatican not allowed the priest Tiso to be active for the Slovakian Fascists. . ? , it was now asked pointedly.

"The Vatican in the service of American reaction," read the title of an official brochure in Slovakia; a campaign began against the nunciature chargé d'affaires. Naturally it did not escape the secret police's attention that Monsignore Verolino, a peripatetic Neapolitan, was traveling around the country visiting the bishops and vesting them with those powers to establish a substitute and underground hierarchy with which we are familiar from other countries. But hardly had Verolino been expelled and the Vatican anti-Communist decree issued than the Czech Stalinists felt able to drop the last restraints. In the fifties almost all the bishops were arrested and replaced by vicars general or capitular, selected by the state (some were bought or blackmailed, others went along in order to save the ministry). Archbishop Beran, whom they did not dare to put on trial, disappeared for fourteen years, interned in village parsonages or cloisters. Monks, nuns, and theology students were locked up by the hundreds in "concentration convents" and "re-education camps." These were actions in which a mixture of Stalinist and Hussite fanaticism was vented with an over-zealousness characteristic of the country.[23]

And at the same time, the emergency measures prepared by Rome came into play: In the Czech region, the Prague chaplain Kajetan Matoušek was secretly consecrated bishop in the middle of September 1949; he escaped arrest temporarily only because he made no use of the office. "You did not become a bishop so that you could hide," he was told one day by a Jesuit novice with forty months in an army penal company behind him. Matoušek secretly ordained him as a priest, and was soon "discovered"; to this day (1978)—although formally suffragan bishop of Prague—he is only allowed to officiate as a priest. Ladislav Hlad of Pilsen, secretly consecrated in 1950, under arrest since 1960, after nine years in prison was pastor in an old people's home—after 1973 even this was forbidden him. Karel Otcenasek, then 30 years old, was secretly consecrated as bishop in April 1956 in Hradec Kralove. Arrested shortly thereafter, he was in prison for over ten years, then worked as a milkman; since 1967 he has been allowed to resume the ministry, but only as a parish priest at Trmice. He was never able to officiate as bishop. Only František Tomašek, secretly consecrated in October 1949, briefly in a penal camp, then active as a pastor, later rose to official episcopal rank—the price for Cardinal Beran's resignation.

In Slovakia, Pavel Hnilica, a Jesuit, was secretly consecrated in the early fifties, and in 1959 conferred the honor upon the Slovakian Jesuit Jan Korec, who worked as a glass grinder and was immediately locked up for seven years (while Hnilica lost his nerve and—to the displeasure of his superiors—crossed the "green border" to the West and settled in Rome). Soon after Jan Korec, in 1961, a Slovakian construction worker in Prague, the Jesuit Petr Dubovsky, was vested with the bishop's rank under the seal of secrecy. He was thereupon put in prison for six years for "endangering the republic." Korec and Dubovsky are still alive today (1979); Korec was allowed to be priest of a children's hospital from 1968 to 1974; since then he has been a transport worker; Dubovsky is a pastor in a little village.

On August 16, 1968, I met one of the Czechoslovakian secret bishops (all are long since known by name to the authorities) in his one-room apartment; at that time he worked in an office as a city employee. In the kitchen corner he had built a little altar at which he used to say the mass. In his opinion, it would make some sense to build up an "underground church" with secret bishops if one believed that "in ten years everything would be over," that is, that the Soviet Communist supremacy in Eastern Europe would be only temporary.

"However, even in this case the attempt was more than dubious," said the bishop, "because the omnipotence of the police was underestimated, as was the risk existing for those who had to perform their duties, such as ordaining priests, administering confirmation, without official permission, if they were to fulfill their episcopal function at all. After 1945, and especially after 1949, the West continually gave us hope of freedom—not only 'Radio Free Europe,' but the Vatican radio station too—of course without ever saying when and how this would come about. Many people here also believed what the official party propaganda argued: that a war between the USA and the Soviet Union was inevitable; and some even hoped for it. This naive belief received its first, almost fatal, blow in 1956, during the events in Hungary [when Soviet troops brutally crushed the rebellion], because the West did not help."

"And what connection did you, as a secret bishop, have with the Vatican? Besides the spiritual authority, did it give you any instruction?" I asked.

"Nothing; we were left to ourselves—everyone for himself; most were inexperienced, young, naive, spiritually afire. We had trouble not hating those who were trying to help themselves and the faithful by compromises because they thought that the conditions were permanent and to be accepted as an act of God. From the Holy Father we now and then heard calls that could be interpreted in several ways. . . ."

"The Roman Pope is represented as an enemy of your people," lamented Pius XII on October 28, 1951, in a message to the Czechoslovakian Catholics.[24] "They go so far as to accuse him of preparing another, more dreadful war, whereas he . . . does not allow any opportunity of furthering peace to slip by. Do not lose courage, any of you, beloved brothers and sons!," the Pope cried to them and promised them the admiration of all the world for their loyalty "when finally all *errors are conquered* and the church is again given its due freedom. . . ."

Agreements in Poland and Hungary: "Embarrassing Concessions"

The Polish bishops in 1949 were more alarmed by the Mindszenty trial in Budapest, by the radical anti-Vatican campaign in Eastern Europe, and not least by the Vatican anti-Communist excommunication decree in July (see p. 271), than by Communist chicanery and "administrative measures" that tended to bounce off strong Polish Catholicism. In the Warsaw government, the Communists alone now set the tone; the Stalinists were just preparing to topple the "national deviationist" Wladyslaw Gomulka.

Cardinal Hlond's far-reaching papal authority, which included negotiations with the government, after his death at the end of 1948 had passed to the new primate, Archbishop Stefan Wyszyński, only 47 years old. He was "no politician, no diplomat," but rather a minister, Wyszyński had asserted right at the beginning. But for that very reason, he considered the Roman decree, which church opponents greeted with great joy, as folly from the pastoral point of view, and—since the Vatican had left the church in Poland to itself anyway—he decided on a rescue action on his own. Speed was of the essence, since the government was already preparing to initiate a kind of "patriotic" movement among the priests, intended to isolate the bishops.

Wyszyński later boasted that he and the Polish bishops had dared to take "the great risk" of supplying the government with "an enormous trump in view of world opinion"; they had "not relied on experiences abroad" and had not "prematurely" assumed a lack of good will on the part of the Communists (*letter to State President Boleslaw Bierut, May 8, 1953*). Wyszyński's courage and his calculation of the risk actually did not arise from a very optimistic, but rather a pessimistic, assessment of the situation. In any case, the agreement that was signed on April 14, 1950, by the episcopal and government members of a so-called "Mixed Commission," to the astonishment of the world, and especially of the Pope, was an event "without precedent," as Wyszyński correctly wrote.

While bishops and priests went to prison in Rumania, Hungary and Czechoslovakia because they refused to take oaths of loyalty to the Communist rulers or at least to distance themselves politically from the Vatican, the Polish episcopate, after relatively short, but harsh, negotiations, signed statements such as these:[25]

"The principle that the Pope is the competent and highest authority of the church refers to matters of faith, morals and ecclesiastical jurisdiction; in other matters, the episcopate is guided by Polish reason of state (*racja stanu*)." (Art. 5)

"Proceeding from the principle that the mission of the church can be realized under various socio-economic systems erected by secular authority, the episcopate informs the clergy that it does not oppose the construction of the cooperatives (*spoldzielczośći*) in the villages, since every cooperative system basically rests on the ethical basis of human nature which is oriented toward voluntary social solidarity and has the general welfare as its goal." (Art. 6)

"True to its principles, to condemn any anti-state behavior, the church will above all oppose any exploitation of religious feelings for anti-state purposes." (Art. 7)

The state's recompense consisted of a promise not to touch religious instruction in the schools, the existence of the Catholic university in Lublin, the existing Catholic associations, pilgrimages and processions, military and hospital ministries, and above all the "absolutely free activity" of religious orders (which were completely liquidated in Czechoslovakia and Hungary).

In deference to the papal authority to make concordats, this arrangement was characterized neither as a "contract" nor an "agreement," but rather as an "understanding" (*porozumienie*). In the Vatican, the document had a shocking effect, as some Monsignori remember even today. If one thinks that Pius XII seven months earlier had still tried to console the Polish bishops with the verse from the Psalms "that in the future too, the way of the ungodly shall perish and their plans profit nothing,"[26] one can imagine with what discomfort the Pope took cognizance of this agreement. This all the more so because, while he had not been consulted, he was addressed on a decisive point of this document, and had to help foot the bill, so to speak, for this *modus vivendi*. For it said:

> "Proceeding from the principle that the recovered territories [the formerly German ones beyond the Oder and Neisse] form an inseparable part of the Republic, the episcopate turns to the Apostolic See so that the church administrations, which are vested with the rights of resident bishops, be changed into permanent ordinary dioceses." (Art. 3)

This was the point at which the Polish Stalinists could re-exert pressure at any time and accuse the episcopate of non-fulfillment of the agreement; for they knew only too well that Pius XII had no intention of meeting the nationalist desires of Poland and giving up consideration of the electors of the German Catholic Chancellor Konrad Adenauer, or of arriving at any final settlements *before* a peace treaty (which lay far in the future). To the indignation of Catholic Poland, the Pope on March 1, 1948, had not only called the forced resettlement of millions of Germans from the Oder-Neisse area politically unreasonable, but also expressed the wish that "what has been done be undone, insofar as it may still be undone."[27] Though the Warsaw government had refused "to recognize" the five apostolic administrators installed by Cardinal Hlond in the Oder-Neisse region (see p. 255), it had nevertheless not ceased to press for a final resolution; now the episcopate gave its assent—but Rome apparently turned a deaf ear.

As early as the summer of 1950, the government used this as an excuse to violate the agreement. It struck on January 26, 1951: all five administrators were ordered to leave their sees. Government officials appeared with the canonical code of law under their arms and ordered the competent cathedral chapters to elect vicars capitular. Although the majority were priests who closely cooperated with the government, Primate Wyszyński recognized their election in order to avoid a split in the church. And—he hastened to Rome to bring the Pope around.

Twice within a two week interval, in April 1951, the Pope received the Polish Primate in private audience. The Pope treated him with cool dignity, subtly letting him know just how greatly he had been shocked by the agreement of 1950. For four weeks, Wyszyński tried to explain to the Roman curia the complicated situation in Poland (with a strong Catholicism and a very weak Communism in a "camp" overwhelmingly dominated by the Soviets). There was some understanding, but more skepticism and at the end only a partial concession from the Pope: the five administrators in the Oder-Neisse region were named titular bishops.

Wyszyński then tried—in a long conversation on May 12, 1951—to make this modest solution palatable to the Polish head of state Bierut as a major step toward the ultimate recognition of the Oder-Neisse border by the Vatican. The final answer came from Moscow, where *Pravda* wrote on July 17, 1951:

". . . The Pope is still negotiating through his double agents. His Polish policy is exclusively determined from the point of view of American imperialists, who are working for world hegemony. . . . The Vatican is declaring itself strongly for the rearmament and the return of the Fascist regime in West Germany. . . . Obedient to the wishes of Pius XII, the episcopate did not agree to Poland's treaty with the GDR [East Germany], in which the Oder-Neisse line is recognized. *Wyszyński's trip changed nothing in this regard.* . . . The clique that leads the Catholic church in Poland completely follows the line of the Vatican, which is an enemy of peace and democracy. . . ."

We have quoted this gem of Stalinistic journalism in detail because it also represented instructions for the Polish Communists. Now the struggle against the church in Poland was really unleashed, although it never attained the violence that it did in Czechoslovakia, Hungary and Rumania. But even now, Wyszyński—whose elevation to cardinal at the end of 1952 was regarded as a provocation by the Communists—was still realistic enough to avoid what would have been in line with Vatican policies, that is, to secretly consecrate the titular bishops who had been rejected by the government in 1951. That took place much later, long after Wyszyński's arrest (1953). Not until autumn 1954 were Bishops Edmund Nowicki (later in Danzig/Gdańsk), Theodor Bensz and Boleslaw Kominek (later cardinal in Breslau/Wroclaw) consecrated in the private chapel of the Bishop of Przemyśl, secretly of course, but without harmful consequences—since after Stalin's death, things had become less dangerous.

"The battle is still raging. . . . The mighty virgin [Mary] and conqueror of the powers of hell will lead you to glorious victories. . . ." With such statements, the Pope thought he could "help" the Polish church (in an apostolic letter of September 1, 1951)[28], after he had involuntarily aided Stalinist efforts to twist Wyszyński's attempted compromise as a historical proof of good will into an instrument against the church.

Wyszyński's unpleasant experiences at that time with Polish Communists as well as with Roman prelates form the most important psychological-historical roots of his later ever-growing pugnacity. This did, of course, in times of extreme threat to Poland—as in 1956, 1970 and 1976—always give way to a conciliatory, diplomatic attitude dictated by the "reason" of state and church.[29] And it was in this regard, above all, that Wyszyński always differed in the last three decades from the Hungarian Cardinal-primate Mindszenty. In contrast to Wyszyński, who during his detention (1953-1956) never saw the inside of a prison, was never mistreated and never brought into court, Mindszenty was deeply humiliated, abused and isolated.[30] Of course, his intellect and his ecclesiastical-diplomatic talents would hardly have sufficed, even with relative freedom of action, to attempt the risky ventures that Wyszyński repeatedly undertook, as with the agreement of 1950, but also later.

However, a year and a half after the Mindszenty trial, Wyszyński's example encouraged the Archbishop Joszef Grösz, the new chairman of the Hungarian episcopate, to attempt a similar undertaking. Like the primate of Poland, he formally possessed the necessary authority from the Vatican; but he, no more than Wyszyński, asked for prior express agreement from Rome. Since the Pope undertook nothing concrete to support the church in Hungary politically and diplomatically, indeed had rather effected the opposite with his anti-Communism decree of 1949, the bishops acted without him. They "only wanted to save what still seemed salvageable, at a time of affliction and isolation," they later wrote to the Cultural Minister Jószef Darvas.[31]

The situation in Hungary was incomparably more threatening and oppressive than in Poland. Since the Mindszenty verdict, the church was increasingly discriminated against. In the middle of June, thousands of monastics were driven from their cloisters overnight. Yet in spite of that—indeed for that very reason—Grösz signed an agreement with Cultural Minister Darvas on August 15, 1950. It differed from the Polish one not only in that it was much shorter and less concrete, but also in that a far greater imbalance existed between the promises of the church and those of the state. Above all: the Holy See, or any reference to the Pope, was not even mentioned. Grösz was only able to attach to the agreement a unilateral accompanying letter in which the conference of bishops declared "that with this agreement it in no way intended to impair the rights of the Holy See. . . ."[32]

The bishops now expressly recognized the new constitution of the People's Republic, condemned all anti-state activity and called upon the faithful to support the five-year plan "with all their strength," including the collectivization of agriculture. In foreign politics, the episcopate promised "to support the peace movement," to condemn war-mongering and the use of the atom bomb.

The government promised what was already in the constitution anyway (and for that reason was not even mentioned in the Polish agreement): namely, freedom of worship. Not a word about religious instruction, but— as a sop—the return of *eight* (of the more than 3000) nationalized Catholic schools as well as financial subsidies for the church (of which the Polish church had no need). Only in those eight schools was the work of the religious orders allowed—otherwise not a word about the fate of the 53 Catholic orders, which were dissolved by a governmental decree literally on the day after the signing of the agreement (while the Polish agreement, in article 19, assured "complete freedom" to the orders).

No wonder that the Vatican was even more unhappy about this agreement than about the Polish one. To be sure, the Holy See could not offer the hard-pressed bishops any alternative, any practical way out—or even an attempt. An original document, the complete Latin text of which is reproduced here (see facsimile below) confirms this almost dramatically. The Vatican had at first not even wanted to believe the report about the agreement. Only when the Hungarian episcopate sent a message by roundabout ways did the Pope order his under-secretary of state Monsignore Angelo Dell'Acqua to write a letter on October 9, 1950 (No. 6990/50), to be delivered to Archbishop Grösz via the Italian embassy in Budapest:

SEGRETERIA DI STATO
b.
SUA SANTITÀ ·

N.6½.:/50

. EX AEDIBUS VATICANIS, die 9 Octobris 1950.

Exc.me ac Rev.me Domine,

Per nuntios radiophonico invento ac diurnis vulgatos, Apostolica Sedes didicit Episcopos istos Conventionem cum Hungariae Moderatoribus iniisse.

Initio rei - ex quibusdam saltem eius adiunctis - nihil veri inesse aestimatum est. At ipsa nuntiis postmodum acceptis pro dolor confirmata est.

Doleo quippe tecum communicare id maeroris haud mediocris causam Augusto Pontifici attulisse. Quod te istosque locorum Ordinarios aegritudine, non tamen stupore, afficere profecto poterit.

Etenim, ceteris, quae considerari possent, omissis, notum est publicas definire ac moderari rationes, quae Ecclesiae cum variis intercedunt Nationibus ad Sedem spectare Apostolicam.Agitur siquidem. de Pactionibus, quae ad Ecclesiae vitam regendam sese referunt in Natione universa, quarum effectus in Ecclesiae condiciones aliarum quoque Nationum recidunt, et, quod pluris est, res indultas ab ecclesiastica potestate non paucas continere solent: quae omnia auctoritatem dioeceseon Praesulum propriam, uti liquet, excedunt.

Verum quidem est - juxta relatos in diurnis nuntios - te in epistula Cultui, ut aiunt, ac Publicae Institutioni praeposito Administro missa, occasione confectae Pactionis, exceptionem interposuisse, quoad jus Sanctae Sedis, cum scribebas: "Episcoporum Collegium animadvertere cupit Pactionem hanc nullum afferre praejudicium Sedis Apostolicae juribus rationes definiendi inter Ecclesiam et Statum". At non videtur exceptionem huiusmodi peculiari consideratione dignam haberi, quandoquidem in cunctis ephemeridibus ac diurnis hungaricis Conventionem nulli subiectam esse dilatoriae condicioni asseritur;quod negatum fuisse ab ecclesiastica potestate ista heic non constat.

Exc.mo ac Rev.mo Domino
MATKO JOSEPHO GROSZ
Archiepiscopo Colocensi
COLOCIAM

Quodsi vero ea, quae Pactione continentur, examinantur, haud minus gravibus animadversionibus locus fit. Ibi equidem onera non levia imponuntur eaque talia ut difficulter cum Ecclesiae doctrina et normis componi possint.

Praeterea Conventio aliquem secum fert assertum violentae et arbitrariae universarum paene Societatum Religiosarum suppressioni, quae in rem a publica civili potestate jam adducitur. Pro perniciosis hisce concessionibus ab Episcopis factis, reipublicae Moderatores non aliud indulgent nisi vagam promissionem libertatem observandi religiosam – ceterum Constitutione ipsa declaratam – ac spondent sese ecclesiasticae potestati restituturos catholicas scholas octo, quae tamen munera sua difficile obire poterunt, ut res postularet.

Vix autem recolere expedit Sanctitatem Suam probe intellegere quibus difficultatibus ac minis Ecclesiae vita istic subdatur. At eae praemissarum animadversionum vim haud minuunt.

Pastoralem sollicitudinem ante oculos habens Beatissimus Pater, qua antehac isti sacrorum Antistites non caruere, eos iterum iterumque hortatur, ut vigili studio sacrosancta Dei animorumque jura tueantur: assidue reminiscantur praeclara Episcoporum Hungariae superiorum aetatum facinora. Omni virium contentione curent, ut secum et cum Jesu Christi Vicario conjuncti permaneant, simulque Clerum suum fidelesque doctrina et exemplis confirment.

Peculiari hoc volvente discrimine, Pontifex Maximus mente animoque prope est dilectum Hungariae populum, nominatimque prope eos qui, ob suam erga Ecclesiam fidelitatem, quoquo modo divexantur, sive ex ordine Cleri sive ex ordine laicorum sint. Praecipue autem Sanctitas Sua paterna conjungitur benevolentia Religiosis Sodalibus, tam duriter discruciatis, qui videlicet hisce temporibus sacra saepta derelinquere atque, veste sua deposita, tristes incertosque exspectare dies coacti sunt vel coguntur.

Sacris istis Praesulibus, Clero, Religiosis Sodalibus fidelibusque universis Augustus Pontifex Apostolicae Benedictionis robur amantissimo corde impertit, in auspicium divinae opis, qua recreati, valeant ardua sua munera explere intaminatumque posteris trasmittere fidei thesaurum, quo tam gloriosus Hungariae jam evasit populus.

Haec tibi dum refero, Sacrum Anulum deosculor, meque profiteor

Excellentiae Tuae
addictissimum

Sac. Angelinus Dell'Acqua
Subsecretarium

". . . I am sorry to inform you that [the news of the agreement] has caused the High Pontifex no small measure of grief. You and the local Ordinaries will note this with sorrow, if not with astonishment. For even if one ignores other considerations, it is a well known fact that it is the Apostolic See's right to define and balance (*moderari*) the political principles (*rationes publicas*) that exist between the church and the various nations. Especially when it concerns contracts that relate to the direction of the religious life of the nation as a whole and affect as well the conditions of the church in other nations and—which is even more [important]—contain not so small concessions by church authorities: all this clearly exceeds the proper authority of the diocesan directors (*auctoritatem dioeceseon Praesulum propriam, uti liquet, excedunt*). . . ."

Archbishop Wyszyński and the Polish episcopate may have received similar critical corrections from Rome after they had signed their agreement in April 1950. But the Hungarian bishops were now especially reprimanded because they had not worked into the contract a single clause referring to the Vatican and because they had practically accepted the arbitrary dissolution of the monastic communities: the counter-offerings of the government were by no means commensurate with these "pernicious concessions," wrote Dell'Acqua.

"His Holiness—as we do not need to remind you—can understand very well the difficulties and threats to church life there. But this does not diminish the emphasis of the aforementioned reproof. . . ." Still, "the Pontifex Maximus is close in heart and soul to his beloved Hungarian people . . . and he sends his apostolic blessing to the bishops, clergy, monastics and all the faithful. . . ."

This document has only become known because it served the Hungarian Stalinists, less than a year later, to bring to trial the man who had been so accommodating over the agreement of 1950: Archbishop Grösz. Under the cover of the leather sofa in his library, the police found Dell'Acqua's letter, together with 2500 dollars—subsidies from Rome. (The Archive of the Vatican Secretariat of State on September 17, 1974, confirmed to the author of this book the authenticity of this letter which was published by the Budapest government in 1951.)

"So they even condemned your hypocritical agreement!" cried the public prosecutor on June 22, 1951, and triumphantly held up this letter from Rome to the accused archbishop.[33] The stage-managers of this trial did not seem to realize that this did not dovetail with the position of their indictment: namely, that the chairman of the episcopate was a puppet of the Vatican and on its orders (naturally together with the US embassy— and with Tito!) had formed a "plot to overthrow the people's democratic government. . . ."

Grösz's fifteen-year sentence at hard labor was suspended five years later; indeed, the government of the National Communist and anti-Stalinist Imre Nagy recognized Grösz again as chairman of the episcopate. In the meantime, of course, the Catholic church in Hungary had been organizationally decimated, humiliated and intimidated. The few bishops still at liberty, who had mostly resigned not only politically but also ecclesiastically, continued to sit in their feudal residences, surrounded by state controllers and by a splendor that in their social environment and in view of their actual impotence had a quite surrealistic effect.

In 1955, Grösz was interned for several months in the castle of Püspökszentlászlo (near Pécs), together with Cardinal Primate Mindszenty, who in the meantime had been released from prison and placed under house arrest. Mindszenty spoke openly with Grösz—and in correspondence as well—although their contacts were limited. As Grösz later reported in private conversations, Mindszenty reproved him strongly because of the 1950 agreement. Even in his memoirs, in which he conceded Grösz's goodness and loyalty, the cardinal accused his colleague of "irresolute behavior." Mindszenty—as we first learned from his memoirs in 1974 (pp. 191-192)—had declined an offer from the government in the summer of 1956: he refused to return to his seat Esztergom because he feared that the Communists would regard him as "more or less one of their own," and because he did not want to watch "the humiliation of Esztergom," which he saw in the fact that the city had lost its rank as county seat. . . . If Mindszenty had at that time—months *before* the Hungarian revolution—reassumed the leadership of the episcopate (like the liberated Polish Primate Wyszyński), perhaps subsequent events would have taken a different turn and Mindszenty, like Grösz, would never have had to go into exile. Of course, this assumes that Mindszenty, like Grösz, would have swallowed his pride and been prepared to come down a peg or two.

Grösz' experiences with compromise had certainly not been good—but what was actually the alternative, he asked himself and the Primate. And what was the real purpose of the church: pastoral work or political resistance? Or had the two perhaps become inseparable as the struggle "for souls" was conducted in the political arena or even—as did the Stalinists—under police pressure? But was it serving the faithful—who wanted to hear the gospel and receive the sacraments—when their shepherds uncompromisingly delivered themselves up to the atheist state power? Was it more heroic for the shepherd to let himself be devoured by the wolves and thus deliver up the flock to them—or denying himself, to howl with the wolves in order to save the flock?

To these questions, contemplated in a Hungarian castle—surrounded by police—not even the Bible (John X, 11-18) gave any final, timeless answer: especially since the gospel was also valid for those people "who are not of our fold." And since "the good shepherd" should only "lay down his life that he may take it up again". . . .

In any case, the Popes since 1917 had never answered this question unequivocally and uncompromisingly (as this book has shown). And Pius XII, that cautious and frightened diplomat on the papal throne, who after 1945 thought he had to overcome his scruples by loud battle cries, would have been the last to raise "uncompromising stubbornness" to a general rule of church-political conduct—except for questions of church doctrine.

Stalin and the West had made it easy for him to join the general trend of the Cold War—just as his predecessor, Pius XI, had followed different political currents in the twenties and thirties. However, after Stalin's death (1953), as a new period in east-west relations, difficult in its own way, began in the middle of the fifties, this Pope too began to utilize the changing tide and warily to look around for new shores.

IX

The Difficult Shift Toward Co-existence, 1955-1964

Unsolicited Reconnaissance: Marcel Reding's Trip to Moscow

"You want to go to Moscow?" Jesuit Father Robert Leiber, one of Pius XII's closest collaborators, whose name never appeared on any Vatican VIP list, thoughtfully wrinkled his brow. Before him stood Marcel Reding, a Catholic theologian from Luxemburg, professor of moral theology in Graz (Austria). On this day in June 1955, during the "Cultural Days" in Florence, the enterprising Christian-Democratic mayor Giorgio La Pira had brought Reding together with Leiber to propose his—for that time— quite unusual plan:

Reding had received a government invitation from the Soviet embassy in Vienna to go to Moscow. Attention had been drawn to Reding, according to embassy counsellor Kudriazev, because he had been the first more or less conservative Catholic theologian in the West to favor a "dialogue" with the Soviet Union. Moscow had also noted that his colleague in Trier, Professor Joseph Lenz, had compared Reding to a sheep wanting to go to the tiger "to strike up a dinner conversation while being eaten."[1] Kudriazev thought that Reding should convince himself that there were no cannibals in Moscow. . . .

The theologian, who had never been active politically, had compared Karl Marx with Thomas Aquinas on December 5, 1952, in his maiden lecture in Graz, printed with permission of his bishop (imprimatur).

285

Reding had come to the surprising conclusion that there were such "deep analogies" (that is, Aristotelian) between the two thinkers that they would have been able to communicate with each other. . . .

"Why can't we?" Reding asked, arguing that "despite all the contradictions between Communism, Socialism and Christianity," a "human dialogue" should be possible.[2] That was "naive optimism," Professor Lenz had answered, to which Reding had replied that we must "at least attempt to alleviate our brethrens' lot, in our own way and without yielding an inch of the Christian doctrine." This debate between theologians was more than two years old. What made it so timely now?

Reding's theses were certainly not new. Back in spring of 1952, the Austrian Jesuit Gustav A. Wetter had discovered formal "inherent points of contact" between Soviet philosophy and Catholic thinking, and his German Jesuit brother Klemens Brockmöller had a year later drawn the conclusion from this which Wetter—as a professor at the Pontifical University in Rome—had avoided: "If Saint Paul had found that many correlations in the heathenist ideas of his time, he would not have hesitated to use them for the Christian message"; the clearer the contrast to Communism, the more open "the way to a meeting of understanding, certainly not between the systems, but between the peoples of these systems."[3]

All this would hardly have amounted to anything more than vague theory, if Stalin had not died in March 1953: the beginning of a new phase in the history of Soviet Communism.

"The struggle against religious prejudices must be regarded today as an ideological struggle between scientific-materialistic and anti-scientific-religious ideologies, . . . whereby the feelings of the faithful and the clergy must not be injured. Oppressive measures damage the goals of the Communist Party and ultimately result in entrenched prejudices. . . ." Thus read a declaration of the Central Committee of the Soviet Communists on November 11, 1954.

The Vatican pricked up its ears; first it spoke disparagingly of "propaganda," then, more attentive now, of a "swing of the pendulum."[4] The revived Leninist slogan of "peaceful coexistence" with the capitalist countries, which now introduced a period of military relaxation in world politics, marked the beginning transition from the "cold war" to a "cold peace," which did not leave untouched internal conditions in the Soviet empire: things solidly frozen began to thaw out, although without any recognizable finality. As always, the Vatican discreetly and flexibly prepared itself for *any*, perhaps even new, possibilities. Pius XII, with his diplomatic sense, but also the caution which he customarily adopted when the outcome of an affair seemed uncertain, in his own way took up the slogan "coexistence".

Since atomic powers faced each other in east and west, the two misgivings of the Vatican in 1943/44 (see p. 238) had become groundless: neither a Third World War nor the withdrawal of the USA from world and European politics was probable. Coexistence had thus become unavoidable—if only out of fear. But, as the Pope asked in his Christmas address of 1954, was this sufficient for a real peace? His answer was:

"To justify this expectation, it must somehow [!] be a *coexistence in truth*. But a bridge between these two separate worlds can be constructed from the truth only if it is based on the *people* living in the one and the other world, and not on the form of government or social system. . . ."[5] Seven months later, however, at the first east-west summit conference in Geneva, an initial rapprochement between the governments (not of the *forms* of government) was reached. At the beginning of June 1955, the new Soviet leadership invited the German Catholic Chancellor Adenauer, whom they considered their most dangerous opponent in Europe, to Moscow—and already on June 27, three days before Adenauer accepted the invitation (after obtaining the endorsement of the USA in the middle of June), Pius XII changed his tune even more:

"The true Christian westerner nourishes thoughts of love and peace toward the peoples of the east, who live within the sphere of influence of a materialistic Weltanschauung supported by state power. If the question of coexistence continues to move the spirit, then we can frankly affirm one kind of coexistence: faithful westerners pray together with those on the other side of the iron curtain who are still stretching out their hands to God—and these are not few in number—that we will become unified in complete freedom. . . ."[6]

This was actually nothing new in principle, it only seemed original in the east-west atmosphere of the time (which was still stamped by the last phase of the cold war), especially as the Pope simultaneously distanced himself somewhat from the world "that is generally called free." The old, only slightly buried policy of "impartiality" again became cautiously visible. And during these same days of June 1955, the Graz Professor Reding approached Father Leiber with his plan to travel to Moscow.

As Pius XII's "private secretary," Father Leiber knew better than most that the Pope was now increasingly upset by the question of how the supranational church should proceed "in this world of Communism, Americanism, and nationalism." Used to thinking almost more with his exalted boss's head than with his own, Leiber believed he sensed something of a "turning point" that would become necessary: the church—like the rest of the world—would have to live in this century and perhaps also in the next *with* Communism, *within* its structures. It would even have to hurry to find a mode of practical coexistence with the Communists before it was too late—before the breath of religious life was snuffed out completely among the millions of Catholics in the east. . . .[7]

These were considerations that perhaps went beyond those of the Pope, yet Robert Leiber not only knew the timid character of the Pope, which with advancing age cloaked itself more and more in a condescending unapproachability, but as a silent observer he had also noted evidence of change within the Vatican: for example, a tug-of-war behind the scenes in the curial apparatus, which always began when a pontificate was nearing its end. Under-Secretary of State Dell'Acqua and Milan Archbishop Montini (whom Pius XII had removed from the curia) had asked Socialist leader and Stalin Prize winner Pietro Nenni to do some non-committal fact-finding on his trip to Moscow. After deliberation, Robert Leiber had told a trusted journalist in Rome of this state of affairs—about which the Pope also knew, and had raised no objections—though not for the sake of gossip; and this although Leiber foresaw that the Vatican would soon publish a denial out of consideration for Italy's Christian Democrats.

So how could Leiber answer the Graz Professor Reding? Would he deter him from the Moscow trip? "Five times between 1945 and 1949 the Russians made inquiries regarding the resumption of diplomatic relations, and each time the Holy See declared its readiness, but nothing more was heard from the Soviets," Leiber told Reding, and at the same time reminded him of the many years of fruitless discussions which the Pope, when still Nuncio Pacelli in Berlin, had conducted with the Soviets until the end of 1927 (see p. 112f.). "One misjudges this Pope if one believes that he ever wanted to slam any door. He never passed up any opportunity to negotiate that arose. If the Russians really want to negotiate again, they can make it known through diplomatic channels."

"Does that mean I should drop the trip?" asked Reding.

"I wouldn't say that!", Leiber retreated. "Ask the Secretariat of State!"

There too, Reding could not get a clear answer. When the Austrian ambassador to the Vatican made inquiries as a mediator, the Vatican referred him to Reding's local bishop, the Graz Ordinary Schoiswohl. And he, after discreet inquiries in Rome, then finally gave his permission— months later.

As Reding flies to Moscow on December 16, 1955, both sides have already prepared the atmosphere for such a non-committal fact-finding tour: on September 7, before an international convention of historians in Rome, the Pope recalled the concordatory policy of the church, which had always been directed toward procuring "the legal security and necessary independence" for its mission. Konrad Adenauer's spectacular journey to the Soviet Union begins the next day. Shortly thereafter, on Sunday, September 11, the German chancellor kneels in St. Ludwig's in Moscow, where the Polish Pastor Buturowicz reads the mass. Adenauer does not know that it is the same pew in which, 19 years earlier, another German

Catholic chancellor, Josef Wirth, attended the mass for a bishop secretly consecrated by Eugenio Pacelli. . . .

"Religion in Soviet Russia is as good as eradicated. . . .One should not have any illusions about that," Adenauer was told.[8] However, clever Kremlin staging assured that this Sunday morning—September 11, 1955—two Catholic bishops could be consecrated for the first time since the war in Soviet Lithuania. Four months previously, right after the Four-Power Agreement about Austria (which marked the first Soviet foreign policy concession to the West), the Vatican—as a test case—had delivered two nominations of bishops to the Vienna Soviet embassy and formally requested endorsement.[9] Again the Vatican's policy toward the East followed in the footsteps of the West. . . .

Marcel Reding was received curiously and politely in Moscow on December 17, 1955. Igor Polianski, the vice-minister in charge of non-Orthodox religious communities at the time in the "Council for Religions," insisted on accompanying the Catholic professor of theology on his two-week air journey: first to Ečmiadzin, to see the leader of the Armenian church, then to Leningrad to the only Catholic church in the city on the Neva. On Christmas morning, Reding (in the presence of Polianski and the head of the Soviet-Lithuanian government!) celebrated a mass in Lithuanian Vilna and visited the newly-consecrated Bishop Julian Steponavicius.[10] In a three and a half hour discussion he tried to convince four professors of the Moscow "Academy of Sciences"[11] of his theory that the atheism in dialectic materialism was only politically determined, but not essential to the system.[12]

However, Reding's last and most important discussion partner was little interested in such philosophical bridge-building: Anastas Mikoyan, then the First Vice-Premier of the USSR and member of the Party Presidium. He received Reding on December 28 for almost an hour of discussions. The professor from Graz told him that he had no instructions from the Vatican, but had come with the knowledge of his church superiors to hold discussions with atheists, to study the religious situation and to ascertain quite privately "whether a *modus vivendi* between the Vatican and the Kremlin would be at all thinkable." Mikoyan, apparently waiting for that cue, assured him (as Reding himself told me eleven years later[13]) that. . . .

". . . the Soviet Union was doing its best to maintain contacts with all peace-loving organizations, including the churches. However, correct relations between the USSR and the Holy See were only possible if the church did not interfere in political affairs. The details of a *modus vivendi* would have to follow negotiations with Polianski. . . ."

This sounded very indefinite, and the theology professor was not experienced enough diplomatically to arrive at a more precise definition.

The report that Reding sent to the Vatican Secretariat of State (through Bishop Schoiswohl) after his return in January 1956 thus offered the opponents of any dialogue new ammunition. Reding himself remained silent and discreet. Even when I visited him in Graz at the end of February 1956, he would say nothing about the contents of his discussion with Mikoyan. Nevertheless, the report that I published at the time in the *Frankfurter Allgemeine Zeitung* (FAZ) about Reding's journey had an inflammatory effect on many Vatican circles.

The *Osservatore Romano*, greatly agitated, had already in December replied to an article in the FAZ in which I observed signs of a Catholic "shift toward coexistence" (without possessing at that time the background knowledge that is presented in this book). Now, in March 1956, Federico Alessandrini, the deputy director of the Vatican paper, sharpened his pen again: referring—without naming names— to a "Catholic engaged in theological studies" (*catolico, cultore di studi teologici*), he compared Reding's journey with that of the curious Polish-American pastor Orlemański who had been received by Stalin in May 1944 (see p. 230). The editorial of the Vatican paper insisted that discussions with the Communists remained impossible even after Khrushchev's de-Stalinization speech (February 1956); besides, nothing indicated that the Soviet government was interested in a concordat. In principle, such agreements were of course not excluded even with totalitarian states, but one would "signify that such a state set limits to its own totalitarianism."[14]

To be sure, the Roman curia had realized that the Soviets were interested in "some kind" of contact. For that reason, Alessandrini had been instructed by the Secretariat of State to work into his polemic the basic preconditions for any concordatory rapprochement. Reding's trip of course was not considered a sufficient indication of serious Soviet intentions. Above all the Pope feared that confusion would arise within western Catholicism: in Moscow's slogan of "coexistence," the ideological and the power-political were none too clearly meshed, therefore "coexistence" could undermine the anti-Communist bastions in which Catholics had so comfortably established themselves—abandoning their "brothers in the East" to silence.

Even while Reding was celebrating the Christmas matins in Vilna before tearful Catholics, the Pope presented a new showpiece of his political-theological balancing act in his Christmas message of 1955: he once again condemned "Communism as a social system," but at the same time warned the West against an "anti-Communism that rests only on the defense of an empty freedom" and against an "*indiscriminate* coexistence with *anyone* at *any* price"—as if anyone in East or West had ever argued for *such* a coexistence!

The Pope must have become aware of the difficult position into which he had thus maneuvered himself when Radio Moscow praised him the very next day. Naturally not for his statements about Communism, which Moscow passed over in silence, but because in the same Christmas address he had for the first time warned of the horrors of an atomic war and further atomic tests.

Attempts at Dialogue, Backlash in Hungary—and Poland's Solitary Course

Was this perhaps the Communists' new tactic: to weaken their opponents by "embraces"? Had they thereby become even more dangerous—or was it *their* weakness, which could now be ruthlessly exploited? Was the whole de-Stalinization which began in February 1956 with the XXth Party Congress only a pretence hiding the "unalteredly brutal face" of Moscow? Or was it the beginning of the end of Communism? All these questions were hotly disputed all during 1956 in the West—and also in the Vatican. And when at the end of this eventful year the Red Army put down the rebellion in Hungary, those now unaccustomed to careful reflection as a result of the "cold war" were confirmed in their opinion of the unchanged nature of Soviet Communism. They did not see that the tragedy of Hungary, which Poland only narrowly escaped, was nothing other than the first reaction to the real, though inconclusive, changes that had begun with the end of the Stalin epoch.

Hopes, erroneous estimates, uncertainties—these are also reflected in the Vatican's behavior in 1956. Though the *Osservatore Romano* in March had lamented the lack of "any kind of gesture" toward the Holy See and especially demanded the release of imprisoned Eastern European bishops and cardinals, the Vatican paper still seemed unimpressed when in April— symptomatic of a rapid process of domestic relaxation—Archbishop Grösz was not only released from prison, but immediately recognized again by the Budapest government as chairman of the Hungarian conference of bishops. Grösz announced in the Hungarian press that he intended not only to be loyal to the government, but also "in accordance with the intention of the Holy Father Pius XII, to stand up for peace." It was the first positive Hungarian press statement about the Pope in years.

In May, the Communist *Unità* in Rome published an interview with the new Lithuanian bishop, Petras Mazelis: he said he was in contact by letter with the Vatican, but thought that in the future, relations between the Holy See and the Soviet Union could be regulated by a concordat "or in some other way." Moscow did indeed seek contact "somehow," although the echo from the Vatican did not sound inviting. For hardly had the anti-

Stalinist agitation in Poland reached the boiling point which on June 28 led to a bloody uprising in Poznan, than the Pope on the very next day appealed directly to the peoples of Eastern Europe with an apostolic message in which he reminded them of the victorious war against the Turks:

> ". . . Today you are again being most grievously and sorrowfully afflicted. . . . It is a matter of your eternal salvation, which today, as a result of the increasing insolence of the atheists, is in grave danger. However, if every individual fights bravely and loyally in this battle of the spiritual, there will only be praiseworthy victims, never any vanquished. . . . Some may lose courage, weaken in zeal, and—which is even more fateful—believe that Christ's teachings must be moderated and, in their words, accommodated to the new times and local conditions. . . ."[15]

Those meant above all were Catholic groups collaborating politically, such as the Polish "Pax" movement,[16] which had for years been a thorn in the side of the Vatican, but which were only now directly attacked as the Polish Communists seemed to be approaching a dangerous crisis: a decree of the Holy Office placed a book by the Pax chairman, Boleslaw Piasecki, on the Index of forbidden books on June 29, 1955.

Moscow, however, remained undeterred from seeking contacts with the Vatican. But for what purpose? In July and August the Soviet ambassador to Rome, Bogomolov, had already put out feelers to the papal nuncio for Italy, Fietta. Then his deputy, Poshdayev, had asked for a meeting with Monsignore Fietta. The Pope hesitated. The nuncio—as doyen of the diplomatic corps—would not have been able to refuse the ambassador a conversation (cf. the similar situation in 1941 in Berlin, p. 204), but he did not have to receive a chargé d'affaires. Pius XII's diplomatic sense, however, overcame his reluctance. On August 21, 1956, Poshdayev presented disarmament suggestions to the nunciature, which the Soviet government was offering all states at the time. The hope was, they said, that the "Vatican state" would also make its contribution to this effort. But Fietta had instructions to leave no doubt that the Pope represented not only a tiny, unarmed state, but a world church: he pointed to the "serious religious situation in the Soviet Union" and to the "necessary guarantees of religious freedom." Poshdayev listened politely—and silently.

This meeting, which aroused much speculation, gave the Pope new occasion for a loud demonstration: ten days later, in a radio message to Cologne, he warned the 77th German Catholic Congress (*Katholikentag*) "against the phantom of a false coexistence."[17] The church was facing "the most dangerous persecution ever"; it could even "be justly proud" of the fact that things had come to a "collision" between itself and the atheists. Did he really want to encourage such pride in those 28,000 East German

Catholics who at that time could still travel almost unhindered to Cologne? There was as yet no wall in Berlin; the Soviet bloc would have to live for five more years with a relatively open GDR border, and "East Germany"—as the Vatican, to the displeasure of Bonn *and* East Berlin, called the GDR at the time—was considered the "great exception" by the Roman curia: nowhere in the East had the Catholic church to date been so little obstructed (see also p. 261). Was it very clever, then, to burden the all-German Catholic Congress in Cologne, in particular, with war cries?

The Pope had thoroughly considered this objection; toward East Berlin especially he had behaved carefully up to now. He had received congratulations on his 80th birthday, in March 1956, from the Vice Prime Minister of the GDR Otto Nuschke, the leader of the East Christian Democratic Union—the only birthday wishes from an Eastern statesman. Nuschke, a faithful Lutheran, had quietly done a great deal for the churches in the GDR, the Catholic included, since 1945. His congratulations were thus no mere formality. Naturally the East-CDU had published Monsignore Dell'Acqua's thank-you note, in order to credit it to its own prestige account. But the editors of the *Osservatore Romano* were not a little astonished when they were instructed in a note from the Pope's own hand to print this thank-you note from Dell'Acqua themselves, and thus give the exchange of letters an official character. Here the blessing of God was called down on Nuschke: "May He illuminate you and strengthen you to full effort so that in your land, which is also dear to Him, the laws of God and the church are recognized and protected."[18]

In this sense, diplomatically balanced, the Pope perceived his message to the all-German Catholic Congress in Cologne: the sharp accusations against the system of political atheism which—if one looked to Poland and Hungary—had apparently entered a crisis, served as a cover for informing the Communists of the conditions of a possible *modus vivendi:*

> "The Catholic church does not compel anyone to belong to it. However, it does demand for itself the freedom to live in the land according to its own constitution and laws, to care for its believers and to be able openly to proclaim the message of Jesus Christ. This of course is its unalterable basis for any honorable coexistence. In the meantime it will fight on—not in the field of politics and economics, as it has always been falsely accused, but with its own weapons: the steadfastness of its believers, prayer, truth and love. . . ."

This papal address of September 2, 1956, was nothing less than a well-packaged cease-fire offer, which was submitted to all of Eastern Europe—not out of weakness, but calculation—in case the opponent, against all expectations, should soften. A week earlier, in Czestochowa, a million Poles, with 34 bishops, had demonstrated peacefully but unmistakably for the liberation of their primate. In Hungary, a wave of Communist self-criticism was flooding the land. On September 12, in Königstein/Taunus, one of the Pope's closest advisors and the co-author of many of Pius XII's speeches, the Jesuit professor Gustav Gundlach, appeared before the "Conference: Church in Distress" and surprised his militant anti-Communist audience:

"Do not believe that the church is being drawn into the problem of coexistence by the journalists! It is in the middle of it by its very nature!", said Gundlach, and argued against those who "would present St. Peter's Square as the Red Square" as well as against those who ascribe to the church "a certain Roman cunning and maneuverability, the course of which can never be predicted." Actually, it was neither a matter of "softening" nor of a crusade, which the Pope would "never want to provoke or bless," but of this:

> "The church, under *any* circumstances, will pursue *every* possibility of assuring a minimum of pastoral care in areas where there is none today. And it will take *any* path that to some degree guarantees this. It will seek *every* means on behalf of souls that are deprived of doctrine, of the sacraments; but that is no real embracing of or shift toward Communism. . . . In all eras, the church has tried, in the most difficult situations, to save what it could, to take paths that were at all passable. . . ."[19]

Such a complicated "differentiation of the concept of coexistence," the Catholic journalist Otto Rögele objected to the papal advisor Gundlach, could "hardly be elucidated to all our intellectuals, to say nothing of the absolute impossibility of explaining it to the simple people."[20] This was not a doctrinal matter, however, but part of the basic pragmatic pattern of all Vatican "policy" toward the East which could be seen shining through its fine-spun web. The fact that a man like Gundlach now in the middle of September 1956, should focus on it (without thereby announcing anything new) was due to the fact that the Catholic people—the intellectuals too—had lost sight of this basic pattern in the turmoil of the cold war.

But now western Catholics had to be prepared for a new situation that seemed to be emerging. For six weeks later, Cardinal Wyszyński returned to Warsaw, and Cardinal Mindszenty freely to Budapest. Not that the Vatican had lapsed into sanguine optimism when at the end of October 1956 Wladyslaw Gomulka in Poland and Imre Nagy in Hungary—two ostracized "National" Communists—seized the rudder. But the Pope did not hesitate to greet all these events publicly as "harbingers of the peaceful reorganization of the two states on the basis of healthier principles and better laws"[21]—and this on November 1. On the evening of the same day, Nagy announced over the radio that the Soviet troops (which had fallen back before the bloody popular uprising) were advancing on Budapest a second time and that Hungary was withdrawing from the Warsaw Pact.

At 8:24 p.m.—hardly half an hour after Nagy—Cardinal Mindszenty came to the microphone of the Budapest station and could do nothing better than to announce that he was now investigating how the means toward a "fruitful development" could be found, and that in two days he would again by radio "appeal to the nation about the way toward a solution."[22]

That was a signal for the Vatican to quickly send nunciature counsellor Corrado Bafile, of the Secretariat of State, to Budapest on the morning of November 2 to exercise a moderating influence on Mindszenty. After all, the Polish Cardinal Wyszyński, on this November 2, had done no more than call for an all-embracing mutual love in his first sermon.[23] Would Mindszenty take advice along these lines and renounce any political speeches? Monsignore Bafile got only as far as the Austrian-Hungarian border, where the president of the "Papal Relief Work," Prelate Ferdinando Baldelli, had negotiated in vain with the commander of a Soviet tank unit. No one was allowed through to Budapest, especially not a Vatican diplomat.

On the evening of November 3, Soviet tanks are twelve kilometers from Budapest. Toward 6 pm Mindszenty tells the German Bundestag representative Hubertus Prince zu Löwenstein:[24] "Be strong, be prepared! Otherwise Hungary's fate could be yours tomorrow. Moscow does not shrink from any act of force. . . .Only greater force can protect against them." Two hours later—and eight hours before Soviet cannon open fire on Budapest!—the Cardinal speaks on the radio[25] and demands "the [immediate] re-establishment of freedom of Christian religious instruction as well as the return of the institutions [and associations] of the Catholic church, including the Catholic press." In the tone of a government program he demands "new elections secured against any misuse, in which every party can participate." The tyrannical regime imposed in 1945 had been "swept away" by the nation; its "heirs should not wish any further proof of that." (This final sentence, which is contained in the tape recording, Mindszenty left out of his memoirs. . . .) The Cardinal polemically emphasizes these "heirs" five times: the government of the Communist Nagy (which will already be out of office the next day). The guilty persons in the toppled regime are to be called to account before the courts, but individual acts of revenge must be avoided, says the Cardinal, and simultaneously asserts: "We are neutral, we give the Russian empire no cause to spill blood. . . . We desire friendship with the great United States of America and with the powerful Russian empire." He instructs the Soviet leaders "that we would respect the Russian people far more if they did not enslave us." He himself doubts whether the Kremlin, which sees its empire threatened, can be pacified;[26] still he does not sense that at this moment his speech can only add fuel to the fire.

To be sure, even a Cardinal more familiar with the virtue of wisdom would no longer have been able to put out the fire—so reasoned the Vatican. The Pope, who (in conversation with his collaborators) made no secret that he considered Mindszenty's behavior imprudent, is astonished when the Hungarian primate, on the very day after his fiery speech, having no desire to become a martyr again (a humanly understandable reaction), flees from the Soviet troops to the nearby American embassy, with which the Communists had always suspected him of "conspiring." "That's all we need!," sighed some prelates in the Vatican, who could see beyond the obvious to other approaching embarrassments.

Since the whole world—even a part of the Communist—was airing its outrage over the Soviet intervention, Pius XII also makes haste so as to avoid the old reproach of silence. In Hungary, "the yoke of servitude has again been forced with foreign weapons upon a suffering people," he laments in a short encyclical on November 5, 1956,[27] and five days later—in a radio message to believers all over the world—his eighty-year-old voice trembles: "Can the world abandon these brothers to the fate of a humiliating slavery?" The Pope now even demands a "firm, open pact" that would send illegal attackers into the "desert of isolation," but at the same time move them to "more moderate decisions."[28]

"If We were silent, then We would have to fear God's judgment much more!" he justifies himself in his Christmas address (1956) against the reproach of contributing to the hardening of the fronts. At this time, the East-West relaxation of tension seems to have been superseded again for an indefinite period by a return to the cold war; Moscow's prestige, indeed that of world Communism, has suffered a blow—but so has the illusion that a Western great power would ever be prepared to guarantee anything other than the European status quo of the demarcation line of 1945. This discordant state of affairs (which soon returned the East-West relationship to the coexistence course) is reflected in the strongest political emotions that Pius XII ever allowed himself publicly:[29]

> "We, as head of the church, have avoided, just as in earlier cases, calling Christianity to a *crusade*. We can, however, demand complete understanding for the fact that, where religion is a living heritage from their forefathers, people view as a crusade the struggle that was unjustly forced upon them by the enemy. . . . We are convinced that even today, the only way we can and will save the peace against a foe who is determined to impose upon all peoples in one way or another a particular and unbearable way of life, is by the strong and unanimous union of all who love truth and goodness."

Never before had the Pope identified so unequivocally with the western alliance. Christians should also not approve a "tactical smoke screen" under the name of "dialogue," he warned. "What use is it to talk to each other without a common language?"

But to draw the conclusion from this that all bridges were to be burnt, on the other hand, was to misjudge the "nature of the church" (Gundlach) and the pragmatic basic principle of all Vatican policy toward the East. The Pacelli Pope, for whom the concept of full equality for the simple laity and even the "lower clerics" could hardly be more than a theological arabesque, forbade dialogue to them; but he reserved it for the high diplomacy of states—and of the church:

> "But it would be good . . . , to maintain the mutual ties, people say. But what the responsible men of politics and state—and not special interests—find necessary for contacts and relations to maintain peace for humanity, is sufficient. And *what the church authority thinks it must accomplish in order to maintain the recognition of the rights and freedom of the church is also sufficient.*"

With this last sentence, the formula was incidentally coined that would make it possible to give a measure of blessing to the *Polish way* that Cardinal Wyszyński was following with the Communist Gomulka at the end of 1956. For just as the Roman curia was embarking on a full cold-war course again, a new understanding between church and state was published in Poland on December 7, 1956:

The communiqué of a common commission of episcopate and government[30] was tied—without expressly mentioning it—to the old emasculated agreement of 1950 (see p. 276). The government, which released all imprisoned clerics, promised "to remove obstructions which arose in the earlier period in the process of implementing the principle of complete freedom in religious life"; the bishops in turn assured their "complete support (*pelne poparcie*) for the government's effort to strengthen and develop the People's Republic of Poland, to achieve conscientious obedience to its laws and to assure the fulfillment of civic duties." In addition, a decree of 1953, which had made appointments to all church offices dependent on state consent, was now replaced by another in which the state claimed only a temporally limited veto;[31] the government now finally agreed to the installation of those five titular bishops in the Oder-Neisse region, whose nomination Cardinal Wyszyński had wrested from the hesitant Pope back in 1951 as a partial solution (see p. 278).

Again—as in 1950—an agreement between church and Communists had emerged without Vatican consultation. Wyszyński had even commissioned as direct negotiator Michal Klepacz of Lodz, the very bishop who on the day of the Cardinal's exile in 1953 had, as the new chairman of the episcopate, cordially entertained with a bottle of wine the head of the Religious Affairs department in the Interior Ministry, Colonel Ms. Luna Brystigerowa (who had delivered the government's confirmation to him). . . .

Klepacz had at that time sworn an oath of loyalty to the government which the Vatican had branded "objectively invalid."[32] After the new decree, published December 31, 1956, diocesan bishops also had to "ceremoniously" pledge loyalty to the People's Republic and its legal order (Art. 6). And on January 15, 1957, Wyszyński even asked Catholic citizens to participate in the *elections* for Gomulka's single-party slate (which however also included, for the first time, eight Catholics of the "Znak" group who were close to the Cardinal). How could this be brought into accord with the ominous Roman decree of 1949 (see p. 271)?

The Vatican was conscious of the embarrassment, but also of the inevitable opportunity of this development. The *Osservatore Romano* had already become cautious: the oppression of the church could be "less severe in certain countries than in others," if—as in Poland—the moral resistance of the Catholics proved to be stronger than the will of their antagonists; "Communism then claims as a merit what is actually its defeat. . . ."[33] Such interpretation—which was intended primarily to take the wind out of the Italian Communists' sails—naturally by no means eased the Polish Cardinal's position.

As a result, Wyszyński was also in no hurry to travel to Rome—and the Vatican made no effort to call him quickly. Not until five months later did he set out for Rome. He was greeted at the railway station in Rome by the ambassador of the People's Republic and—a then third-rate official of the curia (the present special nuncio for Poland, Luigi Poggi). The Pope let the Warsaw Cardinal wait for an uneasy week; in the meantime, Wyszyński received anonymous letters reproaching him for having brought along the "discredited" Bishop Klepacz of Lodz; it was for this reason (the letters said) that the Pope hesitated to receive him. But Wyszyński had deliberately brought along to Rome not only Klepacz, but also the Poznan Archbishop Baraniak, whom the Stalinists had treated particularly badly, and the episcopal secretary Bishop Choromanski. The Cardinal himself wanted to assume "full responsibility" for Klepacz's and Choromanski's compromising behavior; for thereby, he declared to the Secretariat of State, "the unity of the church had been guaranteed" during the primate's internment.

Finally, on May 16, the Polish bishops were admitted to the Pope, who excused the delay as due to a visit from the French state president (which had taken place three days earlier). Even now Pius XII had only 15 minutes free. He made an effort to be formally cordial with Wyszyński, embraced Baraniak as a "dear son and martyr," but treated Klepacz and Choromanski with palpable coolness.[34] Wyszyński, who was given the Cardinal's hat informally, did not hear a single public word of praise. The only sign of a slightly improved atmosphere was the appearance of

Monsignore Dell'Acqua, the representative of the Secretariat of State, at the station on the Cardinal's departure. . . .

On the day of Wyszyński's papal audience, Pius XII had published a very pointed encyclical. It was dedicated to a saint whom we have met before in this book: Andrzej Bobola. The 300th anniversary of the death of this Polish missionary to Russia, who was killed by the Orthodox Cossacks and whose relics Lenin had given to the Pope under a condition that Rome did not observe (see pp. 53 and 191), gave the Pope occasion to impart to Poland once more the role of a "bulwark of Christianity": the more presumptuous the enemies of God were, the more courageously must one confront them "in word and print and good example." He expressly exhorted the Polish episcopate to bravery—of course, a bravery combined with "prudence, ingenuity and wisdom. . . ."[35]

The "Polish exception," as they called it in Rome, was thus regarded with reservations. This was more difficult in the case of *Hungary*. Here the anti-Stalinist Janos Kadar, decried by all the world as a "turncoat," was under Soviet control trying to save whatever he could from the ruins of the bloody autumn of 1956: the very goal toward which Archbishop Grösz was also working again. At the end of May 1957 he succeeded in freeing the discredited "Priests of Peace" organization from its all too strong ideological ties to the Communists under the new name of "Opus Pacis," and neutralized it by joining it himself along with all his bishops. A Vatican decree of September 7 forbade the Hungarian clergy all political activity; in March 1958 the Holy Office excommunicated the clerics Horvath, Mate and Beresztoczy because they remained parliamentary representatives. But that did not hinder either Grösz or later his successor Archbishop Hamvas from keeping a protective hand over their reprimanded clergy.

Was this disobedience toward Rome? Compliance simply out of fear or also from pastoral conviction? Pius XII, in the last year of his life, had to realize reluctantly that anathema—and for that matter every traditional disciplinary measure of the church—was less and less appropriate to the situations confronting the Catholic church in this epoch. Communism per se—as an ideological as well as a political force—increasingly eluded any clear-cut definition. In the Far East, a second Communist great power emerged as a rival to the Soviet Union. On January 11, 1958, Soviet Foreign Minister Gromyko spoke in Moscow before an Italian Communist delegation of "agreement" with the Vatican concerning "various questions of Peace"; this could be the basis for "useful," indeed "official" relations in spite of ideological differences. In Peking, on the other hand, a "Patriotic Catholic Association" was formed at the same time which defamed the Vatican as a "puppet of American imperialism and aggression."

After the expulsion or arrest of all foreign bishops, the few native prelates of China faced the choice of bowing to the regime's command or to the Vatican prohibition which forbade them to consecrate new bishops without Roman bulls of nomination. Thus it was that the first and to date the only open act of disobedience toward Rome by an entire episcopate arose not in Soviet-dominated Europe, but among the 4 million Catholics of China: 30 Chinese bishops were consecrated in 1958 in defiance of canonical regulations—three of them on October 9, the day of Pius XII's death.[36]

Was that really a modern "schism"? In his last encyclical, published on September 9, Pius accused the "false shepherds" of China of arrogance and of rebellion against papal authority. Of course he could not deny that the bishops' consecrations—conducted by prelates recognized by Rome—were valid in the sacramental sense, but he called them "unlawful, that is sinful and sacrilegious," indeed a "serious crime," punishable with "the excommunication reserved especially (*specialissimo modo*) to the Holy See," that is, exclusion from the church, of the consecrated as well as the consecrators.[37]

Thus a sentence of condemnation against the hard-pressed bishops of his own church was the Pacelli Pope's last act—the outer symbol of the impotence and failure of his contradictory pastoral policies toward the Communist powers.

Twelve years later, in 1970, as one of the journalists escorting Paul VI, I was flying toward the Chinese mainland near Hong Kong, and while the Pope was polishing his cautious words for China, I asked attending Cardinal Tisserant what the Vatican thought today about those "uncanonically" consecrated bishops. "We know nothing about them—but we regard them as members of the church," said Tisserant. In the meantime, the little Catholic church of China had been submerged in silence and absolute suppression. In Rome, an "undiplomatic" Pope, John XXIII, had begun a new attempt at dialogue with the modern world, including the eastern one. . . .

Without Diplomacy: Pope John, Khrushchev, and the Cousins Mediation

"Better than a slap in the face, isn't it?" said the Pope to his secretary Loris Capovilla, after reading the letter delivered to him on November 25, 1961. It was from the Soviet ambassador to Italy, and read:

> "In compliance with instructions I have received from Mr. Nikita Khrushchev, may I express my congratulations to His Holiness John XXIII on the occasion of his 80th birthday, with the sincere wish for his good health and success in his noble efforts toward strengthening and consolidating peace in the world by solving international problems through frank negotiations."

"There is something going on in the world. . . . Today We have received a sign of divine providence!" the Pope remarked later, after he had withdrawn for prayer. And on November 27, he sent Nunciature Counsellor Mario Cagna (later nuncio in Belgrade) to the Soviet Embassy in Rome with an answer:

"His Holiness Pope John XXIII is grateful for your good wishes and, for his part, conveys to the entire Russian people his heartfelt wishes for the development and consolidation of general peace through positive understandings brought about by human brotherhood. For this he prays most fervently."[38]

So began a transitional period in Vatican Eastern policies, completely shaped by the personal religious and human style of the man who, although he had served both Popes Pius as a diplomat, had always been regarded by the curia prelates as somewhat naive, as a "strange sort of saint." When the College of Cardinals surprisingly elected the 77-year-old Angelo Giuseppe Roncalli in 1958 as Pius XII's successor, they were all aware that a more moderate climate would now arise in the Roman curia, a milder air in which many monsignori could breath more easily. But for that very reason, no one expected from John XXIII an epoch-making push toward church reform, certainly not any change in attitude toward the Communist world. Even while the new Pope was announcing the Second Vatican Council in January 1959, innovations in Eastern policies were hardly visible; the Pope had several times expressed himself in his usual circumspect way against Communism. What then happened was really not the result of a deliberate diplomacy or planned church policy; it was the expression of spontaneous decisions. They stemmed from an almost "unpolitical" attitude, in which trust in God, worldly piety, and peasant wisdom were combined.

John XXIII began to practice Vatican eastern policies in a manner that will in some respects remind us of the mystically-tinged dilettantism of d'Herbigny. Now, at a point where the confrontation between Catholic church and Communist world—from a pastoral point of view—had led to a dead end and pure *politics* had lost its credibility both within the church and vis-à-vis the East, Pope John succeeded in a breakthrough of church-historical significance, just because of his unconventional style.

Not doctrinaire delimitation, but rather turning to a world whose peaceful unity must be realized as a Christian one—that was the meaning that John wanted to give the council. The method was called "*aggiornamento*": the church's message was to "*be brought up to date*"—not slavishly conforming to the modern, the current fad, but listening attentively. The church was to change from a "militant" church to more of a "serving, loving" one—also in its dialogue with non-Catholics, with non-Christians, with non-believers. Thus the council was to affirm the universality of the Catholic church on a newer, broader basis. To the mere administrators of the means of salvation, it might appear "utopian." However, as so often happens, it was just this utopian impulse that set historical reality in motion, even in directions that were neither foreseeable nor planned.

The establishment in 1960 of a "Secretariat for the Unity of Christians" under the presidency of the biblical scholar (and former confessor of Pius XII), the Jesuit Augustin Bea, was the beginning of an effort to soften the attitude of the "separate" churches, above all the Orthodox, toward the council. The first invitation from Cardinal Bea to the Moscow Patriarchate met with refusal—though a cordially formulated one. The social encyclical *Mater et Magistra* of May 1961, in which John followed the teachings of his predecessors without, however, discussing Socialism and Communism, signaled the new, unpolemical, but also non-intellectual style of the Pope. His call for peace, his appeal to all rulers to be conscious of "the dreadful responsibility before history and, more importantly, before God's judgment" (September 10, 1961), evoked sudden interest in Moscow.

"It is not that we fear God's judgment, in whom as an atheist I do not believe, but we welcome an appeal to negotiate in the interest of peace, no matter where it comes from. Will ardent Catholics like John F. Kennedy, Konrad Adenauer and others listen to the Pope's warning?" Thus responded Soviet Party Chief Khrushchev in an interview for *Pravda* on September 21. He, who kept the world in suspense with policies that were now offensive, now conciliatory, did not hesitate to compliment even the Roman Pope if it had propaganda value. In addition, Khrushchev had a nose for a similar peasant mentality, now that the papal throne in Rome was suddenly occupied not by an "ideologue," but by a man with "good common sense."

And thus, on the Pope's birthday in November, there occurred that unusual exchange of greetings which was widely dismissed in Catholic circles as "a clumsy diversion" (German Catholic Press Agency KNA, January 20, 1962). It was not yet obvious that the "atheist peasant" in Moscow had been taken at his word by a faithful peasant, and would not get off so easily. "A sign of providence. . . !", John had told his secretary. Was it perhaps even an omen of that broad plan known as the "conversion of Russia"—so meditated the Pope. The catchword "Fatima" floated through his thoughts, but he pushed it away; just as at the beginning of 1960 he had rejected a request from the Bishop of Leiria in Portugal and sent his letter to the Holy Office, recommending that it be hidden forever in the archives.

(The letter had disclosed the third prophecy that had been given to three shepherd children of Fatima in an alleged appearance of Mary in 1917, shortly before the Russian revolution. The "vision of hell" of Fatima had been published in 1942, in which the Madonna commanded, "dedicate Russia to my Immaculate Heart"; it will thereby "convert"; otherwise Russia will "engender wars and persecutions of churches" and "many nations" would be destroyed. Pius XII—intent on his neutrality—in 1942 dedicated "to the Immaculate Heart of the Virgin Mother of God," "*all* of humanity," and not until 1952 "the peoples of Russia," but at the same time he distanced himself from thoughts of a crusade.[39])

For Pope John, "conversion" was not simply a "return to the fold of the Roman shepherd"; *conversio* for him meant a conversion (*metanoia*) for the better which the Catholic church itself also had to undergo, especially in the mystical-metaphysical sense, and not only in a church-political one. Almost unconsciously, therefore, John changed the traditional concept of the "conversion of Russia," which was of great concern to him, into both an ecumenical and a "pacifistic" undertaking: peace among the separated churches was also to help build human bridges over the ideological and power-political trenches that separated East and West; ultimately it was also intended to give the Catholics in the East more breathing room.

In August 1962, in Paris and Metz respectively, Monsignore Jan Willebrands, the secretary of the Vatican "Unity"-Secretariat, and shortly thereafter Cardinal Tisserant, met very confidentially with Archbishop Nikodim, the leader of the Foreign Department of the Russian Orthodox church. For the first time in decades, there were objective discussions. It became clear that the Kremlin, out of political considerations, would agree to an observer's role for the Moscow Patriarchate if the Vatican could guarantee that the great assembly of churches would not become an anti-Soviet forum. And the Moscow Patriarchate had recognized the chance—above and beyond theological considerations—of broadening its contacts with the world, especially the western.

Could the Vatican provide the desired guarantees? And in what form? A difficulty in protocol arose for the Pope because he wanted to send the invitation to *all* the Orthodox churches via the Patriarch of Constantinople, Athenagoras, since he was—of course only formally—entitled to the honorary primacy in Orthodoxy. Athenagoras, in turn, had to show consideration for the attitude of the Russian church—not only because it was the largest, but also because it was the *least free* to make decisions among the Orthodox. For that reason—and not, as was later claimed, because of intrigue by the Moscow Patriarchate or delayed telegrams[40]—Athenagoras, on October 8, 1962, four days before the opening of the council, declined to send observers to Rome, after he had received no word from Moscow. It was not until two days later, on October 10, that the Holy Synod in Moscow received permission from the Kremlin—so late that its two observers (Archpriest Witalij Borovoi of Leningrad and Vladimir Kotliarov) could not fly to Rome until October 12, the day after the opening of the council.

Khrushchev was naturally not displeased that at the first session of the council, Moscow could thus exercise a sort of "sole representation" of Orthodoxy. But it was not this which really interested him (much less whether the theological rapprochement between Catholics and Orthodox took place through Moscow or Constantinople); decisive for him was whether the neutralization of Catholic anti-Sovietism could be achieved at the council. And Monsignore Willebrands had been quite unable to offer such absolute assurance when he had come to Moscow for the first time from September 27 to October 4, 1962, to explain the Pope's conception of the council and to smooth over political considerations. The fact that the Pope could not "gag" the council fathers if the council was to fulfill its collegial function was understood in the Moscow Patriarchate, but less so in the Kremlin. When Willebrands flew back to Rome on October 4, nothing was yet decided; Willebrands had promised, however, to lose no time in arranging a special invitation from the Vatican to the Russian council observers in which assurances would be given in writing. On October 6, Willebrands telegraphed the invitation from Rome, after Cardinal Bea, two days earlier, had intimated, in a letter, the possibilities of political temperance at the council.

All this could not entirely dispel the suspicions of the state "Office for Religious Affairs." Nevertheless, three events changed the minds of the functionaries shortly before the beginning of the council and made possible the departure of the Orthodox observers:

1. *A political gesture:* On October 8 the Pope received sixteen Polish bishops[41] who had been allowed to make the trip to the council—at this time the first from the Eastern bloc—after a long tug-of-war between Cardinal Wyszyński and a government casting anxious glances toward Moscow. Even before the press, which only heard of it on October 13, Moscow was informed that at this opportunity the Pope, in his otherwise almost unpolitical address, had spoken of the Polish "western territories regained after centuries" (*ziemiach zachodnich, po wiekach odzyskanych*), thus seemingly confirming the post-war borders on the Oder and Neisse.

2. *A confidential document,* which conveyed an impression of changes in Catholic anti-Communism, at this time landed in Moscow, deliberately launched through East German channels: it was a statement from Cardinal Alfred Bengsch, who resided in East Berlin, to one of the preparatory committees of the council. The Cardinal refused to make an express condemnation of Communism. He warned against using such expressions as "fear of the Soviets" or "iron curtain" in council documents and

generally asked them to "keep silent on the Church of Silence" (the exact text of this document, dated May 4, 1962, is published for the first time in the appendix).

3. *A crisis in world politics*: Khrushchev had provoked acute tensions by establishing rocket bases in Cuba, within striking distance of the USA. During these initial days of the council, the world was steering toward a war, since the western great power seemed to be arming for a preventive strike. It had not escaped the Kremlin, however, that Pope John did not succumb to any "war hysteria," and rejected advice to postpone the council. (In his opening speech on October 11, the Pope spoke out against the "prophets of doom, who always predict disaster as if the world were soon coming to an end.")

Only two weeks later, John XXIII was involved in a delicate mediation. Since "classical" diplomacy seemed to be breaking down in the Cuban crisis, "outsiders" stepped into action as well: on the evening of October 23, after having ordered the blockade of Cuba, President John F. Kennedy telephoned an old acquaintance, the left-pacifist, non-denominational publisher of the *Saturday Review*, Norman Cousins, who was just then participating in a conference of American and Soviet intellectuals in Andover, Maryland; another participant at this meeting was a Belgian Dominican Father, Felix Morlion, who had connections to the Vatican. Kennedy now asked Cousins to speak with the Russians, of whom two, it was known, were well acquainted with Khrushchev, and also to consult with Father Morlion to set in motion a papal mediation.[42]

When Morlion called Rome, he heard that the Vatican was already active. On the morning of October 24, the Pope had his plea for peace delivered to the American and Soviet embassies: "We implore all rulers not to remain deaf to the cry of humanity for peace . . . to reassume negotiations . . . to set in motion, encourage and accept discussions at all levels and at any time is a maxim of wisdom and prudence. . . ."

"This message was the only gleam of hope," Khrushchev said later.[43] On October 26, 1962, when Khrushchev declared his willingness to withdraw the rockets from Cuba, Moscow's *Pravda* printed the Pope's appeal for peace. Perhaps the Vatican then was not the "warm body that no magic formula can bring back to life," as *Komsomolskaya Pravda* had just described it on October 13, at the opening of the council. In any case, it now praised the "realism of the Pope concerning the question of peace."

Could this moment be used for the church in the East? The Pope thought so, but he did not have much confidence in curial diplomacy. It was important to him above all to put the two Moscow observers, whose reports from Rome would certainly also be read in the Kremlin, in a favorable frame of mind. As could be foreseen, there were complications:

already, at the third session of the council on October 20, the Canadian-Ukrainian Bishop Hermaniuk demanded an explanation for the "persecuted, silent church," which of course the Hungarian Bishop Hamvas advised against in the same session, because that could "irritate some governments and thus worsen the situation of the church, which is just showing signs of improvement."[44] In the middle of November a declaration of fifteen Ukrainian exile bishops "bitterly" criticized the presence of Orthodox observers from Moscow and demanded the release of the Metropolitan Josef Slipyj, "the only survivor of the eleven members of the Ukrainian episcopate who died in Communist prisons."

"The Secretariat [of the council] regrets this declaration all the more because it contradicts the spirit of the contacts that have been cultivated with the observers and which are still ongoing; it can only distance itself from this declaration," Monsignore Willebrands stated on November 24.[45] On that day, however, Cardinal Gustavo Testa was already negotiating with the two Moscow guests, whose ikon-like impassivity struck many of the council fathers as almost eerie, about the "Slipyj case." Could the incident of the Ukrainian exiles not have been avoidable if the Soviet Union had made a church-political gesture toward the Vatican—by at least releasing Slipyj?—Testa suggested.

Borovoi and Kotliarov would raise the matter in Moscow when they returned at the beginning of December. In the meantime, Norman Cousins, the American who had already tuned in during the Cuba negotiations, also appeared in Rome, and offered his services. He spoke with Cardinal Tisserant and Monsignore Dell'Acqua, to whom he had been recommended by Father Morlion. "They showed me Vatican situation analyses and also asked me to state my own opinion in Moscow," Cousins later reported.[46]

"I am not an official messenger and do not represent anyone." With these words Cousins entered Nikita Khrushchev's study in the Kremlin on December 13, 1962, at 11:30 a.m. The more than three hour discussion which then developed—with many rambling diversions by the Party leader—can be read in a twenty-page report which Cousins made to the papal Secretariat of State.[47] Here is an excerpt:

> Khrushchev: "What the Pope has done for peace . . . will go down in history."
> Cousins: "But what a Soviet paper wrote—that the Pope had turned his back on the West, on anti-Communism—is a distortion. . . ."
> Khrushchev: "I know that. . . . I cannot convert the Pope. . . . I was religious myself in my youth; Stalin was even in seminary. . . . What we fought against then was not religion as such, but a particular situation in which there was a lot of politics . . . and other things . . . very complicated. The priests were not servants of God, but rather gendarmes of the Czar. . . . Now we

respect the church and have a special government office for it. . . . I am anxious to assure the Pope that I am convinced that he does not want his church used for politics."

Cousins bluntly asked the Party chief whether the Soviet Union wanted relations with the Vatican, for example unofficial ones; Khrushchev affirmed this and agreed to a five-point summary of the results of the discussion:

"1. The Soviet Union values the mediation of the Pope, and Khrushchev agrees that it is not only a question of useful mediation during the final moments of a crisis, but of a lasting effort by the Pope on behalf of peace.

2. Khrushchev confirms that he desires a *communication line* with the Holy See through *private contacts*.

3. Khrushchev recognizes that the church respects the principle of the separation of church and state in various countries.

4. Khrushchev recognizes that the church wants to serve all humanity from the perspective of the higher values of life and is not only concerned for Catholics.

5. Khrushchev recognizes that the Pope exhibited great courage in acting as he did, since he knows that the Pope has the same problems within the church that he, Khrushchev, has within the Soviet Union."

Viewed through a diplomatic lens, this result was modest: it only gained dimension when measured against the previous three decades of Soviet-Vatican "relations." At the end of the discussion, therefore, Cousins sought to bring up more concrete proposals, for example the matter of religious instruction and of religious literature.

"I will have the matter reviewed," Khrushchev answered.

"Would it not be good to give the Pope a sign of good will in the matter of religious freedom, for example by releasing Bishop Slipyj?" asked Cousins.

Khrushchev: "I remember the case . . . but I do not know where he is and whether he is still alive."

Cousins: "I have been assured that no publicity will be given to his release."

Khrushchev: "Oh, it will create an enormous stink! But I will have the matter reviewed, and if there is a guarantee that no political case will be made of it, I would not rule out a release. One more enemy in freedom doesn't scare me. . . ."

A week later, on December 19, 1962, Pope John, greatly moved, held a card with Khrushchev's handwritten Christmas wishes—it was Cousins' "proof" of the authenticity of his report from the Kremlin. The Secretariat of State drew up a diplomatically formal thank-you, but John insisted on *his* humanly moving and pious style: he embellished the answer that the Croatian Jesuit Father Stefan Schmidt carried to the Soviet embassy in Rome on December 22 with warm words—and Latin Bible quotes. . . .

His feelings did not deceive the Pope; by the very fact that he behaved like a sympathetic pastor, he instilled trust and kept the sensitive opening contacts away from the reefs of prestige and protocol. Thirty-five years after the last discussions between Eugenio Pacelli and the Soviets, that was the only method that could perhaps open the way for church diplomacy. . . .

The Council's "Asceticism" and Slipyj's Release: Steps Out of the "Catacombs"?

In a Moscow hotel room at the beginning of February 1963, two Catholic priests struggled for a solution: the Pope's representative Monsignore Willebrands, and Bishop Slipyj, the Lemberg Metropolitan of the Eastern Rite Catholic Ukrainians. After 17 years of confinement, camp and exile in Siberia, he had been "pardoned" at John XXIII's request, although the message that the Soviet ambassador in Rome sent to the Vatican via the Italian Prime Minister Fanfani stated expressly that "nothing had been found that would allow a less severe view of Slipyj's crime against the Soviet people" (see p. 246). The Kremlin did not even hope for a propaganda effect from his release, but only feared what Khrushchev had dramatically called a "stink"; it was hoped that Slipyj "would not be used to the detriment of the interests of the Soviet Union," the note said.

But Slipyj did not want a pardon, he wanted justice, and also he did not want to leave the country. Thirty years earlier, Bishop Sloskans had defended himself with similar arguments against being exchanged for Latvian Communists. But now it was not a question of an exchange, but rather of a new beginning for Vatican eastern policies. The symbolic value of the Soviet gesture, in which the Pope believed, would be voided if Slipyj refused to go to Rome forever. —The age-old dilemma between the church's necessities of life and the witness of those who suffer for it remained insoluble.

Slipyj wanted at least to take his last leave of his bishopric, Lemberg (Lvov). A compromise was reached: the train journey to Vienna and Rome led through Lemberg. As the Metropolitan blessed his city through the window of the express train, he did not yet know that the papal church was in the process of revising its centuries-old concept of "orthodoxy," a move that seven years later would evoke a bitter statement from him (see p. 367); the idea of union in the sense of conversion of the Orthodox, that concept by which the Catholic church repeatedly (and with tragic consequences) had become entangled in the nationalistic quarrels of Eastern Europe, was gradually being filed among the historic documents. The challenge from the eastern state atheism, and the late discovery of tolerance, a long-scorned product of western liberalism, had effected that the solidarity of all Christians was slowly gaining the upper hand over merely denominational interests. The main question became whether the faithful in Lvov had religious freedom—not which Patriarch they were subject to, the Roman or the Muscovite.

Pope John led his church onto this course more intuitively than consciously. Indeed, he himself, who had not simply laid down his triple papal crown nor his life-long concepts, almost opposed the consequences of what he—to the quiet dismay of the curial bureaucracy—had set in motion. Characteristic of this was the course of a visit paid him on March 7, 1963, by Khrushchev's daughter and son-in-law Alexej Adschubej (a journalist and political traveler of short-lived fame). Since this was the first papal audience for a prominent Communist, the event stirred up Italian domestic politics, where elections were approaching, and caused a corresponding annoyance in the Vatican Secretariat of State: the prelates successfully opposed the later suggestion of the Pope to simply publish the minutes of the conversation as the interpreter Father Alexander Kulik had drawn them up—then people could see, the Pope thought, that nothing terrible had happened. Naturally the minutes would have stirred up new debate, but they would also have shown how the Pope had avoided the main political point. Here is the decisive part of Father Kulik's report:[48]

"Mr. Adschubej said that this audience was a historic one: just as Mr. Khrushchev was regarded as reformer of the Communist world, so the Pope was regarded as renewer of the Catholic world. And here he asked the Holy Father whether His Holiness would not consider it opportune to take up *diplomatic relations* between the Soviet Union and the Vatican. Thereupon the Holy Father replied: God in His omnipotence took seven days to make the world; We, who are much less powerful, may not precipitate matters, must proceed carefully (*dolcemente andare*), in stages, must prepare the minds and spirits. At present such a step would be misunderstood."

The frequently and touchingly described scene in which John presented the daughter of the Moscow Party Chief with a rosary only formed the colorful background to a pastoral diplomacy whose tactical finesse, paradoxically, consisted in its trusting more in divine dispensation than in political instruments and religious doctrine.

That is also true of the famous encyclical of April 11, 1963, "*Pacem in Terris*," for which Pope John received applause from all of Eastern Europe, although it contained only ideas that had been thought out in the Catholic church long before by other Popes and theologians, even if they had not always been in the foreground: the differentiation between the "error" and the "erring," between the ideologies and their practices, which changed "with changing circumstances"; the qualified possibility of cooperation and a dialogue with the errant; the recognition that even in error, there can be "something good." New was the simple, generally comprehensible, completely unpolemical language in which the encyclical was written; new was the world-wide effect, beyond the political lines of division. And this was simply because in this encyclical the personal charisma of a peaceable man was truly palpable.

But Pope John hereby also prepared new possible activities for traditional Vatican diplomacy (in which—as this book shows—these basic elements were always present). It produced its first results in the middle of 1963, before the beginning of the second council session: after fact-finding trips by Vienna Cardinal Franz König to Hungary and Poland (in April and May), Agostino Casaroli (since March 1961 papal Under-Secretary of State) flew for the first time to Budapest and through negotiations on May 9, 1963, freed four bishops from enforced residence far from their sees; then he went to Prague to establish preliminary contacts. For the first time, bishops or diocesan administrators came from almost all the Eastern European countries to the council, and finally—after eighteen years—the Vatican again began to establish contact with priests and believers in these countries, and could again gather information on the spot for personnel and pastoral decisions. Millions of Catholics were no longer viewed and treated as adherents or "agents" of the "enemy Vatican," even if their complete civil equality was by no means established.

When Pope John died in June 1963 ("too late," according to conservative cynics, "too soon" for progressive dreamers in the Catholic church), he had during his short pontificate built the necessary bridges between two periods of Vatican eastern policies: that of Pius XII, which stretched from diplomatic attempts at coexistence to sharp fighting, and that of Paul VI, who took up again the last stalled "shift" of Pius XII (see p. 287f.) in a new diplomatic initiative and pursued it in a changed world.

The sixty-six year old Giovanni Battista Montini, who was elected Pope in June 1963, knew the apparatus and the functioning of the Roman curia incomparably better than his predecessor: for more than three decades he had been direct witness and collaborator in the diplomacy of the two Popes Pius. Paul VI thus knew their eastern policies, as they have been described in this book, from the vantage point of the "workshop": he had experienced the eleventh Pius's temperamental, changeable decisions and admired the twelfth Pius's "escatologically" over-refined diplomatic balancing talents—first in 1923 for a few months as attaché in the Warsaw nunciature, then in 1924-25 in the "second section," the so-called Interior Ministry of the Secretariat of State, after 1937 as deputy, after 1952 as pro-secretary of state. From the closest vantage point he saw how two Popes, with the help of the "first section" (the quasi-Foreign Ministry of the curia), most recently under the long-time direction of Domenico Tardini, confronted the Communist world. "In the shadow of Tardini," as his friend Jean

Guiton has delicately described Montini's position, quiet doubts slowly grew in him as to whether the 70 million Catholics in the East were still being served by the weapon of excommunication which Pius XII had used after the Second World War, as the Stalin epoch approached its end.

These quiet doubts had indeed also been held by Pius XII. But: "There is no easy solution for what is difficult by nature: if one is torn, one must, for love's sake, bear being torn," Montini told Guiton on September 8, 1950. And before the Papal Academy, in 1951, Montini gave church diplomacy one advantage over that of secular states—although "either one can run aground"—namely, that "it proceeds from an ideal and strives for one: the universal brotherhood of mankind."[49]

Diplomacy was and remained for Montini—even as Pope—a pastoral instrument, even and especially toward the East, where after all sorts of catastrophes it was often only a matter of "salvare il salvabile—saving whatever they could." However, to think that "Communism" ever was or would be "a hope" for Montini is to misunderstand fundamentally the world of ideas and the church environment in which this Pope actively lived for more than half a century. Also the claim that Montini, back at a time when this was hardly conceivable—and on his own at that—had cultivated contacts with Communists, perhaps with the CPI chief Palmiro Togliatti, comes from a source that has been exposed by historical research as a source of falsifications.[50]

Just as Pius XII's anti-Communism was never "unconditional," neither was Paul VI's attempt to reach a *modus vivendi* for the Catholics with the Communist-ruled countries. One of the basic conditions remained the impossibility of "ideological coexistence." Right at the beginning of his pontificate and even before he continued the Second Vatican Council in autumn 1963, Pope Paul warned against the misunderstanding—which his predecessor's style may have promoted—that the church was changing its judgment about wide-spread errors—"such as about Marxist atheism." The Pope even compared the latter with a "contagious fatal disease." To seek a cure for it meant to "battle it not only theoretically, but also practically, to have the therapy follow the diagnosis, healing brotherly love follow doctrinary condemnation. . . ."[51] At the same time, the Moscow Communists were protecting themselves against "churchmen who are changing their methods to fit the spirit of the times": Iliechev, the director of the "Ideological Commission" of the Soviet Communist Party, on November 25, 1963, named the "hierarchs of the Catholic church" among those whose peaceful, realistic attitude "would lead to a certain, even if temporary, consolidation of the positions of the church"; in Vilna, he said, the deacon of the cathedral had even stated that the Communists' moral codex was based on the Bible. . . . Iliechev demanded a vitalization of atheistic education and propaganda.⁵² The Soviet Communists began to fear the ideological consequences of a relaxation that they needed militarily and politically—a permanently suffered contradiction of their politics during the following decades.

But this was one more reason for Paul VI not to give priority to the theoretical dialogue that was fashionable at this time; doctrinaire polemics could not be allowed to hinder the practical-pastoral actions of the church. —When the council two years later, in autumn 1965, met for its last session, a petition from 297 of the more than 2000 council clergymen demanded that the so-called Scheme 13, which was concerned with the "church in the modern world," also treat the "problem of Communism"—so that the council not be accused of silence, "as for example today, surely unjustly, Pius XII [is accused] regarding the victims of Naziism."⁵³ Two hundred nine suggestions for amendments even demanded an express *condemnation* of Communism. But the council commission rejected all these proposals on the *direct instructions* of Paul VI,⁵⁴ who thereby had to tolerate 251 negative votes in the final ballot about the scheme.

In order to prevent any misinterpretations, the Pope, shortly before the beginning of this last council period, had visited the Roman Domitilla catacombs, where the church had once "not loudly and offensively," but rather "poor, humble, pious, oppressed and heroic," challenged the negative forces of the world, as the Pope said, and then added this programmatical statement:

> "The Holy See is avoiding raising a justified cry of protest and regret more often and more strongly—not because it mistakes or ignores the reality of the situation, but rather from a concept of Christian patience and *so as not to provoke greater evil.* It is always prepared for honest and dignified *negotiations*, for forgiving injustices suffered, also prepared to look into the present and the future and not the recent painful past, whenever it meets efficacious signs of good will."⁵⁵

The basic concepts of Paul's eastern policies were contained in this catacomb address, which referred to well-known positions of the two Popes Pius. It was directed toward a changed world, whose peace—even without Khrushchev, Pope John and Kennedy—rested on a more or less tense atomic balance. Catholics in Communist countries had to reckon with this reality for the rest of the 20th century. And not in a catacomb church, not with secret bishops as in the past, when the papal church thought it only had to "survive the season." At the end of the council, 89 bishops from Eastern Europe had been able to journey to Rome—and back again to those countries where their situations were as varied as "Communism" itself had become in Eastern Europe.

With this East, Pope Paul VI began a diplomatic dialogue in the middle of the sixties: "Not everywhere; not everywhere in the same form and with the same constancy; not always crowned with success. Nowhere easily. But rather decisively and with—one could say—a movement hard to reverse" (Casaroli).[56]

X

Negotiation, Not Condemnation:
Return to the Tradition, 1964-1979

Partial Agreement with Hungary, and
Mindszenty's "Rebellion"

Protesting modestly, Monsignore Agostino Casaroli accepted a glass in order to drink a toast—following international protocol—with his partner Jozsef Prantner, the director of the Hungarian Church Office. What the Pope's "Foreign Minister" and the Communist Minister had agreed upon was not much, but it had great significance: the first written agreement of the Vatican with a Communist government since the Famine Relief agreement of 1922 (see p. 31), was signed on September 15, 1964, in Budapest (see illustrations). To be sure, they had intentionally avoided calling the paper an "agreement"; it was a "document with attached protocol"—and its exact terms were not published. Why?

Negotiations carried on since May 1963, in five rounds of discussions alternately in Rome and Budapest, had soon made it clear "that there are several points in which a complete agreement between the partners is not possible because of principle and for other reasons."[1] Thus, according to good diplomatic custom, they worked toward a *partial* agreement; Casaroli called it *"intesa pratica"* (practical agreement), probably alluding to that *"intesa semplice"* (simple agreement) by which in pre-war Hungary, 1927, the state had secured a far-reaching right of nomination in the naming of bishops that went back to "royal patronage" (the Pope at that time had only been able to choose from the government's list of names).

The Communists, although averse to monarchical customs, had in decrees of 1951 and 1957 made the nomination of bishops dependent on their "prior approval," and in addition demanded a loyalty oath to state and constitution, the text of which did not even mention the religious function of the person swearing the oath.

It was this point that Casaroli latched onto—much to the astonishment of his partners, who at first refused to believe that for the Vatican an oath was not a mere formality nor simply a matter of political significance. They agreed upon the insertion of a clause into the oath which limited the loyalty oath to what was justifiable from a religious point of view: ". . . as is appropriate for a bishop or priest" (*sicut decet Episcopum vel sacerdotem*). On this basis a procedure was then laboriously worked out that represented a compromise between "free nomination" and "nomination with prior approval": in the future, nominations of bishops would be worked out in direct negotiations between the government and the Holy See. As a practical test of the agreement the chairman of the episcopate, Bishop Hamvas (named Archbishop of Kalocsa) was allowed to consecrate *five* new bishops—the first in fourteen years—of whom three were more acceptable to the government, two less acceptable (one had up to then been forbidden to officiate); but all were known to the Vatican as deserving their new dignity.

The "assurances" the Vatican received, as Casaroli freely admitted right after the signing, were "certainly still far from meeting the desires of the Holy See and the necessities of Catholic life"—especially regarding the freedom of action of bishops (of whom some remained under the supervision of strange vicars general installed by the state Church Office, as I observed in Hungary in 1965). But it also concerned the question of the dissolved orders and of religious instruction, which in Hungary—in contrast to Soviet legislation—was possible even in the schools, at the request of the parents, although it was not unopposed. What was important was that the Pontifical Hungarian Institute in Rome (*Pontificio Istituto Ecclesiastico Ungherese*)—financed by the government—was now again subordinated to the episcopate and could accept theology students sent by it (from Hungary)—future prelates, of whose qualities the Vatican could now gain a first-hand impression.

The Roman curia naturally had to refrain from speaking publicly, even by allusion, about the greatest success of this first agreement: namely that the Communist attempt to have the Hungarian church governed by those prominent "Priests of Peace," who had—justly or unjustly—long been compromised in the eyes of the faithful, had been thwarted.

Casaroli spoke of a "basis for future progress." However, this was long in coming: not least because the Budapest government, which had become emboldened shortly before Khrushchev's fall and with his express approval, had gotten "cold feet" when the church-state battle flared up in Poland in 1965/66 (see p. 343) and in 1967/68 when in Czechoslovakia the détente dialogue seemed to assume uncontrollable forms (see p. 334–5). In the shadow of the events in Prague, however, new rounds of probes and negotiations were begun as in March 1968 Monsignore Luigi Bongianino and in September Monsignore Giovanni Cheli were able to look around in Hungary for an extended period, and Minister of State Prantner personally, with his deputy officer Imre Miklos, went to Rome in October. It was a matter of replacing three old bishops who were retiring, and further expanding the episcopate. On January 23, 1969, *four* new titular bishops were agreed upon; four others, who in 1964 had been installed only as apostolic administrators, could now be named residentiary bishops. Among these named at this time was Imre Kisberk, the only Hungarian bishop who in 1951 had refused to take the oath (in the old form).

From the very beginning, whenever the Vatican negotiators demanded greater concessions, especially in the area of pastoral possibilities, they ran into this excuse: the unsolved Mindszenty question. For fifteen years already, the pugnacious Cardinal Primate, who had suffered so much and learned so little, had been sitting in the American embassy in Budapest, a burden to his involuntary hosts (see pp. 295–6). Hungary's Communists, accustomed for decades to grossly overestimating the political importance of religion, church and clergy, of course continued to declare that the nation had long ago forgotten Mindszenty—which was indeed almost the case and which even Vatican investigators, to their astonishment, had established for themselves. But the Hungarian government itself did not believe it. Instead of calmly awaiting a natural solution to the "problem" (for after all, Yugoslavia had also survived a ceremonial funeral for Cardinal Stepinac in 1960), instead of politically neutralizing the "case" through an honorable, historical and legal accounting, they expected the Vatican to come up with a "solution" which—however it turned out— could only stir up the forgotten Mindszenty case.

The current Hungarian Foreign Minister Janos Peter, a former reformed bishop (about whose real credo—so he told me— historians will find interesting revelations in his papers), on April 17, 1971, visited the Pope. The private discussion, conducted in French, lasted forty minutes. Peter openly stated that the "Mindszenty problem" had to be solved if the Catholic church in Hungary was to expect more freedom. When Paul VI still expressed doubts as to the real gravity of the problem, the minister exclaimed that the objective importance of problems sometimes arose from their subjective evaluation. . . . Of course, Hungarian pressure on the Vatican was encouraged by the US government's desire—finally almost an ultimatum—to get rid of its inconvenient embassy guest of fifteen years.

Cardinal König of Vienna, on the Vatican's orders, since 1963 had almost regularly conducted tedious discussions with Mindszenty in the Budapest US embassy once or twice a year, and —like Casaroli in 1964— listened to the Primate's cautionary monologues. When Ambassador M. J. Hillenbrand came to Budapest in 1967 (after the US embassy had been headed by only a chargé d'affaires for ten years), Mindszenty regarded this elevation in the American representation as an insult to his person and thus announced that he would leave his asylum and let himself be arrested by the Hungarian Communists. This was prevented at the last moment only by the Pope's dispatch of the Cardinal of Vienna to Budapest with an urgent command to the contrary; at this time, König traveled "incognito"—with a Vatican passport made out in the name of "Monsignore Finke" (König's mother's maiden name). . . . After these and similar experiences, Monsignore Cheli of the Vatican Secretariat of State now appeared on June 25, 1971. He was accompanied by Monsignore Zágon, a Hungarian curial prelate whom Mindszenty still trusted at this time. In his memoirs published in 1974,[2] Mindszenty described how they tried for three days to convince him to leave Hungary. The government was prepared—like the Soviets in the Slipyj case—to enable the Cardinal to depart unhindered with a formal "pardon." A complicated agreement had been reached, which was kept secret from the Cardinal, according to which Mindszenty would for the time being formally remain Archbishop of Esztergom living in Rome, and would only be released from this office when Hungary had "paid" his departure from Budapest and his silence (which was a condition).

This all too cleverly devised solution, however, did not work, if only because it presupposed real insight on the part of the almost 80-year-old Cardinal into the vital pastoral-political intentions of the Vatican. But Mindszenty insisted on regarding himself as a symbol of anti-Bolshevik resistance and seeing his pastoral function primarily within this framework. He refused to sign a document which among other things prescribed in four points his waiver of statements "which could disturb the relations of the Apostolic See to the Hungarian government." Although he had already written to the Pope that he would bear "the heaviest cross" and leave Hungary, he again pleaded for time to reflect and added conditions of his own to the document: for instance, only the Vatican could decide which of his possible utterances could be "harmful". . . . Since he personally did not sign the document, the Roman curia subsequently did not feel itself bound by it either.

Though events prior to Mindszenty's departure from Budapest are still not completely clear—disregarding his own naturally slanted and fragmentary memoirs—it is evident that curial diplomacy did not take Mindszenty's resistance seriously enough, believing it had overcome it with "pious cunning." The Budapest government, on the other hand, considered the Vatican more unscrupulous than it was. It did not suspect that the papal negotiators, conscious of the embarrassment, had not insisted on written promises from Mindszenty and had intentionally left essential points undefined, in the hope that a cardinal would ultimately do as the Pope wished, even if it was not an order. . . .

The first inkling of what was to happen came when Mindszenty, after his arrival in Rome on September 28, 1971, was respectfully conducted by the Pope himself into the Sistine Chapel for the opening of the Synod of Bishops: he was to be introduced casually to the officiating chairman (since 1969) of the Hungarian episcopate, Jozsef Ijjas, but Mindszenty refused to shake hands with the bishop. Ijjas broke out in tears. Without deigning to look at him, Mindszenty said only: "Pray for Hungary!"

Conversations with the Ukrainian Cardinal Slipyj, who bitterly considered himself a powerless "prisoner" of the curia, strengthened Mindszenty in his decision to escape Vatican supervision as quickly as possible. The excommunication of three clerical parliamentary representatives in Budapest (see p. 299) was lifted on October 15, just three weeks after Mindszenty's departure, and it was left to the Hungarian episcopate in the future to evaluate the political activities of clerics; apparently that was a part of the agreement with the government. This enraged Mindszenty even more. Now he insisted he be allowed to settle in Vienna as he had intended—against the urgent advice of the curia, which however hesitated to detain the Cardinal.

On the morning of Mindszenty's sudden departure, which he especially did not want to postpone because it was the anniversary of the Hungarian uprising (October 23), the Pope at the last moment invited him to his morning mass. At first privately, then in the presence of Monsignore Zágon, Paul is supposed to have assured the cardinal that he would *always regard* him as Archbishop of Esztergom and Primate of Hungary (according to another version, he would *remain* Primate[3]).

This assurance meant that Esztergom, as long as Mindszenty lived, would only be occupied by an apostolic administrator—as was the case. Of course, whether Mindszenty would formally retain the title of Esztergom, the episcopal see he had been away from for 23 years, depended on his conduct. The Pope had spoken expressly of "limitations," but Monsignore Zágon, who did not want to hurt Mindszenty's feelings, had not translated this. . . .

On the whole, what characterized the Vatican's attitude in the Mindszenty case was an insecurity compounded of timidity, annoyance and respect. Thus it happened that, although the Hungarian government had been guaranteed that Mindszenty would restrain himself politically, the Vatican did not dare to demand this unambiguous promise from the cardinal. The "Mindszenty problem" had thus not been eliminated, but rather merely aggravated, thus offering the Budapest government an excuse to delay further steps toward normalization. Mindszenty's own statements from Vienna were in the same spirit with which he also insisted upon the publication of his memoirs: that the situation of the church in Hungary was so dreadful anyway that "hardly anything essential" could still be destroyed. He refused to take cognizance of the fact that church attendance in Hungary is better than in Rome. After him, so to speak, he saw the deluge. . . .

It was thus all the more astonishing that the Vatican negotiators nevertheless succeeded in reaching agreement on the nominations of four more bishops on February 25, 1972, and on the release of a bishop consecrated back in 1951 (Mihaly Endrey) from a ten-year ban on the performance of his duties. For the first time, a group of 300 Hungarian pilgrims was even allowed to go to Rome. Of the eleven Hungarian dioceses, which for the most part had no bishops at the end of the fifties, all were now occupied at least by suffragan bishops and apostolic administrators, some even with regular residentiary bishops. They were by no means "mostly from the ranks of the Priests of Peace," as Mindszenty claims in his memoirs. However, none of them was a "political" priest— whether in the Communist or anti-Communist sense. One of the last nominated, Laszlo Lekai, was even an old friend and secretary of Mindszenty's from his time as bishop in Veszprem, a cleric of whom Mindszenty himself said to a confidant that he was the "only true" bishop.

At the end of 1973, the duty then fell to Lekai to go to Vienna and plead with Mindszenty to renounce his archepiscopal see—or the publication of his memoirs—better yet both, in the interest of the Hungarian faithful. The Cardinal refused both requests. Back in the summer, the Pope, who had read but not condemned the manuscript, had suggested that he think about the consequences of publishing the memoirs. Popes like Pius XI or Pius XII—as this book shows—would in such a case have cut off any further discussion and peremptorily silenced the obstreperous Cardinal. Not Paul VI: patient, tormented, unsure, he tried to convince Mindszenty by letter. For five weeks the Cardinal did not even answer him.[4] In November 1973 the new Hungarian director of the Church Office, Imre Miklos, had been in Rome; then Monsignori Poggi and Sodano had visited Hungary once more: the situation had clearly not developed completely as desired. There were hindrances, especially in religious instruction in the cities, but what had been attained, the securing of a hierarchical ministry and the positively altered climate for the faithful, who at least felt themselves less discriminated against than at any time during the previous 25 years—that was important and also stable enough not to be jeopardized again.

After Mindszenty, on December 8, had bluntly refused to resign, the

Pope—still using indulgent language—informed him that he himself would relieve him of the responsibility and declare the See of Esztergom "vacant." On January 7, 1974, the Cardinal refused in a letter to accept what he called an "extorted" papal decision. No Catholic bishop in this century had dared to claim that a Pope could be "blackmailed," much less write this to Rome. And still Paul VI did not lose his Christian forbearance. "We bow to you with great respect," he wrote to Mindszenty on January 30, but informed him of the imminent publication of the decision.[5]

Nevertheless, the Pope still hesitated to pronounce the dismissal. It was not to be published before a new reply from the Cardinal and especially not before or during a journey by Casaroli to Poland at the beginning of February, where the Vatican had to deal with a Cardinal just as willful, but much smarter and more flexible (see p. 350). Then something happened that finally made the Pope lose patience: on February 5, Mindszenty, through the Vienna "Catholic Press Agency," directed a "proclamation to the world." The occasion was the 25th anniversary of his sentencing at the Budapest show trial. The proclamation, composed in German, not only accused those responsible for the Stalinist judicial farce of 1949, but spoke of Hungary as a country that had been free only "in the *caricature* of the old Yalta agreement and the *new Vienna armaments conference.*" Apparently what he meant was the East-West conference meeting since 1973 in the capital of neutral Austria concerned with a balanced limitation of armed forces (MBFR).

It was not the Cardinal's first political lapse in Vienna, but it was the most embarrassing for the Pope, because it not only disturbed Vatican relations with Hungary, but also placed efforts of papal diplomacy toward European security (e.g. at the Helsinki conferences) in a bad light. Now Paul hesitated no longer: on the same day, February 5, a few hours after the teletype had relayed Mindszenty's message, the Vatican report followed that Mindszenty had been relieved of his archepiscopal see of Esztergom. A new archbishop was not named—as Mindszenty had been promised. But the Budapest government had agreed to the installation of an apostolic administrator in Esztergom: the same Bishop Lekai who had once been Mindszenty's secretary. . . .

In the Mindszenty memoirs that appeared at the beginning of October 1974, quite a different story is told, of course. But even these unwittingly acknowledged that the Vatican had not rendered any "concessions" to the Hungarian Communists, but that the Vatican's eastern policy had only succeeded at the last moment in at least moderating the consequences of a basically unsuccessful settlement of the "Mindszenty case."

In the words of Archbishop Ijjas, speaking before the Roman synod on October 14, 1974, on behalf of the Hungarian Conference of Bishops:

"Whoever is not obedient to the Pope (*non est in oboedienti animo*), but rather rises up against him, becomes a stumbling-block for those who receive the gospel. In our country, the obstacles to the proclamation of the glad tidings are great. One may thus all the less undermine the credibility of the church. . . . May our synod finally silence those who—in speech or writing—injure the evangelization of Hungary." At the same time Ijjas announced that the Budapest government—as the ambassador to Rome had just informed him—was finally permitting religious instruction for youths in churches twice a week. Until then, religion had only been taught, at the request of the parents, as an elective in the elementary schools (by teachers paid by the state); the new regulations now eased parental resolve to send their children to instruction without arousing official displeasure. However, permission was limited to children under twelve.

Still, this was the first objective sign of accommodation on a question that Casaroli had raised repeatedly for ten years in his discussions with Hungary and one that had always been particularly delicate for the Communists (ever since the Soviet ban on religious instruction in the twenties). Did it take Mindszenty's memoirs to move Budapest to make a counter-gesture long demanded in the West—the removal of the Cardinal Primate? For a long time it seemed that Hungary would, on the contrary, use the Mindszenty memoirs as an excuse to refuse further concessions. Finally, however, the Budapest Communists seemed to recognize that their own foolishness was also to blame if, through the difficult Cardinal, the shadow of their own Stalinist past, never quite overcome historically and morally, had risen up against them. A year after Mindszenty's removal from office, they agreed to further steps toward normalization after two rounds of negotiations with the Vatican (November 1974 and January 1975).

On January 10, 1975, the Pope was able to nominate five apostolic administrators in Hungary as residentiary bishops and four priests as suffragan bishops. Thus, for the first time since the agreement of 1964, nine of the eleven dioceses in Hungary were occupied by ordinary bishops (two bishoprics—Esztergom and Györ—the Vatican itself only wanted to staff with episcopal administrators). Characteristically, two of the four newly-consecrated bishops were considered especially pro-regime (without there being any reason to doubt their loyalty to the church). The re-occupation after long vacancy of the bishopric Hajdudorog and the exarchate Mikolc, where 270,000 Uniate eastern-rite Catholics live, was significant (the Uniates in Hungary were not—as in the Ukraine and Rumania—forcibly separated from Rome). As a special gesture of the government, Bishop Mihály Endrey, who had been kept out of office for twenty years, and in 1972 installed only as administrator, was raised to residentiary bishop of

Vac, which was tantamount to his complete rehabilitation. (He died in 1977.) Imre Miklos, president of the State Office of Religious Affairs, now also announced permission for the publication of catechisms and a Bible translation. In 1974, Hungary's five priests' seminaries were allowed to accept 79 theology students (compared with only 38 in 1973).

After Cardinal Mindszenty had died in Vienna on May 6, 1975, the Vatican succeeded in convincing the Budapest government that Mindszenty's one-time secretary, Laszlo Lekai, and not the previous chairman of the Conference of Bishops, Ijjas, should become the new Primate of Hungary. On February 24, 1976, Lekai was ceremoniously elevated to Archbishop in the cathedral of Esztergom; in May he received a cardinalship in Rome. Shortly after his nomination, a diocesan bishop was named in Györ, and thus all eleven Hungarian bishoprics were properly occupied by bishops loyal to Rome.

This then, twelve years after the first Vatican-Hungarian agreement, was the actual situation of a church of which Cardinal Mindszenty had claimed (in a version of his memoirs published in the *Frankfurter Allgemeine Zeitung*, which was moderated in the book) that there was "hardly anything more of importance to be destroyed."

At the beginning of 1975, with the help of Vatican diplomacy, an agreement had been reached between episcopate and government which made possible the reorganization of religious instruction in the individual Hungarian parishes—limited, however, to 160 children between the ages of 6 and 14, once on Sundays and once on weekdays. In 1977 it was possible to relax these restrictions further. Imre Miklos declared the period of "confrontation" ended and wrote that it was "necessary to create contacts between the two partners which do not demand the surrender of their principles but call for a principled debate that is open and shows respect for each other's views" ("*Uj Ember*", March 20, 1977). Shortly thereafter, the government for the first time in thirty years allowed an "ad limina" visit to Rome by eleven Hungarian bishops. "There can today be observed signs that kindle hopes that the religious situation will improve from day to day," said Paul VI to the bishops on April 14, 1977, but also reminded them that he was still awaiting "the solution of various problems."

No one in the Vatican had any illusions about the fact that the relative weakness of Hungarian Catholicism (its traditional loyalty to the state and its susceptibility to secularizing tendencies) also made it easier for the Hungarian Communists to combine an increasing tolerance toward the church with only slightly relaxed control. Thus, church-state relations in Hungary could *not* become a generally valid *model*, but were the most significant *example* for the relative success of a realistic, patient eastern policy in the Vatican. Accordingly, on June 9, 1977, "the Holy Father [received] in private audience Mr. Janos Kadar, the First Secretary of the Central Committee of the Socialist Workers' Party of Hungary, accompanied by his wife Mrs. Maria Kadar and numerous personalities. . . ," as the Vatican protocol report announced. This was, as the Pope said in his address to the visitors, "in effect the endpoint of a long, but uninterrupted, process which in the course of the last 14 years has gradually brought the Holy See and the People's Republic of Hungary closer together after a long period of distance and tensions, *whose echo has not yet quite died away.*"

The declaration of principle which the Pope made on this occasion was not directed only at Kadar, but at all those who had observed Vatican policy "with watchful and not seldom critical or perplexed eyes":

"The Catholic church and with it the Holy See, accustomed to the succession of changing events which characterize the course of their two thousand years, do not shrink from decisions, even bold ones. For they are not led by considerations of temporary advantage and popularity, but by the profound needs of their religious mission. . . . We believe that experience confirms the validity of the path we have taken: it is the path of objective discussion (*dialogo sulle cose*), which pays attention to the protection of the rights and legitimate interests of the church, but simultaneously remains open to understanding the concerns and the activity of the state in its own areas. . . ." (*Osservatore Romano*, June 10/11, 1977).

Agreement with Tito: Model or "Special Case"?

In his spiritual testament, the Croatian Cardinal Stepinac (see p. 259), who died in 1960 as a village pastor—exiled from his see—declared that he would have been prepared at any time to resign his archdiocese Zagreb "if this could have signified an improvement of the church's situation in Yugoslavia. But neither I nor the episcopate is authorized to finalize agreements: this is the province of the state authorities and the Holy See."[6]

When the first ambassador from Yugoslavia ten years later presented his credentials to the Pope, he said: "In a multi-national and multi-confessional country such as Yugoslavia . . . the ecumenical ideas of the Second Vatican Council were received with lively interest and broad acceptance. These ideas have, to a large extent, encouraged the process of normalization of the relations between church and state. . . ."[7]

It was on June 26, 1964—at the same time that in Budapest the partial agreement between the Vatican and Hungary was materializing (see p. 314)—that the first negotiations began between Under-Secretary of

State Casaroli and the Yugoslavian ambassador in Rome. In Eastern Europe, the Khrushchev era was coming to an end, and in Yugoslavia there was recollection of the principle that Edvard Kardelj, the ideologist of Titoism, enunciated back in 1953: "We Communists are atheists, but atheism is not our religion, and thus we are not religiously intolerant." In this summer of 1964, the Italian Communist Party Leader Togliatti attempted shortly before his death to convince the Soviet leaders that "the old atheist propaganda is completely useless." If the Communists did not define the religious problem differently, people would "view the hand offered to the Catholics as simply an expedient gesture and almost a hypocrisy" (Yalta memorandum). Nowhere was the echo of such considerations stronger than in Yugoslavia. Tito was prepared to give certain guarantees to the 6.2 million predominantly Croatian Catholics, almost a third of the citizens of his country, through a formal peace treaty with the Vatican. He thereby also hoped to appease the national tensions that were always smoldering underground, especially now that the Serbian Orthodox church viewed the Catholics less intransigently since Paul VI had exchanged the kiss of peace with the ecumenical Patriarch Athenagoras (January 1964).[8]

Still, the negotiations at first ran into difficulties—somewhat as in Hungary. In four meetings of negotiations in Rome and Belgrade totalling 38 days (over a span of almost two years), they did, however, pragmatically take a rather opposite route from the Hungarian negotiations: not *principles* of relations were emphasized, but rather *questions of detail* (of which there were not very many; for instance, all dioceses were occupied by bishops). Although a model agreement was finally reached, it was not in the form of a concordat or a *modus vivendi*, because the Yugoslav side thought that a formal contractual "special regulation" with a single confession contradicted the constitutional principle of religious equality.

The "protocol" (see text in appendix 6) that was concluded in April 1966 could not be signed until June 25 in Belgrade by Agostino Casaroli and Milutin Moraca, the president of the Federal Committee for Religious Affairs. The Yugoslavian bishops, whom the Vatican had hardly consulted during the negotiations (while the Belgrade government kept the Orthodox synod up to date), felt not only bypassed, but offended: Archbishop Franjo Seper of Zagreb, who hurried to Rome on May 26, implored the Pope above all to remove from the protocol one formulation that—he thought—amounted to an insinuation, in which the "Holy See" condemned "any act of political terrorism or similar criminal forms of violence, no matter who uses them" (Art. II, 2). Tito's government was naturally concerned, after the war experience (see p. 259), that the Vatican in the future put a stop to nationalistic excesses in the clergy as well, and in general to guarantee its de-politicization. In return for this Belgrade allowed the Vatican to exercise its jurisdiction not only in strictly church-religious, but also in "spiritual questions"—in the broader sense.

The Pope replied to Seper's objections that this very agreement also protected the church against false political or criminal suspicions, by relegating any such accusation to *church* jurisdiction ("measures that canonical law provides for in such cases"). Nevertheless, it could not be denied that with longer negotiations, many other formulations could have been moderated. Especially since the powerful second in command and rival to Tito, Alexander Rankovic, who for Serbian nationalist reasons was especially concerned with stemming Catholic-Croatian nationalism, was toppled six days after the signing of the protocol as a "nationalistic Centrist."

But it was precisely Rankovic's fall, the partial abolition of police state methods in Yugoslavia and the further opening of the country toward the West (which slowed again at the beginning of the seventies) that made it possible for the agreement to stand the test. Since the supreme head of the Catholic church for the first time unequivocally "took cognizance" in a legal agreement of the "separation of church and state" which the Popes had always condemned in principle, a condition had arisen that also made it easier for the Communists to take seriously the principle of separation, possibly in the sense formulated by the Italian CP leader Luigi Longo in January 1966: "Just as we reject the confessional state, we are also against state atheism, against the state's granting privileges to any ideology, to any religious belief."[9]

For ruling Communists, who must ideologically justify their monopoly of power, that remains difficult to practice. In Yugoslavia too, Bishop Franic of Split foresaw that "implementation of the agreement will be very convoluted."[10] It soon became noticeable that the Catholic church in Yugoslavia was becoming freer and more active, indeed to a degree that would later worry the Communists.[11] This was encouraged by the exchange of diplomatic representatives: Archbishop Mario Cagna came to Belgrade as apostolic delegate, Viekoslav Cvrlje to the Vatican as envoy to the Holy See. Cagna traveled around a great deal and began to influence the Croatian church within the spirit of the agreement, and not always to the bishops' pleasure. Above all he attempted, naturally on the Pope's orders, to put the brakes on Cardinal Seper, who was zealously trying to extend the opportunities of the church in public life.[12] Given Hungary's experiences, and in view of what was brewing in Czechoslovakia at the end of 1967 (see p. 334), the Vatican advised caution. It was no accident that the hidden tug-of-war between the Roman curia and leaders of the episcopate ended— at the suggestion of Vienna's Cardinal König—with Seper's recall to Rome to become prefect of the Congregation of the Faith on January 8, 1968—

exactly three days before the Yugoslavian Prime Minister Mika Spiljak paid the Pope an official visit. (On the same day, January 11, Seper was sharply criticized in the Central Committee of the Croatian Communists.)

Prime Minister Spiljak assured the Pope "that people can be both good Christians and good citizens of their country"; Paul VI spoke of the value of religion for the state's welfare[13]—the first time this topic was broached in discussions with a Communist "of the highest level." Two years later, on August 15, 1970, contacts had improved so much that both sides decided on "regular" diplomatic relations: Monsignore Cagna was named Pronuncio,[14] Crvlje became ambassador, and the Vatican declared:

> "The church demands no privileges, but it needs—and this it does demand— living space (*spazio vitale*) to execute its mission. The purpose of diplomatic relations between the Holy See and governments is to guarantee—respecting each other's sovereign prerogatives—freedom and collaboration for the welfare of the people. But it is clear that this is all the more effective, the greater the Holy See's opportunities in its own religious-ecclesiastical sphere."

With this comment,[15] the Yugoslavian example was recommended for use by Communist countries; but in reality, the Roman curia was under no illusion that Yugoslavia remained a "special case." Tito alone among Communist dictators took seriously the separation of church and state that was a part of all the constitutions. Of course, even in Yugoslavia the dispute between party and church was never quite settled, and state functionaries and clergy now and then had altercations. However, nearly all the conflicts—including those that flared up temporarily in 1972/73 and again in 1976/77—were kindled more by national than philosophical differences. And what was most significant: not once since Tito's break with Stalin (see p. 259) had there been interference in the church's internal affairs. Even the religious decree of May 22, 1953—enacted a year after the break with the Vatican—was criticized by the *Osservatore Romano* as being "not very far from bourgeois laicism."[16] Pro-Secretary of State Tardini would even have seen issues for negotiations in the decree if anti-Vatican polemics had not just then (1953) been making such waves (because of the "Stepinac case"). Neither then nor later did the Yugoslavian Communists claim any right to participate in appointments to church offices; they needed no loyalty oaths and other state church instruments, demanding of the clergy only the loyalty expected of other citizens. Even the redrafting of the religious law, in March 1965, which limited the "misuse of religion"—until then subject to very loose interpretation[17]—to six clearly described situations, followed this policy of non-interference in internal church life and its administration. And this was confirmed by the new decentralized church legislation of the single republics (according to Yugoslavia's new constitution of 1974.) Through discreet contacts, the papal pro-nuncio in Belgrade, Michele

Cecchini, was able to bring his influence to bear on the new religious laws of the individual republics, and also to strengthen the backbone of the local episcopacy—for example the Zagreb Archbishop Kuharic, who was even able to publish his criticism of a new draft law in the Communist paper *Vjesnik* (March 18, 1977). Thus the religious law which took effect on April 17, 1978, acquired a distinctly compromisory character, and even in the delicate question of religious instruction is more liberal than the Yugoslavian Federal Law of 1953.

From the Vatican's point of view, that meant less when compared with countries where state and church lived together in friendly harmony, but it was a great deal when contrasted with the situation in other Communist-ruled countries, not to mention neighboring Albania, where Enver Hoxha had closed all churches in 1967 and declared the "total liquidation" of religion (which was confirmed by art. 37 of Albania's new constitution in December 1976).

"Monolithic" Communism, the stereotype image of the Popes Pius, had long since vanished. Enver Hoxha, who had studied philosophy at the Sorbonne in Paris, was a Communist. So was Josip Broz-Tito, the former Comintern agent who, accompanied by his wife in a black veil, entered the Vatican palace on March 29, 1971, in tails and top hat to pay his respects to Paul VI (see illustrations). There was a great deal about international politics and world peace in the speeches by the Yugoslavian head of state and the Pope, but little about religion and the church—in Tito's speech literally nothing: a symbol of demarcation. When the Yugoslav bishops came to Rome for an "ad limina" visit on November 21, 1977, the Pope saw no reason to even mention church-state relations. It was the mission of the church, he said, to oppose the influence of the "so-called scientific materialism" in the schools.

Perhaps a "protocol" like the Yugoslav-Vatican one of 1966, which established a few basic points and primarily an "amicable distance" between state and church, was in the final analysis generally preferable to a "fixed *modus vivendi*" or even a concordat? This question, asked by a high Vatican dignitary, was a product of the curia's Yugoslavian experiences and occupied its eastern policies more and more in the early seventies.

Wait-and-See Contacts with Bucharest and Sofia

Without formal negotiations, simply through personal contacts, the situation improved in another country, Rumania, which—although part of the Soviet bloc—began in the sixties to take its own steps in foreign policy. Here, of course—as in the Soviet Union—the fate of the Uniates remained the main obstacle to any Vatican effort. The attempt to protect them from complete assimilation by Rumanian Orthodoxy had failed, just as had efforts to protect the Latin-rite church through secret bishops (cf. Bishop Schubert's fate, p. 263ff.). When Cardinal König of Vienna, at the invitation of Patriarch Justinian, undertook an initial fact-finding trip to Bucharest in November 1967, he hoped to improve the atmosphere by avoiding the Uniate question. However, years later, when he indicated in his acceptance of a second invitation to Bucharest that he could not exclude the problem this time, Rumania declined his visit. . . .

Still, Rumania's Communists seemed to regard the Uniate question more casually after Nicolae Ceausescu had substituted a more moderate, nationally-flavored dictatorship for Soviet Stalinism. Prime Minister Maurer was not deterred from visiting Paul VI on January 24, 1968, because the Pope had, at the beginning of December 1967, publicly honored the Uniate Bishop Hossu, who had been banished to an Orthodox monastery. However, Maurer did tell the Pope that Rumania, "as a sovereign state," wished to establish good relations with all religious communities; that it valued the conciliatory attitude of the Vatican, and that this would also benefit Rumania's Catholics. A month later, on February 29, 1968, Ceausescu received all "religious leaders" of the country, among them the Roman Catholic Bishop of Alba Iulia, Aaron Marton, who had lived under house arrest for seventeen years. In a speech, Marton promised to urge the faithful "to the fulfillment of their civic duties." However, he was not allowed to travel to Rome for two years, and only four years later, on February 13, 1972, did the Rumanian church office for the first time give its express permission to consecrate a bishop: Antal Jakab, a priest who had been in prison for seven years, was consecrated in Rome and appointed Marton's "coadjutor" with the right of succession. On the other hand, an attempt seven years earlier to occupy the diocese of Jasi with a bishop, in a "coup de main" so to speak, had miscarried: the priest Petru Plesca, in Rome on a visit, had been openly consecrated as bishop in December 1965, but the Rumanian church office had only subsequently been informed of this; it refused official recognition to Plesca, but allowed him to perform his pastoral duties. (He died in 1977; and the Vatican was only allowed to nominate a successor who was not a bishop: Petre Gherghel, Vice-Rector of the priests' seminary, became "Ordinarius" in April 1978.) Bishop Adalbert Boros (secretly consecrated in 1951, see p. 266), was also allowed to travel to Rome, but in his Rumanian-German bishopric of Timisoara could only act as assistant chaplain following his release from prison. Konrad Kernweiss, who had been appointed by the government, functioned as ordinary; when he came to Rome in November 1973, he made such a good impression that he was at least named "prothonotary apostolic."

Of course, the Bucharest Church Office director, Dumitru Dogaru, a former Orthodox priest and dogmatic Communist who likes to philosophize and talk about his pious mother, hinted repeatedly that he would negotiate with the Vatican. But Rome hesitated. The attempt to first clarify the Uniate question with the Rumanian Orthodox led nowhere. Monsignore Jan Willebrands met secretly in 1970 with Patriarch Justinian (in Cologne). At the end of 1971, Cardinal Döpfner of Munich, as Justinian's guest in Bucharest, was only able to improve the atmosphere, and even the visit to the Pope by a delegation from the Rumanian Patriarchate brought no substantive, but only more atmospheric, progress.

When Chief of State Ceausescu was also received by the Pope on his visit to Italy on May 26, 1973, there seemed to be some movement. In December the new "traveling nuncio" Luigi Poggi, who had replaced Monsignore Cheli, flew to Bucharest to a UNESCO conference, which incidentally offered an opportunity for discussions with Dogaru. Great mistrust could still be felt. There was even hemming and hawing about an import license for 500 priest's breviaries as if it were a state problem: Why had they been printed in West Germany, not by the Vatican, which was sending them?

Not until January 1975 did Special Nuncio Poggi go to Bucharest for the first official talks, then in October 1976 and July 1977. Although in the meantime, Dumitru Dogaru had been replaced as head of the state Church Office by the more flexible career diplomat Ion Roseanu, the negotiations proceeded only at snail's pace. Five of the six bishoprics remained unoccupied, for the government still officially recognized only two dioceses (Alba Iulia and Bucharest); the Vatican, for its part, could not bring itself to accept Mons. Augustin (see p. 267) as bishop for Bucharest. The ruins of the unsuccessful policies of the fifties were still difficult to remove, even after the death of Orthodox Patriarch Justinian in March 1977. His successor, Justin, was elected by a body which included not only the Holy Synod, but also government representatives. Cardinal Jan Willebrands, who delivered the Pope's congratulations to the new Patriarch, mentioned in a speech that not only historical antagonisms, but also "wounds of the recent past [must be] healed" (*Osservatore Romano*, June 29, 1977). But for Justin, as for the state, the question of the Uniates remained taboo. It remained an obstacle on the path toward a concerted "statute" for the Latin church in Rumania. (Only in July 1979, when Special Nuncio Poggi negotiated in Bucharest, was a draft of such a "statute" prepared—the first without mentioning art. 47 of the 1947 law, which prohibited "foreign" religious jurisdiction on Rumanian territory).

Similar findings also left *Bulgaria* on the periphery of Vatican efforts in the southeast. For the tiny minority of about 65,000 Catholics, whose priests at the end of the fifties were all in prison, the conciliatory tendency introduced by John XXIII (once delegate in Sofia), and especially Paul VI's approaches to the Patriarchs of Constantinople and Moscow, had an almost redemptory effect. The most prominent Catholic bishop, Evgen Bossilkow, who had been sentenced to death in 1952 as a "Vatican spy," but whose execution had never been made public, was not able to escape with his life from the prisons of the Bulgarian Stalinists. Kyril Kurteff, the Exarch of the Bulgarian Uniates, who had only escaped being liquidated according to the Soviet and Rumanian example by reason of their insignificance (hardly 15,000 believers, mostly in villages on the Greek border), returned to Sofia at the end of the fifties; he was allowed to establish communications with Rome. In December 1960 he received permission to consecrate the Capuchin monk Simeon Kokoff as bishop for the faithful of the Latin rite and install him as vicar general in Plovdiv.

Kokoff moved into the sacristy of the "cathedral" of Plovdiv, where I visited him in summer 1965 (see illustrations). After long years in prison, he was deeply bitter and resigned. Even the opportunity to participate in the Second Vatican Council had not mellowed his antipathy toward any innovations in the church. He refused a reconciliation with the Orthodox, whose Patriarch cooperated with the new state as he had with the old. But it was just this conservatism that made him more comfortable for the government than the apostolic administrator of Plovdiv at the time, Bogdan Dobranow, a much younger, modern and active priest, who the government knew had also been secretly consecrated as bishop in 1959. As so often happened in the straits of oppressive circumstances, personal animosities also broke out between the prelates. For the Vatican, however, the only important thing now was to free the surviving hierarchy—especially in such a tiny, defenseless church as the Catholic one in Bulgaria—from any appearance of illegality. On April 27, 1965, the Roman Congregation for the Eastern Church named Bishop Kokoff apostolic administrator for Southern Bulgaria and relieved Dobranow of this office. To those familiar with the local situation, this sounded like mockery when the letter from the Congregation to Dobranow (*Prot. No. 100/49*) read that he could "go to any city of his choice until he was needed again in the vineyard of the Lord."

The removal of Dobranow, whom the authorities did not allow to function as a bishop anyway, was the price for receiving permission to consecrate as bishop the 49-year-old Assumptionist Father Dimitrow Stratiew in Sofia in September 1965. After long years in prison, he was recommended not only by his loyalty, but also by his good relations with the Bulgarian Patriarch. Succession to the almost eighty-year-old Exarch Kurteff was promised to him; when the latter died in March 1971, Stratiew assumed office without difficulty and was even allowed to go to the Roman synods of bishops in 1971 and 1974. After the death of the Capuchin Bishop Kokoff in August 1974, however, the Latin hierarchy was completely extinct.

Quite unexpectedly, a meeting took place a year later that one could call a stroke of luck were it not so obvious that it could hardly have been otherwise, given the pragmatism of the Vatican's eastern policies: the Bulgarian state and party leader Todor Zhivkov, on the occasion of his state visit to Italy, also visited the Pope on June 27, 1975, and asked what his wishes were. With a dictatorial gesture that cost him little (since he was realistically aware of the insignificance of Bulgarian Catholicism), Zhivkov approved, without negotiations, the installation of two new Latin bishops for south Bulgaria (Plovdiv) and north Bulgaria (Nikopolis). Both were the Pope's candidates: the 55-year-old cathedral pastor Vasco Seirecow (who died in 1977), and—even more surprising— Bogdan Dobranow, to whom justice was belatedly done. The Sofia Church Office, which would certainly never accept Dobranow, had thus simply been "run over" by the head of state. In October 1975, the Secretary of the Vatican Congregation for the Eastern Church, Mario Brini, was able to go to Bulgaria himself and consecrate the new bishops, and in November, for the first time, a pilgrim group made up of 28 Bulgarian Catholics was able to go to Rome for the Holy Year. A year later, Agostino Casaroli, the Vatican "Foreign Minister," went to Sofia at the invitation of the Bulgarian Foreign Minister (November 4-8, 1976). This was not only a "diplomatic" but also a pastoral journey: for a whole week, Casaroli visited Catholic congregations all over the country, even the most remote, in order to then bring their concerns before the competent government offices. For the first time in three decades, the Bulgarian Catholics had the feeling that they were not forgotten. . . . And John Paul II, the new Pope, confirmed this on December 14, 1978, when he received the Bulgarian Foreign Minister Petar Mladenov in private audience where he made a speech—unusual in customary Vatican protocol—which was then published: that he was pleased with "the *progress* already achieved [since Zhivkov's papal visit] in giving the Catholic church in Bulgaria the opportunity to fulfil its mission"; that Bulgarian Catholics were not only loyal to the church, but also "exemplary in the fulfilment of their civic responsibilities. . . ." For further developments in 1979, see last chapter of this book.

"Save What Can Still Be Saved": Tug-of-War with Prague

Except for the invisible audience—microphones in the walls of the room in the Prague "Alcron" Hotel, no one heard the old man's soft sighs. He bent over a paper given him by another, younger man, Monsignore

Agostino Casaroli, who had come inconspicuously from Rome a few days earlier. On this afternoon of February 17, 1965, he met for the first time the Archbishop of Prague, Josef Beran, who for sixteen years had not been allowed to enter his residence (see p. 273). Dragged from one place of internment to another, Beran had been "pardoned," but not released, in October 1963, when things finally began to loosen up a little in Czechoslovakia. Casaroli had asked for relief for Beran back during his first discreet visit to Prague, in May 1963, and had been able to report to Pope John a few days before the Pope's death that at least a few clerics were able to come to Rome for the council—but not Beran. In January 1965, almost two years later, he received the news via a registered letter from Rome that Paul VI had named him Cardinal. Officials of the Prague Ministry of the Interior who appeared shortly thereafter at Beran's internment in Radvanov, near Tabor, told him only that appointments of cardinals—in contrast to appointments of bishops—did not interest the authorities. When Beran was called to Prague four weeks later to meet privately with Monsignore Casaroli, the papal negotiator had already had lengthy days of negotiations with the Prague Church Office.

It was a strange "conversation" of mutes conducted this February in the Prague hotel. In order to give away no information to the electronic eavesdroppers in the walls, Casaroli formulated his communications in writing, and Beran wrote his answers on the same paper. This also had the advantage of enabling later church historians with access to the Vatican secret archive to reconstruct the proceeding verbatim. Here only the substance can be reproduced:

Casaroli, on the Pope's orders, submitted two possibilities for Beran's choice, one of which had been worked out with the Czech government:

1. Beran could go to Rome unmolested to accept his Cardinal's hat, participate in the council, and formally also keep his title of Archbishop of Prague until his death; however, he would never be able to return to Prague. His diocese, orphaned for sixteen years, would however receive as apostolic administrator a bishop selected by the Holy See: Frantisek Tomasek, who for years had only been allowed to function as a village parson. Vicar Capitular Stehlik would step down, satisfied to be provost of the cathedral.

2. Beran could refuse this solution, and everything would remain unchanged. The Holy Father would regret this, since negotiations with the government were exceedingly difficult and a first, however modest, result could perhaps lead to opportunities for further action. But Beran could count on the complete understanding of the Pope if he preferred to remain in Czechoslovakia under prevailing circumstances.

Beran asked for time to think; for several hours he wrestled alone with the decision. Then he wrote his "Placet" for solution no. 1 on Casaroli's paper with the remark that it was more important for the Archdiocese of Prague to finally receive a bishop recognized in Rome and Prague and to get rid of Stehlik. He was prepared to make this heavy sacrifice. Two days later, on February 19, 1965, he flew with Casaroli to Rome. The two had waited another day in order to be sure that the Prague government would keep its promise: indeed, Bishop Tomasek already took the prescribed loyalty oath on February 18 and moved into the archepiscopal palace in Prague. While Casaroli and Beran were still en route to Rome, the Ceteka agency announced the Cardinal's departure and the nomination of Tomasek.

Later, in 1968, Cardinal Beran presented these events rather differently—as if the Prague government (or even the Vatican) had duped him into leaving with the promise that he could return after three weeks, and then claiming that he was staying abroad of his own choice.[18] There was of course no question of such a "choice," only of his own decision. This was made easier for both him and the Vatican because the head of the Prague Church Office, Karel Hruza, for the first time held out the prospect of open negotiations with the Vatican concerning "unresolved questions," including the occupation of vacant episcopal sees.[19]

It did, however, take over a year before occasional confidential contacts led to secret exploratory talks. The situation confronting Casaroli in Czechoslovakia appeared nearly hopeless: after twenty years of Stalinism, the unsuccessful experiment with the secret bishops (see p. 273f.) had left only ruins. Large areas of the country were without pastors. The remaining church administration was under direct state control—more completely than anywhere else in Eastern Europe. When in 1960, on a visit to the archepiscopal palace in Prague, I mistakenly opened the wrong door, I discovered that the diocesan administration was a department of the ministry of culture, with party pictures decorating the office. Timid, powerless vicars capitular, often discredited ecclesiastically as well as morally, maintained hardly more than an outward appearance. Some, like Stehlik in Prague or Oliva in Litoměřice, assured the Holy See by circuitous paths of their loyalty, but had lost their credibility. The priest Plojhar, who was minister of health for twenty years and finally could not even prevent those dying in state hospitals from being denied spiritual support, was bound to Rome only by his clerical collar and a "renaissance" lifestyle. . . .

At the second "Congress of the Peace Movement of Catholic Priests," in November 1966, Plojhar alluded to the secret discussions with the Vatican and demanded that the vicars capitular installed by the government be named bishops. When Casaroli thereupon threatened to break off the discussions, government representative Hruza offered a compromise: the Vatican could fill three of the six unoccupied bishoprics with priests of its own selection if it accepted the government's suggestions in the others. Casaroli wanted to "sound out" the candidates. Private conversations were arranged for him in Prague, but in Litoměřice they were stopped at the last moment (because—as Casaroli could not know—the vicar capitular, Oliva, was no longer considered trustworthy by the Communists either. . .). The Bishop of Litoměřice, Stefan Trochta, had been sentenced in 1953 to 25 years in prison (as a "Vatican spy" among other things). Pardoned in 1960, he worked as a locksmith, and after a heart attack, lived in an institution. This man, who like Party Chief Novotny had narrowly escaped death in Hitler's concentration camp Mauthausen, Prague wanted to offer a diocese—but not Litoměřice, where the bishop was popular, and not without the "price" of other unacceptable bishops.

Casaroli broke off advance negotiations over this point in July 1967. However, those who assumed that the Vatican was only waiting for "better times" and speculating about those dramatic changes which in 1968 led to the "Prague springtime," were wrong. The Roman curia knew only too well that even a liberal period might be short-lived. A "humanized" Communism, like that which emerged under Party Chief Alexander Dubcek, would only accelerate a process of secularization already far advanced in the CSSR: even before 1948, almost 30 per cent of the country's citizens were atheists.

It was the state and not the church which hinted for the first time on March 1968, that the nation's faithful should now also receive genuine equal rights. On March 20, the Prague Administrator, Bishop Tomasek, wrote a pastoral letter: "We want no privileges, we are calling, in good conscience, for our rights in this democratic society." On March 22, Minister Plojhar resigned from his office—"with a good conscience," as he attested—and Church Office director Hruza promised "not to interfere." On March 26, Hruza himself was replaced by the more tolerant Communist sociologist of religion Erika Kadlecowa. She explained on April 8 to the Ceteka agency: "It is difficult to predict negotiations with the Vatican, but important changes have taken place in the Vatican too, just as with us. . . ."

When he came to Rome for two weeks at the end of April 1968, Bishop Tomasek was astonished to learn that the Vatican certainly was not in any hurry to "seize, the iron while it was hot," let alone to strike it. The Vatican's motto was: wait and see. Influential prelates and even the Pope himself were reckoning with the fact that the Soviet Union would not tolerate developments in the CSSR, which seemed to be sliding from the Stalinist extreme to the liberal. The Vatican also refused to give in to pressure from Prague Catholics that Cardinal Beran should return quickly; a serious illness of Beran's at the beginning of August made it easier to restrain the Cardinal. Bishop Trochta, however, had returned to his see in Litoměřice at the beginning of August, and was now pressuring Prague to make an offer to negotiate. The Vatican finally named a date—in October.

Procrastination and caution were at first rewarded. After the Soviet intervention in August, which the Dubcek leadership escaped for a half-year's grace, the church remained almost untouched, but the October date with the Vatican was quietly forgotten. "We are happy to see a certain improvement arising in the situation of the Catholic church in Czechoslovakia," the Pope told Slovakian pilgrims on November 13, 1968, after Bishop Tomasek had come to Rome again to set the negotiations in motion. But tension in Prague made the Vatican hesitate further. When the self-immolation of Jan Palach in the middle of January 1969 signaled a high point in the desperate agitation in the CSSR, the 80-year-old Cardinal Beran turned to his Prague diocesans with a message from Rome which the *Osservatore Romano* printed on the front page on January 26:

> "I am weeping with you. . . . He who is speaking to you, as you know, has himself suffered a great deal. But the moment has come to forget the past. Let us not consume our spiritual energies in hatred, but let us direct them toward harmony, work, service to our brothers, toward a new flowering of our land! Lift up your hearts: may you be strong in silence and in hope!"

This last pastoral letter from Beran before his death (May 1969) had a different tone from Hungarian Cardinal Mindszenty's in 1956 (see p. 295). When it seemed for a short time in February 1969 that the Dubcek leadership might last after all, the Pope thought that he should make use of the opportunity; before a thousand Slovakian pilgrims, he expressed for the first time his requests of the government: "No claims of privilege, but rather a legitimate extension of natural rights: good bishops without unseemly restrictions, seminaries, orders, a Catholic press, religious instruction. . . . The good will shown up to now is a good omen," Paul VI said on February 12. Even the dramatic change of leadership in Prague, which in April brought a Slovakian Communist to power in Gustav Husak, who—himself a victim of Stalinism—promised to save the reform movement, did not dash all hope. It was known that Husak was anti-clerical, but also that he supported a normalization between church and state. But the fact that Karel Hruza, the old Church Office director, now returned to head this office, but at the same time told Catholic bishops that he had been "practically compelled" by his superiors to adopt his attitude of the sixties,[20] also made it difficult to draw any firm conclusions.

It was not until more than a year later, on October 13, 1970, that Hruza appeared in Rome in order to renew negotiations with the Vatican that had been broken off three years earlier. Together with embassy counselor Alois Tychy and the Slovakian Church Office Director Karol Homola, he met with the papal "Foreign Minister" Casaroli and his eastern experts Giovanni Cheli and Angelo Sodano in the Italian nunciature (i.e., not in the Vatican).

The Prague negotiators had protected themselves from the suspicious Soviets: in a Moscow journal, Hruza made a kind of confession of sins, denounced the direction of the Church Office of the Dubcek period, dug up old reproaches against the Vatican, indeed even claimed that "papal audiences in Rome usually turn into anti-Czech demonstrations all by themselves."[21] With the callous opportunism that characterizes Communists of this kind, Hruza nevertheless showed not the slightest embarrassment in presenting himself to the Vatican prelates as negotiating partner. . . . The discussions ran aground during the second round, in December, when Prague began to organize a new government-directed priests' movement under the name of *Pacem in Terris*, and they broke off again on March 27, 1971, when the government, in four-day discussions that Cheli conducted in Prague, insisted on unacceptable candidates for bishop.

The Vatican now had to deal less with the arrogance of the Communist dogmaticists than with their self-confidence, severely diminished since 1968/69. Their phobia of political impotence turned into an irrational fear of a church which in truth had quite often resigned not only politically, but also religiously, since its exostructure was nearly broken, or had crumbled. In Bohemia, 1239 pastoral positions out of 2175, more than half, were unoccupied in 1970; prospects for the next generation of priests, which had been revived for a short time in 1968, were again circumscribed in the only two seminaries as a result of the "numerus clausus" (enrollment quota). The remaining superannuated episcopate was almost extinct. Since June 1971 there were no officiating bishops left in Slovakia, and since June 1972 only two in the Czech dioceses, who were forbidden any activity outside their bishoprics. For 23 years no bishop had been openly consecrated, and the time could be foreseen when there would be no one left in the CSSR who could ordain priests and administer the sacrament of confirmation.

This was the situation when Karel Hruza, after an interruption of eighteen months, resumed negotiations with Casaroli in Rome from the 13th to the 16th of November 1972. In contrast to Hungary or even Poland, in Czechoslovakia it was only a matter of "saving what could be saved"—as the Pope formulated it. He was aware that there were more than a few priests and believers in the CSSR who took the standpoint: "Rather no bishop at all than one with the blessing of the Communist state!"[22]

Embittered and isolated in an environment that was largely indifferent to religion (which even politically only paid lip service), these Catholics overlooked something essential: that it would contradict their church's historical principles of existence and survival, and above all its own concept of hierarchical structure, apostolic succession and the transmission of sacramental authority, if it had bluntly rejected the only opportunity that the Prague Communists—for reasons of prestige—were now offering. For the only alternative, the installation of secret bishops, had failed long ago.

Thus it happened that Hruza and Casaroli, in the second round of discussions in this phase of the negotiations—from December 11 to 16, 1972—agreed on four candidates for bishop, of whom not all seemed unreservedly acceptable to the Vatican. A particularly problematical case was that of the proposed apostolic administrator of Olomouc, Josef Vrana. Son of a pre-war politician, since 1971 he had been president of the Czech national unit of the government-directed association of priests, "Pacem in Terris," and as vicar capitular was very controversial among the clergy. In the middle of February 1972 he had come to Rome to deliver documents for the beatification procedure for the Olomouc Archbishop Antonin Stojan, who had died in 1923. The Vatican used the opportunity to explore Vrana's inner orientation and his priestly qualities in long discussions; Archbishop Tomasek, who was in Rome at the same time, was also consulted. It was therefore not as if the Vatican had not gathered precise information about the candidates for bishop. Casaroli also insisted on a confidential meeting with the others.

On January 15, 1973, Monsignore Giovanni Cheli traveled to Czechoslovakia to hold long private discussions with all four prelates in uncontrolled surroundings; in addition, Cheli gathered further information from trustworthy clerics. The Roman curia convinced itself that these were priests unobjectionable in the church-religious and moral sense, but who were of the opinion that under the given circumstances some political engagement, essentially limited to civic loyalty, was unavoidable if the church in the CSSR was not to promote its own isolation—already instigated by atheistic party fanatics—and thus forfeit its remaining pastoral possibilities.

So at the end of February 1973, the Pope named three Slovakian clerics, Julius Gabris, Jan Pastor and Jozef Feranec, as titular bishops and apostolic administrators for the orphaned dioceses of Trnava, Nitra and Banska Bystrica, and Josef Vrana as titular bishop and administrator in Olomouc—the last with the restriction "*ad nutum sanctae sedis*" (which, according to church law, could facilitate a possible future removal from office). The Prague government had agreed that Vrana should give up his office with "Pacem in Terris"; after some hesitation, it had also accepted Rome's condition that the four bishops' consecrations be undertaken in Czechoslovakia by a representative of the Pope, in order to thus document, before the CSSR Catholics, their competence and their connection with Rome.

Thousands of people knelt before the cathedral in Nitra (Slovakia) on March 3, as Agostino Casaroli appeared for the first time in a Communist country in episcopal robes; ceremoniously he consecrated the three Slovakian bishops, then traveled with them to Olomouc, where on March 4—assisted by Bishops Trochta and Tomasek—he also crowned the controversial Josef Vrana with the mitre and gave him the bishop's ring, a gift from the Pope. In his sermon to the new bishops, Casaroli solemnly impressed upon them the religious duties of a bishop, with quotes from the council's decrees: "Be witnesses of faith and love, also toward human and state society!" Never had the pastoral intention and function of Vatican eastern policy been so visibly demonstrated as at this moment, when the top papal diplomat carried out his pastoral, episcopal office there where they had tried for a quarter century to cut off the Catholic church from its Roman center and let it wither away. But since Michel d'Herbigny's times (see p. 83), such an act did not need to be celebrated so in extremis. . . .

Casaroli did not indulge in any illusions, not even about the risk taken by the Vatican. "Many problems remain unsolved," he said after a two-hour discussion with Vice Prime Minister Matej Lucan on March 5 in Prague. On the same day, however, he was able to inform Bishop Trochta in Litoměřice of his elevation to Cardinal and invite him to Rome, but he also heard of the discomfort that the "Catholic performances" in Nitra and Olomouc had caused the nervous Communist dogmatists.

The news was soon out that the new Bishop Vrana had spoken before the "Pacem in Terris" association on March 8 and promised it his "continued full support." Had he then not—as promised—stepped down from the chairmanship of this organization? In the negotiations the evasive formulation had been agreed upon that Vrana's office with "Pacem in Terris" was incompatible with his office as bishop because this organization was based on only a part of the clergy, while the bishop "must be father and shepherd to all believers and priests." Had Vrana broken this agreement? Not until the end of March did he finally inform a journalist in Vienna by telephone that at the session on March 8 he had in fact declared his resignation; the CSSR press had been forced to suppress this, however[23]— a sign of how much the Czechoslovakian Communists thought they had to fear the consequences of a church-political relaxation of tension, in which, at the same time, they were and still are interested—though not less fearfully.

This was shown again when the Prague negotiator Karel Hruza came to Rome in the middle of September 1974 to begin a new phase in negotiations. After the death of Cardinal Trochta in April (a few hours after a violent argument between the Cardinal, who had a bad heart condition, and the North Bohemian Party Secretary Dlabal), eight of the 13 bishoprics in the CSSR were completely orphaned. Except for Bishop Vrana, who could use his political prestige for better pastoral conditions, the bishops felt themselves increasingly hard-pressed by the functionaries. The Communists were still trying to compensate by acts of force for their spiritual impotence or their desperate cynicism, which since 1968 had replaced many people's disappointed convictions; even if only with chicanery toward harmless nuns. When a Prague newspaper described the professional discrimination against a believing, but non-party, little clerk as good and proper, the malicious-servile mockery of a "Good Soldier Schweik" was almost visible, that traditional Czech figure who glorified the absurd in order to take it *ad absurdum.* . . . But did this not contain the ray of hope which the Vatican diplomacy even now did not stop seeking by sitting around a table with CSSR functionaries?

Paul VI hesitated for a long time when the Czechoslovakian government invited the papal "Foreign Minister" Casaroli to Prague at the beginning of 1975—not to discuss problems of the church, but as a visit from "state to state." How could such an invitation be accepted while at the same time state pressure on religious life in the CSSR was steadily increasing? On the other hand: would refusing the invitation not offer new excuses for increasing the pressure further? After tortured consideration of both arguments, the Pope decided to send Casaroli to Prague and to point out, in discussions with Foreign Minister Chnoupek as well as with Vice Premier Lucan, the "close connection between the international problems of peace and the problems of the church in the various countries" (cf. Casaroli's dinner speech in Prague on February 26, 1975).

Nevertheless, after this Prague visit of Casaroli's, the negotiations, which had proceeded without result in two rounds of discussions in 1974 (September 17-20 and December 7-12), continued to stagnate. A journey to Prague by Nuncio Poggi in the summer of 1976 was equally unsuccessful in getting them moving. Only when the Prague civil rights movement with its "Charta 77" drew world-wide attention to the limitations on freedom, including religious freedom, in the CSSR, did a certain interest re-awaken in the Czechoslovakian government. Karel Hruza declared in the CPC newspaper *Rude Pravo* (February 23, 1977) that "religious freedom [was] guaranteed" in the CSSR, and accused Radio Vatican of participating in "defamation campaigns"; but at the same time he admitted that the party was "undertaking a decisive action to eliminate the remnants of religion . . . and to create all necessary prerequisites so that atheism may take root in the consciousness of every citizen. Are there reasons, then, why the believers do not participate in the realization of our party policies?" asked Hruza with an unequalled cynicism, which paradoxically was also the signal for certain gestures of relaxation:

On March 18, 1977, for the first time in thirty years, the Pope was able to welcome five CSSR bishops on a *joint* "ad limina" visit to Rome, and to value their work "under the particular conditions that are known to Us and to you" (*pecularibus in condicionibus, quae notae sunt vobis et Nobis*). This was all the more significant because Hruza, in fear of any joint appearance of the bishops, had even forbidden the formation of the Czechoslovakian Conference of Bishops. Now the Prague government agreed to the announcement at the beginning of June 1977 of Bishop Tomasek's appointment as cardinal (which the Pope had already undertaken earlier "in pectore," i.e., in secret). The CSSR Embassy in Rome even gave a reception on June 27 for the new Cardinal of Prague, whom Party Chief Husak assured in a congratulatory message: "I am interested in the positive progress of the negotiations our state is conducting with the Holy See" (*Katolicke noviny*, 7/24/77).

Tactics or realism?—Father John Bukovsky (SVD), an American of Slovakian descent, who this year had become one of Mons. Casaroli's closest collaborators in eastern policy, was able in the summer of 1977 to travel for several weeks through six of the eight Czechoslovakian dioceses that were lacking bishops. The papal representative was of course constantly shadowed by the police; however he was enabled to conduct unsupervised conversations with the clergy: he brought written answers to written questions back to Rome in his diplomatic luggage. He met 170 priests, among them also "secret bishops" living in the CSSR (see p. 303); all of them, almost without exception, agreed with the persons and the activities of the bishops that the Vatican had appointed in 1973, and only one third of them expressed criticism of the Vatican eastern policy.

Bukovsky also spoke for several hours with the "most prominent," but most dubious, opponent of this policy: Felix Davidek, an almost seventy-year-old psychologically unbalanced Catholic priest living in Brno, who had been consecrated bishop in the sixties by a bishop (unknown to this day) *without Vatican permission* and was trying to build up an "underground church," independent of Rome, in the CSSR. Bishop Davidek had ordained a great number, probably hundreds of priests, among them many *married* men of varied professions, and probably also women—sacramentally valid, but in contradiction to canon law. This was no secret from the Prague government from the very beginning; it used Davidek's "dissident" church as an instrument to promote distrust and schismatic tendencies in the "official" clergy, to cast doubts on their loyalty and to cause the Vatican to intervene in a situation which, under the repressive circumstances of the CSSR church policy, cannot really be clarified. For that reason, the Vatican was also wary of handling the "Davidek case" openly (in the well-grounded expectation that the Prague government, also, was not interested in a public scandal, but only in the exploitation of the case to fit its schemes). The case however symptomized the extreme difficulty with which the often misunderstood Vatican policy must contend especially in Czechoslovakia, in the absence of a pastoral alternative to the arduous quest for a *modus vivendi*.

So finally, after a round of negotiations from the 20th to the 27th of September 1977, a modest new agreement came into being: finally the Prague government agreed to the formal appointment of Cardinal Tomasek (till then active only as apostolic administrator) as Archbishop of Prague, and the Vatican completed the establishment—promised since 1928—of a separate church province in Slovakia (thereby adjusting the ecclesiastical borders to the political borders that had come into being after the First [!] World War after the downfall of the Hapsburg monarchy). Not until months later, January 10, 1978, could the Pope announce this decision—without enthusiasm, for in the meantime the Prague government had refused its (promised) agreement to the appointment of Bishop Gabris as the new Slovakian Archbishop. Gabris had expressed open criticism of the obstruction of religious education in the CSSR at the Roman Bishops' Synod in September 1977, and after his return from Rome had been so reviled by the director of the Church Office in Bratislava, Karel Homola, that he suffered a heart attack. . . .

Should the Vatican have annulled the entire agreement because of that? Would that have helped the Slovakian Catholics?—The answer is not as easy as many Catholics in the West pretend, who prefer to be edified by the "sufferings of our brothers in the East" rather than grasp a papal pastoral policy that went beyond the horizon of their always freshly-painted churches. . . .

"Secure What is Strong": Poland; Its Primate and its Pope

Receiving 38 Polish bishops on November 13, 1965, at the end of the Second Vatican Council, the Pope did not believe his ears when Cardinal Primate Stefan Wyszyński, in a firm, mild voice, gave a summing up that not only broke forms of protocol, but revealed a barely-disguised criticism:

> "We are aware that it will be very difficult, but not impossible, to put the decisions of the Council into effect in our situation. Therefore we ask the Holy Father for one favor: for complete trust in the episcopate and the church of our

country. Our request may appear very presumptuous, but it is difficult to judge our situation from afar. Everything that occurs in the life of our church must be assessed from the standpoint of our experiences. . . .If one thing is painful for us, it is above all the *lack of understanding* among our brothers in Christ. If anything grieves us, it is only the *lack of trust* that we often feel in spite of the proofs of loyalty to the church and to the Holy See that we have presented in *refusing offers of an easy, more comfortable life. . . .*"

Paul VI, who coolly and formally replied that he did not doubt that the Council's decisions would be realized "willingly and energetically" in Poland too, and also "for the good of civil society" (*in civilis etiam societatis utilitatem*), had only his own, and not Wyszyński's, speech published in the Vatican newspaper.[24] He could not quite understand what had induced the Warsaw Cardinal to make this statement. Was it the feeling of isolation to which the Polish episcopate had increasingly succumbed at the Council because it considered the traditional forms and expressions of the church more resistant to state atheism than the Council's innovations and conciliatory readiness to conduct dialogue? —Since the end of the fifties, when it became clear that Poland's "national Communism" would never see a "second stage" under Moscow's shadow, the compromise that Wyszyński had concluded with Party Chief Gomulka had become more and more questionable in this new phase. The quarrel did not assume the dramatic forms of the Stalinist years, but was carried on through a policy of mutual needling, with the church compensating for its political, the party for its spiritual, impotence.[25] Since the Gomulka leadership did not even dare to hope that it could soften Poland's mighty Catholicism by an atheistic frontal attack, it settled for now timid, now hectic and furtive attempts to set in motion a secularization of society— even with the help of old-fashioned anti-clerical emotions. An attitude of coexistence, Wyszyński believed, could only favor this process; open battle—of course never overstepping the *edge* of a breach of relations!— would on the other hand keep Catholic consciousness alert and resistant.

This tactic was favored by two circumstances: by the lack of a clear church-political concept on Gomulka's part, and by the hesitation of the Vatican to canonically sanction Poland's national demands for ecclesiastical normalization in the Oder-Neisse territories (in which Catholics and Communists were of one mind). Friendly words from Pope John (see p. 304) did not change this situation any more than a non-committal allusion about "possibilities of a concordat" that Gomulka's closest collaborator, Zenon Kliszko, made in a lecture in Rome in December 1962.

For the Vatican's eastern policy, therefore, Poland was and is a quite different, much less pressing problem than for instance Czechoslovakia or Hungary. In Poland it was not necessary to undertake any salvage-action.

Here it was at most a question of the timely installation of solid juridical assurances, of legal guarantees of a condition that the Catholic church could not even dream of creating anywhere else in the Soviet sphere of influence: an intact episcopate of more than 70 bishops; no lack of priests; no restrictions on the orders; almost uncontrolled religious instruction in 17,000 catechetical points; more than 30 seminaries; a Catholic university in Lublin. . . .

The Roman curia, however, also inclined to the opinion that the Warsaw Cardinal's tactics would only be successful in the short run; that seen in the long run, the tension and "guerrilla war" between church and state would not encourage but rather exhaust the faithful, indeed would leave them susceptible to the secularization that takes place in a growing industrial society even without the assistance of the Communists. Even during the Council Wyszyński therefore received suggestions from the Vatican admonishing him to be conciliatory. And for that reason the Vatican was also very happy to learn, in the autumn of 1965, of an imminent spectacular step by the Polish episcopate: a letter to the German bishops, which for the first time since the horrors of the Second World War sought to build a bridge to the neighboring Germans. Did this perhaps open a door which would also enable the Vatican to enter into discussions with the Warsaw government through a final settlement of the Oder-Neisse church administration?

Paul VI did not know that Cardinal Wyszyński, the very day on which he had spoken such bold words to the Pope and, so to speak, reserved the right to "family quarrels," had decided to sign that conciliatory letter to the German bishops, the draft of which he had long regarded with great skepticism. Bishop Boleslaw Kominek (of Breslau/Wroclaw), an intelligent, peaceable, although politically inexperienced cleric, who was just as much a Polish patriot as a pro-German Silesian, had composed the original text in German. He had counselled with German bishops in Rome in hopes of a positive answer. Kominek had also—as he told me later— kept Ignacy Krasicki up to date, the only representative of the Communist press at the Council and a confidant of the state authorities in Warsaw. In due course Kominek had given Krasicki a text of the letter under the assumption that the Warsaw government would be heard from if anything displeased it.

Krasicki indeed sent the text to Warsaw, not as a confidential inquiry from Kominek, but rather as a "secret document" that he had obtained via circuitous routes, without the knowledge of the bishops. Whether vanity was involved here, or conscious intrigue, will never be known. The effect in any case was fatal: Gomulka, informed accordingly by the Ministry of the Interior, immediately suspected that the church wanted to "take over

German policies," and was only waiting for the German episcopate's answer, which he could be almost certain would not show any decisive accommodation on the Oder-Neisse question.[26]

In the meantime, Kominek in Rome kept hearing from his middleman Krasicki: Warsaw had nothing against the bishops' letter. Since Kominek feared to the end that the less pro-German Wyszyński might drop the project, he did not tell the Cardinal that he had already directed the text to the Warsaw government. Kominek did not suspect that he himself had been misled by Krasicki. Wyszyński, on the other hand, thought that he could proceed under the assumption that the Communists knew nothing about it; gifted with a sharper political insight than Kominek, Wyszyński had recognized that this "message to our German brothers in the pastoral office" contained many formulations that would act as political traps if they were not regarded with pious innocence, but rather—as the Warsaw Communists would—with critical mistrust. Wyszyński knew the mentality of his Warsaw antagonists well enough (and also that of his German colleagues) to be able to figure out that the sudden publication of the correspondence could only be one of those "thunderstorms" that Cardinal Wyszyński always considered appropriate for "purifying" the atmosphere regarding the church and reminding the Communists that they remained a ruling minority.

So Wyszyński did not mention the ominous letter when on the day before its publication he paid a courtesy call on the Polish ambassador in Rome. The Cardinal also maintained silence toward the Vatican, where no one suspected that instead of a West German-Polish rapprochement (useful to the Vatican's eastern policy), a new quarrel between church and state was now brewing in Poland.

The year 1966, the millenial anniversary of the Christianization of Poland and the establishment of the state, thus began under the sign of a dramatic competition between the two powers. Once again, as so often in the previous almost four decades, Poland, the largest Catholic nation in the East, proved itself a "bulwark"—of course not so much of the Catholic church as of its own national interests in the clash between Russians and Germans. In January 1966 Cardinal Wyszyński was refused the usual diplomatic passport for a trip to Rome. A papal journey to the thousand-year celebration in Czestochowa, still under discussion in 1965, had become impossible. Cardinal Wyszyński was less unhappy about this than most Catholic Poles. He alone—vested with the office of papal legate—now dominated the millenial celebrations, the demonstrations of faith by millions of Poles; he alone passed the new test of strength with the state—and he alone then again concluded the next informal provisional truce.

An analysis of the events ordered by the Pope at the end of 1966 showed clearly how urgent it was that the line established by Pius XII in 1945—that is, to leave the Polish church to itself (see pp. 254–5)—be revised in the interest of the Holy See's *overall* policies regarding the East. Certainly the curia never wanted to circumvent the Polish episcopate, to ignore it, or be played off against it; but it could also no longer abstain from active participation in the regulation of Polish church questions.

This was the starting point for a new phase that began in 1967, after the "millenial quarrel" had abated, with three fact-finding tours by Agostino Casaroli: from February 14 to March 7, March 13 to 25, and March 29 to April 6, 1967, Casaroli traveled for almost six weeks all over Poland, spoke with all the bishops, including those in the Oder-Neisse region, visited churches and cloisters in cities and country, talked with representatives of all Catholic lay groups, even with the controversial "Pax" chairman Piasecki. The government, which after 28 years finally wanted the Vatican to get a direct picture of the situation, allowed Casaroli to choose his own itinerary unhindered and conduct uncontrolled discussions; the government itself did not yet seek any discussions—aside from courtesy contacts. The Cardinal Primate's nervousness, which Casaroli could only with difficulty allay by the friendliest assurances, was thus groundless.

Casaroli was astonished to find that the Polish church was in an even stronger condition than he had expected from what he had heard. The Holy See was "in no hurry," he declared openly on one of his stopovers in Rome. The problems involved here seemed minimal in comparison to those in other countries of the eastern bloc: church construction, church press, greater freedom of publication and opportunities for public action, security of the church as a legal person, facilitation of the authorization procedure in the nomination of bishops, return of church property in the Oder-Neisse region (where it had been secularized as "formerly German").

Foremost among the unsolved problems, however, was still the confirmation of the Oder-Neisse border by an appropriate readjustment of the bishopric borders, through appointments of residentiary bishops. Since a government of the Great Coalition (Christian Democrats and Social Democrats) had emerged in Bonn in 1966, which for the first time no longer claimed "the borders of 1937," but rather declared an appreciation for "secure borders" for Poland, the hope also arose in the Vatican that it could rid itself of this tiresome problem.[27] Carefully, but persistently, it began to use Bonn's slowly emerging "new eastern policy" for its own ends—somewhat as it had followed the German Rapallo policy in the twenties (see p. 34ff.).

Since Gomulka did not yet trust Bonn's new tone, and still preferred to believe in a silent "conspiracy" between the Vatican and the "Bonn revisionists," while on the other hand the curia only intended to proceed "step by step," there were new frictions. In April 1967, Gomulka brusquely forbade a visit by the Polish State Council President Edward Ochab to Paul VI, one that had already been prepared in all its details between the Polish embassy and the Secretariat of State—and this despite the fact that two months earlier Soviet President Podgorny had completed a spectacular papal audience (see p. 360). The reason for the Polish obstinacy was the inscription under a picture in the *Osservatore Romano* which unwittingly injured Polish sensibilities. . . . Insulted in turn, the Pope postponed a step intended to oblige Ochab: not until a month later, on May 28, 1967, did he publish the appointment of four Polish apostolic administrators in the Oder-Neisse region.[28]

Strictly speaking, this was no more than papal confirmation of a legal act undertaken by Cardinal Hlond on his own initiative back in 1945, on the strength of his special powers (see p. 254). (Only in Danzig/Gdansk, which had not been a part of the German Reich in 1937, had the Vatican already undertaken a definitive rearrangement.) The Warsaw government recognized the step without particular enthusiasm; the "main obstacle" had not been removed. And it would take another five years before it was actually cleared away.

During the unrest that ended in December 1970 with Gomulka's fall, Cardinal Wyszyński proved once more that in extreme cases he would always cooperate to save the country (and also the regime) from catastrophe; through Prime Minister Jaroszewicz, the new Party Chief Edward Gierek expressed recognition of the Primate's "patriotic attitude" on March 3, 1971. Since in the meantime the last obstacle to the church's Oder-Neisse regulation had been removed by the border treaty between Bonn and Warsaw (December 1970), the moment for negotiations finally seemed at hand. From Jaroszewicz, Wyszyński had heard a harsh judgment about Gomulka's inconsistent church policies and received assurance that the new leadership wanted to proceed together with the Vatican *and* the episcopate.

But that was still a long way off. The first round of negotiations, from April 27-30, 1971, for which Vice Minister Aleksander Skarzyński, the long-time head of the state Church Office (*Urzad Wyznań*), came to Rome, produced nothing more than an exchange of opinions and wish-lists. Basically, the Vatican negotiators felt that Gierek's church policy did not yet have any clear consistency either and was under both internal party and Soviet pressure. In the summer of 1971, Gierek, without negotiations, made an initial gesture of good will: he returned the church property in the Oder-Neisse territories. In a public speech on October 10, 1971, Minister Skarzyński submitted two fundamental points of a compromise that surpassed all previous Communist church policy and promised the church a *permanent* existence:

"a) The church authority, the episcopate, must—in agreement with the character of its religious mission, as underlined by the Council, which lies beyond political systems (*ponadustrojowym*)—consistently recognize (*uznac*) the socialist order of our country, the political orientation of the People's Republic of Poland, as an inviolable, patriotically superordinate reality.

b) The Republic will respect (*szanowac*) the *permanent* character of the religious activity of the church and the social value of its educational function among religious people."[29]

Skarzyński personally, for whom a Roman tailor measured a tail-coat at the last moment, sat in St. Peter's Basilica on October 17, 1971, almost in a row with the Polish and German bishops, and took part in the beatification of Maksymilian Kolbe, the Polish martyr of Auschwitz. After a subsequent short meeting with the Pope, the Church Office director invited Casaroli to Warsaw for a new round of discussions. But it too, between November 10 and 17, brought no real progress: not only because they got caught up in details (military service for theologians, church construction, school reform, method of taxation etc.) and Cardinal Wyszyński—who was in Rome at the time for a synod of bishops—carefully made sure that the curia "remained firm"; also because in the meantime Poland's Soviet neighbor had become alarmed by signs of Warsaw independence (a Communist at a beatification!) and reacted with traditional suspicion.

Curial diplomacy waited patiently. But it was also—as always— prepared to seize the moment if further waiting could impair the situation: no sooner had the Bundestag in Bonn ratified the border treaty with Poland on June 3, 1972, and the German Cardinal Julius Döpfner encouraged the curia in a speech on June 13, than the Vatican acted: Bishop Dabrowski, secretary of the Polish episcopate, who on June 5 had brought the message to Rome from the Warsaw government that the formation of the new dioceses in Koszalin and Szczecin was "not yet of pressing importance," appeared on June 20 at the Polish embassy to Rome and announced the Vatican's decision that had been demanded and awaited for 27 years.

The one-month waiting period, during which the Warsaw government could object to the reconstitution of dioceses—a right it had reserved since 1956 (see p. 297)—could hardly be observed formally. But was that so important now? Poland's ambassador in Rome did not think so; he was all the more surprised when he had to tell the Vatican that his government wanted to negotiate over the reconstitution of two Pomeranian bishoprics. Did it perhaps—there were signs of this—want to arrive simultaneously at a new ecclesiastical regulation of Poland's eastern borders, in order to pacify the Soviets?[30]

Paul VI ordered the diplomatic *coup de main*: on June 28, 1972, six Polish bishops in the Oder-Neisse region were named residentiary bishops, and the borders of the bishoprics between Poland and the German

Democratic Republic redrawn. The Polish government could do nothing other than put a good face on it, although it felt itself "run over."

Not until three months later, in October 1972, could the bishops of the new Pomeranian dioceses of Szczecin-Kamien and Koszalin-Kolobrzeg ceremoniously enter their cathedrals—honored as well by the local state authorities. But Warsaw's resentment against the Vatican was still felt. What was left to be negotiated? The major tangible problems had been resolved, all the bishoprics were occupied, even "over-occupied," with suffragan bishops; existing local wishes and points of controversy (church construction, school reform, etc.) were questions to be discussed between government and episcopate. Only questions of principle, the most delicate for the Communists, were still to be regulated with the Vatican: for instance, the legal status of the church. The Vatican—as always where Poland was concerned—was in no hurry, especially being aware that the Yugoslavian model of an agreement in principle (see p. 324) could not be repeated in Poland, because here an almost homogeneous Catholic society identifies itself with the nation, and the episcopate feels itself to be the guardian of this image. . . .

After a year of waiting, Archbishop Casaroli and Polish Foreign Minister Stefan Olszowski, met in early July 1973 at the preparatory discussions for the European Security Conference in Helsinki. The Vatican used this forum, where its appearance was viewed with surprise by many, much like the West; Soviet interest in securing the status quo in Europe through a détente offered the opportunity to insert elements of religious freedom (see p. 359). The negotiations simultaneously offered the Vatican an opportunity to cultivate semi-official contacts with prominent eastern politicians. In Helsinki, Casaroli agreed with Olszowski on a new beginning for discussions.

Hands folded, head bowed, visibly impressed by an experience that he had perhaps dreamed of in his youth as an altar boy, but never as a Communist, Minister Olszowski stood before the Pope on November 12, 1973. Colonel Jozefa Siemaszkiewicz of the Warsaw Interior Ministry, a woman conversant in church matters who accompanied the Minister as an expert advisor, remained outside when Paul VI withdrew to his private library with Olszowski, as is customary in such audiences. The atmosphere was so cordial, the matter under discussion—without a single critical word about the Polish episcopate—so concrete, that Olszowski shortly thereafter announced to the press that his visit with the Pope was of "historical significance" (*znaczenie historyczne*). They had—as he said— begun to work out a *modus vivendi*, would have to review a "broad range" of problems to be "solved in discussions with the Apostolic See *and* the church in Poland" and were "not far from the finale." The normalization of relations—"which we would like to institutionalize"—was "naturally the premise for a visit by the Holy Father to Warsaw." When? "I am not a prophet. . . ."[31]

However, Olszowski in his prognosis had somewhat overstepped his bounds. When at his invitation Casaroli flew to Warsaw three months later, on February 4, 1974—for the first time as an official guest of a Communist government—he already knew that tangible results were still not to be expected. Olszowski's Roman press conference had evoked Soviet "frowns" and enraged dogmatic anti-clerics within the Polish party leadership. Several days before Casaroli's trip, a Polish ambassador in a western capitol replied with a simple "no" to the question of whether Warsaw now had a clear church-political conception.

At the same time, Cardinal Wyszyński, with time-tested dual strategy, saw to it that a proper atmosphere was prepared for Casaroli's visit to Warsaw. Although the Pope had previously informed him of what he had also told Olszowski (that "we will make no decision without the agreement of the episcopate"), Wyszyński thought it better to take precautions: "Favorable political situations could arise, but that does not mean that our uneasiness will vanish . . . , for the church takes no holidays," the Cardinal preached. Before a closed meeting of priests in December 1973, he recalled:

> "In 1949 we took the initiative for talks with the state authorities which found expression in the agreement concluded later. If it bore no fruit, that is not the fault of the church. It remains a historical fact that the Polish episcopate took the first steps toward a meeting and at that time was understood by no one; even in certain circles in Catholic countries there was criticism. Today this route is considered positive and useful for the state. . . . It is evident that the episcopate's position from the beginning has been exactly the one assumed by the government at the end of 1973. . . ."

Did Wyszyński thereby want to explain to the Vatican that even now— as in 1950—he would have preferred to manage the agreement alone, without the Vatican? It sounded that way; but the Cardinal did not want to put on the brakes either. So he did what seemed to exclude the possibility of participation offered him by the Pope: he left for Gniezno shortly before Casaroli arrived in Warsaw.—

An honor guard had been drawn up; with some effort, a military band blared the papal hymn into the grey-cloaked Warsaw winter's day. Communist officers saluted, and Paul VI's "Foreign Minister" crossed himself, while two uniformed military chaplains carried his wreath with the pale yellow ribbon to the tomb of the unknown soldier. But neither guest nor host seemed particularly inspired by the scene's conciliatory symbolism. Both had to reckon with a "big brother": with a Cardinal in

Gniezno and with a Party chief in the Kremlin. "The superficial as well as the deeper causes" of the existing difficulties had to be explored, Casaroli said in his first after-dinner speech; they had to be overcome "or at least be prevented from becoming permanent, becoming more acute, or leading to incurable conflicts." This sketched the limited goal of the Vatican's Polish policy. But Casaroli also attempted to make clear to his hosts that the "main theme" of the papal appeals for peace and security (which always met with Communist applause) "is always the real and complete normalization of relations between church and state."

But it was this very theme that Olszowski, at least outwardly, now tried to efface: in a tone quite different from that of his visit to Rome, he spoke in his dinner speeches almost exclusively of European peace, of coexistence between the states. Only in three sparse sentences did he mention the positive contribution made by the "whole church" to the well-being of the country—and mentioned as an example, of all things, the "Pax" organization most suspect to episcopate and Vatican, which for 25 years had enjoyed special Soviet favor. Not a word about the object of the discussions, no optimistic announcements, no more allusions to the third partner in the discussions, the episcopate. The "institutionalization" of relations shrank in the communiqué to "permanent working contacts."

Casaroli understood. In his toast in Jablonna castle, where he gave the customary dinner for his hosts, Casaroli stated: "I believe, Mr. Minister, that I represent a common position, and do not doubt that I echo the thought of the *Polish episcopate* when I say that certainly *no haste* will govern our common labors, but also *no delay* that would be detrimental to the desired understandings. . . ." For the Cardinal Primate, who had expressly refused to sit down at a table with his nation's ministers and had only sent the secretary of the episcopate, all this was reason enough for a rapid return to Warsaw; Wyszyński now took over direction of the second part of Casaroli's visit to Warsaw. The Roman guest now moved from the government guest house to the archepiscopal palace—accompanied to the door by the government's director of protocol. On the evening of February 7, Wyszyński and the papal emissary together celebrated mass in the overflowing Warsaw cathedral. In his own style, Wyszyński commented on the event from the pulpit:

"The present situation is far more difficult than it has ever been. . . .It demands a knowledge of the opposing positions . . . and a comparison (*porownanie*) of the two differing viewpoints: the one represented by the Polish nation, of which the overwhelming majority is faithful, led by bishops and priests through the centuries, and the other of a new Weltanschauung which wants to educate without the gospel, without the help of the church. Does this comparison yield a solid result? It appears that this will take a long time. Just as the church has up to now served the nation, even influencing political life—

although that is not its main duty, but rather an incidental effect—. . . so must we clearly express our point of view, and that the Polish bishops are doing. The Holy Father desires the same thing, in that he has sent his representatives to present the position of the church in our fatherland in discussions with the state representatives so that it is properly understood. Perhaps certain agreements are advancing. . . . But a true normalization must follow from a recognition of the independent, essential mission of spreading the gospel. That is the constant effort of the Holy See. . . . How many discussions have I held with the Holy Father, how many with the state and party authorities (these are not all known, but they are historical facts)—I always found understanding from the Pope. And from this understanding for the solution of difficult matters also arises the high mission of our dear and beloved guest Archbishop Casaroli. We must value his efforts, which are full of patience and skill, and keep in mind that he has come here at the will of the Holy Father. We must therefore trust and pray. . . ."[32]

Wyszyński made clear his reservations and skepticism, diplomatically packaged, but without assuming an obstructive position. In this his behavior differed markedly from that of the Hungarian Primate Mindszenty, whose removal from office by the Pope had been announced in Rome two days earlier (see p. 320). News of this came as a surprise to Casaroli. He feared—as actually happened in the world press—that an immediate connection would be drawn to his mission in Warsaw. For that reason, he carefully avoided answering Wyszyński's subtle warnings, but rather contented himself in his address from the altar of the Warsaw cathedral with pastoral, quite unpolitical remarks; he did not even mention the purpose of his visit, namely talks with the government. Only *one* word contained a sting: the Pope needed not only good will and prayer, "but above all attention and *obedience*." The Polish translation could spare the faithful the second harsh word (*ubbidienza*), for the Primate understood Italian. . . .[33]

But the Warsaw government could not deny its own character so easily either. When five months later, Vice Foreign Minister Jozef Czyrek was negotiating with Casaroli in Rome concerning the "permanent working contracts," he initially agreed to a joint communiqué which spoke of "progress in mutual relations," of "information" that Czyrek had relayed to the Vatican, about problems of normalization, but also about the "will to continue the discussions with the Polish episcopate." This communiqué was already published on the evening of July 6, 1974, when the Polish embassy in Rome—because of a telegram from Warsaw—had to ask the Vatican to withdraw the text and replace it with a laconic 20-line note.[34] Why?

Because Warsaw had to take care not to arouse the impression (so difficult for the Soviets to understand) that it was arranging "domestic affairs" in consultation with a foreign country (i.e., the Vatican). All the more so since it had leaked out that Cardinal Wyszyński had induced the

Vatican to suggest the secretary of the Polish episcopate, Bishop Dabrowski, as papal representative for the planned "working contacts." They finally did agree to supply Luigi Poggi, the new papal "traveling nuncio," with a permanent visa for Poland, while Poland would station a specially authorized diplomat, Minister Kazimierz Szablewski, in its Roman embassy. But the announcement was postponed. At the end of September 1974, Warsaw made a unilateral announcement of Szablewski's appointment—shortly before a trip to the USA by Party Leader Gierek, who averred in an interview with *Time*: "The Catholic church is an essential and positive force in Poland."

It took a second visit by Minister Czyrek to the Vatican (November 5 and 6, 1974) to formalize the "permanent working contacts" with the appointment of the directors of the two delegations and finally get them into gear at the beginning of 1975. Cardinal Wyszyński, who was visiting in Rome, was informed by the Pope himself, although not completely reassured. . . . It was still not certain whether the "trilateral discussions" would function. "We are now waiting for the episcopate. . . . There is no reason for nervousness and harsh words," Party Leader Gierek told Polish journalists on November 20, 1974. However, only a little earlier, on October 1, Cardinal Wyszyński had declared in a secret message to the 4th Synod of Bishops in Rome: "It is impossible to convince those in power that the struggle against religion is not a direct, but rather an indirect, deduction from Marxist doctrine." As a means for providing security for the church in Poland, the Cardinal mentioned first the discontinuation of "unfounded theological opinions" and the "conservation of traditional forms of worship." In Poland too it was a case of "saving what one could," he said, but admitted at the same time: "All this allows us to preach the gospel to a greater extent than before the war." But for the Vatican's eastern policy, Wyszyński counseled that it should introduce "elements of unambiguous Christian courage of confession" into its diplomacy: "Diplomacy must not obstruct the work of spreading the gospel [evangelization]."[35]

In the following years, the Cardinal's critical, reserved attitude toward Vatican diplomacy yielded to a more positive judgment; thus at the beginning of July 1977, for the first time, the Polish Conference of Bishops could officially declare that the annual week-long visit to Warsaw of the papal "special nuncio" Poggi "advanced the regulation of open questions between church and state," whereby Poggi "worked strictly with the episcopate." A contributing factor in this was the fact that the Vatican supported Wyszyński's attitude, which, as firm as it was prudent, proved itself once again in the summer of 1976, when dramatic workers' riots put pressure on the government and introduced a new period of domestic political and economic instability. Without identifying himself with dissident groups or calling for direct opposition and resistance, the Cardinal defended human rights; at the same time, he offered moral support in avoiding—as he called it—"little revolutions," "out of consideration for reasons of state" (that is to say: in order to prevent the danger of Soviet intervention), of course under the condition that the state would reward the patriotic engagement of the church.

The high point of this strategy of cooperation was the first personal meeting between Cardinal Wyszyński and Party Leader Gierek on October 29, 1977, at which—according to the mutual communiqué—"opinions were exchanged about the most important affairs of nation [!] and church, which have great significance for the unity of Poles in their strivings for the prosperity of the People's Republic." Paul VI took up this quote in an address when he received Gierek in a private audience in the Vatican on December 1, 1977: "Today too, the church is prepared to make a positive contribution in Polish society. . . . It does not demand any privileges for itself, but only the right to be itself and the opportunity to fulfil its mission without obstruction. . . ." Gierek had assured the Pope that "patriotic unity beyond any doctrinal differences" was not only a "historical imperative" for the Warsaw leadership, but even (astonishing from Communist lips) "the highest good":

"In following this line we consolidate, in the spirit of the traditional Polish *tolerance*, a state with such characteristics that no situation of conflict between state and church will return. . . . The thing that unites us all—as we have emphasized together with the Primate of Poland, Cardinal Wyszyński—is concern for the welfare of our fatherland. . . ."

This concern had even induced the Cardinal, for the first time in thirty years, to participate in a state reception given by his country on November 29, and to be seen publicly with the Party Leader: in the Grand Hotel in Rome, the two, Wyszyński and Gierek, were to be seen sitting at the *same* table, together with the Italian Christian Democrats Moro and Andreotti, the Communist Berlinguer, and—Archbishop Casaroli. . . . When I asked him about the motive for his participation, Wyszyński told me, "The situation is very serious." Scarcely recovered from a severe illness, he had hastened to Rome in order to harmonize in advance every detail of the meeting of Gierek and the Pope, and every detail of Paul VI's speech.

But were concrete results to be expected from this event? The church in Poland was standing on its own strength and not thanks to "this or that political agreement," Wyszyński had declared to emigré Polish priests in Rome on November 10. When the Vatican installed bishops in other countries (like the CSSR) who could not really govern their dioceses themselves, because the state ruled the church, he said, then a kind of

"Caesaro-papism" resulted. Therefore "we do not want to secure the church in Poland on the strength of political agreements. These have their *significance, but as tiles on the roof* of a building that grows from its own foundations, and it is growing in Poland on the strength of the living faith of the nation. . . ."

The Vatican had also increasingly accepted this "roofing tile" thesis—of course only in the case of Poland; partly because it became obvious, after Gierek's visit to Rome, how circumscribed the Warsaw government's freedom of movement still was. For example, the central question of whether the Catholic church in Poland was to regain the status of public law could not even be discussed seriously; even the permanent establishment of a Vatican representation in Warsaw (in the old, undestroyed nunciature building) was repeatedly delayed. "For now, the formula of working contacts—with the presence of commissions in Rome and Warsaw—is sufficient," said Minister Kakol (interview for *Il Giornale*, June 6, 1978.) In 1978 it appeared that the atmosphere had become further relaxed, and that many concrete problems (for instance, church construction) could be resolved. But Gierek could less than ever afford any sweeping agreements—be it with the Vatican or the episcopate—for Moscow had not without suspicion observed his "flirtation" with the church in 1977.

In this delicate situation, something happened that no one would ever have expected: a Pole became Pope. On October 16, 1978, the cardinals of the Roman Catholic church, unable to agree on any of the "Italian" candidates, elected the Archbishop of Krakow, Karol Wojtyla, as successor of Pope Paul VI and Pope John Paul I, who had quickly followed him in death. For the first time in centuries, a non-Italian was master of the Vatican, not a bishop from the "West," but from that historical "East" so often discussed in this book—indeed, from its most sensitive field of tension in church policy. The 58-year-old Karol Wojtyla, up to then, had not been an actor in this history, neither as priest nor as diplomat. Was it this that predestined him for the highest office of his church? The questions nevertheless raised by his election even in the early hours produced abundant speculation, especially about eastern policy: a Pope for new "crusades" or new "compromises"? The continuity of Vatican policies, as presented in this book, has never been reducible to such simple formulas. And this was also true for Pope John Paul II.

This clever, cautious, rather conservative theologian, who was at the same time an open, popular minister, had always stood in the shadow of Wyszyński, the politically and nationalistically *engagé* Primate, even when Wojtyla—after long discussions in Krakow with papal "Foreign Minister" Casaroli—had received the Cardinal's mitre, the second in Poland.

Absolute solidarity with the Primate was for him, as for all bishops of the nation, unquestioning, even if he himself preferred a more "apolitical" style and neither quarreled very much with the ruling Communists nor was fond of transactions with them. "The legal status of the church must be clearly and exactly defined," he had demanded, nevertheless, on May 25, 1978, for the pending negotiations; however, he always also emphasized the principle of Vatican Council II, that the church cannot identify itself "with any political system or with any political community" (nor with a nation); on the contrary, that it always and everywhere had to represent the "transcendental character" of the individual. Even in his inaugural sermon as Pope John Paul II, Wojtyla stressed this in his own arresting style: "Throw open the doors for Christ! Open the borders of the states, economic and political systems, to his redeeming power. Do not be afraid!" The political undertone of such statements could not be missed, especially because, for the first time in history, they were beamed out directly by the Polish state television network far beyond the borders of Poland, as far as White Russia and Lithuania; indeed, the Pope added greetings in Polish, Russian and Lithuanian.

Thus had "the Socialism of a People's Republic, as its only world-wide sensation in thirty years, produced—a Pope," as Moscow's ambassador to Rome, Rishov, joked bitterly. Still, he, as well as other ambassadors from the Eastern bloc, was sent by his government to participate in the inaugural mass of the Polish Pope. Poland's chief of State, Professor Henryk Jablonski, even sat in the front row of guests of honor, and, with Foreign Minister Cyrek and Director of the Church Office Kakol, was received in a special audience. Friendly and relaxed, the Polish Pope spoke with his Communist compatriots about "the tradition of tolerance in our country which never in its history has burned heretics at the stake." Couldn't that be "exemplary" for the present?, Wojtyla remarked, without touching on the sensitive question of the trip to Poland that he would undertake in 1979.

Thus, in the early hours, the view from the central seat of power of the universal church expanded beyond "provincial" horizons. Wojtyla knew very well the danger that his election as Pope presented to Poland's Communists (and not only to them), he knew how their national pride was mixed with fear of their "big brother" in the east, and also with their worries about Polish Catholicism, now strengthened from outside. In Party Chief Gierek's congratulatory telegram (October 17), these mixed feelings were expressed in awkward formulations:

". . . For the first time in history, the papal throne is occupied by a son of the Polish people, which with the unity and cooperation of all citizens is building the greatness and prosperity of its socialist fatherland. . . ."

Wojtyla, in his thank-you telegram to the "esteemed Mr. Gierek," corrected this diplomatically, but clearly, demonstrating readiness for dialogue as well as referring to spiritual priorities:

"In the spirit of the *dialogue* begun by the great predecessors whose names I bear, may I, with God's help, act for the welfare of my beloved nation, whose history, for a thousand years, has been united with the mission and the services of the Catholic church."

It became evident, even in the first months of the new pontificate, that the prevailing always-complicated "triangle" of episcopate-government-Vatican would change in the case of Poland. This "Polish" Pope could not be played against the episcopate, even less so than any earlier Pope; but neither could the Cardinal Primate any longer doubt the Vatican's understanding of Polish church problems, and determine the line of church policy by himself. In the previous years, the Vatican had to a large extent lost its influence on the selection of new Polish bishops; the Primate ruled the church's "personal policy." Almost every new appointment to a bishopric was preceded not only by a tug-of-war between Primate and government, but also by many difficult discussions with Rome. Agreement on a new archbishop in Poznan (Jerzy Stroba in September 1978) had taken over a year—not least because in the background the question of a successor to Cardinal Wyszyński, 77 years old and suffering from gall bladder problems, had already arisen. The Warsaw Communists had considered Krakow Cardinal Wojtyla "politically unpredictable" as presumed future Primate, because in the last analysis they found Wyszyński's open, but diplomatically dosed, opposition more convenient than Wojtyla's apolitical, pastoral zeal. But now that Wojtyla had become Pope and the universal dimension of his pastoral personality became more evident, something surprising occurred: In the record time of three days, the Warsaw government agreed to the new Pope's suggestion to appoint his closest friend, theology professor Franciszek Macharski, as new archbishop of Krakow (and not, for example, one of the four auxiliary bishops of this diocese). Pope John Paul II seemed to want to address just as ingenuously the delicate question of diplomatic relations when in his first New Year's address to the diplomatic corps (January 12, 1979) he expressed a desire to see more diplomatic representatives at the Holy See—"above all from nations that may be regarded as Catholic." This was also meant as a preparation for the Pope's visit in Poland (see chapter XI).

To leave Poland for any length of time without "roofing tiles" was now less desirable than ever before. For now more than ever—in the era of a Polish Pope—the Soviet concept of "Catholic" fixated on "Polish" (a permanent tendency since the czarist era, as has been repeatedly shown in this book). For that reason, although Vatican eastern policy had the least reason for pastoral concern in Poland, it was here as nowhere else that it could prove its credibility for a *modus vivendi* in the eyes of Moscow.

Late Start to East Berlin

Was this not also the case for a neighbor of Poland, in which the Catholic church—by no means strong, living rather in diaspora—has endured under the dominion of German Communists, who for thirty years have proven to be model pupils of the Soviet Union? The 1.3 million Catholics of the GDR (German Democratic Republic) and their bishops (9 in 1978) were spared major quarrels with the regime. To investigate the deeper reasons for this would go beyond the purpose of this book; they are connected with the overall problem of the gradual division of Germany. Not until this was formalized by domestic German arrangements, and even the fictitious unity of a German conference of bishops could no longer be maintained, did the necessity arise for the Vatican to address the government in East Berlin as a direct partner. Until then, the improvised agreements reached by Bishop Wienken after 1945 (see pp. 261–2) had proven durable. The GDR regime accepted the appointment of bishops without question, even when they were received in the wording of that Reich concordat of 1933, which the GDR did not consider binding upon itself (giving polite and formal notification of this each time). The atmosphere—even during periods of tension—was tempered by the correct coolness of a basically "non-political," only pastorally-oriented cleric.

Cardinal Alfred Bengsch, who at age 40 had been appointed Bishop of Berlin by Pope John a few days after the building of the wall in 1961, did not let himself be pressured into either "progressive" confessions (which some Catholics in East Berlin urged), or collision with the state (which many West Berlin Catholics could have wished from him). Since for him— as he says—"prestige is not a clerical category," his usually frictionless distance from the Communists was easier for him than other church leaders in Eastern Europe (*see also his statement to the Council in Appendix 5*). He protested only on very rare, precisely gauged moments and only for religious concerns: against abortion, against the "consecration of youth" (*Jugendweihe*, a socialist substitute for confirmation and a relic of the petit bourgeois free-thinker movement in German Communism), and on November 17, 1974, against the state's claim to an atheistic monopoly of education. He always had the Vatican's full support for his actions. As a rather conservative theologian, he also thought little of the "local church cult": there is a lot of talk about Roman centralism, "but the danger exists that a new national centralism will arise," he told the Synod of Bishops in Rome in 1969.

The fact that Bengsch was nevertheless rather unpleasantly surprised by a meeting in Rome between papal "foreign minister" Casaroli and East German Communist Politburo member Werner Lamberz (on January 24, 1973) was not least because this Roman event was given excessive interpretation in West German Catholicism. (Lamberz, the most open-minded member of the GDR leadership, died in a plane crash in 1978.) However, more frequent trips to Rome and discussions with the Pope and his diplomats made it possible for Bengsch to assume a more sympathetic position. The conclusion that the Vatican drew on July 23, 1973 from the Basic Treaty between Bonn and East Berlin (May 1973) was discussed in advance, in detail, with Bengsch; the appointment of apostolic administrators *"permanenter constituti"* (canon 315 of the church law codex) in Erfurt, Magdeburg and Schwerin released these pastoral districts from their former West German dioceses and thus not only complied partly with the desires of the GDR government, but also with the pragmatic pastoral needs of the church. Not least, they favored Bengsch's inclination to protect "his" church from "Western theological vogues," to rule his clergy with an even firmer hand, and to decide what would benefit the GDR Catholics. . . . Of course, a papal pronuncio, whose dispatch the GDR government was temporarily pursuing with great zeal in informal contacts in Belgrade, Helsinki and Geneva, could become a hindrance to him. The Vatican was of course interested in activating its eastern policy in regard to the GDR too, in order to guarantee the relatively favorable status quo for Catholics there. But the curia was in no more of a hurry than in the case of Poland—at least much less so than its West German critics accused it constantly between 1973 and 1978.

Even a trip to East Germany that Mons. Casaroli undertook from June 9 to 15, 1975, at the invitation of GDR Foreign Minister Oskar Fischer, had no accelerating effect. In contrast to the Warsaw Primate, Cardinal Bengsch of East Berlin preferred to have as little part as possible in Casaroli's contacts with the government, and to leave "the political things" completely to the Vatican diplomats. Conversely, Casaroli was induced by insensitive West German church circles to demonstrate as extensive a participation as possible on Bengsch's part. Thus Bengsch not only had to make his lodgings available for a dinner to which Casaroli invited his host Fischer, but also, for the first time, had to dine with a Communist Minister. . . . (See Casaroli's after-dinner speech in Appendix 7.) Casaroli did not fail to present his hosts with a long list of the church's wishes, and to give them to understand that the extensive autonomy allowed in practice to the churches in the GDR was also in need of a contractual security, as is provided for in the new 1968 constitution of the GDR (Art. 39). However, Casaroli did not attain any concrete results. The "measured confidence" (*misurata fiducia*) that he attested to after his return to Rome, however, was based on the formal assurance given him by Prime Minister Horst Sindermann in a "friendly discussion": ". . . that the government of the GDR, as before, will continue its proven and constructive policy in ecclesiastical questions on the basis of the constitution and the legal stipulations of the GDR." (ADN report of June 10, 1975). Casaroli realized how little haste was necessary when—accompanied by Cardinal Bengsch—he visited Catholic congregations in East Berlin, Dresden and Erfurt, which demonstrated a vital church life and their loyalty to the Pope in Rome.

For its part, the Vatican only very gradually created preconditions for a future church treaty with the GDR—always intent on carefully overcoming West German sensitivities as well as legal impediments (which could arise from the Reich concordat of 1933). That there were indeed pastoral necessities for this was verified by the former Bishop of Magdeburg (GDR) Friedrich Rintelen (who today lives in West Germany); he pointed out that the independence of the GDR church administration, to which the Vatican aspired through the formation of new dioceses, conformed to the decisions of Vatican Council II concerning pastoral duties of the bishops (decree "Christus Dominus" nos. 22, 23), which provided for the adjustment of diocesan borders to state borders. "If in this matter the wishes of the church and the wishes of the GDR government should coincide, is that grounds for commotion?" asked the bishop (*Deutsche Tagespost*, December 6, 1977).

Not until September 25, 1976, did the Vatican Congregation of Bishops approve the formation of an autonomous "Berlin Conference of Bishops" for the bishops in the GDR, who up to then—even if only informally—had still been connected with the West German Conference of Bishops as a Conference of Ordinaries, "without being able to directly present their experiences, opinions and suggestions," as a Vatican press release stated (*Osservatore Romano*, October 27, 1976). For the first time, the Vatican extensively justified one of its moves in the east in order to anticipate publicly its critics: the activities of the West German Conference of Bishops had "referred to pastoral circumstances which are considerably different from those prevailing in the GDR"; hence the "pastoral necessity and usefulness" of autonomous GDR bishops, without the Holy See "interfering in the unresolved questions between the two German states, such as the national question." While transforming the GDR apostolic administrative units into new bishoprics, the Vatican continued to take its time. In 1973 already, at a meeting with GDR Foreign Minister Winzer during the Helsinki Conference, Casaroli had left no doubt that the Holy See was concerned with the substance and not so much with the protocolary form of a normalization. And this remained the Vatican's line when Winzer's successor, Oskar Fischer, was received by the new "Polish" Pope, John Paul II, as the first minister from the eastern bloc, on October 28, 1978. The new pontiff was pleased that he had not been pressed with requests from his visitor and also he had no great grievances to discuss on this occasion. New contacts would have to wait as well as decisions already prepared (a Polish Pope had to be particularly careful in dealing with German affairs . . .). The East Berlin government, however, was clever enough to nominate in October 1979 a new State Secretary for Church Affairs: Klaus Gysi (b. 1912, graduated in Paris and Cambridge), former ambassador of the GDR in Rome, where he had cultivated friendly contacts with Casaroli—now the new Cardinal Secretary of State for John Paul II.

Cardinal Bengsch, however, had undertaken two trips to the Soviet Union in June 1974, at the invitation of the Moscow Patriarch, and in August 1975 as guest of the bishops in Lithuania. That was quite in line with papal efforts to open doors not only by means of diplomacy, but also through religious meetings. This is important to recognize, since the master key for unlocking all opportunities, be they for the Vatican's or anyone else's eastern policy, was to be found in Moscow, and it was not only political.

Soviet Visits to the Vatican and Papal Travelers to Moscow

As the auto with the red hammer-and-sickle pennant drove up in the Damascus Court of the Vatican, the Swiss guards presented their halberds. It was 1:30 p.m. on January 30, 1967. The man with the order of a Hero of the Soviet Union pinned to his black suit who met the Pope a few minutes later was a head of state, yet he was received with a simplified, unpretentious protocol, because for fifty years there had been no diplomatic or official relations between his country and the Holy See. It was the "planned meeting between the Holy Father Paul VI and His Excellency Mr. Nikolai Podgorny, the chairman of the Presidium of the Supreme Soviet of the USSR." Thus read the first page of the *Osservatore Romano* under the trivial headline, "Our Information."

Among the peculiarities of this audience was the fact that the Pope spoke with the Soviet President at a desk, not from the chair of state; that the chain smoker Podgorny was offered cigarettes (the curial courtiers whispered to each other, shocked!); that—to bridge the mutual embarrassment—the two paid each other banal compliments. For instance, as the Pope offered his visitor a coin commemorating the 75th anniversary of the encyclical *Rerum Novàrum:* "We had them minted as a remembrance of a document that was dedicated to the lot of the workers. We love the workers!" said the Pope. —"Who doesn't love them?! After all, we are all workers!" replied the Soviet President. . . .

But the Czech Father Stefan Olsr of the papal "Russicum," as interpreter, also was able to translate some concrete things. "In the course of the meeting, in which questions concerning the preservation of peace and the development of better relations between peoples were discussed in detail, the Holy Father also called President Podgorny's attention to the problems of religious life and the presence of the Catholic church in Soviet territory," so the communiqué paraphrased the delicate theme, which Podgorny, however, politely evaded.

Was this meeting, which many contemporaries regarded as a revolutionary event—in the good or bad sense—a political breakthrough, a farce—or neither? Were "the heads of the Soviet revisionist group showing an increased interest in pilgrimages to the Vatican" because they wanted "to open the door to capitalism and its capital"? This was the comment of the Chinese agency "Hsinhua" the day after Podgorny's papal audience. The Soviet agency "Novosti," on the other hand, (on January 17, 1967) recalled past events: the Pizzardo-Chicherin discussion in Rapallo, Pacelli's contacts in Berlin.

There was now some progress following the cold war, "not because the papal guards have halberds," the Moscow agency wrote, "but rather [because] it seems that the moral prestige of the Vatican in many countries, especially those in which Catholics form the majority of the population, and certain changes in the Vatican, were taken into account."

As certain as it was that the Pope was trying to use the relaxation of East-West tension for his church, it was just as sure that the Soviets had included his world-wide respect, his appeals for a peaceful settlement of differences, in their political calculations—without either side indulging in "ideological" illusions. As coolly and pragmatically as the Soviet leadership under Leonid Brezhnev proceeded, concerned solely with the security of its empire, it did not consent to any semi-private contacts and agreements, such as those improvised by Khrushchev in John XXIII's time (see p. 300). Nor were they greatly interested in the artificial distinction between the head of the Vatican state and the head of the church. When Foreign Minister Andrei Gromyko came to Rome in spring 1966, the public puzzled for a long time about whether and how he would pay his respects to the Pope. And yet the audience of April 27, 1966, had been prepared quite formally after the minister had already been introduced to the Pope on October 4, 1965, in New York; there he had publicly applauded Paul VI's plea for peace before the United Nations. Gromyko did not hesitate to refer to the Pope as "head of the Catholic church" (and not as sovereign of the Vatican state), but he refused to give any information about the results of the discussions. Otherwise he would have had to reveal what the editor-in-chief of the *Osservatore Romano* only hinted at very indirectly in his low-key commentary on Gromyko's papal audience:

"It is precisely the sorrow and—one could say—the insolubility of certain situations and ideologies that bring about a patient, almost heroic search for other, new, solutions, even if on an unending treadmill."

For with the friendliest countenance, Gromyko had declared himself "not competent" in response to the Pope's question during their 45-minute discussion concerning an easing of the situation for the Catholics in the Soviet Union. Many observers later believed that it had perhaps displeased the Soviet Minister that Paul VI, on the very day before Gromyko's visit, had declared: "The church is not antagonistic toward the *Chinese* revolution; it is prepared to understand the achievements of the present historical phase. . . ." Others even fancied that the Pope had thereby tried to play the hostile Communist powers off against each other. However, his concern at this moment had been to underline his "impartial" position. He was not yet aware that Mao Tse-tung's "cultural revolution" was in the process of completely eliminating the Catholic church organization in China, even the one which had tried to save itself as "national church" (a situation that only seemed to alter in 1978, with the changes after Mao's death).[36] Gromyko, on the other hand, knew very well that the Vatican could expect even less from Peking than from Moscow. His visit to the Pope had no other immediate purpose than to contribute to the political "neutralization" of the Roman curia, which concerned the Soviets greatly in view of Poland—which was especially restive in 1966.

More than four years later, on November 14, 1970, Gromyko again entered the papal chambers, this time for an hour-and-a-half discussion. The *Osservatore Romano* also had to defend this second meeting against misinterpretation: "To assume that a meeting with a Soviet Minister means coming to terms with atheistic materialism, would be to insinuate a moral and spiritual inconstancy that would be against the nature of the Holy See." —Nevertheless, this time Gromyko had not declared himself incompetent, but rather (like Podgorny in 1967) listened in silence.

On February 21, 1974, after another three and a half years, Gromyko paid a third call on the Pope, who welcomed him almost as an old acquaintance. Again Paul VI, after a global political "*tour d'horizon*," began to approach that theme to which the Soviet Minister had always been deaf: the situation of the Catholics in the Soviet Union. Now Gromyko finally at least promised to transmit the requests and suggestions in a favorable light to the competent authorities in Moscow. And the same thing happened on June 28, 1975, during Gromyko's fourth visit. It was a tiny, non-binding step, almost nothing compared to those high expectations which opponents of the Vatican's eastern policy especially liked to use as a standard. . . .

But the Pope and his diplomats had not held such expectations for a moment, even though "hope"—taken as a Christian virtue—was a part of its diplomatic armor. Real progress could also not be measured by spectacular events like visits from Gromyko, but rather by those slow changes, achieved laboriously and usually in silence. The inverse relationship between publicity and the rapidity of change was especially true of the Soviet Union. After all, *six* new bishops had been installed for the seven dioceses in the Baltic countries, in which the church hierarchy had been nearly extinct—installed not in secret, but with the tacit consent or express approval of Moscow, with whose embassy to Rome permanent contacts had existed since Gromyko's first visit.

The Vatican had refused to install as bishops those three Baltic vicars (Krivaitis, Butkus and Baksys) who were allowed to go to Rome for the first time to attend the second session of Vatican Council II; but at the end of the third Council session, when it had been possible to make some personal acquaintance, the Latvian Vaivods was consecrated bishop (for Riga) in Rome on November 18, 1964, and at the end of the fourth session, on December 5, 1965, the Lithuanian Matulaitis-Labukas (for Kaunas), who could then—with Roman and Soviet permission—consecrate as bishops in Lithuania the priest Pletkus (for Telsiai) on February 25, 1968 (he died in 1975), and the priests Povilonis and Kriksciunas (for Vilkaviskis and Panevezys) on December 21, 1969. The appointment of the 38-year-old Kriksciunas was all the more astonishing because he had finished his studies in Rome and only returned to Lithuania in 1963. Povilonis received permission even though he had been sentenced to prison for several years in 1962 for "illegal church construction." In 1973 the Vatican was even able to designate the 64-year-old Povilonis as successor (*coaduitor cum iure successionis*) to Matulaitis-Labukas, who died in 1979. (Povilonis and Kriksciunas were among the first bishops received by Pope John Paul II after his election, on October 24, 1978, in Rome.) On November 10, 1972, the 77-year-old Latvian Bishop Vaivods (Riga) also received a suffragan bishop with the right of succession: the 64-year-old rector of the Riga seminary, Zondaks. Papal "Foreign Minister" Casaroli personally celebrated this consecration in the grotto of St. Peter's in Rome, assisted by Bishops Vaivods and Matulaitis-Labukas, who went to Rome eleven times between 1964 and 1976, and thus could maintain direct contact with the western center of their church. To deprecate this by speaking of surveillance of these bishops by escorts or secretaries loyal to the regime is to underestimate the possibilities the Vatican possesses of testing reliability even where double loyalties are supposedly present (even loyalties that are mutually exclusive). The Pope is in the habit of speaking privately with his bishops. In 1976, for the first time with Soviet permission, several thousand missals, breviers and catechisms printed in the Vatican could be sent to Lithuania.

All this would have been unthinkable without the relaxation of east-west tensions and Paul VI's related Ostpolitik. But it was kept within narrow limits: three Baltic bishops continued to be restricted in their office and could only act as village pastors (Sladkevicius, Steponavicius, Dulbinskis). The number of priests in Lithuania (for 2.3 million Catholics) shrank from 1460 (in 1944) to 708 (in 1979), primarily through aging of the clergy and the state decree limiting admissions to Lithuania's sole seminary, in Kaunas: in 1950, it was fixed at 75 seminarians, reduced to 25 until 1966, and only in 1974 raised to 50, in 1978 to 72. Increasing unrest among the Catholic population, which sharpened dramatically in 1972 after the self-immolation of a young Catholic, was unleashed by anti-religious chicanery (primarily against preparatory courses for the first communion for children), but also by injured national sentiment, and finally expressed itself in a letter of protest to the Secretary General of the United Nations, signed by 17,000 Lithuanians. Even the party organ *Sovietskaya Litva* warned on August 1, 1972: "Irreparable damage can result from administrative measures which injure the feelings of the faithful. . . . It is not their fault that they have inherited the faith." A secret Catholic newspaper (*Kronaka* No. 4/72) let it be known that the Communists had succeeded in sowing suspicion between the faithful and some bishops, about whose loyalty supposedly "the Vatican had been deceived." In the mid-seventies, the Secret Police were increasingly successful in placing confidants among the staff of the "Kronaka" and in endangering the internal cohesion of the church in Lithuania through intrigues and false information. National and religious feelings fused into an explosive mixture, by which the Soviet power had already felt itself threatened in 1944/45 (see p. 247).

The situation in *Latvia* developed somewhat more quietly; here the number of priests had risen from 120 (1944) to 144 (1978), although the number of Catholics—through flight and deportation—had dropped from 476,000 to 252,000. The Bishop of Riga, who is granted a seminary with 20 students (1978) was able to send Latvian priests to the Catholic parishes in Leningrad, in Georgian Tiflis, in Reval (Tallinn) and Dorpat (the only Catholic parishes in Estonia), and in addition four priests in the Ukraine (where, for national reasons, the Soviets do not want any Polish clerics), and two in White Russia.[37] About eighty Polish priests were holding on in White Russia; however, if they belonged to the diocese of Pinsk, they had been without a bishop since 1945; if to Minsk or Mogilev, since the end of the twenties (see p. 46f.). Since here not even a minimum second generation of priests was assured, the Vatican attempted to improve the situation through a direct diplomatic move in Moscow:

The Holy See's formal participation in the Nuclear Non-Proliferation Treaty among the great powers (which took effect in early March 1970) offered the Pope an opportunity to send his "foreign minister" Agostino Casaroli to Moscow for the first time; he deposited the Vatican signature there—as the apostolic delegates were doing simultaneously in Washington and London—in order to document the Pope's desire for peace. Casaroli's appearance in Moscow embarrassed the Soviets; they knew only too well that he was not interested in atomic weapons. . . . One could hardly deny any wishes expressed in conversation by a papal delegate who sat down in the Kremlin with Soviet Vice Foreign Minister Semyon Kosirev, under a picture of Lenin, on February 25, 1971, in order to sign their participation in the treaty.

The western press later claimed that Casaroli had asked in vain for a conversation with Gromyko; but Casaroli had already spoken twice with the "not competent" Foreign Minister in Rome (1966 and 1970). Now he was interested in finally establishing contact with "those who were competent"—for the first time since d'Herbigny's trip to Moscow in 1926 (see p. 95f.). After a quiet mass in St. Ludwig's, where he meditated on all the destinies that had begun here, Casaroli drove to the "President of the Council for Religious Cults of the Council of Ministers of the USSR," Vladimir Kuroiedov (who had succeeded Karpov in 1966). Piotr V. Makarzev, too, who was responsible for the "non-Orthodox cults," also sat at the other side of the table when Casaroli and his companion Monsignore Achille Silvestrini carefully laid out their wishes and offers:

These were the installation of a bishop in the White Russian, formerly Polish, diocese of Pinsk (where about 250,000 Poles with Soviet citizenship are living) and a papal delegate—accredited to the Soviet government or to the Orthodox Patriarchate—with episcopal rank in Moscow; all open questions relating to the religious life of Catholics could be continuously discussed with him and misunderstandings cleared up. The Vatican, for its part, would be prepared later to adjust the borders of the dioceses of Vilna, Lvov and Pinsk to the Soviet-Polish border existing since 1945.

Casaroli's partners in the discussion replied coolly with the old argument that Pacelli had heard 35 years earlier from Chicherin: the Soviet state could only regulate things of this nature on its own sovereignty, "within the framework of the law," and without interference from outside. Casaroli mentioned that the Communist governments of Hungary and Poland had never disputed in principle the Vatican's right to concern itself with the regulation of the bishoprics. But that did not greatly impress Kuroiedov and Makarzev; their thought processes about "the church" resembled the traditional thinking of the czarist era. Catholics actually existed almost solely in the Baltic republics, which had bishops, and competent comrades as well, they said.[38] They were not greatly interested in the division of Catholic bishoprics. Only when they heard that there were episcopal administrators in Poland for parts of the dioceses of Pinsk (in Drohiczyn on the Bug), Vilna (in Bialystok) and Lvov (in Lubaczow) was their attention aroused, but they still did not want to go into the topic any more deeply. Again and again Casaroli heard how greatly the loyal attitude of the Orthodox church was valued, as well as the reconciliation between the Pope and the Moscow Patriarch. . . .

"After fifty years of monologue, we have progressed to dialogue," Casaroli said later on this day in the Hotel "Sovietskaya." However, the historical-psychological barriers were more evident to him than ever. Here one was not dealing with a Hussite inheritance as in Prague, nor with a "Josephite" one as in Budapest, nor the national Catholicism of Poland and the national Communism of Yugoslavia; real progress here presupposed not only a change of mentality in the post-Stalinist bureaucracy, but also a coming to terms with Russian Orthodoxy— without missionary expectations. Nor with any hope for a revival of the Catholic Ukrainians?

This last question remained unspoken in all the discussions. The trauma of 1945, when Soviet Communists had become agents of Orthodoxy and separated the Ukrainian Uniates from Rome, had not yet healed. It

vox potens Synodi olata in favorem et defensionem eorum, qui per-
sucutionem patiuntur, passi sunt ac pariter orationes pro luctan-
tibus inter vitam et mortem fusae, novam vim ad perseverandum usque
ad victoriam finalem infunderunt. Nam pereat mundus, sed fiat ius-
titia !

remained just as vivid for the Soviets, whom it reminded of the ever sensitive national problems in their heterogeneous Union of Republics.

Was the pectoral cross of the deceased Patriarch Alexji, which his successor Pimen sent to the Pope with Casaroli, meant to be a token of reconciliation in this matter too? In 1945, in the Ukraine, Alexji had declared the Union of Brest (1596) invalid; Pimen reconfirmed this act when he was elected Patriarch by the all-Russian synod in Zagorsk at the beginning of June 1971. That fact had escaped Cardinal Willebrands, who represented the Roman Curia at the festivities in Zagorsk as an observer, for linguistic reasons. He nevertheless demurred later, "We cannot share this thesis,"[39] even though he did not protest directly. Still, Cardinal Slipyj, the Archbishop of Lvov who was living in exile in the Vatican, raised bitter reproaches during the 1971 Synod of Bishops because of this incident.

In Slipyj's speech to the synod on October 23, 1971, the tragic fate of eastern European Catholicism, caught in the grip of national, religious and ideological conflicts, arose once again. Slipyj was angry at everyone—the Russians, the Poles, the Communists and the Vatican: "No one defends the Catholic Ukrainians. . . . Now, because of the diplomatic negotiations, they are put aside as embarrassing witnesses of past evils," he said, adding that the powerful voice of the synod would instill the persecuted with new strength to "hold out to the final victory." "For the world may perish, but there must be justice!" (see facsimile.)

This might be the impressive and painful obituary of a world that—as this book shows—had come to an end with the pious, adventurous illusions of Metropolitan Sheptyckyi; but it could not become the motto of a pastoral policy that could do justice to what it could save only if it gave up what it could not. Certainly, of the millions of Uniate Ukrainians who were forcibly separated from Rome at the end of World War II, many may have remained quietly loyal to the Roman church; to what extent an "underground church" exists is hard to ascertain. It was astonishing that the Soviets, in 1972, allowed a secretly consecrated Uniate bishop (of Luck) to journey to the West, via Yugoslavia, and give reports.[40] Among the 1.5 million Ukrainian exiles living in the USA, Canada and Western Europe the demand was repeatedly raised, for nationalistic as well as religious reasons, that the Pope create Cardinal-Archbishop Slipyj Patriarch of the Ukraine, and thereby give a sign to a "church condemned to death, which has been waiting for thirty years for a word of comfort from Your Holiness." Paul VI refused three times to do this, in letters to Slipyj in 1971 and 1975, and on December 14, 1976, in an audience for the Cardinal and six Ukrainian Archbishops:

"You know very well that circumstances independent of the Holy See prevent compliance with your repeated request; because the Holy See follows a very prudent line of action, and this is—as you well know—also in the best interest of the Ukrainian church itself."

Slipyj, far distant from his Metropolitan seat, raised to Patriarch of the Ukraine—this would indeed be taken as a provocation by the Moscow Orthodox Patriarchate as well as by the Soviet government, and would therefore only impair the situation of the Ukrainian Catholics. Wherever it was possible without risk, the Vatican by no means ignored the Uniates. Thus for example it had been possible to induce Bulgarian Party Leader Zhivkov to release a communiqué at his papal visit on June 27, 1975, in which he spoke of "problems of Catholics of both rites." (i.e., the Uniate too—which was of course not forbidden in Bulgaria). During the Belgrade follow-up conference to the Helsinki European Security Conference, Vatican Under Secretary Achille Silvestrini (Casaroli's representative) mentioned on October 7, 1977, "some serious open wounds that we would like to see healed. It is the case, for the Catholic church, of certain communities of the Eastern rite. . . ." (see complete text in Appendix 7).

But not even Pope John Paul II, to whom Cardinal Slipyj, on November 3, 1978, renewed his demand to be "recognized as Ukrainian Patriarch," indeed a revision of the dialogue, "based on false premises," with the Moscow Patriarch (cf. "Kultura," Paris, no. 12/78)—even this Pope "from the East" remained cautious. This became evident on November 23, 1978, when he received the bishops of the Ukrainian Uniates of the USA. Their spokesman, Archbishop Stephen Kocisko of Pittsburgh, declared: "Our hearts go to the land of our forefathers, where today [our brethren] are suffering . . . in Czechoslovakia and in the USSR. We ask Your Holiness's prayers *and intervention,* so that . . . full religious freedom might return to our dioceses of Presov and Uzhorod [Mukacevo]." Pope John Paul II, however, gave a politically reserved, laconic reply: "I *pray* also for your fellow citizens and for your brethren in the countries from which your ancestors came. For most of those countries are close to my own native land." (For further development of this question in 1979 see chapter XI of this book).

The Vatican policy of *ecumenical* overtures to the Moscow Patriarchate was rooted in such considerations—a policy that could not be logically combined with spectacular actions in the Uniate question that would do more harm than good.

Notwithstanding, a theological reconciliation between the Roman and the Russian Orthodox churches which would serve the eastern policy progressed only slowly. Of course, a changed atmosphere enabled individual events to become visible which went almost unnoticed by the general public and extended beyond the purely ecclesiastical; for instance, when Professor Eduard Huber of the Roman Gregoriana, a Bavarian Jesuit who later became director of the Pontifical Institute for Eastern Studies, was allowed to work on Marxism in 1965 and then again in 1968/69 for fourteen months at the University of Moscow; or when Professor Gustav Wetter, who had worked for decades on Russian and Soviet philosophy at the Pontifical University, could go to Moscow for the first time in September 1973 and deliver a public lecture during a scientific symposium. In 1978 the Roman "Russicum," which the Soviets had for decades considered only a "center of espionage and diversion," could for the fourth time take in two young Orthodox theologians from the Moscow and the Leningrad Theological Academy as official guest students. In July 1975, Metropolitan Nikodim of Leningrad visited the Pope; in October 1976, Cardinal Willebrands visited Metropolitan Juvenaly in Moscow and the Armenian "Catholicos" (Primate) Vasgen I in Echmiadzin. In 1977, Father John Long S.J. represented the Vatican "as observer" at the "World Conference of Religious Forces for Peace" which took place in Moscow in June (serving Soviet goals in foreign policy, but also for the first time presenting "religion" to the Soviet public in a positive light, even on TV). At the beginning of July 1977, Jesuit General Pedro Arrupe was a guest of the Moscow Patriarchate and, to his surprise, was allowed to preach during a service; in November, a Vatican delegation led by Archbishop Jerome Hamer, the Secretary of the Congregation for the Faith, journeyed to the Soviet Union and a Russian delegation with Bishop Kyril of Vyborg visited the Vatican. On May 27, 1978, in Zagorsk, Archbishop Ramon Torrella Cascante, the Vice President of the Vatican "Secretariat for Christian Unity," delivered a message of greeting from the Pope (as "Bishop of Rome") at the 60th anniversary of the restoration of the Moscow Patriarchate. And when Paul VI died in early August, 1978, Metropolitan Nikodim hastened from Leningrad to Rome, to participate not only in the funeral ceremonies, but also—on behalf of the Moscow patriarch—in the installation mass of the new Pope John Paul I (Albino Luciani). And there Nikodim was suddenly seen to approach the surprised Cardinal Slipyj and publicly embrace this most implacable opponent of Roman-Russian rapprochement. It was a tragic symbol of the impotence of such a gesture that Nikodim, only 49 (and in the West often unjustly suspected of being an "agent"), was struck down by a heart attack during a candid, pastoral discussion with John Paul I. Thus the Archbishop of Leningrad and Novgorod died literally in the arms of the Roman Pope. . . .

Only someone familiar with the history of the last fifty years, as presented in this book, is able to evaluate the importance of such isolated symptoms of change. If one keeps in mind the centuries-old chasm between

Rome and Moscow, even modest theological debates become events: the first from December 6 to 10, 1967, in Leningrad, where at the end Metropolitan Nikodim took part in Bishop Willebrands' mass in the only Catholic church in the city ("Notre Dame de Lourdes"); the second from December 6 to 10, 1970, in Bari (Italy), where Nikodim celebrated the liturgy at the grave of the legendary St. Nicholas, equally familiar to eastern and western Christians. However, it was not until the third meeting—from June 4 to 7, 1973, in Zagorsk near Moscow—that they succeeded in building a narrow bridge, which was hardly broadened at the fourth meeting in Trento (Italy), July 23–28, 1975. (For further events see chapter XI.)

Fantastical speculations were attached to the communiqué signed by the two churches in Zagorsk which the *Osservatore Romano* published on June 16: that "practical cooperation between the Soviet Union and the Vatican had been decided," indeed that it marked a "turn by Rome toward socialism modeled on Russia."[41] Actually, the document—as participants in the Zagorsk debates credibly testify—was neither prepared by the Vatican, nor was it discussed with the Vatican before the signing. It was the result of a debate conducted in several languages without simultaneous translation which the Jesuit Father John Long laboriously put down on paper together with one of the Russian participants. Of course, there was more agreement in the religious sense than ever, but politically—also in regard to the church's social doctrine—there was agreement only on the *smallest* common denominator:

"A recognition of the fact that in many parts of the world there is a strong tendency toward *certain forms of 'socialism.'* [Note the quotation marks around the ominous word!] The participants in the discussions had *different concepts* of the nature of these tendencies and the level of these values—this was also not an object of discussion—but they agreed that there were *positive aspects* in these tendencies which Christians must recognize and attempt to understand." That man must control and try to change the world— "created as an image of God"—was legitimate, but: "Christians do not reduce humanity and the universe simply to the visible aspect."

These were platitudes that allowed the Orthodox side to demonstrate a minimum distance from the reigning atheism, the Catholic side a minimum approach to a social order whose definition remained unresolved. What the Pope personally thought of "socialism," he had stated clearly a year earlier in a doctrinal document for the 80th anniversary of the encyclical "*Rerum Novarum*" ("*Octogesima Adveniens*" *of May 14, 1971*):

"Differentiations may be made . . . between the various forms (*inter varios modos*) of socialism, that determine a clear choice (*certa selectio).* . . . Even if one can differentiate various aspects in Marxism, it would be illusory and dangerous to forget the inner bond that ties these aspects closely together, and to assume the elements of Marxist analysis without recognizing their relationship to the ideology. . . . A Christian can never become an adherent of ideological systems that contradict his beliefs and his Christian view of humanity. . . ."

In spite of many uncertainties and utopian beginnings that define his pontificate during an epoch of internal church crisis, this policy position by Paul VI has always remained clear: indications of it are contained in his encyclical *"Ecclesiam Suam"* (1964), in which he condemned "atheist systems," but affirmed dialogue even where it "is very difficult, not to say impossible." In his most important social encyclical *"Populorum Progressio"* (1967), which underlined more radically than ever the Catholic engagement in a world in need of reform, he had also not denied this basic position: "All social action presumes a doctrine. But a Christian cannot accept any system based on an atheistic and materialistic philosophy." On the 40th anniversary of Pius XI's encyclical *"Divini Redemptoris"* (see p. 170), the Vatican did declare that since 1917 there had been "profound changes" in international Communism, also "varying interpretations of Marxism," but that Pius XI's diagnosis and admonition remained the "exact criterion" in evaluating these changes (*Osservatore Romano*, March 19/20, 1977). Nor did the rapprochement which took place in 1976/77 in Italy between Christian Democrats and Communists motivate the Vatican to any doctrinal compromises: on July 2, 1977, Paul VI exhorted the bishops of the "red" region Emilia-Romagna to vigilance against a "mighty opponent," which did not put him in contradiction to his eastern policy: the pragmatic principle of Vatican pastoral policy was and is to offer spiritual *resistance* as long as possible against a political seizure of power by atheists, but once the atheists exercise state power, then to negotiate as far as possible, and strive for an *agreement* about a practical security for the existence of the church.

This policy was doubtless put to the hardest test in relation to the Soviet Union. For nowhere else in the Soviet bloc was the existence of the church and religion brought so much into question as in the Soviet Union itself. Just how unchanged in principle the religious policy of the Soviet Communists had remained even in the period of East-West detente was shown on June 23, 1975, when the religious legislation of 1929, for the first time in 46 years, was centralized and formally "modernized," but not moderated, by a new "ukase."[42] Article 52 of the new Soviet constitution[43] of October 7, 1977, to be sure contained (in contrast to Art. 124 of the Stalin constitution of 1936) not only the right "to conduct religious worship," but also again (as in the constitution of 1925) *"to profess* or not to profess any religion." But now too, as expression of "freedom of conscience," only "*atheistic* propaganda," and not the propagation of religion, was guaranteed. Soviet commentators tried to explain the fact that there was no more talk of "*antireligious*" propaganda—as in 1936— as an expression of the "humanization" of atheism: they were no longer fighting *against* the faithful, but *for* them; also the new constitutional principle which expressly forbids "incitement of hostility or hatred on religious grounds" was to be interpreted as protection of the faithful against discrimination (thus *Pravda Ukrainy*, mid-March 1978). Even Vladimir Kurojedov, president of the "Council for Religious Cults," admitted in an interview (with Italian Communist Alceste Santini) that "religion is a complex social phenomenon with strong social roots"; therefore "admonitions, prohibitions and administrative measures [are] useless measures in the struggle against religious ideology" (*Unità*, November 24, 1978). However, the identification of atheism with state ideology remained unchanged, as did the intention to fight for atheism with state means. Measured against this state of affairs, all ecumenical efforts, all Catholic-Orthodox rapprochement, as important as it may have been as a means of self-representation vis-à-vis the state, remained hardly more than a straw of hope.

Nowhere else but here in the Soviet Union was the Vatican confronted with the basic question: how the principles of *peace* and *justice* could be reconciled without the one being sacrificed to the other. Paul VI's policies persistently tried to bridge this dilemma. For—as his "foreign minister" Casaroli said at the end of October 1974—"complete justice within the nations and among them is impossible in actuality without a situation of peace," but peace without justice "carries the seed of its own destruction." In concrete moments, however, Casaroli said, this problem presents itself now and then in a form "that forces one to [make] practical decisions that are not easy."[44] Thus the Vatican participated intensively in the "Conference on European Security and Cooperation" (CESC) in Helsinki, and in its preparation in Geneva. It was primarily the Vatican which insisted on incorporating in the Final Act of August 1, 1975, formulations which Moscow only reluctantly accepted, because they exceed the formulations of the Soviet legislation: "VII. Respect for human rights and freedoms, including freedom of thought, conscience, religion or convic- tion. The participant states will respect human rights and basic freedoms including freedom of thought, conscience, religion or conviction for everyone without regard to race, sex, language or religion. They will promote and encourage the effective exercise of civil, political, economic, social, cultural and all other rights and freedoms, which all arise from the dignity inherent in man and are essential for his free and complete development. Within this framework, the participant states will recognize and respect the freedom of the individual, alone or together with others, to confess and exercise a religion or conviction in agreement with the dictates of conscience. . . . (4/1) They verify that religious confessions, institutions and organizations which act within the constitutional framework of the participant states, as well as their representatives, may have contacts and meetings among themselves and exchange information in the areas of their activities."

Catholics all over Eastern Europe may appeal to these principles signed by their governments—and they do. If in doing so they still often meet with obduracy instead of moderation (cf. the balance two years after the Helsinki Conference, no. 8 in the Documentary Appendix), this is only a proof of the conflict peculiar to all state atheism: it requires a relaxed relationship to the religious citizen, and at the same time must ideologically fear this relaxation. Papal eastern policy, however, is not discouraged by this basic difficulty. In his address to the College of Cardinals at Christmas 1975, Paul VI said:

"If in many cases the results of this dialogue seem to be meager or insufficient, or to be late in arriving, and if others can see a sufficient reason in this to break off this [dialogue], we still see it as our solemn duty to continue wisely and steadfastly along a path that appears to us, most importantly, as distinctly according to the gospel: as a path of patience, of understanding, of love. Still, we do not want to conceal the bitterness and worry that the continuation or the deterioration of more than a few situations causes us, situations that oppose the rights of the church and those of the human being, and we warn against interpreting our responsible attitude as a condoning or as a resigned acceptance of such situations."

The Pope, in the same address, expressly emphasized the observance of the Helsinki promises. He insisted especially on "acceptable agreed-upon solutions" in the interests of the faithful in the CSSR, in Rumania and "certain regions of the Soviet Union." Only a person who mistakes ("or wants to mistake") the spirit of his efforts could accuse him of indifference. But he also admitted that in many cases he could only continue his eastern policies "*contra spem*," against hope, with trust in God.

Two years later, on December 22, 1977, the Pope felt it necessary to deplore the undiminished "suppression and unjust limitation" of religious freedom. "We wish once again to tell all those who suffer that Our ear is not deaf and Our heart—must it be said?—not unreceptive to the laments and cries for help that arise." As example Paul VI named only the most hopeless case: "little Albania, so dear to Us." And on January 14, 1978, at his last meeting with the diplomatic corps in the Vatican, Paul VI asked: "Can a state that declares itself atheist and turns against the belief of a portion of its citizens—even though it claims to respect their personal beliefs within a certain framework—gain trust by this sort of 'negative confessionalism'?"

A year later, John Paul II quoted this statement of his predecessor in a letter to the Secretary General of the United Nations on Human Rights Day (December 10, 1978).

XI

Pope Wojtyla: Continuity and Challenge

It was a spontaneous gesture, sentimental and at the same
time of historic and political significance; as documentation, the picture was transmitted by television
all over the world on June 10, 1978: the Roman Pope, John Paul II, and a
Communist chief of state, Henryk Jablonski, embraced in farewell at the
Balice airport near Krakow. Certainly, it was two Poles who met there, but
also two worlds. Was this the symbol of a turning-point in the history of
Vatican eastern policy, of Communist church policy? A Warsaw party
functionary standing beside me watching on the press platform said of this
scene that now nothing "could stay the way it was." But what really would
change—and how? Thirteen years earlier, in 1966, Poland's Communist
government had refused entry to a Pope; now Jablonski was saying that the
stations of the Pope's visit would remain "in the hearts of all Poles," and —
in a gesture previously unimaginable—the honor guard of a Soviet bloc
army dipped its colors before the Pope. Had historical fantasy overtaken
reality?

There is no doubt that the election as Pope of a bishop from a country
within the Soviet bloc at the time of the Cold War could only have
contributed to a hardening of relations between church and state and
intensified the repression of believers in the East. However, after the years
of cautious pastoral diplomacy by Popes John XXIII and Paul VI, this
choice could mean a new opportunity—not least thanks to the "more
favorable climate created by the Helsinki Conference on Security and
Cooperation in Europe" (thus Silvestrini, the Vatican representative in

375

Belgrade, October 7, 1977). Still, in the tendency of the Helsinki Declaration there also lay a challenge that a Pope from the East could embody better than a "Westerner": Would this Pontiff, permeated with the strength of Polish Catholicism, be less defensive and diplomatic with regard to threatened church structures but more aggressive with regard to religious liberty and human rights? As we have seen in this book, an alternative between diplomatic "transactions" and moral-religious "mission" never had existed; both elements always had been very closely entwined. But this Pope embodied a new dynamic style. This continuity and its new momentum were confirmed primarily by two striking events:

1.   The appointment (May 1, 1979) of Agostino Casaroli, the "architect" of Paul VI's *Ostpolitik*, as Cardinal Secretary of State, and of Achille Silvestrini, Casaroli's closest associate, as his successor as Secretary of the "Council for Public Relations of the Church" (the ministry of foreign affairs of the Roman Curia).

2.   The Pope's journey through Poland (June 2–10, 1979), an event with long-term and unforeseeable effects on the future of religion in Eastern Europe and the Vatican's relations with the East (which were always dependent on general East-West relations). When the Warsaw government, after months of preliminary discussions reflecting hesitation and embarrassment, finally agreed to this papal visit, the Pope wrote a letter to Polish State Council President Jablonski (March 8, 1979) with the programmatic contents:

". . . The themes of peace, coexistence and cooperation among nations and social orders are particularly close to me. I am profoundly concerned for the mission of the Church of Christ . . . In respect for mankind . . . I see the key to the realization of those great tasks which stand before all of humanity. . . . I trust, in conclusion, that this visit will serve to further the development of relations between the state and the church. . . ." (see facsimile).

John Paul II had used even his first trip abroad, to Mexico in early February 1979, to clarify the theological and philosophical basis of his *engagement*. Statements that displeased the leftist Catholic and Marxist opposition in Latin America were more reassuring for the ruling Communists of Eastern Europe:

"The conception of Christ as a politician, a revolutionary, the subversive agitator of Nazareth, is not in accordance with the teaching of the church. . . . Liberation, in the mission of the church, cannot be reduced to a pure and simple economic, political, social or cultural dimension. . . . The church has no need to resort to systems and ideologies to love and to defend man and to collaborate in his liberation. . . . The church wishes to remain *free vis-à-vis opposing systems* so as to opt only for man. . . ."[1]

To be sure, Pope John Paul II left no doubt, in his first encyclical ("*Redemptor Hominis*," March 4, 1979), that he considered the "state totalitarianisms" *(totalismow panstowowych)* of this century[2] as great a threat to mankind as the mechanisms and pressures of the materialistic consumer society; but the "missionary dynamics of the church" that he wanted to mobilize at the same time remain "in the dialogue"—in the pastoral-diplomatic one too. During his first meetings with the diplomatic corps of the Holy See (October 20, 1978 and January 12, 1979), the Pope had declared his determination to employ—as he emphasized—the "proven means" of diplomacy and negotiation.

Diplomatic relations "as a sign of courtesy, discretion and loyalty," he said, are "not necessarily an expression of approval of this or that regime— *that is not my task*—nor are they an expression of approval of all their actions," but rather they indicated the "*willingness* to talk" with people bearing political responsibility. In this, the Holy See in no way intended to overstep its pastoral duties, which consisted in safeguarding the "religious cult" and also the believers' "access as loyal citizens to full participation in social life."[3] John Paul II accordingly made use of even his first meetings with Communist politicians, e.g. with GDR Foreign Minister Fischer and Bulgarian Foreign Minister Mladenov (see chapter X)—in the latter case with visible success: On May 13, 1979, the Pope's desires to set up a diocese in southern Bulgaria (Plovdiv) and to appoint a new bishop for northern Bulgaria (Nikopoli) were granted. What was most surprising was that the government in Sofia accepted for Nikopoli a man with a past that previously had been a hindrance: Samuel Serafimov Djoundrine, a priest trained at the Catholic University of Lyon, who in 1952 had been sentenced to 12 years' imprisonment as a "French spy" and "counterrevolutionary on account of his hatred of the Soviet Union. . . ."[4] The Pope himself consecrated Djoundrine in Rome on May 27, and Nuncio Poggi went to Bulgaria on October 18, 1979, for his inauguration and for negotiations with the government. The new Pope immediately continued contacts with Hungary as well, following the line of previous Vatican diplomacy: In two series of negotiations, at the beginning of December 1978 and in mid-March 1979 in Budapest, Nuncio Luigi Poggi succeeded in facilitating the appointment of four bishops acceptable to both the Church *and* the government, and thus completing the Hungarian hierarchy on April 4. In a letter that the Pope wrote to Hungarian Cardinal Laszlo Lekai on December 2, 1978, Poggi was referred to as the "interpreter of our pastoral care"—a function of Vatican diplomacy that seemed all the more

Szanowny Pan
Prof.Dr Henryk JABŁOŃSKI
Przewodniczacy Rady Państwa
Polskiej Rzeczpospolitej Ludowej

Przekazując niniejszym serdeczne podziękowanie za list
z dnia 2. marca br., pragnę równocześnie dać wyraz mojej
radości, że dane mi będzie w dniach od 2. do 10. czerwca
przybyć do Polski, mojej Ojczyzny. Wyrażam radość,iż będzie
mi dane spełnić w tym czasie doniosłą posługę wynikającą
z mojego urzędu pasterskiego w Kościele.

Na ręce Pana Przewodniczącego składam podziękowanie
dla Władz Państwowych Polskiej Rzeczpospolitej Ludowej za
pozytywne ustosunkowanie się do sprawy mojego przyjazdu,
jak o tym świadczy Jego tak bardzo uprzejmy list.

Motywy pokoju,współżycia i współpracy pomiędzy naroda-
mi i ustrojami sa mi szczególnie bliskie : uważam je za i-
stotne dla posłannictwa Kościoła Chrystusowego - a w posza-
nowaniu dla człowieka, o którym Pan Przewodniczący łaskawie
wspomniał w swym liście,widzę klucz do realizacji tych wiel
kich zadań,które stoją przed całą ludzkością. Polska, która
po doświadczeniach straszliwej drugiej wojny światowej,
szczególnie potrzebuje owego pokoju, przykłada wielką wagę
do tych ogólno-ludzkich zadań. Pragnę,ażeby moje odwiedziny
w Ojczyźnie stały się również tego wyrazem. Pragne, aby odwiedziny te przyczyniły się do umocnienia jedności wewnętrz
nej moich umiłowanych Rodaków, a także do ugruntowania świa
domości tego miejsca, jakie Naród Polski zajmuje w wielkiej rodzinie narodów świata współczesnego. Ufam na ko-
niec, że odwiedziny te przysłużą się dalszemu rozwojowi
stosunków pomiędzy Państwem a Kościołem, co dla Polski
nie przestaje być sprawą wielkiej doniosłości.

Dziękując raz jeszcze za cenne pismo Pana Przewodniczącego i licząc również na możliwość spotkania się
z Nim w czasie pobytu w Polsce, pozostaję z wyrazami
głębokiego szacunku.

Watykan, dnia 8. marca 1979 r.

Jan Paweł II papież

Dear Sir
Professor Henry Jablonski, Chairman Council of State
Polish People's Republic

Transmitting herewith sincere thanks for the letter of the 2nd of March, I hasten at the same time to give voice to my joy, that, on the days between the 2nd and 10th of June, I will be able to come to Poland, my motherland. I express joy, because it will be given to me to fulfill in that time the important service stemming from my Pastoral office in the Church.

Through your hands, Mr. Chairman, I render thanks to the Officers of the Polish People's Republic for positively committing themselves in occasion of my arrival, as I am informed by such a very courteous letter.

Motives of peace, co-existence, and cooperation among nations and social orders are particularly close to me: I regard them as essential for the mission of the Church of Christ— and, in respect for mankind, as Mr. Chairman you kindly note in your letter, I see the key to the realization of those great tasks, which stand before all humanity. Poland, which, after the horrible experiences of the second world war, especially needs this peace, attributes great weight to the universal human tasks. I wish that my visit to the Homeland contributes to the strengthening of the internal unity of my beloved compatriots and to the fastening of the conscience of the place which the Polish Nation occupies in the great family of nations of the modern world. I trust, in conclusion, that this visit will serve to further the development of relations between the state and the church, which for Poland never cease to be a matter of great importance.

Thank you for the valuable letter, Mr. Chairman, and I am counting on the possibility that we shall meet during the time of my stay in Poland, I remain with expressions of deep esteem.

The Vatican, 8 March, 1979

John Paul II
Pope

important to the Pope because the (historically-caused) weaknesses of Hungarian Catholicism make its institutional link with the Roman directorate more imperative than elsewhere. The papal letter to Lekai, which Western Catholic media wrongly "distorted into a letter of warning and reproach" (according to a critical comment from Cardinal König in Vienna),[5] was an exhortation to "pastoral zeal" and contained a greeting "to the whole Hungarian nation." It became evident that the atmosphere was not at all clouded when the Hungarian Cardinal Primate came to Rome on April 1 to participate in the 400-year anniversary of the "Collegium Germanicum et Hungaricum"—together with the Budapest Secretary of State for Church Affairs, Imre Miklos, who (as a small gesture to the new Pope) had allowed the dispatch of two Hungarian theology students to the Roman "Germanicum," for the first time in decades. Lekai afterwards participated in the Pope's visit to Poland; on June 4 he was honored publicly in Czestochowa by John Paul II as a symbol of Polish-Hungarian "brotherhood."

In the autumn of 1979, when Eastern Europe's Communists, especially the Soviets, were undecided as to whether the outcome of the Pope's trip to Poland should be considered positive or negative (and for whom!), the Hungarian Primate made use of an invitation from Moscow Patriarch Pimen for a good-will tour: in Moscow, Leningrad, Vilna, even in Kiev and Zhitomir, Lekai was able to visit Catholic congregations and at the same time to explain the Pope's eastern policy line to the concerned Soviet Communists. . . .

Let's go back, however, to the actual basis of the Soviet fears: the fact that the Pope was now a Pole—and wanted to visit Poland! When Pope John Paul II received Soviet Foreign Minister Andrei Gromyko on January 24, 1979, for an audience lasting almost two hours (the longest of Gromyko's five visits to the Vatican since 1976), he was conscious of the key importance this meeting could have, as "Catholic" and "Polish" have always been identical for Russia—for the Soviet Communist state just as much as for the Czarist Orthodox empire. Although the new Pope spoke more candidly and directly than any of his predecessors about the problems of the Catholics in the Soviet Union (even of the Poles living there), he left Gromyko with a "sensible, balanced" impression— as the latter informed Eastern diplomats. Above all else, the Pope successfully made clear that he knew how to distinguish patriotism from nationalism, strength of principles from intolerance, and that he saw human rights, including religious liberty, preserved only in a peaceful world, not a world torn by conflicts.

Now that a Pole is ruling in the Vatican, there is *"no longer a Russian complex"*—the Pope said in a private conversation at the beginning of May 1979. He was referring to a "complex" of a two-fold nature: both the Vatican's consideration of Poland which had always—in particular from the 19th century onward—frustrated all papal efforts to achieve a *modus vivendi* with the Russian imperium for the Church's pastoral policies, and on the other hand the fear of the Poles (including the Polish church) that Rome might seek an agreement with Russia that would not be in the Polish national interest, that might even be at its expense. A Polish Pope, who sees his duties to the *whole* church, could in fact disregard all such constraints. This was made plain in Pope John Paul II's first discussion with Ukrainian Cardinal Josyf Slipyj. On November 3, 1978, Slipyj had appealed to the Pope as a "Slav," who should know that "Ukrainians and Poles have a common enemy, which today is Moscow. . . . Poles know how Russians make contracts and how they keep their word."[6] Slipyj therefore demanded a review of the "dialog with the Russian Orthodox church, which is based on false premises," and—as he had for years—demanded the formation of a "Ukrainian Patriarchate." But in a conversation with Slipyj on November 20, the Pope—like his predecessors—rejected *both* of the Cardinal's demands. John Paul II hardly wanted to open old wounds; but he also did not believe he could allow them to slip into oblivion—especially since the Pope, as a Pole, was very conscious of the complex historical and moral difficulties. Therefore he thought he owed the Ukrainian Uniates at least a gesture, and wrote a letter to Slipyj on March 19, 1979 (on the occasion of the millenium of the Christianization of the Ukraine—which would, however, not take place until 1988). In it he mentioned the "authority, still in force today" of the Union of Brest-Litovsk (1596)—that is, that union of the Ukrainian Orthodox with the Roman church, which had always stood in the shadow of conflicting nationalisms (and was not achieved without political pressure from Poland, although with the concession that these Uniates could keep their own Slavic rite). Without going any more deeply into this historical reminiscence, the Pope appealed now to the "ecumenical spirit," which—as the Pope now admonished both sides—must be respected today, both by the Uniate church and the Orthodox churches, "whose traditions and formulas the Catholic church and the Holy See regard with the utmost esteem." Not a direct word about the forced liquidation of the Uniates in the Soviet Union (1946), but a direct reference to the principle of religious freedom in the United Nations Declaration of Human Rights of 1948. . . .[7]

Was that cautious enough or had he touched upon a taboo after all? In the Vatican "Secretariat for Christian Unity" (which the Pope had not consulted), the letter evoked dismay and apprehension. Pope John Paul II, who could not offend either Moscow or the Ukrainians living in the West (many of whom were openly threatening schism), continued his balancing act: Against Slipyj's wishes, in September 1979 he named Miroslav Lubachivsky to be Uniate Metropolitan in Philadelphia—a man who had emigrated from the Ukraine in 1937, who had never joined in the polemics of his countrymen against the Vatican's eastern policy—and for that reason provoked intense protest from the American Ukrainians. The Pope's reception by the emigrants in the Ukrainian cathedral in Philadelphia, during his visit to the United States, was proportionately cool. John Paul II now decided to perform Lubachivsky's consecration as bishop personally on November 13 in Rome—assisted by Slipyj. For the 87-year-old Cardinal, whose understanding was impeded by his age and his nationalistic advisors, the Pope had respectful words: "The whole church and the world recognize the uncommon witness you have given by your imprisonment for many years; today you are with us, free for many years . . . and can thus dedicate yourself to your people." The Pope recalled the duty of "mutual loyalty" and assured him that he would "with all my strength, alleviate the trials of those who suffer because of their faith. . . . "[8]

But would it serve this goal if the Pope "seized the iron [of the Ukrainian Uniates] while it was hot," as Slipyj wished? Both Orthodox and Communists in Moscow had received with suspicion the letter the Pope had written on March 17 to the 87-year-old Cardinal, in spite of its appeasing formulations (also because the Vatican diplomacy, with a rather naive cunning, had postponed publication of the letter in the *Osservatore Romano* until June 17, that is until *after* the Pope's trip to Poland!). The Moscow Patriarchate had cancelled, on short notice, a Fifth Theological Colloquium planned for April in Odessa between the Catholic and Russian Orthodox churches. But now Metropolitan Juvenaly, Nikodim's successor as director of the Foreign Office of the Moscow Patriarchate, on September 4, 1979, directed a concerned letter to Cardinal Jan Willebrands, President of the Vatican Secretariat for Christian Unity. Juvenaly threatened "public criticism" if Willebrands did not quickly communicate the "exact meaning" of the papal letter to Slipyj. The main polemical question was whether the Polish Pope really regarded the 400-year-old Union of Brest as the *model* of a future union of Catholic and Orthodox churches, and thus disavowed the ecumenical progress of the Second Vatican Council?

Juvenaly surely had discussed his letter with the state Church Office in Moscow; he emphasized, however, that his "ardent desire to avoid polemics and unnecessary misunderstandings after all the years of brotherly relations" had dictated his inquiry. Willebrands replied on September 22, 1979 with a long letter to Moscow:

"I have called your letter to the attention of the Holy Father and spoken with him about its content and significance. He is aware of the thoughts that I am expressing here, and I am writing to you in his name. The letter addressed to His Eminence Cardinal Slipyj [from the Pope on March 17] had a very limited objective. The Holy Father had no intention of expressing in it his concepts of the relations between the Roman church and the Orthodox church. . . . The unity that we seek is *not the absorption of the one by the other*, but rather full communion between the churches. . . . The Union of Brest has always possessed a special significance for the Ukrainian Catholics. . . . The Pope wanted to dissociate this union *from political and national elements*. He had by no means any intention of presenting it as a model for our relations with the Orthodox church today or for a future union. The Catholic Uniate churches arose under circumstances different from ours, and were inspired by a theology that is no longer current. Within the Catholic church they have been a concrete reminder that the Latin tradition is not the only authentically Christian one. In this sense, their existence has been and still is useful. On the other hand, one must admit that their foundation caused a breach and new tensions. . . . We must profit from the teachings of the past. More than ever, our efforts must be dissociated from every kind of political element and from any intention that is alien to the single desire of fulfilling Christ's will for his church. This is John Paul II's intention. He does not demand that we orient ourselves to a model from the past, but calls for loyalty and obedience to Him who renews everything. . . ."[9]

Like all his 20th-century predecessors, John Paul II too is confronted with the extremely sensitive (almost impenetrable) national-religious problems at the juncture of Polish, Russian and Ukrainian Christianity in atheist-ruled Eastern Europe. Could the religious uncertainties really be "dissociated" from the political ones?—A reconstruction or re-legalization of the Uniates in the Ukraine, in the sense of a "national restitution," would only be conceivable—as so often in history—through violent shifts of power. To hope for this, or to work toward it, the Vatican considered unrealistic as well as immoral. Therefore it was striving for a "reparation" of injustice in a broader sense: through a connection with the common interest of all Christians, the Russian Orthodox included, in a "universal restoration" of religious rights and freedoms. Was freedom for Catholics of the eastern rite in the Ukraine more important than for the Orthodox, in whose few open churches, after all, Catholics too could find religious refuge? Was the future of the Catholic church in the Soviet Union not linked inseparably with the future of the Russian Orthodox church, itself under so much pressure? Such considerations were the base of the Vatican policy of ecumenical overtures to the Moscow Patriarchate, a policy that could not be combined logically with spectacular actions in the Uniate question, that would do more harm than good.

Without a "Russian complex," yet at the same time the "first *Slavic* Pope," who would act as a voice for *all* the nations in the East "who have so often been forgotten in the West," a Pope who would bring to light "the spiritual unity of Christian Europe" and the "great traditions of West and East" (sermon in Gniezno, June 3, 1979)—this is how John Paul II set out on his journey to Poland.[10] But the emotions which were bound to overwhelm this Pope on his "return home," as well as his patriotic-missionary sense (related to 19th century Polish Messianism), also made his message risky. Time and again the Pope was careful to add revisions and amplifications in order to guard against misunderstandings of his speeches: for example, when he emphasized before millions of believers in Krakow on June 9 that "There is no imperialism of the Church"; or when on June 7 he paid his deepest respect in Auschwitz also to the people "of various religions and ideologies, certainly not only believers" who had suffered there, or when he recalled the part the Russian people had played "in the last terrible war for the freedom of the nations" and called on his fellow Poles to treat all people and all nations as brothers. The ideological challenge to Moscow posed by the visit to Poland, however, could not be avoided, and for this very reason the Pope staked everything on the "Polish card." For if it was at all possible to prove it to Moscow, then Catholic, Communist-ruled Poland would have to demonstrate that religion can be a stabilizing factor, a support of civic steadiness and vigor—a "stimulant," not an "opium"—if it only were left in peace; and that the church "is willing to reach mutual agreements with any economic system (*z kazdym ustrojem pracy*) as long as it is permitted to speak to people about Christ" (sermon to workers at the Lenin steelworks in Mogila/Nowa Huta, June 9).

With this in mind the Pope called upon the bishops of his homeland to make their own contribution to the Vatican's *Ostpolitik* when he addressed the Polish episcopate in Czestochowa on June 5. If the Polish episcopate and its Primate Cardinal Wyszyński had formerly tended to doubt the Vatican's competence in the East and to consider church-state relations in Poland as primarily their own affair, here now was a Pope whose knowledge of Poland could not be disputed, who was relying on his primacy and emphasizing the decisive significance of the "*hierarchical constitution and structure*" of the Roman church. Throughout the centuries, he said, the church in Poland had been indebted to the Roman church and its "universal dimension" for its own strength, inner unity and closeness to the nation. "Only if we bear in mind this correct picture of the church and in its organic wholeness that of the Holy See," the Pope taught the bishops, "can we gauge correctly the meaning of something that for some years has been acquiring new significance in Poland, namely the *normalization of church-state relations.*" With detailed quotations from his address to the Vatican's diplomatic corps on January 12, 1979 (see above), the Pope then stressed the importance of Vatican diplomacy, which wished to "be open to every country and every regime." Poland's episcopate had already done a great deal in this direction, the Pope said, it was "not to stop taking these initiatives that are important for the present-day church."

In Czestochowa on June 4, the Pope introduced his (and Paul VI's) Secretary of State Cardinal Casaroli to hundreds of thousands of believers as the man "who knows the roads to Poland, the roads from Rome *to the whole European East,*" who, together with Special Nuncio Luigi Poggi, had expressed Paul VI's "untiring concern for the entire European East," and who "has served and still serves this great and difficult task in the name of the Holy See."[11] On June 9, in a unique gesture, the Pope called Casaroli to the window of the Vatican palace to receive, together with him, the acclamation of the Romans after his triumphant journey to Poland. Thus did Pope Wojtyla demonstratively abolish the personal reservations that he (among many others), as a Polish bishop, had held against Casaroli, but above all he strengthened the line of eastern policy whose basic correctness the new Pope had recognized after studying the internal documents.

Together with Casaroli, he had outlined the address to Polish Party Chief Edward Gierek at the beginning of the trip, on June 2 in Warsaw, as well as the one to State President Henryk Jablonski at the end on June 9 in Krakow. These important documents included programmatic formulations which were chosen in full awareness of the effect that could emanate from Poland:

"When the church establishes religious contact with a person it strengthens him in his natural social obligation. . . . This is a result of the fundamental mission of the church, which endeavors always and everywhere to better a person, to make him more aware of his worth and to make his devotion to the fulfillment of his family, social and patriotic duties more complete. . . . The church does not demand any privilege for its activities in this respect but only and exclusively what is essential for the fulfillment of its mission. This is the direction in which the activity of the episcopate is moving in Poland. . . . If the Holy See is seeking an agreement (*porozumienie*) with the state authorities in this area, it is aware that apart from the association with the creation of conditions favorable for the total activity of the church, this agreement concurs with the historical *raison d'être (racja)* of a nation whose sons and daughters are for the most part sons and daughters of the Catholic Church. In the light of these self-evident preconditions, we see this agreement as one of the elements of the ethical and international order in Europe and the world of today as a result of respect of the right of the nation and of human rights. I take the liberty of expressing the opinion that one may not give up the quest and efforts in this direction" (address of June 2, 1979).

"The visit of a Pope to Poland is certainly an event without precedent, not only in this century but in the whole millenium. . . . This event was undoubtedly an act of *courage* on both sides. In our times, however, just such an act of courage is needed. Sometimes one has to dare to move in a direction which nobody else has taken before. Our times have an immense need for such a testimony, which gives voice to the desire for closeness (*zblizenia*) between nations and systems (*ustrojami*) as an essential *condition for peace in the world* [stressed in the original]. Our times demand from us that we should not shut ourselves into any rigid frontiers when it is a question of the good of mankind. . ." (farewell address of June 9, 1979).

But what does "closeness," what does "normalization" mean? Only "agreement" (*porozumienie*)? This is how the partial solutions were described which Cardinal Wyszyński had twice entered into (1950 and 1956) without consulting the Vatican; but this is also how Pope John Paul II now described his aim. Certainly, neither side was thinking of a classical concordat. On the day before the Pope's visit (May 29), Gierek and Wyszyński spoke, in a communiqué which in its decree of accord put all their previous meetings in the shade, of "new impulses for co-operation (*wspoldzialania*) between church and state and a further development of the relations between Poland and the Holy See." The unresolved specific problems are overshadowed by the main question of whether the church—within the framework of a true separation of church and state—can achieve "permanent" public legal status in Poland. The Vatican could function here as the negotiator, without itself being a party to the agreement.

The "true dialogue" which John Paul II offered in Poland—but with its signal effect beyond Poland!—concerned, as he underlined, the "real application" of religious liberty which is guaranteed in all Eastern European constitutions yet so often is restricted in practice. "We are aware that this dialogue will not be easy because it has to take place between two diametrically opposed views of the world, but it must be possible," the Pope said in Czestochowa. And he expressed this very conviction in even more urgent terms when he appeared before the General Assembly of the United Nations in New York on October 3, 1979:[12]

". . . Even a confrontation between the religious view of the world and the agnostic or even atheistic view, which is one of the 'signs of the times' of the present age, could preserve honest and respectful human dimensions without violating the essential rights of conscience of any man or woman living on earth. Respect for the dignity of the human person would seem to demand that, when the exact tenor of the exercise of religious freedom is being discussed or determined with a view toward national laws or international conventions, the institutions that are by their nature at the service of religion should also be brought in. If this participation is omitted, there is a danger of imposing, in so intimate a field of man's life, rules or restrictions that are opposed to his true religious needs. . . ."

The representatives of all the states, even the Communist ones (with the single exception of Albania's delegation, which had left the assembly hall) applauded John Paul II's speech. This was certainly polite, but hardly a sign of unanimous agreement to this demand for a voice for the church in state religious legislation. But for the first time in the history of Vatican eastern policy, and before an international forum, a readiness for dialogue with atheistic governments too was thus tied to a precise demand for equal partnership. And this in the context of an *appeal for peace*, which sounded different, more radical, from this Pope than from his predecessors. If Paul VI, speaking before the United Nations on October 4, 1965, had clothed his call against war and the arms race completely in the classic formulations of Catholic state philosophy, differentiating for example between "offensive weapons" and "defensive weapons," Pope John Paul II now embraced an almost total pacifism:

"The continual preparations for war . . . show that there is a desire to be ready for war, and being ready means being able to start it; it also means taking the risk that sometime, somewhere, somehow, someone can set in motion the terrible mechanism of general destruction." The Pope thus demanded a "readiness even to renounce one's own particular interests, including *political interests*. It is by *sacrificing these interests* for the sake of peace that we serve them best. . . . Can our age still really believe that the breathtaking spiral of armaments is at the service of world peace? Is alleging the threat of a potential enemy really not rather the intention to keep for oneself a means of threat, in order to get the upper hand with the aid of one's own arsenal of destruction? Here too it is the human dimension of peace that tends to vanish in *favor of ever new possible forms of imperialism. . . .*"

One who speaks thus of the politics of *all* the great powers can of course not be accused of partisanism; but his own interest—in the case of the Pope, the religious—becomes that much greater an ideological challenge for those who—like the Soviet Communists—have incorporated the concept of "peace" into their monopolistic ideology. This, together with the unique charisma with which John Paul II, in the first year of his pontificate, mobilized greater masses of humanity than any political personality of this century—this gradually aroused Soviet skepticism and uncertainty toward this Pope in 1979, in spite of all beginnings toward dialogue and understanding. When the manuscript of this book was concluded, no critical voices had yet been heard from Moscow, but there were symptoms that betrayed how disconcerting and irritating this Pope's spiritual radiance was felt to be:

In 1965, Soviet Ambassador to the United Nations Nikolai Federenko had asked Vatican UN Observer Alberto Giovanetti confidentially for a *private* meeting between Pope Paul VI and Foreign Minister Gromyko in New York (the first meeting of this kind ever)[13]; now, in 1979—Gromyko left New York shortly before John Paul II arrived. For the first time in years, in 1979 not a single Vatican diplomat was invited to the "November reception" in the Soviet embassy in Rome. And Soviet diplomats in Rome used every opportunity to ask why the Pope had to speak continuously about human rights. . . . Had the Pope's "signal" on his trip to Poland not been understood after all, or incorrectly understood?

It was not the Pope and his behavior that were the actual causes of the change in atmosphere, but the general global political situation: the end of the Brezhnev era and the Carter era seemed to be in sight; in the Eastern bloc—not least in Poland—there was unrest, not only among political and religious "dissidents," but also as a result of symptoms of economic crisis and loss of ideological perspective. At the same time, the irrational eruption of an Islamic priest (Khomeini) tempted the Great Powers to compensate for their impotence—spiritual as well as material—with dangerous acts of violence. The horizon of East-West relations seems to have clouded over, and with it—as often before—the prospects for the Vatican's eastern policy.

A Pope like Karol Wojtyla still may hope to overcome "Europe's ideological disunity" by promoting Christian humanism, through dialogue—philosophical and diplomatic. There is certainly a "Utopian" element in this; but papal policy, unlike secular diplomacy, was never under the same "pressure to succeed" as the political powers.

XII

The Endless Dialogue:
A Summing Up

"Le présent est chargé du passé et gros de l'avenir"
Leibniz

Where does Vatican Ostpolitik stand after more than a half-century of confrontation and attempts at coexistence with the Communist-ruled states in Eastern Europe?

This book has tried to present its tactics and strategy, its successes and defeats, its checkered experiences and its constant goal—certainly not in toto, but at the most critical junctures of its activity. The situations confronting this eastern policy have become more diverse from decade to decade, from country to country—even outside Europe. "One" Communism as such no longer exists, but in its diversity it is historically even more impressive, thereby presenting a "challenge" for papal diplomacy as well.

Simultaneously with the Communists' economically and sociologically conditioned need for an "easing of tension" interpreted as a military and political detente, their defensive reflex against the ideologically "heretical" world has grown stronger. The Soviet Central Committee spoke of an "unprecedented intensified ideological struggle" in April 1968, and Brezhnev spoke of a "ceaseless ideological battle" at the XXIVth Party Congress in 1971. And this at a historic moment when Communist church policies in all their uniformity—as we have seen—were increasingly differentiated from land to land. The "unity of theory and practice," so

389

important for Marxists, is thus violated by historio-politically motivated opportunism (and realism). "However, since according to Marx 'freedom is insight into necessity,' the Communists have enough insight to take into account the necessity that arises from religious realities, and concede the church a *minimum* of freedom from which a clever pastor can build a maximum." (Thus Karol Wojtyla, Archbishop of Krakow, to a visitor in 1977). Soon thereafter he was faced as Pope by this basic problem of all Vatican eastern policy of the last six decades.

The Vatican—wherever possible—carefully followed the eastern policies of the western nations: the German, the American, the French, without ever setting a rigid behavioral pattern for itself, and without ever making its activities dependent purely on "profit and loss account" (as many of its critics think it should[1]). "Here years and decades do not count," Casaroli reflected. "The Roman tradition of 'thinking in centuries' has lost nothing of its empirical value. . . . The Holy See makes no claims of infallibility in this area; it only feels entitled to be believed that it stakes everything on acting according to reality as it is, on weighing with Christian wisdom the bearable and the unbearable, what can be given up and what cannot. . . ."[2]

The thrust of Vatican Ostpolitik in the seventies—elastic, adjustable from case to case, but delimited in principle—may be defined by four theses:

1. Classical concordatory policy is no longer a model for agreements with Communist governments, for it presumes a greater degree of mutual accommodation than is desirable for either side. The clear delimitation of church and state, the—harmonious—separation of spheres is to be preferred.

2. Partial solutions, even those unwritten or only of a trial nature—because they can effect concrete results—are to be preferred to universal agreements, which are much more difficult to achieve and then usually remain all too unstable. Therefore, diplomatic relations are neither to be sought as a first step, nor avoided as a last. However, just as the Vatican has never broken off existing diplomatic relations, so it also does not refuse them to nations that request them.

3. It is not positions of prestige, not political resistance nor collaboration that must be secured, but rather the practical ministry of souls. This includes not only freedom of *worship*, but also freedom of *confession* and *instruction*. Since the human right of religious freedom (in this sense) can only be secured in a world at peace, Vatican participation in East-West attempts at relaxation becomes a prerequisite for its eastern policy and its credibility.

4. Theoretically, the relationship to the Soviet Union takes precedence,

although this is the most difficult to regulate. Only if the recognition grows in Moscow that a church whose leader resides abroad is not necessarily a disturbing factor in domestic politics, that on the contrary it strengthens domestic peace (also between nationalities) if it is left in peace—only then would Moscow give the national leaderships of its eastern European allies permission for more far-reaching, stable arrangements.

The only alternative to this Vatican eastern policy, as well as for East-West relations in general, would be a retreat to the positions of the fifties. What they brought the papal church in Eastern Europe has been described in this book. "Have the critics ever asked themselves," Casaroli asked, "what situation the church would be in if the Holy See had not done what it actually has done?"[3] The difficulty remained that the Vatican diplomats could explain themselves publicly only with great care, and were thus often delivered defenseless to their critics. Only since the mid-seventies have these critics—primarily in the German and Anglo-Saxon language areas—gradually noticed that it was rather paradoxical to aim their polemics more at the Vatican than at the Communist church policies. And finally they had to recognize the obvious fact: Without a Vatican eastern policy as established by John XXIII and Paul VI, the cardinals of the church of Rome in 1978 could certainly never have risked electing a Pope from Poland, of all places—John Paul II. Even in selecting that name, he expressed a desire for *continuity*, and in his person—as former Archbishop of Krakow—the primary reproach of many critics was refuted: that the Vatican did not take sufficiently into consideration the "local churches," the local bishops, their knowledge of "the East" and their experiences.

In many countries, however,—as this book shows—the problem was first to get these local episcopates reinstalled at all. Where they are strong and stable—as in Poland—the Vatican took counsel with them, indeed it is post-1964 Vatican policy which alone has enabled them to establish permanent contacts and influence in Rome, though to be sure not without frequent conflicts and differences of opinion. But the "super-ordinate interest of the universal church" (Casaroli) that the Vatican thereby defends is the monarchical central authority of the Pope, which basically has not been touched by any reforms. Even a Polish Pope like John Paul II, who began his pontificate in Autumn 1978 with an avowal of stronger "collegiality" between Pope and bishops, can only alter the personal style, the form of expression, of this authority, not its dogmatically-based principle. It is also the expression of the institutional conception of the church which has remained peculiar to the Roman church—as to no other Christian church—even after the Second Vatican Council, which "has to be seen in the light of tradition and in relation to the dogmatic definitions of the First Vatican Council" [which proclaimed the Pope's infallibility in

1870]—thus John Paul II on October 17, 1978. To discuss this, as I remarked at the beginning of this book, is a subject for theologians, not historians. Of course, the history of the last half century has also taught us that the Catholic church itself was never quite destroyed even where its outer framework nearly disappeared. But for this it always had to thank its attribute of neither admitting defeat, nor battling on to its own destruction. Again and again it answered the challenge of Marxism, of Leninism, of Stalinism, of Post-Stalinism, of the old and the new generation of Communist authorities: not only in defense and negation, but also in examination of its own conscience, with re-consideration, with delimitations and adaptations, with the whole armor of an institution that is—let us not forget—almost forty times as old as Lenin's Soviet Union.

Like all church history, that of the Vatican's Ostpolitik also knows advances, retreats, compromise, the clash of weapons and ceasefires. At its rear march many critics who use the Pontiff as whipping-boy for their short-term political interests, but also many admirers who confuse his fallibility as a historical figure with his supernatural claim as infallible teacher of his church. Vatican Ostpolitik, however, is part of that great historical panorama that stretches back two thousand years: popes went into exile and caesars to Canossa, saints were martyred and heretics burned, new doctrines were condemned and—accepted if the time was right and the earth turned. . . .

But always there was a consciousness or at least a subconscious awareness of the fact that in the Occidental cultural complex no idea, no "doctrine" and no "heresy" can arise that is not bound by an "umbilical cord" to a Christian origin. It can never be broken—as little as can the cycles of fighting and peace.

Notes

Introduction

1. Quoted from König's interview for the Catholic weekly "Rheinischer Merkur" (Cologne), June 23, 1978.
2. Cf. "Religion und Atheismus heute," East Berlin, 1966, p. 135. As Vasily Furov (vice-chairman of the Moscow Council for Religious Affairs) said to editors of the "Bolshaya Sovetskaya Entsiklopedia," 876,000 babies were baptized in the Soviet Union in 1975.
3. Cf. Johannes Chrysostomus [Plaśkevic], "Die Problematik der heutigen russischen Kirche des Moskauer Patriarchats" (Festschrift für Bernhard Stasiewski, Beiträge zur ostdeutschen und osteuropaeischen Kirchengeschichte, Cologne/Vienna, 1975).
4. Texts of the letters of the priest-dissidents in "Ostkirchliche Studien," Würzburg (Vol. 23, March 1974), pp. 40-46. To the question of the Orthodox catacomb churches and their criticism of the Vatican's attitude, see discussion in the emigrant paper "Novoe Russkoe Slovo" (New York), 12/31/77, 1/8 and 2/7/78, and J. Chrysostomus in "Der Christliche Osten" (Würzburg) 1978, no. 2, pp. 52f.
5. Author's taped interview with Alessandrini, Oct. 17, 1972.
6. "Prima la carità, poi la verità, anche nella storia"—First love, then truth, in history too, said Cardinal de Lai to Ludwig von Pastor, who remarked: "If that were right, all historiography would cease" (cf. "Tagebücher" [Diaries], p. 695).
7. Tape interview by the author with Casaroli, March 28, 1973.
8. Quoted from Casaroli's lecture in Milan, 1/20/1972 (in "Civiltà Cattolica"), his interview for "Die Presse" (Vienna), 12/21/1974, his lectures in Vienna on 11/17/77 and in Linz, Austria, on 11/18/77 (complete text in the *Osservatore Romano* of 6/7 Feb. and 17 Feb. 1978; German text in "Oesterreichische Zeitschrift für Aussenpolitik," vol. 6/1977).
9. This summary is based on the Dogmatic Constitution of Vatican Council II, "Lumen Gentium", ch. I no. 8, ch. II no. 9, ch. IV no. 38, on the Pastoral Constitution "De Ecclesia in mundo huius tempore" (The Church in the World), ch. IV no. 40, Pope John Paul II Encyclical "Redemptor Hominis" III, 13, Casaroli's interview in "Die Presse" (cf. note 8) and a lecture of Benelli's in Vienna on May 4, 1976 (French original text in "Documentation Catholique" no. 1677, June 6, 1976).
10. See also H. Stehle, "Some Aspects of State Policy towards Religion and Church Policy" (in "Concilium," May 1977, The Seabury Press, New York).
11. The author was also in the Pope's airplane during John Paul II's travels to Poland, Mexico, and the USA.

Chapter I

1. An eyewitness report by Zofja Licharewa in the Polish Jesuit newspaper *Oriens*, Krakow, August-September 1935, p. 104.

2. Quoted by Gervais Quenard in the *Pages d'Archives*, an internal publication of the Assumptionist Order (Augustinian), Paris 1955.

3. Eduard Baron von der Ropp (1851-1939), born in Liksna. Convert. Pastor in Libau (Lithuania), 1902 Bishop of Tiraspol, 1904 of Vilna, 1905 Duma representative, 1907 exiled, 1917 Bishop of Mogilev, after 1920 in exile in Warsaw; he died there shortly before the beginning of World War II.

4. Sheptyckyj (1865-1944), a member of the Ukrainian aristocracy, Polonized in the 19th century (his brother was a Polish general). 1900 Archbishop of Lemberg (Polish Lvóv, Ukrainian Lviv) and metropolitan of Halyc and Kamieniec for some five million Uniate Ruthenians (Ukrainians) in Austrian Galicia. After the Russian invasion (September 3, 1914) he was arrested and exiled to a convent 200 miles east of Moscow, freed in 1917. He died on November 1, 1944, in Lemberg, which after 1918 belonged to Poland, was occupied by the Russians in 1939, the Germans in 1941, and since July 27, 1944, belongs to the Soviet Union. (Cf. Korolevsjij, Cyrill, "Metropolite Andre Szeptyckyj," Roma, 1964).

5. Leonid Feodorov (1879-1936). Born of a Russian family, converted to the Catholic church in Rome in 1902, entered the Studite order. 1917 Exarch of the Russian Catholics without episcopal rank (acc. to *Annuario Pontificio* of 1930: subordinate to the Archbishop of Mogilev as Vicar General for the Catholics of the Slavic-Byzantine rite). 1923-26 in prison and penal camp, then under house arrest and in Siberian exile, died March 7, 1936. (Biography by Paul Mailleux SJ: Exarch Leonid Feodorov, Bridge-builder between Rome and Moscow, New York, 1964; see also *Oriens*, Krakow 1935.)

6. Polish Professor Stanislaw Trzeciak in the Krakow *Czas*, Nr. 336/1921.

7. Lenin: Ausgewählte Werke in 12 Bänden, Vienna-Moscow, Vol. 11, p. 397ff. (Lenin: Selected Works.)

8. Sammlung der Gesetze und Verordnungen der Arbeiter- und Bauernregierung Nr. 18 (quoted from N. Struve: Die Christen in der UdSSR, Mainz 1965, p. 461.) (Collection of Laws and Regulations of the Worker and Peasant Regime).

9. For text see Struve, p. 374. This also contains an exact description of the situation of the Orthodox church at this time.

10. Resolution of the 5th session of the state Commission on Education of April 24, 1918 (see *Isvestia* of September 5, 1918).

11. This and the following presentation of the events concerning Ropp are based primarily on the "Kronika archidyecezji mohylowskiej," to be found in the Cieplak Archive of the Roman Catholic Union, Chicago. (See also James Zatko SVD: Descent into Darkness, Notre Dame, Indiana, 1965.)

12. See Wilhelm's Memoirs: Ereignisse und Gestalten, 1922, p. 255.

13. Bayerisches Geheimes Staatsarchiv (Bavarian Secret State Archives, BStA), Munich, file 967 (Bayer. Gesandtschaft beim Päpstl. Stuhl); see also *Bayerischer Kurier*, May 13, 1919.

14. BStA, File 967, Päpstl. Stuhl, Reports nr. 139 and 169.

15. Reported by Bishop Michel d'Herbigny in a speech to the 'Circolo di Studi sull 'Oriente cristiana' in Palermo on March 14, 1930. Pius XI (Ratti) later remarked "plus d'une fois" (more than once) to Gervais Quenard, the Superior General of the Assumptionist Order, that he would have preferred going to Kiev and Charkow instead of Poland (*Pages d'Archives*, nr. 11, 1959, p. 381).

16. According to Ludwig von Pastor (Tagebücher [Diaries], p. 818), this is how the Belgian Ambassador Beyens understood it during a papal audience (on September 27, 1924). Eduard Winter (Die Sowjetunion und der Vatikan, Bd. 3, p. 23) quotes this passage incorrectly and writes that Ratti had twice "telephoned" Lenin.

17. Thus Cardinal Gasparri in Autumn 1916 to Roman Dmowski (Polityka polska i odbudowa panstwa, Warsaw 1925, p. 208). Cf. also Andrzej Micewski: Roman Dmowski, Warsaw 1971, p. 227 f.

18. Gasparri said to Ludwig von Pastor, the Peace of Versailles and of St. Germain would "cause ten wars" (Tagebücher, p. 681), and on May 13, 1921, the Cardinal Secretary of State told the Bavarian ambassador that Poland's only chance of existence was to rely on its eastern *or* western neighbors. Since no help could be expected from the east, it was foolish to burn the

bridges to the west; "Poland will someday suffer greatly from this, when Germany has recovered" (BStA, file 980, Päpstl. Stuhl).

19. Ks. Jan Gnatowski: Z Polski do Rzymu—Papiez Pius XI, p. 82-84 (a hymnic biography of Ratti probably published in 1923); in contrast, the unobjectively critical biography by Jaroslaw Jurkiewicz: Nuncjatura Achillesa Ratti w Polsce, Warsaw 1953. The so-called "miracle on the Vistula," the salvation of Warsaw from the Red Army, which Gnatowski ascribes to divine assistance, represented by Ratti, brings Jurkiewicz—in the Stalinistic interpretation—back to the "traitors" Trotsky and Tuchatschevski.

20. Information from Professor Federico Alessandrini, Vatican (see also Curzio Malaparte: Technique du coup d'Etat, Paris 1931 p. 118-119 [Malaparte in 1920 was attaché in the Italian legation in Warsaw]).—For Isaak Babel see: Budjonnys Reiterarmee, dtv-edition, Munich 1961, p. 10.

21. Lenin's speech at the All-Russian Women Workers' Conference on November 19, 1918 (quoted from Schachnovitch, p. 540). Cf. also the list of acts of violence in a warning from the Justice Commissariat of December 1918 (in: Voprossij istorij, Moscow, V, 1958, pp. 16-20).

22. Quoted from Schachnovitch (p. 528), who however is silent on Lenin's reply to the Vatican.

23. The exchange of telegrams was printed in full in the Osservatore Romano of April 2, 1919. Eduard Winter speaks erroneously of only a "short reference," p. 27; the Soviet documentary publication of 1958, from which Winter quotes, omits Chicherin's grotesquely tasteless remarks about the opening of the reliquaries and contains numerous errors in translation.

24. By "Czechoslovaks" is meant members of a "Czechoslovakian Legion" formed of former Austro-Hungarian prisoners of war who fought against the Bolsheviks in Siberia. Admiral A.W. Kolchak (b. 1874, executed 1920) in Siberia, and General A.A. Denikin (b. 1872, d. 1947 in the USA) in the North Caucasus, formed "white" anti-Bolshevik armies. S. Petljura (b. 1879, murdered in Paris in 1926) led the independence movement in 1919 and an anti-Communist army of Ukrainians.

25. See note 26.

26. See Osservatore Romano of December 28, 1919. The version offered in previous literature, that Ropp was exchanged for Lenin's collaborator Karl Radek (in prison in Berlin since January 1919) is not confirmed by the documents. It is also improbable, since Radek was released only in December 1919 in exchange for German "agents." Another assumption by Schachnovitch (p. 528) is also false; according to this, Ropp was exchanged for a group of Communists who had been arrested in Poland and "treacherously murdered" by Polish troops while crossing the border. However, this event took place almost a year earlier, in January 1919, and concerned a Soviet Red Cross delegation which was first interned in Warsaw, was supposed to be banished, but then was shot unexplainedly—by border police or bandits?—(see Kowalski: Zarys Historii Polskiego Ruchu Robotniczego, Warsaw 1962, p. 117-118, and Adam Krzyzanowski, Dzieje Polski, Paris 1973, p. 57). Finally, in Anthony Rhodes' book "The Vatican in the Ages of Dictators 1922-1945" (New York, 1973) (otherwise very superficial) is found the absurd story that Ropp had fled to Tabris with the help of Persian carpet dealers.

27. The Vatican newspaper reporter also thinks that he heard that Ropp was to have been shot the night of May 20, 1919. But the quoted "Kronika" of the Archdiocese of Mogilev, which describes every detail of Ropp's imprisonment, knows nothing about this.

28. See Schlesische Volkszeitung, March 8, 1921.

29. See Zatko, loc. cit., p. 82-88.

30. Ibid., p. 19ff.

31. Feodorov's letter to Lenin of March 30, 1919, and the reply in Bontsch-Brujevitch: Isbranje sotschinenja, Vol. 1, 1959, p. 351ff.—Feodorov's letter to the Pope in Mailleux, loc. cit., Budkiewicz' letter to the nuncio in Zatko, loc. cit., p. 199/120.

32. Statement of the People's Commissariat for Justice of the Ukrainian Soviet Republic (quoted in Codevilla: Stato e Chiesa nell'Unione Sovietica, p. 116).

33. See *Pravda*, April 21, 1921. (Quoted in Schachnovitch, loc. cit., p. 544).

34. See *Oriens*, Krakow, May-June 1935, p. 105. According to the Great Soviet Encyclopedia, Vol. XVI, "Famine," two million people starved at that time.

35. Nansen-Hauptmann-Gorki: Russland und die Welt, Berlin, 1922. In this publication Nansen, who as High Commissioner of the League of Nations for Refugees organized the first famine relief action, first published shocking photos from the disaster area. The most extensive photo documentation of the famine disaster in *Orientalia Christiana* no. 14, April-May 1925.—Michel d'Herbigny SJ: L'Aide Pontificale aux Enfants affamés de Russie. This text was also published in Russian, tr. by Serge Wolkonski. See also Fischer, H. H., *The Famine in Soviet Russia 1919-1923. The Operations of the American Relief Administration*, New York (Macmillan), 1927.

36. Waclaw Vorovski, b. 1871, murdered in Lausanne by Russian emigrants on May 10, 1923 (his monument in Moscow). For Vorovski's personality see D. Schub: Lenin, Wiesbaden 1948, p. 82f. and 311/312. (Lenin: A Biography. Penguin 1976).

37. In Rome, the Archive of the General Offices of the "Societas Verbi Divini" (SVD), among others, is accessible, the so-called Steyler Missionary Order. I am indebted to a collection of sources by the Order's historian Father Johann Kraus, compiled for a work on the participation of the Order in the famine relief, for many references in this book: Im Auftrag des Papstes in Russland, Veröffentlichung des Missionspriesterseminars St. Augustin, Siegburg 1970. From this archive, other important documents for the present book could be utilized, for which I have to thank Father Bornemann. The reports of the German Embassy to the Holy See are very informative; they are available in the Political Archive of the Foreign Office in Bonn (PAAA).

38. Wilhelm von Braun (1883-1941) had several siblings, and was thus not sole heir (cf. "Gotha"-Handbuch 1934). At the beginning of the thirties he was temporarily a novice in the Benedictine Order (in Niederaltaich/Bavaria and Cava/Italy). In 1976, old monks could still remember that Braun had a photo showing him together with Lenin. His unstable life is said to have led him temporarily to China at the end of the twenties. His special protector and friend since 1913 was the later Cardinal Pizzardo. It is documented in portions of his papers (in possession of the von Braun family) that W.v. Braun was arrested in Munich in 1935 "under § 175" (homosexuality), and delivered to the Dachau concentration camp, and died six years later, probably from ill-treatment, in the Buchenwald concentration camp (where he was interned in the so-called "Prominentenbau" [prominent prisoner building]).

39. Johannes Steinmann (1870-1940), distinguished in 1914 with the title of "papal privy chamberlain"; spiritual consultant at the German Embassy to the Holy See from November 1921 to May 1940.

40. Giuseppe Pizzardo (1877-1970) became titular archbishop in 1930, Cardinal in 1937; he was active for almost 50 years in several congregations, and above all also in the Vatican Secretariat of State.

41. See the reports of the Procurator General Carl Friedrich, who was brought into the negotiations, in the SVD Archive, Rome (Kraus, loc. cit., p. 21-24).

42. Copy of the text, covered with added "conditions" and signed by Pizzardo, in the SVD Archive, Rome (Gehrmann papers); see Kraus, loc. cit., p. 190.

43. See Kraus, loc. cit., p. 24-25.

44. See Pastor, loc. cit., p. 711 and p. 717.—On December 29, 1921, Benedict XV told Pastor, the Austrian ambassador to the Holy See: "Now I ask you as a historian of the church: Don't you consider it providential that instead of the Luther jubilee, the Protestant empire has collapsed?"

45. Report by Bishop d'Herbigny SJ in an address in Palermo on March 14, 1930 (printed by the "Circolo di Studi sull'Oriente cristiana," p. 15).

46. This and the following account are based primarily on two detailed, confidential reports by Steinmann (of March 23, 1922 and May 18, 1923) to Ago von Maltzan in the Foreign Office, Berlin; see PAAA, Abt. IV, Russia; Pol 16, Vol. 1, K 480 041-53 and Vol. 4, K480 211.

47. See Nino Lo Bello: The Vatican Empire, New York, 1968. The statement seems all the

more credible as Lo Bello otherwise is more inclined to overestimate the financial strength of the Vatican.

48. Text of the decree of February 26, 1922, in W. C. Einhardt: Religion in Soviet Russia, London 1929, p. 46.—An official Soviet publication openly admitted that the forced delivery of valuable objects of worship was intended to deal "a final blow" to religion, and not only to obtain money to purchase grain (see V. Let Vlastji Sovietov, Moscow 1922, p. 292).

49. The agreement was briefly mentioned—without date or contents—in the *Osservatore Romano* (April 7, 1922), with date in the "Great Soviet Encyclopedia" under the catchword "Gasparri" (Vol X, 261).

50. For insight into the text of von Braun's memorandum the author is indebted to the Archive of the SVD General Office, Rome (a short allusion to it in Kraus, loc. cit., p. 35 note). —Dr. Erich Alexander (b. 1880) was also a member of the Deutsche Orientgesellschaft [German Orient Society].

51. See the thorough monograph of Dr. G. Gerschuni: Die Konzessionspolitik Sowjetrusslands, Berlin 1927. —At the Soviet Congress of Arsamas a peasant cried: "Do not sell our Mother Russia for concessions" (Gerschuni, p. 51).

52. Diego von Bergen (1872-1944) was envoy after 1919, then from 1921 to April 1943 ambassador of the German Reich to the Vatican.

53. Edmund Walsh, b. 1885 in Boston; after his studies, in Dublin, London, and Innsbruck (Austria); professor at Georgetown (D.C.) after 1918; founded a Foreign Service School there; died 1956. His papers in the Archive of Georgetown University (see Gallagher, Louis, S.J., *Edmund Walsh, S.J., A Biography*, New York, 1962).

Chapter II

1. See Archbishop Signori's description to a correspondent of the *Corriere della Sera* (April 30, 1922), and in a letter of Signori's of April 23, 1922, to Monsignore Roncalli (the later Pope John XXIII), quoted in Giancarlo Zizola: L'Utopia di Papa Giovanni, Assisi 1973, p. 176-77.

2. For the personality of Josef Wirth (1879-1956) see Thomas A. Knapp's biographical portrait in: Zeitgeschichte in Lebensbildern. Aus dem deutschen Katholizismus des 20. Jahrhunderts, Mainz 1973 (p. 160ff). For the history of the Rapallo treaty see F.A. Krummacher and Helmut Lange: Krieg und Frieden—Geschichte der deutsch-sowjetischen Beziehungen, Munich 1970, p. 126ff.

3. See Ernesto Buonaiuti: La Chiesa e il Comunismo, Milan 1945, p. 13. —Buonaiuti (1881-1946), as a Catholic theologian, was the leading spokesman of Italian "modernism." Ordained as priest in 1908, he was professor of church history in Rome until 1921 and a friend of Cardinal Gasparri (whose statements he claims to repeat "word for word"). In 1924 Buonaiuti was excommunicated.

4. The "most serious fears" that Cardinal Gasparri expressed to the Austrian Ambassador Ludwig von Pastor about the Rapallo treaty on May 1, 1922, related to the fact that church interests were not yet taken into consideration in this treaty, nor in the Genoa conference in general. Gasparri by no means repudiated the Rapallo policy as such (as Winter claims, p. 63); on the contrary, the Vatican made use of the improved German-Soviet relations from the treaty for years (which Winter does not even mention).

5. For Pastor, see Hof- und Staatsarchiv, Vienna, Papal See, Curia 87, Z113, no. 260. — Winter quotes this statement quite uncritically, without source (cf. note 4).

6. Thus the author Dimitri S. Mereshkovkij (1865-1941) in an open letter to the Pope on May 7, 1922, in which he also spoke of the fact that now "the hands that touch the holy host shake the bloody hands of murderers" (Graham, loc. cit., p. 456). Soviet dissidents raised similar reproaches 50 years later.

7. *Ordine Nuovo*, May 15, 1922, no. 134 (see Togliatti: Opere, Vol. I, p. 137).

8. French original text in the *Osservatore Romano* of May 15/16, 1922.

9. This and the following statement are based on the report (in facsimile on p. 48) of Ago

von Maltzan (1877-1927) of the German Foreign Office (PAAA, Abt. IV; Russia, Pol 16, K 480058), as well as on a private letter of Monsignore Steinmann to Reich chancellor Wirth of May 18, 1922, that was made available to me from Wirth's bequest (which is not yet accessible). See also H. Graf Kessler: Tagebücher, Wiesbaden 1961, p. 317, where a report of Maltzan's is quoted.

10. Georgi Vasilievich Chicherin (1872-1936), son of an aristocratic land holder, 1904 social democrat, 1905-1907 emigrant in Berlin and Munich, 1914 in England, 1917 Bolshevik, 1918-1930 Soviet People's Commissar for Foreign Affairs. Maksim Maksimovich Litvinov (1876-1951), Bolshevik since 1903, emigrant in Switzerland, 1918-1920 diplomatic representative in London, 1921-1930 deputy People's Commissar for Foreign Affairs, 1930-1939 People's Commissar for Foreign Affairs, 1941-1943 ambassador in Washington.

11. Graham, loc. cit., p. 453, and Katholische Kirchenzeitung, Salzburg, no. 20/1922.

12. Struve, loc. cit., p. 38.

13. For the original French text of the correspondence see Osservatore Romano of June 18, 1922. Gasparri used the address V.S.=Vossignoria=Esquire.

14. The originals of both letters as well as a thank-you note from Wirth to the Pope of June 1, 1922, all previously unknown, were made available to me from Wirth's bequest (which is not yet accessible). Wirth later used to show the papal picture, with the dedication relating to Rapallo, to people who suspected him of being "all too leftist" or even a "salon Bolshevik." (The picture disappeared after the German Gestapo searched his Parisian emigrant apartment in 1940—when Wirth had retreated to Switzerland.) Wirth's domestic political course displeased the Vatican; when the chancellor, after the murder of Reich Foreign Minister Rathenau, cried out to the right-radical opponents of Rapallo in the Reichstag: ". . . the enemy is on the right," Cardinal Gasparri criticized this formulation (see report by Pastor in the HStA-Vienna, Papal See/K82/no. 302).

15. Von Bergen's coded telegram of August 9, 1922 (PAAA, Abt. IV, Russland, Pol. 16, Vol. 2, no. 97). Vicar General Budkiewicz' report from Petrograd to the papal nuncio in Warsaw of September 1922. Text in Zatko, loc. cit, p. 196ff.

16. See also the report of the Moscow correspondent of the Berliner Tageblatt, Paul Scheffer, of December 17, 1922: "A gigantic housecleaning . . . tens of thousands of boxes full of church valuables . . . In the provinces . . . many things . . . were senselessly destroyed right there. . . . A strict darkness lies over the fate of these innumerable objects. . . ." (P. Scheffer: Augenzeuge im Staate Lenins, Munich [Piper] 1972, p. 129f.). Up to the middle of 1923, only 700,000 gold rubles from the sale of the church treasures had found their way into foreign trade (see I. Frohberger: Sturm über Russland, Cologne 1930, p. 22).

17. See Michel d'Herbigny: L'Aide Pontificale aux Enfants affamés de Russie, Orientalia Christiana, Vol. IV-1, Rome 1925, p. 27.

18. On June 4, 1922, Pravda had published the first bulletin about Lenin's advancing fatal illness.

19. This and the following according to letters by Fathers Eduard Gehrmann (July 15, 1922) and Heinrich Pöping (August 14, 1922) quoted in Kraus, loc. cit., p. 37-41.

20. The apostolic document was not published in the Osservatore Romano until July 26, 1922, the day of the relief mission's departure.

21. See Kraus, loc. cit., p. 177/178. Of course, it must be remembered that at this time, especially in Germany, inflation severely limited financial options.

22. See Gehrmann's final report of July 23, 1924 for the German embassy in Moscow (PAAA, Abt. 11b, Vatikan, Pol. 3, K624559-K624569).

23. Thus the Catholic Center Party paper Germania of June 27, 1924.

24. A copy of the authorization with the headline "Declaration" is found in PAAA, Geheimakten 320/3, 4/Russia, Pol. 16, Rel. u. Kirchenwesen, K105169.

25. Ambassador von Bergen's telegram of August 9, 1922 (PAAA, Abt. IV A, Russland, Pol 16, Vol. 2).

26. See no. 34/1923 of the party paper Krasni Krim.

27. Report of the Bavarian ambassador Otto Ritter von Groenesteyn from his papal audience of February 14, 1923 (BStA, file 991, Päpstl. Stuhl).

28. See Kraus, loc. cit., p. 95-100.
29. See Zatko, loc. cit., p. 147-149.
30. See McCullagh: The Bolshevik Persecution of Christianity, London 1924 (German edition: Paderborn 1926); Joseph Ledit: Archbishop Cieplak, Montreal, 1963; Zatko, loc. cit., Mailleux, loc. cit.
31. See Feodorov's letter of March 7, 1923 to Archbishop Sheptyckyj in Lemberg (quoted in Oriens, Krakow, May/June 1935). See also p. 393, note 5.
32. See Zatko, loc. cit., p. 148. Text of the amnesty decree in McCullagh, loc. cit., p. 144, also Isvestia of March 30, 1923. Cf. J. Ledit, Archbishop John Cieplak, Montreal 1963.
33. See Isvestia no. 62/1923. The Osservatore Romano of April 14, 1923, quotes this article of Marchlevski's and declares that the Holy See did not want "in the least to interfere in things that did not concern it"; it was only concerned with continuing its relief action for starving Russia.—Marchlevski, b. 1865, father Polish merchant, mother the daughter of a Westphalian officer, Auguste von Rückersfeld. Marchlevski died in 1925 in Bogliasco, Italy; equally prominent in the Russian, Polish and German Communist Parties, he represented "national Bolshevist" opinions and wanted, in his words, to "do it better" than Lenin.
34. This opinion is also held by McCullagh, who personally experienced the trial in Moscow (loc. cit., p. 114 and 117). Lenin had been unable to work since March 3, 1923, because of his third stroke. —Sikorski's speech in the senate session of March 27, 1923 (Sprawozdanie stenogr. XVII 1923, p. 2-4). The Soviet ambassador in Poland was the former Prince Obolenski.
35. The French text of this instruction in a telegram of Ambassador von Bergen of April 9, 1923 (PAAA, Abt. IV, Russland, Pol. 16, Vol. 2, Tel. no. 34).
36. Gasparri to Bavarian ambassador Ritter on April 12, 1923 (BStA, file 991, Päpst. Stuhl, report no. 23) and on April 13, 1923, to Pastor (HStA Vienna, Päpst. Stuhl, K 87, report no. 442)—Winter (loc. cit., p. 71) quotes Pastor's report without an exact source reference, distorting the meaning by leaving out Gasparri's reference to the "blood of martyrs."
37. Cieplak's letter to the Papal Relief Mission in Moscow on December 19, 1922 (Cieplak archive).
38. To Maltzan, May 18, 1923 (PAAA, Abt. IV, Russland, Pol. 16, Vol. 3, no. K 480211). The following description of the conference in the Vatican of May 4, 1923, follows this report in substance (see also Kraus, loc. cit., p. 99/100).
39. Personal letter from Wirth to Maltzan of July 17, 1923 (copy in the author's possession). Wirth repeats Gasparri's quote word for word in French. On this visit to Rome, Wirth "posed as rightist," reports the Bavarian ambassador Ritter (BStA, file 991, Päpst Stuhl, report no. 133). But Ritter also quotes a statement of Wirth's in Rome: "The German worker will again present big industry with a terrible bill."
40. Ulrich Count von Brockdorff-Rantzau (1869-1928), lawyer, before the First World War ambassador in Copenhagen, 1919 Reich Foreign Minister for four months; he resigned rather than sign the Treaty of Versailles. In a note of July 4, 1942, Chancellor Wirth calls Rantzau the "most remarkable man I have ever met." Rantzau had stipulated that he should not be subordinated as ambassador to "the asses" [Scheisskerlen] in the Foreign Office and that he should be allowed to report directly to the Reich President (Ebert); he had roared "like the bull of Uri" that he was going to Moscow to take "revenge for Versailles." —According to a report by Rantzau's personal secretary Andor Hencke (of March 16, 1974) Rantzau admired the Vatican because "law and order" still ruled there, and he hoped to become ambassador to the Holy See someday. (See also E. Stern-Rubarth: Graf Brockdorff-Rantzau, 1929 [new edition: Herford, 1968] and H. Helbig: Die Moskauer Mission des Grafen B.-R. in: Forschungen zur osteuropäischen Geschichte, Vol. 2, Berlin 1955.)
41. Walsh memorandum of June 23, 1923 (A.E.S., Vatican; copy in the Gehrmann papers in the SVD Archive, Rome).
42. Quoted in Kraus, op. cit. p. 133.
43. Some Russian employees of the Vatican mission, but also Russians it had helped, were suspected because of "unproletarian origin" and discredited; the secret police (GPU) watched

the mission continuously. This was very visually described by the secretary of the mission at the time, the former Princess Natalia Volkonska, who later married the German journalist Paul Scheffer and published her memoirs under a pseudonym (Natalia Petrova: Twice Born in Russia. My life before and in the Revolution, New York 1930, p. 168ff.).—On the other hand, how Walsh discontinued the famine relief in summer 1923 follows from statistics contained in a report of the German embassy in Moscow—based on Gehrmann's information (PAAA, Abt. IV A, Russia, Pol. 16, Vol. 3 K624559-K624569).

44. Quoted in Kraus, op. cit., p. 102, note 40.

45. Letter of September 20, 1923 (Gehrmann papers in SVD Archive, Rome).

46. Kraus, op. cit., p. 127, finds this "strange" and does not recognize Walsh's tactics.

47. Rantzau's report of November 26, 1923 (PAAA, Abt. IV A, Russland, Pol. 16, Vol. 3, K480263). The following remark of Chicherin's is also reproduced in this report.

48. Report of SVD procurator general Friedrich of November 15, 1923, from Rome to Steyl (SVD Archive, Rome).

49. See note 47. —It is probable that Rantzau's "reliable source" was Father Gehrmann, who made no secret of his "factual contrast" to Walsh (see Kraus, op. cit., p. 116) and was very close to Rantzau, who even helped him with the composition of reports to Rome (information from Rantzau's secretary Andor Hencke on March 16, 1974).

50. Bergen's report of December 3, 1923 (PAAA, Abt. IV A, Russia, Pol. 16, Vol. 3, K480268/69).

51. Rantzau's report of December 7, 1923 (PAAA, Abt. IV A, Russia, Pol. 16, Vol. 3, K480278). The Moscow ambassador adds that he was "very far from wanting to make myself an advocate for the Soviet government."

52. Gehrmann's report to Steyl of November 24, 1923 (Gehrmann papers in SVD Archive, Rome).

53. The reliquary was kept until 1938 in the Roman Jesuit church "Il Gesu," where a part of the relic (the right arm) remains until today. Bobola was canonized in 1938 by the Pope, and his remains conveyed to Warsaw, where they are interred today in a Jesuit chapel in the street named for the saint, then for a Soviet cosmonaut (Ulica Sw. Boboli, then Komarova Chodkievicza Mokotow) (see also Louis J. Gallagher SJ and Paul V. Donovan: The Life of Saint Andrew Bobola of the SJ, Martyr, Manchester/USA 1939, and Kraus, op. cit., p. 82).

54. Schachnovitch remarks in retrospect: "As the masses turned away from the church, a great interest in religious matters arose among them in the years 1922 to 1928" (op. cit., p. 554).

55. See Schachnovitch, op. cit., p. 562/563 and John Shelton Curtiss: The Russian Church and the Soviet State (1917-1950), Boston 1953 (Munich 1957, p. 194ff).

56. Quoted in S. Shub: Lenin, p. 439.

57. For the reference to Viktor Bede I am indebted to Prof. Federico Alessandrini (Vatican) as well as a report of the German Ambassador von Bergen of August 15, 1929 (PAAA, Abt. II, Vatican-Russia, Pol. 3, Vol. 2). —Bede's first anonymous article appeared in the Osservatore Romano of August 23, 1924: "Pensieri di Lenin sul cattolicesimo," the second as a reply to numerous, probably also critical, skeptical letters on September 24, 1924: "Il problema russo nel pensiero di Lenin." That Bede enjoyed the trust of the Vatican at the time is shown by his position in the preparatory committee for the Holy Year 1925, to which he was appointed by Mons. Nogara, the Secretary General of the Highest Council for Missions (Consiglio Superiore Generale della Pontificia Opera della Propagazione della Fede). Bede died ca. 1930 in San Remo (cf. Hudal, "Römische Tagebücher," Graz, 1976, p. 159/160).

58. Concerning these events see Giorgio Pini: Geschichte des Faschismus, Berlin 1941, p. 198ff. —Alcide De Gasperi: Lettere sul Concordato, Brescia 1971, p. 198—L'Unita of February 18, 1974.

59. Bergen's report of December 3, 1923 (PAAA, Abt. IV A, Russland, Pol. 16, Vol. 3, K480268-69), Pastor's report of December 14, 1923 (HStA-Vienna, K87/Z172/no. 579 and Z177/no. 587). See also report from Warsaw in the New York Times of December 30, 1923.

60. Father Eduard Gehrmann, b. 1888 in East Prussia, d. 1960 in Siegburg/Rheinland. 1922-1924 in Russia, 1925-1945 secretary of the Vatican nunciature in Berlin, 1950-1960 hospital priest.

61. Quoted in Kraus, op. cit., p. 123.
62. Instruction of the People's Commissariat of the Interior of December 22, 1923, no. 461, and "authentic interpretation" of the same of March 16, 1924, no. 18711 (see Codevilla, op. cit., p. 238).
63. Report of December 3, 1923 (see note 59).
64. Ritter's report of November 13, 1923 (BStA, file 991, Papal See).
65. See Pastor's report quoted in note 59 and his report of February 15, 1924 (HStA-Vienna, K87/Z21—no. 615).
66. Letter to Msgr. Pizzardo of January 12, 1924; quoted in Kraus, op. cit., p. 139.
67. So Kraus judges, op. cit., p. 138, while Winter, op. cit. p. 67, tendentiously maintains: "The activity of twelve (!) clerics of the papal relief mission, who were missionaries first and foremost (?) . . . would naturally incite the counter-revolutionary forces in the Soviet Union. . . ."
68. Consistory address of May 23, 1923 (quoted in Graham, op. cit. p. 460).
69. See the confidential report by Giulio Roi SJ to Ambassador Brockdorff-Rantzau of July 31, 1924 (PAAA, Büro Reichsminister, Kurie Vol. 2, D701938-39) and the report of the German ambassador to the Holy See of February 10, 1925 (PAAA, Abt. 11b, Päpst. Stuhl, Pol.3, Vol 1, L233247-48). Cf. Also report of the Austrian ambassador to the Holy See of February 25, 1924 (HStA-Vienna, K87/Z21/no. 615).
70. Gehrmann in a letter to Steyl of January 13, 1924; the instructions to G. in a telegram of January 4, 1924 (PAAA, Abt. IV A, Russland, Pol. 16, Vol. 3, K480292).
71. Giulio Roi, b. 1870 in Vicenza, d. 1924 in Brescia, was rector of the Jesuit College in Milan, later in Gorizia (Görz) and Modena. His papers, like those of the other missionaries to Russia of the Jesuit Order, are to this day not accessible. Roi made himself known to the German ambassador in Moscow as a future Apostolic Delegate (see Brockdorff-Rantzau's report of July 31, 1924, see above note 69).
72. To Austrian ambassador Ludwig von Pastor (see his report of February 15, 1924, HStA-Vienna, K87/Z21/no. 615).
73. See the reports of Friedrich, February 21, 1923 and Gehrmann, July 19, 1924 (SVD Archive, quoted in Kraus, op. cit., p. 117) as well as the reports of the German ambassador to the Holy See of June 28, 1924 (PAAA, Abt. IV A, Russland, Pol. 16, Vol. 4, K480355) and the German embassy in Moscow of February 31, 1924 (PAAA, Büro Reichsminister, Kurie 70, Vol. 2, D701938).
74. To the German ambassador Brockdorff-Rantzau on January 31, 1924.
75. Cf. Kraus, op. cit., pp. 145 and 161.
76. The following is taken from a report of the SVD procurator general in Rome, Friedrich, of March 24, 1924.
77. See PAAA, Büro Reichsminister, Kurie 70, vol. 2, D701897.
78. This and the following are based on Brockdorff-Rantzau's report of March 31, 1924 (PAAA, Büro Reichsminister, Kurie 70, vol. 2, D701903/04).
79. Letter to Steyl of April 7, 1924.
80. Telegram of April 22, 1924. The Foreign Office probably did not relay it to Moscow and noted in the margin: "Unknown here which Braun is intended, and thus whether transmission is harmless." Braun never worked in the relief mission, as Winter erroneously claims. —op. cit., p. 78.
81. Brockdorff-Rantzau's report of April 16, 1924 (PAAA, Büro Reichsminister, Curia 70, vol. 2, D701915).
82. Cf. Lionel Kochan: Russland und die Weimarer Republik, Düsseldorf 1955, p. 94.
83. The Comintern in Moscow at this time supported the Irish nationalists against England. Karl Radek described the background of Cieplak's liberation to the German ambassador (see the latter's report of April 16, 1924). In conversation with the ambassador, Chicherin had already held out hope for Cieplak's release on March 31 (cf. reports D701903 and D701916 in PAAA, Büro Reichsminister, Curia 70, vol. 2).
84. Gehrmann reported this by telegram to the Vatican on May 31, however requested that the information be kept secret (PAAA, Büro Reichsminister, Curia 70, vol. 2, D701932).
85. To Austrian ambassador Pastor (HStA-Vienna, K87/Z39/no 662).

86. The following facsimile is located in PAAA, Abt. IV, Russia, Pol. 16, vol. 3.

87. See PAAA, Abt. IV, Russia Pol. 16, vol. 4, K480350.

88. Kraus, op. cit., p. 155.

89. In conversation with the Austrian ambassador Pastor (see his report in HStA-Vienna, K87/Z2/no. 773 of January 25, 1925).

90. Cf. Franciszek Rutkowski: Archbishop Cieplak, Warsaw 1934, p. 334/335. As late as 1975 [?], censoring instructions of Polish Communists said: "Any information concerning the Archbishop Jan Cieplak, d. 1925, is to be eliminated." (Cf. *Czarna Ksiega Cenzury w PRL,* Aneks, London, 1977.)

91. Cf. Gehrmann's letter of July 19, 1924.

92. See Kraus, op. cit., p. 167-71.

93. Gasparri's telegram to Roi (PAAA, Abt. IV, Russland, Pol. 16, vol. 4, K480355).

94. Brockdorff-Rantzau's report of March 31, 1924 (PAAA, Abt. IIb. Pol. 3, vol. 1, D701938). —Pacelli had travelled from Munich to Berlin on July 25 to meet with Brodovski.

95. Report of the Bavarian ambassador Ritter of April 12, 1924, whom the Vatican assured that Pacelli was negotiating in Berlin only about the mission's remaining and about "a bishopric in Russia"; there "could be no discussion of a rapprochement" (BStA, file 997, Päpst. Stuhl, no. 114).

96. Winter—op. cit., p. 77—repeats Chicherin's statement without exact source reference (Brockdorff's report concerning it is no. D701903), but suppresses Gasparri's dementi that I give here of April 25, 1924 (PAAA, Abt. IV A, Russia, Pol. 16, vol. 3, K480348). Oskar Simmel SJ even states incorrectly that the whole Soviet-Vatican negotiations had run aground on the supposed demands for "Catholic schools" (cf. *Communio* 6/1974, p. 558).

97. Thus according to Francis McCullagh, who saw the Cieplak trial in Moscow and investigated the afflictions of the Catholics: The Bolshevik Persecution of Christianity, London 1924, p. 322.

98. Cf. Zatko, op. cit., p. 183.

99. Cf. Brockdorff-Rantzau's report of November 6, 1924 (PAAA, Büro Reichsminister, Kurie 70, vol. 2, D701957) and Kraus, op. cit., p. 180.

100. Cf. PAAA, Abt. IV, Russland, Pol. 16, vol. 4, K624573.

Chapter III

1. Thus Ludwig von Pastor in a report of July 3, 1924 (HStA-Vienna, Päpst. Stuhl Z92).

2. Cf. Gehrmann's letter from Rome of September 30, 1924 (quoted in Kraus, op. cit., p. 183).

3. On this October 2, 1924, the *Osservatore Romano* announced neither the audience nor the return of the mission to Russia, but only the fact that the mission had left Russia on September 18.

4. Thus to Bavarian Ambassador Ritter on October 13, 1924 (BStA, file 997).

5. Fedukiewicz' letter, dated September 9, 1924, was printed on November 16, 1924, in the party paper *Kommunist*. The German consulate general in Kharkov considered it "if not dictated, at least influenced in its entire content" by the Political Police (cf. PAAA, Abt. IV A, Russland, Pol. 16, vol. 4, K624626-29). The authenticity of the letter, however, is confirmed by the fact that, after serving a prison sentence of eight months, Fedukiewicz committed suicide by self-immolation "in remorse over the letter" (report of the consulate general in Kharkov of May 3, 1925).

6. In the SVD Archive in Rome there is Gehrmann's outline of catchwords prepared for the papal audience: "Chicherin's message; A. text B. my difficulties."

7. Winter, op. cit., p. 79, claims that Gehrmann only wrote such a *political* report, and indeed had "the duty" of sending this sort of material from Russia. A there are (in PAAA, in the SVD Archive and in the Vatican Secret Archive) two more summary reports from Gehrmann (the one 33, the other 23 pages long), which deal with the Russian relief in exhaustive detail and statistics.

8. Cf. Ruth Fischer: Von Lenin zu Mao, Düsseldorf 1956, p. 27-29. After the defeat of the German Communist Party in 1923, the Communist International had met a dead-end; Stalin was fighting for power against both leftist and rightist deviations, i.e. "against the majority of the old Bolshevik cadre." In foreign affairs the "rightists" favored a moderate policy toward the capitalist countries, the "leftists" still believed in the world revolution. "In domestic affairs, however, the two directions were in agreement on many things."

9. Cf. note of legation counsellor Meyer-Rodehüser of January 31, 1925 (PAAA, Abt. IIb, Vatikan, Pol. 3, vol. 4, Vat. 96).

10. Cf. Kraus, op. cit., p. 185/86. —Wilhelm Schmidt (1868-1964) was the founder of the theory of an original monotheism among primitive peoples; he was interested in Communist atheism and the Russia mission—cf. his book, written under the pseudonym "Austriacus Observator": Germanentum, Slaventum, Orientvölker und die Balkanereignisse, Kempten 1917, and F. Bornemann in the journal Anthropos, no. 49/50, 1954/55. —Considering this background to the origin of Gehrmann's memorandum, Winter's claim (op. cit., p. 80) that Gehrmann had developed a "plan of a thirty-years' war [!] by the Vatican against the Soviet Union" seems particularly absurd.

11. Cf. Pastor: Tagebücher, p. 850, note of January 5, 1925. —Francesco Ragonesi (1850-1931) was a friend of Pastor's; Raffael Merry del Val (1865-1930) was a Spanish curial cardinal.

12. Brockdorff-Rantzau's telegram of November 6, 1924 (PAAA, Abt. IV, Russia, Pol. 16 vol. 1, D701957).

13. "Acta Apostolicae Sedis," vol. XVI (1924), p. 494/495. —Winter (op. cit., p. 81) translates "government" instead of "form of government" and "to recognize" instead of "to approve," thereby tendentiously coarsening the statement, which contains diplomatic latitude.

14. Cf. Pastor: Tagebücher, p. 804.

15. When Marx was received by the Pope in Rome in April 1925, he was reproached for it; he justified himself in a letter to Pius XI of July 18, 1925 (copy in the author's possession): "The German Center Party has never regarded political cooperation with Social Democracy as an ideal situation. . . . If the bourgeois parties burn their bridges to this mass party, the process of its de-radicalization will be interrupted and Social Democracy will again be forced more strongly to side with Communist radicalism. . . ."

16. This description and the quotes are based on a letter from Gehrmann to Steyl of February 7, 1925 (cf. "In Verbo Dei," Festschrift for the 50th anniversary of the origin of the missionary priests' seminary St. Augustin, Siegburg 1960, p. 167-194, a study by Johann Kraus about Gehrmann's activity in the Berlin nunciature until 1945).

17. The following presentation is based on a note of the Berlin Foreign Office on the strength of information from a confidant of the nuncio (Gehrmann?), of February 28, 1925 (PAAA, Abt. IV, Russia, Pol. 16, vol. 3, L233249) as well as a report of the German embassy in Moscow of February 10, 1926 (PAAA, Abt. II, Vatikan 153, K011983-84) and personal information from the Archive of the papal Secretariat of State of December 3, 1973.

18. J. M. Bonn, e.g., so describes him on the basis of a personal meeting (cf. his autobiography: So macht man Geschichte, Munich 1953).

19. See the statements of Father Leiber SJ, quoted by Tadeusz Breza: Das Eherne Tor, Munich 1960, p. 82/83.

20. Cf. Wieslaw Myslek: Kosciól katolicki w Polsce, Warsaw 1966, p. 28-33, and Franz Manthey: Polnische Kirchengeschichte, Hildesheim 1965, p. 259/260.

21. See Pastor, Tagebücher, p. 618 and p. 830.

22. These and the following, of course only fragmentary, details of the negotiations of 1925 are based on personal information from the Archive of the papal Secretariat of State of December 3, 1973; on a report from Brockdorff-Rantzau of February 10, 1926 (PAAA, Abt. II, Vatican 153, K011983-84); and on a telegram of Foreign Office advisor Köpke of February 16, 1926 to Brockdorff-Rantzau, in which he also passes on Pacelli's "warmest thanks for past and future mediations" (PAAA, Abt. II, Vatican 153, K011985-86).

23. Anatoli W. Lunacharski (1875-1933) was a Marxist receptive to modern music,

painting and literature. From 1906-1911 he wrote, in Italy, his work "Socialism and Religion." Lenin discussed the theory of "human idolatry" with him and Maxim Gorky on the Isle of Capri. As late as in 1925, Lunacharski regretted that "socialism had only surreptitiously embraced a few elements of the convictions and world views of the great idealists" (cf. Schachnovitch, op. cit., p. 435, 442 and 607). Cf. also an appreciation of Lunacharski in the *Osservatore Romano* of April 8, 1973.

24. The scene is described in great detail by d'Herbigny in "L'Aspect Religieuse de Moscou en Octobre 1925" (*Orientalia Christiana*, no. 20, Rome 1926, p. 222-231). First published in *Etudes* of December 5 and 20, 1925. German edition: Kreuz unter dem Sowjetstern, Illertissen 1926.

25. Michel d'Herbigny, b. 1880 in Lille, d. 1957 in Aix-en-Provence, dedicated his first work to the imperial university in St. Petersburg: Un Newmann Russe, Vladimir Soloviev 1853-1900 (ed. Beauchesne, Paris 1911), D'Herbigny was very productive as a theological writer; an index of 1930 lists 19 book titles. Cardinal Mercier of Mechelen (Brussels) wrote the foreword to his three-volume "Theologie der Offenbarung" (Theology of Revelation).

26. La Tyrannie Sovietique et la Malheur Russe, Paris, 1923, p. 2.

27. On May 28, 1923, the German ambassador to the Vatican reported that d'Herbigny had visited Nuncio Pacelli in Munich to discuss the ministry to Russian émigrants.

28. Cf. Alexander Solzhenitsyn: Der Archipel Gulag, Bern 1974, p. 332ff. (The Gulag Archipelago).

29. Thus states a report of the German embassy in Moscow of January 23, 1926 (PAAA, Abt. II, Vatican 84, L233323).

30. D'Herbigny: "L'Aspect. . . ,", op. cit. p. 189.

31. Ibid., p. 221.

32. Ibid., p. 244/245. "We need Catholic mysticism," said a participant to d'Herbigny, while another protested against Vvedenski's exposition: "That is Catholic, not Orthodox." When d'Herbigny told Archbishop Cieplak about it in Paris on October 20, 1925, the latter remembered: "Yes, even in the years before my trial, Vvedenski recommended frequent communion" (which is not customary for the Orthodox).

33. Cf. report of the German embassy in Moscow of January 23, 1926 (L233324-25).

34. In their newspaper they wrote: "Professor d'Herbigny, director of the Institute for Eastern Studies in Rome, has rendered a great service to the Holy Synod; after he had appeared in Moscow in October 1925, with the special goal of establishing contacts with the Tikhon adherents, he took the side of the Renovation." (Vestnik Sw. Syn. 1926, no. 6.)

35. Cf. *Pages d'Archives* of the Augustinian Assumptionist Order, Nouvelle Serie, no. 3, December 1955, p. 41.

36. D'Herbigny, "L'Aspect. . . ," loc. cit, p. 272-73.

37. Cf. *Völkischer Beobachter*, Munich, of December 10, 1925, which states of d'Herbigny that he knew as much about Russian conditions "as an Eskimo [Polarbewohner] about Chinese grammar" (the editor-in-chief of the NSDAP paper was the Baltic German "Russia expert" and Nazi ideologist Alfred Rosenberg).

38. In conversation with the Bavarian ambassador Ritter (cf. his report of April 13, 1924 [BStA, file 997, Papal See]).

39. Cf. memoir fragments in *Pages d'Archives*, Nouvelle Serie, no. 3, December 1955, p. 40.

40. Intended is the secret cooperation between the Reich army and the Red Army to circumvent the limitations on armaments imposed on Germany by the Treaty of Versailles; apparently the Vatican was informed about this cooperation which had been set in motion by Reichskanzler Wirth and General von Seeckt (cf. also Krummacher-Lange, op. cit., p. 185ff., and Lionel Kochan, op. cit., p. 85ff.).

41. Cf. PAAA, Büro Reichsminister, Kurie 70, vol. 2, no. K011983-87.

42. Cf. "Annuario Pontificio" 1930, p. 322.

43. For information about the events of March 20 and 27, 1926, I am indebted to personal information from the archives of the Papal Secretariat of State on December 3, 1973.

44. The description of d'Herbigny's second trip to Russia is based—unless other sources

are cited—on d'Herbigny's own report "Paques 1926 en Russie Sovietique," Paris 1926; (German: "Seelsorgefahrt in Russland," Illertissen 1929). In this report, of course, essential events—for instance the consecrations of bishops—are omitted. A fragment of previously unpublished memoirs of d'Herbigny, "Soixante ans Jesuite," 1955, was used to close such gaps, as well as memoirs of Father Gervais Quenard: Hier, Paris, 1955, p. 116-126. Cf. *Pages d'Archives*, Nouvelle Serie, no. 3, December 1955 and no. 11, October 1959, also "Annuario Pontificio" 1925 and 1930. See also Paul Lesourd, Le Jesuite Clandestin, Paris, 1976.

45. Report of June 6, 1926 (PAAA, Büro Reichsminister, Kurie 70, vol. 2, no. D702058-61).

46. Personal information from the archive of the Papal Secretariat of State.

47. Cf. Brockdorff-Rantzau's report of August 11, 1926 (PAAA, IIb, Päpst. Stuhl Russland, Pol. 3, vol. 1, no. L233345-46) and Bergen's report of June 16, 1926 (no. 233337-38). See also Curtiss, op. cit., p. 218. Schmidovitch was not an official of the Foreign Commissariat, as Winter claims (op. cit., p. 89/90), and d'Herbigny did not understand Schmidovitch's remark as a "free rein for his plans for building up the church," as Winter writes—to be sure, only in his presentation intended for the West, and not in the East Berlin version (cf. Rom und Moskau, Vienna 1972, p. 319).

48. Cf. decree of the Commissariat of Justice, Aug. 22, 1922, no. 512, and of the Commissariat of the Interior, Feb. 17, 1925. (Quoted in Codevilla, op. cit., 136/137).

49. "St. Louis des Français," built in 1833 in classical style, as a result of a 1789 ukase of Czarina Catherine II, today the only Roman Catholic church in Moscow.

50. Alice Ott (1886-1969), an Alsatian, was sexton of St. Ludwig's in Moscow for 25 years; arrested in 1947 and exiled to Siberia, she was rehabilitated in 1959 and, as a result of de Gaulle's intervention with Khrushchev, released to France in 1960. —Bergera, later an artillery general (d. 1930 in a mental hospital in Palermo), after his return from Moscow was received by Pius XI in 1928 to report on the situation in the Soviet Union.

51. Cf. Bessedovsky: Oui, j'accuse, Paris 1930, p. 138ff. (German: Den Klauen der Tscheka entkommen, Leipzig 1930). —Bessedovsky is a Soviet diplomat who defected to the West at the end of the twenties.

52. Holders of the "Mologa" were the "Rhein-Elbe-Union" and the lumber company "Himmelsbach" in Baden, in which Wirth had interests. "Mologa" was involved in the acquisition of timber in the forest areas near Leningrad (see also note 7 of ch. IV).

53. Retrospective report of Brockdorff-Rantzau's of June 6, 1926 (PAAA, Büro Reichsminister, Kurie 70, vol. 2, no. D702058-61).

54. This and all further details concerning d'Herbigny's 3rd trip to Russia (including all quotes)—insofar as no other source is given—are taken from his report published in *Etudes* (Paris) of July 5, 1927 (German version in: Seelsorgefahrten in Russland, Illertissen 1929, p. 91ff.).

55. According to report of the German embassy in Moscow of August 11, 1926 (PAAA, Abt. IIb, Papal See-Russia, Pol. 3, vol. 1, L233344). —Skalski (b. 1877) came from the Polish minor aristocracy in the Ukraine.

56. Report of Consul Dienstmann (PAAA, Büro Reichsminister, Kurie 70, vol. 2, K01001).

57. Hey's report of August 11, 1926 (PAAA, Abt. IIb, Päpst. Stuhl-Russland, Pol. 3, vol. 1, L233344-46).

58. Telegram of Ambassador Brockdorff-Rantzau from Berlin to his representative Hey in Moscow (PAAA, Abt. IIb, Päpst. Stuhl Russland, Pol. 3, vol. 1, L233351).

59. Hey's report see note 57.

60. The date of the consecration of Malecki and other secret bishops is entered incorrectly in the "Annuario Pontificio" of 1930 (where their names are mentioned for the first time); for the correct dates as well as other details not reported by d'Herbigny, I am indebted to reports from Bishop Boleslas Sloskans (Louvain).

61. Barthelemy, b. 1888 (as Nikolas F. Remov), was consecrated bishop by Patriarch Tikhon in 1921, converted to Catholicism in 1932; his rank of bishop was recognized by the Pope on Feb. 25, 1933, and he was authorized to keep his conversion to the Catholic church

secret indefinitely. He met with d'Herbigny and also later kept up a correspondence with him, through Neveu and the French Embassy in Moscow; on February 6, 1934, Barthelemy was arrested, and executed on July 31, 1935 (*cf. Pages d'Archives*, Nouvelle Serie, no. 3, December 1955, p. 49).

62. For the reference to this third meeting between d'Herbigny and Schmidovitch I am indebted to a report from the archive of the Vatican Secretariat of State of December 3, 1973.

63. The originals of the four documents are in the Neveu-papers ("Archivio dei Padri Assunzionisti," Rome). I am indebted to Prof. A. Wenger, A.A., for the insight. —Winter's claim (op. cit., p. 92) that d'Herbigny did not until this occasion, September 5, publicly consecrate Neveu as bishop, is wrong.

64. "Consolanti solennitá a Mosca" (cf. *Osservatore Romano*, September 7, 1926).

65. Cf. Lesourd, op. cit., p. 125. Intervening with the Pope in June 1923, Ledochowski had also prevented Father Edmund Walsh (who at that time had interrupted his stay in Moscow to come to Rome) from being consecrated as bishop (see Louis J. Gallagher: Father Edmond Walsh, p. 46/47). Probably in order to forestall Ledochowski's objections, Pius XI had also had d'Herbigny's consecration performed by Pacelli in Berlin rather than in Rome.

66. D'Herbigny: Seelsorgefahrten. . . , op. cit., p. 104.

67. PAAA, Büro Reichsminister, Kurie 70, vol. 2, K012004-05.

68. Two decades later, on June 23, 1946, Radio Vatican stated in reference to the consecration of bishops in 1926: "They were kept secret until it was certain later that the Soviet authorities knew about them" (quoted in: *Tablet*, London, July 13, 1946).

69. Ambassador von Bergen's report quoted in note 67 expressly points to Father Gehrmann as initiator. —Cf. also Gehrmann's Promemoria for Pizzardo, quoted in Kraus, op. cit., p. 184.

70. Cf. *Pages d'Archives*, Nouvelle Serie, no. 11, October 1959, p. 373.

71. To the Superior General of the Assumptionists, Gervais Quenard, see *Pages d'Archives*, op. cit., p. 371.

72. *Osservatore Romano* of November 20, 1926 ("Un grande sogno svanito").

73. For the date and a short description of the document I am indebted to information from the archive of the Vatican Secretariat of State, December 3, 1973.

74. Personal information from the Vatican Secretariat of State. Cf. "Traduction des Documents Officiels du Commissariat du Peuple a la justice" (NKVD, 5th Section) in: Orientalia Christiana, no. 18, 1925.

75. Cf. Brockdorff-Rantzau's report of August 29, 1927 (PAAA, Büro Reichsminister, curia 70, vol. 2, K012053).

76. According to personal information from Andor Hencke, personal secretary of Brockdorff-Rantzau, of March 16, 1974, Chicherin was more than once indignant over d'Herbigny's "underhanded actions."

77. P. Giduljanow: Odelenie cerkwi od gosudarstwa, Moscow 1926, (IX, 6).

78. The seminary had been established on the initiative and through the negotiations of the Moscow Lutheran bishop, Meyer, without the assistance of the German official authorities.

79. Schweigl, b. 1894 in Flauring, d. 1964 in Frascati, had earned his doctorate with a thesis on "The Soviet Marriage Project" (cf. *Orientalia Christiana*, no. 26, 1926), was later a professor in the "Collegium Russicum" and at the "Gregoriana" in Rome, and is the author of numerous works on Sovietology.—Ledit, b. 1898 in Montreal, was until the fifties "Curator for the Russian mission" of the Jesuit Order. In the thirties he published the anti-Communist *Lettres du Rome*, in Rome. He now (1977) lives in Montreal. On June 14, 1974, I had a long conversation with him in Rome.

80. Ritter's report of November 14, 1926 (BStA, file 1005, Papal See, no. 127).

81. Cf. the reports of the German Consul General Dienstmann in Odessa of October 30, 1926, the German chargé d'affaires Hey in Moscow of October 30, 1926, and the German Consul General Walther in Leningrad of February 5, 1927 (PAAA, Abt. IIb, Päpst. Stuhl-Russland, Pol. 3, vol. 1, L33360, L33357, 133368).

82. Schweigl in: *Civiltà Cattolica* of February 21, 1948, p. 243.

83. See Embassy Advisor von Tippelskirch's memorandum of April 27, 1927 (PAAA, Abt. IIb, Päpst. Stuhl Russland, Pol. 3, vol. 1, L233385).

84. Quoted in Mailleux SJ: Entre Rome et Moscou, Paris 1966, p. 101. —Ledit and Schweigl, however, were not travelling "in civilian clothes," but wore Catholic priest's ("clergyman") clothing; of course, they were even more noticeable this way, wherefore Schweigl disguised himself with a top hat (!) (so Father Ammann SJ, who died in 1974, remembered a story of Schweigl's in Rome).

85. This and the following excerpt from the trial are taken from Sloskans' "Diario" (Diary), note of September 17, 1927 (manuscript in the library of the "Papal Institute for Eastern Studies—Pontificio Istituto Orientale," Rome).

Chapter IV

1. Ernst Count von Rantzau (1869-1930), the twin brother of the ambassador, was a councillor in the former royal house of Hohenzollern and at the time active in the estate trusteeship of the exiled ex-Kaiser Wilhelm.

2. The following according to a tape recording of a conversation with Andor Hencke on March 16, 1974. Hencke, b. 1895, was finally Secretariat of State in the Foreign Office, Berlin, until 1943, then ambassador to Madrid. In 1939 he accompanied Ribbentrop as interpreter to Moscow for the signing of the Hitler-Stalin Pact (cf. ADSS, vol. 7, Doc. no. 95).

3. The quoted documents: PAAA, Abt. II, Vatikan, telegram from Brockdorff-Rantzau of January 12, 1927 (K012006-07), letter to Zech of January 14, 1927 (K012008), Brockdorff-Rantzau's report of January 23, 1927 (cf. Isvestia of January 22, 1927), letter to Gehrmann (K012033-35), Gasparri's letter (L233373, L233371-72), Steinmann's letter (K012025-30).

4. Chicherin—according to Brockdorff-Rantzau's report of November 25, 1926 "very ill (six per cent [blood] sugar)"—stayed in German sanatoriums almost the entire first half of 1927.

5. Connivance: the legal designation for tolerating punishable actions of subordinates.

6. PAAA, Geheimakten 361, 9, vol. 73, H114430-36.

7. As shareholder and chairman of the board of directors of "Mologa," Wirth had strongly supported the credit assistance that the faltering timber enterprise received in July 1926 in the amount of 5 million Marks from the Reichskreditgesellschaft; within three months the "Mologa" could no longer pay wages. Brockdorff-Rantzau reported on January 2, 1927 that the entire German capital in the company (total investment 34 million Marks) was lost if another 20-25 million Marks were not spent for the restoration of this "symbol of German-Russian cooperation." The government of the Catholic Center Party's Chancellor Marx declared itself willing if the Soviets would grant better conditions (more acquisition of timber, less firewood). Since these guarantees were not offered, Mologa was liquidated in the spring of 1927 with great losses for the Reich treasury (PAAA, Russland, Handakten, vol. 33/36, Mologa).

8. Ambassador von Bergen sent this Osservatore Romano article (no. 132) to Berlin with the note that this was also the Pope's opinion.

9. Quoted from Kochan, op. cit., p. 115.

10. Cf. the ambassador's report of August 29, 1927 (PAAA, Büro Reichsminister, Kurie 70, vol. 2, K 012051-55).

11. Complete text see Patriarch Sergij i ego duchovnoe hasledstvo, Moscow, 1947, pp. 59-63.

12. See note 10.

13. Zech's telegram of September 8, 1927 to the embassy in Moscow (PAAA, Büro Reichsminister, Kurie 70, vol. 2, K 012056).

14. To Dirksen, Director of the eastern section (PAAA, Geheimakten 361, 9, vol 73, H 114409).

15. See note 18.

16. Herbette's report no. 501 of August 19, 1927 (text published in 1943 by the Historical

Commission of the Foreign Office from documents looted from Paris, "Ein französischer Diplomat über die bolschewistische Gefahr," p. 36).

17. Winter, op. cit., p. 139.

18. According to personal information from the archive of the Papal Secretariat of State of December 31, 1973.

19. According to confidential information from the Secretariat of State to Ambassador von Bergen of May 24, 1927 (PAAA, Büro Reichsminister, Kurie 70, vol. 2, K 012074). Personal information from the archive of the Papal Secretariat of State confirmed the contents to me on December 3, 1973. —Winter, op. cit., ignores this important document, which cannot have escaped him in his studies of the documents if only because he quotes other documents from the same volume of the PAAA.

20. Personal information from Henke on March 16, 1974.

21. This connection between forced collectivization and the system of terror was attested to later, for example, by the Polish Communist party chief Wladyslaw Gomulka (cf. his address to the XXIst Soviet Party Congress in *Trybuna Ludu* no. 323, 1961).

22. See Stalin: Soltschinenija, vol. X, p. 131ff and 324 (cf. Curtiss, op. cit., p. 199).

23. Herbette, op. cit., p. 50. Cf. Stalin's dialogue with American workers on 9/9/1927 (Werke, vol. X, p. 131ff).

24. Personal information from the archive of the Papal Secretariat of State, December 3, 1973.

25. The following is quoted from Sloskans' diary notes of October 18, 1927 and April 6, 1928 ("Diario" manuscript in the library of the "Pontificio Istituto Orientali," Rome).

26. Sloskans mentioned that he received a Polish translation of the "Meditations" of the French Jesuit Pierre Chaignon (d. 1887) from the GPU library to read.

27. Cf. *Osservatore Romano* of February 2 and 10, 1928, as well as the reports of the German embassy to the Holy See of January 21 and February 2, 1928 (PAAA Abt. II, Vatikan, Pol. 3, vol. 2, no. 192 and Abt. IV, Russland, Pol. 3, vol. 1, no. 698).

28. Cf. report of May 9, 1928 (PAAA, Abt. II, Vatikan, Pol. 3, vol. 2, no. 478).

29. Cf. Alcide De Gasperi: Lettere sul Concordato, Brescia 1970, p. 157.

30. Cf. De Gasperi, ibid., p. 93 (letter of March 28, 1929).

31. Cf. De Gasperi, ibid., p. 62-66 and 93 (letters of February 12 and 29, 1929).

32. Address to theology students, March 12, 1929 (cf. Graham, op. cit., p. 443).

33. See *Germania* of March 10, 1929.

34. Report of the German chargé d'affaires in Moscow, Hey, of March 30, 1929. (PAAA Abt IV, Russland, Pol. 3, vol. 1, no. 2111).

35. Back on August 15, 1929, the German embassy to the Vatican had told the Foreign Office that "Bede is not acting on orders from the Vatican" (PAAA, Abt. II, Vatikan, Pol. 3, Vol. 2, K503440-47). —Winter, op. cit., p. 136, who mentions a "mission of Msgr. Bede from Katowice" without more precise information, ignores the documented circumstances. —See also ch. 2, note 57.

36. "Extremely dubious and undesirable," notes the Foreign Office (signed D., probably Dirksen) on July 13, 1927 on the newspaper clipping of the Kaas article from the *Reichspost* of June 29, 1927.

37. *Weltbühne*, Berlin, February 12, 1929.

38. *Osservatore Romano*, October 4, 1929.

39. In the Apostolic Constitution "Quam curam" (AAS, October 1, 1929).

40. Pastor A. Hessenbach (with "Imprimatur" of the Augsburg episcopal office, March 6, 1929).

41. Cf. *Germania*, December 11, 1929.

42. See Bergen's report of February 21, 1928 (PAAA, Abt. II, Vatikan-Russland, vol. 2, no. 38).

43. In the Bulgarian capitol d'Herbigny met the apostolic delegate Roncalli, later Pope John XXIII.

44. Quoted in a lecture that d'Herbigny gave on December 11, 1927, in the presence of the Polish and French ambassadors in Rome (text in *Etudes*, Jan. 20, 1928).

45. Cf. *Pages d'Archives* of the Assumptionist Order, Nouvelle Serie, no. 3, December 1955, p. 47.

46. Neveu's papers, above all his correspondence with d'Herbigny, are being examined and evaluated by Prof. Antoine Wenger A.A. (Strassburg/ Rome) for a planned biography of Neveu. I am indebted to Prof. Wenger and the archive of the Assumptionist Order in Rome for examining these documents.

47. Cf. Sloskans' notes ("Diario" manuscript in the library of the "Pontificio Istituto Orientale," Rome).

48. Matulionis (b. 1873) was released in the exchange in 1933, was later Bishop of Kaisiadorys (Lithuania); condemned to ten years imprisonment in 1946, in 1956 in office again, but restricted. He died at 90 in 1962 and was ceremoniously buried in the cathedral of Kaisiadorys (Soviet Lithuania).

49. Complete text of the decree in "Kommunističeskaja partija i sovetskoe pravitelstvo o religii i cerkvi," Moscow, 1959, pp. 78-93; see also Struve, op. cit., p. 462. The last (unmoderated) version of the decree, which only limits the competence of the local authorities in favor of the Moscow central and recognizes the church directorate as legal persons, was enacted on July 3, 1975 (Vedomosti Verchovnego Soveta RSFSR, XIX, 1975, no. 572 p. 487-491). Cf. also Gerhard Simon's analysis in "Herder-Korrespondenz" (Freiburg) no. 6, 1976, p. 295ff. and Giovanni Codevilla, *La Communità Religiose nell'URSS. La nuova Legislatione sovietica*, Milan, 1978.

50. No. 11 of February 21, 1930. See also the detailed report of the German ambassador in Moscow, Dirksen, about the religious situation, February 27, 1930 (PAAA, Abt. IV, Russland, 1457).

51. January 22, 1930, to the Secretary General in the French Foreign Ministry, Berthelet (see Herbette, op. cit., p. 149/ 150).

52. In conversation with Ludwig von Pastor on March 9, 1928 (cf. Pastor: Tagebücher, p. 89).

53. For text see *Osservatore Romano*, February 9, 1930.

54. Documentary note from legation counsellor Schubert of February 15, 1930 (PAAA, Abt. II, Vatikan, Pol. 3, vol. 2, K 503461).

55. Bergen's report of March 1, 1930 (PAAA, Abt. II, Vatikan, Pol. 3, vol. 2, no. 59).

56. D'Herbigny in a lecture on February 27, 1930 (cf.: La Guerre Antireligieuse en Russie Sovietique, Paris 1930).

57. Ambassador Bergen's report of April 9, 1931 (PAAA, Abt. IV, Russland, Pol. 3, vol. I, no. 76, Ru. 1989). Winter, op. cit. p. 138, suppresses Bergen's important sentence quoted here, and tries to ascribe to the Vatican the absurd intention of "starting the war." Bergen's report with the quoted argument was occasioned by a report of the German embassy in Moscow, in which a statement of Litvinov's was repeated: that the driving forces behind a war against the Soviet Union are France and the Vatican.

58. Cf. *Pravda*, February 16, 1930. Sergius had Rome informed immediately that he had so spoken "on the one hand under pressure from the GPU, on the other to save the lives of many prisoners" (see d'Herbigny in *Revue des Deux Mondes*, July 15, 1930, p. 210).

59. See *Pravda*, July 15, 1930 (German version of the pamphlet with the title: "Warum Päpstlicher Kreuzzug?" from Carl Heym-Verlag, Hamburg-Berlin 1930).

60. *Besboshnik* no. 12, February 28, 1930.

61. From Herbette's report of February 26, 1930 (see Herbette, op. cit., p. 164).

62. The long-time Moscow correspondent of the *Berliner Tageblatt*, Paul Scheffer, was one of the few contemporary observers to see through this. (Cf. Scheffer, op. cit., p. 419-428).

63. *Pravda*, March 15, 1930.

64. Herbette, op. cit., p. 168.

65. Report by Ambassador Dirksen, February 21, 1930 (PAAA, Geheimakten 320, Pl. 16, K 105194).

66. Documentation about this entire episode in BStA, File 1027, Papal See.

67. *Isvestia*, April 23, 1930.

68. This and the following are based on a note of the Foreign Office in Berlin for

Ministerial Director Trautmann of June 17, 1930 (PAAA, Abt. II, Vatikan, Pol. 3, vol. 3, K503469).

69. Cf. Sloskans' diary notes of November 1 and 8, 1930 ("Diario" manuscript in the library of the "Pontificio Istituto Orientale," Rome).

70. See *Osservatore Romano*, April 14 and 15, 1930 (German version in the *Augsburger Post Zeitung* series, Heft 8, 1930).

71. Cf. Ambassador Dirksen's report of April 10, 1930 (PAAA, Abt. IV, Russland, Pol. 3, no. A/625).

72. With the Motu propio "Inde ab initio Pontificatu" (cf. "Annuario Pontificio" 1931).

73. Bergen's report of April 22, 1930 (PAAA, Abt. II, Vatikan, 356, no. 104).

74. "Acta Apostolicae Sedis" XXIII (1931), p. 177-228.

75. Cf. *Oriens*, Krakow, Marzec-Kwiecien 1933, p. 57f.

76. Quoted from d'Herbigny's memoires in Lesourd (op. cit., p. 151).

77. Skrzyński reported to the Polish Foreign Minister on March 11, 1933, about his audience with the Pope and the latter's flaring up (Pius uniósl sie). —Skrzyński's report (no. 489138/33) text in Jaroslaw Jurkiewicz; Watykan a stosunki polsko-niemieckie w latach 1918-1939, Wybór materialów, Warsaw 1960, p. 52ff.

78. Cf. *Osservatore Romano*, February 2, 1933.

79. Thus Jurkiewicz in a note (op. cit., p. 52).

80. Thus Winter in the "western" version of his book: Rom und Moskau, Vienna 1972, p. 339. In the East Berlin edition of his book, however, (p. 121) Winter drops the same justification.

81. Cf. A. Deubner: La traduction du mot χαύολιχήν dans le texte slave du symbole de Nicée-Constantinople, in: *Orientalia Christiana*, Rome 1929, no. 55. It deals with the acceptance of the Greek word "Catholic" from the Nicean Creed into that of the Eastern church.

82. Cf. Michel d'Herbigny et Alexandre Deubner: Evêques Russes en Exil. —Douze ans d'epreuves (1918-1930) in: *Orientalia Christiana*, vol. XXI, no. 67, 1931.

83. This and the following are taken from a thoroughly-documented investigation by M. Cappuyns OSB: Dom Lambert Beauduin (1873-1960), in: *Revue d'Histoire Ecclesiastique*, Louvain 1966, vol. 61, p. 761ff.

84. Cf. Osteuropa-Handbuch "Polen," Cologne 1959, p. 103-118. For the so-called revindication trials cf. Myslek, op. cit., p. 114-122.

85. Henryk Ignacy Lubieński: Droga na Wschód Rzymu, Warsaw 1932, in the author's own publishing house (a brother of Konstanty Lubieński, who was a representative from 1957 until his death in 1977 for the Catholic "Znak" group in the Sejm of the People's Republic of Poland.) The book was forbidden for Catholics by Archbishop Kakowski, Warsaw, on Rome's intervention, and today is not even found in the library of the Papal Institute for Eastern Studies in Rome.

86. They gathered around the bi-monthly journal *Oriens* published by Father Jan Urban and had a Russian missionary center in Albertyn near Slonim (East Poland).

87. According to Czarneckyj's own statements to the Polish Foreign Ministry (cf. Myslek, op. cit., p. 171 and 186).

88. For this event and its background cf. Zatko, op. cit., p. 184-188.

89. This was confirmed later by a letter of Bishop Neveu's; he stated that Alexander Deubner's mother had been in the Kremlin and visited her sister-in-law, who after her divorce had married Clara Zetkin's son (Neveu's letter of July 31, 1933, to d'Herbigny in the Neveu papers of the Roman "Archivio dei Padri Assunzionisti"). Clara Zetkin (b. 1857), Communist member of the German Reichstag, had fled to the Soviet Union after Hitler's seizure of power and died in Moscow on June 20, 1933.

90. D'Herbigny gives numerous references in his letters to Bishop Neveu in Moscow for Okolo-Kulak's decisive participation in the staging of the Deubner affair (personal information from Prof. Wenger out of the Neveu papers in the "Archivio dei Padri Assunzionisti," Rome).

91. Monsignore Filippo Giobbe, the secretary of the Commission for Russia, in 1937 told

Jesuit Father Josef Ledit that documents had indeed disappeared from the Commission (pers. information from Ledit of June 14, 1974). In posthumous notes, d'Herbigny accused the then 28-year-old priest Eduard Prettner-Cippico from Triest, who had been installed as archivist of the Russia Commission at the end of 1932, of having passed photos of documents from the Vatican Secretariat of State to the Soviets (cf. Lesourd, op. cit., p. 161). Prettner-Cippico, who worked for 15 years in the archive of the Secretariat of State, was involved in 1948 in a trial concerning financial irregularities, suspended from church duties and laicized (cf. *Osservatore Romano*, March 7, 1948 and *La Croix*, March 10, 1948). Pope John XXIII rehabilitated Prettner-Cippico, but did not reinstate him in the Vatican service; he lives (1978) in Rome as a Catholic priest and works for a so-called "Research and Information Service" of "TRI-International Ltd.," an investment company with holdings based in Luxemburg and Bermuda (President: Ernest Csendes, Texas Republic Industries, Inc., Director: Curtis E. LeMay, Chief of Staff U.S. Air Force 1960-65). —Prettner-Cippico protested in writing against the accusations in Lesourd's book, but has taken no legal action. In a conversation on Jan. 18, 1978, Prettner-Cippico told me that he had never heard of any vanished documents; but he did remember that d'Herbigny had been officially reprimanded several times for making documents from the Commission on Russia available to the Jesuits of the "Istituto Orientale" and the "Russicum."

92.   Personal information from Father Alfons Maria Mitnacht OSA (Würzburg) of March 7, 1973. Mitnacht spoke with Deubner several times in 1938 in Prague about the events of 1932/33. (Mitnacht died in 1977.)

93.   Reference is to Father Siegbert Riedmeister SJ (d. 1936 in Berlin).

94.   From the minutes of the meeting on January 19, 1933, of the "Papal Relief Work for the Russians in Germany" (Gehrmann papers in the SVD archive, Rome). At this time there were four thousand Orthodox Russian emigrants in Berlin, among them 50 Russian-Catholic families. The Relief Work also sent packages and books to priests in the Soviet Union, for the last time at Christmas 1934.

95.   *Oriens* (Krakow) I. 4 of August 1933, p. 127.

96.   Cf. Fest: Hitler, Frankfurt 1973, p. 665-667.

Chapter V

1.   Cf. Theo Pirker: Utopie und Mythos der Weltrevolution. Zur Geschichte der Komintern 1920-1940, p. 46-77 and 166.

2.   Quoted by his advisor Father Leiber SJ in *Stimmen der Zeit*, no. 167, 1961, p. 215.

3.   Cf. Heinrich Brüning: Memoiren 1918-1934, Munich 1972 (paperbook edition), p. 144 and 378-380. Brüning sees a contradiction in the statements of the Pope and Pacelli; he fails to recognize that both were concerned primarily with the supposed "restraining" effect.

4.   *Osservatore Romano*, March 13, 1933, in an article signed F. (Monsignore Giuseppe Frediani).

5.   Jurkiewicz, op. cit., p. 57.

6.   Cf. Skrzyński's reports of February 10 and 27, 1933 (quoted in Jurkiewicz, op. cit., p. 44-49).

7.   Cf. Hans Roos: Polen und Europa, Studien zur polnischen Aussenpolitik 1931-1939, Tübingen 1957, p. 117-155.

8.   Cf. the document publication of the Kommission für Zeitgeschichte (Comm. for Contemporary History) of the Catholic Academy in Bavaria: Kirchliche Akten (Ludwig Volk) und Staatliche Akten (Alfons Kupper) zu den Reichskonkordatsverhandlungen 1933, Mainz 1969. See also: Klaus Scholder, Die Kirchen und das Dritte Reich, vol. I (1918-1934), Frankfurt/Main, 1977.

9.   Cf. Karin Schauff: Erinnerungen an Ludwig Kaas, Pfullingen 1972, p. 12, and also according to pers. information from the author (wife of the Center party Reichstag representative Johannes Schauff, who emigrated in 1933, first to Rome). In fact the Nazis did

step down "later"—after 12 years—but the Reich concordat, favorable to the Vatican, was still in force 35 years later.

10. Papen's speech to the Catholic Academic Union in Maria Laach on July 22, 1933, and Hitler's letter to Cardinal Bertram of April 28, 1933 (quoted from "Das christliche Deutschland 1933-1945," Katholische Reihe, Heft 1, Freiburg 1946, p. 39).

11. De Gasperi, op. cit., p. 29 and 64.

12. Cf. Joseph Goebbels: Vom Kaiserhof zur Reichskanzlei, Munich 1934, p. 271.

13. Bergen's report of February 18, 1933 (PAAA, Abt. IIa, Vatikan, Pol. 19, no. 38). Received in Berlin on February 27, 1933. The report is stamped: "The Prussian Ministry of Interior has got directly 2 copies of this report" (cf. also PAAA, Secret Documents, Abt. IV, Russia, vol. 4, Pol. 15, Erlass no. 855—charred documents).

14. Information from the Prussian Ministry of the Interior to the Foreign Office acc. to decree of the Foreign Office to the German embassy to the Vatican of May 26, 1933 (PAAA, Secret Documents, Abt. IV, Russland, vol. 4, Pol. 15, no. Ru 2348—by war damaged, charred documents).

15. Letter of March 18, 1933 (Neveu papers, AA Archive, Rome).

16. Gehrmann's minutes of the April 11, 1933, session of the Papal Relief Work for the Russians in Germany, in Berlin (Gehrmann papers, SVD Archive, Rome).

17. This and the following are taken from Skrzyński's reports of February 11, March 11 and April 9, 1933 (complete text in Jurkiewicz, op. cit., p. 46, 54 and 62).

18. Pers. information from Father Alfons Maria Mitnacht OSA (Würzburg) on March 7, 1973.

19. Thus the Pope to the Polish ambassador Skrzyński (quoted in Jurkiewicz, op. cit., p. 63).

20. Tablet no. 4859, June 24, 1933. —In Poland only Oriens (Krakow), no. 4, 1933, took notice of Deubner's statement; Ambassador Bergen mentions the Tablet text in a report of August 19, 1933.

21. Cf. d'Herbigny's letter to Neveu of June 11 and July 5, 1933 (Neveu papers, AA Archive, Rome) as well as personal information from Father Ledit SJ of December 19, 1972.

22. From PAAA, Abt. IV, Russia, Pol. 3, vol. 1.

23. Text of the secret addendum agreement that exempted theologians from military service (except in case of general mobilization), see "Documents on German Foreign Policy" (C, I. Doc. 371, p. 618-679).

24. The document is kept in the "Istituto Gramsci" in Rome (cf. L'Unita, Rome, of January 20, 1967.—Gramsci, b. 1891, died in 1937, three days before his release.

25. Bergen's report no. 247 of October 12, 1933 (PAAA, Abt. II, Vatikan, Pol. 3, vol. 3, K 503490).

26. Bergen's report of December 6, 1933 (PAAA, Abt. II, Vatikan, Pol. 3, vol. 3, no. 328).

27. Archbishop Gröber (Freiburg) in a record written in 1947 about the concordat negotiations (Diocesan archive, Freiburg, Gröber papers, file 77).

28. Cf. Foster Rhea Dulles: The Road to Teheran: The Story of Russia and America, 1781-1943, Princeton 1944.

29. Cf. Pages d'Archives of the Assumptionist Order, Nouvelle Serie, no. 3, December 1955, p. 44.

30. Father Leopold Braun (1903-1964) came from New Bedford. His grandfather came from Lorraine. Braun was active in Moscow until October 1945.

31. D'Herbigny to Neveu (Neveu papers, A A Archive, Rome).

32. In the following, insofar as documentary sources are not given, I am indebted for references to lengthy, sometimes numerous conversations with the following gentlemen—clerics and scholars—whose names are given here in alphabetical order without titles: Alessandrini, Ammann, Bernard, Bornemann, Brini, De Vries, Graham, Ledit, Lesourd, Mailleux, Martini, Mitnacht, Moreau, Olsr, Slipyj, Sloskans, Schasching, Schneider, Schultze, Wenger, Wetter.

33. Cf. F. Charles-Roux: hiut ans au Vatican, 1932-1940, Paris 1947, p. 175.—How much the secrecy surrounding d'Herbigny's fall stirred the imagination is shown in a novel by Josef Martin Bauer: Kranich mit dem Stein, Munich 1958, p. 532/33, where fiction and half-truths

are mixed without the name of d'Herbigny being mentioned. The same can be said about the novel of John Gallahue, *The Jesuit*, New York, 1973 (cf. also note 77, p. 415).

34.　Report of January 6, 1934 (PAAA, Abt. II, Vatican, Pol. 3, vol. 3, no. 5).

35.　This and the following proceed from a letter of d'Herbigny to Neveu of September 30, 1933 (Neveu papers, "Archivio dei Padri Assunzionisti," Rome).

36.　Carlo Margotti (b. 1891) was secretary of the Commission on Russia until March 8, 1930, then apostolic delegate in Athens and Constantinople. After d'Herbigny's fall Margotti became Bishop of Gorizia at the end of 1934.

37.　The original is found in the d'Herbigny papers now deposed in the "cabinet de manuscripts" of the Bibliothéque National in Paris. (Cf. Lesourd, op. cit., p. 174 and 237).

38.　Cf. *Le Temps* (Paris) of November 29, 1930; *L'Avvenire d'Italia*, December 21, 1930; *Oriens* (Krakow), February 1, 1934; *Schwäbischer Merkur*, February 10, 1934.

39.　Bergen's report of December 6, 1933 (see note 26).

40.　Cf. Sloskans: "Diario" manuscript in the library of the "Pontificio Istituto Orientale," Rome, entry of November 1, 1930; see also d'Herbigny's letter to Neveu (Neveu papers, A A Archive, Rome) of April 26, 1930: "They wrote Awglo that he should stay." For Awglo cf. Leopold Braun: Catholics behind the Iron Curtain (in: *Worldmission*, December 1950, p. 93).

41.　Letter of September 26, 1933 (Neveu papers). Cf. Lesourd, op. cit., p. 144.

42.　Cf. Beauduin's letters of December 8 and 13, 1933 and January 4, 1934 (see M. Cappuyns: Dom Lambert Beauduin, in: *Revue d'Histoire Ecclesiastique*, Louvain 1966, vol. 61, p. 790/791). The Polish embassy counsellor at the time in Rome, Witold de Bronowski (d. 1975 in Rome), told me on April 4, 1975: "We disposed of d'Herbigny."

43.　Cf. Beauduin's letter of December 8, 1933: that d'Herbigny had tried to become a member of the Academy after the death of Henri Bremond (b. 1865, d. August 17, 1933), by suggesting that this would please the Pope.

44.　Cf. Lesourd, op. cit., p. 174.

45.　Cf. the memoirs of the French ambassador to the Vatican, Charles-Roux, op. cit., p. 212ff.

46.　Cf. Raske: Der totalitäre Gottesstaat (Dokumentation), Düsseldorf 1970, p. 56/57.

47.　Cf. Wilhelm Corten: Kölner Aktenstücke zur Lage der Katholischen Kirche in Deutschland 1933-1945, Cologne 1949, doc. 130, p. 156-161.

48.　See *Kommunistitscheskij International* of October 1935 and *Völkischer Beobachter* of December 10, 1935: "Moskau als Freund der Jesuiten in Deutschland." (Moscow as friend of the Jesuits in Germany.)

49.　Complete text in Friedrich Muckermann SJ: Es spricht die spanische Seele, Colmar 1937, p. 15/16.

50.　Cf. Jurkiewicz, op. cit., p. 81.

51.　Alois Hudal (1885-1963) was rector of the German-Austrian college "Santa Maria dell'Anima" in Rome from 1923. In 1933 he was named titular bishop. His book "Die Grundlagen des Nationalsozialismus," Leipzig-Vienna 1937, was completed on July 11, 1936, a week before the beginning of the Spanish Civil War; although it appeared without the church's imprimatur, Pacelli prevented its getting on the list of forbidden books; the *Osservatore Romano* distanced itself only very slightly from the book (cf. Hudal, "Römische Tagebücher," Graz 1976, p. 129 and 131). Hudal dedicated a copy of his book to Adolf Hitler: "Dem Siegfried deutscher Grösse: (To the Siegfried of German Greatness); this copy is in Hitler's private library, today to be found in the Library of Congress, Washington. (On Hudal's memoires cf. Franz Wasner, "Torso aus der Anima," in Theologisch-praktische Quartalsschrift, 1978, no. 1).

52.　Hudal, op. cit., p. 245.

53.　Cf. Charles-Roux, op. cit., p. 177.

54.　For the text of the encyclical "Mit brennender Sorge" [With burning sorrow] (original text in German) see "Das christliche Deutschland 1933-1945," Katholische Reihe, vol. 1, Freiburg 1946, p. 1-24.

55.　For text of the encyclical "Divini Redemptoris" see Emile Maurice Guerry: Chiesa cattolica e communismo ateo, Rome 1962, p. 264ff.

56.　Krestincki was not rehabilitated until 1963 (see the headline in *Isvestia*, September 27,

1963: "A true statesman" and Maiski: Memoiren eines Sowjetbotschafters, East Berlin 1967, p. 256).

57.   "Under President Cardenas (1934-1940) the tensions relaxed between church and state. . . . Of course the Catholic church was completely ousted from the political stage, but . . . religion is very much alive" (Kath. Staatslexikon, vol. V, p. 688/689).

58.   "Mit brennender Sorge," op. cit. (see note 54), p. 49.

59.   Ibid., p. 53ff.

60.   Cf. Guenter Lewy: The Catholic Church in Nazi Germany, Christian Classics 1964 (Die katholische Kirche und das Dritte Reich, Munich [Piper] 1965, p. 227-234.)

61.   See Der Angriff, October 28 and December 15, 1937.

62.   Communication from Father Ammann SJ (Rome), who spoke about Deubner with Archbishop Sheptyckyj in Lemberg in 1938, also from Father Mitnacht OSA (Würzburg), who as pastor of the Uniate congregation in Prague met with Deubner in Prague, 1937/38, and from Father Horacek SJ (Wildbad-Einöd, Austria), whom Deubner asked in 1943/44 during World War II to intercede with the archbishop of Prague so that he could read the mass again "for my poor Russian people."

63.   See "Annuario Pontificio" of 1937.

64.   Cf. Michel d'Herbigny: Le Message du Christ et de l'Eglise aux civilisations (Chronique Sociale de France, Paris).

65.   Cf. the description of the Lisieux celebrations in the memoires of Charles-Roux, op. cit., p. 223/224.

66.   This representation is based on Lesourd, op. cit., p. 186-233, on the Neveu papers (Prof. Wenger, Rome), also on information from Father Moreau SJ (Rome), who met d'Herbigny in Mons. Cf. also Lesourd's representation (op. cit., p. 186-233). Jesuit General Ledóchowski's authoritarian behavior is confirmed by Friedrich Muckermann SJ (1883-1946) in his memoirs (Im Kampf zwischen zwei Epochen, Mainz, 1973, p. 628-635). The dossier on d'Herbigny in the archive of the Jesuit General Offices is not available; according to information from F. Johann Schasching of the Jesuit General Offices (letter to the author of Jan. 7, 1978), even the publication of Lesourd's book could not bring the Order to open the dossier.

67.   Cf. the short Latin obituary by Bishop Giuseppe Mojoli in: Acta Pontificii Instituti Orientalium Studiorum, 1958, p. 19/20. The requiem could only be celebrated "pro sacerdote defuncto," not "pro episcopo." Not until the 50-year jubilee of the Eastern Institute, 1967, was d'Herbigny's name called forth from oblivion in an illustrated jubilee publication: "The Institute owes great thanks to hits first Jesuit president, Msgr. d'Herbigny. . . . The Institute was revived primarily through the energy and the unconquerable optimism of Father (later Bishop) d'Herbigny. . . ."

68.   Personal information from Cardinal Archbishop Slipyj (Rome), Dec. 6, 1971.

69.   The Motu Proprio "Quam Sollicite" of Dec. 21, 1934, was published in the March, 1935, issue of the Acta Apostolicae Sedis.

70.   Cf. Bergen's reports no. 108 and 124 of March 12 and 26, 1935 (PAAA, Abt. II, Vatican, Pol. 3, vol. 3).

71.   The Red Book of the Persecuted Church, by Alberto Galter, Westminister 1957, stated: "With the year 1933 a new, relatively quiet period of cease-fire began" (p. 55 of the German edition, Rotbuch der verfolgten Kirche, Recklinghausen, 1957).

72.   "Actes et documents du Saint Siege Relatifs a la Seconde Guerre Mondiale" (up to now 9 volumes, Vatican 1965-1975), vol. 5, p. 242. This publication of documents from the Vatican secret archives will hereafter be abbreviated "ADSS".

73.   Cf. L. Braun in Worldmission, vol. I, no. 42, December 1950, p. 92.

74.   Amoudru (b. 1878) lived 25 more years in retreat and mentally ill in a convent in Pensier near Fribourg (Switzerland), and died on October 12, 1961 in Onzain/Dep. Loire (France). An unprinted autobiographical report of Amoudru ("Les catholiques sous la terreur a Petrograd, Rome 1936) is found in the archive of the General Offices of the Dominican Order in Rome (cf. A.Esser OP in "Archivum Praedicatorum," Vol. XL (1970), p. 277f.).

75. Cf. Rudinskij: Swoboda sowesti w SSSR (Freedom of Conscience in the Soviet Union), Moscow 1961, p. 35. The author points out the difference, however thinks that there is "no substantial" difference between the concepts "confession" and "acts of worship."

76. The figures for 1936 come from Schweigl: Il Communismo e la Religione, Rome 1937; for 1937 from *Osservatore Romano*, April 11, 1937; for 1939, from Braun in *Worldmission*, vol. I, no. 2, December 1950.

77. Cf. Walter Ciszek, "With God in Russia," New York, 1964.—A supposedly historical novel by the former Jesuit John Gallahue ("The Jesuit," New York 1973), which describes a secret mission of a bishop in Russia, is based "on a compilation of partial events in various Jesuit communities at various times, mixed with phantasy and subjective interpretation" (communication from the Jesuit General Offices in Rome of Jan. 7, 1978).

78. Winter, op. cit., p. 205.

79. Ciszek, op. cit., p. 20.

80. Charles-Roux, op. cit., p. 122/123.

81. See *Der Angriff* of October 28, 1937.

82. Charles-Roux, op. cit., p. 129.

83. It was Emilio Sereni and Ambrosio Donini (cf. Paolo Spriano: Storia del Partito Comunista italiano, vol. III, Turin 1970, p. 240). In the publication of the CPI, *Stato Operaio*, the December 1938 issue said: The worker's movement has in the past made mistakes regarding the Catholic workers, but the Communists were innocent of that; their "outstretched hand" was neither borrowed nor imitated.

84. Cf. ADSS, vol. 2, p. 424 and 408.

85. See Eugenio Pacelli: Discorsi e Panegirici, 1931-1938, p. 738ff.

86. ADSS, vol. 2, p. 435.

87. ADSS, vol. 2, p. 413 and W.A.Purdy: The Church on the Move, London 1968 (German: Die Politik der Katholischen Kirche, Gütersloh 1966, p. 94.)

88. Cf. The description in Louis Gallagher and Paul V. Donovan: The Life of Saint Andrew Bobola of the SJ, Martyr, Manchester/USA 1939, p. 191-201.

89. Cf. Myslek, op. cit., p. 116 and 158/159; also G.J.Perejda: Apostle of Unity. The Life of Andrew Sheptytsky, Winnipeg, Canada, 1960, p. 33.

90. Cf. Pastuszek: Z filozofii i psychologii komunizmu, Lublin 1938.

91. See the CPP publication *Czerwony Sztandar*, no. 56, dated May 1938, which appeared at the end of June 1938 (cf. Z Pola Walki, no. 3, 1968, p. 45).

92. ADSS, vol. 1, doc. no. 34.—For general background cf. Walther Hofer: Die Entfesselung des Zweiten Weltkriegs, Frankfurt/Main 1964.

93. Cf. "Documents on British Foreign Policy," 3rd Series, vol. V, p. 435 ff. and ADSS, vol. 1, doc. no. 19.

94. ADSS, vol. 1, doc. no 29.

95. ADSS, vol. 1, doc. no. 47.

96. ADSS, vol. 1, doc. no. 109 and 116.

97. ADSS, vol. 1, doc. no. 113.

98. ADSS, vol. 1, doc. no. 125, 144, 152, 153, 165, 166.

99. ADSS, vol. 3, doc. no. 18.

Chapter VI

1. Letter of October 7, 1939; ADSS, vol. 1, doc. no. 21.

2. ADSS, vol. 1, doc. no. 13.

3. AAS, XXXI (1939), 413-479.

4. AAS, XXXI, (1940), 435-445.

5. ADSS, vol. 1, doc. no. 257.

6. ADSS, vol. 3, doc. no. 26.

7. G. Perejda, op. cit. p. 35, mentions the name of the courier, who is not named in the ADSS (cf. vol. 3, p. 15).

8. ADSS, vol. 3, doc. 375, and esp. note p. 565. Josef (Kubernyckyj-) Slipyj, b. 1892 in Tarnopol, studied in Innsbruck (Austria) and Rome, 1925 rector of the priests' seminary in Lviv, 1945 arrested, 18 years in Soviet prison cavps. In Rome since 1963. (Cf. Milena Rudnycka, The Invisible Stigmata, Rome-Munich-Philadelphia, 1971.)

9. Ciszek, op. cit., p. 26.

10. ADSS, vol. 3, doc. no. 52.

11. Cf. ADSS, vol. 3, doc. no. 158, 159, 160, 167 and note p. 135.

12. ADSS, vol. 3, doc. no. 105.

13. Cf. Etudes, Paris, of December 5, 1939, and the eye-witness description of the Soviet entry in the eastern mission station of Albertin in Ciszek, op. cit. p. 22.

14. ADSS, vol. 3, doc. no. 79.

15. ADSS, vol. 3, doc. no. 44, 47.

16. Cf. the nunciature report in ADSS, vol. 3, doc. no. 41. —See also the memoirs of the Vilna Communist (and wife of the later Polish Foreign Minister) Anna Jedrychowska: Zygzakiem i poprostu, Warsaw 1965. Stefan Jedrychowski, who came from a leftist Catholic student group in Vilna, was the contact to the Red Army.

17. ADSS, vol. 1, doc. no. 313.

18. ADSS, vol. 3, doc. no. 158 and 159.

19. ADSS, vol. 3, doc. no. 185.

20. ADSS, vol. 3, doc. no. 214.

21. ADSS, vol. 3, doc. no. 187.

22. ADSS, vol. 3, doc. no. 191.

23. ADSS, vol. 3, doc. no. 199.

24. ADSS, vol. 3, doc. no. 241.

25. Letter of September 20, 1941, in ADSS, vol. 3, doc. no. 310.

26. For documentation about the Profittlich case see ADSS, vol. 3, doc. no. 217, 219, 245, 251, 487, 504. Eduard Profittlich SJ (b. 1890 in Birresdorf near Trier) was in Estonia since 1930 and after 1935 possessed Estonian citizenship in addition to German. The Vatican tried in vain in 1942/43 to make inquiries of the Soviets concerning Profittlich through American intervention. Twenty years later, in 1963, there was a report from Estonia that Profittlich was still living in Siberia (cf. report of the 13th Congress 'Church in Crisis,' Königstein 1964, p. 71).

27. ADSS, vol. 4, doc. no. 227. —W. G. Dekanosov had appeared in Kaunas in June 1940 as Soviet Vice Foreign Minister and had prepared the "annexation" of Lithuania; he was a high functionary of the secret police, later Minister of the Interior of the Georgian Soviet Republic, and in 1953 was shot, together with Stalin's chief of security Beria, in the course of the de-Stalinization (see Pravda, December 24, 1953).

28. Cf. ADSS, vol. 4, p. 60 (reference to an 'appunto of Mons. Tardini' of 1946). In all probability the informant was a Jewish-Catholic journalist in Rome by the name of Sigfried (alias Gabriel) Ascher, who was a contact to the German military Secret Service ["Abwehr"] officer Josef Müller (the later politician and founder of the Bavarian Christian-Social Party [CSU] (cf. Josef Müller, "Bis zur letzten Konsequenz," Munich 1975, p. 153, and F. Muckermann, op. cit., p. 643).

29. Cf. Walter Hagen (pseudonym of German Secret Service Officer Wilhelm Hoettl): Die geheime Front, Linz 1950, p. 454.

30. ADSS, vol. 2, p. 221.

31. Cf.: Das politische Tagebuch von Alfred Rosenberg, Göttingen 1956, p. 116.

32. Bergen's telegram no. 9 (PAAA, Büro Staatssekr. Vat. 1941).

33. The claim by East Berlin historian Winter that the Vatican had "consorted with the monster (Naziism)" (op. cit., p. 196) is based on Walter Hagen's suggestions (op. cit., p. 453), but suppresses Hagen's conclusion that the negotiations between Ledóchowski and the German secret service failed.

34. ADSS, vol. 2, doc. no. 74.

35. ADSS, vol. 3, doc. no. 257 and 262. Cardinal Antonio Samorè, who was an attaché in the Vatican Secretariat of State during World War II, reported on June 22, 1977, in a lecture in Rome, that Tardini returned a draft of a protest note against the German occupation policy

in Poland to him fourteen times for correction because the note was not written cautiously enough. Finally Tardini ordered that the word "Poland" was not to be used.

36. Complete text in Struve, op. cit., p. 402ff.
37. Cf. Gordon Zahn: Die deutschen Katholiken und Hitlers Krieg, Graz 1965, p. 213. (German Catholics and Hitler's Wars. Sheed Andrews & McMeel, 1962).
38. ADSS, vol. 5, p. 9 and doc. no. 151.
39. Telegram no. 40 (PAAA, Büro Staatssekr. Vat.).
40. ADSS, vol. I, doc. no. 257 (Tardini's description of the report given him by the Pope).
41. ADSS, vol. 5, p. 8.
42. ADSS, vol. 5, p. 4.
43. Address to the diplomatic corps on February 25, 1946, and in a "Letter to the Peoples of Russia" of July 7, 1952 (cf. Paul Duclos: Le Vatican et la seconde Guerre Mondiale, Paris 1955, p. 131).
44. Archbishop Skvireckas reported proudly from Kaunas: "Lithuania has been freed from the Bolshevist yoke by the German army, which armed Lithuanians (cum armis in manibus) supported to the best of their ability" (ADSS, vol. 3, doc. no. 316).
45. ADSS, vol. 4, doc. no. 432.
46. ADSS, vol. 5, doc. no. 8.
47. Menshausen's report no. A 479 of August 23, 1941 (PAAA) and Weizsäcker, "Papiere," Berlin 1974, p. 264.
48. ADSS, vol. 5, doc. no. 182.
49. Text of Roosevelt's letter in ADSS, vol. 5, doc. no. 59.
50. ADSS, vol. 5, doc. no. 74.
51. ADSS, vol. 5, doc. no. 79
52. ADSS, vol. 5, doc. no. 75.
53. ADSS, vol. 5, doc. no. 82.
54. The differences of opinion among Catholic bishops in the USA had in part assumed dramatic forms and were aired in public: Bishop Hurley (St. Augustine, Florida), who had been employed until 1940 in the Vatican Secretariat of State, most decisively supported aid to the Soviet Union and declared that Naziism was a greater evil than Communism; on the extreme opposite side stood Bishop Beckman (Dubuque, Minnesota), who declared in radio talks: "It is time to stop differentiating between Red Army and Soviet state. The Red Army is the Soviet state, as long as it obeys godless tyrants." Beckman was as the only bishop who had to be pressured by the Papal Nuncio to agree to sign the balanced joint statement of the bishops at the US entry into the war at the end of December, 1941 (cf. ADSS, vol. 5, doc. no. 131 and 181). See also "America" (New York), of July 12, 1941 and Sept. 6, 1941.
55. ADSS, vol. 5, doc. no. 78 and 93.
56. ADSS, vol. 5, doc. no. 131.
57. See Reinhold Schneider: Verhüllter Tag, Cologne 1954, p. 174.
58. Rolf Hochhuth: Der Stellvertreter. Ein Schauspiel, Hamburg 1963, p. 154-177 (The Deputy, Winston, Richard and Clara Winston, tr., Grove Press 1964).
59. Letter of March 4, 1944 (ADSS, vol. 2, no. 119). —Author's emphasis.
60. Letter to Archbishop Kolb in Bamberg (ADSS, vol. 2, no. 121).
61. ADSS, vol. 2, no. 76.
62. Letter of June 21, 1940 to Archbishop Gröber in Freiburg (ADSS, vol. 2, no. 49).
63. Letter of January 31, 1943 to Cardinal Faulhaber in Munich (ADSS, vol. 2, no. 96).
64. Through a report from Pater Pirro Scavizzi (1884-1964), who on several occasions accompanied a hospital train of the Knights of Malta into the occupied zones of Poland and the Soviet Union as a military chaplain, and who had also been appropriately informed by Cardinal Innitzer on the trip through Vienna (cf. ADSS, vol. 8, no. 374).
65. ADSS, vol. 3, no. 406.
66. ADSS, vol. 8, no. 493, and "Foreign Relations of the U.S.," 1942, vol. III, p. 775f.
67. ADSS, vol. 8, no. 496.
68. ADSS, vol. 8, note p. 669 and La Parrochia, May 1964.
69. ADSS, vol. 8, no. 507. On June 15, 1944 Mons. Mario Martilotti, a Vatican diplomat

of the Apostolic Delegation in Bratislava, had a secret meeting (in the Slovakian Piarist Monastery of Svaty Jur) with two persons who had succeeded in escaping from the Auschwitz extermination camp: Rudolf Vrba and Czeslaw Mordowicz. Martilotti interviewed both for six hours and transferred their written report to Rome. On June 25, the Pope, by telegram, asked Hungary's chief of state Admiral Horthy to stop the deportation of Hungarian Jews [to Auschwitz]; and Horthy did so on July 6 (See John S. Conway in "Vierteljahrshefte für Zeitgeschichte No. 2/1979 and J. Levai, Hungarian Jewry and Papacy, London 1968, p. 26).

70. ADSS, vol. 2, no. 105. Mons. Tardini noted on August 20, 1943: "Complaints, suggestions and protests are completely useless if they remain secret" (ADSS, vol. 9, no. 297).

71. June 11, 1940, to Cardinal Suhard (Paris). The letter was discovered by the German security police after the occupation of Paris (today in the Bundesarchiv, Koblenz, Bestd. Reichskanzlei/Frankreich, R 43 II/1440 a) and was first published by Eberhard Jäckel (cf. Geschichte in Wissenschaft und Unterricht, Stuttgart, vol. 15, January 1964).

72. Cf. Paul Duclos: Le Vatican et la seconde Guerre Mondiale, Paris 1955 and A. Giovanetti: Der Vatikan und der Krieg, Cologne 1961.

73. Cf. ADSS, vol. 3, no. 241 and vol. 4, no. 257.

74. ADSS, vol. 4, doc. no. 433 and vol. 5, doc. no. 4.

75. Regarding this complex question cf. the well-documented essays by Robert A. Graham SJ (one of the editors of the Vatican documentary publication on the Second World War) in: Civiltà Cattolica no. 2937 and no. 2939, November/December 1972, as well as his discussion with the East Berlin historian Winter, who still maintained his false claims of 1962 in 1972 (cf. Winter, op. cit., p. 211). —Maglione's denial in ADSS, vol. 5, doc. no. 298; Orsenigo's reports in ADSS, vol. 3, p. 29.

76. Weizsäcker's note of November 11, 1941 (PAAA, Microfilm, Serial no. 535, p. 24099).

77. Bergen's report of November 29, 1941 (PAAA, Microfilm, Serial no. 535, p. 240126).

78. Cf. "Internationaler Militärgerichtshof," [Nuremberg Trial] vol. XXXVIII, 1086-1094, doc. 221-L and von Papen's private correspondence to Graham in: Civiltà Cattolica, no. 2937, p. 248, note.

79. Cf. "Gegenwärtiger Stand der Organisation der katholischen Kirche," July 1941, printed in RSHA, Geh. no. 17 (MIT-Documents, doc. no. PS-1815 [unprinted]), NA-T-988, Reel A 219, 092860031. Cf. also the secret report "The Status of Religion in the USSR" of 1944 by the American Secret Service OSS (Hoover Library, Stanford University).

80. Legation counsellor Fischer's note of December 4, 1941 (PAAA, microfilm, serial no. 335, p. 240100-101). —In the ADSS vol. 5, p. 273, note 3, the first part of the quote from this document is not mentioned (!).

81. Orsenigo to Maglione, October 22, 1941 (ADSS, vol. 5, doc. no. 125). Cf. Pietro Leoni SJ, "Spia del Vaticano," Rome 1959, p. 34.

82. ADSS, vol. 3, doc. no. 355.

83. For the quoted reports of Sheptyckyj see ADSS, vol. 3, doc. no. 297, 324 and 406; Slipyj's report doc. no. 375.

84. Cf. Ciszek, op. cit., p. 47ff.

85. ADSS, vol. 5, doc. no. 94.

86. Harriman's report in "Foreign Relations of the U.S., Diplomatic Papers," 1941, I, p. 1001-02 and ADSS, vol. 5, doc. no. 481. —For Losowski's explanation see Pravda, October 5, 1941.

87. Manuscript in the archive of the "Assumptionist Provincial house," New York City (cf. esp. p. 376-385; 67). —See also Dennis J. Dunn in: The Catholic Historical Review, vol. LIX, no. 3, 1973; cf. also David J. Dallin: The Real Russia, 1947.

88. ADSS, vol. 5, doc. no. 481.

89. ADSS, vol. 5, doc. no. 484.

90. ADSS, vol. 5, doc. no. 166 and 171.

91. Bishop Slipyj reported from Lvov to Rome on April 12, 1942. as follows: "Notitiae sparsae de litteris Stalin ad Sanctissimum Patrem missis, in quibus libertatem ecclesiae in Unione Sovietica profitetur gubernium Kioviae moverunt, ut ecclesiam nostram iterum aperiat" (ADSS, vol. 3, doc. no. 375).

92. ADSS, vol. 5, doc. no. 274, 284, 287, 288. —Avro Manhattan, e.g., took the false report seriously: "The Catholic Church and the XXth Century" (a tendentious production that went through 27 editions in west and east and is full of false data; German in East Berlin 1958).

93. Cf. Marina's report of August 5, 1942, in ADSS, vol. 8, doc. no. 442. Stanislaw Kot (1885-1975) belonged to the Polish Peasants' Party (SL), was Poland's ambassador to the Quirinal in Rome from 1945-1947, then emigrated to Paris.

94. ADSS, vol. 4, doc. no. 430 with note.

Chapter VII

1. ADSS, vol. 3, doc. no. 391 and 264 (Gavlina's report to Rome).

2. The bishops from the Baltic and Poland had repeatedly informed the Vatican of mass deportations. While East Berlin historian Winter speaks of "mythical" deportations (op. cit., p. 206), reported by Sheptyckyj, today even Communist publications in Poland admit the facts of this forced displacement (cf. W. Sokorski: Polacy pod Lenino, Warsaw 1971, p. 126).

3. ADSS, vol. 8, doc. no. 125.

4. ADSS, vol. 3, doc. no. 391. Thirty years later, one of these Polish clerics, Wladyslaw Bukowinski (1893-1971), who made it through the summer as a night watchman and spent the winter in prison, was still legally active in Kazakhstan and usually spent his vacation in Krakow (Poland) with a Soviet passport. (See report of Valentina Dötzel in "Russia Cristiana" [Milan], no. 1, 1978).

5. Roncalli—the later Pope John XXIII—in a report to Rome of April 7, 1943 (ADSS, vol. 9, doc. no. 138), describes how the Soviet consul received him "graciously" (con garbo), and among other things declared that the Orthodox Church "no longer alarmed" the Soviet State, "which is why a position which respected freedom of conscience could now be assumed." Ivanov promised to pass on the question concerning the prisoners of war to his embassy in Ankara. However, at a second meeting with Roncalli on March 29, he reported that he had been forbidden any further contact regarding this question (cf. also ADSS, vol. 7, doc. no. 282 and vol. 8, no. 125, 344, 336).

6. ADSS, vol. 7, no. 253.

7. Wlodzimierz Sokorski, in his book: Polacy pod Lenino (p. 13, 17, 126ff), for the first time described details about the tense relations within the Kościuszko division and within the "Union of Polish Patriots" in Moscow as an eye- and ear-witness. (Cf. also Werth, op. cit., p. 484-489).

8. Cf. Ciszek, op. cit., p. 105/06.

9. Documents on Orlemański (1899-1960) have been published in a Polish-Soviet document publication: Dokumenty i Materialy do Historii stosunków polsko-radzieckich, vol. VIII, Warsaw 1974. It contains the text of Orlemański's Moscow radio address (p. 135). Cf. "War Correspondence between Stalin and Roosevelt," Moscow 1960, no. 182, 183, 190. See also Alexander Werth, op. cit., p. 615-617 and Dennis J. Dunn in: The Catholic Historical Review, vol. LIX, no. 3, 1973, p. 420/421; for the Orlemański press conference see the New York Times, May 13, 1944 and Pravda, May 14, 1944.

10. ADSS, vol. 3, doc. no. 503.

11. ADSS, vol. 3, doc. no. 567. —Cf. also E. Lauterbach: These are the Russians, New York 1943, p. 277.

12. Quoted in Dallin: The Real Russia, p. 234.

13. "Prawda o Religii w Rossij" (the German in Zurich, 1944).

14. Cf. unpublished Braun Memoirs, op. cit., p. 382.

15. ADSS, vol. 5, no. 477, note 695.

16. Cf. note in ADSS, vol. 7, p. 161.

17. Telegram no. 347 of December 27, 1942 (PAAA, Büro Staatssekr. Vat.).

18. ADSS, vol. 7, no. 113.

19. ADSS, vol. 7, no. 126.

20. Cf. Senatro's statement in a public discussion in Berlin on March 11, 1963. —(Cf.

"Summa iniuria oder Durfte der Papst schweigen," documentation by Fritz J. Raddatz, Hamburg 1963, p. 104).
21. ADSS, vol. 7, no. 143, 144, 148 and note 2 on p. 276.
22. ADSS, vol. 7, doc. no. 150.
23. ADSS, vol. 7, doc. no. 173, 216, 217, 315.
24. ADSS, vol. 7, doc. no. 153 and annex.
25. ADSS, vol. 7, doc. no. 277, 278. Ernst von Weizsäcker (1882-1951). Cf.: Die Weizsäcker-Papiere 1933-1950. Pub. by Leonidas Hill, Frankfurt/Main 1974, p. 339-341.
26. Weizsäcker's telegram no. 271 of July 5, 1943 (PAAA, Staatssekr. Italien).
27. ADSS, vol. 7, doc. no. 372 and note 2. Cf. Weizsäcker-Papiere, op. cit., p. 364 and 369.
28. ADSS, vol. 2, doc. no. 115.
29. Cf. Pius XII's radio message of September 1, 1943 and the Christmas addresses of 1943 and 1944 (German in "Gerechtigkeit schafft Frieden. Reden und Enzykliken Pius' XII," ed. W. Jussen SJ, Hamburg 1946).—Cf. also Prof. Walter Becker (Augsburg) in: "Geschichte in der Gegenwart. Festschrift für K. Kluxen," Paderborn 1972, p. 316/317.
30. Cf. "Weizsäcker-Papiere," op. cit., p. 399-405 and "Magic"—Diplomatic Summary No. 1065 Feb. 23, 1945 (War Department Office of A.C. of S. G-2 (SRS-1587) Here full text of Ribbentrop's "speech directive."
31. ADSS, vol. 3, doc. 586 and Galter, op. cit., p. 96.—A Soviet report of the burial by W. Belajew: Kto tieba precal, Moscow 1969.
32. Original in the "Centralni Istoritscheskji Archiv, Lviv." Published in a study by Edward Prus (cf. Zycie Literackie, Krakow, of July 23, 1972.—Cf. also Widomosti (News) of the Archdiocese of Lemberg (Lvov), Jan.-Feb.-Mar. 1944, p. 16/17.
33. ADSS, vol. 3, doc. no. 605.
34. Letter to Pius XII of May 26, 1946 (ADSS, vol. 3, doc. no. 605).
35. Cf. Galter, op. cit., p. 96/97, and Borys Lewitzkyi: Die Sowjetukraine 1944-1963, Cologne 1964, p. 38/39.
36. Complete text in J. Schweigl: Il nuovo Statuto della Chiesa Russa, Rome 1948, p. 94 ff. Cf. also the evidence of the Italian Jesuit Pietro Leoni, who stayed in Odessa in 1944 when the city was re-occupied by the Soviet army. After a short period of amity, Leoni came into conflict with the Orthodox Bishop Sergej Larin and was arrested in April 1945 as a "Vatican spy." He did not return to Italy until 1955. (Leoni, "La spia del Vaticano," Rome, 1959).
37. Cf. G. Kostelnik: Nova doba nashoj Cerkwi, Lemberg 1926.—Kostelnik, whose three sons had died in the war, was murdered on September 21, 1948, by Ukrainian nationalist partisans.
38. E.g. Johann Chrysostomus OSB: Kirchengeschichte Russlands der neuesten Zeit, Munich 1968, vol. 3, p. 198.
39. Cf. Galter, op. cit., p. 108-114.
40. Cf. M. Gelzinis: Christenverfolgung in Litauen, Königstein 1955, p. 54 and 39.
41. Charles de Gaulle: Memoiren (Taschenbuchausgabe), Gütersloh, n.d., p. 177 (Memoirs).
42. Cf. a report (Pol. XV, 860) of the German embassy to the Vatican sent by the Foreign Office in Berlin to the Ministry for Ecclesiastical Affairs on December 16, 1944 (Deutsches Zentralarchiv, Merseburg, GDR).—See also Osservatore Romano of July 23, 1944.
43. Cf. an interview with Soviet General Koravnikov in Zycie Literackie, Krakow, no. 806, p. 8.
44. See note 42.
45. Ibid.
46. Cf. Tablet, London, June 17, 1944. Secretary of State Cardinal Maglione died on August 22, 1944 (b. 1877). Pius XII left the post unoccupied and performed the duties himself.
47. Cf. Osservatore Romano, August 14, 1944.
48. ADSS, vol. 3, doc. no. 591 and 598; cf. also doc. no. 568.
49. Jasinski made himself so unpopular that he had to resign in December 1946 and go to a cloister, where he died in 1962. (cf. Polityka, Warsaw, January 23, 1971, and ADSS, vol. 3, doc. no. 475 and 585).

50. Cf. Francois Fetjö: Die Geschichte der Volksdemokratien, Graz 1972, vol. I, p. 60. [English see note 54.]

51. Casaroli's lecture in Milan, January 20, 1972 (*Civiltà Cattolica*, no. 2920).

52. Cf. Graham, op. cit., p. 479/480. In Moscow, Flynn only spoke with functionaries of the city government (information from P. Graham).

53. ADSS, vol. 7, doc. no. 505.

54. For the following see Z.K. Brzezinski: The Soviet Bloc—Unity and Conflict, Harvard, 1960, and Francois Fetjö: Die Geschichte der Volksdemokratien, vol. I, p. 187-191 (A History of the People's Democracies: Eastern Europe since Stalin, London, Pall Mall, 1971.) In Italy at the time, the Communist Party Chief Togliatti spoke of the "Italian path" to socialism and laid the foundation for what would later be called "Euro-communism."

55. ADSS, vol. 3, doc. no. 602.

56. Complete Latin text of the decree in Jan Zaborowski: Kościól nad Odra i Nysa, Warsaw 1969, p. 53.—The original Vatican decree with the plenary powers for Hlond was signed by Tardini (Prot. No. 41-167/1945); it is preserved in the Archbishops Archive in Gniezno (see "*Acta Hlondiana*" t. VI) Cf. St. Kosinski in "*Chrzescijanin w Swiecie*" No. 81/1979.

57. Complete text in: Polozenie Prawne Kościolów w PRL, Warsaw 1961, p. 127/128.

58. Msgr. Breitinger had made himself an advocate of persecuted Poles and lamented the Pope's silence in a letter to Rome (cf. ADSS, vol. 3, doc. no. 444). Bishop Splett, on the other hand, had been chastised by the Vatican for forbidding confession in Polish under pressure from the Gestapo. "One may not bow to the demands of worldly authorities when it concerns unjust commands," the Vatican wrote him (cf. ADSS, vol. 3, doc. no. 222). Cf. the essay by A. Martini SJ in *Civiltà Cattolica*, April 7, 1962.

59. Cf. Alfons Sarrach: Das polnische Experiment, Augsburg 1964, p. 65.

60. AAS, XXXVIII (1946), p. 172.

61. This representation is based on private information from F. Alessandrini (Vatican) of September 9, 1974, as well as on Claude Naurois: Dieu contre Dieu?, Fribourg/Paris 1956, p. 156 ("Naurois" is the pseudonym of Maria Winowska, a confidante of Cardinal Wyszyński).—Ksawery Pruszyński (b. 1907) had been connected with the London exile government and at the time of this probe was a press attaché with the Polish embassy in Washington. He died in 1950 in Holland, where he was ambassador of the Polish People's Republic. He was probably proposed as Vatican ambassador earlier. (Cf. also "Studium," Rome, June 1949).

62. Kardinal Mindszenty warnt.—Reden, Hirtenbriefe, Presseerklärungen, Regierungsverhandlungen 1944-1946, St. Pölten 1956, p. 64.

63. Mindszenty, op. cit., p. 64.

64. *Tablet*, London, September 22, 1962.

65. Mindszenty, op. cit., p. 53.

66. Mindszenty, op. cit., p. 59. In his memoirs the sentence about the "legal abyss" is deleted.

67. Mindszenty, op. cit., p. 91 and 95.

68. The most extensive version of the facts (including sources)—although with a very one-sided analysis and without contemporary background—is found in Albert Galter: Redbook of the Persecuted Church, Westminster, 1957.

69. Interview for the Catholic newspaper in Budapest, *Uj Ember*, December 30, 1945.

70. Mindszenty, op. cit., p. 125. Cf. also Mindszenty: Erinnerungen, Frankfurt/Main 1974, p. 86/87 (Memoirs).

71. Cf. Carlo Falconi: Das Schweigen des Papstes. Eine Dokumentation. Munich 1965 (the Croatian archives are utilized here).—See also ADSS, vol. 5, doc. no. 224.

72. AAS, XXXVIII (1946), p. 391.

73. Cf. *Nova Pot*, vol. I, no. 2.

74. Quoted by Msgr. Casaroli in his lecture in Milan (*Civiltà Cattolica*, Feb. 19, 1972).

75. Cf. P. Mathas' letters to the Superior General of the Assumptionist Order of January 1948 and March 4, 1948 (AA Archive, Rome, 2 DZ, no. 181 and 183).

76. Cf. the memoirs of Josef Müller (Bis zur letzten Konsequenz, Munich 1975), p. 330-333.

77. Bishop Wienken had already conducted the negotiations with the Hitler government and was among the proponents of a "modus vivendi." He burned all his papers before his death (cf. Walther Adolph, Die katholische Kirche im Deutschland Hitlers, Berlin 1974, p. 177).

Chapter VIII

1. In addition to my own investigations in Rumania and the Vatican, the following presentation—insofar as sources are not cited—is based on a privately printed book that contains many dates, but aside from that more emotion than historical analysis—Hieronymus Menges: Joseph Schubert, 1890-1968, Biographie eines rumänischen Bischofs, Munich 1971.

2. O'Hara (1895-1963) was last the apostolic delegate in London.

3. For general background, cf. Stephen Fischer-Galati: The New Rumania, Cambridge, Mass., 1967 and Paul Lendvai: Der Rote Balkan, Frankfurt/Main 1968.

4. The names of the secret Uniate bishops in Rumania (all known to the authorities, but not listed in the "Annuario Pontificio") are: Joan Ploscaru, Joan Chertes, Alexandru Todea, Jon Dragomir, Juliu Hirtea (died 1978), and Liviu Chinezu (who died in prison).

5. Alexander Cisar (1880-1954) was of Czech-Polish origin and was allowed to return to Bucharest shortly before his death.

6. AAS, XXXIX, 1947, p. 493.

7. AAS, XLI, 1949, p. 9.

8. Exhortatio Apostolica of Feb. 11, 1949 (AAS, XLI, 1949, p. 58).

9. Encyclical "Orientales Omnes" (AAS, XXIII, 1946, p. 33).

10. Apostolic letter of March 27, 1952 (AAS, XLIV, 1952, p. 249).

11. AAS, XL, 1948, p. 254.

12. AAS, XLI, 1949, p. 29.

13. Cf. Mindszenty's version in his memoirs (Macmillan, New York, 1974, p. 117ff.).

14. AAS, XLI, 1949, p. 41.

15. See note 14.

16. AAS, XLI, 1949, p. 74.

17. Cf. Casaroli's lecture in Milan of Jan. 20, 1972, in: Civiltà Cattolica no. 2920, p. 372.

18. Cf. Rude Pravo, July 17, 1949.

19. Tiso (b. 1887) was executed in 1947.

20. ADSS, vol. 8, doc. no. 426.

21. The complete original text of the pastoral letter is in Katolicke Noviny of April 26, 1942; an Italian translation is in the report of Papal Nuncio Burzio (ADSS, vol. 8, doc. no. 360); cf. also the publication cited in note 24, p. 69/70—for general background, see also Wolfgang Venohr: Aufstand für die Tschechoslowakei, Hamburg 1969, p. 150.

22. ADSS, vol. 8, doc. no. 334 (cf. Galter, op. cit., p. 168, 206 and 209).

23. AAS, XLIII, 1951, p. 768.

24. Cf. also A. Michel: Religiöse Probleme in einem Lande unter kommunistischer Herrschaft, Königstein 1955, where a noteworthy self-criticism of the church's behavior is expressed (p. 51/52).

25. Cf. Polozenie Prawne. . . , op. cit., p. 128 (complete Polish text).

26. Letter of Sept. 1, 1949 (AAS, XLI, 1949, p. 450).—Cf. Psalms 1,8 and Proverbs X, 3.

27. Cf. Der Papst an die Deutschen, ed. Bruno Wüstenberg and Joseph Zabkar, Frankfurt/Main 1956, p. 138/139.—Pius XII himself inserted the skeptical, cautious conclusion in the draft text written for him by his German advisor, Robert Leiber SJ.

28. AAS, XLIII, 1951, p. 775.

29. Cf. Hansjakob Stehle: The Independent Satellite.—Society and Politics in Poland since 1945, New York 1965, p. 60ff.

30. Cf. Mindszenty's Memoirs, p. 83-138.

31. Cf. "Documentation catholique," 1951, col. 94.
32. See note 31.
33. Cf. Proces de Joszef Grösz et ses Complices [published by the State Editorial House in Budapest 1951] p. 49. In these court records, translated into French and circulated in numbered copies, there is also a French translation of the Dell'Acqua letter.

Chapter IX

1. Cf. *Trierer Theologische Zeitschrift*, vol. 63, no. 3, p. 180.
2. Cf. Reding: Thomas von Aquin und Karl Marx, Vorträge im Rahmen der Grazer Theologischen Fakultät, 1st issue, 1953.
3. Cf. G.A. Wetter: Der dialektische Materialismus, Freiburg 1952 (new version of a work by Wetter which appeared in Turin in 1948) (Dialectical Materialism, Peter Heath, tr., Greenwood 1973), and Klemens Brockmöller: Christentum am Morgen des Atomzeitalters, Frankfurt/Main 1953.
4. *Osservatore Romano*, Nov. 13 and 24, 1954.
5. *Osservatore Romano*, Jan. 3, 1955.
6. Letter to the Bishop of Augsburg on the occasion of the millenial of the battle of Lechfeld (*Herder-Korrespondenz*, vol. 9, p. 525f).
7. Cf. Leiber's remarks, quoted by Tadeusz Breza: Das eherne Tor, Munich 1962, p. 86/87. Robert Leiber (1887-1967) confided to a co-resident in the Roman "Collegium Germanicum" shortly before his death that he had never seen himself as well "understood" as in Breza's book (private information from Dr. Heinz Joachim Fischer, Rome).
8. Cf. Konrad Adenauer: Erinnerungen 1953-1955 (Taschenbuchausg.), p. 519.
9. It concerned the Bishops Julijonas Steponavičius (b. 1911) in Panevezys and Petras Mazelis (1894-1966) in Telsiai. Both were consecrated by the 80-year-old Kasimir Paltarokas, at that time the only free Catholic bishop in the Soviet Union.
10. Steponavicius has not been recognized by the authorities since the early sixties; he lives (1979) in Zdanovo/Joniskio as a pastor.
11. Participants were the former theologian K.W. Ostrovitianov (Vice President of the Academy) and Professors A.S. Fedosseiev, A.P. Gagarin, Omelianovski and Shapershnikov.
12. Cf. Reding: Der Politische Atheismus, Graz 1957.
13. Private correspondence from Reding of Feb. 9, 1967. —Cf. also *Pravda*, Dec. 29, 1955 about Reding's reception by Mikoyan. —Reding was called at the end of 1956 to the chair for Catholic theology at the Free University in Berlin, although Msgr. Pizzardo, the Prefect of the Vatican Congregation for Studies raised objections with the Berlin vicar capitular Prange (cf. Reding's maiden lecture: Der Sinn des Marxschen Atheismus, Munich 1957).
14. Concerning my controversy at the time with Prof. Alessandrini, which was carried out between the *Frankfurter Allgemeine Zeitung* (of which I was editor) and the *Osservatore Romano: FAZ* Nov. 12, 1955, *OR* Dec. 1955, *FAZ* Dec. 21, 1955 and Mar. 13, 1956, *OR* Mar. 23, 1956 and Apr. 8, 1956, *FAZ* Apr. 12, 1956, *OR* May 27, 1956 and June 29, 1956. My information came partly from Josef Schmitz Van Vorst (1949-1979 Roman correspondent of the "Frankfurter"), who was in close contact with the Jesuits Leiber and Gundlach.
15. AAS, XLVIII, 1956, p. 549.
16. For background to Piasecki and the "Pax" see Stehle, The Independent Satellite, New York 1965, p. 102ff., Lucjan Blit, The Eastern Pretender, London 1965, and Andrzej Micewski, Katholische Gruppierungen in Polen, Mainz 1978.
17. Speech of Sept. 2, 1956 (AAS, XLVIII, 1956, p. 622). Cf. also *Osservatore Romano*, Sept. 9, 1956.
18. Cf. *Osservatore Romano*, Apr. 27, 1956 and *Neue Zeit*, East Berlin, Apr. 25, 1956.
19. For text of the Gundlach report see minutes of the congress "Church in Crisis," Königstein/Taunus 1957, p. 11ff.
20. Ibid., note 19, p. 153.
21. Circular of Nov. 1, 1956 (AAS, XLVIII, 1956, p. 745).
22. Cf. George Mikes: The Hungarian Revolution, London 1957, p. 132 and Die ungarische Revolution—Rundfunkdokumente, Regensburg 1957, p. 98.

23. Cf. Cardinal Wyszyński: Für Freiheit und Menschenwürde (Addresses), Limburg 1966, p. 44ff.

24. Cf. Löwenstein's report in *Rheinischer Merkur*, Nov. 30, 1956.

25. Cf. the complete text of Mindszenty's speech in his "Memoirs," p. 331ff and in Kalman Konkoly and Aurel Abranyi: Ein Land in Flammen, Munich 1956, p. 146ff.

26. Mindszenty, op. cit., p. 358. —The bracketed portions of the quote were omitted in the Mindszenty Memoirs, but kept in the shorthand report of the tape of the Munich publication.

27. AAS, XLVIII, 1956, p. 748.

28. AAS, XLVIII, 1956, p. 787.

29. AAS, XLIX, 1957, p. 5.

30. For text see *Trybuna Ludu*, Dec. 8, 1956.

31. Cf. text of the decree of Feb. 9 in *Dziennik Ustaw*, no. 10 (1953), poz. 32, and of the decree of Dec. 31, 1956 in *Dziennik Ustaw*, no. 1 (1956), poz. 6. —The regulation of 1956 is in effect to this day (1975).

32. *Osservatore Romano*, Dec. 20, 1953.

33. *Osservatore Romano*, Sept. 9, 1956.

34. This version is based on confidential notes of a friend of Wyszyński's who died in 1968, Prelate Wladyslaw Kulczycki.

35. AAS, XLIX, 1957, p. 321.

36. Cf. Louis Wei Tsing-sing: Le Saint-Siege et la Chine, Paris 1968, p. 259ff. (Here a complete list of the names of the 43 bishops consecrated between 1957 and 1962 without Rome's approval, but theologically valid.) Cf. also François Dufay, "En Chine—L'Etoile contre la Croix" (Paris, 1954).

37. Cf. encyclical "Apostolorum Principis," dated June 29, 1958. —The decree of excommunicatimn, that was now in effect, had already been issued by the Holy Office on April 9, 1951 (cf. AAS, XLIII, 1951, p. 217-218).

38. Only three weeks later, on Dec. 17, 1961, did the *Osservatore Romano* publish the two messages.

39. Cf. AAS, XLIV, 1952, p. 505 and Pius XII's letter to the Portuguese of Oct. 31, 1942 (ADSS, vol. 5, doc. no. 507). The Jesuit Josef Schweigl (who had been in the Soviet Union in 1926 on d'Herbigny's orders), at the end of November 1956 published as his "private interpretation" (his words) the thesis that there was a "complete parallelism between the events at Fatima and those of the political and religious history of the Soviet Union"; he even related Stalin's death to the Pope's act of dedication (cf. Schweigl: Fatima e la Conversione della Russia; pub. by the "Pontificio Collegio Russico"). —See also Odilo Flagel OSB: Fatima Heute, Feldkirch-Altenstadt 1966.

40. Thus one of Reinhard Raffalt's false conclusions in his book: Wohin steuert der Vatikan? —Papst zwischen Religion und Politik, Munich (Piper) 1973, p. 130-133.

41. Soon after the arrival of the observers from the Moscow Patriarchate in Rome, the Warsaw government allowed nine more bishops for whom Wyszyński had made travel applications to take part in the Council.

42. Cf. Giancarlo Zizola: L'Utopia di Papa Giovanni; Assisi 1973, p. 15-20. Zizola, however, whose information comes from the former secretary of the Pope, Capovilla, overrates the importance of Cousins and Morlion in the papal mediation on Cuba. (See also Norman Cousins, The Improbable Triumvirate. John F. Kennedy, Pope John and Nikita Khrushchev, New York 1972).

43. To Norman Cousins, who reported this in a news special on April 29, 1973 on the "Zweiten Deutschen Fe nsehen" (second West German TV station) by Luitpold A. Dorn.

44. Cf. "Notiziario" no. 2, in: Il Concilio Vaticano II, Rome 1968, pub. by *Civiltà Cattolica*, vol. II, p. 47.

45. Ibid., p. 202.

46. See Note 42.

47. Excerpts from the report in Zizola, op. cit., p. 188ff.

48. Complete text in Zizola, op. cit., p. 217ff.

49. Cf. Jean Guiton: Dialog mit Paul VI., Vienna 1947, p. 31, and Montini's address of April 25, 1951, (quoted in Graham: Diplomazia Pontificia, Rome 1960, p. 50ff.).

50. Cf. Raffalt's claims (op. cit., p. 124-126) identical to a document of the American "Office of Strategic Studies" (OSS) published in the weekly *Il Borghese* (March 3, 1974). This talks about a meeting between Montini and Togliatti, where a Communist-Christian Democrat collaboration and a Vatican-Soviet understanding were planned; this "secret information" also reached the news agencies (like United Press), since they as well as the OSS subscribed to the "Notiziario", an information service of Virgilio Scattolini. Scattolini, who in the thirties was with the *Osservatore Romano* and was later known for pornographic novels, in 1948-1949 published in Switzerland supposed Vatican secret documents (Documenti segreti della diplomazia vaticana, Lugano 1948); they were still used in 1972 as a serious historical source by the East Berlin historian Winter (op. cit., p. VIII). However, Scattolini was sentenced by a court back in 1949 as a fraud and forger. He supplied the American, German and Soviet secret services with his clever inventions (cf. Graham: "Il Vaticanista falsario" in *Civiltà Cattolica* no. 2958, Sept. 15, 1973 and no. 2970, March 17, 1974, p. 569).

51. Cf. Il Concilio Vaticano II, vol. III, p. 13.

52. Cf. *Kommunist* (Moscow), no. 1/1964 and *Partijna Schisn* no. 2/1964.

53. Text of the petition of Sept. 29, 1965, in: Il Concilio Vaticano II, vol. V, p. 119.

54. Cf. Il Concilio Vaticano II, vol. V, p. 402/403. —See also G. Scantamburlo: Perche il Concilio non ha condannato il Communismo, Rome 1967.

55. Address of Sept. 12, 1965 (cf. Il Concilio Vaticano II, vol. IV, p. 520 and vol. V, p. 116).

56. Lecture in Milan, Feb. 19, 1972 (cf. *Civiltà Cattolica*, no. 2920/1972). —Agostino Casaroli, b. 1914 in Piacenza as son of a tailor, graduated in 1940 from the Pontifical Diplomatic Academy, since 1937 in the Vatican's Secretariat of State, first as "archivista," since 1961 Under Secretary of the Congregation for Extraordinary Affairs, since 1967 Secretary of the "Council for Public Affairs of the Church" (Foreign Ministry) and titular bishop of Carthago. Since 1979 Cardinal and Secretary of State of Pope John Paul II.

Chapter X

1. Thus M. Wesselenyi in *Studien*, vol. III, Budapest 1968, p. 126. See also Casaroli's explanation in *Osservatore Romano*, Sept. 19, 1964.

2. Cf. Mindszenty's "Erinnerungen," p. 396ff.

3. Cf. Mindszenty, op. cit., p. 402 (in the pre-publication of the memoirs by the *Frankfurter Allgemeine Zeitung*, Sept. 18, 1974, there were documents on this theme that were left out of the book).

4. Cf. Mindszenty, op. cit., p. 411.

5. *Osservatore Romano*, Feb. 6, 1974.

6. *Osservatore Romano*, Feb. 11, 1970.

7. *Osservatore Romano*, Nov. 13, 1970.

8. Winter's claim (op. cit., p. 323) that Athenagoras had said after his meeting with Paul VI: "It was a kiss of Judas," may be a misunderstanding. According to a private report from Cardinal König (Vienna), Athenagoras said to the Vienna bishop about the meeting: "Hardly anything separates us any more."

9. Cf. Communisti e Cattolici, Stato e Chiesa, 1920-1971, Rome 1971, p. 82.

10. In an interview for *Die Furche* (Vienna), no. 6/1967.

11. Cf. "Church-State Coexistence in Yugoslavia Improving" (RFE Research Paper of Feb. 27, 1967), and "Growing Tension in Relations Between Churches and State in Yugoslavia" (RFE Research Paper of Nov. 9, 1972).

12. Cf. Seper's interview for *Glas Koncila* (Zagreb), Feb. 19, 1967.

13. *Osservatore Romano*, Jan. 11, 1968—cf. also the exchange of telegrams between Tito and Paul VI (*Osservatore Romano*, Feb. 12, 1967).

14. The papal representative is called "pronuncio" where he does not carry out the function of a dean of the diplomatic corps as provided for in the Vienna Convention (especially in non-Christian countries).

15. *Osservatore Romano*, August 15, 1970.

16. *Osservatore Romano*, Dec. 6, 1953; cf. also *OR* of December 31, 1953.

17. Cf. The Legal Status of Religious Communities in Yugoslavia, Belgrade 1967, p. 19ff. Text of the new Decree of 1965 in "Kirche und Staat in Bulgarien und Jugoslavien: Gesetze und Verordnungen," Witten, 1971, pp. 22-25.

18. Cf. Beran's interview for the Prague magazine *Student*, no. 19, May 7, 1968.—On August 30, 1965, in a speech in Assisi, Beran had reported more correctly that he had already been told in Prague that he could not return (cf. *Frankfurter Allgemeine*, August 31, 1963).

19. Cf. Hruza's interview for *Agence France Press* of Feb. 25, 1965.

20. Cf. *Kathpress* (Vienna), Sept. 26, 1969.

21. Hruza's article appeared in *Znanie, Serija estestvoznanie i religija* (Moscow) no. 5/1970.

22. Cf. Angela Nacken's report from Prague in the *Frankfurter Allgemeine Zeitung* of Jan. 21, 1973.

23. Cf. *Katolicke Noviny* (Prague) of March 18 and 25, 1973 and Vrana's statement to the correspondent of the Spanish paper *La Vanguardia*, Estariol (*Kathpress*, Vienna, of March 27, 1973). See also *Osservatore Romano* (German edition) of March 30, 1973.

24. Cf. *Osservatore Romano* of Nov. 14, 1965. —The text of Wyszyński's speech was passed out by the Cardinal himself on stationery of the Council Press Office.

25. Cf. H. Stehle, Nachbar Polen. Erweiterte Neuausgabe, Frankfurt/Main, 1968, p. 132f.

26. For the German-Polish bishops' correspondence, cf. the two contradictory, both well-documented presentations, which proceed from two extremely one-sided positions: Otto B. Rögele: Versöhnung oder Haas? Ein Briefwechsel der Bischöfe Deutschlands und Polens und seine Folgen, Osnabrück 1966; and Oredzie Biskupów Polskich do Biskupów Niemieckich, Warsaw 1966. —New background documents I have published in Herder-Korrespondenz No. 1/1979.

27. Cf. H. Stehle: Nachbarn im Osten, Frankfurt/Main 1971, p. 219ff. 241ff and 275ff.

28. Cf. *Europa-Archiv*, no. 17/1967 (H. Stehle: "Neue Aspekte und Methoden Vatikanischer Ostpolitik").

29. Cf. *Slowo Powszechne* (Warsaw) of Oct. 4, 1971. Vatican specialist Ignacy Krasicki (see p. 343f.), who quoted this speech of Skarzynski's in an article in the weekly *Argumenty* (Warsaw, April 23, 1972), suppressed the part about the "permanent character" of church activity.

30. Cf. *Europa-Archiv* no. 16/1972 (H. Stehle: "Der Vatikan und die Oder-Neisse-Grenze." With documentation).

31. Quotes according to author's own tape recording in Rome on November 11, 1973.

32. According to author's own tape recording in Warsaw, Feb. 7, 1974.

33. The translator was the Polish curial prelate Andrzej Deskur, president of the Vatican Commission for the Mass Media, who soon thereafter was made bishop.

34. For text of the withdrawn communiqué see *L'Avvenire*, July 7, 1974; for the reduced text see *Osservatore Romano*, July 8, 1974.

35. From the author's own translation from the Latin text. (Another German translation was published in "KIPA-Backgrounds" on October 15, 1974).

36. At the 5th National People's Congress in Peking on Feb. 26, 1978, two missing Chinese bishops unexpectedly appeared as delegates: the 81-year-old archbishop of Mukden, Ignacius Pi Shu-shih, who—himself appointed by Pius XII—had consecrated twelve bishops without papal approval in 1957-1960, among them the Jesuit Chang Chia-shu accompanying him now, who was declared bishop of Shanghai. (Archbishop Pi died in the spring of 1978.) On May 21, 1978, Italian Christian Democrat Minister Vittorio Colombo met in Peking with the chairman of the "United Patriotic Catholics of China," Bishop Yang Kao-Jen (of Changteh/Hunan) and held a two-hour "informal contact discussion" with him on behalf of the Vatican. At this time, the bishop interpreted the emergence of the Catholic church from the underground as a sign of hope. The precondition for diplomatic contacts between Peking and the Vatican, of course, was that the Vatican end its diplomatic relations with Nationalist China (Formosa). Therefore even when Prime Minister Hua-Kuo-feng visited Rome in 1979 he did not see the Pope.

37. The Polish emigrant monthly magazine gave precise data on Catholic parishes in seven Soviet republics: "Kultura" (Paris), no. 5/1978. Here a tangible, if relative, mitigation of the situation is noted: in 1977, primarily in Kazakhstan, official permission was given in several cases for the conversion of private residences into chapels for religious ceremonies.

38. Vladimir Kuroiedov, the Chairman of the "Council for Religious Matters in the Council of Ministries of the USSR" (b. 1906, teacher by profession), in a brochure printed only in German ("Kirche und Religion in der UdSSR", Moscow 1977) dedicated 18 lines to the Catholic church. "The congregations of the Roman-Catholic church, which exist in 10 of the 15 republics of the USSR, are united by single religious administrations—curias—independent of each other. In the Lithuanian SSR, for example, the Catholic congregations are led by six religious centers," the archepiscopal diocese of Vilnius and the episcopal dioceses of Panevezys, Telsiai, Kaunas, Kaisiadorys and Vilkaviskis. In the Latvian SSR, the Catholic congregations are united in the archepiscopal diocese of the Roman-Catholic church in Riga. In Transcarpathia (city of Ushgorod, Ukrainian SSR) there is a vicariate of the Roman-Catholic church. The curias direct the religious life of the congregations, nominate and transfer clerics, etc. The directors of the curias, who are named by the Vatican, undertake regular canonical visitations to the congregations and control their activities." (p. 38).

39. Cf. L'Avvenire of July 4, 1971 and Giovanni Caprile: Il Sinodo dei Vescovi (1971, p. 826ff).

40. Vasyl Velickovsky, a Redemptorist monk who spent the years 1946-1957 in prison camps, was in 1963 secretly consecrated bishop without Vatican nomination, was arrested in 1969; early in 1972, very ill, he received a tourist visa to visit his sister in Yugoslavia, then came to Rome, where he was received by the Pope. He died June 30, 1973, in Winnepeg, Canada. Cf. his memoirs: Vasyl V. Velickovski, Episkop-Ispovidnik, Norkton, Saskatchewan, Canada, 1976.

41. Thus R. Raffalt, op. cit., p. 288.

42. Cf. note 49, Ch. IV and Gerhard Simon, "Das sowjetische Religions-gesetz vom Juni 1975" (Berichte des Bundesinstituts für ostwissenschaftliche und internationale Studien, Cologne, no. 14/1976).

43. For official English translation of the constitution see "New Times," Moscow, no. 41/1977.

44. Casaroli's lecture on "L'anno Santo e la pace nel mondo" (The Holy Year and World Peace), October 31, 1974, to the "Banca di Roma" (cf. L'Avvenire of Nov. 1, 1974).

Chapter XI

1. See La Documentation Catholique (Paris), Feb. 18, 1979, pp. 164-172.

2. The Pope wrote the encyclical in his mother tongue.

3. French text of these speeches in the Osservatore Romano, Oct. 19, 1978 and Jan. 13, 1979.

4. See Rabotnitchesko Delo (Sofia), Sept. 21 and 30, Oct. 3 and 4, 1952.

5. See König's statement to Kathpress (Vienna), Feb. 23, 1979. Latin text of the Pope's letter in Osservatore Romano, Jan. 14, 1979.

6. Text of Slipyj's statement in a Polish translation authorized by the "Chancellory of the Patriarch" ["Kanzlei des Patriarchen"] (sic) in Kultura (Paris) No. 12, 1978.

7. For text see Osservatore Romano, May 17, 1979.

8. See Osservatore Romano, Nov. 14, 1979.

9. The full text was first published in the Neue Züricher Zeitung, Nov. 11/12, 1979. Text of the French original see "Documentation catholique" (Paris) No. 1774 (18.11.1979)—This letter exchange soothed the doubts of the Moscow Patriarchate to such an extent that it was ready to delegate its representatives to the "Catholic-Orthodox Mixed Commission for Theological Dialogue" which was agreed on November 30, 1979 during Pope Wojtyla's visit to the Ecumenical Patriarch Dimitrics I. in Istanbul (see "Osservatore Romano" Dec. 1, 1979). In spring 1980 Cardinal Willebrands was invited to Moscow and Odessa, where the fifth theological meeting (March 13-23) could take place after an interruption of almost five years. At the

same time, during a special Ukrainian Synod in Rome (March 24–27, 1980), the Pope appointed Miroslav Lubachivsky as future successor ("coadjutor cum jure successionis") of the 88 year old Cardinal Slipij—against the Cardinal's desire.

10. For the Polish text of the papal addresses (in the originally prepared version) see *Osservatore Romano*, June 3–10, 1979; and for the tape-recorded version see *Chrzesijanin w Swiecie* (Warsaw), No. 80, 1979.

11. Taped by author in Czestockowa.

12. See *Osservatore Romano*, Oct. 4, 1979 (English text).

13. See Giovanetti's exposure of Fedorenko's sudden telephone call in *Corriere della Sera*, Sept. 16, 1979.

Chapter XII

1. Vatican diplomatic relations with Communist and Catholic Cuba, for example, were never interrupted; however, the nunciature in Havana was occupied by only a chargé d'affaires for a long time in the sixties, when Castro restricted the freedom of the church. On a one-week visit to Havana, in a late-night discussion on April 5, 1974, the papal "foreign minister" Casaroli came to an agreement with Castro on a normalization which included the regime's refraining from anti-religious measures. Cesare Zacchi, who had prepared this development, was the first pro-nuncio in Havana, until he was named president, in 1975, of the papal Diplomatic Academy in Rome. Since June 1976, Archbishop Mario Tagliaferri has been pro-nuncio in Cuba, and since 1976, José Antonio Portuondo Valor has been Cuban ambassador to the Holy See.

No Vatican relations have arisen with Communist Vietnam, but the archbishop of Hanoi, Trinh Nhu Khue, who was named cardinal in May 1976, was allowed to travel to Rome; after his return, on Sept. 1, 1976, he delivered a paper from the Vatican to Vietnam Premier Pham Vàn Dong. In October 1977, the cardinal was again able to go to Rome for the Synod of Bishops, accompanied by the archbishop of Saigon (Ho Chi Minh City), Paul Nguyen Van Binh, who pleaded for an accommodation to the new situation on the part of Vietnamese Catholics. The Cardinal was again in Rome in 1978 for the election of two Popes, and died shortly after. His successor, Trinh văn-Căn (born 1921) visited the Vatican in 1979.

2. On the lively discussion that arose especially in the German-speaking areas about Vatican eastern policy cf. Cardinal Franz König: "Das grosse Gespräch" (*Europäische Rundschau*, Vienna, 2/74); Heinrich B. Streithofen O.P. in: Diskussion um den Frieden, Stuttgart 1974; H. Prauss: "Einige grundsätzliche Aspekte vatikanischer Ostpolitik" (*Informationsdienst des katholischen Arbeitskreises für Zeitgeschichte*, Bonn, no. 52/1972); Oskar Simmel SJ: "Vatikanische Ostpolitik" in: *Communio—Internationale Katholische Zeitschrift*, no. 6/1974). Characteristic of the climate of discussion is the polemic of J. G. Reissmüller in the *Frankfurter Allgemeine* against Prof. H. Vorgrimmler (*FAZ* of November 19, 1974) and the latter's reply (*FAZ* of December 4, 1974). Also the polemic of Rudolf Krämer-Badoni, in: *Die Welt* of December 27, 1974 and the reply of the former bishop in Magdeburg (DDR), Rintelen, in *Die Welt* of January 10, 1975.

3. Casaroli to Otto Schulmeister in an interview (*Die Presse*, Vienna, December 21, 1974).

Sources and Bibliography

1. Archives and Document Publications consulted (Abbreviations used in the notes are in parentheses)

Archivio del Generalato dei Verbiti ("Societas Verbi Divini") Rome (SVD)

Archivio del Generalato dei Assunzionisti ("Augustiani ab Assumptione") Rome (AA)

Archivio della Congregazione degli Affari Ecclesiastici Straordinari, Vatican (AES)

Bayerisches Geheimes Hauptstaatsarchiv, Munich (BStA) [Bavarian Secret State Archive]

Hof- und Staatsarchiv, Vienna (HStA) [Court and State Archives]

Politisches Archiv des Auswärtigen Amtes, Bonn (PAAA) [Political Archives of the Foreign Office]

Acta Apostolicae Sedis (AAS)

Annuario Pontificio, 1921-1978 (AP) [Pontifical Yearbook]

Il Concilio Vaticano II (ed. G. Caprile) vol. 1-5, 1966-1969

La Saint Siege et la Guerre en Europe. Actes et Documents du Saint Siege Relatifs a la Seconde Guerre Mondiale, Città del Vaticano, vol. 1-9, 1965-75 (ADSS)

Traduction des Documents officiels du Commissariat du Peuple a la justice, Rome 1925 (Orientalia Cristiana, no. 18).

Kirche und Staat in der Sowjetunion. Gesetze und Verordnungen. Witten, 1962.

Kirche und Staat in Bulgarien und Jugoslawien. Gesetze und Verordnungen. Witten, 1971.

2. Publications on the theme of this book

For general background the *Kirchengeschichte Russlands der neuesten Zeit* by Johannes Chrysostomus [Plashkevič] may be used (3 vols., Salzburg 1968), which however only treats the Orthodox church.

429

Equally useful is Giovanni Barberini's work, *Stati Socialisti e Confessioni Religiose* (Milan 1973), which is based on thorough, comparative legal studies in all Communist-ruled countries (see also *Church within Socialism*, ed. Erich Weingartner, based on the work of G. Barberini, IDOC International, Rome, 1976). Closer to our theme is the two-volume work by Eduard Winter, *Russland und das Papsttum* (to 1917) (East Berlin, 1960/61), which is based on intensive source studies, however inclines toward one-sided interpretations; Winter, a former priest, Professor in East Berlin, and Austrian citizen, produced a third volume in 1972, *Die Sowjetunion und der Vatikan* (East Berlin, Akademie-Verlag), and at the same time an abridged, "westernized" version, *Rom und Moskau* (Vienna, Europaverlag). Winter used some of the sources that I have also utilized for the present volume; however, Winter alters and distorts them frequently in order to support his biased conclusions (often giving incorrect sources or none at all; this is pointed out individually in the notes of this book). Still, Winter's presentation—often conceptually confused—offers more than the very few books on this theme that have appeared in the West:

Maxime Mourin, *Le Vatican et l'URSS* (Paris 1965), a very fragmentary, superficial work with no sources, of which the author himself says that the central problem remains "au delá des limites de notre investigation."

Ulisse A. Floridi, an Italian-American Jesuit (from Wilkes-Barre, Pa.), in 1976 dedicated a book to Vatican eastern policy under the title of *Detente versus Dissent?*, that as yet has only been published in Italian (*Mosca e il Vaticano. I dissidenti sovietici di fronte al "dialogo"*, Milan 1976). Floridi gives extensive information about the religious dissidents, but suppresses—with false or tendentiously distorted quotes—motives inappropriate to the Vatican (precedence of peace before "the laws of God" and thus "collaboration with the oppressors"). The historical basis of the book is superficial and narrow. This is also true of the collection of material by Józef Mackiewicz, *Watykan w Cieniu Czerwonej Gwiazdy* (The Vatican in the Shadow of the Red Star) London, 1975—sharply criticized by M.K. Dziewanowski in "Problems of Communism" Vol. XXVII, no. 1/1978.

Wilfried Daim, *Der Vatikan und der Osten. Kommentar und Dokumentation* (Vienna 1967) (*The Vatican and Eastern Europe*, Alex Gode Tr., Ungar 1970), offers in addition to 250 pages of "documents," which are primarily newspaper clippings from 1964-66, only a hasty and superficially written "analysis" full of false data and conclusions. For

him the Vatican is politically too far to the right, while for
Reinhard Raffalt, *Wohin Steuert der Vatikan?* (Munich 1974), the Vatican
is too far to the left; Raffalt, of course, makes no historical-documen-
tary analysis, but rather is trying to proclaim his theses; insofar as they
are supported by false data that touch upon our theme, this is noted in
the footnotes.

Dennis J. Dunn, *Détente and Papal-Communist Relations, 1962-1978.*
(Boulder/Colorado, 1979), an extensive, careful collection and synop-
sis of published facts and figures. Almost ignoring the historical background of the Vatican *Ostpolitik*, its continuity and its exclusively pastoral, non-political motivation, Dunn looks to its efficacy in terms of
"reciprocity" and general East-West power balance. So he underesti-
mates the usefulness of Papal peace engagements for its claims to religious freedom, overestimates Soviet interest in "seeking a modus
vivendi with the church" and misunderstands the exceptional case of
Yugoslavia as a "model".

3. Frequently Cited Works (For further publications concerning
    particular events and for general historical-political background see
    notes.)

Charles-Roux, François: *Huit ans au Vatican, 1932-1940,* Paris 1947.

Ciszek, Walter: *With God in Russia,* New York 1964.

Codevilla, Giovanni: *Stato e Chiesa nell'Unione Sovietica*, Milan 1972.

Curtiss, John Shelton: *The Russian Church and the Soviet State 1917-
1950,* Boston 1953.

Galter, Albert: *The Red Book of the Persecuted Church,* (Tr.),
Westminster, 1957.

Giovanetti, Alberto: *Pio XII parla alla Chiesa del Silenzio,* Milan 1959.

Herbette, Michel: *Ein französischer Diplomat über die bolschewistische
Gefahr,* Berlin 1943.

d'Herbigny, Michel: *L'Aspect Religieuse de Moscou en Octobre 1925,*
Milan 1959.

d'Herbigny, Michel: *Paques 1926 en Russie Sovietique,* Rome, Paris, 1926.

Jurkiewicz, Jaroslaw: *Watykan a stosunki polsko-niemieckie w latach
1918-1939,* Wybór materialów, Warsaw 1960.

Kraus, Johann: *Im Auftrag des Papstes in Russland,* Siegburg 1970.

Lesourd, Paul, *Le Jesuite Clandestine. Mgr. Michel d'Herbigny,* Paris
1976.

Mailleux, Paul: *Exarch Leonid Feodorow, Bridgebuilder between Rome
and Moscow,* New York 1964.

McCullagh, Francis: *The Bolshevik Persecution of Christianity,* London
1924.

Pastor, Ludwig von: *Tagebücher, Briefe, Erinnerungen, 1854-1928*, Heidelberg 1950.

Quenard, Gervais: *Hier. Souvenirs d'un octogenaire*, Paris 1955.

Shachnovitch, M. I.: *Lenin und die Fragen des Atheismus*, East Berlin 1966.

Simon, Gerhard, *Die Kirchen in Russland*, Munich 1970.

Struve, Nikita: *Les Chrétiens en URSS*, Paris, 1963 [German: Mainz, 1965].

Die Weizsäcker-Papiere, 1933-1950, ed. Leonidas Hill, Frankfurt/Main, 1974.

Zatko, James J.: *Descent into Darkness. The Destruction of the Catholic Church in Russia, 1917-1923*. Notre Dame, Indiana, 1965.

4. General Literature on Vatican Policy

Breza, Tadeusz: *Das Eherne Tor. Römische Aufzeichnungen*, Munich 1962.

Duclos, Paul: *Le Vatican et la Seconde Guerre Mondiale*, Paris 1955.

Falconi, Carlo: *Il Silenzio di Pio XII*, Milan 1965.

Friedländer, Saul: *Pius XII und das Dritte Reich*, Hamburg 1965.

Giovanetti, Alberto: *Der Vatikan und der Krieg*, Cologne 1961.

Graham, Robert: *Vatican Diplomacy*, Princeton 1959.

Kolarz, Walter: *Die Religionen in der Sowjetunion*, Freiburg 1963.

Lama, Friedrich: *Papst und Kurie in ihrer Politik nach dem* [*ersten*] *Weltkrieg*, Illertissen 1925.

Leist, Fritz: *Der Gefangene des Vatikans. Strukturen päpstlicher Herrschaft*, Munich 1971.

Nichols, Peter: *The Politics of the Vatican*, London 1968.

Nikodim (Metropolitan of Leningrad): *Johannes XXIII.—ein unbequemer Optimist*, Zurich, 1979.

Purdy, W.A.: *The Church on the Move.* The Character and Policies of Pius XII and John XXIII, London 1966.

Rhodes, Anthony: *The Vatican in the Ages of the Dictators (1922-1945)*, New York-London 1973.

Sejnmann, Michail: *Vatikan meždu dvumja mirovymi vojnami*, Moscow 1948. [German: *Der Vatikan im Zweiten Weltkrieg*, East Berlin, 1954].

Wall, Bernard: *Report on the Vatican*, London 1956.

PAPAL INSTITUTIONS IN ROME that are significant to the eastern policy of the Vatican, and their directors (1978)

Secretariat of State (Cardinal Villot); since 1979 Cardinal Casaroli

Council for the Public Affairs of the Church (Archb. Casaroli; since 1979

Silvestrini)—before 1967 the Sacred Congregation for Extraordinary Ecclesiastical Affairs.

Sacred Congregation of the Oriental Churches (Archb. Brini)—founded 1917; the entire Church of the Eastern Rite is under it (Uniate), as well as the Latin Church in Albania and Bulgaria.

Commission for Russia (Archb. Casaroli)—founded 1926 (under d'Herbigny), independent 1930, after 1934 competent only for the faithful of the Latin Rite and subordinate to the Congregation for Extraordinary Ecclesiastical Affairs.

Pontifical Institute for Eastern Studies (F. Eduard Huber)—founded 1917; part of the Pontifical Gregorian University.

Pontifical Russian College (Russicum), founded 1929 (F. Mailleux SJ)

Pontifical Polish College, founded 1866 (Msgr. B. Wyszyński)

Pontifical Polish Church Institute, founded 1910 (Msgr. Maczyński)

Pontifical Polish Institute of Ecclesiastical Studies, founded 1958 (F. Fokciński)

Pontifical Ukrainian St. Josafat College, founded 1897 (F. Mudryj)

Pontifical Lithuanian St. Kasimir College, founded 1948 (Msgr. Tulaba)

Pontifical Bohemian St. Neponuk College, founded 1930 (Msgr. Planner)

Pontifical Rumanian College (founded 1930)

Pontifical Croatian College, founded 1901 (Msgr. Kokša)

Pontifical Slovenian College, founded 1960 (Msgr. Jezernik)

Pontifical Hungarian Church Institute, founded 1940) (Msgr. Bagi)

Documentary Appendix

1. *The Secret Agreement of 1922*

A facsimile copy of the only written agreement to date between the Vatican and Moscow—damaged by traces of fire—was found in the files of the Political Archive of the German Foreign Office in Bonn (PAAA, Geheimakten 320/3,4, Russland, Pol. 16/Nr. K105166 to 68); it was procured and sent to Berlin in July 1922 by the spiritual consultant of the German embassy to the Vatican, Monsignore Steinmann. The following translation (from the French original) also relies on a transcript in the Gehrmann papers (Archive of the "Societas Verbi Divini" Order, Rome):

ACCORD BETWEEN THE HOLY SEE AND THE GOVERNMENT OF THE SOVIETS ON THE DISPATCH OF AGENTS OF THE HOLY SEE TO RUSSIA

§ 1. The envoys of the Holy See shall not be members of nations or political formations hostile to Soviet Russia.

§ 2. The envoys shall swear to abstain from any political activity that is contrary to the existing government, directly or indirectly, in Russia or abroad.

§ 3. Except for any political propaganda, the envoys of the Holy See shall have complete freedom to dedicate themselves to the relief of the people (relèvement du peuple) by distributing foods to the hungry. (*Crossed out in the original draft*: through agricultural, artisan or professional schools, etc., as well as through their moral and religious education.)

§ 4. The names of the envoys of the Holy See, with the curriculum vitae of each, shall be presented for approval to the Government beforehand, through the mediation of the Delegation in Rome.

§ 5. The approved envoys of the Holy See shall immediately establish contact with the civil authorities in the place where they wish to exercise their activity and afford them the opportunity for effective control.

§ 6. The envoys of the Holy See shall conform their activity to the decrees and orders in force in Russia.

§ 7. The sphere of activity of the Holy See's envoys shall be previously established by agreement [*par une entente*] between the Holy See and the Russian Delegation in Rome, and may subsequently be modified in agreement with the local Soviet organs.

§ 8. All envoys of the Holy See admitted to Russia shall enjoy the protection of the law and the authorities. They are granted unlimited right of relocation (*déplacement*), with reservation to the observance of the previous paragraphs.

§ 9. The Government reserves the right to demand the recall of any envoy of the Holy See if it finds that his activity opposes the interests of the State.

§ 10. Envoys of the Holy See who wish to leave Russia or whose presence is considered undesirable shall be enabled to leave Russian territory freely, insofar as they have not committed a crime stipulated in the Penal Code.

§ 11. The government pledges to provide gratis lodgings and offices for envoys of the Holy See who have come to Russia for charitable purposes and to facilitate the rental of lodgings and offices for the others.

§ 12. Loading and transport of objects intended for the needy populations shall be done at state cost whenever on Russian territory.

§ 13. Rights and privileges of the envoys of the Holy See shall be more precisely regulated by additional paragraphs; they must correspond in their basic lines to the rights and privileges of the missions of Mr. Nansen and the German Red Cross.

§ 14. Prepared in duplicate and signed by the authorized Representatives of the Holy See and the Soviet Government in Rome:

The Vatican, March 12, 1922   (signed) Pietro Cardinal Gasparri
                                      Vorovski, Representative of the
                                      Republic of Russia

2.   The Vatican's "Rapallo Concept"

The following note of the Spiritual Consultant of the German embassy to the Holy See, Monsignore Johannes Steinmann, was sent on March 30, 1922, by Ambassador Diego von Bergen "requesting confidential treatment," to the ministerial counsellor in the Foreign Office, Ago von Maltzan, who was at the international conference in Genoa and became one of the main initiators of the Rapallo treaty between Germany and the Soviet Union (Source: PAAA IV, Ru, Pol. 16, Vol. 1, Document Nr. K480041-53—excerpt—):

"The plan for a systematic missionization of Russia is probably more due to the present [Vatican] initiative than that of Archbishop von Ropp. As we know, the plan here excludes the French and the Polish. The latter must have learned of this and are now trying—apparently through Ropp— to destroy the whole plan in the Vatican, which they also temporarily succeeded in doing. Meanwhile, the Vatican soon convinced itself that Ropp's plans were utopian, with the consequence that, as was remarked confidentially, 'Ropp had dashed out of the Vatican full of anger.' The judgment of the Russian representative here about Ropp is interesting: 'Ropp is a sly fellow, who is hard to get at because he does not conduct himself as a Pole, but rather as a Russian, and is very concerned not to lose his Russian citizenship. But his whole plan, although it pretends to be purely Catholic, is purely Polish in the eyes of the Bolsheviks. He wants the return of Catholic schools, libraries, church properties etc., which however were and will remain confiscated not as Catholic, but rather as Polish institutions.'

So far, the *Congregatio pro ecclesia orientali* has only made plans on paper for Russia (cf. the confidentially reported guidelines at the time), i.e. actually only determined the Orders to be involved in the missionization of Georgia and Russia, and prescribed the Ukrainian-Uniate rite for them (Basilians, Uniates). An apostolic delegate, reputedly a Dominican, is supposedly already resident in Georgia; but the actual missionary activity has not yet been taken up, much less so in Greater Russia itself, which now, as aforementioned, is the responsibility of the Secretariat of State, which deserves the credit for having created the possibility of a missionization of Greater Russia in the negotiations with the Soviet representatives that I began in the interest of Germany [Deutschtum].

. . . The Soviet authorities, may I add, believe that the Orthodox Patriarch Tikhon, whom they greatly fear, is now negotiating with the Holy See concerning recognition of papal primacy. That is not true, and would also be premature; for it would be an arbitrary act by the Orthodox church authorities and would be opposed by the people for the present. Later, of course, when the Catholic church has inclined the Russian people more favorably by its acts of charity, it is not impossible that such a step will take place, one desired by the people themselves and felt by them to be an earned right of the Catholic church, with firm prospects of permanency.

In conclusion, may I report the following about the present state of the planned undertaking by the Holy See in agreement with the Soviet representatives here:

The agreement mentioned at the time has met with approval from the Moscow government with the modification that the words 'membres des missions' be replaced with the words 'délégués du S. Siege' [not quite correct; in the text of the treaty it is 'envoyés,' see pp. 30, 435-6], and actual teaching which is a state monopoly, is excluded from the activity of the delegates, after the Vatican, on request, had made a declaration that the earlier Czarist representation still present at the Holy See would not represent the present government of Russia. Thereupon the contract between the Holy See and the Russian representatives was signed by both sides. In addition, the Soviet representative here, Vorovski, gave the Holy See a document in which the latter was promised land concessions. The Holy See does not intend to make use of this for the time being. Further, the Vatican gave the resumés of the Patres traveling as delegates of the Holy See—3 Steyler missionaries, 3 Salesians and 3 Jesuits, of whom the first deserve our particular attention because of their purely German character—to the Russian representatives, who telegraphed them to Moscow, whose approval is expected in the next few days. Thereupon the passports will be issued, and all 9 Patres will travel together to Novorossijsk, where the Russian government has already made preparations for the reception of the papal delegates and their continued journey to Samara. According to the latest papal orders, the papal delegates, given 1 1/2 million lire for the present by the Holy See, will go to Russia only as 'esploratori' (scouts) for purely charitable purposes without any missionary duties for the time being. This is why the Holy See does not want to make any immediate use of the Russian concessionary offers, and has forbidden its delegates to seek any concessions. It wants to convince the Russians that the church is acting not out of egoistic motives, but from Christian love, and has no intention of allowing charity to degenerate into exploitation.

In case the delegates' reports sound favorable for actual missionary activity, then the Pope will appeal to the faithful all over the world on behalf of Russia. But the Holy See is already turning to all bishops, and the Jesuits to their rich American establishments, correctly recognizing that the Russian mission is also a major financial problem. It should be mentioned in connection with this that the American relief mission to Russia, which includes the Jesuit Father Walsh as a secular priest, has already spent over 20 million lire. Jesuit General Pater Ledochovsky has placed this Father, who can offer valuable services with his knowledge of Russian and other languages, at the complete disposal of the Holy See, and in view of the importance of the matter, it is conceivable that he may be employed in a department for Russia which the Holy See wants to create in the papal Secretariat of State.

It would be in Germany's interest to support the Steyler missionaries. The Steyler missionaries are a missionary society composed almost solely of Germans and Dutch, founded in 1875 by the German Pater Jansen, which has its mother house in Steyl in Holland, and numbers about 1200 German students in its houses in Germany. . . ."

Ambassador von Bergen writes in his accompanying letter to this assessment by Monsignore Steinmann that financial assistance to the Steyler mission will be given

". . . if use can be made by the missionaries of the concessions offered by the Russian government. However, that will only be possible with the participation of wealthy German financial circles in the Catholic missionary undertaking. As I hear, Dr. Jur. von Braun, a German living here, who spent a long time in Russia and has played an important advisory role in the whole missionary undertaking contemplated by the curia, has already interested the Director of the German Orient Bank Inc., Dr. Alexander, in this."

Ministerial Counselor von Maltzan only transmitted Steinmann's report to the Foreign Office in Berlin on April 25, 1922, nine days after the conclusion of the Rapallo treaty and two weeks before the meeting of Pizzardo and Chicherin (see p. 40), with the remark: "An appropriate contact with competent Catholic circles here has been taken up by the Russians."

3. *The End of the Dialogue 1927*

This report by the German ambassador in Moscow, Count Brockdorff-Rantzau, about a conversation with Soviet Foreign Minister Chicherin, was written after the break in diplomatic relations between Great Britain and the Soviet Union and after the last meeting between Chicherin and Nuncio Pacelli in Berlin (see pp. 115–16). At the ambassador's suggestion, only the two bracketed [] paragraphs of the report were read orally to papal nuncio Pacelli (original in the Political Archive of the Foreign Office, Bonn, Büro Reichsminister, Curia 70, Vol. 2, K012051-55).

TELEGRAM (GEH. CH. V.)

Moscow, August 29, 1927 12:57 pm

Arr. August 29, 1927 9:40 pm

No. 1009, of August 28.   SECRET!

The pastoral letter of Metropolitan Sergius (Tel. Nr. 981, 8/19) gave me opportunity to ask Chicherin whether this ostentatious declaration of loyalty by the prince of the Orthodox church had anything to do with the reconciliation between the Vatican and the British government recently mentioned to me by the People's Commissar. Chicherin replied characteristically that "he did not consider it out of the question." When I remarked that world opinion would probably not consider the Metropolitan's declaration completely "voluntary," Chicherin replied, without commenting more fully on this point, that the development of the Orthodox church had gone through three stages here under the regime of the Soviet government. The first was at the time of the Genoa conference. At that time Pius XI had flirted with the rulers in Moscow in the hope that they would "demolish" the Orthodox church, and indulged in the hope that the Roman church would win over the disappointed faithful. The period of favorable relations between Vatican and Soviet government, however, had been of only short duration, for soon the second phase began, in which Jesuit Father Walsh had become very active. The emigrants at that time had actually converted in great numbers to the Catholic faith; to Walsh had fallen the responsibility of arranging communications between them and the members of the Orthodox church who had stayed in Russia, especially through generous monetary contributions. Rome had hoped to establish close contacts in this way between the emigrants and their relatives who had remained in Russia, in order thereby to lead the latter to the Catholic church.

The support that the Vatican had from the emigrants abated, however, when the Soviet government decided to proceed less rigorously against the Orthodox church within the Union.

Chicherin agreed with my remark that the harsh, often repulsive actions against the religious sensitivities of the people that I had observed in the first years of my activity here were impolitic, and continued that the third period had now begun. "The Orthodox church here is now independent"; the Vatican could not, as previously, therefore rely on the converted emigrants, and had given up hope of winning over the "lost lambs" through them. The People's Commissar declared that under these circumstances the Vatican had apparently decided to proceed with the strongest measures; after having realized that the Soviet government was not going to do the Vatican's business, it was now trying to fight it politically. This also explains the rapprochement with the British government.

When I remarked that perhaps some friendly advance by this government could pull the rug out from under the Holy See regarding the rapprochement between Rome and London, the People's Commissar replied without annoyance that [the Soviet government was prepared now as ever to negotiate with the Vatican; however, it did not intend to conclude a concordat, but was not disinclined to agree on a "circular" with Rome, by which the legal position of the Catholic church in the Soviet Union would be regulated and guaranteed. Serious negotiations in this direction had already taken place earlier. About a year ago Brodovsky had given Nuncio Pacelli certain communications in this regard, although not extensive ones; an answer from Rome was however still outstanding, although Pacelli, on his last visit to Berlin, had promised him he would expressly work in Rome on the answer to the Russian communications. It was obvious that the Russian government, if not considered worthy of any answer at all in almost a year, could not attempt on its own to begin new negotiations.]

My report that leading German Catholic circles were disturbed about the relations of the Soviet government to the Vatican (your top secret document of August 20 Nr. IV Ru. 5169) did not fail to make an impression on Chicherin. So far as I can judge, the People's Commissar was trying to be objective from his view point in the discussion regarding relations with the Vatican; I have no desire to suggest that we should try to influence the Holy See to give the overdue reply to the Soviet government and thus create the possibility of renewed negotiations. I do not consider it impossible that Rome regards any further negotiations with the Soviet government as hopeless, and I have always refused to give unsolicited advice; I have not the slightest inclination to advise the Holy See to be yielding or conciliatory. [However, I regard it as my duty to describe the situation as objectively as possible, as I see it here, and thus I must in truth emphasize that I did not find any animosity toward the Vatican in Chicherin; on the contrary [I] received the impression that he is by no means disinclined toward negotiations with the Vatican—and not from fear of the rapprochement between Rome and London, or in view of the break with England—for the purpose of final legal regulation of the position of the Catholic church in the Union.]

Whether and to what degree it may be useful in this matter to inform Nuncio Pacelli or the ambassador to the Vatican in strict secrecy, I shall leave to your discretion; caution is recommended in any case. In my opinion, at all events only extracts read orally to the nuncio or the Vatican through our embassy should be considered. I feel justified in this judgment, after having worked continuously since taking over the post in Moscow, in spite of many disappointments, on an understanding between the Soviet government and the Vatican to create at least a tolerable *modus vivendi* for a Catholic church under great pressure here.

Rantzau

4. *Exile Orthodox: With Hitler Against Moscow—and the Vatican*

Berlin, 8/22/43

To the Ministry for Ecclesiastical Affairs, Berlin
Regarding: Propaganda activity of the Vatican station.

Enclosed I am sending you for your information a translation of the letter of 7/25/43, by His Eminence the Metropolitan Anastasius, of 7/25/43.

Heil Hitler!
The Orthodox Bishop of Berlin and Germany:
Metropolitan Seraphim

SERAPHIM

Metropolit
ß Orthodoxen Mitteleuropäischen
Metropolitankreises
und
orthodoxer Bischof
ın Berlin und Deutschland

Nr **558/43**

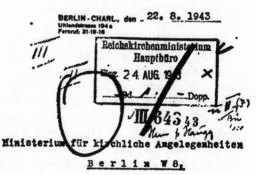

BERLIN - CHARL., den **22. 8. 1943**
Uhlandstraße 194 a
Fernruf: 31-19-16

Reichskirchenministerium
Hauptbüro

Eing. **2 4. AUG. 19**   ✕

Bd. _____ Dopp.

III/64343

An das

Ministerium für kirchliche Angelegenheiten

B e r l i n W 8,

Leipzigerstr. 3

Betrifft: Propagandaaktion des Vatikansenders.

In der Anlage übersende ich Ihnen eine Uebersetzung des
Briefes Sr. Eminenz, des Metropoliten Anastasius vom 25.7. 43
zur Kenntnisnahme.

H e i l · H i t l e r !

Der orthodoxe Bischof von Berlin und Deutschland :

Mp. 19. Vbr   *Mtr. Seraphim...*

Translation

Chairman of the Synod of
Bishops of the Russian
Orthodox Church Abroad

His Eminence
the Very Reverend Seraphim,
Metropolitan of Berlin and
Germany

Your Eminence, Very Reverend Bishop

The newspapers here have printed a report that the Vatican radio station is making broadcasts in the Russian language. One must assume that these broadcasts represent Catholic propaganda for the liberated Russian territories. In connection with this, I request that you call the attention of the German authorities to the danger of this propaganda, especially the attempt to introduce Catholicism among the Russian population, and the necessity of setting up something to oppose it. I assume that missionary broadcasts should be made over the German radio as a countermeasure.

Up to now they have not taken up religious questions, but from an official source we have received information that a change was possible.

Your Eminence's faithful Brother in Christ
Metropolitan Anastasius

5. *Cardinal Bengsch: Silence About the "Church of Silence"*!

The document published here for the first time (translated from a signed copy of the Latin original) was presented confidentially at the 6th session of the Central Commission for the preparation of the Second Vatican Council, which met May 3-4, 1962, in Rome. It relates to Chapter 6 of Part II, entitled "Ministry of Souls in Particular" (*De Animarum Cura in Particulari*), concerning the description of the bishops and their pastoral duties (cf. *"Praecipuae de animarum cura questiones," propositum a Commissione de episcopis et de dioeceseon regimine, Typis Polyglottis Vaticanis, MCMLXII*).

Archbishop Alfred Bengsch   Rome, May 4, 1962
Remarks

concerning the treatment of the draft decree that the "Commission on the Bishops and the Diocesan government" has proposed for the theme "Ministry for Christians infected by Communism" (*De cura pro Christianis communismo infectis*).

I do not agree (*Non placet*)

Certainly the church has the right and the duty to condemn in candid language any heresy, especially atheistic Communism. Beyond that, it must be especially confirmed that—just as the whole church, with an active conscience, bears in mind the danger of Communism to the world—the intention of the Right Reverend Fathers who proposed this draft is also praiseworthy.

In spite of this, I would briefly like to explain why I, exercising my office of Archbishop in East Germany, thus under the reign of the Communists, do not like the proposed draft.

1. It is very well stated in the draft that the activity of the church must be clearly differentiated from political or economic anti-Communism, for Communism, even in areas where it is official (*publica*) ideology, is only one form of atheism or materialism. There are in fact very many people who have accepted the above-named ideology—in short, Communism— that is, the so-called dialectic materialism, only to a small degree but who are still adherents of a practical or liberal materialism.

However, if the Holy Synod now, in view of this situation, ceremoniously proceeds exclusively against Communism, it could become almost impossible, as is so well said in the draft, to successfully withstand such a difficult intellectual battle. The Communists would have an easy opportunity, very welcome to them, to misuse the words of the Council in their propaganda and prove to the inexperienced that the church is engaging in political actions. I therefore suggest that we condemn *every* materialistic ideology that has crept in—in this or any other manifestation—all over the earth and attempts to intrude into Christian life.

For the nature of materialism seems to me to be almost completely independent of the borders of nations or nationalities. As I have often witnessed in the western part of my diocese, i.e. the politically free sector of the city of Berlin, materialism or liberalism raises a number of difficulties concerning the schools or sciences, just as in the church administration.

2. The dignity of the Council demands that the draft not use certain expressions and words which are used frequently—and there correctly—in the political arena or in the language of the mass media:

"Fear of the 'Soviet Power' "

"Free nations"

"Hatred of Communism"

"Iron Curtain"

3. Article III about the "Church of Silence" should be *completely deleted*. It not only does not help the bishops and faithful who live under the rule of the Communists in any way, but also will absolutely surely occasion new oppression and give the Communists opportunity and cause to reopen the struggle against the church. In addition, the bishops who exercise their office in regions that are under Communist domination, and who can probably only participate to a limited extent in the council, will meet with new difficulties on their return to their dioceses. Quite certainly the bishops and the faithful who live in the Communist areas will be thankful for any help that the church can afford them. The proposed article about the Church of Silence does not offer such help; it will only intensify the persecution. The expression "Church of Silence" is only relatively accurate in regard to the freedom of publications or propaganda in other areas of the globe. Even then the church is not altogether silent, but rather to this day conducts its spiritual battle through sermons and teachings. It would be considerably more helpful in this battle if the church in other nations would *keep silent about the Church of Silence*.

And because of this—in conscience bound—I have come to the above-expressed "non placet."

a) The suggestions of the draft do not absolutely have to be circulated in the church by means of a decree of the Council; they can be taught in other ways which do not reveal so clearly to the enemies of the church the methods the church will use to conquer these, its worst adversaries.

4. Are two drafts about the ministry and about Communism necessary? I fail to understand why, in this matter of such great importance, the suggestions of two commissions cannot be coordinated. The model presented by the commission on "the discipline of the clergy and the Christian people" seems to me much better, because it delineates more clearly the pastoral orientation, avoids expressions of a political nature, and condemns not only Communism, but also all other heresies of our time. Therefore—after certain improvements—it will also be able to serve even for the ministry in areas under the dominion of the Communists.

signed +A

6. *The Yugoslav-Vatican Agreement of 1966*

(Official English translation in: *The Legal Status of Religious Communities in Yugoslavia*, Medunarodna Stampa-Interpress, Beograd, 1967, pp. 84-86.)

PROTOCOL

OF DISCUSSIONS BETWEEN THE REPRESENTATIVES OF THE SOCIALIST FEDERAL REPUBLIC OF YUGOSLAVIA AND THE REPRESENTATIVES OF THE HOLY SEE

With a view to the settlement of relations between the Socialist Federal Republic of Yugoslavia and the Catholic Church, the representatives of the Government of the Socialist Federal Republic of Yugoslavia and of the Holy See held discussions in Rome from 26-th June to 7-th July, 1964, in Belgrade from -5-th to 23-rd January and from 29-th May to 8-th June 1965, and again in Rome from 18-th to 25-th April, 1966.

I

Within the general cadre of subjects which came up for discussions, the representatives of the Socialist Federal Republic of Yugoslavia presented the following attitudes of the Yugoslav Government:

1. The principles upon which the regulation of the legal status of religious communities is based in the Socialist Federal Republic of Yugoslavia and which are guaranteed by the Constitution and laws of the Socialist Federal Republic of Yugoslavia are as follows: *freedom of conscience and freedom of religion; separation of the Church from the State; equal status and equal rights for all religious communities; equality of rights and duties of all citizens whatever their creed and religious worship, freedom to found religious communities*; recognition of the status of a legal person to the religious communities.

With the cadre of these principles, the Government of the Socialist Federal Republic of Yugoslavia guarantees to the Catholic Church in Yugoslavia the free performance of religious functions and religious rites.

The responsible organs of the social-political communities (the commune, the district, the republic, the federation) ensure to all citizens, without any discrimination, the consistent application of the laws and other regulations serving to safeguard respect for the freedom of cor. cience and the freedom of religious worship guaranteed by the Constitution of the Socialist Federal Republic of Yugoslavia.

The Government of the Socialist Federal Republic of Yugoslavia is prepared to consider the cases which the Holy See may deem necessary to indicate to it in connection with this matter.

2. The Government of the Socialist Federal Republic of Yugoslavia admits the *competencies of the Holy See in the exercise of its jurisdiction over the Catholic Church in Yugoslavia in* spiritual *matters and in matters of* ecclesiastical *and* religious *character in so far as they are not contrary to the internal order of the Socialist Federal Republic of Yugoslavia.*

Also in future bishops of the Catholic Church in Yugoslavia shall have guaranteed to them the possibility of *maintaining contacts* with the Holy See, deeming that such contacts have an exclusively religious and ecclesiastical character.

The Holy See—while adhering to the demands which it presented for its part in the course of the discussions in connection with the *complete* regulation of relations between the Catholic Church and the Socialist Federal Republic of Yugoslavia—*noted* the declarations on the attitudes of the Government of the Socialist Federal Republic of Yugoslavia expressed in Points 1 and 2 above.

II

Within the general cadre of subject which came up for discussions, the representatives of the Holy See presented the following attitudes of the Holy See.

1. The Holy See reaffirms the principled attitude that the activity of Catholic priests, in the performance of their clerical duties, should proceed within the religious and ecclesiastical framework and that, consequently, they may *not abuse their religious and ecclesiastical functions for ends which would actually have a political character.*

The Holy See is prepared to consider the cases which the Government of the Socialist Federal Republic of Yugoslavia may deem necessary to indicate to it in this respect.

2. The Holy See—consistently with the principles of Catholic ethics— does not approve and *condemns every act of political terrorism* or similar *criminal* forms of violence, whoever its perpetrators be.

Consequently, should the Yugoslav Government appraise that Catholic priests have participated in an action of such a kind to the detriment of the Socialist Federal Republic of Yugoslavia, and should it deem necessary to indicate such cases to the Holy See, the Holy See is prepared to *consider* such indications with a view to instituting proceedings and eventually taking appropriate measures provided for by *Canon Law* for such cases.

The Government of the Socialist Federal Republic of Yugoslavia—while adhering to the demands which it presented for its part in the course of the discussions in connection with the *complete* regulation of relations between the Catholic Church and the Socialist Federal Republic of Yugoslavia—noted the declarations on the attitudes of the Holy See expressed in Points 1 and 2 above.

III

Both sides express their readiness for mutual consultation also in future, whenever they deem it necessary, on all matters affecting the relations between the Socialist Federal Republic of Yugoslavia and the Catholic Church.

IV

With a view to facilitating further mutual contacts, the Government of the Socialist Federal Republic of Yugoslavia is prepared to facilitate the stay in Belgrade of an Apostolic Delegate who would simultaneously possess the function of envoy to the said Government, with the proviso that it reserves the right to designate its envoy to the Holy See.

For its part the Holy See is prepared to receive the envoy of the Government of the Socialist Federal Republic of Yugoslavia and to send its apostolic delegate to Belgrade.

Drawn up in Belgrade on the June, 25-th of 1966, in two original texts, in the Serbo-Croatian and Italian languages, with the proviso that both texts shall be equally authentic.

For the Government
of the Socialist Federal
Republic of Yugoslavia,
Milutin Morača, signed.

For the Holy See,
Agostino Casaroli, signed.

7. *Casaroli on morals and politics*

Excerpts from the text of the toast Archbishop Agostino Casaroli made at a dinner given by GDR Foreign Minister Oskar Fischer on June 9, 1975, in East Berlin in honor of his Vatican guest:

"The Holy See thinks it is able, as an exclusively moral force, to make a valuable, if modest, contribution to the cause of peace. But in order to collaborate in the control of mistrust between peoples and powers, it needs, on its part, the open confidence of both sides, so that its constant appeals for respect for the law and morals be better received among the peoples and in international relations. . . . This explains the readiness of the Holy See for dialogue with those who desire it, which naturally does not mean that the Holy See is overlooking or underestimating ideological and doctrinaire divergences, or that it accepts especially existential questions of the church and of Catholics remaining unsolved in those nations with which it is taking up dialogue about problems of peace and of international cooperation. The Holy See, rather, is convinced that the greater its credibility in the area for which it is directly responsible, the greater its authority will be in the world of believers and non-believers and the more effective its actions as a moral factor in the area of peace and cooperation between peoples. . . ."

Excerpts from Archbishop Casaroli's toast at a dinner he gave for the GDR Foreign Minister Fischer on June 10, 1975, in the archepiscopal palace in East Berlin, in the presence of Cardinal Bengsch, Bishop Schaffran (Meissen) and Bishop Braun (Magdeburg):

"Experience shows: the greater is technical progress, the more necessary it becomes to consolidate moral structures, which alone can give progress a human dimension. In social relations, these moral structures consist in the rejection of egoism, in the spirit of human solidarity, in respect for the same dignity, the rights, the legitimate interests and the freedom of individuals and of peoples. Without these provisions, material, technological, scientific and even cultural progress not only becomes the advantage of one without a corresponding advantage for the others (indeed to their disadvantage, which is morally unacceptable), but excites and maintains reactions of revolt, which form the basis of social conflicts and wars. . . ."

8. *"Far from Cold War—and from normal freedom"*

In autumn of 1977, a 5-man Vatican delegation participated in the Belgrade Follow-up Conference of the "Helsinki Conference on European Security and Cooperation" (C.E.S.C.). On October 7, the Under Secretary for the Public Affairs of the Church, Mons. Achille Silvestrini, made an introductory declaration, which among other things contained a sort of account of Vatican Ostpolitik since the Helsinki Final Act (of August 1, 1975). The following excerpt is taken from the official translation from the English-language weekly edition of the *Osservatore Romano:*

. . . Mr. President, already during the preparatory consultations of Helsinki, in March 1973, the Holy See felt it its duty to take an initiative for the respecting of *religious freedom.* Its proposals were received with favour by several delegations and with consideration and respect by all of them. Outside the conference they were supported by the major European religious groups, and in the first place by the Conference of European Christian Churches.

The Final Document accepted a substantial part of these proposals in careful formulations, in the context both of the seventh principle on human rights and fundamental freedoms and of cooperation in the humanitarian sector. It is to these formulations, since their publication, that constant reference was and is made, sometimes with warm and passionate appeals, from many quarters in Europe and also in the rest of the world.

The seventh principle which commits every country to respect for human rights and fundamental freedoms, has aroused in public opinion an interest that has gone beyond many expectations. This is due, in our opinion, to the fact that the same principle recognizes the "universal significance" of human rights; recognizing that their respect arouses echoes of solidarity in the hearts of all men, from one country to another, because the aspiration to see it acknowledged and practised is common to all. . . ."In this context", the text of the seventh principle states, "the participating States recognize and respect the freedom of the individual to profess and practise, alone or in common with others, a religion or a creed, acting according to the dictates of his own conscience". A simple, plain, almost bureaucratic formula, which contains, however, something really important and essential! This is confirmed by the interest it aroused, when the text of the final document was published, in millions of believers—Catholics, Orthodox, evangelical Christians, Jews, Moslems and members of other faiths or confessions, both individually and in groups and communities spread throughout every region of Europe. These felt understood and interpreted by the Helsinki declaration, thus finding themselves involved in a great historic event owing to a common aspiration for freedom.

It is natural, therefore, that the Holy See should examine with special attention the practical consequences of the Final Document in this particular sector. It is, in fact, pressed from many sides to speak out, to formulate a judgment. It wishes to do so with a sense of responsibility, that is, adhering to the truth and with the intention of offering a constructive contribution. . . .

In particular, as regards the Catholic Church, it is a reason for satisfaction to note that a certain number of *positive facts* have certainly taken place from this standpoint. In the first place, there has been a wider flow, sufficiently constant, of facilitations granted for *journeys for religious motives*: for the "ad limina" visit of the bishops to Rome (which they must pay to the Pope every five years; this year it is the turn specifically of the European countries), or likewise for the presence of bishops and other ecclesiastics at important Holy See meetings: for the participation of religious men and women in their own general chapters, or other meetings, in Rome or in other localities of Europe and America: for the participation of bishops, priests, and groups of faithful in important religious events— such as the Holy Year in Rome in 1975 and the international Eucharistic

Congress in Philadelphia in 1976—or for pilgrimages to European sanctuaries.

Furthermore, there are more frequent meetings and exchanges of visits between representatives of episcopates of various countries, more numerous *permits for emigrant priests* to visit their relatives in their homeland, and the sending of a certain number of young ecclesiastics to attend study courses in institutes of culture and theological formation in Rome or elsewhere.

In the same way, in the sector of the media of communication and information, mention should be made of permits given to religious communities to print locally a certain number of prayer books and catechisms, consent given to the *sending of some thousands of religious publications* (gospels, bibles, catechisms) or liturgical publications (Mass-books, rituals for sacraments, prayer books for priests and religious) or collections of prayers to Catholic communities which up to then were unable either to have them printed or to import them: furthermore the reception, *no longer disturbed*, of certain radio religious programmes, such as the broadcasts of the *Vatican Radio*.

These measures correspond to commitments of the final document and have begun to change—even if still partially and not to the same extent for every place—a preceding situation which, on the plane of communications and relations between one country and another, was of rigid and discouraging closing.

Mr. President, it is more difficult, delicate and complex to speak of *religious freedom within States*. Here appeals, testimonies, and requests continue to multiply, some pressing and distressing, because the situation in various regions is *still far from a normal life of sufficient freedom*.

Complaints are made, in particular, about difficulties with regard to the religious practice of given categories of persons and to the religious education of the young, limitations as regards the formation of aspirants to ecclesiastical life, *restrictions on the freedom of pastoral action of bishops and priests*. There are also some serious open wounds that we would like, with a hope that we cannot abandon, to see put right and healed.

It is the case, for the Catholic Church, of *certain communities* of faithful of the *Eastern rite* which in the past, had a flourishing religious life rich in centuries-old traditions and which, in the new juridico-political post-war regimes have lost the civil right to exist. This is all the more painful because it concerns specifically a central point of religious freedom, which is to profess a faith "according to the dictates of one's own conscience".

Of course, the Holy See considers it right and opportune to continue to reserve the treatment of the concrete problems that concern the Catholic Church to *bilateral dialogue*: further intensified these years thanks to the atmosphere favourable to more numerous contacts and to more intense cooperation promoted by the C.E.S.C.

But it can be hoped, however, that "the spirit of Helsinki" will gradually bring to light the necessity of recognizing new spaces of freedom, especially to ensure the essential conditions of spiritual life of some millions of believers and their communities.

Far from making the Helsinki Final Document a polemical subject for deplorable returns to cold war tensions, our delegation wishes to renew here an expression of confidence that the work of interpretation and mediation which Government authorities are called to carry out in every country in order to put into practice the great principles proclaimed and subscribed to at Helsinki, will come, with enlightened far-sightedness, to accept these aspirations which are of vital significance and claim priority.

Mr. President, we do not believe that a wish formulated in this way is improper, far less utopian. It springs from confidence in a truth which is at all times within man and which then spreads at first almost imperceptible, and then more and more powerful and moves the world and history.

9.   *Ghetto or catacombs—an alternative?*

Excerpt from correspondence between the author of this book and an editor of the journal *Russia Christiana* (Milan, No. 5, Sept./Oct. 1976) after the appearance of the German edition of *Ostpolitik des Vatikans 1917–1975:*

Dear Mr. Modesto,

. . . You write that the heroism and the martyrs of the church of the catacombs are "practically ridiculed" by me. That is not true. One who reads my book without prejudice will find full respect for the sufferings and the human tragedies and also for the theological necessity of martyrdom. I do believe, however, that no one has the moral right to incite others to resistance to the point of martyrdom (while he himself enjoys all the fruits of freedom) and then to leave them in the lurch, even diplomatically (as has occurred not seldom in the history of Vatican Ostpolitik). The catacombs are an "ultimo ratio," but they have never been the pastoral centers of a living "church of the people." Certainly, a pastoral policy like that of the Vatican today can be nothing other than a search for possibilities of changing the "status moriendi" of the church in certain countries into a "status vivendi"—not in heaven, but in the existing Communist societies. A "post-Communist" society unfortunately does not exist; it can thus be an object of prayers, but not of a policy understood as an instrument of the possible.

Hansjakob Stehle

Dear Dr. Stehle,

. . . You trust exclusively to diplomacy, to save what can be saved, I appeal to the prophetic strength of the Church. . . . You reduce the actions of the Church to an (egoistical?) effort to survive, I challenge it to collaborate effectively for a future better society. You close the church into a ghetto, I want her active in a society seeking new ways. My position may be accused of naïveté and exaggerated optimism. I reply: it is precisely the attitude of the engaged Christians in the Soviet Union . . . those who are thinking not only of the survival of the church in the present, but of its responsibility for the future. . . .

Pietro Modesto

Chronology of important dates in recent Vatican Eastern diplomacy (1961–1977)

1961

Nov. 27—John XXIII thanks Khrushchev in a telegram for his birthday congratulations to the Pope.

1962

Sept. 27-Oct. 2—Mons. Willebrands of the Vatican "Secretariat for the Unity of Christians" in Moscow.

Oct. 23—Papal mediation between Moscow and Washington in the Cuba crisis.

Dec. 13—Norman Cousins presents Khrushchev, in Moscow, with the papal plea for the release of Archbishop Slipyj.

1963

Feb. 5—Mons. Willebrands brings Slipyj from Moscow to Rome.

March 7—John XXIII receives Alexei Adshubej, Khrushchev's son-in-law.

April—Cardinal König (Vienna) feels out the situation in Budapest.

May 9—Mons. Casaroli begins the first of five rounds of discussions in Budapest.

1964

June 26-July 7—Casaroli begins negotiations with Yugoslavia.

Sept. 15—Signing of a first partial agreement between Vatican and Hungary, in Budapest.

1965

January 5-23—Continuation of negotiations with Yugoslavia.

Feb. 19—Casaroli brings Cardinal Beran from Prague to Rome.

April 29—Cardinal König (Vienna) makes probes in Poland.

Oct. 4—Pope Paul VI meets Soviet Foreign Minister Gromyko at the United Nations in New York.

1966

April 18-25—Casaroli's third round of negotiations with Yugoslavia.

April 27—Soviet Foreign Minister Gromyko in private audience with Paul VI.

Summer—Casaroli's secret negotiations in Prague.

June 25—Agreement between Yugoslavia and Vatican signed.

June—Vatican diplomat Mons. Cheli in Bucharest.

1967

Jan. 30—Nikolai Podgorny, Soviet Head of State, in private audience with Paul VI.

Feb. 14-Mar. 7—Casaroli's first exploratory trip through Poland.

Mar. 13-25—Casaroli's second exploratory trip through Poland.

Mar. 29-Apr. 6—Casaroli's third exploratory trip through Poland.

1968

Jan. 11—Yugoslavian Prime Minister Spiljak in private audience with Paul VI.

Jan. 24—Rumanian Prime Minister Maurer in private audience with Paul VI.

1970

Aug. 15—Diplomatic relations assumed between Yugoslavia and Vatican.

Oct. 13—Czechoslovakian Director of Church Office makes probes in Vatican.

Nov. 14—Soviet Foreign Minister Gromyko in private audience with Paul VI.

December—Vatican diplomat Cheli makes probes in Prague.

1971

Feb. 25—In Moscow, Casaroli signs the Nuclear Disarmament Treaty and negotiates with the Soviet Director of the Church Office Kuroidev.

Mar. 25—State visit by Tito to the Pope.

Mar. 27—Discussions with Czechoslovakia broken off.

Apr. 17—Hungarian Foreign Minister Peter in private audience with Pope.

Apr. 17-30—Polish Director of Church Office Skarzynski negotiates in Vatican.

June 25—Mons. Cheli negotiates in Budapest.

Sept. 28—Mons. Cheli brings Cardinal Mindszenty from Budapest to Rome.

1972

Nov. 13-16—Vatican-Czech negotiations in Prague.

Dec. 11-16—Vatican-Czech negotiations in Rome.

1973

Jan. 15—Cheli tests candidates for bishop in Prague.

Jan. 24—Discussion between Casaroli and the East German Politburo member Wernher Lamberz in Rome.

Mar. 3-4—Casaroli himself completes three consecretions of bishops in the CSSSR.

Mar. 5—Casaroli received by Prague Vice Premier Lucan.

May 26—Rumanian Party Leader Ceausescu in private audience with Paul VI.

Summer—Casaroli speaks with Eastern European foreign ministers at the European Security Conference in Helsinki.

Nov. 12—Official visit by Polish Foreign Minister Olszowski to Paul VI.

1974

Feb. 21—Soviet Foreign Minister Gromyko in private audience with Paul VI.

Feb. 4—Casaroli in Warsaw at the invitation of Foreign Minister Olszowski.

Apr. 5—Casaroli in Cuba with Fidel Castro.

July 6—Polish Vice Foreign Minister Czyrek in Rome agrees with Casaroli on the formation of "permanent working contacts" (Nuncio Poggi-Minister Szablewski).

Sept. 17-20—Prague Director of Church Office Hruza in Rome for a new phase of negotiations.

Dec. 7-12—Second round of negotiations between Vatican and Czechoslovakia.

1975

Jan.—Nuncio Poggi takes exploratory trip to Rumania.

Feb. 26—Casaroli in Prague at invitation of Czechoslovakian Foreign Minister.

June 9-15—Casaroli in East Berlin at invitation of Soviet-German Foreign Minister Fischer. Casaroli visits bishops and congregations in the GDR.

June 27—Bulgarian State and Party Leader Zhivkov in private audience with Paul VI.

June 28—Soviet Foreign Minister Gromyko visits Paul VI at the Vatican.

Aug. 1—Casaroli signs the Helsinki Final Act for the Vatican.

Nov. 13—Hungarian Prime Minister Lazar

1976

Nov. 4-8—Casaroli in Sofia, guest of Bulgarian Foreign Minister. Visits Bulgarian Catholics.

Oct.—Nuncio Poggi negotiates in Bucharest

Nov. 3-10—Casaroli in Bulgaria; visiting all Catholics.

1977

June 9—Hungarian Party Leader Kadar received by Pope in official audience.

Summer—Vatican diplomat Bukovsky on exploratory trip in Czechoslovakia.

June 29—Cardinal Willebrands in Rumania (for installation of new Patriarch).

Sept. 27—Czech-Vatican partial agreement about appointment of Cardinal Tomasek as Archbishop of Prague and about new diocesan borders.

Oct. 7—Mons. Silvestrini, in Belgrade, criticizes the incomplete fulfilment of the Helsinki accords.

Dec. 1—Polish Party Leader Gierek in audience with Paul VI.

1978

Apr. 20-27—Nuncio Poggi and F. Bullovsky negotiate in Prague with CSSR-government—without results.

June 20-27—Special Nuncio Poggi negotiates with the Rumanian Church Office in Bucharest.

Oct. 16—Polish Archbishop Karol Wojtyla becomes Pope John Paul II.

Oct. 22—Polish head of state Jablonski and delegations from all nations of the Soviet bloc (except Rumania) at the Pope's inauguration mass.

Oct. 28—East German Foreign Minister Oskar Fischer received by Pope John Paul II.

beg. of Nov.—Special Nuncio Poggi in Budapest.

Dec. 14—Bulgarian Foreign Minister Mladenov received by Pope.

1979

Jan. 12—Pope John Paul II offers diplomatic relations with all countries; Poland's representative Szablewski at New Year's reception in the Vatican for the first time.

Jan. 24—Soviet Foreign Minister Gromyko's fifth visit to the Vatican; first meeting with the Pope from Poland.

June 2-9—Pope Wojtyla in Poland.

July 9-22—Nuncio Poggi negotiates in Rumania.

Oct. 3—John Paul II addresses the United Nations in New York.

Oct. 18—Nuncio Poggi in Bulgaria for bishop's inauguration.

Index